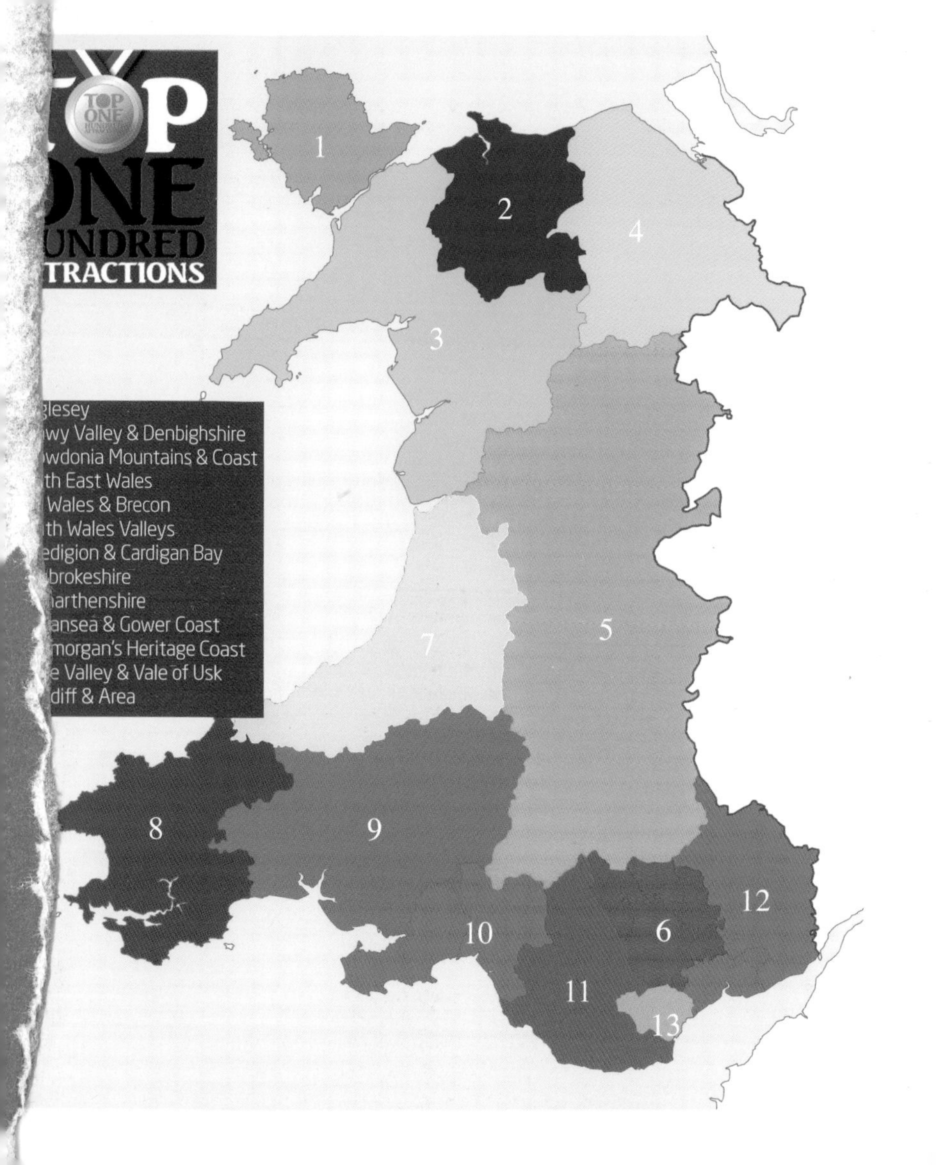

TOP
ONE
UNDRED
TRACTIONS
glesey
wy Valley & Denbighshire
wdonia Mountains & Coast
th East Wales
Wales & Brecon
th Wales Valleys
edigion & Cardigan Bay
brokeshire
arthenshire
ansea & Gower Coast
morgan's Heritage Coast
e Valley & Vale of Usk
diff & Area
1
2
3
4
5
6
7
8
9
10
11
12
13

2020 Edition by Plasma Media Ltd,

Plasma Media Ltd
Company Reg No. 07327527

Address for Plasma Media Ltd
can be found by visiting
www.top100attractions.co.uk
www.plasmamedia.org.uk

A CIP catalogue record is available for this book,
and other in Plasma Media titles from the British Library.

Author: Joshua Stevenson
Designed by Gordon Milton
Edited by Joshua Stevenson
Design Manager: Gordon Milton
Photos: Joshua Stevenson, Neil lambert, Kevin Hughes, Tim Richmond, John Millar
Arnhel de Serra, David Levenson, Paul Harris, Matthew Antrobus, Ben Hall, Chris
Walling. Gordon Milton.

Because of the dynamic nature of the Internet, any web addresses or contact
details in this book may have changed since publication and may not be valid.
All telephone numbers, addresses, contact details and opening times were
correct at the time of going to print.

ISBN: 978-0-9571957-3-8

Foreword

Ve are grateful to you for picking this book from many of the fantastic books that are available on the great ountry of Wales. For many of you that have bought this book, I'm sure it was because you have been to Vales on many occasions, and like me, the country has left you with some very happy memories. For those of ou that have bought this book because you haven't yet visited this magical land, then you are in for a pecial treat. Whatever your reasons for buying this book, we are sure that you will not be disappointed with s content. We at 'Plasma Media Ltd' have brought you the Top 100 of the very best Attractions within Vales and its borders, and with a sprinkle of some of the very best in places to sleep and eat, we are positive hat you will want to visit many of the areas, and attractions that we have featured.

would also like to inform you that not one business featured within this publication have paid any dvertising fees whatsoever. The places to visit, sleep and eat are all endorsed by us because they all offer oth visitor experience set against value for money. This statement is quite a rare one to make nowadays as nost publications have to rely on advertising to survive. All of our profits solely rely on the sales of all of our ooks, which just adds to the credibility of the decisions on who to feature.

inally, this book is just one of what will be 12 of its kind. We will be bringing the Top 100 Attractions from he four corners of England, throughout the length and breadths of Scotland and finally, attractions from all he 32 counties of Ireland. We have taken on the difficult task of looking at, visiting and determining which ttractions are worthy of a Top 100 title. Also, if you have visited an attraction that left a long lasting imprint n your mind, why not visit www.top100attractions.co.uk and tell us about which attraction it was, where is, and why you feel it should be considered for inclusion as being a Top 100Attraction. If after inspecting hat attraction, we determine it too be worthy of a Top 100 title, we will with your permission, publish your ame alongside that attraction's page.

sit the Top 100 Website for further information on all the Attractions, Accommodation, and Restaurants within this book.

www.top100attractions.co.uk

CONTENTS

Various Attractions have earned what we have called 'Hidden Gem' status. Please see below a list of those gems and what they represent.

- Historical Importance
- Gardens & Parklands
- Family Fun
- Heritage

ANGLESEY

Anglesey is one of those places that remains just as magical and mysterious as it did since it was nvaded and made part of the Roman Empire 1,934 years ago. Ever since visiting here with the school nany years ago, I've always had a soft spot for this geologically complex island. The island has several mall towns dotted around it, Llangefni, Menai Bridge, Holyhead just to name but a few. But each one of the towns that you will come across on Anglesey has something very unique to offer the thousands of visitors the island gets on a yearly basis. When you ask people what immediately springs to mind vhen they hear the name Anglesey, they would immediately associate it with getting the ferry from Holyhead to Ireland. But when you ask many others, they too have many fond childhood memories of he place.

During the writing and compiling of this book and whilst living in Beaumaris for a couple of years, I got o meet so many interesting people, some I would definitely like to meet and others maybe not so, but ve met people from all walks of life, and a whole host of varied backgrounds. Whether it's a day on the beach you're after, or a trip to many of its great locations, Anglesey has it all! Anglesey also has a Coastal Path that spans some 200-kilometres (124) miles and boasts some absolutely spectacular views, no natter what kind of weather is thrown at you. All in all you will not be disappointed with your visit here, nd once your holiday has come to an end, why not pop onto our website www.top100attractions. om and tell me and our thousands of other readers what you thought. I hope you have a great time isiting this timeless island.

James Pringle Weavers

t: 01248 717171 e: simplythebest@ewm.co.uk
www.ewm.co.uk

Come and visit Llanfairpwllgwyngullgogerychwyrndrobwllllan-tysiliogogogoch, in store we have a split level licensed restaurant serving hot and cold food, tea for two and outside picnic tables. Two large car/coach parks front and rear of the store. The big name made the village famous now the shopping is even bigger! This truly is a unique shopping experience with everything from luggage to lingerie, welsh whisky to wellingtons, you will surely find something for everyone in our large retail area, Welsh gifts, Hornby shop, clothing, souvenirs, shoe shop, golf shop and so much more. Our newly refurbished restaurant serves traditional Welsh fayre, hot meals, snacks and refreshments all day every day. The New Welsh gifts section cannot be rivalled.

AUTHOR'S REVIEW

If anyone has ever wondered what Wales has in common with its Celtic neighbours of Ireland & Scotland, it has to be their love for high quality garments! James Pringle Weavers is one of The Edinburgh Woollen Mills flagship stores and has a vast array of quality clothing, including Cashmere, fashions, performance Outerwear, kids clothing, homewares, golf and shoe shop. There's also a great Welsh gifts shop and a Whisky & Real Ale shop (try before you buy!) The restaurant serves everything from Bara Brith to delicious Sunday lunches. I enjoyed my time at James Pringle Weavers that much, that I am going back very soon.

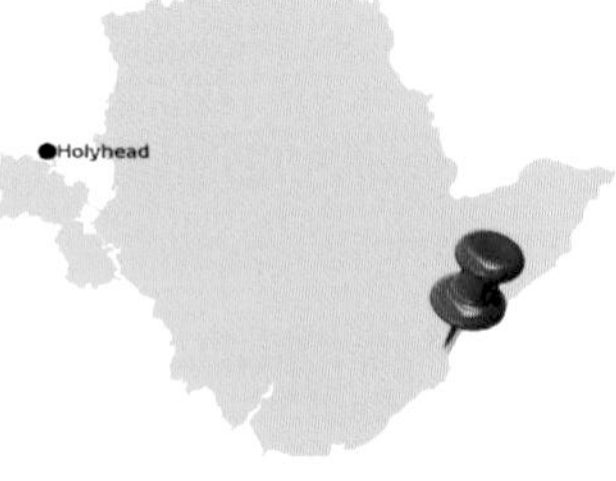

The Station, Llanfairpg, Anglesey, LL61 5UJ

Anglesey Riding Centre

t: 01248 430377
e: angleseyriding@gmail.com
www.angleseyridingcentre.co.uk

Set within Anglesey's AONB and alongside the beautiful Menai Straits with stunning views of Caernarfon Castle and the Snowdonia mountain range beyond, you won't find horse riding in more involving surroundings. Our 5 miles of private bridleways will give you a fantastic, safe introduction to riding, and we're sure that more experienced riders will find plenty here to challenge them too. We cater for all abilities, from the complete beginner to those who've been at it for years. Our indoor riding school is the perfect environment to hone your skills and get you ready to tackle whatever challenge you set your sights on, whatever the weather. Anglesey Riding Centre is fully approved by the British Horse Society (BHS) and by the Pony Club as a Pony Club Riding Centre. It is also a BHS approved Livery Yard and the home base for the Anglesey Riding for the Disabled Association (RDA).

AUTHOR'S REVIEW

One of the worlds most used and loved animals is the horse. From needless battles, to farming our great lands, this great creature has been one of humanities most trusted animals. Here at the Anglesey Riding Centre, you can put that statement to the test by spending some quality time with one of their many horses. With their own network of bridleways, coupled with the stunning beaches on offer here in this corner of the world, a visit to the riding centre will most certainly not disappoint Whether you are a beginner, or a seasoned rider, the staff here at the Anglesey Riding Centre can tailor make your ride depending on your level of confidence. They also have what they call their Unicorns group. This group is specially tailored to children between the ages of 4 and 7 years old and are designed to break them in gently, excuse the pun.

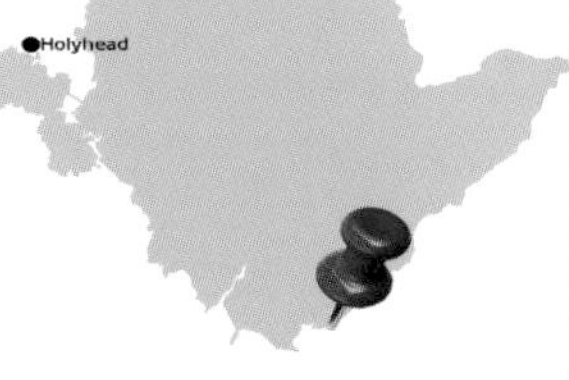

Llanfairpg, Dwyran, Anglesey, LL61 6LQ

RibRide

t: 0333 1234 303
e: info@ribride.co.uk
www.ribride.co.uk

We are Wales' best adventure boat tour company. Our skippers are your fast and fun guides to the natural history of Anglesey. Ride a RIB on the Menai Strait or join us on a Bear Grylls adventure boat tour to the islands and high cliffs of the north Anglesey coast. Come with us for an unbeatable adventure. Our bookings office and main departure location is in Menai Bridge next to the fabulous Dylans Restaurant at post code LL59 5DE. From here we run year round tours to Puffin and Llanddwyn Islands and the infamous Bridges and Swellies. From Easter to October we also operate from Beaumaris, Caernarfon and Holyhead. Trips last from one hour, require no skill and are suitable for ages 4 and up. We also offer private charter for groups up to 11 per boat. These can be from one hour up to an entire day around the Island -a trip of a lifetime!

AUTHOR'S REVIEW

RibRide is a new addition to our Top 100 Attractions books, and after winning their much earned 'Anglesey Tourism Award' they have earned with pride their place in our popular Wales edition. In my honest opinion, although Anglesey in itself, is a huge attraction and brings hundreds of thousands of visitors every year to this ancient Celtic island.

Anglesey is still very lucky to have been chosen by RibRide as its base for all of its activities. This is not just a thrill seekers type of attraction, and even if you're not confident on the water, their trained and informative staff will very quickly put your mind at ease. This attraction really does allow you to see this part of the North Wales coast in a totally different light, and for that very reason, RibRide offers total value for money.

Menai Bridge LL59 5DE   Holyhead-Sat Nav post code LL65 1YA.

Anglesey Transport Museum

t: 01248 440344 e: email@angleseytransportmuseum.co.uk
www.angleseytransportmuseum.co.uk

Walk back in time and see over 130 gleaming classic cars and vehicles from the 1920s onwards. Set in a replica of a 1940s cobbled village street, you can view an assortment of vehicles including motorbikes, cars, vans, military and agricultural vehicles, some of which have even been used in films!
We have a Cafe on site featuring local produce, a play area with outside seating and panoramic views of Snowdonia.
We are a disabled friendly venue and have received positive reviews from www.disabledholidayinfo.org.uk along with other websites and previous visitors.
We also have electric hookup for caravans and shower facilities!
Dont forget to keep an eye on our facebook page for all upcoming events!

AUTHOR'S REVIEW

During my time as a travel author I have travelled to many attractions, some being of course transport museums. From the British Leyland museum in Lancashire, to the Transport museum in Gaydon, they have all made their way into one of my books, but one such Transport museum that took me completely by surprise, was the Tacla Taid Transport Museum based in Newborough, Anglesey, which is based to the west of the island. As seen on TV, this museum lives up to its reputation and whether or not you are a lover of Motor vehicles, there is literally some-thing for everyone here. This attraction despite its greatness, is still very much a family run business and all of the effort that goes into the restoration of each vehicle, goes into making your visit a most memorable one. I also found the entrance fee to be very reasonable and most definitely worth every penny.

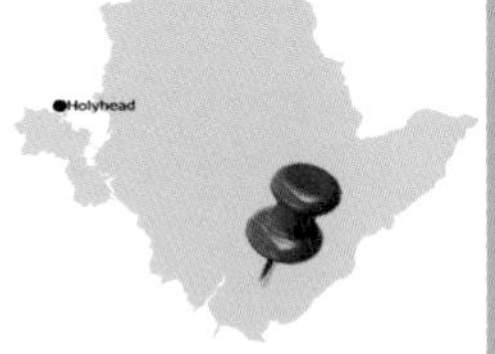

Tyddyn Pwrpas, Newborough, Anglesey, LL61 6TN

Anglesey Circuit

t: 01407 811400 e: admin@angleseycircuit.com
www.angleseycircuit.com

Set on the west coast of Anglesey, overlooking the Irish Sea and the Snowdonia mountain range beyond, Anglesey Circuit provides visitors with a challenging and exciting circuit in a breathtaking location. Whether you are visiting the Circuit as a competitor, spectator, for driving instruction or as part of a corporate activity day, you are assured of a day to remember. It is one of the few circuits to be designed and constructed with an entirely new concept. Full advantage has been taken of the the undulating landscape and created a circuit with imaginative cambers, a blend of fast sections, technically challenging mid range corners complimented with two hairpin bends and a 10% banked corner. The alternative circuit configurations enable Anglesey Circuit to offer the ideal facility for a wide variety of events.

AUTHOR'S REVIEW

It is no hidden secret that there are many people that don't know Anglesey has a world class racing circuit, but after next year that will all be history. Soon to be hosting Formula 3, Anglesey Circuit is set to be put on the racing world map. I was very fortunate to be shown a few laps in a sports car, around this amazing track and that experience will be one I will never ever forget. Travelling at speeds in excess of 100mph I was taken into the world of Jenson Button and Lewis Hamilton. But these are not impossible dreams; these are dreams that can be made to come true at Anglesey circuit.

Holyhead

Anglesey Circuit, Ty Croes, Anglesey, LL63 5TF

Anglesey Sea Zoo

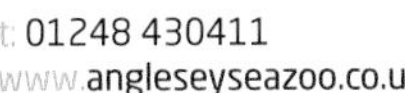

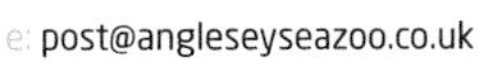

t: 01248 430411 e: post@angleseyseazoo.co.uk
www.angleseyseazoo.co.uk

Anglesey Sea Zoo is a unique aquarium with over 40 tanks displaying the best of British marine wildlife! Don't expect to see large sharks, tropical fish or sea turtles – instead you'll find fascinating creatures from around the coasts of the UK, such as octopus, lobsters, seahorses, conger eels and small British catsharks! You'll also learn about British marine habitats and the research and conservation work which is helping to save them. As well seeing all our animals, you can learn all about British marine habitats and the research and conservation work which is helping to save them, both here and further afield, including our British seahorse breeding programme and the Lobster Hatchery of Wales. Explore British marine habitats including incredible invertebrates in the No Bone Zone, the wolf fish lair, a real crashing wave, a creepy shipwreck and a kelp forest full of big huge fish.

AUTHOR'S REVIEW

The Anglesey Sea Zoo has become the very fabric of what Anglesey is all about. Owned and ran by Frankie Hobro, the Sea Zoo isn't just a local attraction, it has become an important conservation centre, that has Britains Sealife at its very core. Every time I visit the Sea Zoo, I can't get over how I see something that I didn't spot the last time. I find the staff very knowledgeable and approachable and they will always go out of their way to answer any questions you may have. Nothing is ever too much trouble. Now that's what I call a Top 100 Attraction! The Sea Zoo's main months are of course during the season, but their work is endless and as you make your way around the centre, all of the hard work they do on a daily basis becomes ever so apparent, I love this little attraction and I know you will too!

Brynsiencyn, Anglesey, LL61 6TQ

Oriel Môn

t: 01248 724444
www. orielynysmon.info

Since opening in 1991 Oriel Môn near Llangefni has established itself as one of Wales's leading art venues. The contemporary spaces showcase the work of well-known and emerging artists whilst the Kyffin Williams Gallery shows the work of one of Wales's best loved artists and regularly provides an opportunity to view the work of other famous individuals from private and national collections. Celebrated as one of the greatest wildlife artists of the 20th century the largest collection of work by the multi-talented Charles Tunnicliffe is held at the Oriel.
The museum which includes the Discovery Den gives an introduction to Anglesey's history. With regular children and adult workshops, talks and events, a well-stocked shop and a busy café there is something for everyone.

AUTHOR'S REVIEW

This new edition of the Top 100 Attractions in Wales book is even bigger and better than before, mainly down to the great attractions that are featured within its pages. One of those great attractions and one that is absolutely huge on Anglesey, is that of Oriel Môn, and in Welsh, Oriel means gallery. This purpose built, bright and modern building is really reflective of the type of art you can expect to find here. Despite being a modern building, Oriel Môn has a certain warmth about it, and this certainly has the gallery staff to be thankful for. All of Anglesey's culture and heritage through art is based within its walls and no visit is complete without taking a break in its well stocked Blas Mwy Café, translated into English, Blas Mwy simply means 'more flavour' No matter your level of love for art, you will really enjoy your visit here.

Rhosmeirch,Llangefni,Ynys Môn, LL77 7TQ

RSPB South Stack

t: 01407 762100 e: southstack@rspb.org.uk
www.rspb.org.uk/southstack

Dramatically located within Anglesey's Area of Outstanding Natural Beauty, RSPB South Stack is the place to experience breathtaking landscape, fascinating history, and wonderful spectrum of wildlife and marine life. Stroll along the trails and you'll see the iconic South Stack lighthouse, huge seabird cities crammed onto the sheer cliffs, and heathland of heather, gorse and wildflowers.

Look out for the charismatic choughs - on windy days their acrobatic flying is a fascinating sight, whilst peregrine falcons, the world's fastest bird, can be seen dropping prey in mid-air for their young to try and catch. Get an even closer view of the spectacular seabird city at Ellin's Tower where up to 10,000 seabirds make their home. You'll be able to watch puffins, razorbills and guillemots raising their young and also spot porpoises, dolphins and seals from viewing points and on live cameras.Young ones will love our play area. You can scramble your way to the top of the climbing frame; try to keep a steady balance on the log stumps; hop onto the see-saw then jump onto our basket swing which arguably has one of the best views in Wales.

AUTHOR'S REVIEW

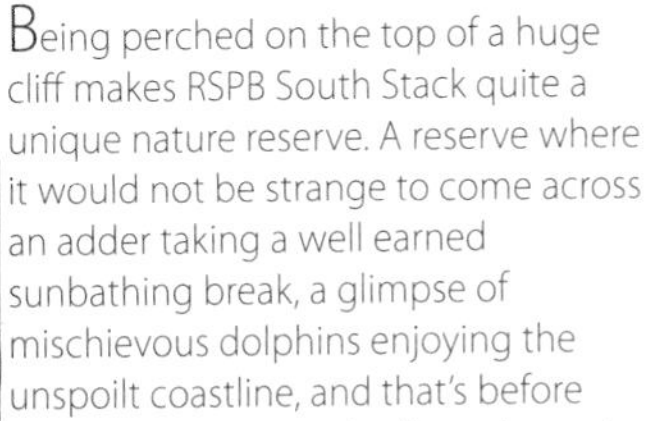

Being perched on the top of a huge cliff makes RSPB South Stack quite a unique nature reserve. A reserve where it would not be strange to come across an adder taking a well earned sunbathing break, a glimpse of mischievous dolphins enjoying the unspoilt coastline, and that's before we have even started talking about the huge range of birds that south stack has visiting its reserve on a regular basis. All in all I had a wonderful time here at South Stack, and this reserve certainly fits in with our 'value for money being set against visitor experience criteria. Finally the staff were all so friendly, which just adds to the enjoyment of visiting this great site!

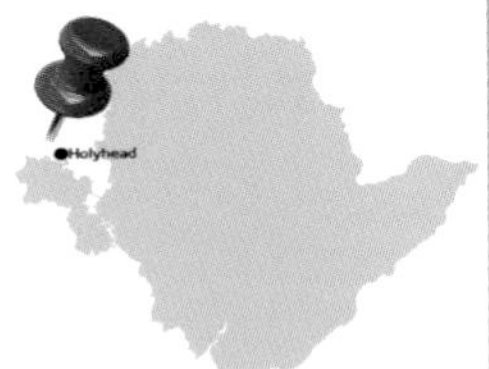

Nr Holyhead, Anglesey, LL65 1YH

Funsport & Surf Cafe

t: 01407-810899 e: info@funsportonline.co.uk
www.funsportonline.co.uk

Funsport is a Windsurfing and water sport shop, mainly dealing in windsurfing, kite surfing and surfing accessories, but we also provide our customers with surf-wear and water-sport accessories such as wake-boarding. During windy weekends, hordes of windsurfers and kitesurfers will come down to Rhosneigr from all over Great Britain. They enjoy extremely good conditions for every level of sailing in a friendly and radical atmosphere! Rhosneigr is no doubt one of the best spots in the UK for the intermediate to advanced windsurfer and kitesurfer. We are here to make it the spot with the best atmosphere both on and off of the water.

Windsurf: At the shop we have all levels of windsurfing equipment from beginners and intermediate to advanced boards and sails.All our equipment comes from world renowned companies such as: Simmer Sails & Boards, Tabou, Gaastra, Fanatic, Mistral and many more...

AUTHOR'S REVIEW

North Wales has become the adventure capital of the United Kingdom and one of the attractions that makes that statement all the more true, is Funsport here in Rhosneigr. With decades of experience between them, all of the staff here at Funsport, are some of the most experienced water sports instructors that North Wales has to offer. When it comes to choosing our attractions, a lot of time and effort goes into making sure all of our readers receive value for money, set against visitor experience and that's before we talk about lasting memories.

Funsport, along with their many affordable water based packages has all of those in abundance. Also on-site, is their well stocked surf shop and the food at the Surf Cafe really is second to none. With locally sourced produce and all at very reasonable prices, I wouldn't recommend you eat anywhere else after your session.

1 Beach Terrace, Rhosneigr, Anglesey, LL64 5QB

Pili Palas Nature World

t: 01248-712474
www.pilipalas.co.uk

e: info@pilipalas.co.uk

A day out at Pili Palas can be a magical experience for all the family, whatever the weather! So come along, enter a steamy environment full of lush vegetation and waterfalls with LIVE butterflies flying all around you. This is the magical world of Pili Palas. But there's a lot more than just butterflies to see. You'll meet Charlie, Elvis, Jake and a host of other feathered friends in our birdhouse. We have plenty of snakes and lizards of all kinds, and you're sure to be able to get up close to some of them in our popular animal handling sessions. If someone in your family likes bugs then they'll have the time of their life in our bug-zone, home to our hissing cockroaches, millipedes, locusts, giant snails and much more. Then we dare you to visit the tropical lair of tarantulas, scorpions and fire-bellied toads. Don't forget pets' corner where you can meet the rabbits and guinea pigs. Take a walk through our farmyard where our pygmy goats Milly and Molly live happily with Bert and Ernie.

AUTHOR'S REVIEW

We were just as selective in our selection process of the attractions here on Anglesey, as we were in any of our other areas, but one attraction we just had to have in, was Pili Palas. With new additions being added every year, it's not hard to see why this attraction gets thousands of visitors every season. With the addition of the ever popular Meerkats, it just goes to show, the management here at this attraction, really have their fingers on the pulse when it comes to knowing what additions to make year in year out. I know it sounds a bit of a cliché, but this really is a place for all ages young or old. I will be visiting here again soon, and maybe this time, I just may get to see the Meerkats a bit closer than those on TV!

Penmynydd Road, Menai Bridge, Anglesey, LL59 5RP

Anglesey Adventures

t: 07896 239951 e: info@angleseyadventures.co.uk
www: angleseyadventures.co.uk

Anglesey Adventures is an adventure activity company that provides adventure days and breaks on Anglesey and throughout North Wales. If you are looking for an outdoor experience with a difference then our adventure breaks will not disappoint you.

We regularly run Coasteering, Kayaking and Climbing days so get in touch if you'd like to book any of these activities. We also run regular Mountain Days in Snowdonia and are now taking bookings for 2020 for a Guided Walk up Snowdon for just £40 per person and a Mountain Hike across the Glyderau range for just £55 per person.

The Isle of Anglesey is an absolute playground for the adventure enthusiast with a huge range of activities to choose from. Our location on Holy Island provides a stunning coastline, towering sea cliffs and numerous award winning beaches.

AUTHOR'S REVIEW

Having featured Anglesey Adventures in previous editions of this Wales book, we are no strangers to the amazing activities available to you when entrusting them with your outdoor adventure. Despite now being under new ownership, Steve Miles has worked for the company for many years and has probably single handedly been the driving force behind the companies success, so much so, he and his partner Lynn, since buying the business have turned Anglesey Adventures into the best activity business on the island. But don't be fooled by the name, their reach also stretches out into Snowdonia itself and whether your a seasoned outdoor activity goer or just a novice, their team of experienced staff are able to put you at ease and work to your level with the greatest of ease, so what are you waiting for, hop onto their website and see if they have an activity for you!

Ffordd Beibio, Holyhead, Anglesey, LL65 2EN

Tregoegan Holiday Accommodation

Tregoegan, Pencarnisiog, Ty Croes, Anglesey, LL63 5SE

T: 01407-810378 www.bedandbreakfast-anglesey.com E: tina12345@hotmail.co.u

Tregoegan sits in an acre of semi wild garden which won a wildlife award in 2008. It is a haven for wildlife birds and butterflies. We are approximately two miles from the popular watersports beach 'Rhosneigr' where watersports equipment such as canoes are available to rent. Windsurfing and kite surfing lessons can be booked or your own equipment can be used.There are cafes and restaurants serving food to suit most tastes as well as shops and pubs. Other beautiful sandy 'blue flag' beaches such as Cable Bay and Aberffraw are within close proximity.We have been complimented on our hea traditional breakfasts, made from fresh local produce, sure to fill you up for the day. Vegetarian options available.

Tal y Foel Farm B&B

Dwyran, Anglesey, LL61 6LQ

T: 01248-430977 www.tal-y-foel.co.uk E: judy@tal-y-foel.co.uk

Welcome to Tal-y-Foel, with spectacular views over the Menai Straits, where you can have a break tha a little bit different! You can not only relax in our luxury WTB-approved four-star farm accommodation (we have two rooms with ensuite whirlpool baths!) and also a caravan in a private paddock. You can go fishing or birdwatching, or enjoy horse-riding in the adjacent Anglesey Riding Centre. They can offer you bespoke packages for riding holidays including Bed & Breakfast for horses. Some of our guests come to ride, but most just come to enjoy a peaceful rural location. Enjoy what can only be described as our breathtaking view over the Menai Straits towards the historic Caernarfo Castle. Sit back, relax and watch the world go by in this simply outstanding location.

White Lodge Caravan Park

Penlon, Newborough, Isle of Anglesey, LL61 6RS

T: 01248-440 230 www.whitelodgecaravanpark.com E: info@whitelodgecaravanpark.cc

Only five minutes by car to Llanddwyn Beach or 30-40 minute walk from the site (1.4 miles) through Newborough Warren and Forrest. White Lodge lies in around 2 acres of peaceful flat pasture land. Sheltered from the prevailing winds by conifer trees, the camp field enjoys views towards Caernarfon and the Snowdonian mountain range. Our small family site is fully equipped with two ladies and gen toilets, and two ladies and gents showers, a dish wash area with two sinks, electric hook-ups, childrer play area, table tennis room and on-site cafe.

We are open every day of the year, we cater mainly for families, well behaved dogs are welcome, but ask that you keep your dog restrained whilst on site, and to walk them off the campsite.

Parc yr Odyn Farmhouse Accommodation

Penlon, Newborough, Isle of Anglesey, LL61 6RS

T: 01248-450566 www.parcyrodyn.com E: parcyrodyn@yahoo.com

Parc yr Odyn is a modern Anglesey farmhouse that commands panoramic views of the Snowdonia mountain range and is an excellent base for exploring the island, touring North Wales and convenien for the ferry crossing to Ireland. We have created a traditional Welsh farmhouse ambience together w all modern comforts. The warmth of the welcome is guaranteed regardless of the weather and we are happy to share our home. We have created a traditional Anglesey farmhouse ambience together with all modern comforts. Every effort is made to ensure the comfort of guests, while maintaining the trad tional feel of a Welsh farmhouse. The warmth of the welcome is guaranteed regardless of the weathe and we are happy to share our home with others who want to enjoy peaceful and lovely surrounding

The Prince Llewelyn

Abberffraw, Ty Croes, Anglesey, LL63 5YU

T: 01407-840090   www.princellewelynanglesey.co.uk   E: bookings@princellewelynanglesey.co.uk

The Prince Llewelyn is an 8 bedroom Bed and Breakfast situated on the west coast of Anglesey, in the small village of Aberffraw, and owned by Charles & Theresa. We are close to Rhosneigr, Malltraeth & Newborough and also the Anglesey Circuit (Trac Mon). With plenty of places to visit, things to do and beaches to relax on, Aberffraw really is the perfect location to base yourself when exploring the Isle of Anglesey. For those of you participating, spectating or marshalling at Trac Mon (the Anglesey Circuit), we are only 2 miles away.Walkers and cyclists are well catered for with facilities to hang and dry wet clothing and boots, along with space for bike storage. For those of you walking the Anglesey Coastal Path, we are just a couple of hundred yards from the path, extremely well situated on your route.

Arlanfor B&B and Self Catering Accommodation

Moelfre, Anglesey, LL70 9PZ

T: 01248-410555   www.arlanfor.co.uk   E: enq@arlanfor.co.uk

Enjoy one of the best views you will ever see when you stay at Arlanfor. The light and spacious bedrooms, with seating areas, all have panoramic sea and mountain views. After a fabulous night's sleep in our luxurious beds you can enjoy a Welsh Continental breakfast served in the dinning room or on the deck, overlooking the sea. Located right on the coast in Moelfre we are ideal for walkers, bird watchers, fishermen, beach lovers, families or people who just want to watch the world go by. The sea is literally on our doorstep. We also have 2 luxurious self catering apartments.

Minffordd Luxury Caravan Park

Moelfre, Anglesey, LL70 9PZ

T: 01248-410555   www.minfforddcaravanpark.com   E: enq@minfforddcaravanpark.com

Our Award Winning 5* Caravan Park is a quaint garden park of only 10 caravans, each with its own outside area. The park is sheltered and peaceful, surrounded by trees, bushes and flowers, with ample space between caravans. Wooden tables and benches are positioned near each caravan for enjoyable 'al fresco' meals. There are plenty of recreational areas, including a small play area with swings, a slide, climbing frame and sand pit for young children to enjoy. An adjoining paddock is provided for ball games and other activities. Minffordd Caravans all come fully equipped enabling you to relax and enjoy your holiday knowing everything is to hand.

Cremlyn Farm B&B

Cremlyn, Beaumaris, Anglesey, LL58 8YR

T: 01248-810420   www.cremlynfarm   E: od.jones@btinternet.com

Cremlyn farmhouse, built in the year 1859, is spacious and full of character. The house is set in 460 acres of prime agricultural land on which sheep, beef cattle and cereals are produced. Superb location for a relaxing break in the countryside. A warm and friendly welcome awaits you. Cremlyn is only 1½ miles from the historic town of Beaumaris, with attractions including the Castle, Gaol, golf course, walks, beach, children's playing areas, fishing trips or shopping. Beaumaris is probably the best town on the island to go out for a meal, with excellent restaurants and brasserie, etc. The lounge has a large bay window overlooking the large garden, and there is a patio area with a barbeque. Excellent breakfasts, made with local produce whenever possible, are served from 6:30 to 9:30am.

Rhosboeth B&B

Amlwch Road, Benlech, Anglesey, LL74 8RU

T: 01248-853957 www.rhosboeth.co.uk E: ruthtebach@gmail.com

Being over 300 years old -and the first building to be listed by CADW- Rhosboeth has a wealth of character and original features. However, all our rooms are a successful marriage of traditional and modern, that provides our guests with very comfortable but unique accommodation. Our Tea Rooms have been regarded as being amongst the top ten Tea Rooms on the Coastal Path of Wales. Both bedrooms have all the facilities expected from a 4 star establishment: tea making facilities with complimentary homemade cake or biscuits and Welsh bottled water, flat screen television, hair dryer, i-pod docking, digital clock radio and hairdryer . An honesty fridge is placed just outside the bedroor with a supply of soft drinks and chocolate!

Ingledene B&B

Ravenspoint Road, Treaddur Bay, Anglesey, LL65 2YU

T: 01407-861026 www.ingledene.co.uk E: info@ingledene.co.uk

Situated in the heart of Trearddur Bay with magnificent sea views to the front and towards the Snowc nia mountain range from the rear, Ingledene is an ideal base for your holiday or short break. Walkers the Anglesey Coastal Path need only turn in at the gate as we are situated on the Path. For a comforta and relaxing stay, we offer a choice of guest rooms, many with ensuite and all rooms at the front of th house have stunning sea views. Binoculars are provided in all sea view rooms. Relax and watch the g rious sunsets, wake up to the sound of the waves. To the rear of the main house is our holiday cottage "Ingledene Bach". Originally the servants' quarters, the cottage is light and airy and although it has no direct sea views, is still close to the beach and provides the perfect base for a traditional seaside holid

Nant Yr Odyn Country Hotel & Restaurant

Turnpike Nant, Llangefni, Anglesey, LL77 7YE

T: 01248-723354 www.nantyrodyn.co.uk E: nantyrodyn@gmail.com

Tastefully converted from an 18th Century farm complex, Nant-yr-Odyn is situated near the centre of the picturesque Isle of Anglesey and is within easy reach of the commercial and administrative centre of Llangefni just 1 mile to the north and only 500 metres from the newly completed A55 Euro route Chester to Holyhead. All our light & airy bedrooms are en-suite and are individually furnished in a country style with colour television, direct dial telephone, radio alarm, and tea & coffee making faciliti business users will find our rooms have plenty of space to work with ample light, while ground floor accommodation is available for our less able guests.

Craig Eithin B&B

Caergeiliog, Valley, Anglesey, LL65 3HR

T: 01407-749355 E: scull1.dw@googlemail.com

Craig Eithin B&B is a cosy single-storey B&B, surrounded by lovely gardens and fields, located in a prim position to experience and explore the wonderful island of Anglesey. The accommodation:
The bedrooms are newly converted, modern and comfortable.
1 double-bed room with full en-suite shower (garden view)
1 twin-bed room with full en-suite shower (garden view)
All rooms have new smart TVs, free fast WiFi and, tea and coffee making facilities
There is a single lounge and dining room for guests to share

Blackthorn Farm B&B

South Stack Road, Penrhosfeilw, Treaddur Bay, Anglesey, LL65 2LT

T: 01407-765262 www.blackthornfarm.co.uk E: enquiries@blackthornfarm.co.uk

Blackthorn Farm is an award winning family run Bed and Breakfast, Camping and Touring site. Situated in an idyllic spot on peaceful Holy Island in North Wales, it is set in 18 acres of outstanding unspoilt beauty with panoramic views encompasing the Irish Sea, the Snowdonia mountains, and the breathtaking coastal views of the Isle of Anglesey. Within walking distance of Blackthorn Farm is a beautiful local beach and peaceful coastal trails where you can enjoy the peace and quiet, and more often than not catch a glimpse of some of the local wildlife.

Within a few minutes drive is the famous South Stack lighthouse as well as the town of Holyhead which offers rail facilities to the rest of North Wales and high speed ferry services to Ireland.

Blackthorn Farm Self Catering & Camping

South Stack Road, Penrhosfeilw, Treaddur Bay, Anglesey, LL65 2LT

T: 01407-765262 www.blackthornfarm.co.uk E: enquiries@blackthornfarm.co.uk

This property is 10 minutes walk from the beach. Award-winning Blackthorn Farm is set in an Area of Outstanding Natural Beauty, 10 minutes' walk from Porth Dafarch Beach in Holyhead. It offers a self-catering cottage and comfortable rooms, most with fantastic sea and countryside views.

Cosy rooms include tea and coffee making facilities and a flat-screen TV with DVD player. The charming cottage has 2 bedrooms and includes an open-plan kitchen and lounge, dining area and a private garden. Free Wi-Fi and free parking are provided. Set in 18-acre headlands, Blackthorn Farm has a great location for walking, fishing, bird watching and sailing. The town centre and Ferry Terminal are 5 minutes' drive away and Holyhead Train Station is 2 miles away.

Castellor Bed & Breakfast

Cemaes Bay, Anglesey, LL67 0ND

T: 01407-10789 www.cemaesbaybandb.com E: castellorbandb@btinternet.com

In a stressful, busy world, the sea calms and connects us. Imagine how relaxing it will be when you wake up and see this view. Our boutique bed and breakfast is for discerning Grown Ups Only. We opened in summer 2016 - the grand Georgian house has been completely renovated by your hosts Neil and Lavinia and is now one of the most lavish guest houses on the island. We have five charming rooms, all on the ground floor, each with free WiFi, Sealy Posturetech Geltex pocket sprung beds and 600 thread count Egyptian cotton linens. The rooms provide high standard en-suite facilities with Duck Island toiletries and the largest three rooms having power showers. Homemade cake is waiting for you in your room to revive you after your journey. There's also chilled, filtered water, fresh milk and a range of loose leaf teas or freshly roasted coffee.

Maen Hir B&B

Pentraeth Road, Menai Bridge, Anglesey, LL59 5RW

T: 01248-716077 www.maenhir.co.uk E: maenhir61@yahoo.com

Featuring free WiFi, a restaurant and a terrace, Maen Hir offers accommodation in Menai Bridge, 15.5 miles from Llandudno. Guests can enjoy the on-site restaurant. Free private parking is available on site. All rooms are en-suite and have a flat-screen TV with Sky channels including sports and movies. You will find a kettle with tea, coffee and fresh milk in the room. For your comfort, you will find free toiletries and a hairdryer. here is a shared lounge for guests to use during their stay. There is a choice of restaurants nearby in Menai Bridge town.

Maen Hir is situated within easy reach of the A55 for Holyhead port also Bangor University. You can engage in various activities, such as golfing and cycling.

The Valley Hotel

London Road, Valley, Isle of Anglesey, LL63 3DU

T: 01407-740203 www.valley-hotel-anglesey.co.uk E: booking@valley-hotel-anglesey.co.u

Established for 21 years, the family-run Valley Hotel, located on the beautiful island of Anglesey. A wic choice of scenic beaches are merely ust 10 minutes away by car. Free WiFi is available in the main pub area. The bright and airy accommodation offers traditional features complemented by modern facilities. Each room includes a TV, work desk and full private bathroom. Much of Anglesey's coastline designated an Area of Outstanding Natural Beauty and offers excellent walks just a few minutes' drive from the hotel. The Valley Hotel's friendly bar serves local and national cask ales, and the hotel restaurant provides an extensive à la carte menu. Guests can enjoy their food and drink in the large garden.

Boltholes & Hideaways - Anglesey Holiday Cottages

T: 07918-901843 www.boltholesandhideaways.co.uk - E: info@boltholesandhideaways.co.

Escape to Anglesey with stunning coastal scenery, sandy coves, rock pools and clear dark skies ready star gazing. From town boltholes to coastal hideaways, our Anglesey holiday cottages have everythin you need for a break away from it all. Each of the cottages in our collection has its own unique person ality and we focus on making your stay feel relaxing and special. Enjoy unrivalled sea, countryside or roof top views whilst relaxing with friends and family. We have cottages with open fires, wood burnin stoves, under floor heating, hot tubs, whirlpool baths, roll top baths - and of course the views we all love to write home about. Anglesey holiday cottages are a very popular choice for self catering breaks This diverse island with its wonderful coastline, that is now so accessible due to the Anglesey Coastal Path, and an interior that is a green treasure trove of small villages and market towns.

North Wales
Holiday Cottages

North Wales Holiday Cottages

39 Station Road, Deganwy, Conwy, LL31 9DF

T: 01492-582492 www.northwalesholidaycottages.co.uk info@northwalesholidaycottages.co.

North Wales Holidays Cottages is a holiday letting agency in the beautiful region of North Wales. We act on the behalf of the owners of a wide variety of privately-owned holiday properties in all parts of the area. Our properties allow you the freedom to come and go as you please, allowing you to experience the delights of North Wales at your own pace. The Isle of Anglesey (Ynys Mon in Welsh) is a beautiful part of Wales set apart from the Welsh mainland by the Menai Strait. Ynys Môn has somethir to suit every taste from the numerous water sports, coasteering and fishing opportunities along the coast to the fast paced world of motor sport at Trac Môn, fun and learning at the Anglesey Sea Zoo an Pilli Palas and much, much more making it the perfect location to start your self-catering holiday in North Wales.

Holland Hotel

London Road, Valley, Isle of Anglesey, LL63 3DU

T: 01407-238181 www.hollandhotel.co.uk

Situated in Llanfachraeth, Holland Hotel features a garden and a bar. This hotel offers free WiFi. There is a restaurant. The units in the hotel are fitted with a kettle. Every room comes with a private bathroom with a bath, free toiletries and a hairdryer. At Holland Hotel each room is fitted with a desk and a flat-screen TV.Guests at the accommodation can enjoy a Full English/Irish breakfast. Holyhead is 4.3 miles from Holland Hotel. This property also has one of the best-rated locations in Llanfachraeth! Guests are happier about it compared to other properties in the area.This property is also rated for the best value in Llanfachraeth! Guests are getting more for their money when compared to other properties in this town.

Holland Arms Hotel

Pentre Berw, Gaerwen, Anglesey, LL60 6HY

T: 01248-421651 www.hollandarmshotel.com E:hollandhotel1@gmail.com

Holland Arms Hotel is a bed and breakfast located in Gaerwen. This 3-star bed and breakfast features free WiFi and a garden. Guests can make use of a bar. All rooms in the bed and breakfast are fitted with a kettle. All rooms are fitted with a private bathroom with a bath. The rooms in Holland Arms Hotel are equipped with a flat-screen TV and free toiletries.

A vegetarian, Full English/Irish or continental breakfast is available daily at the property.

Holyhead is 14.9 miles from the accommodation. This property also has one of the best-rated locations in Gaerwen! Guests are happier about it compared to other properties in the area.

Tafarn y Rhos

Rhostrehwfa, Llangefni, Anglesey, LL77 7YU

T: 01248-724404 www.robinsonsbrewery.com/tafarnyrhos E: tafarnyrhos2018@outlook.com

The Tafarn Y Rhos is situated in the Anglesey village of Rhostrehwfa some 2 miles from the market town of Llangefni and conveniently located just off the A5. There is always a warm welcome here where customers can choose from our traditional locally sourced food menu. You can also enjoy a pint (or two) of our award-winning cask ales. We have 11 en-suite letting bedrooms and are an ideal base for guests to stay whilst enjoying the beauty of the nearby Snowdonia National Park or the Anglesey coastline. Make a night of it! With super-comfy beds available, and those little home comforts, we're sure you'll have a great night's sleep.

Sandy Mount House

High Street, Rhosneigr, Anglesey, LL64 5UX

T: 01407-253102 www.sandymounthouse.co.uk E: info@sandymounthouse.co.uk

Sandy Mount House is a contemporary beach house restaurant & bar set in the relaxed seaside village of Rhosneigr in Anglesey. A home from home to eat, gather & sleep. Think cosy corners, log fires & stylish interiors. Sandy Mount House will be passionate about delivering the simple pleasures done well – design, warmth, great food and hospitality with a side of fun. We are creating seven individually designed guest rooms at our new venue – five of them oversized (with some interconnecting ones, perfect for family visits), the other two with spectacular sea views. Stylish, thoughtful, spacious and above all, seriously comfortable. Check in:15:00 till 23:00 Early check-in available on request

Check out:11:00 . Late check-out available on request. Child Policy:No preference.

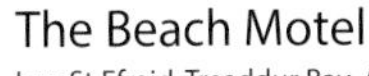

The Beach Motel

Lon St Ffraid, Treaddur Bay, Anglesey, LL65 2YT

T: 01407-860332 www.thebeachmotel.co.uk E: info@thebeachmotel.co.uk

We are a family run motel that offers great value accommodation in the heart of Trearddur Bay, Anglesey. We are just short stroll from Trearddur Bay's beautiful blue flag beach and only a 10 minute drive from nearby Holyhead. We have clean, modern rooms that are all en-suite with tea &coffee making facilities, a flat screen TV, hair dryer with free wifi and parking. Our bathrooms are fitted with showers and whirlpool spa baths, perfect to relax in after exploring the island or a day on the beach. Our Driftwoord Restaurant & Bar serves delicious homemade food, local cask ales and our famous traditional carvery on a Sunday. For those using the ferry, we are happy to arrange late arrivals and early departures prior to your stay with us.

Jolly's

5 Bulkeley Terrace, Beaumaris LL58 8AY

T: 01248-811111 E: jollysbeaumaris@gmail.com

Located on the waterfront and a short stroll away from the Beaumaris Castle, Jollys Coffee House and Patisserie serves up a variety of sweet and savoury treats along with afternoon teas. This quaint little eatery is decorated with floral wallpapers, plush leather sofas and chandeliers bringing together elements of both traditional and contemporary design.

Review 5 Star Fantastic. Came in fifteen minutes before closing and the staff there were more than welcoming to let us sit in. Was pleasantly surprised all tea and coffee and cake selections were availab even though it was so close to closing. We had a chai tea latte and mocha and a selection from the pa serie which was absolutely gorgeous! Will definitely be back, and will recommend to friends!

Pier House Bistro

Seafront, Beaumaris, Anglesey, LL58-8BS

T: 01248-811055 www.pierhousebistro.com E: robertcharlton1983@gmail.com

Pier House Bistro is situated on the seafront, Beaumaris, set in idyllic North Wales. From our bistro and terrace, enjoy stunning views of the Menai Straits and the breathtaking Snowdonia mountain range. Our culinary influences are eclectic, inspired by flavours from around the world with our own unique twist. We source fresh local ingredients that are expertly infused with flavours known, loved and trusted. Our dishes are homemade with much care and attention. We offer a tasty selection of sweet bites and deserts for your fancy. To compliment our food we have a wide range of high quality teas ar coffees, or, if you prefer, choose from our selection of wines and beers.

Tredici Italian Kitchen

13, Castle Street, Beaumaris, LL58 8AP

T: 01248-811230 www.tredicibeaumaris.com E: tredici@outlook.com

Welcome to Tredici Italian Kitchen, an inviting restaurant based in the heart of Beaumaris. Tredici was born out of sheer passion for Italian cooking. We aim to use quality ingredients with traditional and modern cooking methods to bring you colourful, vibrant and rich flavours of Italy. Here at Tredici we offer fine Italian cooking in beautiful surroundings. An intimate setting with a warm atmosphere, perfect for a romantic meal or to relax with friends and enjoy Italian cuisine at its best. We pride ourselves on our authentic Italian chef who produces a wide range of homemade breads and pizza dough. Our menu boasts a wide selection of antipasti, pasta and pizza.
Various booking options available, please contact us for reservations and more information.

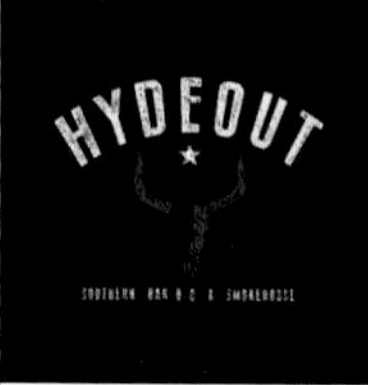

The Hydeout Bar-B-Q & Smokehouse

1 Coronation Road, Menai Bridge, Anglesey, LL59 5BD

T: 01248-345956 www. hydeoutbbq.com E: howdyhydeout@gmail.com

Hydeout was born out of the sheer love of American barbeque. The word originally means a social gathering with food. We aim to offer you true american barbecue smoked low and slow enjoyed in the relaxed surrounding of a Texan Bar-B-Q joint. We smoke our meats fresh, here, everyday over hickory a fruit woods, we also use a charcoal Inka oven for steaks and burgers, all this bringing you toe wiggling flavours from across the southern states.

Trip Advisor Review -5 Stars. Superb

Had a lovely meal when I visited the other day,waitress Amy treated me like a queen and the food was die for. Definitely calling back soon!! ,the service was brill and the staff was kind.

Quays Cafe

Machine Street, Amlwch, Anglesey, LL68 9HA

T: 0786-793-1014 www.quayscafe.com E: info@quayscafe.com

Situated in the beautiful historic port of Amlwch, The Quays Café is in a prime location to cater to your needs whether you intend to spend your day on the golf course, out at sea fishing or just walking along the coast admiring the breath-taking views. The Quays has been established in the port for a number of years now. Family run and offering only the highest of quality in food, drinks and service, lovingly prepared on the premises and served with a smile. Daily specials are available, as is free Wi-Fi.
Opening hours are Mon – Fri: 9am – 6pm Sat: 9am – 4pm Sun: 10pm – 4pm

Nant Yr Odyn Country Hotel & Restaurant

Turnpike Nant, Llangefni, Anglesey, LL77 7YE

T: 01248-723354 www.nantyrodyn.co.uk E: nantyrodyn@gmail.com

Delicious cuisine to suit most tastes is offered by our chef in the attractive beamed restaurant where a la carte meals using the finest local Welsh beef, lamb & dairy produce are complimented by our range of fine wines & spirits. Vegetarian & special dietary needs also catered for. Our Function Room is equipped for seminars and presentations & will accommodate 40-45 delegates comfortably and a variety of packages are available including morning coffee, lunch & afternoon tea. Overnight accommodation is also available at a discounted rate. Private parties, family gatherings, & smaller weddings up to 50 guests can also be catered for with menus to suit all occasions.

The Crown

33-35 Bodorgan Square, Aberffraw, Anglesey, LL63 5BX

T: 01407-840222 www.thecrownaberffraw.com E: Landlord@thecrownaberffraw.com

The Crown Aberffraw is located in the village square visible from both the A4080 and the estuary/beach car park. Our bar offers a range of beers, lagers, wines and spirits.We pride ourselves on the real ales we offer, Conwy, Purple Moose, Cwrw Llyn & Heavy Industry are just a sample of the local breweries who's ales we are proud to serve. Our new kitchen is fully operational.We have invested in all new equipment and our experienced chef has everything he needs to ensure good quality food is served consistently. Due to the limited size of our dining room booking is recommended. The Crown.........a lovely place to come to after a day on the fantastic beach, at the end of a walk along the coastal path, or for a relaxing drink after a hard days work. We are a DOG FRIENDLY Pub.

Ann's Pantry

Moelfre, Anglesey, LL72 8HL

T: 01248-410386 www. annspantry.co.uk E: enquiries@annspantry.co.uk

Ann's Pantry is a family run café and restaurant in the picture postcard village of Moelfre. We strive to serve quality local produce in a relaxed atmosphere. We are well known for our homemade cakes for which we use only free range Welsh eggs, and fresh real flavours such as lemon and freshly ground coffee. These are made regularly on the premises. Our homemade scones are the quintessential holiday treat, served with fresh cream of course. On a good day you can enjoy the weather in one of our popular outside areas, from our lovely walled garden, a sunny courtyard area and a lovely corner cushioned area under our palm tree, and not forgetting our bbq shed.We are also dog friendly.

The Midland Tapas & Wine Bar

38 Castle Street, Beaumaris, Anglesey, LL58 8BB

T: 01248-810429 www.themidlandtapas.com E: bookings@themidlandtapas.co

We have had always had a passion for creating a restaurant. We wanted our restaurant to be in cont to the towns more traditional venues, creating a modern, vibrant environment and exciting food. At Midland, you'll discover authentic and modern tapas… Our dishes that always start with the best ingredients to create gourmet tapas with seasonal specials based around local produce. The combina of good wine, good food and a stylish, vibrant restaurant combines to make a great experience.At T Midland, you can eat lunch, dinner, get something to share or pop in for a glass Cava or a cocktail. We are looking forward to welcoming you to The Midland tapas restaurant and bar.

Gwesty Gadlys Hotel & Restaurant

Llanbadrig, Cemaes Bay, Anglesey, LL67 0LH

T: 01407-710227 www.gadlys.co.uk E: Richard@gadlys.co.uk

The Gwesty Gadlys Hotel can be found on the beautiful Isle of Anglesey, on the edge of Cemaes Bay the most northerly village in Wales. Surrounded by wonderful countryside, a couple of minutes wal from the beach and the coastal footpath, the hotel is the perfect base for exploring Anglesey. The h has been completely renovated and rejuvenated without compromise, and all our rooms have mod ensuite facilities. The focal point of the hotel, the bar and restaurant have been totally redesigned w a modern and comfortable style. With stunning views across the grounds and the bay there is no be place to while away time enjoying a refreshing cocktail before choosing from our menu, and daily specials. With local produce and seafood there is wide choice on offer.

Catch 22 Brasserie

London Road, Valley, Anglesey, LL65 3DP

T: 01407-238220 www.catch22brasserie.co.uk E: info@catch22brasserie.co.uk

Catch 22 Brasserie is a casual family run restaurant that opened early April 2017 in Valley. Our menu focuses on using locally sourced produce to create Mediterranean dishes with a few international inspirations. We are open all day long 7 days a week. With the combination of our friendly staff, varie menu and relaxed decor, we have tried to create a space that is 'a home away from home' for our customers, whether it be for a quick coffee or a three course meal. Il our dishes, including the bread puddings, cakes and ice creams are prepared by the Catch 22 team completely from scratch using t most local ingredients available.Neil and the chefs are constantly challenging themselves to come u new and fresh recipe ideas for you to try and enjoy.

Sea Shanty Cafe

Lon St Ffraid, Trearddur Bay, Anglesey, LL65 2YR

T: 01407-728200 www.seashantycafe.co.uk E: info@seashantycafe.co.uk

Stacey 4th March 2017 **Fantastic**

Big thank-you to everyone at The Sea Shanty who helped today for my sisters baby shower. The foo was perfect, staff were very helpful and polite and I would highly recommend here for any occasion Everyone enjoyed their visit and we will definitely be returning in the future. Thanks again.

Malcolm Lee 22nd January 2017 Llangefni **Fantastic Night**

Took a party of eight there on Saturday evening 21 January. The food was fantastic and the service f the staff was warm and friendly. We could not have wished for a better place to spend the evening. Will definitely call again and will have no hesitation in recommending the Sea Shanty to my friends.

Trearddur Bay Hotel

Lon Isallt, Holyhead, Anglesey, LL65 2UN

T: 01407-860301 www.trearddurbayhotel.co.uk E: enquiries@trearddurbayhotel.co.uk

The Trearddur Bay Hotel is situated in a prime position overlooking the beach on the North-West coast of Anglesey. The Bay Restaurant offers a classic menu in delightful surroundings. Enjoy a range of dishes, freshly prepared with an emphasis on locally sourced ingredients. We serve a great pint of cask ale and being owned by a brewery means we serve some of the finest ale in the area. We're also pretty good at serving up a G&T or a glass of fizz, plus we have a fantastic wine cellar offering a choice of specially selected wines from around the world. Our Inn at the Bay pub is the popular choice for our locals and offers a relaxing atmosphere where you can enjoy hearty, seasonal pub classics such as beer battered fish & chips and signature burgers from our new Spring menu before heading out to explore.

The Valley Hotel

London Road, Valley, Isle of Anglesey, LL63 3DU

T: 01407-740203 www.valley-hotel-anglesey.co.uk E: booking@valley-hotel-anglesey.co.uk

We here at the Valley Hotel work hard to be attentive without being intrusive, engaging without being over the top. The hotel has character and a heartbeat and we will do all we can to help you enjoy your time in Anglesey. If you are looking for a traditional Inn or Tavern with a good atmosphere and genuinely friendly people, the Valley Hotel is for you. There is always an interesting blend of Welsh and English accents and a real, friendly, convivial pub atmosphere. Our Bar and Grill provides the perfect place to socialise with friends, enjoy a quiet drink or treat yourself to a taste of our home-made food. Our Head Chef, Charlie Diamond and his team has been with us for many years and they are justifiably proud of the Valley's reputation for providing quality food at affordable prices.

The White Eagle

Rhoscolyn, Anglesey, LL65 2NJ

T: 01407-860267 www.white-eagle.co.uk E: white.eagle@timpson.com

Completely rebuilt in 2007 The White Eagle is a fond Anglesey landmark for both residents and visitors. A Free House with all the freedom that the term implies, The White Eagle is a pub with attitude, to be enjoyed by anyone who likes good food, beer and wine in a relaxed atmosphere with fantastic views. Owner and Chief Executive, Alex Timpson has created her ideal pub and one for the whole family. The pubs inviting character together with its warm and friendly atmosphere, will ensure that your visit to The White Eagle is more than memorable. In its idyllic surroundings, the pub is perfect for a refreshing pint during one of the many coastal walks, or a long relaxing evening meal.

Pot Jam

25 High Street, Menai Bridge, Anglesey, LL59 5EF

T: 01248-714444 www.potjam.cymru E: nia@potjam.cymru

A brand new cafe in the bustling town of Menai Bridge. This is a first time venture for Nia and the family from Llansadwrn, inspired by her late father, Elfed Hughes. Offering an array of light meals and home-made cakes, afternoon teas and fresh bread, there is something to suit everyone's tastes. The cafe's ethos is to offer a range of local foods and produce, for example Poblado coffee and Morgan's Brew teas, as well as a range of tempting treats by Bys a Bawd, Central Bakery Beaumaris, cakes from The Bakehouse Tregarth and Rhyd y Delyn cheese company. Pot Jam is also a licensed cafe, and regional wine and beer such as Pant Du and Gogarth Brewery can be enjoyed. Up to 35 guests can be accommodated, making it a perfect venue for a special occasion, birthday or baby shower. A warm welcome awaits you at Pot Jam. Public parking nearby. Baby changing facilities available.

Langdons

Holyhead Marina, Beach Road, Newry Beach, Holyhead, Anglesey, LL65 1YA

T: 01407-762415 www.langdons.restaurant E: colin@langdons.restaurant

Langdon's, a new family-run restaurant based next to Holyhead Marina, on Newry Beach. Our name stems from Langdon ridge, which is a submerged rock between the Skerries Lighthouse and Holyhea Harbour. The ridge is marked by a West Cardinal Mark which is where the Langdon's Logo comes fron So come down for a drink or two whilst enjoying stunning sea views and sample some delicious, distinctive, homemade food with Holyhead Mountain as a beautiful backdrop. Open all day for hot and cold drinks. Open for lunch from 12:00 to 2:30 and dinner from 18:00 to 21:00 Thursday through t Saturday. Sunday Lunch Special served from 12:00 until 16:00.Langdons Afternoon tea (24 hours noti required). We look forward to seeing you soon!

Dylan's Restaurant

St George's Road, Menai Bridge, Anglesey, LL59 5EY

T: 01248-716714 www.dylansrestaurant.co.uk E: menaibridge@dylansrestaurant.co.

Dylan's restaurant sits at the water's edge, alongside the Thomas Telford bridge in the small town of Menai Bridge, Anglesey. The restaurant serves locally sourced, seasonal produce, specialising in freshl baked pizza and seafood. A passion for baking has driven us to create a range of specialist breads and pizza, made on the premises using traditional baking techniques and the finest flours.
Dylan's menu also includes some of the very best seafood sourced directly from the Strait such as our world famous Menai mussels, lobster and Anglesey sea bass. Our menu is a celebration of the abundant seafood and farm produce available to us on and around Anglesey - The Mother of Wales.

Bocca Italian Pizzeria

9 Wood Street, Menai Bridge, Anglesey, LL59 5AS

T: 01248-713 008 www.boccaitalian.co.uk E: info@boccaitalian.co.uk

Bocca is set down a secluded back street in Menai Bridge just off the local square
We offer all our customers a warm welcome in a comfortable ambient atmosphere serving a great tasting range of pizzas & pastas, Italian beers, wines & spirits. Bocca is ideal for families or a romantic meal for two.
Booking Recommended.(We don't take email bookings)
Please e-mail info@boccaitalian.co.uk or call 01248 713 008
Open from 17:00 Tuesday to Saturday-Closed Sunday & Monday
Open selected Sundays - please enquire for details.

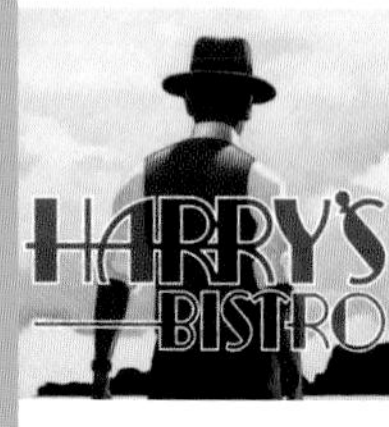

Harry's Bistro

Henllys Hall, Henllys, Beaumaris, Gwynedd, LL58 8HU

T: 01248-812976 www.harrysbistro.com E: enquiries@harrysbistro.com

Chef Simon Doyle and front of house partner Nia Roberts are a well-known Anglesey combination. Th unique styles of bistro-style food and service have built the reputation of Harry's being amongst the best restaurants on the Island.
We are passionate about our food and will offer you a special dining experience. You will find us just outside beautiful Beaumaris on the Island of Anglesey. Harry's is situated within Henllys Hall, a famou old mansion house set in the most stunning scenery with wonderful views across the Menai Strait to mountains of Snowdonia. Come and relax at Harry's - you'll find our restaurant a unique and unhurrie place to enjoy our bistro style food, our award winning desserts and our specially selected wines.

The Oyster Catcher

Maelog Lake, Rhosneigr, Anglesey, LL64 5JP

T: 01407-812829 www.oystercatcheranglesey.co.uk E: oyster.catcher@timpson.com

The last rays of the sun are dappling a stunning vista stretching from the indigo of Lake Maelog to the sand dunes of Broad Beach, and here we are sipping post-dinner coffee in a beach hut. Not any old beach hut, though, It is one of several little pastel-coloured sheds (with their own heaters) newly erected on the large verandah behind The Oyster Catcher restaurant at Rhosneigr in Anglesey. The Oyster Catcher food is superior gastro pub fare – stolid mains such as a burger and chips or Cumberland sausage and mash, pizza, pasta, salads, and some more imaginative dishes such as meatballs with mustard seed macaroni or braised rabbit .

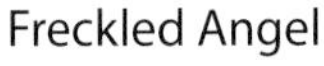

Freckled Angel

49 High Street, Menai Bridge, Anglesey, LL59 5EF

T: 01248-209952 www.freckled-angel-fine-catering.co.uk E: freckled-angel@outlook.com

A great party is something to look back on for a long time. As a private chef for North Wales and the surrounding area, we do more than just provide you with a variety of high-quality meals to suit your requirements.We're also happy to offer our organisational skills, staff and equipment to make organising the entire event easier for you.

Be it a family celebration in your own home or a large party at a rented venue, our experienced team will work out a culinary programme to accompany your event and the very best ideas to make your celebration an unforgettable experience.

The Four Crosses Inn

Pentraeth Rd, Menai Bridge, Anglesey, LL59 5RP

T: 01248-712230 www.robinsonsbrewery.com/fourcrossesinn E: fourcrossesinn@btconnect.com

The Four Crosses Inn is a large family run pub situated in Menai Bridge after crossing the Brittannia Bridge onto The Isle of Anglesey. It is a popular pub with locals, tourists and holidaymakers alike who visit the nearby campsites and caravan parks. There are six cask beers available at any one time including Robinsons award-winning Old Tom on draught... at 8.5% ABV drink with caution; you've been warned. We get extremely busy during the summer months and our traditional homecooked food menu is always a favourite with customers. We also have specials of the day including our famous Sizzler dishes.

The Pilot House Cafe

Black Point, Penmon, Nr Beaumaris, Anglesey, LL58 8RP

T: 01248-490140 www.pilothousecafe.com

Come & see some of the most glorious views that Anglesey has to offer, here at Penmon Point. Set on the Eastern Peninsular of this magical island with stunning sea views overlooking Puffin Island, The Great Orme & Mount Snowdon. Throughout the morning and afternoon we offer a selection of hot & cold snacks, ice-creams, speciality coffees & a variety of mouth-watering cakes. We also serve delicious Welsh cream teas. So whether you're a fisherman, a birdwatcher, a walker or would simply like to catch glimpse of a Puffin, seal, dolpin or beautiful sunset, then feel free to come & visit us here at Penmon Point. Families and dogs are welcome plus we also have a small souvenir shop. Wheelchair access is also available. We have indoor & outdoor seating so you can watch the world go by at your leisure.

The Kinmel Arms

Moelfre, Anglesey, LL72 8HH

T: 01248 -410231 E: kinmelarmsmoelfre@gmail.com

Popular sea-view pub with nautical-theme interior, four Robinsons ales and generous helpings of enjoyable traditional food from sandwiches and baked potatoes up, friendly service; dogs welcome, picnic-sets on paved front terrace, open all day. Come enjoy a quality ale or a warm fresh coffee along with a meal. **What a pub!! Reviewed 13 March 2017**

We stayed in Moelfre last week for my Father's surprise 50th getaway. We all met at the pub to surprise him on his birthday!! Later that night we went down for a few quiet drinks... and I must say this has to be one of the best pubs I've been in. Traditional decor, reasonably priced and damn good beer and food!

Tafarn y Rhos

Rhostrehwfa, Llangefni, Anglesey, LL77 7YU

T: 01248-724404 www.robinsonsbrewery.com/tafarnyrhos E: tafarnyrhos2018@outlook.co

The Tafarn Y Rhos is situated in the Anglesey village of Rhostrehwfa some 2 miles from the market to of Llangefni and conveniently located just off the A5. There is always a warm welcome here where customers can choose from our traditional locally sourced food menu. You can also enjoy a pint (or tw of our award-winning cask ales. Feeling peckish? Come dine with us! We offer Great British homecook dishes served with a smile… and best of all no washing up! With an impressive wine list, spirits range and award-winning cask ales; we have just the tipple for you. For opening times please give us a call. Food service times: Mon - Sat 12:00pm -2:30pm & 5:00pm-8:30pm, Sunday: All day.

Sandy Mount House

High Street, Rhosneigr, Anglesey, LL64 5UX

T: 01407-253102 www.sandymounthouse.co.uk E: info@sandymounthouse.co.uk

Sandy Mount House is a contemporary beach house restaurant & bar set in the relaxed seaside village of Rhosneigr in Anglesey. Think cosy corners, log fires & stylish interiors. Sandy Mount House will be passionate about delivering the simple pleasures done well – design, warmth, great food and hospita with a side of fun. Whether you're looking to grab a quick bite in the bar from our selection of small plates, or enjoying a more indulgent dinner with friends, we can promise generous cooking and robu flavours, using the very best locally sourced produce. Comfortable and informal, our dining areas are family-friendly and dogs are welcome in the bar and on the front terrace. From our light-filled roof lantern dining area, you can see our chefs at work in the open kitchen and during the summer month we fold back the glass doors to our covered and heated outdoor dining terrace with cosy fireplace.

The Driftwood Restaurant

Lon St Ffraid, Treaddur Bay, Anglesey, LL65 2YT

T: 01407-860332 www.thebeachmotel.co.uk E: info@thebeachmotel.co.u

We are a family run motel that offers great value accommodation in the heart of Trearddur Bay, Anglesey. We are just short stroll from Trearddur Bay's beautiful blue flag beach and only a 10 minute drive from nearby Holyhead. Our Driftwood Restaurant &Bar always offers a warm welcome to customers. We serve delicious homemade food and local cask ales with our traditional carvery on a Sunday. Where possible we source locally, and have most recently incorporated a delicious Welsh rose wine to our new wine list.We show live sporting events from Sky Sport and BT Sport, so you can put your feet up and cheer on your team.Our conservatory will seat up to 70 people making it the ideal location for functions, family, celebrations, wedding parties, birthdays and Christmas parties.

CONWY VALLEY & DENBIGHSHIRE

/lost of the areas that we have featured within this Wales book and the Top 100 website all stand one, but then there's some of the thirteen areas that are featured, we have merged together, as ley are so great, they all need showing off. This particular section in the book and website is a crime kample of what I am talking about. The huge area that makes up the Conwy Valley & Denbighshire gion, spans from Prestatyn to Penmaenmawr and features some great little towns along the way. ke Llandudno for instance, once crowned the Queen of all Welsh holiday resorts, this once great ctorian destination did, and still does manage to pull in the crowds from far and wide. Speaking of ılling in the crowds from far and wide, that leads me very nicely onto Conwy. This walled Bastion of town, complete with its quaint fishing quay always seems to have visitors come rain or shine.

ıen there is Rhyl, this end of the pier style holiday destination with its sandy beaches and nusement arcades, has them flocking from all over the Midlands and the Northwest primarily and huge regeneration project is underway that is going to see this small seaside great once more. Not rgetting of course the unsung hero that is Llangollen. This small town, as far as I am concerned is e jewel in Denbighshire's crown, a town that can still manage to pull in the crowds most weekends the winter, has to be applauded. So you see, you cannot fail to be hugely spoilt for choice in this ea. Not only has it got some great attractions to visit, but the locations themselves truly are tractions in their own right! So, no matter what you chose to do, don't forget to take this book with ɔu!

Bodafon Farm Park

CARTWHEEL CAFE, BAR & BBQ.

t: 01492-549060 e: info@bodafonfarmpark.com
www.bodafonfarmpark.com

Bodafon Farm Park is only a stone's throw from the sea front in beautiful Llandudno, and is very easy to find – it's just off the Promenade towards the Little Orme by the fields.
Come and experience life on a genuine working farm. There's lots to do at Bodafon farm or just come and relax in our cartwheel cafe and courtyard where our unique BBQ is situated.
For the children we have ride on tractors and an adventure playground where adults can sit on our sunset terrace and watch the kids play. We have a wide variety of animals which you can feed or take a tractor trailer ride around the fields. We also offer pony rides and we are home to the North Wales Bird Trust with a large collection of owls and unusual birds to walk around. We also have stunning views over Llandudno Bay, so come and enjoy a day out with great food and a relaxed atmosphere.

AUTHOR'S REVIEW

Combining both coast and countryside, Bodafon Farm Park really does have a lot to offer. They have one of the biggest birds of prey areas that I have seen at a farm park, which was a sheer delight to see, Owls, Hawks just to name but a few and all very friendly I found. As I walked around the farm park all the animals seemed to make their way to where I was standing, I was beginning to think I must be a kind of Dr Doolittle figure, when I suddenly remembered that people can feed these animals by buying feed in the cafe, so it clearly wasn't me they were interested in, but merely what I may have had in my hand! Story of my life! Ha!
Another thing that really impressed me was that since 2013, it is totally free to visit Bodafon, so what are you waiting for?

•Conwy

Bodafon Road, Llandudno, Gwynedd, LL30 3BB

WELSH MOUNTAIN ZOO

t: 01492-532 938 e: info@welshmountainzoo.org
www.welshmountainzoo.org

The Welsh Mountain Zoo is set in North Wales, high above Colwyn Bay with panoramic views and breathtaking scenery. Its beautiful gardens are home to this caring conservation zoo. Roam the wooded pathways, relax on the grassy slopes and spend a lovely day learning about many rare and endangered species from Britain and around the world including Snow Leopards, Chimpanzees, Red Pandas and Sumatran Tigers! Enjoy our Penguin Parade, Chimp Encounter, Bear Falls, Lemur Lookout, Condor Haven and the Children's Farm plus much more. Visit 'Sea Lions Rock' and watch our Californian Sea Lions being trained. Enjoy the exciting and extensive Jungle Adventureland and Tarzan Trail Adventure Playground. For the more technically inclined, visit our Media Centre, where you can do a virtual tour of the Zoo and play some great educational games. OPENING HOURS: April to October: Gates open at 9.30am, last admission just before 5.00pm, Zoo closes at 6.00pm. November to March: Gates open at 9.30am, last admission just before 4.00pm, Zoo closes at 5.00pm. Closed Christmas Day.

AUTHOR'S REVIEW

Visiting all the attractions that makes Wales such a special place is truly an honour. Not only is it an honour for the attractions to make their way into these books, but the memories they have given me will stay with me for the rest of my life. I say this now because I have some very fond memories of my visit to the Welsh Mountain Zoo. There is no zoo on this earth that offers the same views as can be found here, and the magnificent range of animals they have, really did put a smile on my face. Open all year round, this attraction offers amazing value for money by way of its annual pass, and the idea of being able to be a 'keeper for the day ' truly excited me! This attraction owes itself to its founder, the late Robert Jackson who opened the zoo back in 1963. It is also my opinion that Colwyn Bay owes a debt of gratitude to Robert Jackson's vision, and to his family for continuing to keep that vision alive.

Colwyn Bay, Conwy, North Wales, LL28 5UY

Adventure Parc Snowdonia

t: 01492-353123 e: info@surfsnowdonia.co.uk
www.surfsnowdonia.co.uk

The Surf Snowdonia Adventure Parc is an exciting new adventure destination located in the beautiful Conwy Valley of North Wales. Set in the foothills of the Snowdonia National Park, Surf Snowdonia is a world-first inland surf lagoon and a place which has equal appeal for beginner through to expert surfers. Its revolutionary design and technology simultaneously generates different wave profiles – from knee high to head high – in different zones of the lagoon. Guaranteed to roll every 90 seconds, the consistency and regularity of the waves will fast-track your progression far quicker than is possible in the sea. You can take a lesson with the Surf Snowdonia Academy or access the waves independently. Surf Snowdonia also offers onsite glamping accommodation and regularly plays host to events, festivals and competitions. A 50-metre glass-fronted café bar and viewing gallery allows visitors to enjoy food and drink whilst watching the surfing action close-up. There is also a Surf Snowdonia shop s elling high quality surf equipment, clothing and accessories, and a kiddie's soft play zone for the nippers. Parking and spectator entry to Surf Snowdonia is free.

AUTHOR'S REVIEW

Formerly Surf Snowdonia, this attraction has truly gone from strength to strength and due to its popularity and success, the attraction has had to rebrand itself to encompass everything it offers its visitors and once you've visited, you'll see that surfing isn't all you can do here. If you have a love of the outdoors, looking for something that's just that little bit different, I cannot recommend Adventure Parc Snowdonia enough. Another thing I like so much about this attraction, is that you can tailor your own activities and package your own visit clearly to suit your needs and with amazing little Glamping pods, this place has truly become a resort in its own right and you can even hook up for your own camper van here, truly awesome. I have always believed this attraction would be a huge success and I was not wrong, now all that's left to do, is for you to go and see for yourself .

Conwy

Conway Road, Dolgarrog, LL32 8QE

Venue Cymru

t: 01492-872000 e: info@venuecymru.co.uk
www.venuecymru.co.uk

Venue Cymru is situated on the coast of undoubtedly one of the most beautiful settings within the British Isles. Lying at the centre of the North Wales coast, Venue Cymru is easily accessible with fast, efficient transport links connecting Liverpool, Manchester and London to the venue.

Situated in Llandudno and with a unique and outstanding sea-front location which never fails to charm, Venue Cymru is one of the UK's leading receiving theatres with a continual diverse programme of events, covering virtually every form of live performance from opera and West End shows, to dance and live music gigs, to comedy and pantomime. It also houses and provides professional, modern, purpose built and affordable conference facilities for anything from 5 to 5000 delegates with a full range of rooms and services available for events and conferences of all sizes.

AUTHOR'S REVIEW

Venue Cymru has to be the brightest jewel in the Queen of British holiday resort's crown. Llandudno isn't only a seaside from Victorian times gone by, but the town is also home to one of the most modern and vibrant theatres Wales has to offer. Venue Cymru isn't just a theatre but a very busy conference centre and live music arena to boot. Playing host to a wide variety of artistes such as Stereophonics, Manic Street Preachers, Mike Peters, Status Quo, Ian Brown, Duffy, The Kooks, Feeder, Pendulum and many more.As I was being shown round Venue Cymru I was gobsmacked to realise just how diverse the venue is and how important the theatre is to not only North Wales but also to the hundreds of thousands of visitors to North Wales on a yearly basis.

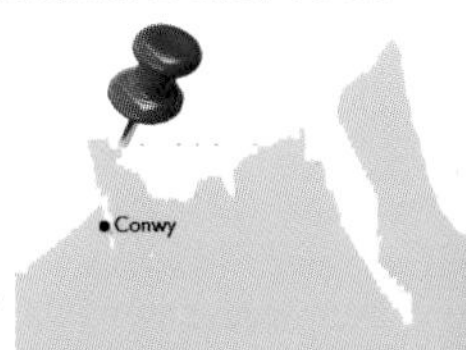

The Promenade,Llandudno, LL30 1BB

Manorafon Farm Park

t: 01745-833237 e: jules@manorafon.co.uk
www.manorafon-farm-park.co.uk

Manorafon Farm Park offers an opportunity to meet a large array of cute, not so cute, small and large farm animals, so why not come and see what we have to show you. Grab some feed from the shop and take a stroll around the farmyard trail and into the Old Dutch barn. Come and grab a cuddle at Cwtch corner, we offer small animal handling sessions every day. For handling times please visit www.manorafon-farm-park.co.uk. Whenever you visit, we always try to ensure that we have young and new-born animals on the farm, from orphan lambs to sheepdog pups and lots of little piggies. Burn off some energy in our new play barn which offers children aged up to 10 years the opportunity to explore 2 storeys of fun, whilst children aged under 4 years can enjoy playing in our soft play toddler area. Visitors both young and old will be made to feel welcome, we also cater for groups, schools, birthday parties and also offer bespoke experiences for those wanting to get closer to the action!

AUTHOR'S REVIEW

Having visited a huge number of farm parks whilst writing my range of books, I have been privileged to have visited some great sites and have grown to really love this type of attraction. Thinking that I knew North Wales like the back of my hand, someone recommended an attraction that I hadn't actually heard of, Manorafon Farm Park. Being a new kid on the block I wasn't actually expecting too much, but I couldn't of been more wrong. It was totally clear to me that the owners of the site, Jules and Wil really are passionate about the animals on their farm and everything goes into making sure your visit is one to remember. I found the staff to be really professional, knowledgeable and they all had smiles on their faces which was really clear to me that they really enjoyed what they do. The admission price is very reasonable and for the experience that is on offer, Manorafon Farm Park offers huge visitor experience over value for money, so a huge Top 100 thumbs up to Will, Jules and their great team.

Llandulas Road, Abergele, Conwy, LL22 8ET

Cae Dai 50's Era Museum

t: 01745-817004 e: caedaitrust@btconnect.com

The Cae Dai Trust is based in the countryside just 1 mile outside the market town of Denbigh. After the closure of North West Wales largest psychiatric hospital in 1994, the Cae Dai Trust was established to provide support for vulnerable adults. Cae Dai is able to give limited temporary accommodation; which provides the"umbrella" of support required to enable the beneficiary's time to gain confidence, self esteem and life skills essential to moving on and living independently in the community. The main source for this support is the 1950's museum, a fantastic resource and attraction for the local and wider community. The museum has a collection of classic cars, sport, music, film and crime memorabilia. Our beneficiaries also enjoy looking after the animals on our farm and a spot of gardening in the woodland and community orchard. Please visit Cae Dai and help us to continue.

AUTHOR'S REVIEW

The 50's museum here in Denbigh is one of those little hidden gems you will hear talked about a fair bit in this book! Having seen fire destroy one of the main buildings last year due to an arson attack, like a Phoenix from the ashes Cae Dai 50's Museum bounced back to its former glory again since April 2012. You will be able to enjoy looking around such vehicles as the original lorry that was used in the real 'Great Train Robbery'. Also featured at the museum, is the car that belonged to 'Christine Keeler' the 50's & 60's model that sparked the whole 'Profumo' scandal that rocked the then Conservative government, plus many more treasures from the 50's era. So whether you're a 50's enthusiast or just somebody who appreciates the past, do not overlook this amazing little museum.

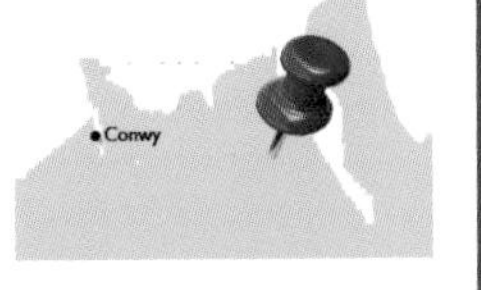

Cae Dai Trust, Cae Dai, Denbigh, LL16 4SU

RSPB CONWY

t: 01492 584091 e: conwy@rspb.org.uk
www.rspb.org.uk/Conwy

Situated on the banks of the Conwy estuary, with magnificent views of Snowdonia and Conwy Castle, this reserve is delightful at any time of year. RSPB Conwy is a great place to get close to wildlife, to spend time with family and friends, or just take time out in fantastic scenery that embraces 4,000 years of human history. There's a network of pushchair-friendly trails with viewpoints and hides to make the most of your visit and plenty of information about the species that you may see. Perhaps you'll meet one of our friendly volunteer wildlife guides who can help you discover just a little bit more? In our Visitor Centre, our warm welcome will ensure you have exactly what you need for your visit. We have activities that involve the whole family, such as Wildlife Bingo, encouraging you to look out for nature as you walk the trails. Immediately behind the Visitor Centre, an area we call Y Maes, has lots of opportunities for wildlife discovery and natural play, and it's not just for kids; we see plenty of older people trying the hula-hoops too! Our coffee shop is the ideal place to relax and enjoy our bird friendly coffee and delicious cakes. You can also pick up some wonderful gifts in our shop or some treats for the wildlife that make your garden their home.

AUTHOR'S REVIEW

The nature reserve here in Conwy has to be one of the best situated nature reserves the UK has to offer. With Conwy Castle as a back drop it's not hard to imagine why. Within walking distance of Conwy, and Llandudno Junction train station and adjacent to the main A55 trunk road, RSPB Conwy is totally accessible by any form of transport. The views from the purpose built coffee shop are tremendous and with the location of the reserve being one of the driest places in North Wales they don't get a lot of rain anyway, so there is always a good chance you'll be able to get to have a good walk around. The cakes are good too! 'Nudge Nudge''Wink Wink'...

Conwy

Junction 18 A55, Llandudno Junction, Conwy, LL31 9XZ

Llyn Crafnant Lakeside Cafe & Fishery

t: 01492-640818 e: russell245@gmail.com
www.llyn-crafnant.co.uk

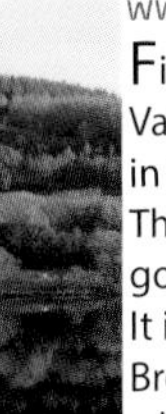

Fish for Trout in Natural Surroundings in a Stunning North Wales ValleyLlyn Crafnant is one of the most beautiful and unspoilt spots in North Wales, nestling in a tranquil valley high up in Snowdonia. The lake is three quarters of a mile long and covers 63 acres, has good access and is well sheltered on all banks.
It is regularly stocked with Rainbow trout supplementing the Wild Brown trout and can be fished from all banks or by the privacy of a boat.
Or why not visit our lakeside Cafe or Tea Garden and enjoy a delicious light meal and homemade scones and cakes after a walk around the lake or nearby hills.
Seating available inside the Cafe, or outside on our Tea Garden on the shore of the lake
Apple parking and toilet facilities.

AUTHOR'S REVIEW

There is a place that is that well hidden, you would hardly know it's there. A place where peace meets beauty and a place where time just stands still, or at least that's what it seems. That place is Lyn Crafnant, a lake perfectly nestled within the Conwy Valley and one that is abundant with the likes of Rainbow and Wild Brown Trout, which can easily be fished from the banks of the lake with a boat hired from the Cafe. As if that really wasn't enough, the lake also plays home to a cute little cafe ran by the very charismatic Caroline Williams. Caroline has bought the cafe and really infused some much needed life into the place, with a great little menu to suit all tastes and budgets and with a great personality, she will be telling you all the local stories within no time!

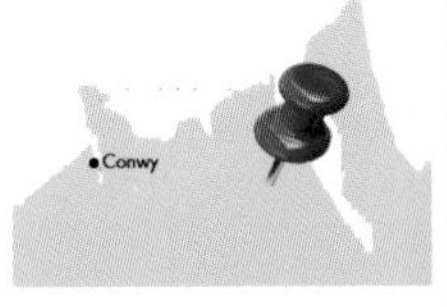

Cynllwyd Fawr, Crafnant Road, Trefriw, Conwy, LL27 0JZ

Llyn Brenig Visitor Centre

t: 01490-420463 e: llynbrenig@dwrcymru.com
www.llyn-brenig.co.uk

Discover beautiful Llyn Brenig – a forested site with trout fishery and visitor centre, cafe and cycle hire in north Wales.
Visiting makes for a full, enjoyable and fun packed day out. Our visitor centre is open all year round with extended opening during the fishing season. The restaurant and shop offer panoramic views of the reservoir - one of the largest areas of inland water in Wales. Offering fun for families, we have an adventure playground and picnic area, and the walk-through exhibition tells the story of Llyn Brenig lake and all it has to offer. Cycling conditions are perfect at Llyn Brenig which is why it's one of the most popular places to ride a bike in North Wales.
Llyn Brenig Lake is now recognised as one of the best top-of-the-water fisheries in the UK. With its 23km of shoreline, it's one of the best places to go fishing in Conwy. Enjoy the thrill of the open water in a variety of ways. Perfect for sailing, the site is at altitude and experiences frequent windy conditions for the budding and adventurous sailor.

AUTHOR'S REVIEW

Welsh Water are the company that own the Llyn Brenig Visitor Centre and more often than not, journalists only ever report on Water Companies when there are bad things to say, but I'm going to turn that around now and tell you about one of the many good things they do, one of them being here at the Llyn Brenig Visitor Centre. Water Activities, Fishing and a great cycling route are just some of the many positives on offer here at the centre and as if that wasn't enough, they have a great little cafe also. The vista around Llyn Brenig are truly breath taking and will remind you of exactly why you chose Snowdonia as the destination of choice. Now lets talk about the cafe, with its amazing Bara Brith, a wide selection of food and great coffee, it's worth just calling in and when you do, you'll be able to enjoy a wide angled view that is unrivalled.

Llyn Brenig, Cerrigydrudion, Conwy, Wales, LL21 9TT

acksons Garden Centre

t: 01745-570680 e: info@jacksonsgardencentre.co.uk
www.jacksonsgardencentre.co.uk

Jacksons "Boutique" isn't any ordinary Garden Centre it has been described as many as a ' Hidden Gem' From the moment customers enter the shop they are blown away by the vast amount of different items that we have on offer, ranging from plants to home accessories. The store is open seven days a week and is easily accessible situated less than ten minutes away from the A55. We are confident that you will not be disappointed with a visit to Jacksons garden centre in North Wales, it's a great day out for all the family young and old with every age and style being catered for. Jacksons is today as it always has been a family run Business. Founded in 1967 by Stanley and Marjorie Jackson the same family still remain and now the third generation are working on site. We have always produced good hardy plants here and although over the years our Retail has outgrown our production side we have never lost sight of our roots. Plants still form a hugely important part of our business along with our horticulture experience which enables us to help our customers with any gardening queries.

AUTHOR'S REVIEW

Garden centres have now become more than what they say in their name, they are now places to meet, peruse and learn a thing about what's in and what's not, take Jackson's Garden Centre for instance. This little boutique garden centre on the North Wales coast may seem small as you drive into its well laid out car park. but looks are completely deceiving. Once in the Jacksons Tardis, a whole world of home, clothing and food delights are on offer. As I walked around the business I was taken aback at just how much was on offer here and if all that wasn't enough, they've got a wonderful restaurant, serving a full culinary array of different foods. I remember Jackson's when it had a small tea room, this is still there, but a tea room would now be an understatement. Booking a table ahead is seriously advised as they get very busy and their cakes, sandwiches and pastries truly are to die for!

Trelawnyd, Denbighshire, LL18 6EB

Nantclwyd Y Dre

t: 01824-706868 e: heritage@denbighshire.gov.uk
www.denbighshire.gov.uk

Take a trip through the seven ages of Nantclwyd y Dre, Wales's oldest dated timbered town house. The house was started in 1435 and has been added to, updated and upgraded throughout the centuries. Nantclwyd y Dre has been beautifully restored to demonstrate the changing fashions and the lives of its residents. Visitors can observe a colony of Lesser Horseshoe bats in the attic rooms via 'bat cam', participate in a quiz and use interactive media screens to learn more about the house and its inhabitants. Come and visit the fully restored Lord's Garden. Admission to the Lords Garden is included in the entry price to the house. You can hire Nantclwyd y Dre parlour rooms for events, parties and meetings, with space for up to 60 guests. Nantclwyd Y Dre is open from April through to September (See Website for details and prices)

AUTHOR'S REVIEW

Nantclwyd Y Dre is in my opinion, one of Denbighshire's biggest hidden gems! So much so, it's won many awards for that very reason. With over 500 years of rich history, this house has survived so well, where many others haven't in the town. A trip around the house is an absolute must, as there is room after room of rich history through the centuries of what has been a very vibrant past here within these walls. Whilst your'e here and within your ticket price, your able to visit the houses small garden, which really is a treat! As you make your way around the gardens to the back of the property, you can marvel at how the volunteers and staff have put their time into renovating not only the gardens but the house also. Whilst visiting Ruthin, no trip to the town is compete without visiting the old Gaol, which is only a five minute walk away from Nantclwyd Y Dre.

Castle St, Ruthin, LL15 1HP

North Wales Garden World

t: 01745-338222 e: support@northwalesgardenworld.com
www.northwalesgardenworld.com

Situated in North Wales in Kinmel Bay we have recently undergone a refurbishment – making us the place to visit! Offering beautiful products for both garden and home. From trees and shrubs and beautiful blooms for outdoors to giftware, outdoor & indoor furniture and specialist aquatic knowledge. We also have a loyalty card where card holders can benefit from special monthly offers. Established more than 25 years ago and still a family run business, we welcome you to our independent garden centre. Our 5 acre site makes a great run out for all the family with something to interest everyone. Let us help you make your garden a captivating outdoor living space to cherish, relax, entertain and enjoy.We have everything you need to make your garden special and enable you to make the most of your precious garden moments. If the weather is wet, we have extensive showrooms and areas under cover with plenty of ideas for the home.We are positioned on the North Wales Coast, two minutes off the A55 with plenty of car parking and easy disabled access.

AUTHOR'S REVIEW

Garden Centres have become a huge hit with the people of the British Isles and here in North Wales, you just have to see the standard of the garden centres to see just how popular they have become. Take North Wales Garden Centre here in Kinmel Bay for instance. Michael Boote, the managing director of Garden World has invested a huge amount of capital into making sure Garden World isn't just your usual run of the mill garden centre, but more as the name suggests, more of a garden world. A place where you can have food to die for, ice cream that is made with the upmost quality and a place that stocks all you could think of, for not only the garden, but your home also. Its very hard to express in just 150 words, just how good this place is, but mark my words, once your here, you'll be here for a while!

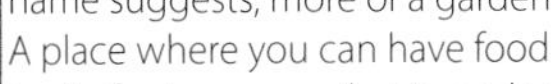

St Asaph Ave, Kinmel Bay, Rhyl, LL18 5TU

Conwy Garden World

t: 01492-562755

Situated in North Wales in Glan Conwy on the A470 we have recently undergone a refurbishment – making us the place to visit! Offering beautiful products for both garden and home. From trees and shrubs and beautiful blooms for outdoors to giftware, outdoor & indoor furniture. We also have a loyalty card where card holders can benefit from special monthly offers. We are also home to Conwy Ice cream World with over 50 flavours of ice cream and the Lavender café which serves full welsh breakfast and delicious afternoon teas. Conwy Gardenworld is a great day out for all the family with something to interest everyone. Let us help you make your garden a captivating outdoor living space to cherish, relax, entertain and enjoy. We have everything you need to make your garden special and enable you to make the most of your precious garden moments. If the weather is wet, we have showrooms and areas under cover with plenty of ideas for the home!

AUTHOR'S REVIEW

I won't go too much into the history of Garden World as I've covered this on the Kinmel Bay sites page, but what I will say is, that Garden World here in the Conwy Valley is a new edition to the fold as it were. Just a tad smaller than its sister site in Kinmel Bay, it still has all the trappings of an excellent garden centre. The team are really friendly here and I witnessed them going the extra mile for their customers, which in my books goes a long way! I choose my attractions based on visitor experience, set against value for money and here at Garden World, they have both in abundance. What I also picked up on was just how knowledgeable each member of staff is. If you ask them a question, they really do go out of their way to answer it. All in all, Garden World has really become one of the best garden centres in North Wales, but don't just take my word for it, go and see for yourself!

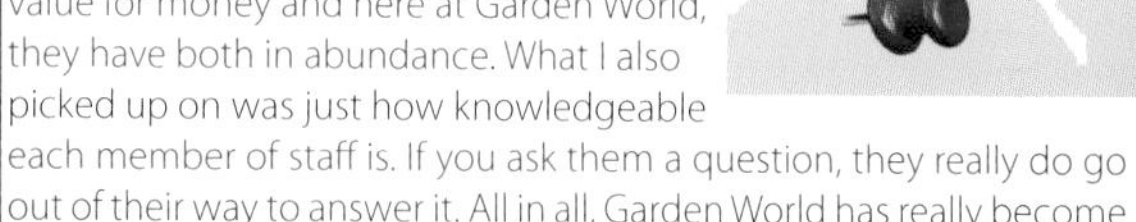

Llanrwst Rd, Conwy, LL28 5TH

Ruthin Gaol

t: 01824-708281 e: heritage@denbighshire.gov.uk
www.denbighshire.gov.uk

Ruthin gaol is the only purpose-built Pentonville style prison open to the public as a heritage attraction. People can spend time exploring its nooks and crannies and learn about life in the Victorian prison system. See how the prisoners lived their daily lives: what they ate, how they worked, and the punishments they suffered. Explore the cells including the punishment, 'dark' and condemned cell. Find out about the Welsh Houdini and William Hughes who was the last man to be hanged there. It ceased to be a prison in 1916 and was used as a munitions factory during the Second World War, before becoming home to the Denbighshire Archives, who remain based there to this day. Suitable for all ages. Audio guide available. Children's crafts and activities available.
You can hire Ruthin Gaol for events, parties and meetings for up to 60 guests. We are open April until September please (see website for details).

AUTHOR'S REVIEW

Ruthin is one of those small Welsh towns that not everyone gets to hear about, well not as much others in Denbighshire anyway. However, when you start to scratch away at the surface, Ruthin has just as much to offer as any other town or area in Wales. Steeped in history, Ruthin's Gaol offers a great insight into the penal system of the Victorian age and as you make your way from cell to cell, there is an eerie feel that just transports you back to the days when this old Gaol would have been full of reprobates and maybe even worse types of prisoners, including tales of the 'Welsh Houdini'. I really had a great experience whilst being shown round. Although not the biggest prison tour you can go on, there is so much history to learn and whilst you are visiting the prison, I would highly recommend a visit to its sister site, Nantclwyd Y Dre a medieval house also in the town centre.

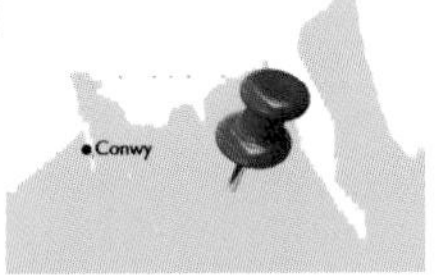

Clwyd St, Ruthin, LL15 1HP

Smallest House in Great Britain

t: 01492-573965 e: info@thesmallesthouse.co.uk
www.thesmallesthouse.co.uk

The Smallest House in Great Britain is a tourist attraction on the quay in Conwy, North Wales. The 3.05 metre by 1.8 metre (10 feet by 6 feet) structure was used as a residence from the 16th century until May 1900. As its name indicates, it is Britain's smallest house, as mentioned in the Guinness Book of Records. The last tenant was a 6ft 3 inch (1.9 metre) fisherman called Robert Jones. The rooms were too small for him to stand up in fully and he was eventually forced to move out when the council declared the house unfit for human habitation.
At the time the house was condemned, it was owned by a prominent local land owner, confusingly also called Robert Jones and the house is still owned by his descendants. The house is currently red and it is built up against the Town Walls. People can enter for £1.00 (50p for children). Recorded information about the house plays inside and a Welsh lady stands outside when the house is open. The upstairs is so minute that there is room only for a small bed and a bedside cabinet. Visitors can't walk about on the 2nd floor, but can view it from the access ladder. Downstairs there is just about enough room for a stove, a water tap, and a settle to sit on.

AUTHOR'S REVIEW

I met with Margaret Williams the then owner of the smallest house in Conwy, for a coffee and a chat about the life and times of this house, past owners, her family and her passion for this cute little house on the quay in the charming walled town of Conwy. First however, I had the fortunate chance to have a good look round this historic property. With the last inhabitant living there in 1900 it is quite easy to see that even though this house is so small, for the time period that people would have lived there, the house itself would have been a very cosy place to live. With poverty all around them, whoever would lived here and there were many, they would have considered themselves very well off indeed! No trip to North Wales is complete without a trip to the smallest house in Great Britain, and that's a fact!

10 Lower Gate Street, Conwy, North Wales, LL32 8BE

SC2

t: 01745 -77562
www.sc2rhyl.co.uk

SC2 is Wales' newest and most exciting leisure attraction, with both indoor and outdoor water play and Wales' first TAGactive arena. Visitors will delight when doors open in Spring 2019.
The amazing water park offers water play for all ages and abilities. With breath-taking feature flume rides, beach style paddling, a splash pad and slides for all ages, there really is something for everybody. There are themed cafés and catering outlets, along with an outdoor bar and terrace (open seasonally).
TAGactive is a fantastic indoor multi-level play zone that challenges your mental and physical ability, skill and strategy, whilst the junior TAG structure is available for 5-7 year olds*. The additional Cyber Tower allows you to race against your friends up a timed vertical obstacle course. SC2 offers something for every visitor, whether you're a thrill seeker, a paddler or just want to put your feet up and relax. See www.sc2rhyl.co.uk for more information. *height restrictions apply.

AUTHOR'S REVIEW

Having featured the original Rhyl Sun Centre in our very first edition of the Top 100 Attractions in Wales book back in 2012, then its eventual closure just a few years later, I've followed the plans of SC2 with great anticipation, in fact, Top 100 Attractions has been following the whole regeneration project to turn Rhyl's waterfront back into being a thriving visitor attraction once again. But here we are in 2019, SC2 is now open and with an anticipated 350,000 visitors per year, they will all be able to enjoy this £15 million water park that is set to make more water fun memories as did its predecessor for decades. I found the prices very reasonable and if you book online, you'll be able to avail of even better prices. Talking about online, SC2 has a really good user friendly website and together with its opening times, all the information you need to know is on there, so what are you waiting for? Get your swimming kit packed!

SC2 Rhyl, West Parade, Rhyl, Denbighshire, LL18 1BF

The Homefront Museum

t: 01492-871032 e: info@homefrontmuseum.co.uk
www.homefrontmuseum.co.uk

In this unique living history museum, take a self guided tour and explore 6 years of war on the home front captured in shops, room displays and tableaux.

- Take time to reminisce and wallow in nostalgic memories
- Discover how the war was won on the 'kitchen front'
- Gas masks, Ration books, Dig for Victory - its all here!
- Yesteryear memories brought back to life!
- Browse for presents in the gift shop

OPENING TIMES
Daily, 10am - 4.30pm,
Sunday 10am - 2pm
Mid March to November

ADMISSION
Adults £3.50
Children £2.10
Senior Citizens £3.25
Family (2+3) £10.00

AUTHOR'S REVIEW

Situated in the queen of seaside resorts, sits the World War 2 Homefront Experience and to be quite honest, I can't think of a better town for it to be based. This may be a unique little museum, however, it has got a massive personality and as you walk around it's many exhibits, you can instantly be taken back to the 40's and with the added extra of the sounds and smells, this instantly transports you back to those days where life wasn't as colourful as it is today. Adrian the owner of the museum, has put everything into making sure your visit to this amazing little museum is one that will be a most memorable one and believe me it really does deliver. I found the interpretation to be of the highest standard and the entrance fee on par to many other museums of its type, is quite nominal really.

New Street, Llandudno, Denbighshire, LL30 2YF

.landudno Monkey Man

Facebook: @LlandudnoMonkeyMan

One of Llandudno's most recognisable residents has married his "soulmate", and the whole town and his fans from across the world joined in on the celebrations. Since "adopting" his monkey from a charity shop six years ago, Samuel Peters - also famously known as the Monkey Man - has toured the country with his cuddly toy, dancing all the while. Recently, his fiancee Amanda Newman has joined him as part of the act, dancing with him and singing hit songs from musicals. They don't receive money for their act. Samuel, who has suffered from a variety of health problems for a number of years and is bipolar, has tried to take his own life numerous times but says his toy monkey saved his life. "I have no idea why, but I bought the monkey and just started to talk to him as I had nobody else to talk to at the time," said Samuel, 62. "In Birmingham, where I'm from, I'd often go to my local police station just for a chat, and I started taking the monkey with me. "Instead of being laughed at, the police started encouraging me and the act started from there. Monkey Man routine has won him fans from all over the world.

AUTHOR'S REVIEW

Llandudno maybe the Queen of Holiday resorts, but there is a new king and queen in town, and they are Llandudno's very own Monkey Man, Sam Peters, complete with his wife and entertaining partner, Amanda Newman and they have dedicated their whole lives to making people smile and quite frankly, I wish the world had more Sam and Amanda's! With dozens of costumes and his 'adopted' monkey, Sam and Amanda can often be seen on Llandudno's thoroughfares and often with a huge procession of holiday makers and locals in tow. Brought back from the brink of depression, Sam and his monkey moved from Birmingham's Kings Heath, where I can assure you he is sorely missed, but he exchanged the cold brummie streets, for the popular holiday destination that has helped him make tens of thousands of holiday goers smile with admiration. So if you're lucky enough to see them, be sure to give them a wave will you!

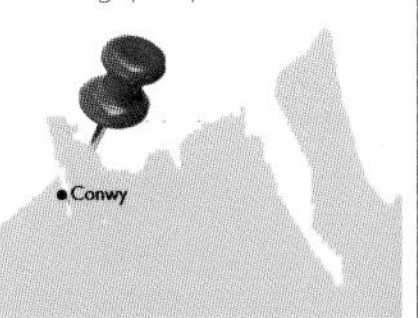

.andudno, Denbighshire

Gwrych Castle

t: 01745-826023 e: info@gwrychcastle.co.uk
www.gwrychcastle.co.uk

Gwrych Castle is a Grade I listed country house in North Wales, being for of the first attempts at replicating true medieval architecture in Europe. It stands in 250 acres of gardens and grounds and has extensive views over former parkland and the Irish Sea.Gwrych Castle Estate is being restored following half a century of neglect. A significant portion of the castle is accessible and family focused with onsite parking.

Gwrych Castle is dog friendly but dogs are to be kept on leads. Visit one on the wonders of Wales and learn a wealth of history about life in a gothic revival castle built in honour of ancestry and as a homage to medieval architecture. Discover Iron Age hillforts, Roman Shrine, medieval battle sites and poignant stories of Welsh history and nationhood. Explore terraced gardens and a. designed picturesque landscape that features banqueting towers and viewing platforms. Learn about the rescue of one of Wales' most endangered buildings and witness the process of restoration in action.

AUTHOR'S REVIEW

Gwyrch Castle has been brought back from the brink and I have to say, it was about time! A new preservation trust has been set up to look after the castle's estate and future and I have to say, they are already doing a brilliant job! With a huge history of entertainment and hospitality, this once beautiful castle is set to be lovingly restored as best as is possible, to its former glory. As humble as he is, the reason why this once much loved castle is now in safe hands, is mainly down to Mark Baker and his team. Mark from a very early age has always had a passion for Gwyrch, this passion, is one that can only be rivalled by one other and that is Countess Winifred Cochrane, Countess of Dundonald, the castles initial owner. The castles Trust has lovingly restored a small portion of the castle and it has some amazing walks. A castle not to be missed!

Llanddulas Road, Abergele, Conwy, North Wales, LL22 8ET

uthin Castle & Medieval Banquet

t: 01745-826023 e: info@gwrychcastle.co.uk
www.gwrychcastle.co.uk

Our banquets are renowned, starting with an introduction in the Presence Room where all guests assemble and partake of bread and salt, age-old symbols of hospitality. Fully costumed Ladies of the Court and the Court Steward then lead you into the candlelit Banquet Hall with its heavily laden tables. Ladies of the Court, The Court Steward and the Jester entertain, sing, jest and lead the feasting with only dagger and fingers accompanied by a tasting of mead from clay cups and wine quaffed from pewter goblets. The Medieval Banquet includes a 4 course banquet. You're welcome to wear costumes if you wish. It's an event not to be missed!

The Medieval Banquet Menu

Peasant Pottage with herb dumplings served with fresh breads and salted butter
Platter of Course pate, homemade meat pies, pickles, rocket and chutneys
Whole roasted chickens with Royal ribs in apple and cider served with roasted root vegetables and potatoes.
Selection of seasonal desserts including fruit pies and creamy custard.
Vegetarian, Pescetarian, Vegan and all other dietary requirements available by prior arrangement.
(menu items subject to seasonal changes)

AUTHOR'S REVIEW

Firstly, let me tell you about the Medieval Banquets that are held here at Ruthin Castle twice monthly. Being a huge fan of these types of events and frequenting many whilst writing my Irish book, I am hugely critical, however, having been to a banquet here in Ruthin. I can tell you. there is not much to be critical of. Great food, first class medieval entertainment and all set within a truly authentic setting, you couldn't be in better company and all for a very reasonable price. Then of course, Ruthin Castle is also a Hotel and with some very sumptuous suites, each with their own name and a selection of luxurious rooms, you'll not be disappointed with your stay at all! Finally, the hotel has two options for you to dine in. There's Berties, which is the hotels main restaurant and if fine dining isn't what you're looking for, there is always the library bar, but no matter what, you'll not be disappointed with either.

stle Street, Ruthin, Denbighshire, LL15 2NU

Gwynfryn B&B

4 York Place, Conwy, LL32 8AB

T:01492-576733 www. bedandbreakfastconwy.co.uk E: info@gwynfrynbandb.c

Gwynfryn B&B and Refrectory is situated in a converted 19th Century Welsh Methodist Chapel locat within the cobbled streets of the historical walled town of Conwy, designated an UNESCO World Heritage Site. Offering Visit Wales 4 Star Boutique Bed and Breakfast accommodation in the convert Chapel House and the Chapel Vestry. Our rooms have been beautifully furnished to offer comfortab yet stylish accommodation each with its own eclectic decor. The Refectory is in main Chapel area w has been renovated to a high standard whilst still retaining a wealth of its historical features includir the organ, pulpit, ornate balcony and the pews which have been modified into banquet style tables seating. Here you will be served your full Welsh breakfast .

Conwy Valley Cottages

Tan-y-Bryn, Hen Efail, Tyn-y-Groes, Conwy, LL32 8SR

T:07788-418795 www.conwyvalleycottages.co.uk E: info@conwyvalleycottages.co.u

Conwy Valley Cottages are nestled in the beautiful area of Conwy, close to the edge of Snowdonia National Park. These unique self catering stone built cottages are situated around the original Victor house with ample scenery to enjoy whilst staying close to all that Conwy has to offer. All six self cate ing cottages are refurbished Victorian farm buildings that offer the charms of a bygone era and are equipped with the modern conveniences of today. Each provides you with private garden space tha offers a picnic atmosphere for you to enjoy all year round. The open and spacious living area has a fu sized kitchen with all of the modern appliances you can expect in a self catering facility with wonderfully cosy open fires to take the chill off on cool evenings.

Tan yr Onnen Guesthouse

Tan-yr-Onnen, Waen, St. Asaph, Denbighshire, North Wales. LL17 0DU

T: 01745 583821 www.northwalesbreaks.co.uk E: tanyronnenvisit@aol.com

Tan-yr-Onnen Guest House offers quality bed and breakfast (B&B) accommodation near St. Asaph at the head of the Vale of Clwyd in North Wales. Tan-yr-Onnen offers quality comfortable non-smoking bed and breakfast accommodation. All rooms have been recently refurbished to a high standard. Th are six bedrooms. Four are ground floor king-size rooms with ensuite superior bathrooms. These roc enjoy the benefit of French windows opening onto a terrace, for you to enjoy the beautiful view on a summer's evening with a cool glass of wine. Upstairs there are 2 luxury suites, with a spacious comfo able sitting room and large bathroom. All rooms are furnished to a very high standard and all of the offer colour TV/DVD/Freeview & free wi-fi internet access.

Lymehurst Bed & Breakfast

5 St Andrews Place, Llandudno, Conwy, LL30 2YR

T: 01492-878631 www.lymehurstbandb.co.uk E: lymehurst@live.co.uk

Come and enjoy relaxing, friendly accommodation at Lymehurst Bed & Breakfast. Lymehurst is situa in a quiet centrally situated cul-de-sac in Llandudno. Light, airy guest bedrooms, recently refurbishe provide modern, comfortable accommodation for guests. They have larger than standard en suites. Both rooms can be booked as double, twin or triple. One double room has an interconnecting singl room that has proved popular with couples travelling with a teenager, parent or friend. Each room h central heating, satellite television, tea and coffee making facilities, hair dryer and Wi-Fi access as we other extras such as tissues, sweets, solitaire & playing cards. A full cooked Welsh Breakfast, that incl Edward's of Conwy award winning sausages, and local free range eggs, vegetarian or continental br fast is served in our Breakfast Room that looks out onto the garden.

The Castle Hotel

High Street, Conwy, LL32 8DB

T: 01492-582800 www.castlewales.co.uk E: castle@innmail.co.uk

Set in a 300 year old coaching inn, Castle Hotel is a mile from Conwy Marina. Offering free parking and free WiFi, the hotel has elegant bedrooms and a traditional restaurant.Rooms at the Castle Hotel have period features and a private bathroom with a hairdryer. Rooms also feature a TV, tea/coffee making facilities and a work desk, and some have views of Conwy Castle.Dawson's Restaurant serves traditional Welsh cuisine using fresh, local produce. The bar offers a range of beverages and snacks, and generous cooked breakfasts are served daily, with continental options also available.Standing on the site of an ancient abbey, Castle Hotel is just a few yards from the scenic River Conwy. Llandudno Golf Club is within a 10-minute drive, and Conwy Castle is just 350 yards away.

Escape B&B

48 Church Walks, Llandudno, Conwy, LL30-2HL

T: 01492-877776 www.escapebandb.co.uk E: info@escapebandb.co.uk

Welcome To Escape. Llandudno's Premier Boutique Bed & Breakfast, offering exclusive, stylish and luxurious accommodation in a unique Victorian Town Villa.

Contemporary in style & offering 9 individually designed rooms with luxurious features such as, Flat Screen TV's, Bose iPod docking stations, Blu-Ray DVD players and high speed wireless broadband access. Situated near the beach, this luxury bed & breakfast is within a 10-minute walk of Great Orme Tramway, Llandudno Museum, and Home Front Museum. Llandudno Pier and Llandudno Tourist Information Centre are also within 10 minutes.

Manorafon Touring & Camping

Llanddulas Road, Abergele, Conwy, LL22 8ET

T: 01745-833237 www.manorafon.co.uk E: booking@manorafon.co.uk

Nestled between countryside and coastline with views over Gwrych Castle; Manorafon is only a short walk away from the town of Abergele, which can offer all the facilities associated with a small but lively town. Llandudno, Snowdonia and the historic castle town of Conwy are all within a 30 minute drive. From action packed to chilled out and peaceful the surrounding coastline and dramatic countryside won't let you down!

Within Gwrych Castle Estate • A stroll away from local inns and grocery stores • On the North Wales Coast • 15min walk to the beach • Modern Facilities • Woodland & Farm walks from the site • Warm welcome • Great Views

Pen y Bryn Farm & Holiday Cottages

Betws Yn Rhos, Abergele, Conwy, LL22 8PL

T: 01745-822344 www.holiday-cottages-north-wales.co.uk E: penybryncottages@gmail.com

Our comfortable self catering holiday cottages and farmhouse make a great base for exploring all that North Wales has to offer. Family friendly, our holiday cottages are located on 25 acres of private land for you to relax and enjoy. Situated just 3 miles from J24 - A55 we are within easy reach of all the top attractions in North Wales. We have over a mile of walks within our boundaries for guests to enjoy and our wildlife ponds are a popular place with the local wildlife and with guests enjoying bird watching or a nice picnic. If you are staying with us in our self catering holiday cottages or Farmhouse then you may also like to hire our Wood-Fired Eco Hot Tub which is available to rent on a nightly basis and is a great way to relax and unwind after a long day.

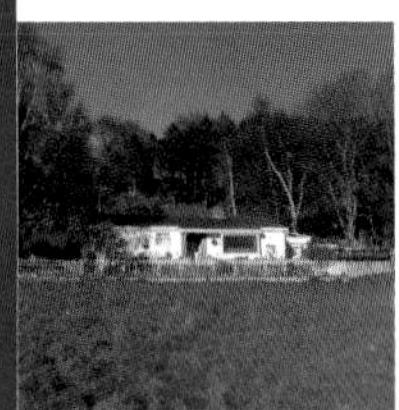

Padog B&B

Padog, Tanlan, Llanwrst, Conwy, LL26 0TY

T: 01492-640942 www.padogbandb.co.uk E: padogbandb@live.co.uk

Padog B&B is a 4* Bed and Breakfast accommodation situated in a beautiful and quiet elevated settir with picturesque views of the Conwy valley and river Conwy. Louise and Elwyn offer a warm and friendly welcome to their B&B, which is non-smoking throughout for your safety and comfort.Padog has 3 high quality bedrooms (1 double and 2 twin rooms which can also be re-arranged to doubles if required), at ground floor level. All rooms have en-suite facilities with complimentry toiletries, central heating, remote control LCD television, tea and coffee making facilities, alarm clock/radio and hairdry Wireless internet access is available free of charge. Children are welcome and a travel cot is available upon request. Secure off road parking and a lock up stone building for bikes is available.

The Lodge Hotel (Conwy)

Tal-y-Bont, Conwy, LL32 8YX

T: 01492-660066 www.thelodgeconwy.uk E: thelodgeconwy@outlook.com

THE LODGE
BAR RESTAURANT HOTEL

Set in the luscious Conwy Valley The Lodge is a brilliant venue and hotel to meet your needs, whatev they may be. From a range of rooms to an excellent venue to host Christenings; Birthday's; Weddings etc. we also serve food on a daily basis, with children welcome. As a place to stay The Lodge has 10 rooms of differing variety as well as a self-catering cottage, which sleeps 4 people. Please see accommodation section for further details. Given its central location on the banks of the Afon Conwy The Lodge represents the ideal location from which to explore North Wales. Under new management we want to make The Lodge one of the leading local businesses in the Conwy area, we feel the best v of doing so is by developing strong and long lasting customer relationships.

Cae Eithin Cottage

Victoria Park, Colwyn Bay, Conwy, LL29 7YY

T: 07711 169 458 www.caeeithin.com E: danmas56@gmail.com

This cottage is a quaint step back in time; the perfect place for a quiet retreat in the Welsh countrysid family adventures at the seaside, or simply an escape away with friends. It can accommodate 8 guest total. Up the wooden staircase you will find 4 bedrooms: 2 king size, 1 double and 1 twin. The propert also features 2 bathrooms (1 upstairs and 1 on the ground floor), both with quality shower and toilet facilities. The cottage is set in a naturally woody area, surrounded by tall trees and flowering plants. Located on a lane, it is a place of respite from the hustle of nearby tourist towns. Other facilities: Ironi board, fully equipped kitchen, T.V. with Freeview and DVD player, towels/bedding/sheets provided, o road parking for 2 vehicles, welcome pack with local Welsh produce, information pack for surroundin area.

Eyarth Station Guest House

Eyarth Station, Llanfair DC, Rhuthin, Denbighshire, LL15 2EE

T: 01824 703643 www.eyarthstation.com E: stay@eyarthstation.com

Eyarth Station Guest House is a former Railway station located near to Ruthin, the county town of Denbighshire in North Wales. We offer country guest house style accommodation set in an elegant ru location, considered to be an area of outstanding natural beauty. We have a variety of rooms offering views of the Clwydian mountains and scenic farmlands.

Bed and breakfast is available daily and the secluded gardens and magnificent scenery make it a perf place to stay if you are visiting North Wales and the surrounding areas.

We pride ourselves on being one of the friendliest places to stay and recommend booking early to av any disappointment.

Tir y Coed Country House

Rowen, Conwy, LL32 8TP

T: 01492 650219 www.tirycoed.com E: reception@tirycoed.com

Tir y Coed Country House is a haven of peace and tranquillity, nestled in over an acre of mature landscaped gardens.On the edge of Rowen, one of the Conwy Valley's most delightful villages, the Tir y Coed is within the boundaries of the Snowdonia National Park. The far-reaching views from Rowen extend to the magnificent mountains beyond. The medieval walled town of Conwy is just 4 miles away, as is the coast. The house has many large windows, filling it with a warm, bright and welcoming light. All of the bedrooms are beautifully appointed and individually designed, with luxurious fabrics and attention to detail ensuring that each room becomes the perfect retreat. All rooms have a TV, refreshment tray, clock radio and an immaculate en suite bathroom or shower room.

Penmaenmawr Bed & Breakfast

Rocklands, Brynmor Terrace, Penmaenmawr, LL34 6AN

T: 01492 623 555 www. northwalesbreakfast.co.uk E: contact@northwalesbreakfast.co.uk

All rates are per room per night including a scrumptious breakfast of your choice. Please check the availability on-line for current prices and any special offers. You can choose from two spacious double rooms and/or a single room, all with sea views across the beautiful bay towards the Great Orme and Puffin Island. Each of the welcoming rooms has been individually designed with your comfort in mind, for specifics, please see the room descriptions below. All are non-smoking. Whatever your choice of breakfast it'll be lovingly presented to you at a time of your choice (provided you let me know the evening before) in the comfortable breakfast room where you can enjoy stunning views. This is a dog friendly place.

Osborne's Cafe & Grill

Promenade, 17 North Parade, Llandudno, LL30-2LP

T: 01492-860330 www.osbornehouse.com E: sales@osbornehouse.com

Luxury all suite boutique hotel located on promenade with glorious sea views. All suites are spacious and romantic with super king size Hypnos beds, marble bathroom plus walk in shower, sitting room with a squashy sofa in front of a Victorian fireplace. Full air conditioning and free WIFI throughout. Stunning Osborne's Café/Grill an extravagant belle époque style bistro open all day and in the evening lit with a multitude of candles - just perfect for that romantic meal.

Free parking at rear. Ideal for touring Snowdonia, Portmeirion Italianate village, medieval castles, stately homes and the world famous Bodnant Gardens.

Trem Gwydir Holiday Village

Betws Road, Llanwrst, Conwy, LL26 0HE

T: 01492 641 543 www.tremgwydir.co.uk E: info@tremgwydir.co.uk

Whether you bring your bikes or your boots to explore the Gwydir Forest just across the bridge or bring your children to enjoy the brilliant beaches of North Wales. Or maybe you just want to relax, enjoy the scenery and watch the birds and wildlife on the river. But whatever your style of holiday, don't forget to bring your curiosity, because there's so much more to explore, from historic castles to iconic 60's TV. Whether you prefer action and adventure, or peace and tranquillity, you'll find everything you need for a brilliant value holiday at Trem Gwydir. Trem Gwydir is great for groups due to our special designed quadrangle area where 6 chalets are all together, perfect for a large party who wish to stay in 2 berth individual accomodation whilst having the atmosphere of all being together.

Paysanne Accommodation

147 Station Road, Deganwy, Conwy, LL31 9EJ

T: 01492-582079 www. paysannedeganwy.co.uk E: paysannecuisine@yahoo.cc

We are now offering up two holiday properties for you to enjoy a well-earned rest. The apartment abc Paysanne has now been renovated into a four star holiday flat for four guests, with breathtaking view across the river into Conwy and Snowdonia. Two bedrooms (1 twin, 1 double en suite), one bathroom spacious lounge and dining area with sensational views across the river Conwy and over to Snowdoni One large kitchen and a terrace area for alfresco relaxation. Our popular, French bistro is located beneath. A secluded beach is 5 minutes walk away. Ours is a relaxing base from which to explore som truly breathtaking and memorable sights, including the dazzling Bodnant Gardens, the Victorian pror enades of Llandudno, the rustic walks and rivers of Betws y Coed,

Sychnant Pass Country House

Sychnant Pass Road, Conwy, LL32 8BJ

T: 01492 596868 www.sychnant-pass-house.co.uk E: info@sychnantpasscountryhouse.co.

Located at the edge of the Snowdonia National park, in three acres of beautiful gardens, Sychnant Pas Country House features an indoor swimming pool and an outdoor hot tub. Each room, individually de orated with luxurious furnishings, and warm, comforting tones, features a private bathroom, includin bathrobes and slippers. The rooms are also fitted with a flat screen TV, refrigerator, hairdryer and iron, and coffee/tea making facilities. Along with the indoor heated swimming pool, Sychnant Pass Country House also has a sauna and a well-equipped small gym. The AA award-winning restaurant features a seasonal menu with food locally sourced wherever possible and cooked to order. It is complemented a small but beautifully formed wine list and well-stocked bar.

Storehouse Cottage

Glanwydden, Conwy, LL31-9JP

T:01492-546570 www.queensheadglanwydden.co.uk E: enquiries@queensheadglanwydden.co.

Bed and Breakfast / Self Catering Holiday cottage suitable for romantic weekend breaks close to the popular Victorian seaside town of Llandudno.

Charming, cosy, sleeps two.

Lovingly and sympathetically restored, The Old Storehouse standing opposite The Queen's Head in th village dates back to the early 18th century and was once the original storehouse of the Llangwstenn Parish. Every attention to detail has been taken to ensure a comfortable and decadent stay. Superb accommodation for self catering or bed and breakfast.

Minimum of 2 nights stay.

Yr Hafod Country House Bed & Breakfast

Trefriw, nr Betws-y-Coed, Conwy, North Wales, LL27 0RQ

T:01492 642444 www.hafod-house.co.uk E: enquiries@hafod-house.co.uk

A centuries old Welsh former farmhouse, nestling in the Conwy valley, that has been welcoming gues to Trefriw since 1906, Yr Hafod offers bed and breakfast accommodation in beautifully presented en-suite bedrooms. Leila and Shaun Hamilton-Hunter offer you a warm Welsh welcome. Leila is a born ar bred, Welsh speaking Trefriw girl and Shaun has been in the Conwy Valley for nearly 40 years. Togethe they've overseen the full refurbishment of Yr Hafod in a bid to create a warm and welcoming getaway destination in their beloved North Wales. Yr Hafods' rooms have been styled with comfort and quality mind.Each with its own entrance providing the freedom to come and go as you please and own terra with seating. The rooms are centrally heated, double glazed and are non-smoking.

The Grafton

14 Craig-y-Don Parade, The Promenade, Llandudno, Conwy, LL30 1BG

T: 01492 860054 www.thegraftonhotel.com E: info@thegraftonhotel.com

The Grafton is situated on Llandudno's Promenade and offers stunning sea views, rooms with modern en-suites, free WiFi and free parking. A wide choice of breakfast is served in the modern sea view dining room. Llanduno`s many amenities are within minutes stroll along the Victorian Promenade. The en suite rooms at The Grafton all include flat-screen TVs, a seating area, and alarm clocks. Hairdryers and tea/ coffee making facilities are also provided and some rooms have sea or Snowdonia National Park views. Each room has towels and toiletries.

A variety of cereals, toast and fruit juices, as well as cooked options, are available for breakfast. There is a variety of shops, cafes, and restaurants within a 2-minute walk.

Cleave Court Guest House

1 St Seriol's Road, Llandudno, Conwy, LL30 2YY

T: 01492 877849 www.cleavecourt.com E: info@cleavecourt.com

Heather and Colin welcome you to the Cleave Court Guest House website and hope that you spend a while exploring what we have to offer. If you need further information or availability please contact us on the details above.

Cleave Court offers quality accommodation in the Victorian Resort of Llandudno and is a short walk to the town centre and tourist attractions. There are 5 en-suite rooms, guest lounge, ample off-road parking, garden and free WiFi.Cleave Court makes every effort to offer a home from home, where guest can relax, enjoy a comfortable holiday getaway and delight in all Llandudno has to offer. So, if you are visiting Llandudno for pleasure or business we will provide comfort and quality for your stay.

North Wales Holiday Cottages

39 Station Road, Deganwy, Conwy, LL31 9DF

T: 01492 582 492 www.northwalesholidaycottages.co.uk info@northwalesholidaycottages.co.uk

North Wales Holiday Cottages is a Visit Wales accredited holiday letting agency based in Deganwy, Conwy. We have a wide range of properties around Conwy and across the whole of North Wales from small single bedroom apartments to large houses and remote locations to town centres. All of our team live locally, visit the properties and have a good knowledge of the area so feel free to call us for help and advice planning your holiday in this beautiful part of Wales. You can also find detailed information on our website for all the cottages as well as suggestions on things to do during your stay. Call us now or visit our website to find your perfect place to stay in Conwy.

The Empire Hotel & Spa

Church Walks, Llandudno, Conwy, LL30-2HE

T: 01492 860555 www.empirehotel.co.uk E: frontdesk@empirehotel.co.uk

The Empire Hotel in Llandudno comprises of a main building with 54 rooms, 2 restaurants, bar, health spa, gym, indoor and outdoor heated swimming pools with sauna, steam room and whirlpool. Immediately next door, No. 72 is a separate building with just 8 large rooms and the facilities provided by the main building (This building does not have a lift). This property has Free Car Parking. Empire Hotel, No 72 and Osborne House all have their own unique style and are located in very close proximity to each other. All guests can make use of the excellent facilities provided by both Empire Hotel and Osborne House.

The Queens Head

Glanwydden, Conwy, LL31-9JP

T:01492-546570 www.queensheadglanwydden.co.uk E: enquiries@queensheadglanwydden.co.

The Queen's Head is a most remarkable country pub in terms of good food, wine, beer, welcome and character.Priceless chefs who have a passion for local produce, excellent staff, effortless charm and a warm welcome. The bar, with its relaxed atmosphere and roaring log fire, is a lovely pre-dinner drink venue. The original styling of The Queens Head provides the perfect ambience for lunch or dinner. Situated on Cycle Route 5. The idyllic country village of Glanwydden is just a 5 minute car journey to t Victorian seaside town of Llandudno and the A55. Perfect for long country walks, cycling, or a day on the beach, it's a great location close to all amenities. The Queen's Head offers a warm welcome to pre theatre dinner guests with Venue Cymru just a 5 minute drive away.

Osborne's Cafe & Grill

Promenade, 17 North Parade, Llandudno, LL30-2LP

T: 01492-860330 www.osbornehouse.com E: sales@osbornehouse.com

Osborne's Cafe and Grill is open every day from 10.30am to 10.00pm (Sunday 9.00pm)
Lit by a multitude of candles, with opulent drapes and dazzling chandeliers, gilt edge mirrors and original art. This romantic bistro/cafe with brasserie style food has a diverse a la carte menu prepared and presented in a modern way with an air of informality. Osborne House has six luxurious large suite (500 sq.feet) with wonderful sea views. Elegantly furnished with antiques and fine paintings. Our siste hotel Empire Hotel is located just 200 yards away around the corner from Osborne House. Empire Ho is larger than Osborne House and has 60 rooms, an indoor heated swimming pool, gym, spa and two popular restaurants.

The Rabbit Hole

3/4 Trinity Square, Llandudno, LL30 2PY

T: 01492 330600 www.therabbitholecafe.co.uk E: welcome@therabbitholellandudno.co.uk

The Rabbit Hole is a contemporary cafe, that believes a healthy body can help improve and retain a healthy mind. We promote healthy, nutritious food including vegetarian, vegan and gluten free along with our regular menu. The Rabbit Hole is a Social Enterprise, set up in 2013 by Aberconwy Mind the Mental Health Charity, every penny spent in our café goes back into mental health services for our community and providing employment opportunities for those in recovery from mental ill health. We also offer outside catering service for: Business Meetings, Training Courses, and Private Functions created from our buffet menu and custom Vegan celebration cakes we have room hire at our café too.

The Beach Cafe

118 Glan y Mor, Penrhyn Bay, Conwy, LL30 3PR

T: 01492-549297 E: the-beach@outlook.com

We are a newly refurbished cafe-bar located right opposite the beach in Penrhyn Bay. We are open for breakfasts, lunches, snacks, pancakes, afternoon teas and coffees and our bar is always open if you'd simply like a drink. Come in and enjoy our friendly atmosphere, redecorated cafe and new bar! Relax outside on our new decking and take in the wonderful sea view!

Dawsons Restaurant

The Castle Hotel, High Street,Conwy. LL32 8D

T: 01492-582800 www.castlewales.co.uk E: mail@castlewales.co.uk

Our Head Chef, Andrew Nelson is ably supported by his team of young aspiring Welsh chefs being mentored in all that's good about Welsh food. Consultant Chef/Director Graham Tinsley is the Manager of the Welsh Culinary Team and as you can imagine, passionate about his food! Peter Lavin and Graham have worked together for over 25 years and have always shared the belief that a good hotel must have good food. Dawson Bar's great new look is now complimented by the new look lounge and garden courtyard with an even better atmosphere and range of hand pulled beers & fabulous wine list.

Bistro Bach

22a-24 Mostyn Avenue, Craig-y-Don, Llandudno, Conwy, LL30 1YY

T: 01492-582800 www.bistrobach.co.uk E: mhj.legatte@gmail.com

For an outstanding quality, sumptuous French feast, we can highly recommend the Bistro Bach in Llandudno. This beautifully decorated restaurant is a fine dining experience not to be missed. From light snacks such as confit of shredded duck, to sumptuous sandwiches and an unforgettable dinner menu; there is something superb here to appease just about any palette. Slow-braised Conwy Valley lamb shoulder and Fillet of Sea Bass are among the array of beautifully cooked and stunningly presented locally-sourced and traditionally prepared dishes that you can expect from this exceptional establishment. All have been prepared to the highest standards, with service to match – ensuring you the ultimate dining experience. The meals are reasonably priced, especially considering their degree of excellence, which many a great online review is testament to.

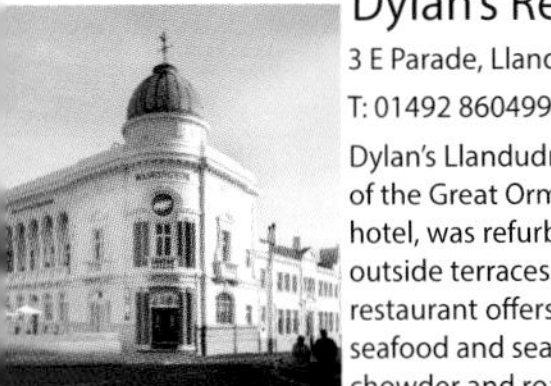

Dylan's Restaurant

3 E Parade, Llandudno LL30 1BE

T: 01492 860499 www. dylansrestaurant.co.uk E: llandudno@dylansrestaurant.co.uk

Dylan's Llandudno is located on the waterfront at the far end of East Parade, providing stunning views of the Great Orme and Llandudno Bay. The fabulous Grade II listed building, formerly the Washington hotel, was refurbished by Dylan's in 2017 and re-opened as a 250 seat restaurant over two floors and outside terraces. A bespoke stand alone cocktail bar is located under the building's iconic dome. The restaurant offers a family friendly, relaxed dining experience. The menu features locally sourced fish, seafood and seasonal farm produce served creatively in dishes ranging from artisan pizza to seafood chowder and roasted Welsh lamb rump. All our restaurants are are open from 11am-11pm, 7 days a week, throughout the year (except for Christmas Day).

The Cottage Loaf

Market Street, Llandudno, Gwynedd, LL30 2SR

T: 01492-870762 www.the-cottageloaf.co.uk E: info@the-cottageloaf.co.uk

The Cottage Loaf has all the character, charm and looks of a traditional village inn, rather oddly though you'll find it nestled down a back street in the centre of Llandudno…

With its roaring log fire and its warm and inviting interior, it is the perfect place to escape from the long winter months. Its large, bright and colourful gardens are the perfect place to enjoy those ever too brief summer months too. At the Cottage Loaf we pride ourselves on our homemade traditional dishes. Pub food has a style of its own and we like to think that we add our own twist to the classic dishes. Our talented and creative Chefs also love to try out their new and original flavours so be sure to try some of the "not-so-typical" dishes on the menu.

The Mulberry Conwy

Conwy Marina, Ellis Way, Conwy, LL32 8GU

T: 01492 583350 www.mulberryconwy.pub E: info@mulberryconwy.pu

With its imposing castle and extensive town walls, Conwy boasts some of the finest military architectu in Europe. The castle and the town it dramatically overlooks both date from the late 13th century, and were laid out on the orders of King Edward I following his victory over the Welsh Prince Llywelyn ap Gruffudd. Whatever the occasion, we promise to make it one that you and your guests will remember for many years to come. With a full banquet menu along with a tailored one-to-one service to your tastes and budget, The Mulberry is perfect venue for weddings, civil partnerships, christenings, birthdays and wakes. Soak up the sunshine and enjoy a tipple in our beer garden. Drop us a line & tell about your experience in our pub.

Y Bedol

Conway Road, Tal-y-Bont, Conwy, LL32 8QF

T: 01492-660164 E: y-bedolinn@outlook.com

The Bedol Inn at Tal y Bont is a lovely example of a truly traditional Welsh pub. This family run establishmnet is popular with locals and visitors alike, Y Bedol Inn is set in the heart of the Conwy Valle and enjoys sensational mountain views, as well as a pretty river running alongside. With open fires, rea ales aplenty, and a good hearty menu, you are assured of a warm welcome and sustenance galore.

Trip Advisor Review

Really lovely food in a very cosy setting with friendly and helpful staff. The lamb dinner was lovely and the rib eye steak perfect served with home made chips - no frozen veg used here. Followed by jam rolypoly and custard - mmmm - and home made Creme caramel. I'll be going back.

Paysanne

147 Station Road, Deganwy, Conwy, LL31 9EJ

T: 01492-582079 www. paysannedeganwy.co.uk E: paysannecuisine@yahoo.co

After 27 years, we have shaken things up a little. With our chef of eight years, David Hughes, we have started serving Sunday lunch for the first time. We're also allowing you the chance to start the weeken early with our new Friday lunch menu. We have over a quarter of a century's experience in the art of wining and dining our guests. We hope very much that you'll join us soon. We have over a quarter of a century's experience in the art of wining and dining our guests. We hope very much that you'll join us soon.

We are now offering up two holiday properties for you to enjoy a well-earned rest. The apartment abc Paysanne has now been renovated into a four star holiday flat for four guests, with breathtaking views across the river into Conwy and Snowdonia.

Tapps Micropub

35 Madoc Street, Llandudno, Conwy, LL30 2TL

T: 01492-870956 E: smoothmobilebars@ymail.com

TAPPS is a micropub in Llandudno, North Wales, serving real local ales, craft beers and ciders from numerous fantastic microbreweries. We offer a friendly, relaxed atmosphere in which you can indulge some of North Wales' (and beyond) finest offerings. We provide a good beer and cider selection for ou guests, with several of our taps changing constantly, along side the beer we also stock a variety of fine Welsh spirits, as well as International ones, and a select wine list. So join us for a beer and a bar snack whilst listening to some gentle vinyl in the back ground, we even have a book exchange and selectior of games to while away the time. We open from 12 noon every day, well behaved dogs are also welcome, so we look forward to seeing you soon!

Johnny Dough's Wood-Fired Pizza- Llandudno

129 Mostyn Street, Llandudno, LL30 2PE

T: 01492 871813 www.jdoughspizzas.co.uk E: info@jdoughspizzas.co.uk

Here at Johnny Dough's we strive to bring you the best in wood-fired pizzas. We put a lot of time into creating a menu that offers that something for everyone. We have new school pizzas for those who fancy something a little different, but we also pride ourselves in showing a lot of love and care to those old favourites. So, whatever your flavour, please come and join us in appreciating some proper pizza, crackin' service all in chilled surroundings.
We look forward to meeting you soon!

Coast Cafe & Gift Shop

71 Rhos Promenade, Rhos on Sea, Conwy, LL28 4EN

T: 01492-544358

Coast Café & Gift shop located alongside the beautiful seafront of Rhos on Sea, Family run established as an iconic café & gift shop within the area. Whatever you are looking for, from an early breakfast to a late lunch or a light snack to afternoon dinner, we have the perfect dish on offer.
Enjoy it with a nice pot of our refreshing hot or cold drinks. Open seven days a week 9am until 6pm with our famous cake table and luxury Belgian chocolates counter - Highly proud of our kitchen & its cleanliness which has earned us a 5 Star Hygiene Rating & an amount of outstanding ratings across our Trip Advisor page.

The Tal Y Cafn

Tal Y Cafn, Conwy Valley, Colwyn Bay, LL28 5RR

T: 01492-650016 www.talycafn.com E: info@talycafn.com

Welcome to the Tal-Y-Cafn, a modern day Coaching Inn turned Bistro, with a delicious locally sourced menu, local beers, spirits and a carefully selected wine list. Enjoy the fantastic atmosphere and warm welcome of your host Graham Higgins and Head Chef Dylan Timperley, in this recently redeveloped 200 year old inn set in one of the most beautiful locations in the Conwy Valley. Just a short drive from Betws-y-Coed, Llandudno, Conwy and the North Wales coast – Tal-Y-Cafn sits right at the centre of some of the best days out in North Wales. Whether you fancy a day out in the Snowdonia National Park, action packed adventure underground at Go Below, flying through the air at Zip World or catching a wave at Surf Snowdonia – the Tal-Y-Cafn is a great place to stay or relax, eat and drink.

The Holland Arms

Trofarth, Nr Abergele, Conwy, LL22 8BG

T: 01492-650777 www.thehollandarms.co.uk E: info@thehollandarms.co.uk

The Holland Arms, a charming 17th century coaching inn on the edge of the SnowdoniaNational Park in North Wales. It has a substantial beer garden with stunning views of the countryside, a lounge bar, public bar and a relaxing restaurant. Lynnette and Cherie the proprietors will welcome you and the head chef Darren are all on hand to make sure you enjoy your visit. We open with a Lunch time Menu with Bar meals being served. Staff can take your evening bookings for the restaurant please book early to avoid disappointment.We cater for all and have great meals for children to choose from. The Family can enjoy our varied menu from fresh local produce with a fine selection of wines, beers, and the local beer from Conwy Brewery and Orme Brewery, we are sure you will find something to your taste.

Chandlers Brasserie

Chandlers Brasserie, Trefriw, Conwy, LL27 0JH

T: 01492 642458 www.chandlersbrasserie.co.uk E: info@chandlersbrasserie.co.uk

Arwel is fluent in the Welsh Language & was born in the village of Trefriw. He is a well-established Local Chef with 32yrs experience and a large local trade following. His cuisine has a Seafood & Portugese influence from his days at The Lord Newborough in Dolgarrog & the Jersey Channel Islands where he worked for many years. Anna was also born in North Wales & moved to Cardiff with her family when she was 5yrs old. She has gained 28yrs experience in all areas of the hospitality business trade.
We had a vision & a dream to have our own restaurant & found this very special gem in the beautiful village of Trefriw & so here we are...... To all who visit us we want to warmly welcome you to our piece of paradise & hope you enjoy.

Amser Da Café Bar

Heol yr Orsaf, Llanrwst, Conwy, LL26 0BT

T: 01492 641188 www.blasarfwyd.com E: amserda@blasarfwyd.com

We have two sides to our company – first we serve the public on the high street of Llanrwst through our Delicatessen and Wine Shop. Amser Da is our Café Bar, it is the ideal place to relax and sample great coffee, home produced savoury foods and delightful desserts made in house. Lastly, we also offer bespoke catering services, having catered for a number of events from weddings to film sets. Amser Da Café Bar is the ideal place to relax and sample great coffee, home produced savoury foods and delightful desserts made in house. We offer an assortment of wines and spirits at Amser Da which can also be found across the road at Blas Ar Fwyd, our delicatessen, which houses a fantastic selection of deli produce, wine, cheese, meats and more.

The Kinmel Arms

Llandyrnog, Denbigh, Denbighshire, LL16 4HN

T: 01824 790 291 www.kinmelarms.com

The Kinmel Arms Pub in Llandyrnog is a traditional free house, country pub in an idyllic location at the foot of The Clwydian Range. From our beer garden we have superb views looking over Moel Arthur and Pen y Cloddiau. Nestled between the two historic market towns of Denbigh and Ruthin and just 10 minutes off the A55, or a short detour off the Offa's Dyke path … a perfect place to drop in for a pint of quality cask ale by our roaring log fire (or in our stunning beer garden … if the sun is out!!!) or for some quality freshly prepared, home cooked food, from bar snacks, sandwiches and light lunches to whole hearty meals with locally sourced produce and home cooked specials that are freshly prepared on a daily basis. Here at The Kinmel Arms we pride ourselves on the quality and freshness of our food.

The Groes Inn

Llanrwst Road Conwy North Wales LL32 8TN

T: 01492 650545 www.groesinn.com E: groes.inn@jwlees.co.uk

The oldest licensed pub in Wales, The Groes Inn is a owned by the JW Lees family, and is a traditional Inn perfectly nestled between the beautiful Conwy estuary and the stunning Tal Y Fan mountain. It offers panoramic views combined with a warm cosy welcome, fresh seasonal food and a great range of quality ales and wines. The perfect place to relax and unwind in Wales. We're dog friendly at The Groes Inn, because your best friend deserves a holiday too. The Groes Inn is all about the food. We have two dining areas: a handsome restaurant with a bright, airy conservatory, and a heart-warming, snug and welcoming pub with cosy log fires. Our menus feature a range of freshly prepared seasonal dishes that have been made using fine, locally sourced ingredients.

L's Coffee & Books- (Conwy)

7 High Street, Conwy, North Wales, LL32 8DB

T: 01492-596661 www.lscoffee.co.uk

Here in L's Coffee & Bookshop we are in a prime location, located halfway up the left hand side of the high street. Here you will discover a wonderful array of delicious mouth watering foods fit for a king and L's Coffee and Co carries on in that tradition today. A tradition that means L's is the sort of place that even Royalty would feel at home.Whether your coming in for a coffee on the go, breakfast on the run, lunch with the family, or just an afternoon tea with your friends, L's has a great menu of food and drink to tempt you back at anytime of the day. Children and dogs are always welcome here and with free doggie treats and plenty of water, we'll look after your four legged friend just as well as we would look after you.

Johnny Dough's at The Bridge

Rose Hill Street, Conwy, LL32 8LD

T: 001492-572974 www.johnnydoughs.com E: info@johnnydoughs.com

As the reputation of Johnny Dough's spread, the time came to look for another premises from which more pizza-love could be spread! So when a pub in nearby Conwy became available, Johnny partnered with the four local breweries that owned The Bridge and re-opened it as Johnny Dough's at The Bridge. The combination of the excellent range of drinks from the four local breweries and Johnny's signature style, quality and speed of service made for a winning combination and very quickly this second location became a thriving restaurant, serving amazing food and drink to impressed locals and happy tourists alike.

Tu Hwnt i'r Bont Tearoom

Nr Inigo Jones Bridge, Llanrwst, Conwy, LL26 0PL

T: 01492 642322 www.tuhwntirbont.co.uk E: sales@tuhwntirbont.co.uk

For visitors to North Wales generally (and the Conwy Valley, Betws-y-Coed in particular), Tu Hwnt I'r Bont is itself, in this idyllic setting, an obvious 'must see' tourist attraction; offering as it does, a truly authentic and hugely enjoyable 'taste' of North Wales and its culture. Comfortably accommodating 50 people inside in traditional style, we seat a further 30 outside in our lovely tea garden, including full waitress service. By prior arrangement, groups of 20 to 80 people are welcome.

We have our own private car park situated at the rear of the building, suitable for 30 cars.

Tu Hwnt I'r Bont Tearoom and Restaurant is open: 10.30 – 5.00 (waitress service)

L's Coffee & Co

71B Conway Rd, Llandudno Junction LL31 9LT

T: 01492-592020 www.lscoffee.co.uk

Our Llandudno shop is all about community and welcoming new customers together with our excellent artisan coffee, coupled with a considered menu, everything we do is lovingly made, from the freshly baked pastries and delicious sandwiches, to our great tasting slow roasted coffee which goes along with our all day breakfast just nicely. We're not only famous for our all day breakfast, we have a concise menu to suit all tastes. Alongside our craft coffee we also have an extensive selection of healthy smoothies and juices. We want you to enjoy a moment of peace; whether you're meeting friends or just having time out. The team at our Llandudno Junction shop hope to see you soon.

Characters Tea HouseTea House

11 Llwelyn Avenue, Llandudno, Conwy, LL30 2ER

T: 01492-872290 www.charactersllandudno.com E: info@charactersllandudno.co

Welcome to Characters Teahouse and curiosity shop. We are a family run business with the idea of bringing back the past time of sitting down for Afternoon Tea, whilst also being able to mooch aroun and take a look at the quirky items we have for sale. Whilst being enchanted by our old boutique style Teahouse, to accompany your visit, we have a variety of our vintage teas and delicious cakes and pastries. If you are catching up with old friends or simply want to sit and watch the afternoon roll away.Characters teahouse brings you the a warmth and comfort that can only be found in your own home.

Llindir Inn

Llindir Street, Henllan, Denbigh, Denbighshire, LL16 5BH

T: 01824 -90291 www.thellindirinn.com

The Llindir Inn is a thatched pub situated in the heart of the Welsh countryside in a village, Henllan. Th pub boasts tremendous character with a thatched roof, a large outdoor seating area and colourful flo ers surrounding. Inside, you approach a warm copper bar with a suspended copper wine rack and cor fortable chesterfield arm chairs in front of the open log fire. There is a large selection of real ale from t village's multi award winning brewery 'Heavy Industry Brewing' as well as a fantastic wine list providin wines from around the world. The Llindir has a huge variety of gins and whiskeys and will be providin cocktails at the start of summer 2017. The Llindir only started serving food from December 2016 but i was worth the wait. The young and talented chef has trained for more than 7 years and has a number welsh culinary awards. The menu provides traditional pub food but expect some italian influence.

Penrhyn Arms

Pendre Road, Penrhyn-side, Llandudno LL30 3BY

T: 01492 549060 www.penrhynarms.com

Penrhyn Arms is a warm and welcoming village pub in the heart of Llandudno. Set in a newly renovated period building, it boasts homely tables and a cosy atmosphere with fireplaces to ward off the cold. In summer, you can enjoy a choice of indoor and outdoor eating areas, with a beautiful oasis of palms, tropical ferns, olive and lemon trees, and a water feature making it very easy on the eye. Perhaps the most noteworthy feature is their pizza oven. Their wood fired pizzas are an absolute treat as their many rave online reviews will attest to. They serve real ales, ciders, gin and spirits for those who enjoy a liquid beverage. In fact the Penrhyn Arms has been featured in the Daily Telegraph as one of the best cider pubs in Wales. An excellent choice should you wish to enjoy a hearty, home-made meal in a traditional, clean setting. As an added bonus, this pub is also dog-friendly.

Barratt's of Tyn Rhyl

167 Vale Road, Rhyl LL18 2PH

T: 1745-344138 www.barrattsattynrhyl.co.uk e: ebarratt5@aol.com

A period Country House set in its own grounds approximately a half mile from the seafront. With a renowned restaurant that uses fresh Welsh produce. The house is full of character - old oak panelling, comfortably furnished and dates back to 1672. You would be forgiven for thinking that Rhyl is something of a gastronomic desert - until, that is, you have sampled the cuisine at Ty'n Rhyl. It's not ju the quality of the food that comes as a pleasant surprise. Ty'n Rhyl is a double gabled house, and is of great historic interest. Without altering its character it has been transformed into a beautiful restaurar with rooms by award winning chef David Barratt and his wife Elvira. Our well appointed, completely non-smoking restaurant has a reputation for quality, home cooked cuisine.

SNOWDONIA MOUNTAINS & COAST

have travelled to many places in the UK and abroad, and have seen some fantastic scenery along e way, but none more beautiful than that of Snowdonia. It's sometimes rugged but Spectacular ountain ranges are simply breathtaking at times, and one can't fail to see why millions of people vel to the area every year, either on holiday, for the weekend, or as I do on many occasions simply t for the day. I have become to know the area just like the back of my hand and when that ppens, then you can truly say how magnificent a place is. But enough about me. You are truly oilt for choice when it comes to Activities, Attractions, Quaint Villages, and Blue Flag Beaches, owdonia, Mountains & Coast simply has the lot! But don't just take our word for it; the proof is erely in the pudding as they say.

owdonia certainly has its biggest hot spots, Llanberis, Betwys-y-Coed, Beddgellert and that is only t a few of the great villages that you can come across along the way. There are also great towns o, like Caernarfon, Bala and the university city of Bangor, which, despite its disappointingly run wn high street, it is still worth a visit. Easy to get to and with a great road system running through very veins, Snowdonia has to be one of Wales most visited areas, so I would always consider oking accommodation well in Advance. You will always find something to suit all tastes and dgets within our wide selection and we have included a great line up of amazing attractions, nazing accommodation providers and restaurants that are absolutely top notch, so there you have get reading, get booking and have a fantastic time whatever you decide to do first.

Plas Glyn-y-Weddw

t: 01758 740 763 e: info@oriel.org.uk
www.oriel.org.uk

One of Wales' most picturesque & oldest art venues. A gothic styled mansion built in 1857. Exhibition changes every 6-8 weeks. Tea room + craft shop on site. Adult + kids art workshops, concerts, lectures, craft fairs along with many other activities held throughout the year. Arts Centre located within a Grade II* listed Victorian Gothic Mansion, with magnificent views of Cardigan Bay and the mountains of Snowdonia. Residential Arts Courses including watercolours, oil paining and more. Permanent exhibition of Swansea and Nantgarw porcelain. Licensed tea room, paintings for sale, craft shop. Licensed for Civil Weddings. We also cater for business meetings, conferences and private functions. Self catering apartment sleeping 10+ also available. With free entry to the gallery and an award winning tea room and craft shop to enjoy there is something for everyone at this most relaxing of locations.

AUTHOR'S REVIEW

Wales is no stranger to all things old, so it won't come as a surprise to hear that Plas Glyn-y-Weddw is Wales' oldest art gallery. The minute I walked through the door I felt a good vibe about the place, a feeling that I had been here before, even though I hadn't, such is the warmth of this amazing arts centre. Our decision to feature Plas Glyn-y-Weddw wasn't just about this great gallery. There is an amazing woodland walk to be found here which in part includes the Wales Coastal Path. During my visit I learned about the new amphitheatre that is located within the onsite woodland, regular performances throughout the summer are on offer and a full list of what's on, can be found by visiting the web address above. Finally, but I think important to mention, the gallery has a great little coffee shop with the best 'lemon drizzle cake' I've ever tasted!

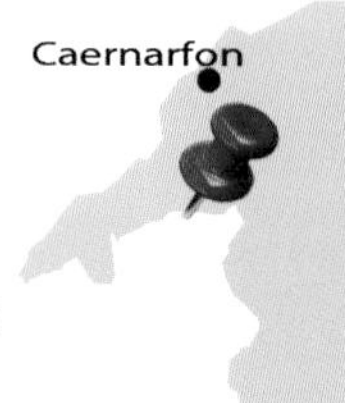

Llanbedrog, Pwllheli, Gwynedd, LL53 7TT

ɢypsy Wood

t: 01286 673133 e: info@gypsywood.co.uk
www. gypsywood.co.uk

We're a must North Wales attraction for all animal, train, nature and fairy lovers - There's lots to do and see for the whole family. Gypsy Wood is an enchanting outdoor attraction for the whole family and is situated in the foothills of Snowdonia, North Wales. Set in 20 acres of natural beauty, visit us and discover one of Wales's best kept outdoor secrets. enjoy the parks ¾ km Train Ride – explore the wood and find the fairies and make a wish. If you feel adventurous, bring your wellies to explore the wetland walk. Bring a picnic – Gypsy Wood offers light refreshments and afternoon teas. Finish off your visit by taking home a little keepsake from our gift shop. Gypsy Wood is filled with friendly animals of many different types – our animals will be pleased to make friends with you – come and see where we live and you can watch us play in our beautiful Gypsy Wood home! Hop on Woody's train and enjoy one of our fabulous adventure play areas.

AUTHOR'S REVIEW

It's not often, that you get to visit a Top Attraction and, use an award winning loo all in the same day! But with a visit to Gypsy Wood that is exactly what you will be doing! I knew this site was going to be great before I got here, but just how great, I did not know. It's no big secret that this attraction is predominately for twelve's and under, but I have to say that adults find it hard not to share in the magic that this enchanting attraction has to offer. I dare say the owners wouldn't have known how popular this attraction would be to all of its visitors, but in my professional opinion, not only should this attraction be winning this award, as one of Wales's Top 100 Attractions but so should its owners, for their creativity, and ingenuity, in the sheer brilliance that is, Gypsy Wood.

Caernarfon

Bontnewydd,Caernarfon, Gwynedd LL55 2YA

Pant Du Vineyard

t: (01286) 880806 / 881819 e: post@pantdu.co.uk
www: pantdu.co.uk

Pant Du Vineyard and Orchard is situated on the stunning slopes of the Nantlle Valley, Snowdonia, North Wales. The vineyard and orchard has been planted on the south facing glacial slopes of the valley, at the foothills of Snowdon.

Pant Du is a family run business with a café, shop on site. Spectacular views of the magnificent Snowdonia mountain range can be seen to the North East, and panoramic views of the sea to the West, Pant Du is an idyllic location to enjoy the spectacular natural beauty Snowdonia has to offer.

Since producing the first bottle of wine in 2010 the company has established a reputable name for themselves in producing award winning wines, and high quality cider and apple juice.

The company's latest venture is premium still and sparkling bottled water. The project arose back in January 2013 following the discovery of spring water under the land at Pant Du.

AUTHOR'S REVIEW

Who would of ever known that there is an award winning vineyard perfectly situated on the west coast of North Wales. Well there is and it came as a great surprise even to me! So I put on my coat and gloves and went to investigate for myself and what I found was just that, an award winning vineyard on the West coast of North Wales. Pant du is far more than just that. There is the usual wine tasting sessions that comes with every visit to a vineyard, but with a great cafe and their all year round vineyard tours, this has now been turned into one of North Wales must see attractions. I had a very pleasurable tour around part of the vineyard, by its owner Richard Huws, who in his own right, is a BAFTA award winning TV and Film Cameraman. Richard took me to see the well, where he knew and believed there was water underneath, this resulting in the addition of still and sparkling water to the Pant du Family.

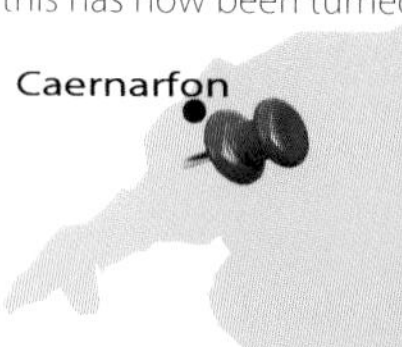

County Road, Penygroes, Caernarfon, Gwynedd, LL54 6HE

Felin Uchaf Centre

t: 01758 780280
www.felinuchaf.org
e: felinuchaf@hotmail.co.uk

The Felin Uchaf Centre is a social enterprise on the Llŷn Peninsula that provides training courses and volunteering opportunities specialising in traditional and eco-skills from thatching to wooden boatbuilding. In addition to running short skills courses: they host an exciting year-round programme of cultural events, storywalks and nature activities; enabling people to enjoy the rich variety of ancient sites and wildlife areas on the surrounding peninsula – from breakfast walks in the spring woods to sunset suppers and stories on the Iron Age Hill forts. Visitors to the 23 acre centre can walk around the footpaths and watch the ongoing eco-building projects, enjoy a picnic in the community gardens and visit the farm shop for organic veg and fine woodcrafts. A Centre for Living Arts & Science is opening soon, crafted of local natural materials such as oak and straw bale and built by trainees and volunteers it will host an eco-visitor centre, exhibition gallery and organic café.

AUTHOR'S REVIEW

At Top 100 Attractions we are not only impressed by visitor numbers, and size of facilities, we judge all of our attractions mainly on visitor experience and value for money. The Felin Uchaf Centre, here on the Llŷn Peninsula has both of the aforementioned qualities in abundance. Hundreds of volunteers from all over the world have dedicated thousands of hours toward creating a whole range of traditionally inspired buildings using locally sourced natural materials from thatched Celtic roundhouses to a mediaeval barn and boatbuilding workshop. A magical event that happens here, is the programme of fire-lit storytelling evenings that take place regularly throughout summer in the subterranean earth-house. This attraction couldn't be in anyway better placed, for the Llŷn Peninsula is steeped in ancient history, and thanks to this centre's founder, Dafydd Davies-Hughes, Celtic roundhouses can be seen. on this beautiful part of the Welsh coast.

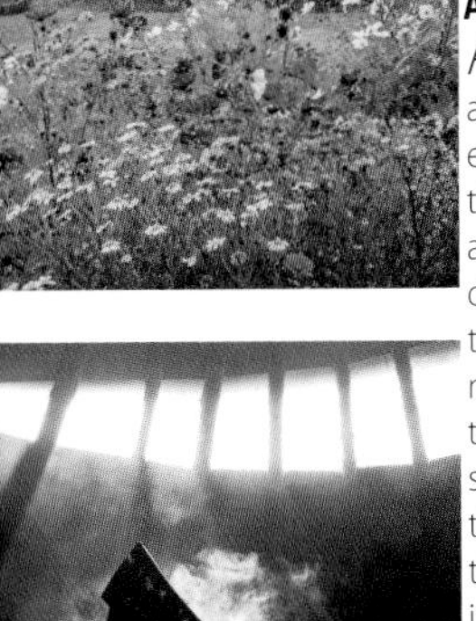

Caernarfon

Rhoshirwaun, Pwllheli, Gwynedd, LL53 8HS

Conwy Falls Forest Park

t 01690-710336 e manager@conwyfalls.com
www conwyfalls.com

The spectacular Conwy Falls runs though the deep gorge of the Fairy Glenn, set in nearly 10 acres of SSSI designated ancient forest. Laced with paths, viewpoints and glades, the Forest Park can be enjoyed by placing a £1 coin per person in the turnstile next to the cafe. You are welcome to bring picnics and well behaved dogs to this special corner of the National Park.
The spacious and attractive Conwy Falls Café was designed by Sir William Clough Ellis to compliment the architecture of Portmerion. It is open from 9am until 5pm every day of the week, serving hot and cold food, cakes, snacks and drinks. They also host events throughout the year.
There is plenty of free parking, ample seating inside and outside with panoramic views, and free Wi-Fi is available over much of the land via outdoor access points. Toilets with a shower facility are available.

AUTHOR'S REVIEW

The cafe here at the Conwy Falls Forest Park is steeped in history, as it was originally built by Sir Clough Williams-Ellis of Portmeirion fame and when you look at the building head on, you can certainly see his influeneces and what a wonderful job he did. The cafe is now owned by the same company that runs the very popular attraction 'Go Below' and the same standards they adopt over there, is replicated within the cafe. Great customer service, fantastic locally sourced food and a good atmosphere, all goes towards making this a very popular place. Then, there is the Conwy Falls Forest park itself, with acres of lush forest and plenty of things to see and experience, a visit to this wonderful and often magical forest park is most certainly a must. Even though this has Conwy in the name, it is very much within the Snowdonia National Park.

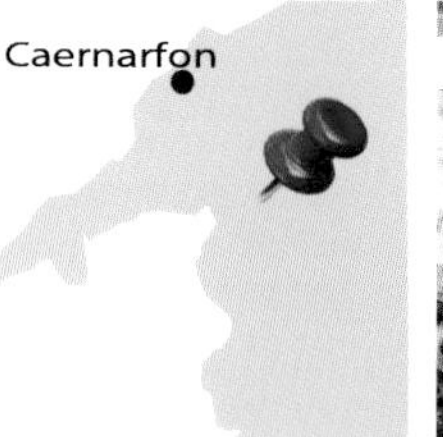

Pentrefoelas Road, Penmachno, LL24 0PN

Go Below - Underground Adventures

t: 01690 710108 e: ask@go-below.co.uk
www.go-below.co.uk

Test your nerve by journeying through a mountain via a series of exhilarating challenges on one of Go Below Underground Adventures' 3 epic trips.Try your hand at zip-lining through enormous caverns on the world's longest and deepest underground zip ride, boat across a glistening underground lake, traverse over a giant void, scale a waterfall and abseil your way down to the deepest point in the UK in the largest slate mine in the world! Think you can handle that? Then challenge yourself to the leap of faith; jump off a 70ft ledge into an abyss on the world's first and only underground free fall! On all our adventures, our knowledgeable trip leaders can show you old artefacts and share info on the mine history. It's 100% raw and genuine adventure! Go Below is open 7 days a week, all year round.

AUTHOR'S REVIEW

Just when you thought Frodo in the Lord of the Rings trilogy had a tough journey, your adventure has only just begun! The mines explored are in the local area and you'll be transported there to take part in one of their varied trips. Challenge, Hero Xtreme and Ultimate Xtreme are a just few of their popular adventures, which offer increasing levels of difficulty. Go Below also has their popular "Mine to Mountain" trip. This exciting trip involves taking a boat across a flooded underground cavern, travelling across a zip line to your next destination. Then, with the company of your colleagues, you abseil down an underground cliff face to reach a further awe inspiring chamber, certainly not for the faint hearted. After lunch, your group leader will take you on a waterfall climb and your ascent back to Terra Firma is via a steep climb up the mine shaft! And if that isn't enough to get your pulse racing, their newest underground adventure lays on even more challenging roped activities.

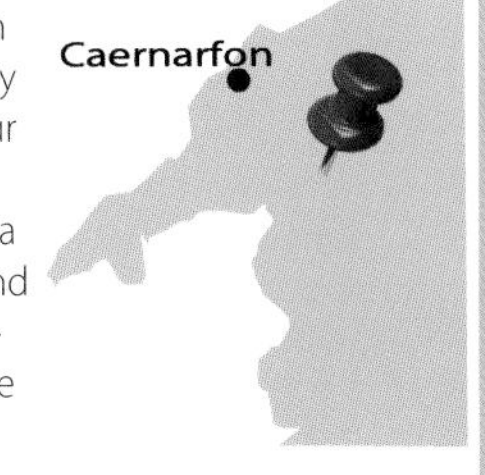

Penmachno, Betws-y-coed, Conwy, LL24 0PN

Geo Helicopters

t: 01286 830 800
e: info@geohelicopters.co.uk
www. geohelicopters.co.uk

This is a fantastic opportunity to experience the magic of flight in a way that only a helicopter can provide before committing to a full course.

Flight Discovery Day:
This is an undeniably magical day, involving 2 full briefings and 2 full training flights, including a demonstration of how a helicopter really is a unique aircraft.

Private Pilot's Licence:
GEO Helicopters provide the full PPL(H) with a structure and timetable to suit all individual requirements. All flight training, ground school, ground exams and flight test are conducted at our facility in Caernarfon Airport.

AUTHOR'S REVIEW

Caernarfon Airport is home to Her Majesty's Coastguard Rescue Team, but there is another helicopter team based at the airport and they are quickly becoming one of Wales's must do experiences. Geo Helicopters have become one of Snowdonia's trusted Helicopter pleasure flight operators and with the backdrop of the area they have to work in, this all adds to the magic of taking a flight with them. Geo Helicopters offer not only pleasure flights around Snowdonia and Anglesey, but they also give helicopter flying lessons as well. With trained pilot Captain Gareth Owen at the helm, you wouldn't be in safer hands. I found Geo to be a very organised and professional business and this is backed up by the service they provide to all of their passengers. So if you want to see Snowdonia in a totally different and very unique perspective, what are you waiting for? about the absolutely stunning scenery which will surround you along your trek. No matter what time of the year you're visiting the area, there is always something beautiful about these mountains.

Caernarfon

Snowdonia Riding Stables

t: 01286 479 435 e: snowdoniaridingstables@gmail.com
www. snowdoniaridingstables.co.uk

Located in North Wales between Snowdon and the sea, Snowdonia Riding Stables offers you superb riding amongst some of the best mountain and coastal scenery in the British Isles, whether you are a complete beginner or a competent rider. With miles of traffic free bridleways we have access through spectacular scenery amongst the foothills of Snowdon. Pony Trekking & Riding with Snowdonia Riding Stables: We have carefully selected horses and ponies to provide a range of sizes, types and temperaments to suit riders of all abilities (or none at all!) We have been established over 30 years with a wealth of experience, and some of our customers are third generation! Snowdonia Riding Stables is an approved British Horse Society Riding School and Trekking Centre and is approved by the Pony Club.

AUTHOR'S REVIEW

After visiting Ireland recently whilst putting together some pages for my new Irish book, I took a horse ride on the beach in Sligo. I had such a great time, and enjoyed myself that much, that I vowed when I re-wrote my Welsh book, I would hunt down and feature the best riding stables Wales has to offer, and after much research, I uncovered Snowdonia Riding Stables. Nestled perfectly under the magnificent Snowdonia Mountain range, these stables have been operated by the same family for decades, and in my opinion, coupled with their professionalism and what they have to offer, makes them one of the top riding stables in Wales. Then of course I must tell you about the absolutely stunning scenery which will surround you along your trek. No matter what time of the year you're visiting the area, there is always something beautiful about these mountains.

Caernarfon

Waunfawr,Caernarfon, Gwynedd, LL55 4PQ

Dyfi Distillery

t: 01654 761551 e: danny@dyfidistillery.com
www: dyfidistillery.com

Dyfi Distillery produces artisan gins crafted with wild Welsh botanicals foraged in the Dyfi Biosphere. Based at Corris Craft Centre, near Machynlleth and this locally produced gin has been recognised in the Great British Food Awards 2017 for the best gin produced in the UK. The prestigious award is for its Pollination Gin, which the judges described as "seriously beautiful". Dyfi Distillery is one of nine studios at the Corris Craft Centre, run by brothers Pete and Danny Cameron. They established the first commercial gin distillery in Mid Wales in 2016. Pete has lived, worked and foraged in the Dyfi Valley for 35 years, while Danny is a long standing drinks industry professional and international-standard judge. While they are a tiny distillery, they welcome curious and enthusiastic gin-hunters. They don't offer formal tours or events, but rather welcome all visitors equally, and if you'd like to chat to the family, taste what they do, or just browse around the information boards and see through the glass screen between our cellar door shop and the distillery, they would love to see you.

AUTHOR'S REVIEW

Gin is fast becoming one of the UK's most popular drinks and here at Dyfi Distillery and also with being a family run business, it was always in the stars that brothers Pete and Danny would team up to create this award winning distillery. On the day I visited the them on that cold January morning, I was fortunate to see Pete at work in his white coat, it was almost like watching watch a scientist at work in his lab, in fact to be honest, that's exactly what it is. There are no tours around this istillery, but most days you will be lucky enough to witness the guys at work and with so much hard work that goes into distilling their award winning Gins, there is always something going on in there. With a well stocked shop and very clued up staff, there is always someone on hand to ask any questions you may have, no matter how big or small.

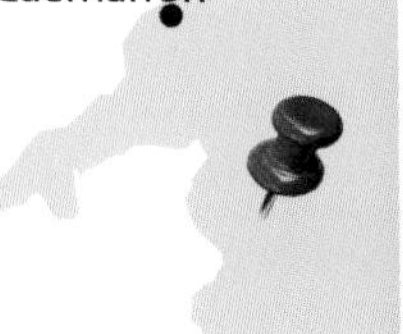

Unit 5, Corris Craft Centre, Machynlleth, Powys SY20 9RF

he Slate Caverns

t: 01766 830306 e: bookings@llechwedd.co.uk
www.llechwedd-slate-caverns.co.uk

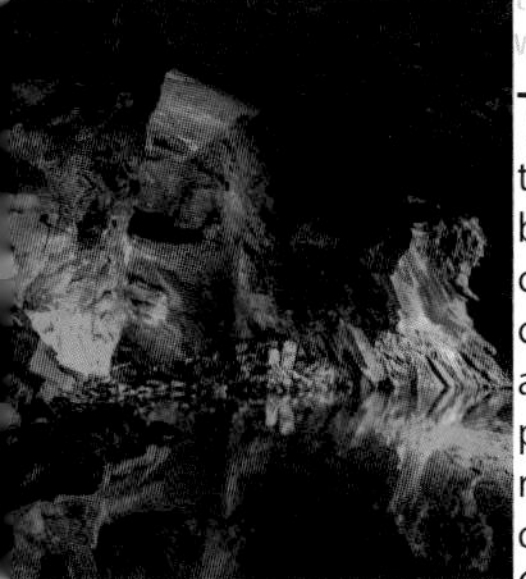

The Llechwedd Deep Mine Tour is a family friendly interactive tour with new technology, amazing effects and features a beautiful projection over the underground lake. It is a place children use miner's primitive drills and hang by chains from the chamber walls just as the men would have done over 150 years ago. They lay fuses setting off powerful blasts using a Victorian plunger - which is proving to be very popular! Visitors gasp at the real life dangermen as they bring to life one of the most death defying elements of Victorian health and safety!
Customers access the caverns using Britain's steepest cable railway to levels of 500ft underground and the passionate tour guides – many of whom have local connections with the mine and whose families can be traced back to Blaenau's past – creates great memories for our visitors.
Our Quarry Explorer is an off road adventure that will take you right into the heart of Llechwedd's man-made mountains. Travelling in a military 4 x 4 truck you'll drive up high to the top of the quarry and into some of the massive craters that were made by blasting the tops off our hundred-year-old caverns.

AUTHORS' REVIEW

The Slate Caverns really is an attraction within an attraction! What I really like about the caverns is it's ability to be as much of an interesting indoor attraction as well as an outdoor one. There is a well stocked Gift Shop as well as The Quarryman's Tavern, with it's restaurant offering great food at even greater prices, it makes sense to have lunch here too. I would most definitely allow a good few hours to be able to see and experience everything at The Slate Caverns with it's many varities of tours and workshops. There is something for every member of the family here and in saying that The Slate Caverns are really a value for money attraction.

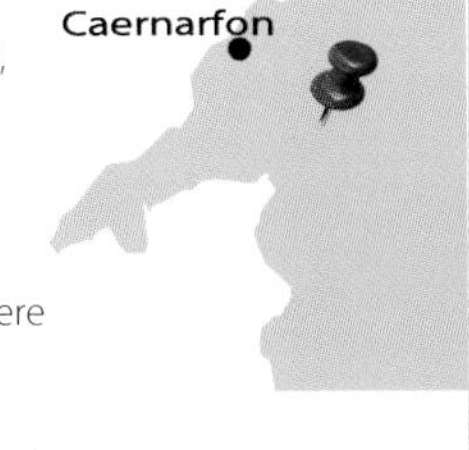

Blaenau Festiniog, Gwynedd, LL41 3NB

GreenWood

t: 01248-671493 e: info@greenwoodforestpark.co.uk
www. greenwoodforestpark.co.uk

Voted Best Family Attraction in North Wales for seven years running, days out don't get much better than this! GreenWood is set in 27 magical acres, and it's easy to see why it's a full day out - discovering woodland adventure, awesome attractions and forest family fun. Make a splash on the UK's only solar powered water ride, Jump aboard the world's first people powered roller coaster or zoom down the longest sledge run in Wales! Children will love discovering the super bouncy Giant Jumper, exploring the turrets of TreeTop Towers, taking their shoes and socks off for the BareFoot Trail or aiming for gold at Archery.We have those rainy days covered too! The Enchanted WoodBarn is full of the latest indoor play with a separate area for the under 3s.
Prepare to be dazzled in the Forest Theatre where during the school holidays you will find our fabulous entertainers, including: Smarty Marty the Clown, Harley's Showtime and Erwyd the Jester- they just can't wait to make you laugh.

AUTHOR'S REVIEW

Snowdonia is the ultimate outdoor destination, and with many of the tourist attractions within this area having an outdoor theme, there is no way you can ever get bored visiting here. GreenWood is a great example of that outdoor fun I speak about, fun that can be enjoyed by all ages of the family. Nestled in a prime location between Bangor & Caernarfon, GreenWood really was an attraction that took me by surprise. I visited here late in the summer of 2018, and was very impressed with what I saw. The staff were friendly, helpful, and there was hardly any litter on the floor whatsoever, which tells me an awful lot about an attraction! I know I talked a lot at the beginning of this review about outdoor fun, but I was so surprised at the amount of indoor fun here as well! Definitely worth a visit!

Bush Road, Y Felinheli, LL56 4QN

Centre for Alternative Technology

t: 01654-705950 e: visit@cat.org.uk
www.cat.org.uk

Nestled in the foothills of Snowdonia, the Centre for Alternative Technology (CAT) is a world-renowned eco centre that researches and supports greener ways of living. With seven acres of hands-on displays, examples of environmentally responsible building, renewable energy, organic gardens and family holiday activities, there is something for everyone at CAT. Follow CAT's interactive Zero Carbon Britain Trail to explore what an environmentally friendly world with reduced emissions will look like or pull on your boots and stomp up through the CAT woodland to discover breath-taking views of the Snowdonia National Park from the Quarry Trail. New for 2018 – explore the new CAT garden displays and discover what you can do to make yours wildlife friendly whilst ensuring a good crop of vegetables. Inspired to learn more about sustainability? CAT offers a wide range of exciting and informative short courses that explore subjects from eco-crafts to environmental building and renewable energy.

AUTHOR'S REVIEW

From the minute you arrive in the car park of this attraction, it hits you that you've arrived somewhere completely different. The excitement starts to build as you journey up to the centre on a water-pumped cliff railway - one of only a handful in the world. As I walked around CAT, it hit me just how much we take for granted and many questions were answered along the way. Questions like, 'how would we cope without electricity, gas' just a few of the many daily elements we take very much for granted. There is so much to see, too much to tell you about in just a short amount of words, but what I can say is, you will definitely not be disappointed with your visit here. But you don't need to just come for the day, the attractions website will guide you to all the many courses they have available here.

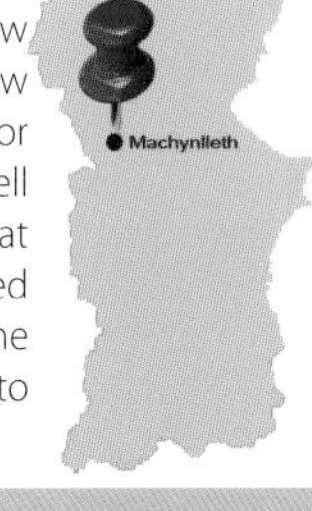

Llwyngwern Quarry, Pantperthog, Machynlleth, Powys, SY20 9AZ

Zip World (Velocity)

t: 01248 601 444 e: info@zipworld.co.uk
www. zipworld.co.uk

Penrhyn Slate Quarry, located near Bethesda in North Wales, is now home to Zip World Velocity, the fastest zip line in the world and the longest in Europe. Enjoy the view of adrenaline seeking zippers from our viewing area or take on Zip World Velocity itself! Our new Adventure Terminal is now open, enhancing the Velocity experience in so many ways. Check in and kit up are now in the new building, where there are lockers to store your belongings whilst you fly. Upstairs is our new Blondin Restaurant with spectacular views over the quarry lake, where your loved ones can grab something to eat and drink whilst they watch you zip over head on the viewing platform. Sit down, relax and refuel after your adventure with our delicious dishes which have been developed by celebrity chef, Bryn Williams. The slate quarry is the largest in the world and has been at the centre of UK natural stone quarrying and it's heritage since the thirteenth-century and a major operation for over 400 years.

AUTHOR'S REVIEW

Snowdonia has been waiting for this attraction for so long now, partly because of the magnitude of this attraction's size, and mainly because Zip World is the second largest Zip Wire in the world, the largest one being in South Africa, which then, makes this the largest Zip Wire in the Northern Hemisphere. Because of my great fear of heights, I have not sampled this particular attraction, but I have visited the site, and it is absolutely breath taking to see. In my opinion the Ogwen Bank side of Snowdonia is the rugged brother of the area which means the terrain lends itself very well to this attractions charm. Taking a trip in the military vehicle up to the summit will make the hairs on the back of your neck stand on end, and this once in a lifetime opportunity will then become very real!

Bethesda

Penrhyn Quarry, Bethesda, Bangor,Gwynedd, LL57 4YG

Zip World (Titan)

t: 01248 601 444 e: info@zipworld.co.uk
www.zipworld.co.uk

Zip World is all about offering a unique range of attractions, that means families, adventure seekers and everyone in between, can experience world-class experiences at any one site. The newest member to Zip World, Zip World Titan is situated near the historic slate mining town of Blaenau Ffestiniog, at the world famous Llechwedd Slate Caverns, making North Wales the Zip Line Capital of the World. Zip World Titan will have riders flying high over Moor, Mountain and Mine whilst flying down eight kilometers of wire in unison of teams of four, reaching up to 70mph speed. **The summer experience** at Zip World Titan encompasses all ZipWorld Titan three zip lines – Anarchy, Bedlam and Chaos! Totalling over 8km of zip lines to race down while taking in the surrounding views. **The winter experience** at Zip World Titan offers riders the opportunity to take part in the last two zip lines, Bedlam and Chaos only, as the first zip line, Anarchy, is the most susceptible to bad weather.

AUTHOR'S REVIEW

After the huge success of Zip World Velocity, it was no surprise to me that there was to be a second site in the planning. What was a huge surprise, was the speed at which this happened. Zip World has become one of the biggest attractions to hit Wales in years and the slickness in the way they run these attractions is awe inspiring. Your experience at Zip World Titan will last around two hours, with around 8 kilometres of zip lines, you'll have two hours of pure adrenalin fuelled fun. Don't get me wrong, travelling down all of these zips lines is amazing and it will be one of the best experiences you've ever had, but I have to say that the views and the scenery which is on offer over the Llechwedd Slate Caverns is absolutely staggering. Zip World has a great website, so what are you waiting for?

Blaenau Festiniog, Gwynedd, LL41 3NB

Talyllyn Railway

t: 01654 710472 e: Enquiries@talyllyn.co.uk
www: talyllyn.co.uk

The Talyllyn Railway is a historic narrow-gauge steam railway, set in the beautiful Mid-Wales countryside. Running from Tywyn to Abergynolwyn and Nant Gwernol, the line passes the delightful Dolgoch Falls and there are excellent forest walks at Nant Gwernol. Experience the nostalgia of historic steam trains in some of Wales' finest countryside. The railway starts on the coast at Tywyn, snakes through the foothills of Cader Idris to Dolgoch Falls, Abergynolwyn and Nant Gwernol. The train clings to the hillside as it passes through woodland and over ravines. The trip takes about an hour each way. Your ticket allows you to break your journey and extend your day. You could take a country walk, explore wooded paths, discover waterfalls or visit the beach. Tywyn Wharf station is home to the Narrow Gauge Railway Museum, which tells the story of little railways across Britain, and King's Cafe which has hot and cold menus, lunch time specials and a licensed bar. Quarryman's Tea Room at Abergynolwyn serves a range of refreshments and light bites.

AUTHOR'S REVIEW

Being hidden on the west coast of Wales, you could be forgiven for missing The Talyllyn Railway. But now I've told you about Talyllyn there can be no forgiveness for not visiting it. This railway has everything the bigger named railways have, and if truth be known just as bigger history to boast. Taking you from the coast to the countryside, you get to see a short glimpse of what Wales is all about. When doing my research on this attraction I visited every station along its route, and I found every member of staff to not only be totally professional, but the stations were totally immaculate right down to the public toilets. In today's day and age these things matter and the management and staff realise this and its clear to see that they care about every single one of their passengers. A true breath of fresh air!

Caernarfon

Paintball Wales

t: 01248 340000 e: info@PaintballWales.com
www.PaintballWales.com

Centrally located in the woods between the sea and the mountains, at the foot of the beautiful Snowdonia National Park. Perfectly situated for North and Mid Wales, the Wirral, Chester, and the Liverpool and Manchester area. Even if you're coming from outside the area, our prices, fun 'n' party atmosphere and beautiful location merely 5mins from the picture postcard pretty village of Llanberis at the foot of Mount Snowdon are well worth the short trip to make a day out of it!

Firmly established for over a decade, and attracting major nationwide events such as BBC Radio 1's Six Weeks of Summer with Top Chart Show DJ's, PaintballWales.com have got years of valuable experience working with schools, universities, colleges, youth clubs, community groups, charities and corporate groups, as well as with Birthday Parties, Stag & Hen Do's and individuals looking to have lots of fun.

AUTHOR'S REVIEW

What denotes a "Top 100 Attraction in Wales" are mainly two principal criteria: Visitor experience set against value for money; and the big bonus criteria is always the memory of visiting that attraction pleasantly staying with you at the forefront of your mind for at least one or two weeks after you've visited it. If it ticks both of the above, well then it certainly falls within our Top 100 Attractions in Wales! There are very few outdoor activity attractions that can genuinely claim that as PaintballWales.com . First of all, we can truly say that "Affordable Paintball has Arrived!" Fitting straight into our first criteria, and indeed as their own motto highlights: "Play VIP-Style, without the VIP Pricetag!", they have the "Best Prices.. by a Long Shot!!" (if you pardon the pun!)

Secondly, and as we can see from both their website (which is simply the same as their name!) and indeed from the wonderful customer feedback and comments on their Facebook Page (www.facebook.com/Paint-ballWales) from thousands of repeat players, they are still talking and remain excited about their experience for literally weeks after their visit, and keep commenting on, tagging themselves and sharing the pictures which are posted on PaintballWales.com's FB Page after every session!

Caernarfon

"Warrior Woods", Nr. Llanberis, Snowdonia, LL55 3AX

Galeri Caernarfon

t: 01286 685 250 e: post@galericaernarfon.com
www. galericaernarfon.com

The award winning £7.5m building includes:

- 394 seat theatre and cinema
- Workspace units
- Art Space (exhibiting a mixture of work by local, national and international artists)
- Rehearsal studios and soundproof rooms
- Meeting rooms
- DOC Café Bar (serving a fresh, local home-cooked menu)

Galeri has over 400 events on an annual basis, ranging from workshops, music concerts, theatre / drama, film screenings, dance and comedy.
International stars often perform at Galeri, from Llŷr Williams to Bryn Terfel and Lee Evans, Rob Brydon and Alan Carr.

AUTHOR'S REVIEW

The building of this state of the art theatre and conference centre couldn't have come at a better time. Caernarfon itself has always been famous for its castle and if you were to ask anyone else that would be it. The c ompany (Galeri Caernarfon Cyf) that owns the centre have been responsible in my opinion for giving Caernarfon a lease of new life, and a visit to this theatre only goes to strengthen that. Since 2005, the award winning centre has been pulling in the masses with such names as top UK comedian 'Lee Evans' and the Welsh opera singer 'Bryn Terfel'. Check out their website above and book your tickets, sit back in luxury and enjoy the show!

Doc Victoria, Caernarfon, Gwynedd, LL55 1SQ

Ffestiniog & Welsh Highland Railway

t: 01766 516000 e: enquiries@festrail.co.uk
www.festrail.co.uk

The Ffestiniog and Welsh Highland Railways are two of the Great Little Trains of Wales, together offering a wide variety of travel options through Northern Snowdonia. The Ffestiniog Railway runs between Blaenau Ffestiniog and Porthmadog. Built to carry slate from the quarries, the little steam trains now haul carriages of passengers through the beautiful Vale of Ffestiniog. The newly reopened Welsh Highland runs through from Caernarfon to Porthmadog sharing a station with Ffestiniog. The impressive Beyer Garratt locomotives haul modern comfortable carriages on this coast to coast journey through the Snowdonia National Park. The scenery is breathtaking as the train crosses the lower slopes of Snowdon before plunging through the forest and alongside the river in the Aberglaslyn Pass on its way to Porthmadog. Refreshments are available with hot snacks on many Welsh Highland services. Trains run daily from late March until the end of October plus selected dates in winter.

AUTHOR'S REVIEW

There are 5 railways featured within this book and each one deservedly so. The task we undertook choosing which 5 railways we would feature wasn't an easy one. The Ffestiniog & Welsh Highland Railway is a slick operation with some of the best scenery routes Wales has to offer. With three main stations in Snowdonia you'll never be far away from catching one of these great little trains, and with the schedules being the way they are, it's quite easy to do both the Ffestiniog Railway & Welsh Highland Railway in one day. The reason I say this is because both routes here in Snowdonia like our other trains featured in this book have something completely different to offer. So whether you're a train enthusiast or not, you will not be disappointed here. What we also liked about this attraction was its restaurant Spooners' serving anything from a fresh sandwich to a full Sunday dinner all at prices that are totally affordable.

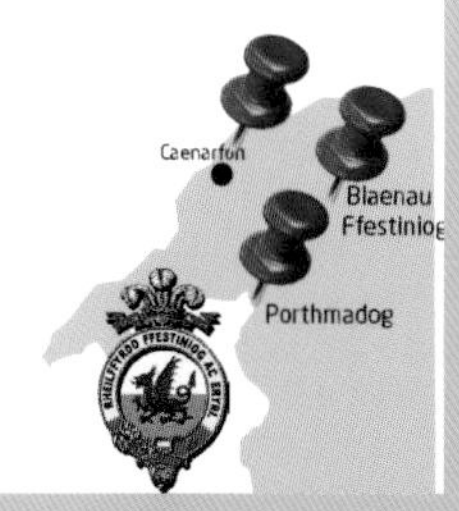

ernarfon, LL55 2YD-Blaenau Ffestiniog, LL41 3HE-Porthmadog, LL49 9NF

Airworld Aviation Museum

t: 01286-832154 e: info@airworldmuseum.co.uk
www. airworldmuseum.co.uk

Airworld Aviation Museum is based at the former RAF Station Llandwrog, which is now Caernarfon Airport, on the beautiful seafront at Dinas Dinlle. The museum tells a fascinating tale with real planes, models, displays and a mini cinema, screening 20 minute shows. This museum is unique, in that visitors are welcome to sit in the cockpits of early post war jet fighters, and training aircraft, and experience the real thing. Parental supervision required! We also have an interesting airport shop, selling aviation memorabilia. On the same complex, is the original control tower, airport reception (where you can book pleasure flights over Snowdonia and the Llyn Peninsula) a modern café and runway viewing area, where you can enjoy watching planes take off and land, microlightsand sometimes a helicopter.

AUTHOR'S REVIEW

Exploring through this particular section of our book will alert you that Snowdonia, without doubt, has its fair share of tourist attractions to go beyond the expectations of tourists of any age, to embrace and relish to their heart's content. For any one of you, with even the slightest love for all things ying, then a trip to Snowdonia, certainly would not be complete without learning what the Airworld Aviation Museum has to offer. Prepare yourselves for an unforgettable visit to the magical and wonderful place, that has the backdrop of a fully functional airfield. This makes the all-round experience an even more exciting and realistic one! Observing and admiring the design and functions of these amazing planes taking off and landing, could have definitely entertained me for hours on end. To my astonishment, I learnt that this museum in particular, provides their tourists with the opportunity to sit in a cockpit of one of their exhibitions. This unique experience makes Airworld so different to any other aircraft museum becauseyou feel as if YOU are the pilot making all those difficult decisions faced by today's modern day pilots.

Caernarfon

Caernarfon Airport,Dinas Dinlle, Caernarfon, LL54 5TP

Pleasure Flights

t: 01286-830800 e: info@caernarfonairport.com
www.caernarfonairport.com

Caernarfon Airport is located in the heart of Snowdonia,operating scenic and training flights all year round. With an on-site aviation museum, Cafe, home to the Wales Air Ambulance and the HM Coastguard Helicopters operated by Bristow.

The airport was originally opened in 1941 and known as RAF Llandwrog. The base was primarily used for training gunners, radio operators and navigators and later was the home for the RAF Mountain Rescue. Please use the navigation bar at the top of the page to navigate your way around the site. The trial lesson can be your first step into a career in aviation. If its not the career you are after and you just want to experience the thrill of flying an airplane…that's fine. Flights are available in 30 minute or 60 minute sessions.

Helicopter Trial Lessons:

This is a fantastic opportunity to experience the magic of flight in a way that only a helicopter can provide before committing to a full course.

AUTHOR'S REVIEW

I have to be totally honest with you, with me having a total fear of heights I haven't been up on one of the pleasure flights yet, or taken a flying lesson, but I have spoken to people at the airport that have and the reviews are outstanding! There is literally no better way to see Snowdonia or Anglesey, either by plane or by helicopter and at Caernarfron Airport, you can experience both! I also couldn't get over how inexpensive it is to take a 20 minute introductory flight, but if you ask me, for just a few extra pounds, you'd be far better to go for the 40 minute experience, as once your up there, you just won't want to come down. With a great little cafe and a really friendly team, Caernarfon Airport really does embody what this book is all about. A huge Top 100 Attractions thumbs up!

Caernarfon

Caernarfon Airport,Dinas Dinlle, Caernarfon, LL54 5TP

Ropeworks Active

t: 01286-871114 e: hello@ropeworksactive.co.uk
www. ropeworksactive.co.uk

Set in beautiful woodland with breath-taking views of lakes and mountains, Ropeworks Active is a memorable experience for all ages. Join us to explore our Ropes Courses, or why not try out our Offsite Adventure Activities.

High Ropes Session

Two hours of adventure. including treetop challenges, giant swing, leap-of-faith and abseil. Why not join us for an extended session and fit in activities like our external climbing wall.

Low Ropes Session

Lots of fun to be had on our low ropes adventure course traversing rope bridges, balancing on beams, sliding through tunnels and fimish off zipping in the trees.

Offsite Activities

Book our fully qualified guides for your offsite adventure in Snowdonia. Trek and scramble through the mountains or explore underground mines. Challenge yourself to gorge walking where you explore the spectacular gorges of North Wales with exhilarating jumps, thrilling ascents and challenging scrambles.

AUTHOR'S REVIEW

This Book is full of massive attractions, and there is a good chance you have already heard all about them. There is a large portion of the attractions that are called our hidden gems and they all deserve their place within this book. Take Ropeworks Active for instance. This is an attraction that caters literally for everyone, adults through to children. All are looked after and they do this with the addition of their low ropes as well as their high ones. Whether you want to swing eloquently like a monkey, or by coming to grips with the popular spiders web, there is literally something for everyone. But with the addition of Gorge & Hill Walking and Climbing to their portfolio, Ropeworks Active is fast becoming one of Llanberis's best activity attraction. But don't take my word for it, pay them a visit and see for yourself!

Caernarfon

Gifach Du, Padarn Country Park, Llanberis, Gwynedd, LL55 4TY

The Fun Centre

t: 01286-671911 e: info@thefuncentre.co.uk
www.thefuncentre.co.uk

The Biggest indoor play area in North Wales, with two giant drop slides, swinging ropes, dark maze, tumble tower, spining discs and so much more, we cater for children from toddlers to 12yrs old even the adults can join in!!

We have an under 5's soft play area, 5yrs and over play are, cafe, Go Karts, Lazer shooting, museum, and patio area.

Why not have your childrens birthday parties with us, we do childrens parties, teenage parties, even adult parties e.g hen do's, stags, 18th, 21st, 40, 50th etc... The main play area features a giant 25ft high drop slide and a 25ft high double drop slide plus, ball pools, swing over nets, tumble towers, spinning steps, dark maze squeeze rollers and much more.Take the wheel of a Go Kart with a variety of different vehicles ranging from a Ferrari to an American truck and then test your driving skill on the Fun Centre's oval track. While the children wear themselves out in the play area why not refresh yourself in the licensed family friendly restaurant which offers a wide variety of freshly cooked food.

AUTHOR'S REVIEW

I don't feature a huge amount of Fun Centres in my books, as they're either done really well, or not that well at all? So after making that statement, you can imagine, that the inclusion of 'The Fun Centre' located in the heart of Caernarfon, this is one that is actually ran very well. I would go as far as to actually say, that the Fun Centre is probably one of the best I have ever visited! Established in 2001, within what was once Caernarfon's main church, Christchurch, this Play Centre was designed with both children and parents in mind and the owner Mr Stuart Crisp, really does know his stuff when it comes to designing Play Centres, in fact, he also inspects play centres, for the actual body that governs these kind of attractions. With great facilities and really good coffee, this attraction really did take me by surprise.

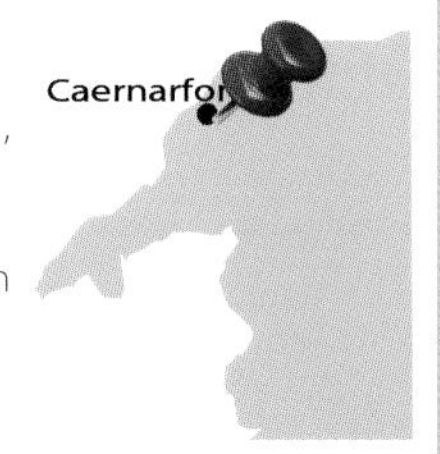

Electric Mountain

t: 01286-870636 e: info@electricmountain.co.uk
www. electricmountain.co.uk

Have you ever wondered how electrical appliances we rely on most in our day to day lives are powered? Or how does the National Grid cope during periods of exceptionally high demand? These questions plus much more are answered as you witness the creation of electricity at Electric Mountain.Visitors can take a guided tour around Dinorwig Power Station starting with a sound and vision spectacular at Electric Mountain, illustrating the role that pumped storage plays in ensuring the country's electricity demands are always met, before descending deep inside the ancient Elidir Mountain's labyrinth of dark and imposing tunnels. Electric Mountain's friendly and knowledgeable guides show you the main features of the complex, from the massive main inlet valve chamber to closeup views of the world's fastest response turbine-generators. These units have a dynamic response capacity from zero output to full power within seconds, and are housed in Europe's largest man-made cavern.

AUTHOR'S REVIEW.

I took a tour inside the Electric Mountain, knowing exactly what to expect, as I have taken a tour inside this world famous power station on many occasions. What you will find for those who also have been before, is that every time you take a trip inside the mountain, you notice or learn something new every time. You cannot fail to be amazed by the ingenuity of this power station and the importance it places in our everyday lives from making a cup of tea in the adverts of 'Corrie' to turning the hoover on, the electricity you are using has a good chance of coming from the Electric Mountain, set in the beautiful and picturesque village that is Llanberis. Why not have lunch in their newly refurbished restaurant, they have a wide selection and the staff are really friendly! Finally, the visitor centre itself has gone through a refurb and so, this means the experience at the visitor centre is now even better!

Caernarfon

Electric Mountain, Llanberis, Gwynedd, LL55 4UR

ach Ventures

t: 01286-650643 e: info@bachventures.co.uk
www.bachventures.co.uk

We offer bespoke courses to families and friends, schools and youth groups and skills courses in Kayaking / Sea Kayaking and Rock Climbing. We have a passion for developing everyone's enjoyment and knowledge of our area and the exciting activities we offer.Our staff are experienced and hold National Governing Body qualifications in the activities they run. We are happy to provide you our Risk Assessments and Operating Procedures should you wish them. We tailor our courses to your requirement having first discussed 'what you want to do / learn / get out of it'. We do not just make you fit into a pre-planned session of activity. This is as relevant to an introductory sea kayaking course to a school group walking up the mountains looking at glaciation effects.Our instructors allow you to discover Yourself – 'what you can do / achieve' Community – 'the benefits of working with others' New skills

AUTHOR'S REVIEW

Bach Ventures is a new addition to the many fantastic attractions and experiences that you will find within this great little book. Run by Karen and Gordon Neil, Bach Ventures have got well over twenty years of experience under their belts and this really does show when you look at their credentials. With activities such as Kayaking, Climbing and Coasteering just to name but a few, I know youre in safe hands with these guys. Then of course, you have Pentre Bach Bunk House and Camping Site. Ever wondered what it's like to stay in an atmospheric Alpine bunkhouse, well now you can experience it for yourselves. Together with their camping site and one of the most scenic areas in Snowdonia, I can guarantee that you will not be disappointed with what Bach Ventures has to offer. They have a great website, so hop on there now and see for yourself just exactly what I'm talking about.

Caernarfon

Pentre Bach, Waunfawr, Gwynedd, LL54 7AJ

Llanberis Lake Railway

t: 01286-870549 e: info@lake-railway.co.uk
www. lake-railway.co.uk

Discover the timeless appeal of our narrow-gauge steam trains - a more leisurely way to travel and the perfect way to savour the grandeur of Snowdonia. Our little steam engines take you on a five-mile return journey alongside Lake Padarn, right in the heart of Snowdonia.
The journey takes you past the 13th century Dolbadarn Castle, across possibly Britain's shortest river and past Llanberis' twin lakes. From Llanberis the train runs non-stop through the Padarn Country Park, joining the 1845 slate railway route to run along the shores of Lake Padarn to Penllyn, and giving stunning views of Snowdon, the highest peak in England and Wales. The five mile return trip takes around 60 minutes, and all advertised trains are scheduled to be hauled by one of our vintage steam engines rescued from the nearby Dinorwic slate quarries and lovingly restored.

AUTHOR'S REVIEW.

Llanberis is rich in industrial heritage and the Llanberis Lake Railway is at the pinnacle of that time in history, where Britain was becoming the leader in the worlds Industrial Revolution. This five mile journey along the very pretty Padarn Lake, this little steam train has the heart of a thousand steam trains. This journey takes around 60 minutes and views are absolutely stunning as you wind your way through the trees, flora and fauna, that make this popular railway journey one for all ages groups. I also liked the little cafe that can be found next to the Slate Quarry museum and with a great little gift shop, you'll be spoilt for choice. As far as steam railways go, they have a great little website that is both informative and very easy to book tickets. Finally, the Llanberis Lake Railway is excellent value for money and I'm sure once you've been on it, you won't want to go home, without taking another trip!

Caernarfon

Gilfach Ddu, Llanberis, Caernarfon, Gwynedd, LL55 4TY

t: 01286-677322 e: info@beaconclimbing.com
www.beaconclimbing.com

Rain or shine, come and climb! Beacon Climbing Centre is an exciting all weather venue, with fun activities suitable for the whole family. It's great fun for kids and the perfect antidote to boring gym regimes for adults!

Conquer our high roped walls for an unbeatable sense of achievement, experience the freedom of climbing without using a rope in our low level bouldering areas or try something that's entirely off-the-wall: CrazyClimb featuring a series of wacky climbing challenges!

No previous experience is required and anyone can have a go. Spectators can watch for free, there is an awesome café on site, and free WiFi is available throughout the centre.

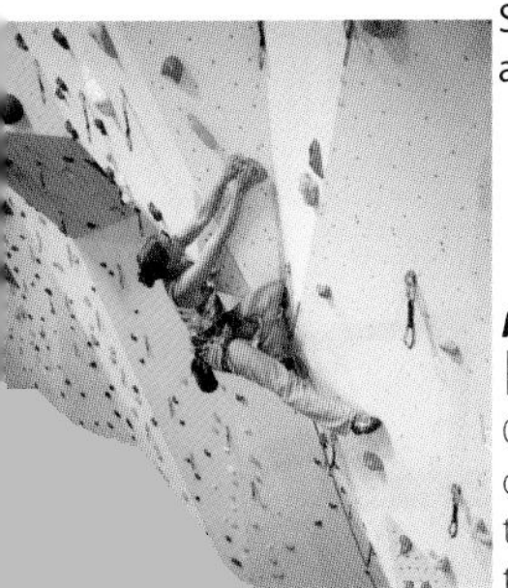

AUTHOR'S REVIEW

Being one of the UK's major indoor climbing centres, Beacon Climbing Centre along with their CrazyClimb facility, I could not have done this Snowdonia Mountains & Coast Chapter without including them. This state of the art climbing facility is an outright leader in their field and whether you are an experienced climber or a total novice, the staff at Beacon are totally dedicated to making sure that you get absolutely everything out of your visit to them. The team of experienced instructors can be as hands on or hands off as you need them to be, with climbing walls of varying heights, you really do get to experience the highs and thrills of a mountain climb, but all indoors. Finally, one thing that I was impressed with, was the admission prices not being as high as I would have expected, in fact if you're over 80, you pay nothing, now that's value for money!

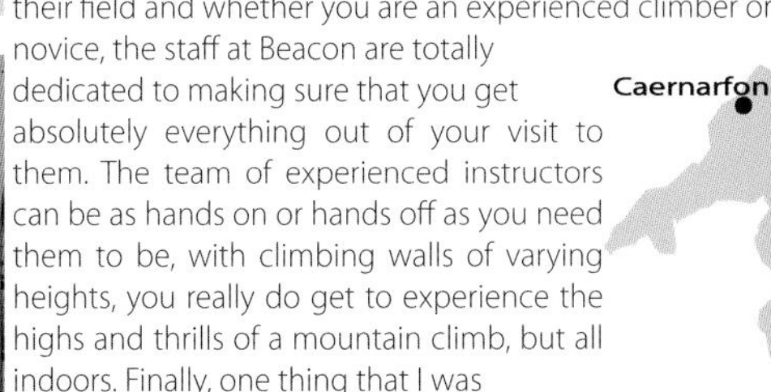

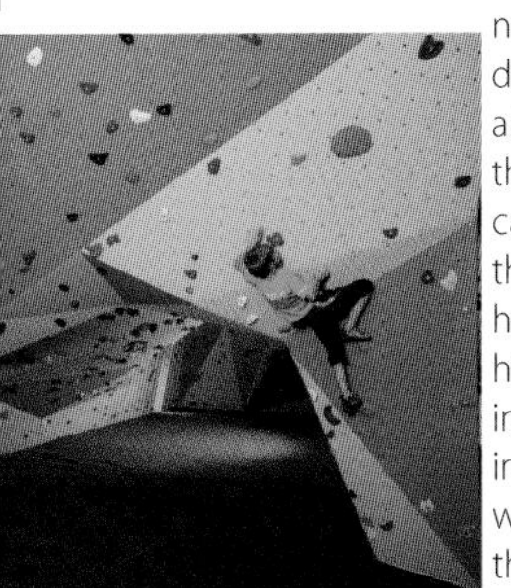

Cibyn Estate, Caernarfon, Gwynedd, LL55 2BD

Plas Dinas Country House

t: 01286-830214 e: info@plasdinas.co.uk
www. plasdinas.co.uk

The family home of Lord Snowdon dates to the 1600s and stands in 15 rural acres with an avenue of oak sweeping you up to the house. Princess Margaret often stayed and much of what fills the house belongs to the family: striking chandeliers, oils by the score, gilt-framed mirrors – an Aladdin's cave of beautiful things. There's a baby grand piano in the drawing room, where you find a roaring fire and an honesty bar, but potter about and find masses of memorabilia framed on the walls (make sure you visit the private dining room). Bedrooms – some with views across fields to the sea – mix a graceful past with modern design. You get four-posters, period colours, bold wallpapers, a sofa if there's room. A cute room in the eaves has mountain views, all have hot-water bottles, Apple TVs and excellent bathrooms, some with showers, others with free-standing baths. Good food waits in the restaurant.

AUTHOR'S REVIEW.

Ever wondered what it would be like to be royalty? Or being lord and lady of the manor? Well a visit to Plas Dinas, will answer that very important question for you. Once being the family home of Lord Snowdon, this private residence, dating back to the mid seventeenth century is the epitome of luxury and all at a very reasonable price. With a wide selection of sumptuous rooms, Plas Dinas is a house that is not only rich with history, but with character also. On the night that I stayed at Plas Dinas, I checked in at around 7pm and was greeted by the hotels owner.

After I was given a brief tour, we were shown to our room, which I have to say blew me away. It had all fixtures and fittings of any hotel room, but the little luxuries that you would need with a night away from home. With a fantastic restaurant, that both your evening meal and breakfast is served from, I was really impressed with the food offerings.

Caernarfon

Bontnewydd, Caernarfon, LL54 7YF

King Arthur's Labyrinth

t: 01654-761584 e: info@kingarthurslabyrinth.co.uk
www.kingarthurslabyrinth.co.uk

King Arthur's Labyrinth is time travel at its best as you're swept, by underground boat, through the magical veil of a waterfall into a mythical world filled with dragons, giants, fierce battles and the legendary King Arthur. Set in the deepest of the Dark Ages, Welsh legends unfold as you explore the vast underground caverns and winding tunnels of the Labyrinth with your guide – a hooded Dark Age Boatman. Brave the waters of Dragon River an exciting new finale to this underground adventure. Suitable for all ages in all weathers.
Open daily 10am to 4.45pm (last boat leaves reception) from Easter to the beginning of November. Find us deep in the mountains of Southern Snowdonia, an area steeped in myths and legends. King Arthur's Labyrinth starts from the Corris Craft Centre which is also home to 9 craft studios and other attractions.

AUTHOR'S REVIEW

This attraction is both unique and diverse as it isn't just the one attraction here its several. Let me start with King Arthur's Labyrinth. Steeped in legend and mystery, this attraction has it both in abundance. As you take a journey back in time you can't help but get caught up in it all! The Labyrinth's main aim is achieved within a very short time. It's both exciting and mysterious and I promise that once you come back above ground you will want to go back down. Then of course if that wasn't enough, there are more stories to be found in Lost Legends of The Stone Circle, a self-guided tour that allows you to take as long as you need to navigate the paths of a simple maze to find intriguing characters, the stone circle and stories of olde. There's a quiz, based around the stories with medals to be won! With this attraction you can go at your own pace making a visit to King Arthur's Labyrinth and surrounding attractions a value for money day. Now that can't be bad can it!

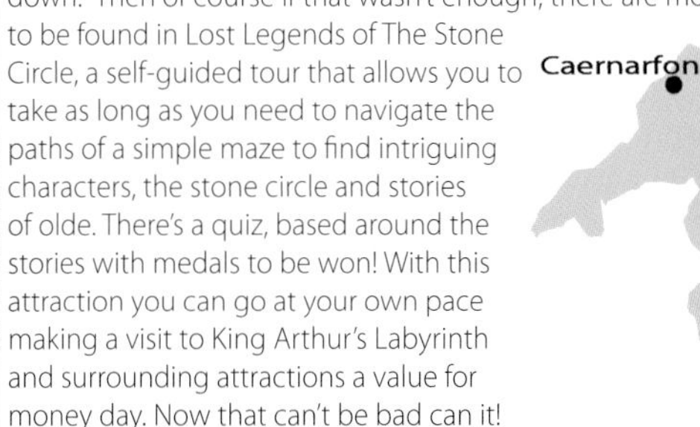

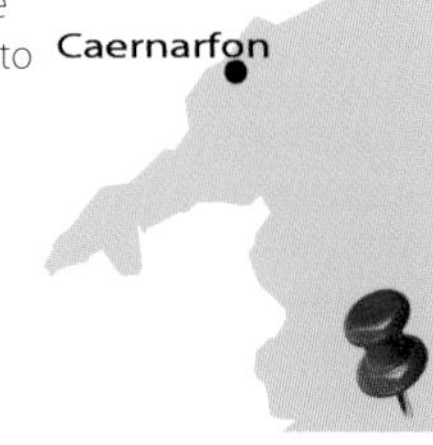

Corris Craft Centre,Corris, Machynlleth, Powys, SY20 9RF

Fairbourne Minature Railway

t: 01341 250 362 e: office@fairbournerailway.com
www. fairbournerailway.com

Travels the two and a half miles between Fairbourne and Penrhyn Point where it connects with a ferry which takes passengers across the Afon Mawddach to Barmouth. Some of the trips they allow footplate passengers, who can ride up front throughout with the driver! At the station there's also an extensive model G-Scale Railway which kids and enthusiasts will love to have a look at. Independent of the Railway, the Barmouth Ferries operate when trains run from Easter onwards so you could potentially add a little jaunt on the water to your transport day out! Take the bus to get there and then all you've got to do for a full house is find some way of getting airborne! Nearby located near to Beach Halt in Penrhyn Corner Pay-and-Display car park there is a children's playground with regular play equipment ok for kids around 2 to 10. So it's a nice little stop on it's own with smalls, or with slightly bigger kids who demand a bit more it's good in conjunction with the amusements and the golf. An easy day!

AUTHOR'S REVIEW.

Wales has many great steam railways, some are small and some are big in nature but, no matter the size, they all have the same aim and that's to give you the best experience they possibly can and one such Railway that is delivering that great experience, is the Fairbourne Miniature Railway. Established in 1916, this particular steam railway has decades of history that saw the dawn of the industrial revolution that Wales played a huge part in. Now in recent years, this small railway carries thousands of passengers every year and all leave with very fond memories of their short time on this very special little attraction. We at Top 100, look for visitor experience, set alongside value for money and this railway, based in sleepy Fairbourne, has both of those qualities and more. With a great team, headed by a great general manager, this small charity run steam railway is an absolute must when visiting this area of Wales.

National White Water Centre

t: 01678-521083 e: info@ukrafting.co.uk
www.ukrafting.co.uk

The National White Water Centre is set on the banks of the River Tryweryn, near Bala. The Tryweryn is dam controlled ensuring great water conditions all year round and the centre prides itself on providing the best white water rafting experiences in the UK. The NWWC pioneered commercial rafting in the UK in 1986 and remains the country's most popular white water rafting destination. Experience the thrill of the Tryweryn for yourselves, with rafting sessions ideal for groups, individuals and families, as well as the brand-new tandem kayak and canyoning sessions. For a more relaxed view of the river, take a walk along the delightful Tryweryn Trail as you explore mossy oaks and delicate willows in this magnificent setting. Or simply enjoy a warming cup of tea in the new riverside cafe; Caffi Celyn as you watch your friends and family whizz past you! Call the centre on 01678 521083 for more details or to book.

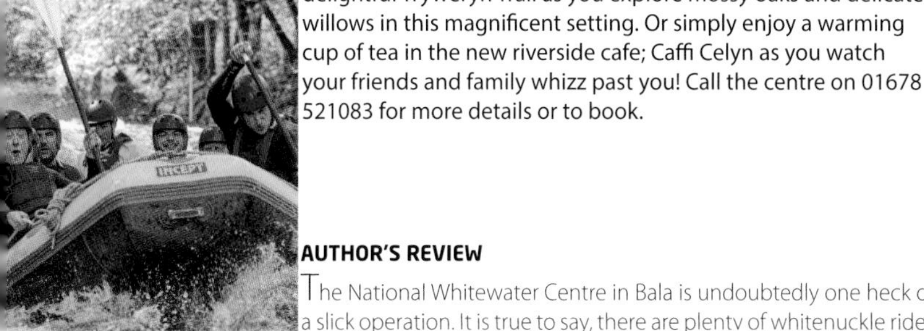

AUTHOR'S REVIEW

The National Whitewater Centre in Bala is undoubtedly one heck of a slick operation. It is true to say, there are plentv of whitenuckle rides to be enjoyed in various theme parks dotted across the UK, but what this attraction has to offer, far surpasses anything man made that is on offer at any of them! When I visited this attraction only recently, I was given a guided tour by the manager Bleddyn, who is clearly very proud of what they have achieved with this attraction, and so he and his team should be! Whether you are a hardened rafter or a novice, the team will look after you all just the same, and if the rapids don't take your breath away the scenery in its surrounding location will do!

Caernarfon

nolfan Tryweryn, Frongoch, Bala, Gwynedd, LL23 7NU

Beics Brenin

t: 01341-440728 e: mail@beicsbrenin.co.uk
www.beicsbrenin.co.uk

Welcome to Beics Brenin, a full service bike shop & rental centre, located within the iconic Coed Y Brenin forest in North Wales. As the UK's first & largest dedicated mountain bike trail centre, Coed y Brenin not only has miles of exceptional singletrack for experienced and expert riders, but also great family and intermediate trails for all abilities. We stock a wide range of accessories and bikes, to ensure that you get the most out of your visit to Coed y Brenin and, right next door, the visitor center café serves a great range of drinks and home cooked cakes and meals. There are showers and 24hr toilets on site and all trails are way-marked and clearly graded. We stock a wide range of trail essentials like tubes, repair kits, pumps and energy products. We also carry essential spares, accessories to enhance your ride alongside apparel from leading brands like Fox, Dakine and Endura. Our store opening hours are 9am to 5pm, 7 days*.We do our best to help keep you rolling and offer friendly advice on making the most of your visit to Coed y Brenin.

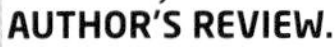

AUTHOR'S REVIEW.

Beics Brenin is speedily becoming one of Snowdonia's musts do's when visiting the region. Nestled perfectly within the Coed y Brenin Forest, Beics Brenin are the leaders in Bike hire and with being situated in one of Snowdonia's iconic forests, the back drop couldn't be better. Open 7 days a week, Beics Brenin and it's widely experienced team are on hand to not only supply you with a top of the range bike, they are also available to give out advice and to ensure that your experience at Coed y Brenin is one that will reach its maximum. On the day of my visit, I was truly impressed at the set up here and the level of customer service that was handed out whilst I was there. As far as costings are concerned, value for money, set against visitor experience is one of the many attributes that helped my decision to make this attraction a Top 100 Attraction.

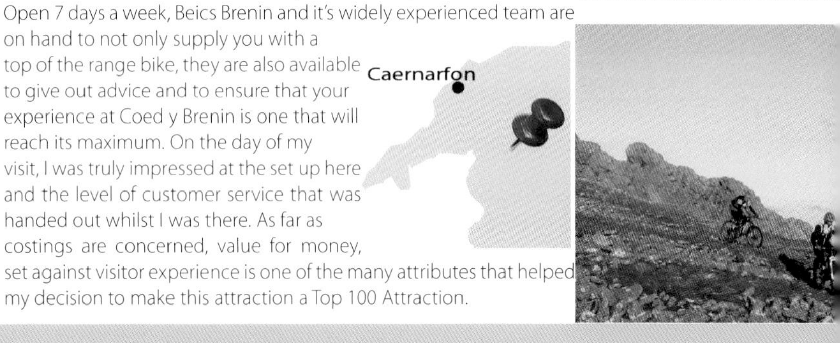

hell Island

t: 01341-241453

e: enquiries1@shellisland.co.uk

www. shellisland.co.uk

Based in North Wales and boasting stunning views of the unspoilt Welsh countryside, including Cardigan Bay and the Snowdonia National Park, Shell Island is one of Europe's largest Campsites. Catering for all the family and with excellent facilities Shell Island will make your camping experience one to remember. From Shell Island on a clear day, you will have fantastic views of the North Cardigan Bay. Looking out across the bay is the Llyn Peninsula, with Abersoch, Pwllheli and Criccieth on the facing shore. To the North lies Snowdon (3559ft), the highest mountain in England and Wales. With its snow capped peak in the,spring, walkers from all over the UK ascend it throughout the year. Harlech castle, stood prominent on the hill at Harlech is clearly visible, and to the right of it, the Rhinogs Mountain range. Looking south towards our sand dunes lies Cader Idris, and the Cambrian mountain range, with the coast extending all the way down to Pembrokeshire.

AUTHOR'S REVIEW.

I went to visit Shell Island at the height of the season, and towards the end of the season, and the place was a hive of activity on both occasions. Now, with their newly built Reception area, the island itself has lot's to offer all ages and all walks of life. Shell Island has got great facilities and all at affordable prices too. I just couldn't get over the atmosphere of the place, everybody speaking to each other like they were all part one big family. I was astonished to find the management at this site doing the types of jobs you wouldn't see management at a lot of resorts doing! Shell Island is certainly a one off and gets a massive thumbs up from us all here at Top 100 attractions in Wales.

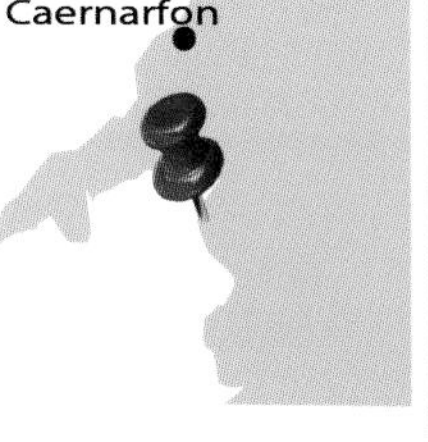

Cae Gethin, Llanfair, Harlech, Gwynedd, LL46 2SA

Portmeirion Village

t: 01766-770000 e: post@portmeirion.wales
www.portmeirion.wales

VISIT Portmeirion Village is a holiday resort situated on its own private peninsula on the southern shores of Snowdonia. Portmeirion is one of Wales's premier visitor attractions offering day visitors complimentary guided walking tours, free forest train and 20-minute video on the history of the site, in addition to seasonal exhibitions. Surrounding the village is 70 acres of exotic woodlands featuring 20 miles of woodland and coastal paths. Portmeirion was created by Welsh architect Clough Williams-Ellis to demonstrate how a naturally beautiful space could be developed without spoiling it. Famous for its colourful buildings, central piazza and Italianate design, Portmeirion is a flavour of Italy on the coast of Snowdonia. Portmeirion is open daily from 9:30am – 7:30pm. Closed for Festival No 6 and Christmas Day. Unfortunately, no dogs (except assistance dogs) are allowed on-site.

AUTHOR'S REVIEW

Portmeirion has been a hotel and visitor attraction since 1926 and many generations of families have enjoyed walking through the streets of this famous Italianate village. I myself have visited here on many occasions and everytime feels like the first! The village has a strange pull on its visitors and its not hard to see why they return time upon time to these famous cobbled streets! People always associate Portmeirion with the Cult Tv series 'The Prisoner' but the site was a popular tourist destination long before the show started filming there and it's all down to the forward thinking of Sir Clough Williams-Ellis who started building and creating Portmeirion from 1925 to 1975 a strong testament to a strong minded man. I would highly recommend a visit to Portmeirion, and see for yourself what makes this place so special and why it leaves such a strong mark on all those who visit!

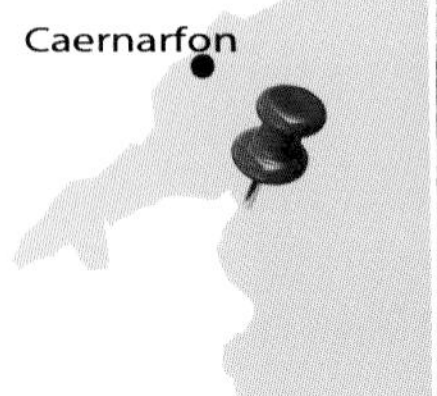

PORTMEIRION, Minffordd near Porthmadog, LL48 6ER

ortmeirion Village

STAY

Experience the magic of staying in Portmeirion. Stay in one of two luxury 4-star hotels – The Hotel Portmeirion or Castell Deudraeth – or choose a suite in the middle of the village. Portmeirion also offers 13 charming self-catering cottages accommodating up to 8 guests.

EAT

With 2 award-winning restaurants and 5 cafes on-site, you will be spoilt for choice at Portmeirion. Dining options include the fine dining Art Deco restaurant at The Hotel Portmeirion, the more relaxed Brasserie at Castell Deudraeth, the Italian eatery Caffi Glas and several cafes serving classic fayre. Portmeirion is also home to Angel Ices, a quirky Italian gelateria featuring unique flavours. Enjoy FREE ENTRY to Portmeirion Village with a 2-course lunch or Afternoon Tea in Castell Deudraeth or The Hotel Portmeirion.

SHOP

Portmeirion is more than just a place that sells pottery. The village is home to a variety of gift and bookshops selling an eclectic range of gifts, books, homeware, toys and more. Portmeirion also boasts an art gallery showcasing stunning watercolours of the village and surrounding mountain and coastal views by talented local artist, Rob Piercy.

RELAX

The Mermaid Spa at Portmeirion offers a wide range of treatments including aroma massages, body wraps, facials and manicures. Relax in a haven of tranquillity in the centre of the village while enjoying coastal views over the Dwyryd Estuary. Spa packages are available. Enjoy FREE ENTRY to Portmeirion Village with any spa treatment.

PORTMEIRION, Minffordd near Porthmadog, LL48 6ER

Snowdon Mountain Railway

t: 0844 493 8120 e: info@snowdonrailway.co.uk
www snowdonrailway.co.uk

Let Snowdon Mountain Railway take you on a journey of a lifetime to the rooftop of Wales. Snowdon, at 3,560ft dominates the landscape of Snowdonia National Park in North Wales. Claim this mountain peak, the highest in Wales, as a lifetime's achievement. With stunning scenery and awe-inspiring views it's all part of a great day out for you and your family in North Wales. The new visitor centre is a uniquely designed structure built of granite with large views from the "window on the world" wall of glass which makes up the front of the centre. It acts as a terminus for the Snowdon Mountain Railway providing refreshment facilities, toilets and interpretation of the mountain, its history and ways to enjoy it. Much of the interpretation is built into the structure.

AUTHOR'S REVIEW

This railway needs no introduction, for those of you that have walked Snowdon, or even taken the train, you will be familiar with this unique railway service. The railway has been servicing Snowdon since 1896 and hasn't stopped since! Every year the railway sees more and more visitors and once you've taken a trip on this famous little narrow gauge railway it's easy to see why. I personally like to walk up Snowdon and get the train down, but no matter what your preference, upon your visit to Snowdon, no trip is complete until you've closed that carriage door and smelt the steam coming through your windows. No matter how many times you've ridden the train the views just get better and better, so what are you waiting for?

Caernarfon

Tyddyn Sydney Bach

Treborth, Bangor, Gwynedd, LL57 2NJ

T: 01248-355180 www.tyddynsydney.co.uk E: info@tyddynsydney.co.uk

Discover self catering in Wales at Tyddyn Sydney Bach. A delightful Visit Wales 5* garden studio cottage sleeping 2 with its open wooden beams and high ceilings. It has an open plan kitchen /lounge/ bedroom with separate bath room furnished and equipped to high standards. Towels, bed and table linen are included. Outside there is garden furniture complete with parasol. Tyddyn Sydney Bach has invested in Far Infrared heating panels. Far Infrared heat is healthier, more comfortable, and a more efficient method than any other source of domestic heating. Upon your arrival, Tyddyn Sydney Bach welcomes you with tea, bara brith, and fresh flowers.

Glan Soch Cottage

Glan Soch Road, Llangian, Abersoch, Gwynedd, LL53 7LT

T: 01758-712565 www.glansoch.co.uk E: emma@glansoch.co.uk

A quaint rural 2 bedroomed coastal cottage that can comfortably sleep up to 4/5 persons located in the self contained converted 17th century stable wing of the property.Situated in the heart of the glorious Lleyn Peninsula some 3.3 miles west of the cosmopolitan, bustling seaside resort of Abersoch with its numerous restaurants, bars, shops and wonderful sandy beaches and 1 mile east of the magnificent 3 mile long beach of Porth Neigwl (Hells Mouth) famous for its surf and wonderful unspoilt location. A 17th century stable tastefully converted into comfortable country style accommodation boasting stunning countryside views from all rooms. Sleeps up to 4 /5 persons in 2 good sized first floor bedrooms.

The Boatyard Inn

Garth Road, Bangor, Gwynedd, LL57 2SF

T: 01248-362462 E: theboatyardbangor@outlook.com

Situated on a small road leading to the Pier, the Boatyard Inn of Bangor, North Wales offers guests just as warm a welcome today as it probably did for many sea workers, sailors and fishermen years ago. Almost sitting upon the water's edge, the pub embodies the character and atmosphere of a traditional sea-side tavern.. There are 3 basic rooms above the pub, all sharing a hallway bathroom.

Full breakfast is served in the cosy, traditional pub which also serves a seafood-based menu. There's a furnished patio with sea views and free parking is available. The pub is also listed in the CAMRA (Real Ale) guide as pub of the season for Gwynedd and Anglesey.

Dinas Farm Holidays

Dinas, Caernarfon, Gwynedd, LL54 5UB

T: 01286-830537 www. dinasfarm.co.uk E: rhian@dinasfarm.co.uk

A warm welcome to the Dinas Farm Holidays web site. We offer self-catering and B&B holiday accommodation based approximately three miles from Caernarfon and near to Snowdonia..On your approach to Dinas Farm, you'll be able to fully appreciate the location and setting of our working farm, we are set in stunning countryside with lovely rural and coastal views. Dinas Farm offers a unique holiday experience; a relaxing environment, with beautiful views. Yet we are on the doorstep of the Snowdonia National Park with all that Snowdonia has to offer - from active adventure activities, to castles, history, culture and of course the steam railways North Wales is famous for. We offer single-occupancy self-catering and B&B accommodation options for up to six people in our spacious and comfortable farmhouse wing.

Porth Tocyn

Bwlchtocyn, Abersoch, Gwynedd, LL53 7BU

T: 01758-713303 www.porthtocynhotel.co.uk E: bookings@porthtocynhotel.co.u

Sitting on the headland beyond the sailing village of Abersoch, with stunning views across Cardigan Bay and out to Snowdonia, the hotel is furnished with country antiques. It exudes a warm & friendly atmosphere which draws guests back time after time. Porth Tocyn has 17 individually designed bedrooms with antique furniture & luxurious Egyptian cotton linen. Most boast super king sized bed & captivating sea views with the dramatic backdrop of the Welsh mountains. Some bedrooms are interconnecting which is ideal for families. If you want the freedom of self catering but a taste of Port Tocyn & its stunning outlook, Louise Fletcher-Brewer runs a lovely self catering cottage; 'Bwthyn Bach & a Shepherds hut; 'Ty Cwtch' within the hotel grounds. These are available all year round.

Bron Eifion Lodges

Criccieth, Gwynedd, LL52 0SA

T: 01766-523512 www.broneifion.com E: carole@broneifion.com

Here at Bron Eifion Fishing Lakes and Lodges we can offer you a tranquil holiday base for exploring t Snowdonia National Park and the Lleyn Peninsula. Our family run lodges and fishing lakes are perfec for a peaceful break at any time of the year.

Our nine log cabins all enjoy lake side views and stand in the heart of 40 acres of beautiful mature woodland, a real haven for wildlife. Bron Eifion is a paradise for the angling enthusiast and a perfect location for the energetic; ramblers, cyclists and water sport lovers. All our Lodges are spacious, furnished to a high standard and have lake and countryside views. We have nine lakeside lodges for you to choose from with different room and bed arrangements: Dwyfor, Teigl, Seiont, Glaslyn and Cedron

Min-y-Don Guest House

Promenade, Llanairfechan, Gwynedd, LL33 0BY

T: 01248-680742 www.min-y-don.co.uk E: minydon1@aol.com

Situated on the beautiful North Wales Coast, On the Promenade, Noted for its outstanding views in a directions. We are in the perfect location for you to start your adventure in Snowdonia and surroundi areas. Classed as the Gem of North Wales, Llanfairfechan has one of the largest Blue Flag beaches, sa soft golden sands for miles, A recreation area close by has a model yacht pond, swings, and a childre paddling pool. A gentle stroll will take you to the Nature Reserves. There are two cafes on the promenade for ice creams and snacks, the beach is popular with families and wind surfers, along with sma sea craft. We are close to all the major outdoor attractions in North Wales being in a 20 mile radius of Beaumaris, Caernarfon, Conwy & Penrhyn Castles. Zip World, Mount Snowdon, Surf Snowdonia, Colw Bay Zoo, all just a short drive away.

Lodge Dinorwig & Cafe

Dinorwig, Gwynedd, LL55 3EY

T: 01286-871632 www.lodge-dinorwig.co.uk E: info@lodge-dinorwig.co

Our Hostel is located in North Wales, just on the edge of the Snowdonia National Park. Our bunkroor is popular with friends, families and individuals alike. If you are looking for a base for your adventures in Snowdonia or if you are looking for an accommodation after finishing the Three Peaks Challenge t is the perfect place to rest your head, with bespoke beds, curtains for privacy, cosy bedding and com mattresses. Our cooked breakfast is inclusive and provides the perfect fuel for your day. Packed lunch and home cooked two-course dinners are available if booked in advance, preferably at the time of b ing your accommodation.

Cae Gwyn Farm Holidays

Cae Gwyn, Trawsfynydd, Nr Blaenau, Gwynedd, LL41 4YE

T: 01766-540245 www.caegwynfarm.co.uk E: enquiries@caegwynfarm.co.uk

Cae Gwyn ('White Field') is a sheep farm in the south of Snowdonia National Park with a farming history dating back over 200 years. Even to this day very little has changed over the centuries. The only differences perhaps are that today we run the 140 acre hill farm., and that Cae Gwyn now welcomes you to experience a close to nature holiday. We offer bed and breakfast, camping, and camping barn facilities in an unspoilt natural environment. Our aim is to offer flexible holiday opportunities to suit everyone, and whether you are here to enjoy mountain-biking, walking, climbing, fishing, canoeing, reading novels, or simply just for the breath of fresh air, we hope you will be able to find your own ideal holiday at Cae Gwyn.

Ty'n Y Cornel Hotel

Tal-y-Llyn, Tywyn, Gwynedd, LL36 9AJ

T: 01654-782282 wwwtynycornel.co.uk E: enquiries@tynycornel.com

Located on the banks of the beautiful Tal-y-llyn Lake, the Ty'n Y Cornel Hotel sits in the heart of the stunning mountain scenery of Mid-Wales. We pride ourselves on having dedicated and attentive members of staff who want to ensure that your stay is a memorable one – and one you will want to repeat. Our Hotel is the perfect base for everyone who wants to explore the many local attractions, whether it's climbing Cader Idris, or simply relaxing by our glorious lake. If you're a keen walker or just want to enjoy the spectacular views, we have a wide variety of walks and activities for you to choose from. The Tyn-Y-Cornel Hotel offers guests individually designed rooms that are among the best in Mid-Wales. Available as Double, Twin, Family, Superior and Bridal.

Heulwen Guest House

Llanfachreth, Dolgellau, Gwynedd, LL40 2EB

T: 01341-423085 www.heulwen.co.uk E: stay@heulwen.co.uk

Heulwen Guest House is a 4 star guesthouse which lies on the outskirts of Llanfachreth, a tiny village close to the centre of the Snowdonia National Park 3 and a half miles from the old market town of Dolgellau. It is owned and run by Heulwen and Andy Watts, who established the business in 1985. The spacious south-facing bungalow is set in its own landscaped garden with magnificent views of the mountains and forests. This tranquil setting offers you the choice of forest walks, hill climbing, fishing, mountain biking or just touring the area by car. The accommodation consists of 3 large south facing bedrooms, all with stunning views of the surrounding mountains. Two of the bedrooms have en-suite facilities (shower, toilet and hand basin) and patio doors leading into garden. There is also a twin/double room available with hand basin.

Aberdunant Hall Country Hotel *

Prenteg, Porthmadog, Gwynedd, Wales, LL49 9SR

T: 01766-512001 www.aberdunant.com E: info@aberdunant.com

Situated within Snowdonia National Park, Aberdunant Hall Country Hotel is a 17th-century property set within 200-acres of woodland on an idyllic upmarket Holiday Home Park. With free onsite parking, it retains many original features, such as beamed ceilings, fireplaces and stained glass. Guests can relax in the garden or on the terrace. All rooms at Aberdunant Hall have a flat-screen TV, en suite bathroom and complimentary tea/coffee facilities. In the mornings, guests can enjoy continental or full Welsh breakfast in the Glaslyn Lounge. Al fresco dining can be enjoyed on the terrace, which boasts panoramic views of the mountains. Family meals and Sunday lunches are served in The Glaslyn Lounge, and intimate dining is available in Y Bistro. A carvery is served every Sunday.

The Waterloo Hotel

Holyhead Road, Betws y Coed, Snowdonia, LL24 0AR

T: 01690-710411 www.waterloo-hotel.info E: reservations@waterloo-hotel.info

The ideal base to explore and discover the breath taking scenery of Snowdonia's beautiful countrysic and coast. Situated on the grounds of the hotel are our modern, spacious lodge style rooms which come complete with own parking space. Rooms are also available in the main hotel. Extensive menu dominated by locally sourced produce at the Bridge Restaurant. All our guests receive complimentar use of our leisure facilities which include indoor heated pool, jacuzzi, sauna, steam room and fully equipped gym. Complimentary WIFI throughout.

Ty Mawr B&B & Tearoom

Rhyd Ddu, Nr Beddgelert, Gwynedd, LL54 6TL

T: 01766-890837 www.snowdonaccommodation.co.uk E: menno.van.boven@btinternet.c

Emma and Menno welcome you to their warm and cosy Bed & Breakfast and Tea room Tŷ Mawr, idea situated for a holiday in the mountains of the Snowdonia National Park. Tŷ Mawr has three double rooms (they are all located on the first floor). All rooms have free internet access, freeview television, central heating, hairdryer, radio/alarm clock and a hospitality tray with tea, coffee and home made cakes or biscuits. Our rooms are not suitable for young children; the minimum age is 8 years. In the Tea room we serve several sorts of tea, sandwiches, toasties, homemade soups, baguettes, omelettes etc. Menno's Dutch pancakes are recommended for the hungry walker!!! We are located opposite Mt. Snowdon and the Rhyd Ddu Path to the summit starts in the village.

Llety Brynawel B&B

Tower Rd, Pennal, Gwynedd, SY20 9DP

T: 01654-791 206 www.lletybrynawel.co.uk E: info@lletybrynawel.co.uk

Our gorgeous Georgian guest house is in the pretty southern Snowdonia village of Pennal between Aberdyfi and Machynlleth (it's the ultimate coast and country location). We have 4 bedrooms at Brynawel. Each of the four guest bedrooms have been individually furnished with lush fabrics and collections of our artwork which give them their own charm and character. All rooms are en-suite, within the bedrooms are luxury toiletries, Television, hairdryers, hospitality tray, complimentary mineral water, complimentary wifi. Enjoy a freshly cooked breakfast in the comfort of our restaurant Glan Yr Afon/Riverside which is a 2 minute stroll away, enjoy reading the daily news in front of a roaring fire on colder mornings.

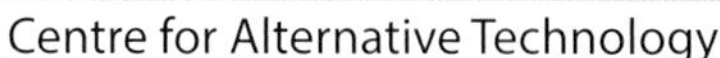

Centre for Alternative Technology

Machynlleth, Powys, Wales, SY20 9AZ

T: 01654-704973 www.visit.cat.org.uk/residential-visits E: cabins@cat.org.uk

We have a range accommodation options available for groups. Make the most of your stay by combining it with one of our inspiring short courses, which range from willow weaving to straw bale building. Tours of CAT and various workshops are available from our Education team, and talks about our pioneering research project Zero Carbon Britain 2030 are also available. and its 4 star group accommodation is also available for groups looking for somewhere unique for their residential stay a CAT, we can also accommodate bed & breakfast bookings. and its 4 star group accommodation is alsc available for groups looking for somewhere unique for their residential stay at CAT, we can also accommodate bed & breakfast bookings. The Eco Cabins are two green roofed cabins overlooking Roger's Field.

Plas Bodegroes

Pwllheli, Gwynedd, LL53-5TH

T: 01758-612363 www.bodegroes.co.uk E: gunna@plasbodegroes.co.uk

Plas Bodegroes stands in its own secluded grounds (just a mile from the beach!) on the wild Llŷn Peninsula, on the far north west of Wales. The Llŷn Peninsula is one of Britain's first designated Areas of Outstanding Natural Beauty. With mile upon mile of open sandy beach, glorious gulf stream light, tranquil seclusion and a coastal path edging the whole peninsula, this is a wonderful, unspoilt region well worth a visit. Our bedrooms are all individually designed, and overlook the gardens. All are non-smoking with ensuite, Flatscreen digital TV with 40 Freeview channels, phone and CD Player. All mattresses are pocket sprung, bedlinen is Egyptian cotton and duvets are goose-down.

Bron Menai Guest House

Ffordd y Gogledd, Caernarfon, Gwynedd, LL55 1AY

T: 01286-675589 www.bronmenai.co.uk E: enquiries@bronmenai.co.uk

We are situated near the Menai Straits and only a few minutes walk takes you to Caernarfon's town centre with the Historic Castle and many points of interest in & around Snowdonia including the Welsh Highland Railway, numerous shops, restaurants & bar facilities. This family run four star Licensed Guest House has a relaxing ambiance to offer their guests. We previously ran a Guest House in Caernarfon for 14 years till 2001 when we moved to this beautiful Victorian house desperately in need of renovation. Bron Menai is a Victorian residence on the edge of Caernarfon Town dating back to the 1830`s. We have a residential Lounge Bar and Free wi-fi access.

The Waverley Hotel

Station Road, Bangor, Gwynedd, LL57 1LZ

T: 01248-370 819 www.waverleybangor.com E: thewaverleybangor@outlook.com

One of Bangor's biggest hotels - The Waverley Hotel Bangor; boasting a wide variety of spacious rooms suiting single, twin, double or family rooms that suit your every need. Hayley and the team have recently taken over the Waverley Hotel (formerly The Regency Hotel) in July 2014 with the aim to totally transform and restore it to its former glory. We have 16 main rooms (with 14 en-suite), boasting free Wi-Fi, Freeview TV, tea/coffee facilities and other amenities available on request. Our hotel also caters for functions including weddings, Christenings, birthdays and funerals with a large restaurant/function room conversion. Please ring us for a quote today. We also cater for outside catering.

Caerwylan Hotel

Beach Bank, Criccieth, Gwynedd, LL52-0HW

T: 01766-522547 www.caerwylan.co.uk E: reception@caerwylan.co.uk

The Caerwylan is a friendly, privately owned 3 star hotel, with wonderful sea views. We are the ideal base to explore Criccieth, Llyn Peninsula and Snowdonia. We have renovated the hotel to a high standard and now have 24 individually designed en-suite bedrooms, a tranquil sea facing lounge and a contemporary bar. Our elegant Tonnau Restaurant is open to residents and non residents for dinner 7 nights a week and at Sunday lunch time, when we serve traditional Sunday roasts.
Visit www.caerwylan.com for more information.

Ty Mawr Farm B&B

Ty Mawr Farm, Llanddeniolen, Caernarfon, Gwynedd, LL55 3AD

T: 01248-670147 www.tymawrfarm.co.uk E: jane@tymawrfarm.co.uk

In this charming 17th Century farm, there are two very spacious en-suite rooms, which can be made into double or twin bedrooms according to your preference. Relax in the character lounge with original oak beams or the TV lounge with a wood burner in an inglenook fireplace. You will be invite to eat in the panelled dining room where a home produced menu and mouth watering desserts will be served. Located between Llanberis and the historical Royal town of Caernarfon in North Wales, commanding magnificent views of the Snowdonia mountain range just 3 miles away. Situated just 10 minutes drive from Anglesey, 20 minutes from Llandudno and 10 minutes from Caernarfon, it is a great location for exploring this stunning part of the country.

Ty Mawr Farm Cottages

Ty Mawr Farm, Llanddeniolen, Caernarfon, Gwynedd, LL55 3AD

T: 01248-670147 www.tymawrfarm.co.uk E: jane@tymawrfarm.co.uk

The stone built granary has been converted to four luxury holiday cottages full of character with inglenook fireplaces, woodburning stoves and exposed beams. The cottages are in their own groun with ample parking area and gardens. Gas Barbeque and Swings, Slide & a 16ft Trampoline available for your use. All beds in the self catering cottages are 3ft single Slumberland beds, they may be zipp up together to make a 6ft queen-bed. All beds will be made up ready for your arrival.
There is ample supply of towels available.
All cottages are fitted with a washing machine, tumble drier & dishwasher. The cottages are heated with Gas Central Heating and the water is heated with a Combi Boiler for 24 hour hot water.

Cae Berllan Holiday Cottages

Tyn Lon, Llandrwrog, Caernarfon, Gwynedd, LL54 5SN

T: 01286-830818 www.caeberllan.co.uk E: anncaeberllan@aol.com

At Cae Berllan we offer three converted stone properties with all the needs of modern day living. Th self catering cottages enjoy a splendid rural location situated at Llandwrog a small village three mile outside of Caernarfon, convenient for easy access to the historic coastal town and majestic castle as well as the Snowdonia National Park. On the farm we have horses and ponies, a few sheep and a few chickens. We have a orchard of about 70 trees which is a ideal area for picnics and for children to pla For our younger clients there is a play/sitting area to the back of the cottages which is covered in ch bark and has secure gates. We are ideally situated for those looking to explore this magnificent part of Wales.

Capel Siloh

Pontllyfni, Caernarfon, Gwynedd, LL54 5EF

T: 07879-012122 E: capelsiloh@gmail.com

Newly converted chapel offering spacious accommodation with upstairs open plan living room kitchen and dining. Living room has 58" Smart TV with Play Station console, blue ray DVD and a larg selection of movies and games. Downstairs there are three spacious king size bedrooms, 32" TV, all with private en-suite with large shower. Bedroom 2 en-suit also has a separate bath.Outdoor area nicely furnished summer sun trap and winter sheltered, has SS gas BBQ. The property is nicely furnished and cleverly combines the traditional and period features with modern living. The vaulted celling's and original A frame beams in the 11 meter by 7 meter open plan living, dining and kitchen provides a spacious communal area perfect for families to interact and converse about their day.

Plas Gwyn B&B

Plas Gwyn, Cader Road, Dolgellau, LL40 1RH

T: 01341-388176 www.plasgwynbandb.co.uk E: plasgwynbandb@gmail.com

Based in the pretty little town of Dolgellau we are ideally located for a huge variety of activities which include cycling, walking, horse riding, fishing, boating, climbing, and lots more. We have 3 rooms in the bed & breakfast, all ensuite. They include a small fridge with fresh milk and bottled water, freesat tv, free Wifi and tea & coffee making facilities. The bathrooms have heated towel rails so your fluffy towels will be nice and warm in the morning!

Plas Gwyn Holiday Cottage

Our holiday cottage is located next door to us and is fully equipped for all your needs and includes free Wifi, a cosy wood burning stove and a decked garden with a BBQ.

Isfryn House

Cader Road, Dolgellau LL40 1RH

T: 01341-388176 www.plasgwynbandb.co.uk E: plasgwynbandb@gmail.com

Isfryn House has been very recently renovated to create a comfortable and stylish holiday home whilst still retaining the original features you would expect to find in a 250 year old listed cottage. With two double bedrooms (1 ensuite) and a single bedroom and family bathroom upstairs, there is a large double aspect lounge with wood burning stove and comfortable farmhouse style dining kitchen on the ground floor. Window seats can be found in the lounge and kitchen. A utility room with butler's sink, washing machine and tumble dryer is at the rear of the property and there is a down stairs cloakroom. The house is pet friendly with steps leading up to an enclosed lawned garden with flower borders with further steps up to a BBQ patio area which is also a great sun trap.

The Old Farmhouse B&B

Tyddun Du, Penrhiw, Dyffryn Ardudwy, Gwynedd, LL44 2DW

T: 01341-242711 www.theoldfarmhouse.com E: timandsally@theoldfarmhouse.com

Enjoy the comforts of a hotel with the friendliness and informality of our renovated farmhouse. It is an ideal centre for touring Snowdonia, walking or just total relaxation by our large heated outdoor swimming pool and hot spa (open seasonally from April to September) whilst enjoying the breathtaking views of Snowdonia and the coast. For guests wishing to take advantage of the tranquil nature of The Old Farmhouse and adjacent stream, our two garden rooms Rhiannon and Seren offer the visitor magnificent views over Cardigan Bay and the Llyn Peninsula and of course the impressive sunsets.
All rooms offer flat screen TV's with built in Freeview and DVD's.
Guests are welcome to take advantage of the extensive gardens, swimming pool and hot tub.

Golden Fleece Inn

Market Square, Tremadog, Gwynedd, LL49 9RB

T: 01766-512421 www.goldenfleeceinn.com E: info@goldenfleeceinn.com

Welcome to The Golden Fleece Inn – a hotel quality B&B situated just 1 mile from Porthmadog in the beautiful Tremadog. Our restaurant and bar serve a variety of fresh food and real ales every day.
Our B&B accommodation is conveniently located Nr Porthmadog for both the Ffestiniog and the Welsh Highland Railway. We are also close to the Italianate village of Portmerion, Snowdonia and the Llyn Peninsula we offer 17 Comfortable en-suite hotel quality guest rooms as well as a self catering cottage all located around Tremadog's picturesque village square.The Golden Fleece Inn boasts a variety of single, twin, double and family en-suite bedrooms on a bed and breakfast basis. Our prices are competitive for the area (starting at just £39) and prices advertised on the site all include breakfast.

Hotel Port Dinorwic

Ffordd Siabod, Y Felinhelli, Gwynedd, LL56 4XA

T: 01248-671122 www.hotelportdinorwic.co.uk E: info@hotelportdinorwic.co.u

The Hotel Port Dinorwic is an informal and friendly hotel with a varied selection of accommodation types. These include double rooms, twin rooms, suites, apartments and cottages, all at affordable pric es. Its location overlooking the Menai Straits gives it un-paralleled panoramic sea views. Each room a the Hotel Port Dinorwic is individually styled and laid out. Room capacity varies from single occupan double rooms, to six person suites. All accommodation is en-suite, with tea and coffee making facilities, free view TV and free WIFI. Please note that not all rooms have a sea view. The hotel also boasts a range of facilities, such as a heated swimming pool, sauna, restaurant and function rooms. The hotel perfectly situated between the university city of Bangor and the historic town of Caernarfon.

Bryn Elltyd Eco Guest House

Tanygrisiau, Blaenau Ffestiniog, Gwynedd, North Wales, LL41 3TW

T: 01766-831356 www.ecoguesthouse.co.uk E: info@ecoguesthouse.co.

Powered, completely by RENEWABLE energy. High -tech, eco greets a balance with nature at this externally accessed, award winning, sustainable eco guesthouse. Nestling at the foot of the Moelwyn mountains in a curve of the Ffestiniog Steam Railway beside a hydro lake. All of our rooms meet our high standards for sustainability and comfort but we are particularly proud of our two double/twin, detached, turf-roofed rooms. The sheep's wool insulation of The Hobbit and Twlc Mochyn provide a cosy sustainable environment while local slate and wood exterior blend into the landscape. For simil stunning views of the lake and surrounding environment we have the double Manod Mawr Room.Th Moelwyn Bach Room and the Wrysgan Room both provide a super king size beds.

Tyn Hendre Farm B&B

Tyn Hendre Farm, Aber Road, Bangor, Gwynedd, LL57 3YP

T: 01248-362871 www.tynhendrefarm.co.uk E: bookings@tynhendrefarm.co.u

Situated just off junction 12 (Tal Y Bont) off the A55 expressway on the outskirts of bangor, this is an ideal location for business or pleasure. The house is situated behind Hendre Hall. This 100 year old former penrhyn estate managers house is an imposing building overlooking the Menai Strait Lavan Sands opposite Beaumaris. Delightfully decorated retaining many original features, the rooms provid spacious accommodation for all.

Home to Anita and Alun Thomas, Tyn Hendre Farm B&B is well established and has 3 letting rooms op all year round. All prices include a full breakfast.

TV and tea/coffee facilities in each room.

Llwyn Onn Guest House

Rhydlydan, Pentrefoelas, Betws-y-Coed, Ll24 0TW

T: 01690-770124 www.llwynonnguesthouse.co.uk E: reception@llwynonnguesthouse.cc

Situated at the gateway of Snowdonia's National Park, this small, family-run B&B is set within an area of natural beauty, amidst the rolling heather moors of the Hiraethog. Llwyn Onn is a former Victorian Watermill sympathetically restored into a modern welcoming guest house. Nestled amid 2.5 acres of land, the house boasts beautiful views, a natural lake to the front, with ducks and local wildlife, and open fields leading up to the Berwyn Mountain range behind. Over the past decade the guest house and glampsite have been transformed into the attractive, welcoming accomodation it is today.

As with all accomodation we strive to maintain our guest house to the highest standard and are constantly making improvements.

The Hut

Rhydlydan, Pentrefoelas, Betws-y-Coed, Ll24 0TW

T: 01690-770124 www.llwynonnguesthouse.co.uk E: reception@llwynonnguesthouse.co.uk

Situated at the gateway of Snowdonia's National Park, this small, family-run B&B is set within an area of natural beauty, amidst the rolling heather moors of the Hiraethog.
Llwyn Onn is a former Victorian Watermill sympathetically restored into a modern welcoming guest house. Nestled amid 2.5 acres of land, the house boasts beautiful views, a natural lake to the front, with ducks and local wildlife, and open fields leading up to the Berwyn Mountain range behind. The Hut is a Sheperds Hut that has a double bed, tv, toiletries,dressing gowns, towels and a full breakfast hamper. You can even collect your own fresh eggs in the morning. Within easy reach of Clocanog Forest and Llyn Brenig, which is popular for fishing and boating.

Glanllyn Lakeside Caravan & Camping Park

Bala, Gwynedd, LL23 7SS

T: 01678-540227/540441 www.glanllyn.com E: info@glanllyn.com

Glanllyn-lakeside caravan and camping park is situated alongside Wales' largest natural lake - Llyn Tegid, in the south of the beautiful Snowdonia National Park. Our site is graded 4 star by Visit Wales. There is WiFi on the site. Glanllyn-lakeside caravan and camping park offers extensive views of the nearby Aran and Arenig mountains and the 16 acres of level parkland makes it the ideal spot to pitch a caravan, motor-home, tent or trailer tent. Glanllyn-lakeside has modern facilities including a modern shower block with free, hot, all-day showers. There is a launderette and dish-washing area.
We have plenty of electric hook up points for caravans motor-homes and tents. The well stocked camp shop sells basic supplies, gas, maps of local walks etc.

Glanllyn Lodge

Bala, Gwynedd, LL23 7SS

T: 01678-540227/540441 www.glanllyn.com E: info@glanllyn.com

Situated near Wales' largest natural lake in the Snowdonia National Park, Glanllyn Lodge is a historic gatehouse lodge, completely renovated and furnished and equipped to the highest of standards. It has been awarded a 5 star grading by Visit Wales (originally the Wales Tourist Board). The Lodge sleeps up to 5 and comprises of one en-suite double bedroom, one twin bedroom and one single bedroom. Bed linen and towels supplied. The large oak kitchen/diner has a dishwasher, washer/dryer, microwave etc. There is a superb luxury bathroom with a whirlpool bath....Go on - spoil yourself! The comfortable lounge is furnished to a high standard and to enhance your stay, it is equipped with sky TV & a DVD player. Glanllyn Lodge has Wi-Fi / Broadband.

Bryn Tyrch Inn

Capel Curig, Gwynedd, LL24 0EL

T: 01690-720223 www.bryntyrchinn.co.uk E : info@bryntyrchinn.co.uk

We are an independently owned Four Star Inn with 12 en suite bedrooms, situated in the heart of the Snowdonia National Park. Located in the village of Capel Curig, we are in easy reach of the many mountain ranges, bike trails and activities including Zip World and Surf Snowdonia. The Bryn is a great base to explore and enjoy all the area has to offer and is just a few minutes drive from Betws y Coed. Our bar and bistro," Y Bryn" (meaning "The Hill") has views of Mount Siabod and the Snowdon Horseshoe, making it the perfect place to relax after a busy and rewarding day. We provide Welsh cask ales, fine wines and cocktails plus a range of soft drinks and hot beverages. Our food is carefully sourced and freshly prepared by our team of chefs to an AA one rosette standard. We look forward to welcoming you at Y Bryn restaurant.

Pentre Bach Bunkhouse & Camping

Pentre Bach, Waunfawr, Gwynedd, LL54 7AJ

T: 07798-733939 www.pentrebachbunkhouse.co.uk E: info@bachventures.co.uk

Our Bunkhouse in North Wales, is just outside the village of Waunfawr and only a 5 minute drive from Mount Snowdon and the footpaths of Snowdon Ranger and Rhyd Ddu. We converted our stone barn in 2001 to provide self catering accommodation for outdoor enthusiasts into an alpine style bunk-house and with a "Real Ale" pub only a 10 minute walk from the bunkhouse. The bunkhouse is split over two floors; the ground floor has a cooking area (with gas burners, microwaves, fridge and freeze all pots/pans cutlery provided), seating and a dining area. The second floor is used for sleeping and can accommodate up to 16 on mattresses on five sleeping platforms 2(5)s 1(4) and 2 (1)s. Bed linen and pillow case provided you just need your sleeping bag. There is also a campsite.

Yr Hen Fecws, Fresh Food, Comfy Rooms

15-16 Lombard Street, Porthmadog, Gwynedd, LL49 9AP

T: 01766-514625 www.henfecws.com E: info@henfecws.com

Many of the traditional architectural features have been retained with exposed beams and stonewor which are perfectly complimented by contemporary and tasteful decor and furnishings. This style ha been carried through to our well appointed and renowned bistro that oozes character and is bursting with freshness and flavour. Porthmadog is the perfect place from which to explore the beautiful Snow-donia National Park and its magnificent surrounds. There is an abundance of activities and things to do and see, no matter what your energy levels. All this make Hen Fecws the perfect place for relaxing and exploring. Comfy 7 comprises of seven 4 star rooms which have been uniquely and lovingly cre-ated and come on a bed and breakfast basis.

Plas Gwyn Caravan, Camping & B&B

Llanberis Road, Llanrug, Caernarfon, Gwynedd, LL55 2AQ

T: 01286-672619 www.plasgwyn.co.uk E: info@plasgwyn.co.uk

Plas Gwyn Caravan & Camping Park is a peaceful, family run, caravan and camp site set within the grounds of Plas Gwyn House. Situated near Llanrug (mid-way between Llanberis and Caernarfon) the park boasts outstanding views over Caernarfon, Anglesey and Snowdonia.
Plas Gwyn caters for touring caravans, motor homes and tents. Plas Gwyn also offers five static holida caravans, a Timber Tent and Bed & Breakfast, all available for short breaks or weekly hire.
The Park has its own private drive off the A4086. A regular bus service can be caught from the end of the drive giving excellent access to Caernarfon, Bangor and Llanberis.It is a great base to discover the many attractions that North Wales has to offer.

Dol Aur B&B

Old Llanfair Road, Harlech, Gwynedd, LL46 2SS

T: 01766-781312 www.dolaur.com E: dolaur@outlook.com

At Dol Aur you will be sure of a warm welcome from Peter and Angela. Our aim is to provide you with all you need to make your stay with us a memorable one. Featuring outstanding sea views, Dol Aur Bed and Breakfast offers free WiFi throughout and free onsite parking. Situated in Harlech, it also has a large sun terrace with seating. Each room includes a flat-screen TV, fridge and tea and coffee makin facilities. The rooms benefit from a private shower room. Some rooms have views of the sea and othe overlook the garden. An array of activities can be enjoyed in the area surrounding Dol Aur Bed and Breakfast, including golfing. Harlech Castle is just 13 minutes' walk away. Llandanwg Railway Station i a 5-minute drive away.

Ty Mawr Hotel & Restaurant/ Bar

Llanbedr, Harlech, Gwynedd, LL45 2NH

T: 01341-241440 www.tymawrhotel.com E: info@tymawrhotel.com

Ty - Mawr means 'Big House' in Welsh, but also 'Big Welcome' in any language! A family run hotel restaurant and bar with a relaxed, warm and friendly atmosphere. Jane and Steve, a brother and sister team run Ty Mawr in a relaxed warm and friendly atmosphere. Rooms are spacious, and welcoming, each with individually designed decor, and the lounge is cosy and relaxing, guaranteed to make you feel at home. Whilst you are here why not mingle with the locals in the public bar or simply soak up the atmosphere and enjoy a drink from our excellent selection of very well kept beers, real ales, wine and spirits. Bar meals and the restaurant menus have an excellent reputation with both residents and locals alike. In the Summer, the garden is a great place for families to relax.

Estuary Lodge

Talsarnau, Harlech, Gwynedd, LL47 6TA

T: 01766-771155 www.estuarylodge.co.uk E: mail@estuarylodge.co.uk

The Estuary Lodge Hotel and Restaurant boasts 10 en suite rooms, all of which are located on the ground floor. Rooms are individually decorated with luxurious fabrics and natural colours, and each has a flat-screen TV with DVD player, work desk and tea/coffee facilities. Following a refurbishment in the winter of 2013, the property now includes upgraded bathrooms. The Estuary Bistro serves a delicious menu featuring fresh, local produce including eggs from their own chickens and ducks, vegetables from the garden and meats from the local butcher. The Coffee Shop offers traditional coffees, a selection of snacks and indulgent homemade cakes. The village of Talsarnau has its own railway station and is only a 5 minutes drive from the nearest shops, pubs and numerous restaurants.

The Slate - Y Llechan

Talybont, Bangor, LL57 3UR

T: 01248-355500 www.theslate.co.uk E: post@theslate.co.uk

The premises has been totally refurbished from top to bottom with some internal modifications to make the most of the space available and to create a coherent and fulfilling place to work, rest and play. Parts of the original building are doubtless quite old (this is after all a former coach house) with thick walls and beamed ceilings, but gone are the dark rooms of yore - the choice use of fitting colours lifts the mood dramatically, with tasteful decor and the general presentation shouting quality, comfort as well as functionality. With a westerly aspect and outdoor seating, you'll be able to relax in the afternoon sunshine after a day out and enjoy some excellent food and drink. With 11 bedrooms, free internet Wi-Fi throughout the building, every room featuring a shower en-suite and much much more, make sure your next stay is with The Slate.

St Curig's Church

Capel Curig, Betws-y-Coed, Gwynedd, LL24 0EN

T: 01690-720469 www.stcurigschurch.com E: alice@alicedouglas.com

St Curig's Church is a quirky and wonderful self-catering property which in quiet periods also offers Bed & Breakfast. It's probably true to say that there's nowhere else quite like Mountain Church in North Wales. Ancient and modern stylishly combine in this beautiful home set within a 19th century church in the mountain village of Capel Curig. Where else can you sleep beneath a carved stone pulpit, enjoy a hot tub under the stars or play table tennis beneath a fabulous 19th century mosaic ceiling? And all with lovely views of Snowdonia's mountains from every window. And as well as a peaceful retreat in the heart of Snowdonia, St Curig's Church is also a fantastic venue for outdoorsy stag or hen weekends. Please don't hesitate to contact us to discuss your needs.

Tyn y Fron B&B

Llanrwst Road, Betws-y-Coed, Conwy, LL24 0HD T: 01690-710449

www.snowdoniabedandbreakfast.co.uk E: welcome@snowdoniabedandbreakfast.co.u

This country house B&B is just a short walk from the centre of Betws-y-Coed, the Gateway to the Snowdonia National Park. We have been awarded a 5 Star Grading and Gold Award for Excellence by Wales (the Welsh Tourist Board). The house is set in grounds of nearly an acre and guests are welcom relax in the garden at the end of the day. On site parking is available for the exclusive use of guests. a restful night's sleep in one of our individual comfortable bedrooms you can sit and enjoy a traditio cooked breakfast whilst admiring the spectacular views of our garden, across the Conwy Valley and t mountains of Snowdonia. We are keen walkers and cyclists and like to share our local knowledge of area to help you plan an action packed day or a breath taking sight seeing tour of this stunning area have plenty of maps and guide books for you to borrow.

North Wales Holiday Cottages

39 Station Road, Deganwy, Conwy, LL31 9DF

T: 01492-582492 www.northwalesholidaycottages.co.uk E:info@northwalesholidaycottages.c

North Wales Holiday Cottages is a Visit Wales accredited holiday letting agency based in Deganwy, Conwy. We have a wide range of properties around Conwy and across the whole of North Wales from small single bedroom apartments to large houses and remote locations to town centres. All of our te live locally, visit the properties and have a good knowledge of the area so feel free to call us for help and advice planning your holiday in this beautiful part of Wales. You can also find detailed informatic on our website for all the cottages as well as suggestions on things to do during your stay. Call us no or visit our website to find your perfect place to stay in Conwy.

Tan y Foel Country House

Capel Garmon, Llanwrst, Conwy, LL26 0RE

T: 01690-710507 www.tanyfoelcountryhouse.co.uk E: stay@tanyfoelcountryhouse.co.

Our boutique B&B is a place to relax, unwind and escape the hustle and bustle. Set in two acres and surrounded by woods and farmland, we are just five minutes by car from Betws-Y-Coed and within e reach of the mountains and the coast. We have just six luxurious en-suite bedrooms, all decorated wi imaginative flair. The Loft, Four Poster and French Rooms are all located within the main house and a have spectacular views over our gardens to the mountains and Conwy Valley. The Retro room is loca to the rear of main house and has a more limited view over roofs to the surrounding trees. All of our bedrooms are furnished with both bath and shower facilites, complimentary tea/coffee trays, direct dial telephones, DVD/CD, colour televisions and free Wi Fi . Bathrobes, hairdryers and toiletries provi thoughtful touches in the en-suite bathrooms.

Dwy Olwen B&B

Coed-y-Fronallt, Dolgellau, Gwynedd, LL40 2YG

T: 01341-422822 www.dwyolwyn.co.uk E: dwy_olwyn@hotmail.co.uk

Dwy Olwyn bed and breakfast in Dolgellau, is a spacious family run guest house, which has offered b in Snowdonia for over 20 years. Accommodation consists of double, family and twin bedded rooms, of which are centrally heated and have TV, and tea & coffee making facilities. Some are en-suite. Dwy Olwyn Bed and Breakfast has a large comfortable guest lounge overlooking Dolgellau, with a patio v seating for guests to relax and take in the scenery. A good selection of guide books, maps and broch for guests use, can be found in the lounge. Facilities Guest lounge, TV in all rooms, , Secure cycle stor Tea and Coffee making facilities, Hairdryers in all, Parking, Garden, Drying facilities for walkers, room.

Bistro Bermo

6 Church Street, Barmouth, Gwynedd, LL42 1EW

T: 01341-281284 E: bistrobermo@gmail.com

Discreetly hidden behind an aqua-green shopfront, this intimate restaurant delivers a sophisticated menu chock-full of Welsh farm produce and fresh fish. Featuring dishes such as red bream with scallops and seafood bisque, the cooking is classical, rather than experimental, and generally excellent. There are only half a dozen tables, so book ahead.

Mark Williams -Daily Post

It isn't down to just one single factor; it is a combination of elements such as freshly prepared food, great wines and an unbeatable atmosphere that show this restaurant is getting things just about right. In fact it just might be worth a drive there alone in its own right.

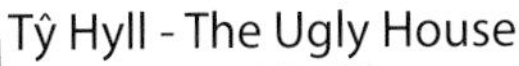

Tŷ Hyll - The Ugly House

Capel Curig, Conwy LL24 0DS

T: 01286 685498 www. theuglyhouse.co.uk E: info@snowdonia-society.org.uk

Shrouded in mystery, Ty Hyll (the Ugly House) is some 3 miles west of Betws-y-Coed, on the A5 towards Capel Curig.Its origins allegedly go back to 1475, when two brothers built themselves a hideaway in the Snowdonia forest and carving the date over the fireplace.

Today the house is in the ownership of local charity the Snowdonia Society, and run as a visitor centre and cosy cottage tearoom.

Visitors can enjoy home baked local produce and also learn about the legends of the house and the local environment, particularly the honeybees and wildlife garden that give the tearoom its name.and beyond.

Tu Hwnt i'r Bont Tearoom

Nr Inigo Jones Bridge, Llanrwst, Conwy, LL26 0PL

T: 01492 642322 www.tuhwntirbont.co.uk E: sales@tuhwntirbont.co.uk

For visitors to North Wales generally (and the Conwy Valley, Betws-y-Coed in particular), Tu Hwnt I'r Bont is itself, in this idyllic setting, an obvious 'must see' tourist attraction; offering as it does, a truly authentic and hugely enjoyable 'taste' of North Wales and its culture. Comfortably accommodating 50 people inside in traditional style, we seat a further 30 outside in our lovely tea garden, including full waitress service. By prior arrangement, groups of 20 to 80 people are welcome.

We have our own private car park situated at the rear of the building, suitable for 30 cars.

Tu Hwnt I'r Bont Tearoom and Restaurant is open: 10.30 – 5.00 (waitress service)

The Glyntwrog Inn

Llanrug, Caernarfon, Gwynedd, LL55 4AN

T: 01286-671191 E: theglyntwrog@gmail.com

A friendly local village pub in the heart of the Welsh countryside, offering a great selection of real ales, beers, wines, cocktails and soft drinks. Serving hearty, homemade food using locally sourced, fresh ingredients. Open every day from 11am till late. Food is being served 12am till 3pm and 5pm till 9pm. Wednesdays it is Burger and a drink all day. You get a 6oz burger, from the local butcher, with your choice of any 2 toppings served with homemade chips & salad and a free drink of your choice, restrictions apply, for £9.50! Thursdays it is Steak Night - The famous 8oz sirloin, again from our local butcher, cooked to your liking served with all the trimmings, homemade chips & salad and your choice of free drink, restrictions apply, for only £13.50On Thursdays it is also quiz night, starting 9.30pm.

Ty'n Y Cornel Hotel

Tal-y-Llyn, Tywyn, Gwynedd, LL36 9AJ

T: 01654-782282 www. tynycornel.co.uk E: enquiries@tynycornel.com

Located on the banks of the beautiful Tal-y-llyn Lake, the Ty'n Y Cornel Hotel sits in the heart of the stunning mountain scenery of Mid-Wales. We have a superb restaurant at Ty'n Y Cornel, our chef has designed a menu that sees a variety of local delicacies along with popular British dishes. If there are dietary requirements you have, let us know and we'll be able to assist. We also aim to create exceller seasonal menus, if you're looking to stay with us and wish to know what will be available at the time please feel free to contact us and we'll be able to help you. The menus at Tyn n Cornel change seasonally and are composed with the very best produce sourced locally where possible. Please not our menus may vary daily based on seasonal produce availability.

Ysgethin Inn

Talybont, Gwynedd, LL43 2AN

T: 01341-247578 www.ysgethin.com E: ysgethin@outlook.com

A warm and friendly country inn, in the idyllic settings of the Ysgethin river and forest. We serve fresh home cooked food 6 days a week and In seasonal times 7 days a week. We have 2 servings of 12.00-2 and then 6.00-8.30 and on a Sunday a traditional roast.

Review 5 Star Trip Advisor - What a find

Well what a place, was looking for a local pub for some honest food and a drink for my family and I a we stumbled on this gem.Great fresh cooked food, with local ingredients, that saw my kids and my w and I leave clean plates. We had two portions of the pulled beef chilli and 2 of the shefs special burg great tasting, good portion sizes and great value for money.

Salt Marsh Kitchen

6, College Green, Tywyn, LL36 9BS

T: 01654-711949 www.saltmarshkitchen.co.uk E: saltmarshkitchen@gmail.c

Proud little restaurant set in Tywyn Wales. We pride ourselves on using the very best produce to crea exciting and delicious food that wont break the bank. A comfortable and easy place to visit and dine Scott Paterson runs the front of house and is manager of Salt Marsh Kitchen. Bryony Davis is Head C Jim Paterson is our Soux Chef and pizza wiz. Serving the best quality food, made from the wonderfu produce we are lucky enough to have growing & breed locally. Meat that has been born, bred and butchered in Wales, and fish plucked from our beautiful Cardigan Bay. Daily delivery's from our local food heroes and crafted from scratch each day by the Salt Marsh Kitchen team.

Number Twenty One

21 Heol, Maengwyn, Machynlleth, Powys, SY20 8EB

T: 01654-703382 www.numbertwentyone.co.uk E: info@numbertwentyone.co

Using the finest locally sourced Welsh ingredients, we offer an exciting mix of traditional and moder cuisine, served in a relaxing, contemporary venue situated in the historical town centre.
Pop in and and try our coffee selections and freshly baked cakes, which are offered throughout the c alongside our lunchtime and evening meals.

We look forward to your visit!

The Slate - Y Llechan

Talybont, Bangor, LL57 3UR

T: 01248-355500 www.theslate.co.uk E: post@theslate.co.uk

The Slate is located in Bangor, North Wales, featuring an on-site restaurant and bar. Free WiFi and free private parking is available.It's not only the restaurant & hotel that's undergone a total refurbishment but the bar too. If you want a real ale then you're in luck as this is just the place to sample some locally produced beer,spirits & wines. Bespoke lighting has been incorporated into the bar to highlight the exciting range of cocktails, spirits and gins on offer. One of our passions at The Slate is Gin. We've sourced some amazing gins, both local and from further afield, to highlight this diverse spirit. The Slate is 1.7 miles from Bangor Cathedral. Bangor railway station is 3 miles from the property, with a junction from the A55 junction 1.4 miles away.

Castell Deudraeth Brasserie

Portmeirion, Minffordd, Penrhyndeudraeth, Gwynedd, LL48 6ER

T: 01766-772400 www.portmeirion.wales E: castell@portmeirion.wales

This warm and friendly restaurant has been flying the flag for Welsh fare for years. At its heart are exceptional service and a series of simple but stunning dishes which never fail to please. Sit in the light and airy conservatory or in the open and spacious dining room overlooking the surrounding countryside and Victorian gardens. Castell Deudraeth has several tables outside on the terrace for drinks and meals in fine weather, and we have a special children's menu available for children under 12.Lunch Service 12pm - 2:30pm, Dinner Service 6:30pm - 9:30pm (last order 9:15pm) Enjoy FREE ENTRY to Portmeirion Village with a two-course lunch at Castell Deudraeth (not including sandwiches and light bites). Please contact the Castell on 01766 772400.

Ristorante Pulcinella

Pier Promenade, Garth Road, Bangor, Gwynedd, LL57 2SW

T: 01248-362807 www.pulcinellabangor.co.uk

Opened in 1998, this family run business is a well established Italian restaurant and a rm favourite with both locals and visitors worldwide. Located in the city centre just a stone's throw from Bangor Pier, enjoy breathtaking views of the Menai Straights in a warm and relaxing environment where Yasmin and sta venture to provide a welcoming, friendly e cient service.
Owner and talented Italian Chef Mario, creates beautifully modern and traditional home cooked Italian cuisine, using high quality local produce and carefully sourced Italian products - direct from Italy! From Lasagna to stone baked pizza and gorgeous seafood dishes, not forgetting the ever popular homemade Tiramisu, Mario and Yasmin strive to bring a piece of Italy to Bangor!

The Slate - Y Llechan *

Talybont, Bangor, LL57 3UR

T: 01248-355500 www.theslate.co.uk E: post@theslate.co.uk

Modern dishes that capture the flavours of the season, with local produce, at the slate.
Often its not just ambiance, decor and general feel of a restaurant that make a night out but also the quality of staff, the courteous and helpful nature and most definitely the quality of food, plentiful choice and of course presentation. It all goes a long way in our perception of what a night out should be like and we don't mind spending that little bit extra either as it's often the small things that all add up to make an enjoyable experience.

Galeri Cafe Bar

Pier Promenade, Garth Road, Bangor, Gwynedd, LL57 2SW

T: 01286-685200 www.galericaernarfon.com E: cegin@galericaernarfon.com

Following a period of renovation and upgrading our facilities and equipment, the new look café ba means that you can now fully take advantage of our unique waterfront location with amazing view: Victoria Dock and the Menai Straits. It offers a perfect place to socialise with friends, to meet with co leagues and clients, to wind down with a glass of wine or to enjoy a family meal in a warm and welcoming atmosphere. Our new head chef, Robbie Worgan has devised a menu that showcases th very best of fresh, seasonal, locally sourced produce – from land and sea. Robbie comes to Galeri fol lowing a period working at kitchens across the United Kingdom and in France. These include: The Clive, Ludlow | Rhodes 24, London| Seiont Manor, Llanrug.

Pant Du Cafe & Restaurant

County Road, Penygroes, Caernarfon, Gwynedd, LL54 6HE

T: 01286-881819 www.pantdu.co.uk E: post@pantdu.co.uk

A warm Welsh welcome awaits you at Pant Du Café. Indulge in our delicious homemade cakes, fresh prepared lunches, speciality coffees or why not treat someone special to our afternoon tea? Come a enjoy the spectacular views of Snowdonia from the new Pant Du café, overlooking the vineyard anc orchard.

Pontoon Pwllheli

1 Marinaland, Pwllheli LL53 5AY, UK, Pwllheli LL53 5AY

T: 01758-228346 www.pontoonpwllheli.com E: info@ pontoonpwllheli.co

We are a very small creative, warm and inviting family-run business. Our team are committed to delivering world flavours with our 'Chef Crango' changing his Mexican, Middle Eastern and Caribbea inspired menus most weeks. Chris and Anna take inspiration for the menu, cocktails, artwork and interior from their travels around Mexico and pride themselves in bringing an authentic and memorable experience to all their customers in North Wales.

The Boatyard Inn

Garth Road, Bangor, Gwynedd, LL57 2SF

T: 01248-362462 E: theboatyardbangor@outlook.com

Reviewed 5*****

Beautiful Food

Came across this lovely pub whilst visiting Bangor pier, and when we called in to have a look at the n we couldn't wait to come back later for our food.Luckily we managed to get a table but it may be wis to ring ahead and book just in case.Had the lamb shank for our main it was cooked to perfection and tasty on top of a bed of creamy mash.We followed that up with amazing deserts Erin mess cheesecak for me and sticky toffee pudding and custard for my partner, we will definitely be back again.

Plas Bodegroes

Pwllheli, Gwynedd, LL53-5TH

T: 01758-612363 www.bodegroes.co.uk E: gunna@bodegroes.co.uk

In the 25 years since we first opened Plas Bodegroes, our restaurant has gained top awards from all of the leading guides, including (for 14 years) Michelin Star, Egon Ronay Star, and UK Restaurant of the Year in the Good Food Guide. Our reputation is based upon the modern interpretation of traditional dishes, concentrating upon the superb local ingredients. In addition, we try to source our fish as sustainably as possible, and do not use endangered wild species. As a result some of our fish is now farmed from sustainable sources. These include Icelandic cod, Norwegian halibut and Shetland organic salmon and sea trout.

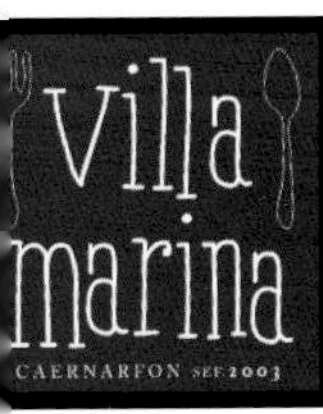

Villa Marina

9 Segontium Terrace, Caernarfon, Gwynedd, LL55 2PN

T: 01286-677290 www.villa-marina.co.uk E: enquiry@villa-marina.co.uk

Enjoying good food and wine are two of life's great pleasures...we are inspired by Mediterranean food, source our ingredients as locally as possible & enjoy the tradition of family meals around the kitchen table. We welcome walking boots, beach gear, the smartest attire & anything in between...it's all about the food, friends, family & time spent eating together. The restaurant is set in a grade II listed building on the impressive Segontium Terrace overlooking Caernarfon Castle and the harbour full of boats. Once owned by a wealthy ship's captain during the heyday of the booming slate trade of the last two centuries, Villa Marina combines rustic charm with Georgian architecture & a dash of shabby chic vintage decor. All our food is made with the season's freshest ingredients & cooked from scratch by our chefs every day.

Tonnau Restaurant

Caerwylan Hotel, Beach Bank, Criccieth, Gwynedd, LL52 0HW

T: 01766-522547 www.caerwylan.co.uk E: reception@caerwylan.co.uk

Experience our new fine dining Tonnau Restaurant, overlooking Cardigan Bay and Criccieth castle. Our contemporary restaurant has an unpretentious approach to quality cuisine with the varied menu changing everyday. Our experienced Chefs source as much as possible from local suppliers. We also have an extensive wine list which perfectly compliments the flavours our menu offers. After dinner relax over coffee in one of our deep settees in the sea facing lounge.

The Port Cafe & Deli

High Street, Porthmadog, Gwynedd, LL49 9LP

T: 01766-513760

The restaurant offers a wide variety of dining options from early morning breakfast for a hearty start to the day, through lunchtime with daily specials available and Sunday Roast to late afternoon dinning, we also offer a Junior Menu for our younger customers. The Port Cafe & Deli offers the option of a lighter meal or snack, with the deli section within the cafe having a vast array of takeaway available and picnic hampers. Favourites from the deli section include the home roasted meats, pies, salads, with special requests catered for. For those summer days we have outdoor seating available. Special occasions are catered for in the function room and outdoor catering is also provided.

Oceans Bistro

The Promenade, Llanfairfechan, Gwynedd, LL33 0BY

T: 01248-681700 www.oceans-llan.co.uk E: contact@oceans-llan.co.u

Located on The Promenade in Llanfairfechan, Oceans offers great food and drink against the backdrc of the North Wales coastline. With views of Puffin Island, the Great Orme and Anglesey across the Me Straits you are guaranteed a great outlook.
We pride ourselves in good food and drink and a friendly atmosphere. We cater for families, couples and larger parties. Our experienced chef attracts great reviews on Tripadvisor.
Open both in daytime and evenings (see seasonal times on this site) we offer a wide choice on our menu. Bookings are advised in busy times........
We look forward to seeing you.

The Waterloo Hotel

Holyhead Road, Betws y Coed, Snowdonia, LL24 0AR

T: 01690-710411 www.waterloo-hotel.info E: reservations@waterloo-hotel.info

The Bridge Restaurant is a fantastic venue for dining, functions and weddings. Our menu has a dedicated emphasis on local seasonal produce. We work closely with local suppliers to ensure we deliver you the freshest quality ingredients on the plate. Offering a modern and contemporary venu Bar 1815 is the ideal place to drink and relax after a busy day out and about in North Wales. After you meal at the Bridge Restaurant unwind on our sofas in front of the fire with a nightcap, but beware … many have been known to fall asleep at this point!

The Black Boy Inn

Northgate Street,Caernarfon, Gwynedd, LL55 1RW

T: 01286-673604 www.black-boy-inn.com E: reception@black-boy-inn.com

We strive to provide a personal service. From the moment you arrive our friendly inn staff are always on hand to assist and share their local knowledge. Since the early 16th Century The Black Boy Inn hc has been welcoming weary travellers and visitors to the Town of Caernarfon and region of Snowdor Some things don't change, whether you want to drink, dine or unwind, you will find The Black Boy Inn the perfect base to explore the beautiful Snowdonia Mountains of North Wales and Anglesey. W have thirty nine comfortable guest rooms all with private bathrooms and all individually styled and furnished. Free Wi-Fi is available for all our guests throughout the entire hotel. Our celebrated restaurant is awarded a Visit Wales Bronze Award and has a menu to suit all tastes.

Voltaire

25 Garth Road, Bangor, Gwynedd, LL57 2SE

T: 07415-619267 E: voltairevegan@yahoo.com

Come and join us at Voltaire. Experience food from a modern vegan perspective. its healthy, its delic and it means we can all live happily ever after!

Trip Advisor 5 Star Review

This little restaurant is a little gem in Bangor, North Wales. The restaurant is fully vegan and the men is packed with a wonder of food to get your mouth watering. The selection of burgers in particular i mind boggling. The service is friendly and the ambience is wonderful with no over bearing music w allows you to relax enjoy the food and the conversation.

Glan Yr Afon Riverside

Pennal, Nr Machynlleth, Gwynedd, SY20 9DW

T: 01654 791285 www.riversidehotel-pennal.co.uk E: info@riversidehotel-pennal.co.uk

The Glan Yr Afon/Riverside is a family run country pub; we very much lean towards being a restaurant. Glyn and I (Corina) bought the freehold in May 2010, are pleased to have been trading successfully for the last three years and long may this continue. Our restaurant seats 50 guests in one sitting, we aim to take two sittings at weekends and during busy periods. We take luncheon & dinner bookings in the restaurant, bar and cwtch. Booking advisable Friday and Saturday evenings and Sunday lunch times to avoid disappointment. All food is freshly prepared on the premises by our team of Chefs who only use the best quality meat, fish and vegetables sourced locally. We are happy to discuss reduced and set menus to suit your requirements and pocket should you wish to book a group in for lunch or dinner.

The Royal Ship Hotel

Queens Square, Dolgellau, Gwynedd, LL40 1AR

T: 01341-422209 www.royalship.pub E : royalship@outlook.com

The Royal Ship Hotel is a 19th century Coaching Inn in Dolgellau. We are ideally situated to explore North and Mid Wales. Located in Snowdonia National Park, the Hotel is surrounded by mountains, rivers and lakes and is a few minutes drive from the coast. The Hotel offers 23 bedrooms. You can choose between Single, Double, Twin or Triple rooms. Some of our rooms have an attractive view over the Town Square and Cader Idris. All rooms are well equipped with tea & coffee facilities, TV and local tourist information. Pets welcome. We have an on site restaurant and bar. The Royal Ship Hotel Restaurant serves a great range of freshly prepared dishes using local produce where possible. Our main menu offers a wide selection of traditional favourites along with lighter options including salads and sandwiches.

Dylan's Restaurant

Esplanade, Maes y Mor, Criccieth LL52 0HU

T: 01766 522773 www.dylansrestaurant.co.uk E: criccieth@dylansrestaurant.co.uk

Dylan's Criccieth, which opened in May 2015, is located in the iconic Morannedd building designed by Portmeirion architect Sir Clough Williams-Ellis. Sitting right on the edge of the water, all tables boast panoramic views of Cardigan Bay and of the town's famous castle. For sunnier and warmer days, there is an outside dining area with direct access to the beach. The restaurant offers a family friendly, relaxed dining experience. The menu features locally sourced fish, seafood and seasonal farm produce served creatively in dishes ranging from artisan pizza to seafood chowder and roasted Welsh lamb rump. All our restaurants are are open from 11am-11pm, 7 days a week, throughout the year (except for Christmas Day).

Bwyty Lleu Cafe

Dinas Dinlle, Caernarfon, Gwynedd, LL54 5TW

T: 01286-831816 www.bwytylleu.co.uk

Bwyty Lleu is located on the promenade in Dinas Dinlle, Caernarfon, Gwynedd. It is a family run Café/ Restaurant, Shop and Bar. We are open 7 days a week peak season and always open on Weekends all year round. Locally famous for our Sunday Lunch, and the use of locally produced ingredients of the finest quality wherever possible. The restaurant caters for a wide range of events, including weddings, birthday parties, private events and Christmas parties. We also cater for coach parties and we undertake outside catering. With the royal town of Caernarfon only 6 miles away, Bwyty Lleu is in an ideal location for tourists, day visitors, those who have been following the coastal path around the Lleyn Peninsula and to those traveling along Lon Eifion the cycle path that is only a stone's throw away. Caernarfon Airport is also located in Dinas Dinlle.

SNOWDONIA Mountains & Coast

Golden Fleece Inn

Market Square, Tremadog, Gwynedd, LL49 9RB

T: 01766 512421 www.goldenfleeceinn.com E: info@goldenfleeceinn.com

The dining room at The Golden Fleece Inn is one of the most popular restaurants in Porthmadog an Tremadog. Managed under the watchful eye of our experienced and cultured Head Chef, we offer o diners excellent quality food in a relaxed environment using the very best ingredients, the majority which are sourced locally. For formal dining, we take reservations in our restaurant, but for larger bookings we may need more notice to ensure that we can accommodate your party. However, you also choose to have your meal in our rustic cellar/bar, which is a little more informal but boasts muc more of a relaxed environment to dine in. As such, there is no need to make a reservation in the bar just simply turn up, enjoy a drink, find your table of choice and browse our vast array of dishes.

Country Cooks Cafe

Two Gates, Ty-Nant, Corwen, Conwy, LL21 0PT

T: 01490 420628 E: countrycooks@btconnect.com

Country Cooks is situated beside the A5 at Ty Nant, one of the main routes into Snowdonia and is fa run with local staff. It has stunning views of the countryside, an outside seating area and a large car There is an easily accessed entry ramp and is 'Dog Friendly'. The menu which is available all day rang from simple snacks and homemade soup to breakfasts and grills. 'Salads and Things' are a speciality served with a large variety of fruit and salad vegetables. The homemade Steak Kidney pie, Chicken p ,Lasagne, Cottage Pie etc and the Local Beef and Welsh Black Beer are made in the traditional way us our local butchers produce.A variety of pancakes are available all year as are a selection of homema puddings from old school favourites Jam Roly Poly and Spotted Dick to fruit pies and others in betw

The Moorings Bistro

4 Ivy Terrace, Borth-y-Gest, Porthamadog, Gwynedd, LL49 9TS

T: 01766-513500 www.moorings-bistro.co.uk E: melanie@mooringsbistro.co.u

Overlooking the beautiful and tranquil bay of Borth'y'Gest' the Mooring's Bistro team welcomes you friendly and relaxed atmosphere

Offering an inventive menu prepared to order with the freshest local ingredients available' the restaurant is open for breakfast lunch and dinner'

In addition to the cosy fireplace inside our heated terrace allows you to make the most of the stunni views' even in the winter'

Please check opening hours' Bookings recommended but not neccessary

Yr Hen Fecws, Fresh Food, Comfy Rooms

15-16 Lombard Street, Porthmadog, Gwynedd, LL49 9AP

T: 01766-514625 www.henfecws.com E: info@henfecws.com

Porthmadog is the perfect place from which to explore the beautiful Snowdonia National Park and its magnificent surrounds. There is an abundance of activities and things to do and see, no matter what your energy levels. All this make Hen Fecws the perfect place for relaxing and exploring. Hen Fecws is set in Porthmadog, a bustling harbour town with an appealing array of shops and attractior and some of the most beautiful and breathtaking scenery that Wales has to offer. Our food is freshly prepared, cooked to order and sourced locally whenever possible. We are happy to cater for dietry requirements. We look forward to welcoming you to Yr Hen Fecws soon!

NORTH EAST WALES

hroughout our Top 100 Attractions books Apps & Website, we have we think, put a lot of hought into the attractions that have been featured. The reason for that simply lies with the huge xpectations that me and my team come to expect when we go on our holidays. If you were ravelling abroad, there would be a good chance you are going for the sun and on that basis, vouldn't be as focused on attractions as a main reason for picking your holiday destination. olidaying in the UK however, because we don't normally see the types of temperatures ommonly associated with those abroad, we base our UK holidays a lot of the times on what o see and do! The reason I bring this up in this particular section of the book, is because in the Velsh borders area, we don't have a wide array of beaches as it is a land locked region.

is therefore a huge fact that the tourist attractions are a very important part of a visit to this ocality. We have chosen a great selection of attractions for you to visit and I'm sure you will not be isappointed with them one tiny bit. Whether it's a trip on a train, visiting a popular farm park, or ust a relaxing visit to one of the many and outstanding National Trust properties within the area. here is something to literally wet all your tourist taste buds. The magic of the Welsh borders ection is that even if you are staying in great places such as Roman Chester or medieval hrewsbury, a trip across the border is one that you could and must make without a doubt and it vill certainly be a trip that will help you plan your next holiday, a holiday in Wales for sure.

Greenacres Animal Park

01244-531147 info@greenacresanimalpark.co.uk
greenacresanimalpark.co.uk

Set in 80 acres at the gateway to North Wales, Greenacres Animal Park is the perfect venue for a fantastic day out for families and groups.
Explore our website to find out more about our supervised animal petting area, and domesticated, zoological and wildlife animals and reptiles around the Park. Take a look at our fantastic amusement and funfair rides, tractor tours, pony rides and magical children's shows taking place throughout the year.

We have established a high reputation for educational visits from schools, nurseries and groups within a fifty mile radius. Please take a look at the facilities, information and price packages on offer.

AUTHOR'S REVIEW

I first wrote my first Top 100 Attractions in Wales book in 2011 and it was first published and hit the shops in 2012, from then on it is re edited every three years, just so we can bring you the most up to date news on all of Wales's best attractions.
This leads me nicely on to this attraction. I look for Visitor experience over value for money and Greenacres has both of these qualities in abundance. As I made my way around the park, it was clear to see that the staff here all love the animals that they all find themselves caring for on a daily basis and I found the few staff that I spoke to, very knowledgeable when I stopped to asked them a question. I couldn't get over how big the actual site is and how much there actually is to do here.

WREXHAM

Cottage Lane, Mancot, Deeside, CH5 2AZ

t: 01978-860324 e: info@llangollenmotormuseum.co.uk
www. llangollenmotormuseum.co.uk

We try to be interesting and informative but most of all to demonstrate the charm and character of our motoring past. The museum is not just two rows of old cars quietly rusting away. Most of our vehicles are on the road. The collection includes a model"T"Ford, a 30/98 Vauxhall, several Austins and Citroens. Among the motor bikes are most of the names that bring back memories of "British Bikes". The Norton, the Triumph, the Ariel, the Sunbeam and the B.S.A.. An experience not to be missed.
More than 60 vehicles from cars to invalid carriages and pedal cars, a 50's village garage scene complete with owners quarters, the cars that grandad used to drive. our experience when visiting this lovely museum will be interesting and informative but most of all it demonstrates the charm and character of our motoring past and in itself, it is a charming place, oozing with character.
The museum is a much loved family run bussiness, We are very welcoming and love to here your stories of your memories.

AUTHOR'S REVIEW

Llangollen Motor Museum is probably Llangollen's best kept secret. Hidden just a mile out of the town, going out towards the Abbey and the Horseshoe Pass, blink and you could miss the entrance, but miss this attraction and you could be missing out big time! Apart from being a big fan of Top Gear I wouldn't say I was a huge car or bike enthusiast, but this attraction has the power to be able to stir up that interest very quickly! Every vehicle on display here has been tender lovingly restored and are a credit to the family that have owned this attraction for many years.

WREXHAM

Pentre Felin, Llangollen, LL20 8EE

Kerry Vale Vineyard

01588-620627 info@kerryvalevineyard.co.uk
kerryvalevineyard.co.uk

Kerry Vale Vineyard is a small, family run, English vineyard situated on the Welsh / English border of rural Shropshire. Planted in 2010 and covering six acres of farmland, on what was the Roman Fort of Pentrheyling, the vineyard resides at the eastern tip of the Vale of Kerry - an area of exceptional beauty, just 3 miles south of the charming town of Montgomery. We run vineyard tours three times a week and our Wine Café and Cellar Door shop are open throughout the season for morning coffee, lunches and afternoon tea. Tasting wines and understanding how they are made is all part of the experience at Kerry Vale Vineyard. Whether you are looking for an interesting place to visit or a gift, our tours are perfect for anyone who enjoys wine. Open Wednesday - Sunday, 10 - 4pm (Mid March - December)Vineyard Tours: Thursdays, Saturday and Sunday 11am (Easter - November). Pre booking recommended.Try our Award Winning Wine! Wine tasting available every day (closed Monday and Tuesday) Free children's trail available on request.

AUTHOR'S REVIEW

We have a wide selection of tourist attractions within this new edition of the Top 100 Attractions in Wales. We have castles, gardens, farm parks and that is just to name but a few. But we have a new type of attraction to the book and that is vineyards. Vineyard tours are normally associated with Italy and the South of France, but you don't actually have to travel that far anymore. Wales really is putting itself on the map when it comes to vineyard tours, and it is all thanks to businesses like the one here just a stone's throw from Welshpool. Kerry Vale Vineyard in my opinion is a slickly run operation from start to finish. With self guided tours running daily, and more specialised tours available also, Kerry Vale is wine heaven. Being a family run business, they have not let this business run away with them, and with a well stocked cafe, I would estimate at least half a day here!

Pentreheyling, Shropshire, SY15 6HU

Rhug Estate

t: 01490-413000 e: contact@rhug.co.uk
www.rhug.co.uk

The history of Rhug, can be split into chapters – the first, being the largest, and spans from earliest times to coming into the hands of the Salusbury family of Bachymbyd. Rhug was then left to the Vaughan family of Nannau and finally it came into the Wynn family in the 19th century, and so to the present Lord Newborough. Our Farm Shop stocks almost 3,000 products from local suppliers and small businesses. All of these are carefully selected by our team to ensure the best quality in everything we sell and to provide our customers with the best of Welsh produce. Of course, this also includes the sale of our own products. Our in-store butchers counter stocks all of our organic meat and a deli counter which showcases some of the finest pastries, cheeses and other items that we have to offer. We have a large collection of Organic wine and spirits. These are also accompanied by some of the best craft beers and ciders in the UK. We stock a wide range of gifts in store and pride ourselves on our diverse stock.

AUTHOR'S REVIEW

For the past six years and because it's food is truly fantastic, Rhug Estate has appeared in the restaurant section of the North East Wales Chapter of this book and for every six of those years, I have seen Rhug Estate Farm Shop along with its Bison Grill Restaurant, turn into a huge attraction in its own right. Lord Newborough, the owner of the Estate, has had huge vision when developing Rhug and has spared no expense in bringing his vision to life and is now why you find Rhug Estate as one of our attractions as well as the restaurant section. Thousands of visitors flock here yearly, not only to be wowed by the farm shops many items of produce, but because of the service and dedication to quality that it brings to its many visitors on a Daily basis. I really like this attraction and I know you will to!

Corwen, Denbighshire, LL21 0EH

Llandegla Fishery

01978-755851 info@llandeglafishery.com
Llandeglafishery.com

Llandegla Fishery is ideally situated for mountain biking and walking with a wealth of outdoor activities available within the magnificent environment of the Welsh hills. We are adjacent to one of the most popular mountain bike centres in the Wales (Coed Llandegla mountain bike centre's entrance is 100 yards from our gate). There is also an RSBP centre within the forest and walks around the reservoir, home to black grouse. We are one mile away from Offa's Dyke path. Llandegla shooting ground, gliding club and horse riding centre are all within a three mile radius. The family team at Llandegla Fishery aim to provide you with a warm welcome in a relaxed atmosphere. The family team at Llandegla are very proud of the cafe. Since teaming up with Home Farm in Overton, we think we are offering one of the most truly 'free range' breakfasts in north Wales. We offer a large bed and breakfast accommodation with self-catering facilities and room to sleep 8 over three rooms. We also have camping facilities as well as a self catering option.

AUTHOR'S REVIEW

Having passed LLandegla Fishery a number of times, I always meant to stop by and see just exactly what it is they have to offer here and what I found, took me by surprise. Firstly the Fishery is situated in a really idyllic spot and its owner Simon Harrison and his sister before him really have created a wonderful haven for anyone who is even just remotely that bit interested in fishing, let alone someone who is a keen fan. With state of the art accommodation and a wonderful onsite cafe, LLandegla Fishery really has everything you need for a relaxing break away from the hustle and bustle of everyday life. On the day I visited, it had just had a snowfall and if I didn't know any better, I could of been forgiven for thinking that I was in Canada. The cute little cafe situated on site is starting to really get a name for itself for its remarkable food and I hear their breakfast is to die for!

WREXHAM

Casgan Ditw, Llandegla, Wrexham, LL11 3AA

ark Hall Countryside Experience

t: 01691-671123 e: info@parkhallfarm.co.uk
www.parkhallfarm.co.uk

Discover the delights of Park Hall Countryside Experience, the national award-winning farm attraction. There's a day packed with animal antics, action, fun and adventure waiting for all the family. Get up close to your farmyard favourites with a regular schedule of interactive events. Bottle feed lambs, groom ponies, or lead the heavy horses. Try hand milking a real cow or cuddle gorgeous bunnies, and don't miss the spectacular pig racing event each day. This all-weather attraction has two massive indoor play barns, including a science illusion zone and a fabulous role play village, while outside there are adventure courses, climbing areas, play houses and great walks for all the family. The Brickworks Construction Zone and the innovative Sand and Water play area will challenge and develop children's skills. Best of all for the kids are the brilliant driving experiences for different ages. The junior driving school, and the 4x4 land-rovers are amazing and the barrel train ride to the woodland is also a must!
At a more sedate pace visit the wonderful heritage exhibits, the Victorian School, the Welsh Guards Museum, the Iron Age Roundhouse and the WW1 Trenches.

AUTHOR'S REVIEW

After featuring a few Children's Farm parks in this book, I thought I knew what I would be expecting. I couldn't of been more wrong! This attraction has everything whether it is indoor or outdoor activities you seek, this attraction has it all!
Just when I thought I had seen it all, there was something else to see, from an indoor Victorian museum to educational farming and Welsh Guards Museum, this site certainly has everything. In the short words I am allocated in this book I simply cannot tell you everything that Park Hall has to offer you! But one thing I can say is that when it comes to simple value for money this site cannot be beaten.

Park Hall, Oswestry, Shropshire, SY11 4AS

Plas Madoc Leisure Centre

01978-821600 info@plas-madoc.com
www. plas-madoc.com

Plas Madoc Leisure Centre reopened to the public in December 2014 thanks to the hard work & dedication of the Splash Community Trust & volunteers from the local community. Plas Madoc is best known for its Leisure Pool, referred to as the "Tropical Lagoon", with it's incredible wave machine, like none other in the north Wales area. The pool features a fantastic elephant and snake slide for the younger children alongside the centre's infamous crocodile! The Pool features a large spiral water slide for older children and Big Kids! The pool runs regular fun sessions in the school half terms, Aqua Classes and 50+ swims are also available. The centre also features a cafe area with soft play, Climbing Wall, Squash Court, Aerobics studio, Gym with functional training room and a large multi use sports hall. Plas Madoc Leisure Centre is truly fun for the whole family!

AUTHOR'S REVIEW

I don't usually feature leisure centres in my books as they tend to be more of a local facility and not one that is quite suitable to tourists visiting the area. But there is always an exception to the rule and in this instance, it is the Plas Madoc Leisure Centre. With state of the art facilities which include a huge family fun swimming pool, gym, play area and not forgetting its very popular climbing wall, all of these features is what sets this Leisure Centre apart from its rivals. I think it is also worth mentioning that although I talked about the family fun swimming pool, this pool has something for everyone. With a very flexible pool timetable, whether your looking for a little swim with your little ones, fun for all of the family, or a relaxing swim in relative piece and quiet, Plas Madoc has it all!

WREXHAM

Llangollen Road, Acrefair, Wrexham, LL14 3HL

Whizzard Helicopters

t: 01938-555860 e: info@whizzardhelicopters.co.uk
www.whizzardhelicopters.co.uk

From Welshpool airport your pleasure flight will take you over some of the most stunning scenery in Britain. Welshpool is not far from the English border, the scene of many conflicts years ago, and the many hill forts and castles you can see form the air is evidence of this. 10, 15 and 30 minute flights are available. Do you want a career as a helicopter pilot ? Do you want to know that you will be offered paid flying work on completion of your flying training ? Then our Career Pilot Program will be of definite interest. At the end of your professional training you will be offered a mix of Commercial Charter, Photographic Flights, Pleasure Flying and Instructional work. Designed specifically for those individuals wanting a career as a helicopter pilot, the training also involves a structured hour building package and offers a minimum of 80hrs paid flying work for those candidates enrolled onto the course and who complete the course to the satisfaction of the Chief Pilot.

AUTHOR'S REVIEW

Whizzard Helicopters are probably one of the most unique and thrilling attractions within this book. With flights throughout Mid Wales & Snowdonia, just to name a few, I couldn't imagine any better way to see these stunning parts of Wales. Even though they do set flights over each area, another great thing I liked about Whizzard Helicopters, is they can tailor make a journey to suit your requirements. Whizzard's professional and well trained pilots are just about the best in the pleasure flight business, and they really do add to the experience, and with state of the art helicopters you really couldn't be in better hands. Despite an attraction being big, we still look for visitor experience set against value for money when choosing our Top 100 Attractions. Whizzard Helicopters doesn't only have both of these criteria, they also offer a once in a lifetime and unrivalled experience, who could ask for more?

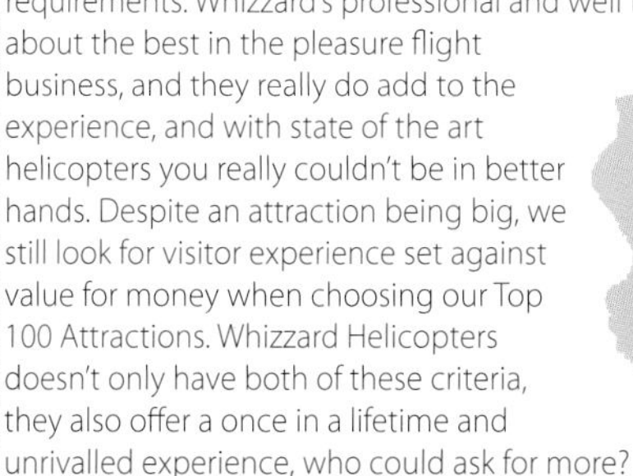

Mid Wales Airport, Welshpool, Powys, SY21 8SG

TNR Coaching (Activities & Training)

t: 01691-897188 e: Hello@tnrcoaching.co.uk
www: tnrcoaching.co.uk

We want to give you the perfect time. We aim to do all we can to offer you great coaching, in great kit, in fantastic locations delivering thrills, spills adventures and learning. On top of that though we want to be able to offer you all the add ons that make your time away special and memorable. We will find you great accommodation, offer you amazing food, and why not a wonderful sauna and massage to help with the aches? s we are a small company who are passionate about what we deliver. We strive to ensure that each Session, Adventure, and Activity that you book with us is tailored to suit you. YOU- will always be first, no easy off the shelf options for us. For all bookings we will find out what it is that you want, what you need and we will ensure that you get the adventure and time with us that is perfect for you. On top of that we will run all our activities with small instructor to client ratios, so you get more time on activity and input from our staff.

AUTHOR'S REVIEW

There are new kids on the adventure block and they come in the guise of TNR Coaching. I originally featured the Boathouse Restaurant, the base of this attraction, back in my previous edition of this Wales book and ordinarily I would be sad to see a restaurant owner go. However, on this occasion, I am pleased to see new the owners, who have completely transformed this business into what is going to be North East Wales's leading activity centres. I don't make that prediction lightly, but after visiting, I was so impressed with the set up here and once visited, I'm sure you will be too. Gorge Walking, Canoeing, Kayaking, even Target Sports are on offer here and that's just to name but a few. With decades of experience between them, all of the instructors here are leaders within their field and I guarantee you are in totally safe hands.

oathouse, Chirk Marina, Chirk, Wrexham, LL14 5AD

Welshpool & Llanfair Light Railway

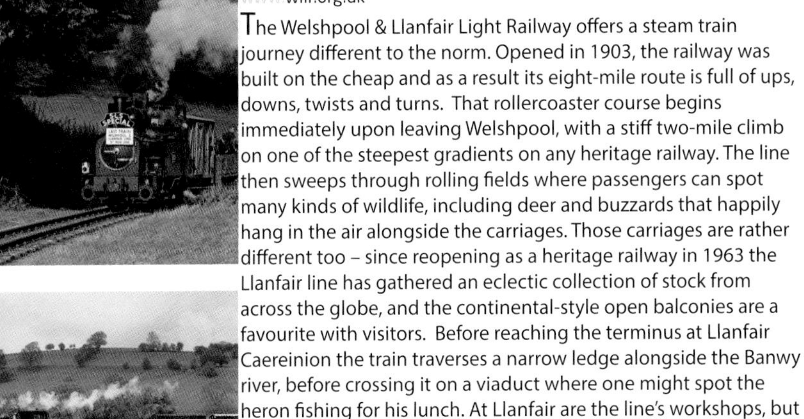

t: 01938-810441 e: info@wllr.org.uk
www.wllr.org.uk

The Welshpool & Llanfair Light Railway offers a steam train journey different to the norm. Opened in 1903, the railway was built on the cheap and as a result its eight-mile route is full of ups, downs, twists and turns. That rollercoaster course begins immediately upon leaving Welshpool, with a stiff two-mile climb on one of the steepest gradients on any heritage railway. The line then sweeps through rolling fields where passengers can spot many kinds of wildlife, including deer and buzzards that happily hang in the air alongside the carriages. Those carriages are rather different too – since reopening as a heritage railway in 1963 the Llanfair line has gathered an eclectic collection of stock from across the globe, and the continental-style open balconies are a favourite with visitors. Before reaching the terminus at Llanfair Caereinion the train traverses a narrow ledge alongside the Banwy river, before crossing it on a viaduct where one might spot the heron fishing for his lunch. At Llanfair are the line's workshops, but passengers mostly head straight for the Edwardian-style tea room, renowned especially for its tempting slices of cake!

AUTHOR'S REVIEW

In this book we have the greatest steam trains in not only Wales, but throughout the world. The Welshpool & Llanfair Light Railway is one of Mid Wales's biggest attractions and it doesn't even have to try. As I travelled the eight and a half mile journey, I had a smile on my face from beginning to end. The beautiful countryside along the journey is just one of the many advantages of visiting this railway, and I have to say that this attraction is run as a really slick operation. The cafe is not only well stocked, but Immaculately clean.They have a great gift shop and the staff uniforms were faultless. The carriages may not be traditionally from the area, but each carriage has come from either Hungary or Austria, and will undoubtedly have been used during wartime, and so, has huge historical importance, let alone historical significance.

WREXHAM

Llanfair, Nr Welshpool, Powys, SY21 0SF

Strawberry Skys Yurts

t 01938-811308 e anya@strawberryskysyurts.co.uk
www strawberryskysyurts.co.uk

It's a pefect combination. Beautiful countryside and cosy yurts, woodburners and campfires. We have four yurts in total set in one of the most beautiful parts of Wales. With three tradtional Mongolian yurts and one all-wooden yurt we offer a no stress, crowd free glamping holiday. We are passionate about glamping and glamping holidays, and were extremely proud to have Strawberry Skys Yurts included in The Guardian's Ten Best Glamping Sites 2011 after only three years after opening. In the same year we hosted a retreat for Druids and Bards from all over the UK which remains a memorable highlight from our early years. We love welcoming guests to Strawberry Skys Yurts and we are extremely fortunate that over a third of the guests we welcome back each season are returning guests and it is both an honour and privelege to see them return and in many cases meet their new additions as we see families grow over the years.

AUTHOR'S REVIEW

Strawberry Yurts isn't your usual attraction, but nevertheless, I had to feature it as one of our hidden gems as what they offer here, is a perfect introduction into the world of glamping. Set just a few short miles away from the small Welsh town of Welshpool, Strawberry Yurts offer a much needed escape from it all. Situated within an idyllic location, Anya and Eric the owners, have created a quite unique experience here. Each Yurt is totally individual and even though your stay will provide a much needed escape from reality, they have all your usual mod cons, once of them even has USB charging ports for your mobile or tablet device. About the surrounding area. You can either BBQ outside your own Yurt, if you decide not to, there are more than enough fantastic places to eat and Eric or Anya will point you in the right direction of those.

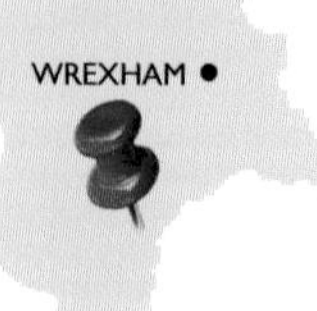

Clynlarth Cottage, Cyfronydd, Welshpool, Powys, SY21 9H

Bike Hire

t: 01352 810841 e: richard@guestinourhouse.co.uk
www. guestinourhouse.co.uk

Fantastic area to cycle with lots of quiet roads with breathtaking scenery. Ride the canal paths of Llangollen over the horseshoe pass with it's magnificient vistas, the Clwydian range hills whith its hill forts , or ride along the River Dee cycle path to visit the beautiful city of Chester our location offers so much and more. There are plenty of pubs and coffee shops along the way to stop and refuel human and electric battery alike. We stock a wide range of e-bikes available for hire. Have a look through the different models and find the right bike to suit you. You can click through on different bikes for more information. To hire our ebikes you have to be over 14 years of age and provide a photo I.D. e.g. Photo Driving Licence, Passport or Identity Card.

AUTHOR'S REVIEW

This book is just as much about Wales's hidden gems, as it is about the bigger more impressive attractions. At E Bike Hire North Wales, so much work has gone into making sure your experience is one that you will cherish for ever. Having done an awful lot of research into these electric bikes and the service that E Bikes provide, I have to say I am quietly impressed, but not as quiet as what these bikes are. You would actually never know you was riding an electric bike they are that quiet. I also want to mention, the accommodation based at this attraction, Glan Llyn B&B. Richard & Paola, the owners really have excelled with this place. The rooms are of a very high standard and the way they do their breakfast is just short of amazing. So many things on offer, it's hard to know where to start.

WREXHAM

Glan Llyn Farm, Pant Du Road, Mold, Clwyd, CH7 4DD

Llangollen Wharf

T 01978-860702 E bill@horsedrawnboats.co.uk
www. horsedrawnboats.co.uk

Llangollen Wharf is one of the major attractions in the North Wales market town of Llangollen. From the Wharf you can embark on either a horse drawn boat trip along the feeder for the main canal, or a motorised aqueduct cruise which takes you across the famous Pontcysyllte Aqueduct built by Thomas Telford. Both these trips take in the magical sights and sounds of the beautiful Llangollen Canal. Longer horse drawn trips can be arranged for large groups. Lunches and cream teas can be pre-ordered for the aqueduct trips. The whole canal in this area is now a World Heritage Site.
We also have a self steer day hire boat for groups of up to 10 people, on our purpose built 32' narrow boat the "Dydd Un". This is an ideal way to take a leisurely cruise along the Llangollen Canal and across the unforgettable Pontcysyllte Aqueduct. This is a perfect way for a family, group of friends or a corporate team to have their own private boat for the day.The Tea Room and Gift shop at Llangollen Wharf is located in the old canal warehouse. All our food is prepared and cooked on the premises so that you know it will always be fresh.

AUTHOR'S REVIEW

The Llangollen Horse Drawn Boats has something to offer everybody, whether you want a relaxing stroll along the canal side in Llangollen or a leisurely cruise across the famous Aqueduct built by the industrial genius himself "Thomas Telford". I actually took a trip across the aquaduct and enjoyed a scrumptious Welsh Cream Tea. I have to be totally honest with you I was a bit concerned about how high the aqueduct might be as I don't really have a head for heights. But after being on the boat ten minutes and listening to the speech perfect vocal commentary by the boats very able captain I truly forget how high I was and just sat back at ease and enjoyed the rest of the cruise.

Wharf Hill, Llangollen, Denbighshire, LL20 8TA

Hawarden Estate

t: 01244-533442 e: manager@hawardenestate.co.uk
www.hawardenestate.co.uk

The Farm Shop is surrounded by 25 acres of its own fields, orchards and woodlands, through which we have signposted a mile-long nature trail. It's a 40-minute walk if you take a questionnaire to do en route, and you will need wellington boots (not suitable for a buggy). We have devised two sets of questions, which you can pick up from the Farm Shop before you venture out. One is aimed at the under-fives, which includes a scavenger hunt (find a piece of ivy or a feather; draw a picture of your favourite animal etc) and one for children of six and over. An ideal way to spend time with your young children or grandchildren, helping to open their eyes to the delights of the natural world. As part of a day out at the Farm Shop, you will spot our flock of chickens in their pen by the play fort. The pig pen is another popular attraction for younger visitors to the Farm Shop. Piglets are born all year round, come to us quite young and stay for a few months: rarebreed saddlebacks, Gloucester old spots and Oxford sandys.

AUTHOR'S REVIEW

Throughout the United Kingdom we have some of the world's prettiest and most historic villages. So much so, it should come as no surprise to see I have featured one such village in this new edition of the Top 100 Attractions in Wales book. Hawarden Village is not only cosmetically pretty, it just has history oozing around every corner. I chose Hawarden Village out of all the Welsh villages I have visited, merely because there is no better example of just how important villages like this one are to British tourism, let alone Wales. Hawarden has everything from a wonderful farm shop, a great pub, which I may add is the backbone of any Great British Village. There is also the Gladstone Library, which was founded by the great Victorian statesman and politician, William Ewart Gladstone. Being located a stones throw from the gateway to Wales, Hawarden is most certainly worth a visit.

WREXHAM •

Chester Road, Hawarden,Flintshire, CH5 3FB

The Little Yurt Meadow

t. 01948-780136 e. bookings@thelittleyurtmeadow.co.uk
www. thelittleyurtmeadow.co.uk

The Little Yurt Meadow is a small family run yurt 'glamping' site. A tranquil place to holiday, located in the beautiful countryside in a little village called Bronington, on the borders of North Wales, North Shropshire and South Cheshire. Our lined yurts, with their AGA Logburners, are warm and cosy whatever the weather. A comfortable large bed and beautiful furniture create a relaxing and luxurious (but quirky) holiday home. The Little Yurt Meadow is all about peace and quiet, just the sound of the fresh air, the birds and occasionally a bit of mooing from the adjacent farm. Glamping is a perfect get away holiday break - a chance to enjoy the simplicity of a camping holiday without having to pitch your tent. Our yurts offer this fusion of traditional camping with the luxuries of home, making it the ultimate glamping experience.

AUTHOR'S REVIEW

We don't measure our attractions in how many visitors they get, how big they are, or how many awards they may of won, we look for visitor experience and their value for money is at the heart of our decision making process. The Little Yurt Meadow is at the heart of that very statement. Situated perfectly between the bordering counties of North Shropshire and South Cheshire, let alone skirting quite close to North Wales, the Little Yurt Meadow offers a great place to stay and one that you won't forget about in a hurry. The Yurts themselves are built to a very high standard and everyone has a small welcome hamper in their yurt when they arrive. The owners themselves have given every thought in what you will want from your stay and they are such a lovely family, I know you will love every minute of your glamming experience.

WREXHAM •

2 Baytree Barns, Mill Road, Bronington, Shropshire, SY13 3HJ

The West Arms

Llanarmon Dyffryn Ceiriog, Nr Llangollen, Wrexham, LL20 7LD

T: 01691-600665 www.thewestarms.co.uk E: info@thewestarms.co.uk

The West Arms is a 16th century Inn, built in 1570 and for the first 100 years operated as a Drovers Inn. All of the rooms at The West Arms are unique. From the character rooms in the original part of the building to more contemporary rooms at the rear, you will find all of the rooms offer a great degree of comfort. The hotel boasts two large Suites, a Four Poster Bedroom, Character Rooms, Superior Rooms, Standard Rooms and a Chauffeur's Wing.Our Suites include the Bunny Warren and the Willow Suite. The Bunny Warren is a lovely split level Suite with exposed beams throughout whilst the larger Willow Suite offers a six foot bed, a roll top bath and views of the village. All prices are for the room when occupying two people, including full breakfast.

Bron Y Graig

Bron-y-Graig 1888, Corwen, Denbighshire, North Wales. LL21 0DR

T: 01490-413007 www.north-wales-hotel.co.uk E: info@north-wales-hotel.co.uk

Bron-y-Graig is a luxurious 9-bedroom Victorian house in North Wales with tranquil river and mountain views. Set in the beautiful Dee Valley, it is the ideal base for exploring Snowdonia, Chester and North Wales castles and coast, and offers: En-suite bathroom * King-size or twin beds * TV with Freeview channels and DVD player * Free broadband internet access for your laptop * Tea & coffee tray.
Each of our spacious bedrooms is sumptuously decorated to recall the Victorian age, and most retain original fireplaces and bellpushes. Most bedrooms have luxurious sofa, superb views of woods or river, and some have room for additional child beds. All rooms have ensuite bathrooms with bath, shower, toiletries and towels. Bron-y-Graig has a residents' licence.

The Royal Oak Hotel

The Cross, Welshpool, Powys, SY21 7DG

T: 01938-552217 www.royaloakwelshpool.co.uk E: royaloak@innmail.co.uk

The Royal Oak Hotel, Eatery and Coffee House is a Grade II listed building which began its life in the 18th century. A Coaching Inn on the main route our function room, The Powis Suite, was one the stables where travelers would hitch their horses during their stay. The Hotel was formerly the manor house of the Earl of Powis until 1927. The Royal Oak Hotel has 25 Bedrooms and have a great range of room types to choose from. All rooms are individual in shape, size and decoration. Our rooms have kept their historic feature and are well equipped with everything you need in the modern world.Take advantage of our great Dinner, Bed and Breakfast Offers. Choose anything from our restaurant menus with no restrictions to be enjoyed in any of our dining areas.

The Buck House

High Street, Bangor-on-Dee, Wrexham, LL13 0BU - T: 01978-780336

www.thebuckhousebangorondee.co.uk E: enquiries@thebuckhousebangorondee.co.uk

Nestled on the banks of the River Dee in the picturesque village of Bangor on Dee, North Wales, the Buck House offers excellent food, drink and accommodation and boasts a unique riverside setting. The Buck has 7 letting Bedrooms, all comfortably furnished with en-suite bathrooms. With some boasting views over the village and large windows making all the rooms light and airy with a home away from home feel. All have tea and coffee making facilities and can be booked on a room only or bed and breakfast basis. The Buck House makes the idyllic location for accommodation near to the famous Bangor-on-Dee Racecourse, with minibus services to the racecourse at only £1 per person for our residents.

Glasgwm Bed & Breakfast

Abbey Road, Llangollen, LL20 8SN

T: 01978-861975 www.glasgwm-llangollen.co.uk E: glasgwm@llangollen.co.uk

Glasgwm is a Victorian townhouse run by John Spicer and Heather Petrie, located close to the centre of the historic town of Llangollen. Just a short walk from all of the town's many attractions, Glasgwm offers plenty of off-road parking at the front of the property. The four en-suite bedrooms have views, either across the beautiful valley at the front of the property, or into a quiet, terraced garden at the back. Glasgwm is ideal for those wishing to explore the wider attractions of North Wales, and also the border counties of Cheshire and Shropshire (Chester is only 30 minutes drive and Shrewsbury 40 minutes drive away).

The Bridge End Hotel

Mill Street, Llangollen, Denbighshire, LL20 8RY

T: 01978-860634 www.bridgeendhotel.com E: bridgeendhotel@gmail.com

The Bridge End is a family-run hotel overlooking the River Dee in the centre of charming Llangollen, just across from the 16th Century Llangollen Bridge and around the corner from the wharf at Llangollen Canal. This 3-star hotel is a five-minute drive from Valle Crucis Abbey and around half an hour's drive from the Snowdonia National Park. All rooms here have en-suite bathrooms, colour TVs, free Wi-Fi and tea & coffee facilities. Free parking is available at the rear of the hotel, which can also b hired out for events. Full cooked breakfasts are included in the price of staying, the restaurant serves hearty Welsh cuisine and light meals, and the busy bar has a wide range of beers and wines. The Bridge End is one minute's walk away from the Llangollen Railway terminal and ideally located.

The Trevor Arms at Marford

1 Marford Hill, Marford, Wrexham, LL12 8TA

T: 01244-579418 www.trevorarmsmarford.com E: info@trevorarmsmarford.co

Set in a 17th-century coaching inn, the Trevor Arms is located in the countryside village of Marford, North Wales. It offers spacious rooms and an elegant restaurant serving home-cooked food. Rooms at the Trevor Arms Hotel feature TVs and tea/coffee-making facilities. Wi-Fi is available in public areas of the hotel. With oak wood flooring, exposed brick walls and beamed ceilings, the Trevor Hotel combines period features with modern interior design. Each room is tastefully decorated and has a private bathroom with bathtub or shower. Special care has been taken in the concealment of light, the quality of the bedding, the soft soothing colors and the selection of fabrics to provide guests wit a private and cozy setting for a peaceful night's sleep.

Bwch yn Uchaf B&B

Llanuwchllyn, Y Bala, Gwynedd, LL23 7DD

T: 01678-540983 www.bwch-yn-uchaf.co.uk E: post@bwch-yn-uchaf.co.u

Bwch Yn Uchaf Bed & Breakfast is situated at the edge of a beautiful village of Llanuwchllyn on the edge of Snowdonia National Park, providing comfortable en-suite bedrooms. The 1800's stone build house was built to go along side the railway when it was part of the main line. The bed and breakfast was once a hotel, village pub, flats and a farm house. A great place to start any walk, as we are at the foot of Aran Benllyn Mountain and the Mary Jones walk in the near hills and only 10 minute drive to the Bala Lake. Situated right next to the house is Bala Railway Station where you can catch the train into Bala and enjoy the beautiful scenery over looking Bala Lake (Llyn Tegid) and Snowdonia National Park.

Oakenholt Farm Guest House

Chester Road, Flint, Flintshire, CH6 5TE

T: 01352-733264 www.oakenholtfarm.co.uk E: oakenholtfarmbandb@gmail.com or.co.uk

The Hulme Family at Oakenholt Farm have been welcoming guests from all over the world since 1985. This small 20 acre sheep farm is situated in a quiet, rural location surrounded by a lovely country side. Guests are welcomed on arrival by our friendly sheep dog Rex who always wants a friend to play ball. There is a beautiful garden with a pond and elegant fountain to the side to relax by on summer days. The farmhouse dates back to 1450, but has been sympathetically renovated to provide all modem facilities expected of a 4 Star Guest house.. All our rooms in the house offer the following: Ensuite with shower • Tea and coffee facilities • Colour TV's with freeview • Radio • Chair • Hair dryer, iron & board available on request • Ensuite with shower • Tea and coffee facilities • Colour TV's with freeview • Radio • Chair • Hair dryer, iron & board available on request

Worthenbury Manor

Worthenbury, Wrexham, LL13 0AW

T: 01948-770342 www.worthenburymanor.co.uk E: enquiries@worthenburymanor.co.uk

Worthenbury Manor is a charming Manor House which offers a true country manor experience at Guest House prices. Both rooms have all you will need to feel right at home, including a beautifully decorated sitting room complete with TV, not that you'll need it as there are a wide selection of books on offer, if all you want is a relaxing evening, either in the sitting room or in the beautiful garden that sits at the back of the house. The two owners Ian & Elizabeth, have done everything to ensure your stay is both a pleasurable and memorable one and I promise, once visited, never forgotten.

The Hand Hotel & Restaurant

Church Street, Chirk, Wrexham, LL14 5EY

T: 01691-773472 www.thehandhotelchirk.co.uk E: info@thehandhotelchirk.co.uk

Located in the picturesque edge of the Ceiriog Valley, Chirk is the perfect choice for visitors wishing to explore the many attractions it offers all year round. The Hand Hotel is conveniently located right next to Chirk railway station and public transport links within the area are excellent; thus giving easy access to neighbouring towns such as Llangollen, Wrexham, Oswestry and Whitchurch. The Hand Hotel are delighted to offer various room types to suit your individual requirements and if necessary can also accommodate an extra bed (ideal if you're travelling as a family or as a group of friends). Simply let us know when you book and this can be arranged for you. Our room types are as follows and all include a hearty English breakfast.

Broncoed Uchaf Farmhouse B&B

Nercwys Road, Nercwys, Mold, Flintshire, CH7 4ED

T: 07875-662981 www.broncoeduchaf.com E: polly@broncoeduchaf.com

Located close to the Welsh-English border, Broncoed Uchaf Country Guest House is A beautiful 18th Century former farmhouse and set within its own courtyard and gardens. just 2 miles outside the historic market town of Mold. Set against the backdrop of the Clwydian Range, an Area of Outstanding Natural Beauty. Free private parking and free WiFi are provided. All bedrooms have a Superking-size double or twin beds with luxury bedlinen, en-suite facilities and Freeview TV. The traditional open fires and exposed oak beams bring character alongside modern luxuries, the guest house offers all you'd expect, and more. Broncoed Uchaf is the perfect venue for your wedding, with it's beautiful rustic setting and views of pure countryside.

Eithinog Hall

Cyfronydd, Welshpool, Powys, SY21 9ED

T: 01938 811200 www.eithinoghall.co.uk E: getaroom@eithinoghall.co.uk

Croeso (welcome) to Eithinog Hall – a beautiful, countryside bed & breakfast surrounded by the green rolling hills of idyllic Mid Wales. Open year-round, this stunning Georgian house sleeps up to six guests in three luxurious suites, and offers a wealth of delights for guests to discover. Enjoy priva woodland walks, exclusive fly fishing and sumptuous home-made meals. From outdoor pursuits to i door indulgences, it's a rural retreat for those looking to escape and relax. Designed with you in min Eithinog is perfectly equipped and laid out to ensure maximum comfort. The interior has a grand bu friendly feel that you sense as soon as you walk through the front door. So what are you waiting for? Make the journey and we'll take care of the rest. We promise it'll be worth it.

Top House B&B & Self Catering

5 B4388, Welshpool SY21 8LU

T: 07967-150992 E: jaxe1@btinternet.com

Featuring free WiFi throughout the property, Top House is located in the Kingswood area of the villa of Forden. Offa's Dyke path and The Cock pub are 200 yards away.
Rooms are en suite and are equipped with a flat-screen TV, a chair and tea/coffee making facilities with fresh milk.There is a shared lounge with a wood-burning stove. There is space to park 4 cars on site.Welshpool is 3.8 miles in one direction and Montgomery is 3 miles the other way. Welshpool Tra Station is 4 miles away. National Express coaches also stop in Welshpool. The nearest large airport is Liverpool John Lennon Airport, 70 miles from the property, but Mid Wales Airport is 2 miles away, where helicopter and plane trips can be booked.

Glan Llyn Farmhouse

Pant Du Road, Mold, Denbighshire CH7 4DD

T: 01352 810841 www.guestinourhouse.co.uk E: richard@guestinourhouse.co.

Ancient and peaceful, the natural beauty of this hidden corner of North Wales is far removed from today's bustling lifestyle. The landscape feels rural yet it is only four miles from the market town of M half an hour from the historical town of Chester and one hour from Liverpool and Manchester. Come and enjoy the beauty, space and tranquility with all the comforts of a home away from home. house dates from the 1850's, we have completely renovated it, maintaining plenty of 'olde worlde' ch while utilising all the latest eco – green technologies. Each room is uniquely and artistically styled w an en-suite wet room, free WiFi, TV, fridge, hair dryer. So if your looking for Hotels in Mold Denbighsh try Glan Llyn Guest House.

The Dudley Arms

High Street, Llandrillo, Denbighshire, LL21 0TL

T: 01490-440223 www.dudleyarms.wales E: julie@dudleyarms.wales

The Dudley Arms is a traditional Welsh village inn nestled within the Berwyn mountain range in picturesque Llandrillo on the B4401 between Corwen and Bala. The Dudley Arms is full of character and charm with many period features and exposed oak beams. The stone walls and tiled floors alon with cosy fires help make your visit a special one. There are many walks to enjoy and also further afie fantastic places to visit such as Llangollen, Snowdonia and Chester are not too far. The old Bakehous our 2 bedroom self-catering cottage to let. You can stay in the cottage which has a kitchen with fridg hob, washing machine, dining space and TV. We now have 2 double en-suite bedrooms above the p and restaurant with WIFI – please ring or email for availability.

The Alyn Riverside Country Pub

Station Road, Rossett, Wrexham, LLl2 0HE

T: 01244-570368 www.thealyn.co.uk E: enquiries@ thealyn.co.uk

Nestled on the banks of the River Alyn in the picturesque village of Rossett, North Wales, The Alyn Riverside Country Pub is the perfect destination for excellent pub food, quality wines and real ales. We open for food at noon, which is served all day, every day. Our menu is coeliac friendly and offers plenty of choice, whether you want to enjoy lunch with friends, a business dinner with colleagues or a family get together over a Sunday roast. As well as a delicious choice of dishes, we offer an award-winning wine menu and a wide range of beers and case marque approved real ales. We can accommodate small and large parties, and our attentive and friendly staff will do everything they can to create a memorable occasion.

Glan yr Afon

Dolphin, Holywell, Flintshire, CH8 8HE

T: 01352-710052 www.glanyrafoninn.com E: glanyrafoninn@gmail.com

Enjoy a meal from our great menu in the pleasant atmosphere of our comfortable restaurant or in one of our bar areas. Traditional freshly cooked food to satisfy a wide variety of tastes, our produce is freshly sourced and prepared to order. Our children's menu also ensures that the whole family is properly catered for. With 14 rooms all en-suite you will be sure of a comfortable stay. There is also a two bedroomed static caravan available, with a double bed and two single beds, bathroom, linen included. This is based at the rear of the pub and is accessed by a staircase. All rooms have digital TV, Tea & Coffee making facilities and separate night time access.

The Crown Inn

Cilcain Road, Pantymwyn, Mold, Flintshire, CH7 5EH

T: 01352-740462 www.crowninnmold.co.uk

Since becoming a free house in April 2012, The Crown Inn is going from strength to strength. Customers are assured of a warm welcome from Martin Peters and team. The Crown is a comfortable and friendly pub/restaurant in a beautiful rural setting, with a strong family-friendly ethos. It is a 1930's building which has been extensively refurbished and modernised inside. Our team of chefs take great pride in their menus which are based on freshly prepared food, most of which is cooked to order. Their cooking and presentation skills are acclaimed by our customers who tend to return regularly. The Chef's Specials are a culinary masterpiece which always go down well.The Restaurant is especially busy at weekends, so booking is recommended to avoid lengthy waiting times.

The Druid Inn Gorsedd

Carmel Road, Gorsedd, Flintshire, CH8 8QZ

T: 01352-713975 www.druidinngorsedd.co.uk E: thedruidinn@gmail.com

Located in rural North Wales in the picturesque village of Gorsedd, The Druid Inn is a little gem of a country pub offering fantastic home-cooked food, quality cask ales and the warmest welcome in the area. With low beams, roaring log fires and cosy nooks to curl up in, the Druid Inn is a great traditional North Wales country pub. However, don't let our quaint appearance fool you, we offer a lively and fun atmosphere, making us a popular pub with the local community and visitors. Come and join us for pub food as it should be; simple, hearty and home-cooked. Take a peek at our menu pages to see what takes your fancy. You can wash down your dinner with one of the cask ales we offer or a glass of wine? Our bar offers a wide range of quality drinks to be enjoyed in our beer garden or curled up in-front of our log fires on a chilly winter evening.

The Hand Hotel & Restaurant

Church Street, Chirk, Wrexham, LL14 5EY

T: 01691-773472 www.thehandhotelchirk.co.uk E: info@thehandhotelchirk.co.uk

We warmly welcome both residents and non-residents into our relaxing bar areas which are open fr 11am to 11pm Monday to Thursday, 11am to midnight on Friday and Saturday and 12 noon until 11 on a Sunday. It's certainly a great place to kick back and relax after a day spent exploring the local ar or simply catch up with the latest results on our Sky Sports channel. Throughout the week our Chefs showcase their culinary expertise with various themed evenings starting with our ever popular Curr Night on a Monday, a 3 course set menu on Tuesdays (with a further 10% off for pensioners), and a S Night on Wednesday (complete with a FREE bottle of wine!)

The Dragons Rest Cafe

St Asaph Rd, Lloc, Nr Holywell, Flintshire, CH8 8RF

T: 07860-643214 Opening times: 8.30am - 4.30pm - 6 days a week. (Closed Tues)

Here at The Dragon's Rest Café, a family run business, we offer the best in home cooked food. Being conveniently located just off junction 31 of the A55, The Dragon's Rest Café truly is the gateway to W culinary delights. We offer all types of home cooked food, from snacks, all day breakfasts, daily speci to roast dinners, made from locally sourced produce. Our homemade cakes and Welsh ice creams a to die for as well. You will receive a very warm welcome from our staff, then place your order and rel Whether outside on the patio taking in the views over the Clwydian Range or inside surrounded by collectables and memorabilia to while away the time or even waiting for your car to be washed by Speedy Dragon's Valet Centre.

The Bison Grill

Rhug Estate, Corwen, Denbighshire, LL21 0EH

T: 01490-411100 www.facebook.com/rhugestate Twitter: @RhugEstate

The Bison Grill Bistro produces all its meals from scratch using Rhug Organic's own award winning meat and was named the "Best on Farm Restaurant" in the UK by the FARMA organisation. Our chef has created a Menu with a real focus on seasonal produce reflecting local products and our own fres organic meat where possible. In addition to breakfast, brunch and lunch dishes we serve our delicio Sunday Lunch Menu using our own Rhug Estate meat and seasonal vegetables every Sunday. We have a carefully-selected wine offer each bottle being hand-picked for their compatibility with our menu, taste, quality and value for money.Our Takeaway, On the Hoof, offers our award-winning Rhu organic meat to those wanting food on the go.

The Eagles Inn (Tafarn Yr Eryod)

Llanuwchlyn, Bala, Gwynedd, LL23 7UB

T: 01678-540278 www.yr-eagles.co.uk E: eagles-inn@btconnect.com

The Eagles Inn (Tafarn Yr Eryod) is a wonderful stone built building, even older than the village church! With a well stocked bar including real ales, inglenook fireplace, beer garden, fine wines and a dining room boasting a menu which would be the envy of many a restaurant, the family run Eagle Inn is in Llanuwchllyn the headquarters village of the Lake Bala narrow gauge railway. And here, you are definitely on the right tracks! The excellent menu of home cooked dishes is complemented by a small but impressive wine list. Such is the popularity of the food served at the Eagles Inn that advan booking, particularly at weekends, is strongly advised.

The Boathouse

The Boathouse, Chick Marina, Chirk, Wrexham, LL14 5AD

T: 001691-772493 www.theboathouseatchirk.co.uk E: info@theboathouseatchirk.co.uk

Here at the boat house we are very proud of what we can offer as a venue. We have 250 parking spaces, 120 seater restaurant, Log burning stove in our Bar, which is stocked with a large range of drinks and local real ales. A conference room that can seat 60, easily. Plus an outside bar, camping for up to 50 tents, a canal side location and masses of green space for adventures and marquees. When it comes to food we have one mission at the Boathouse. Great seasonal ingredients sourced from Wales wherever possible. We work tirelessly with our suppliers to source the finest Welsh meat, fish and game. Beautifully cooked by our amazing team with meals for every budget. We aim to use local prduce as much as possible, we feel it gives that extra little wow.

Try Thai Shop & Noodle Bar

37-39 St George's Crescent, Wrexham, North Wales, LL13 8DB

T: 01978-266586 www.trythainoodlebar.com E: trythaishop@gmail.com

Many of the ingredients we use in the Noodle Bar are available in the shop. People enjoy browsing the shop while waiting for noodles, while others have noodles when they come shopping. Please note that it can often be very busy in the week at lunch time, so do try and call before 11.30am for lunch time collection. Local delivery is available depending on driver availability, but please ensure your orders are over £20. Why not have your food delivered by our TWIZY... We have the authentic ingredients readily available in the shop and authentic Thai chefs cooking the food as it's done in Thailand.
We have many regular customers who love the food and shop together with new people finding us all the time.

The Dudley Arms

High Street, Llandrillo, Denbighshire, LL21 0TL

T: 01490-440223 www.dudleyarms.wales E: julie@dudleyarms.wales

The Dudley Arms is full of character and charm with many period features and exposed oak beams. The stone walls and tiled floors along with cosy fires help make your visit a special one. There are many walks to enjoy and also further afield, fantastic places to visit such as Llangollen, Snowdonia and Chester are not too far. At the Dudley, our real ale (Station Bitter) from the Award Winning Stonehouse Brewery and fine wines from Momentum Wines are plentiful alongside freshly cooked food. Our meat is supplied by our friendly butcher T J Roberts of Bala and our fresh vegetables are delivered by Dee Valley Fruit and Vegetables in Llangollen. Our food is home-cooked and hearty and we change the menu regularly to reflect food in season. However, one item always on the menu is the home-made Steak and Ale pie – a proper plate filler and very popular through all the seasons!

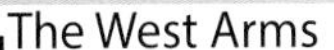

The West Arms

Llanarmon Dyffryn Ceiriog, Nr Llangollen, Wrexham, LL20 7LD

T: 01691-600665 www.thewestarms.co.uk E: info@thewestarms.co.uk

The love of serving up delicious food and drink is as old as the human race, and it's a love which is at the very heart of what makes the West Arms so special. For our chef Grant Williams, making sure that each and every plate we serve is pretty much perfect is a vocation. To call cooking his passion would be an understatement, just like saying that he loves his kitchen would be putting things mildly. You might have seen him doing his thing on ITV or the BBC, and you can't miss him in the Good Food Guide because he makes sure we're included every year. Grant takes influences gathered whilst travelling the globe and turns them into stunning seasonal treats, using locally sourced ingredients. Great food and drink is at the heart of warm hospitality, so at the West Arms we offer options throughout the day.

The Grouse Inn

Carrog, Corwen, Denbighshire, LL21 9AT

T: 01490-430272 www.thegrouseinncarrog.co.uk E: info@thegrouseinncarrog.co

A warm welcome or, Croeso, as we say in North Wales. Staff have been welcoming locals and visitors The Grouse Inn since the 19th century, before which it was a farmhouse. Open all year round, and w our own sizeable car park, we serve locals, hikers, cyclists, dog walkers, tourists and campers alike. W offer traditional pub fare, from curries and stews to full Sunday lunches. Well known favourites inclu fish & chips, gammon steak and whole grilled trout, and we have an in-depth understanding of lact and gluten free catering. We don't do 'posh' food, just great food cooked with care. The surrounding of Outstanding Natural Beauty is breathtaking, and The Grouse Inn overlooks an ancient stone bridg five arches, spanning the River Dee.

The Royal Oak Hotel

The Cross, Welshpool, Powys, SY21 7DG

T: 01938-552217 www.royaloakwelshpool.co.uk E: royaloak@innmail.co.uk

The Eatery at the Royal Oak is so named because it offers a comprehensive, but not overwhelming, menu available to dine from both in the newly refurbished main restaurant and main bar area. The r menu is reviewed regularly by our kitchen team who source ingredients locally, but also travels furt afield to obtain the ingredients that go into making our delicious dishes. Whether you are meeting w friends and family to unwind, or looking for somewhere to celebrate a birthday or anniversary, the R Oak is perfect. We offers a large selection of food for you to choose from. It doesn't matter if you are looking for a full three course meal or just a snack, the team have created a patisserie cabinet with t that change daily, including chocolate fudge cake, muffins, pastries and scones.

The Royal Oak

High Street, Bangor-on-Dee, Wrexham, LL13 0BU

T: 01978-781602 www.theroyaloakbangorondee.co.uk E: enquiries@theroyaloakbangorondee.co

Nestled on the banks of the River Dee in the picturesque village of Bangor on Dee, North Wales, the Royal Oak offers excellent quality of food, it boasts this unique riverside setting with a warm and frie welcome which all combine to make it a cut above the average village pub. Inside is cheerful and contemporary with cosy armchairs and log burning fires as well as plenty of space for diners. Outsid there is terracing providing an idyllic setting on a sunny day, where you can enjoy a meal, coffee, gla wine or pint and just listen to the gentle rippling of the water and watch the world go by. At The Roy Oak you can be sure of great food, a wide selection and of finest beers and wines, a relaxing ambien and friendly helpful staff. Whether you're out fishing, walking or enjoying a pre/post race day drink c meal, we'll do our best to make you feel right at home. We look forward to seeing you!

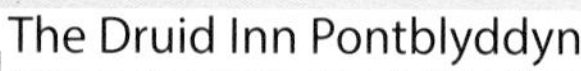

The Druid Inn Pontblyddyn

Wrexham Road, Pontblyddyn, Nr Mold, Flintshire, CH7 4HG

T: 01352-770292 www.druidinn.co.uk E: enquiries@druidinn.co.uk

In the heart of the pretty Welsh village of Pontblyddyn, the Druid Inn combines a traditional stone bu pub with restaurant standard modern British food. Wooden beams, open fires and original features g the Druid a cosy feel, matched by the warmth of the welcome you'll receive.

- Fantastic food, a great atmosphere and brilliant service
- Wide selection of wines and beers
- Lovely beer garden with "jumbrellas" (just in case!)
- Delicious roasts every Sunday
- Special offers throughout the week offering exceptional value.

The Bunbury Arms

Little Stanney Lane, Stoak, Chester, Cheshire, CH2 4HW

T: 01244-301665 www.bunburyarmschester.com E: info@bunburyarmschester.com

The Bunbury Arms at Stoak, Chester enjoys an ideal location – just off both the M56 and the M53 and a mile from the Cheshire Oaks shopping centre at Ellesmere Port. It has its origins back in the seventeenth century as a rustic ale house serving the local farming community and over the years it has grown gradually, but always sympathetically, into the cosy and welcoming place it is today. The fantastic Bunbury team, lead by Janet alongside her 3 children, have maintained and championed the strong Bunbury focus on quality real ale and fresh, hearty home cooked meals served with a smile. This, along with the beautiful Cheshire countryside setting, Summer beer garden, roaring Winter coal fire (and The Bunbury family ducks and chickens!) makes The Bunbury Arms as much the hidden gem as it ever was.

The Trevor Arms at Marford

1 Marford Hill, Marford, Wrexham, LL12 8TA

T: 01244-579418 www.trevorarmsmarford.com E: info@trevorarmsmarford.com

Welcome to Trevor Arms restaurant, it is elegant, traditional and offers family style food and service. Broasted chicken, pot roast, steaks and pork chops along with classic hamburgers, wraps and generous salads are all on the menu. We will offer specialty selections including a lighter options and smaller portions for a children's menu. Set in a 17th-century coaching inn, the Trevor Arms is located in the countryside village of Marford, North Wales. The restaurant has oak furniture and high ceilings and serves traditional cuisine using fresh local ingredients. Guests can relax in the bar area and lounge areas, which have deep leather sofas and mood lighting.The Trevor Arms Hotel is a 10-minute drive from Wrexham. Wrexham and Clay Fram golf clubs are both within a 3 miles radius of the hotel.

The Crown & Liver

The Highway, Ewloe, Deeside, CH5 3DN

T: 01244-531182

Flamboyant decor, huge drinks selection, super cool food and the best outdoor terrace around, bring together a fusion of locals pride and city center coolness! The multi-award winning 'Crown' is an imposing public house in the tourist honey pot of Hawarden - although it would not look out of place in any major cosmopolitan city!

Trip Advisor 5 Star Review A great family meal...

Visited the Crown and Liver for a family meal this afternoon. As usual a lovely friendly welcome, and a cheeky pint of Bombardier while we perused the menu. There were four of us and we all chose a different meal from the menu. The meals were delicious, not a scrap left on the plates! We were so full we were not going to have a dessert, but well.... it would be rude not to!!

The Aqueduct Inn

Holyhead Road, Froncystllte, Llangollen, LL20 7PY

T: 01691-777118 E: theaqueductinn@hotmail.com

Standing beside the busy A5 the pub reopened in 2013 as a freehouse and has been revitalised as a consequence. It's a simple three-roomed affair with small central bar, small games room and comfortable lounge with wood burner. Rear verandah decking offers panoramic views not least of the Llangollen canal as it approaches the eponymous world famous aqueduct. Food includes Sunday lunches and is very popular. Additional parking down the lane. Passing bikers are welcome.

The Wynnstay Arms

High Street, Ruabon, Wrexham, LL14 6BL

T: 01978-822187 www.robinsonsbrewery.com/wynnstayarms E: info@wynnstayarms.

Located between Wrexham and Llangollen, the Wynnstay Arms has been welcoming people throug doors for centuries whether to simply enjoy a quiet drink, a delicious bite to eat or to celebrate milestones in their lives and we are delighted that you are considering us to host your very special d We have two rooms that can be hired exclusively for celebrations, parties, meetings and events. At the Wynnstay Arms we're passionate about serving hearty pub classics using the freshest ingredi Don't forget to check out our delicious Sunday Roast! Our 12 newly-refurbished bedrooms offer a c night's sleep in beautiful surroundings; perfect for couples, solo travelers, families and their four-leg friends!

Lot 11 Cafe & Hideout

11 Hill Street, Wrexham, LL11 1SN

T: 01978-361177 www.lot11wxm.co.uk E: lot11cafe@gmail.com

Located on Hill Street, Lot 11 is a 'hideout' which offers a range of coffees and cakes alongside an extensive menu that we think is offering something quite unique in Wrexham, including bang on tr proper smashed avocado! The main focus of the menu is brunch – something which the owner of L 11, Sarah Baker, says was inspired by her time in Australia. Offering a twist on traditional breakfast it the cafe's menu features a full Welsh breakfast, smashed avocado and poached eggs on sourdough toast, cereals and 'proper baked beans' in chunky tomato sauce. The cafe also offers freshly made sandwiches, cakes / muffins and a range of coffees and teas. In the future the cafe will be looking br out by offering pop-up nights, baby showers and afternoon teas.

The Celtic Arms

Northop Country Park, Mold, Flintshire, CH7 6WA

T: 01352-840423 www.thecelticarms.co.uk E: info@thecelticarms.co.uk

Set in the beautiful surroundings of Northop County Park, the Celtic Arms seamlessly blends traditic and elegance to create a very unique dining experience. Of all the restaurants to choose from in the surrounding North Wales landscape, few offer the scenic views and panache of The Celtic Arms. The Celtic Arms is a traditional restaurant that you need to experience for yourself, at least once, if you a visiting North Wales. For locals, we look forward to welcoming you time and time again. We take pri in the staff that we employ at The Celtic Arms. They are passionate, enthusiastic and provide attentic to detail in everything they do, ensuring that you feel warm and welcome when you visit. The exper of our kitchen team is unparalleled. They work consistently and effortlessly to create new menus an dishes throughout the year to provide variety across all of our menu offerings.

The Fat Boar

17 Chester Street, Mold, Flintshire, CH7 1EG

T: 01352-759890 www.thefatboar.co.uk E: enquiries@thefatboar.co.uk

The Fat Boar is an independently owned and run pub and restaurant in Mold, North Wales. We open in 2015 after spending months gutting the old pub and creating a new venue which is contemporar welcoming and somewhere that we hope you will want to spend a lot of time with family and frienc We've got delicious food, with a large menu featuring lots of fresh, locally sourced and seasonal ingr dients. It seems like everyone says that these days, but the difference is that ours is really good. We h an excellent selection of ales and wines, with something to enjoy whether you're a connoisseur or ju need of a cold glass of something after a long day. We provide service which can't be rivalled or bea That's a big claim, but one we intend to live up to.

MID WALES / BRECON

one of the three Welsh National Parks, the Mid Wales/ Brecon section of the book and website
ɜds no extra introduction. With not as many attractions featured here as some of the many other
as on this around Wales, the reason being quite simply, is the Brecon National Park is the biggest
action itself. That being said, we've assembled an excellent cast that guarantees to be a big crowd
aser. Whether you're a keen walker, nature enthusiast, avid historian or just simply someone who
ted the Mid Wales/ Brecon area as a child, there'll not be enough hours in the week to take it all in!
ybe you should book two weeks instead? Because in my book, website and app, we have
cifically focused on the tourist attractions of the thirteen main great areas of Wales, we just haven't
ɜn able to focus on some of the great walking routes the Brecon Beacons and other areas play
ne to.

ether you're visiting Mid-Wales or the Brecon Beacons area, or in fact both during your trip, you
n't be stuck for things to do. Take Pen-y Fan for instance, this is South Wales's highest mountain.
s area of Mid Wales also takes in the surrounding Black Mountain to the west and the wider Black
untains to the East. In addition to our obvious selection of amazing Mid Wales attractions, you
also blessed with the fact that there are in and around 20 hillforts for you to also visit, some quite
essible and some, just that harder to get to, but no matter what, this all just adds to the Mid-Wales/
con Experience. All in all, if you go prepared and have a huge sense of adventure, you'll absolutely
e this region, just as I did!

MOMA - Machynlleth

t: 01654-703355 e: info@moma.machynlleth.org.uk
www.moma.machynlleth.org.uk

The Museum Of Modern Art, Wales (MOMA WALES) has grown up alongside The Tabernacle, a former Wesleyan chapel which in 1986 reopened as a centre for the performing arts. MOMA WALES has six beautiful exhibition spaces which house, throughout the year, MODERN WELSH ART (Wales' top artists), The Tabernacle Collection and The Brotherhood of Ruralists. The adjacent auditorium has perfect acoustics and pitch-pine pews to seat 400 people. It is ideal for chamber and choral music, drama, lectures and conferences. The Machynlleth Festival takes place in the auditorium in late August every year. For the rest of the year the centre can be hired for performances, rehearsals and gatherings. A number of classes are held each week in the Green Room, which is also equiped as a Language Laboratory. Ty Llyfnant is equipped with music teaching rooms and an artists' studio.

AUTHOR'S REVIEW

A lot of thought goes into the process of choosing all of the attractions within any of our range of books. That process couldn't be more present, than in those we have chosen for our Top 100 Attractions in Wales book. The Museum of Modern Art (MOMA) based here in Machynlleth, couldn't be better situated than where it stands today. You see, Machynlleth was the seat of Owain Glyndŵr's Welsh Parliament in 1404, and for that very reason, claims to be the "ancient capital of Wales". I just love it here, the building itself has a really warm and inviting feel to it, and the amount of art on display here means you'll need a good couple of hours to see it all. Of course I've also included in those two hours, time to grab lunch or just a coffee and cake in their amazing little tearoom.

Y Tabernacl, Heol Penrallt, Machynlleth, Powys, SY20 8AJ

Dragonfly Cruises

t: 07831-685222 e: info@dragonfly-cruises.co.uk
www.dragonfly-cruises.co.uk

Spend a delightful few hours cruising through some of the most beautiful scenery in Britain, lying within the Brecon Beacons National Park.
The Monmouthshire and Brecon canal hugs the mountainside above the valley of the River Usk. Through the four seasons there are fine views and an abundance of wildlife to be seen.
200 Years of History.
Travel on this historical waterway, a fantastic feat of engineering, built before roads and railways. Cruise through a canal lock and over an aqueduct carrying the canal over the River Usk.
Saloon seating for 50 - Refreshment bar - Catering available
P.A. System - Toilet - Souvenirs - All Weather - Wheelchair Lift (2 chairs maximum)

AUTHOR'S REVIEW

Dragonfly Cruises is one of only two canal cruises featured within this book of Wales Top 100 Attractions. I have to say that a trip on this fine vessel is worth every penny. There are many of these canal style boat trips throughout the UK, all offering a good trip. But what I liked about this particular cruise, is that this is a family run business that's operated in a very professional way. Also what sets this particular Canal Cruise apart from many others, is its beautiful setting. Running two trips a day up and down this very beautiful part of Wales. You can just turn up on the day, but booking ahead is very advisable due to the popularity of this particular canal. Also what really impressed me was the adaptation of this boat to accommodate disabled visitors which I saw in action on the day of my visit.

Canal Wharf, Brecon, Powys, Mid Wales, LD3 7EW

Llangorse Multi Activity Centre

t: 0333-6002020 e: action@activityuk.com
www.activityuk.com

We're Wales' Premier Award-Winning Indoor and Outdoor activity and training centre, set in the stunning Brecon Beacons National Park, Mid Wales. For over 55 years, we have offered a cross section of exciting activities for people of all abilities - unrivalled anywhere else in the UK. We attract a broad spectrum of visitors to our centre, including individuals, families, schools and colleges, groups, companies large and small as well as the armed forces. We have many different activities on-site; our popular Indoor Multi-Activities (suitable for ages 6 years and over) gives a taste of Rock Climbing, Bouldering, Rope Bridges, a Zip Line, Caving and Abseiling! Outdoors, we have recently added a new tree-top Junior Challenge Course with many challenging obstacles for 6 - 12 years olds. Or from 12 years why not tackle the the larger Outdoor Multi Level Challenge Course, or zip through the air from platform to platform on a tour of Sky Trek?

AUTHOR'S REVIEW

The Activity centre here at Llangorse is not only an award winning activity centre, but one that is run at the highest levels I have seen in all the years I have been writing my travel guides. The site has been open since 1958, where Mr John Thomas, a man who had a huge passion for horses started his riding school.
Moving the business forward, his son Kevin Thomas who had a love for all things adventurous, started the activity centre as we see it today. The centre is now in the hands of Kevin's son Ryan, and still remains a family run business. This in my opinion is part of the recipe for success here at Llangorse, and as I walked around every inch of the activity centre it was clear to see that the whole business is run as a very slick operation, one of the best in Wales, if not the United Kingdom!

The Gilfach, Llangorse, Brecon, LD3 7UH

Dragonfly Day Boats

t: 07831-685-222 e: info@dragonfly-cruises.co.uk
www.brecondayboats.com

Spend a delightful few hours cruising through some of the most beautiful scenery in Britain, lying within the Brecon Beacons National Park.The Monmouthshire and Brecon canal hugs the mountainside above the valley of the River Usk. Through the four seasons there a fine views and an abundance of wildlife to be seen. The launches carry up to eight people and can be hired for up to 3 hours to the lock and return, with landing points at both ends. The boats have plush seating with picnic tables, the boats are steady in the water with easy to use electric start engines. In case you experience rain, they also have rain covers.
The boats travel through to the lock at Brynich and give a safe steady and relaxing ride, with easy controls. The deeper design also makes it safer for children. Tuition is given at the start of the hire and we are always close to hand in the event of problems.
So come and relax for a morning, afternoon or early evening boat ride and take in the historic beauty that the Monmouthshire and Brecon canal has to offer.

AUTHOR'S REVIEW

Having already reviewed and featured Dragonfly Cruises in my Welsh book for the past six years, I had no doubt in my mind, that the latest addition to their fleet would be any lesser of an experience as their popular cruises. This family run business is probably one of the Brecon Beacons most popular attractions and by taking a cruise on one of their day boats, you get to be the captain this time. Even if the weather isn't quite as good as you expected, you can still take a trip on the day boats, as they have their very own, fully functional rain covers, making them an all weather attraction without a doubt. I found their prices very reasonable indeed, given the fact that you can actually fit 8 passengers onto each of the boats. On the whole, a visit to the beacons is not complete unless you've taken to the water in one of these very enjoyable craft.

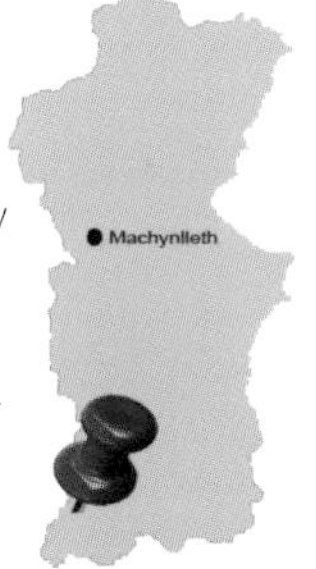

Canal Wharf, Brecon, Powys, Mid Wales, LD3 7EW

Gigrin Farm

Red Kite Feeding Station & Rehabilitation Centre

t: 01597-810243 e: chris@gigrin.co.uk
www.gigrin.co.uk

The Red Kite feeding station at Gigrin Farm attracts as many as 600 of these beautiful birds of prey, together with buzzards, ravens and other species. Five permanent hides, three of which are wheelchair friendly, allow the visitor to see their stunning aerial displays as they dive out of the sky to pick up the food. Specialist hides for photographing and filming are also available. Gigrin Farm attracts a variety of rare and interesting birds, as well as otters, polecats, badgers and hares, and the spring and summer flowers are breathtaking. The farm has an interpretive centre where visitors can use interactive computer displays, see into a red kite nest and watch video recordings of the farm's badgers. Feeding takes place at 2pm in winter and 3pm in summer (kites don't know that we change the clocks!) But except for Christmas day, the farm is open from 12.30pm every day.

AUTHOR'S REVIEW

The Powell family that own Gigrin Farm would never have known just what they were starting back in the early 90's when the late Mr Powell had the foresight in accepting the RSPB's request to make the kite feeding at Gigrin Farm a permanent fixture. A visit to see the kite feeding at Gigrin will make the hairs on the back of your neck stand on end and confirm to you a sight that you've never seen before. If you are a bird enthusiast or not you can't help fall in love with these birds of prey and see just how easy a decision it was all them many years ago for the late Mr Powell to set up this now very important feeding station and rehabilitation centre. Thats right, the centre allows kites, that have fallen ill or been injured, to recuperate after having any required veterinary care elsewhere. Forget your binoculars at your peril! New for this year is their Café that serves hot and cold food and drinks.

Gigrin Farm, South Street, Rhayader, Powys, LD6 5BL

RSPB Lake Vyrnwy

t: 01691-870278 e: vyrnwy@rspb.org.uk
www.rspb.org.uk/lakevyrnwy

Breathtaking scenery and an abundance of wildlife makes RSPB Lake Vyrnwy a magical and unforgettable day out for the whole family. Our visitor centre and shop is the ideal place to start your visit. Enjoy stunning walks and trails around one of the most beautiful lakes in Wales. You might see and hear pied flycatchers and redstarts, while dippers nest by the lake and rocky streams. Great crested grebes and goosanders bob on the water, and above you ravens, buzzards and perhaps a peregrine can be seen soaring in the sky. You can also watch spring's new arrivals being born on a trip to our organic farm. Children can explore the animal puzzle trail and minibeast area or why not visit our natural play area which has been specially developed using natural features from the RSPB Lake Vyrnwy estate to provide a unique play space to inspire children and their families with the beauty, brilliance and astonishing world of nature. There are log beams to walk on, tree stumps to jump from, bird's nests to play in, branches and leaves for den building, a mud kitchen to cook tasty treats, and much more.

AUTHOR'S REVIEW

RSPB Lake Vyrnwy is so much more than a nature reserve that dedicates its time to the conservation of wildlife and birds. With having an organic farm based here also, the site almost feels responsible about the surrounding nature that makes this countryside reserve so popular. From March to the end of November, you can get the chance to see lambs going through all of their stages from being newborn, to almost teenager, and they are so friendly that it is almost in their genes to not be afraid of us curious humans. With a huge range of birds of prey located at this site, it almost seems that RSPB Lake Vyrnwy is three tourist attractions in one, now that's value for money! Having three or four other reserves close by, it's really possible to visit two of these sites in a day, three at a real push!

Machynlleth

Bryn Awel, Llanwddyn, Oswestry, Shropshire SY10 0LZ

National Showcaves Centre for Wales

t: 01639-730284 e: info@showcaves.co.uk
www.showcaves.co.uk

Wales' top award-winning visitor attraction the National Showcaves Centre for Wales, is the most breathtaking Showcaves complex in Northern Europe. Every year tens of thousands of visitors step back in time, as they walk within the limestone rocks, and deep into the subterranean world.Above ground there is plenty to see and do - come face to face with some of the largest animals ever to walk the Earth in our Dinosaur Park, one of the biggest collections of life-sized dinosaur models in the world! Down on the farm, children will have a great time in the covered play areas should there be any excess energy waiting to be used up before the journey home! One ticket gets you into 10 attractions:• Dan-yr-Ogof Showcaves• Cathedral Cave• Bone Cave• Museum• Mr Morgan's Farmyard• Dinosaur Park• Iron Age Village • Shire Horse Centre• Barney Owl's Play Area • The Millennium Stone Circle.

AUTHOR'S REVIEW

The National Showcaves Centre for Wales here at Dan-yr-Ogof is truly one of the most impressive set of caves that I have visited so far on my travels. When I wrote my Top 100 Attractions in Wales book for the first time in 2011, I had visited the Showcaves and remember being that impressed, although my last book was full at that point, I knew even back then that I had missed out one of Wales biggest attractions. I have so many different things that I could share with you about this attraction, but one that really stands out is their app which is available through the 'Apple' App Store. This app brings dinosaurs such as the famous Raptors to life by pointing your iPhone at one of the huge display boards that are dotted around the attraction, I have never seen this done in any of the hundreds of attractions I have been to in the British Isles.

Abercrave, Swansea, SA9 1GJ

Gregynog Hall

t: 01686 -650224 e: enquiries@gregynog.org
www.gregynog.org

Gregynog is a historic house with Grade 1 listed gardens set in the heart of rural Montgomeryshire. One of Wales' premier country estates, and the former home of art collectors and public benefactors Gwendoline and Margaret Davies, it offers a welcoming setting in which people of all ages and abilities may discover, experience, participate in, and be inspired by the arts and natural environment. It is one of Wales's most unexpected hidden treasures, whose name has echoed down the years since the first elusive references to it by the 12th century poets of the Welsh princes. The creation of the Gregynog Trust will open up many exciting new opportunities for regenerating the hall and estate, many new developments, all to be harnessed in the creation of an inclusive identity which will have a crucially important part to play in the future of a sustainable Wales. See the all year round events programme the website. Even though the Hall is not open to the public, there are regular tours throughout the summer. See website for dates.

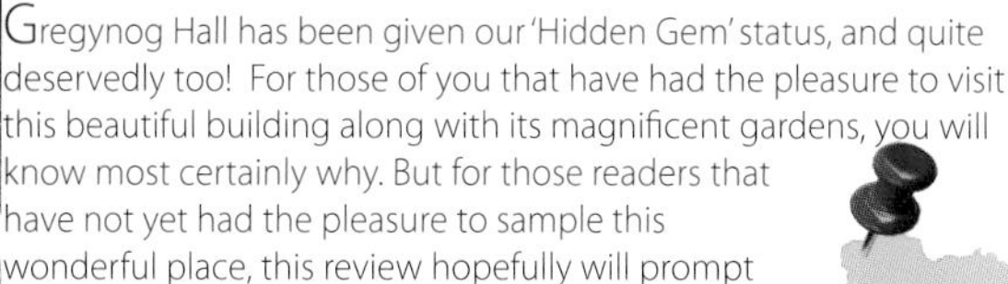

AUTHOR'S REVIEW

Gregynog Hall has been given our 'Hidden Gem' status, and quite deservedly too! For those of you that have had the pleasure to visit this beautiful building along with its magnificent gardens, you will know most certainly why. But for those readers that have not yet had the pleasure to sample this wonderful place, this review hopefully will prompt you to do so now. With history oozing out of every crevice at Gregynog, complete with an art gallery fit for any palace, I just kept saying 'Wow' around every corner, and just when I thought I had seen it all, I was then shown the bedrooms within the accommodation section of the hall, which I have to say, have really been updated to a very high standard indeed. On the whole, I was taken aback by just how professionally run Gregynog Hall is, and I cannot wait to return and spend even more time here.

Machynlleth

Tregynon, Near Newtown, Powys, SY16 3PW

Dyfi Osprey Project

t: 01654-781414 e: enquiries@dyfiospreyproject.com
www.dyfiospreyproject.com

The Dyfi Osprey Project is run by the Montgomeryshire Wildlife Trust on the Cors Dyfi Nature Reserve near Machynlleth. Between April and September each year the reserve is home to a breeding pair of Ospreys, one of just five pairs in Wales. Visitors can wander through the peaceful reserve on boardwalks that lead to the fantastic 360 Observatory to view the Ospreys in the heart of the Dyfi Valley. In the 360 Observatory staff and volunteers are on hand to show visitors the ospreys, point out other wildlife and answer questions.

The reserve is also home to around 100 species of birds, over 500 species of moths, otters, lizards, grass snakes, royal fern and a wealth of other plants and animals.

AUTHOR'S REVIEW

Wales doesn't only get millions of human visitors visiting its shores on a yearly basis, wildlife also makes a beeline for this beautiful and fertile land at various times of the year. One of those beautiful creatures that keeps making its way back to North West Wales, is the Osprey. Almost pushed to extinction a hundred years ago, this magnificent creature has fought its way back from the brink and with the help of decades of various experienced teams at the Dyfi Project, they have managed to learn far more about this fascinating bird of prey than they ever did before and their work is vital. To get a sneak preview of this amazing creature, you can watch a live feed on the Dyfi Osprey Projects Website, I found this truly fascinating and I guarantee that once you've seen this, you'll be packing your bags and off there this weekend!

Cors Dyfi Reserve, Derwenlas, Machynlleth, Powys, SY20 8SR

ambrian Safaris

t: 01974-261 425 e: richard@cambriansafaris.co.uk
www.cambriansafaris.co.uk

Discover the Wild Tranquillity of Wales with us.
Cambrian Safaris offer tours of the Cambrian Mountains (all day or half day) or all of Wales in a Land Rover Discovery.
We aim to show you places you will want to go back to again and again.
Discover the 'Picturesque Hinterland' of Ceredigion's uplands, including locations used in the BBC series 'Hinterland'. Farming, forestry, moorland, small lakes, the historic estates of the Ystwyth and Rheidol Valleys and surrounding area with numerous old mines. Tour the wider Cambrian Mountains byroads, drover's roads and the Elan Valley reservoirs.
Your guide has extensive knowledge of local areas, so CONTACT US to arrange a tour for you to enjoy spectacular landscapes, local history, wildlife and one view after another. A relaxing day out with no pressure of time, we can pick you up from your accommodation if you wish.
Tour All of Wales with us for 2 or more days.

AUTHOR'S REVIEW

Little is known nationwide, let alone worldwide about the Cambrian mountains, as they can sometimes get overshadowed by their big brother the Snowdonia mountain range. Thanks to a selective amount of people this is now being corrected. Two of those selective few are both Richard & Hester Smith, together they have both established 'Cambrian Safaris'. When I first heard about this great idea I had to investigate further. After spending some time with Richard, it was clear to me that not only would it be great to feature them in this new edition of the Top 100 Attractions in Wales book, but it would be a huge honour. I have not met anyone that is as passionate and enthusiastic as what Richard isabout this special part of Mid Wales. I can assure you, that the onlyway to see this area of Wales is by taking a Cambrian Safari.

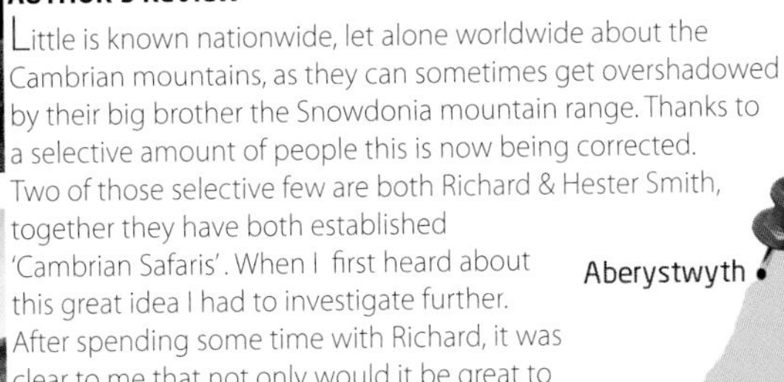

Tan Felin, Llanafan, Aberystwyth, Ceredigion, SY23 4BD

Welsh Overland Safari

t: 01982-552140 e: rjdavies.mint@googlemail.com
www.welshoverlandsafari.com

Almost every region in Mid Wales has something interesting to discover - quiet villages, stunning scenery, historical buildings lost in the countryside...so before rushing to visit the most popular regions why not think about somewhere else for a change? You can avoid the crowds and still have a great time discovering the 'real' Mid Wales! Welsh Overland Safari is an independent guided tour company offering unique overland guided tours of some of the most beautiful, unspoilt landscapes in Europe, as well as rare natural habitats for wildlife. One of Wales's best kept secrets, the region has a rich and diverse history dating back to well before Roman times. Exploring the rugged mountains, lakes, waterfalls and forests of the area. With over 20 years' experience, the founder Richard Davies started Welsh Overland Safari because he wanted to share his passion for the area and share his knowledge with like-minded adventurers.

AUTHOR'S REVIEW

Wales has so many extraordinary places to visit and to be honest, it's very hard to see it all, or to even know which places are worthy of seeing first, second or third, but there is a company who can take the worry out of those decisions and they are the Welsh Overland Safari team. Headed up by husband and wife team, Richard & Jane Davies, they have a vast and rich knowledge of the area and this shines through when on a tour with them. Another thing I think worth mentioning is their holiday cottages. Richard and Jane also own Pwllgwilym Holiday Cottages, these cottages are of a very high standard and if you've not already found somewhere to stay whilst your visiting this part of Wales, I can't endorse these cottages enough. A perfect base during what will become a perfect holiday, what are you waiting for? Get booking your next trip!

Pwllgwilym, Llanafan Road, Cilmery, Builth Wells, Powys, LD2 3NY

Dovey Shooting Ground

t: 01650-511252 e: info@doveyvalley.com
www.doveyvalley.com

Situated high above the Dovey Valley in Central Wales, our 350 acres provide the ideal setting for an exhilarating shoot. We can offer a variety of different activities tailor-made to suit your requirements. In short, this will be a day to remember for either your co-workers or your clients. Complete beginners are particularly welcome and will receive first class tuition plus all the equipment necessary to enjoy this exciting pastime. We have the privilege of Exclusive rights to the Brynmelin Estate, this is a very full intense fun day for the experienced shot. The day is very similar to a game day consisting of a number of drives in the picturesque Welsh mountains. Looking to try out something new, brush-up your old skills or improve your technique? We offer a shooting school of dedicated professional instructors, incorporating some of the most experienced game shots as well as world-class Olympic clay shots.

AUTHOR"S REVIEW

Featuring this attraction was a must for me and I couldn't think ofbetter setting for a shooting ground of this type. Exciting times are also afoot for this attraction, as its owner Richard Jones has a huge legacy to protect as he brings it into the 21st century, speaking of which, it was actually his grandfather who first set the business up back in the 70's and he himself had a huge vision when developing this site to be Mid Wales's go to place to clay shoot. Having met Richard and hearing all about the great plans that he has for this site, I can say with hand on heart, that whether your an experienced clay pigeon shooter or not, you'll come away from DSG having had an amazing experience and one that you'll want to repeat time and time again. So what are you waiting for, hop onto their website and book your space now.

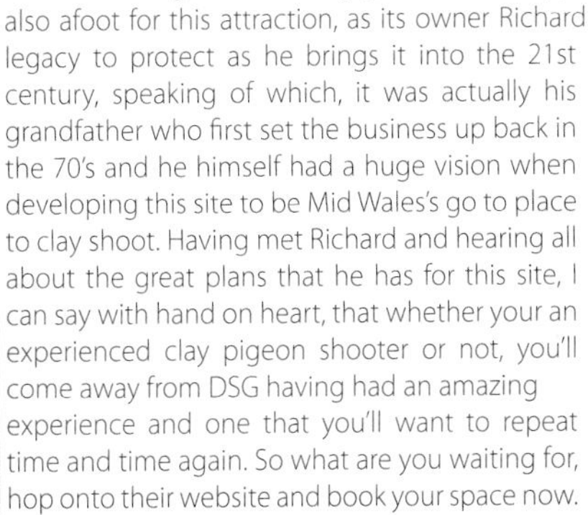

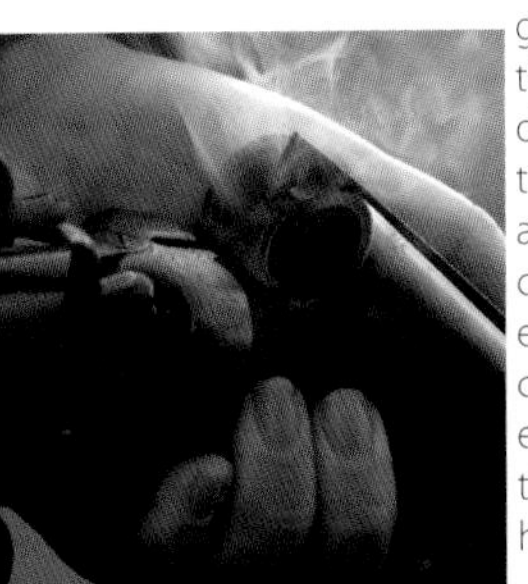

Llanwrin, Machynlleth, Powys, SY20 8QJ

Mid Wales Arts Centre

t: 01686-688369 e: office@midwalesarts.org.uk
www.midwalesarts.org.uk

Mid Wales Arts Centre is home to a unique permanent collection of large scale enamels and sculptures by international artist Stefan Knapp and stone carvings by the late John Paddison. The gallery and sculpture trail, set within the characterful house and beautiful gardens, holds changing exhibitions and events that promote and provide opportunities to artists living and working in Wales. MWAC is the home of Sculpture Cymru, the national association of sculptors in Wales. As well as exhibitions and workshops, MWAC can also host your meetings and events in a gallery setting. Stylish 4 Star residential en-suite B&B rooms are available on site. Courses are run by professional artists in a supportive and friendly environment.Enjoy walking in beautiful scenery and discovering over 100 extraordinary and varied pieces of original sculpture from Wales.

AUTHOR'S REVIEW

Having written several of my Top 100 Attractions books around the British Isles, I thought I had seen and experienced everything that the world of attractions has to offer and even though this comment maybe true, there are places that still really take me by surprise, take the Mid Wales Arts Centre. Dating back to 1526, the house itself charmingly sits on the road to Llandrindod Wells. Its owner, Cathy Knapp is an art guru and her wealth of knowledge of the art world and her keen eye for talented artists seeps through with every exhibition on display here. It has to be said however, that along with the art centre, Cathy runs a charming little B&B and within the art centre complex, Cathy runs a simple but fine little cafe, serving only locally sourced food and along with her own home baked cakes, offers a true culinary delight with every bite.

MWA, Maesmawr, Caersws, Powys, SY17 5SB

Wales Ape & Monkey Sanctuary

t: 01639-730276 e: info@ape-monkey-rescue.org.uk
www.ape-monkey-rescue.org.uk

We are located in the lovely Brecon Beacons National Park area of South Wales. The Park has been officially designated as a Geopark because of its unique geological formations. Formerly a traditional Welsh hill farm, the sanctuary now rescues and provides a home for many types of unwanted animals. especially primates, such as chimpanzees, baboons, spider monkeys, capuchins and marmosets. Visitors are welcome to see the animals and the work we do. We undertake a number of rescues from zoos and laboratories where animals have suffered mistreatment and deprivation or are no longer wanted. As they are not equipped for survival in the wild we can only endeavour to make the rest of their lives as enjoyable and stress free as possible. We have always been encouraged by the support that we receive from the public, but this year has been especially gratifying. Not only have more visitors come to see our animals, but they have been generous with their praise for the work we do .

AUTHOR"S REVIEW

When I wrote my first edition of the Top 100 Attractions in Wales book, I have to say with a red face that the Wales Ape and Monkey sanctuary went completely under my radar. Had I of known about this place back then, I would have featured them in my last book in a heartbeat. Ok, the site may not be as big as Longleat or Dudley Zoo, but Jan & Graham are the ones they call when theyneed a home for such an animal, and their love for all things primate is second to none. Just talking to one of the co founders Jan, I could clearly see that she is not only very passionate about these wonderful creatures, but they are hers and her husband Graham's life! They have dedicated their entire life to provide a wonderful home environment for each and every primate resident here at the sanctuary, and I urge you to pay them a visit.

Merthyr Tydfil

Caehopkin Road, Abercrave, Swansea Valley, SA9 1UD

Shakespeare Link

t: 01597-811487 e: info@shakespearelink.co.uk
www.shakespearelink.co.uk

Shakespeare Link was founded in 1992 by Artistic Directors Susanna Best and Philip Bowen, whose extensive professional experience in theatre includes years with the Royal Shakespeare Company, the English Shakespeare Company, the Royal Opera House and the Old Vic. The Company has had charitable status since 1994. Shakespeare Link has toured worldwide, enthralling audiences and students alike from Utah to the Philippines, and from Budapest to Singapore. The Company has enjoyed strong support from the British Council, and has been highly praised by overseas hosts, audiences, and press. Now based in mid-Wales, we offer a quality resource for the local community and beyond. Our work is flexible and client-led and adapts to the needs of a diverse range of students and teachers, using the medium of Shakespeare to bridge gaps of language and cultural difference, with exceptional results. Our focus now is on broad based community work and we welcome new audiences as well as the contacts and friends we have made at home and abroad to the Willow Globe.

AUTHOR'S REVIEW

Having travelled the world with their theatre company, it was always in the stars that both Phil and Sue Best would settle somewhere and I can't think of anywhere better than Mid Wales to set up their highly acclaimed Willow Globe. Although a scaled down version of the Globe in London, the shows on offer here are in no way scaled down. Painstakingly woven out of the finest willow, this organic building stands majestically for all to see. Having been recommended to me by several other attractions locally, I couldn't really not feature Shakespeare Link and the Willow Globe into this latest edition of the Top 100 Attractions in a wales book.

he Hall at Abbey-Cwm-Hir

t: 01597-851727 e: info@abbeycwmhir.com
www.abbeycwmhir.com

Mid Wales most unique, remarkable and beautiful stately home/ historic house. A 52 room, Grade 11* Gothic Revival mansion in 12 acre gardens overlooking the ruins of the 12th c cistercian abbey. Daily guided tours available to the public. Visitors enjoy the combination of outstanding architecture, stunning interiors, fascinating collections and magnificent gardens. 15 mins from Llandrindod Wells/Rhayader/The Elan and Wye Valleys. 30 mins from Presteigne/ Builth Wells/Knighton/Kington. 1hr from Ludlow/Hay/Hereford/Shrewsbury/Aberystwyth.

Original features include:

23 marble and wrought iron fireplaces; gothic widows and shutters; Maw and Co tiled floors; slate slab surfaces and Rococco and stained glass ceilings etc. The house bursts with interior design ideas: images handpainted on to wallpapers; rooms themed to trains/castles/the 1930`s; a billiards room celebrating The Arthurian Legend and the Garden Room with its 136 enamel signs.

AUTHOR'S REVIEW

The Hall at Abbey-Cwm-Hir is not only in Wales but also in a different world! My visit to The Hall left me spelbound - 52 rooms stylishly furnished with the greatest possible attention to detail. The house and gardens are open throughout the year, with Paul and Victoria decorating each of the 52 rooms to individual themes for Christmas (Nov.1st-6th Jan) and Easter (the month of April) annually. Something unique in the UK.The tour left me with warm feelings for days, and I really cannot wait to go back. But don't just take my word for it! The Hall at Abbey-Cwm-Hir is set for great things, so take a tour yourself, and be amazed and astonished.

Andrew Logan Museum of Sculptur

t: 01686-640689 e: almos@andrewloganmuseum.org
www.andrewloganmuseum.org

ALMoS is a wonderland, a fantastical jewelled treasure trove in Mid Wales housing a glittering selection of artist sculptor Andrew Logan's signature works: jewellery, original costumes and memorabilila from his Alternative Miss World, the 4m tall Cosmic Egg, a 'shrine' to the late Divine and much, much more.
Museum, cafe and shop opening times:
June to the end of September, Saturdays and Sundays 12pm- 4pm.
Plus Easter weekend and August Bank Holiday Monday.
Annual Grand Re-opening and Jewellery Extravaganza every August Bank Holiday Sunday!
Open at other times by appointment. Free activity trails available.
Available for hire or as a marriage ceremony venue, for private hire and workshops. Please contact us for further information.

Image 1Design by David Hand

Photo by David Hand

AUTHOR'S REVIEW 

The Andrew Logan Museum of Sculpture really does epitomise the strap line found on the front of this book, 'Same Country, Different World' Infact as proud as we are to have all of our massive attractions within this book, we also pride ourselves on endorsing those attractions that are maybe just that little bit quirky or a hidden gem, this museum is both of those. Set up in 1991, Andrew & Michael Davis had a vision for a quirky little museum in a little Welsh village that was probably just as quirky as he is and from then on, the museum and the village have coexisted together with great harmony. From the moment you walk in, you are immediately teleported into the mind and soul of Andrew Logan, which is both a fantastic, yet a scary place to be, only scary because after spending some time here, you start to understand all of the amazing pieces on display here, now, you can't get any more scarier than that!

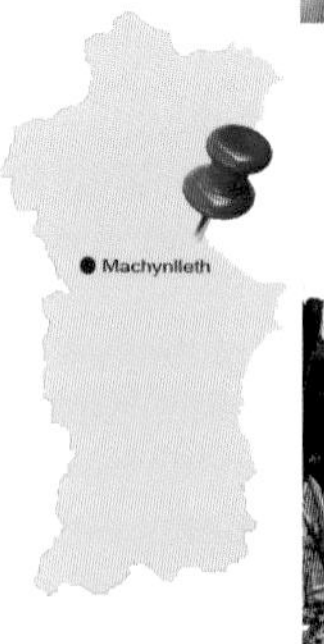

Aqueduct Road, Berriew, Welshpool, Powys, SY21 8PJ

enderyn Distillery

t: 01685-810651 e: visitorcentre@welsh-whisky.co.uk
www.penderyn-distillery.co.uk

At the dawn of the new millennium, a group of friends from the beautiful country of Wales set out with a simple vision. As the first Welsh distillers in more than a century, we were determined to break with convention and pledge to realize our dream. Today, Penderyn is home to the award-winning Single Malt Welsh Whisky, Brecon Gin, Five Vodka and Merlyn Cream Liqueur. We offer distillery tours, enabling our visitors to experience for themselves the sights, sounds and aromas of our working distillery. Learn about the malting, mashing, fermenting, distillation and maturation processes, then try for yourself in our dedicated Tasting Bar. We also offer evening tours and corporate tours.
Nestled in the Brecon Beacons, around 40 minutes from Cardiff, the distillery Visitor Centre is open to the public from 9:30am until 5pm each day, including Bank Holidays (opening hours may vary over the Christmas and New Year period). Booking is essential.

AUTHOR'S REVIEW

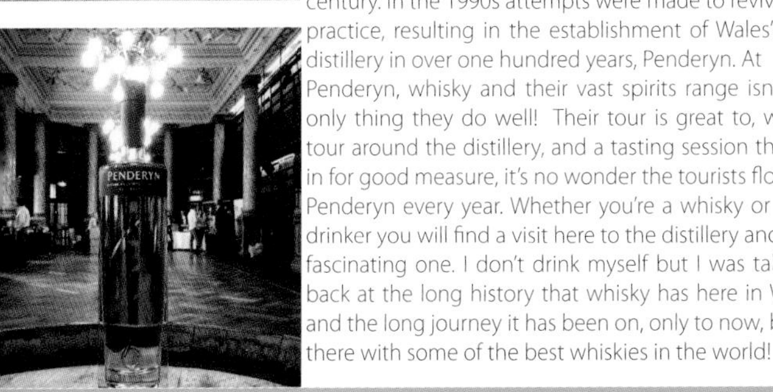

Not widely known but Whisky has now been distilled and enjoyed in Wales since the Middle Ages, but production died out in the late 19th century. In the 1990s attempts were made to revive the practice, resulting in the establishment of Wales's first distillery in over one hundred years, Penderyn. At Penderyn, whisky and their vast spirits range isn't the only thing they do well! Their tour is great to, with a tour around the distillery, and a tasting session thrown in for good measure, it's no wonder the tourists flock to Penderyn every year. Whether you're a whisky or spirit drinker you will find a visit here to the distillery and fascinating one. I don't drink myself but I was taken a back at the long history that whisky has here in Wales and the long journey it has been on, only to now, be up there with some of the best whiskies in the world!

The Welsh Whisky Company, Penderyn Distillery, Penderyn, CF44 0SX

Hawk Adventures

t: 01558-668878 e: info@hawkadventures.co.uk
www.hawkadventures.co.uk

Providers of Outdoor Activities since 1990, we are dedicated to providing exciting and enjoyable adventure activities, corporate events and team building events. Our outdoor activity centre is perfectly placed in the beautiful Brecon Beacons and we deliver the activities across a wide range of locations throughout South Wales, Swansea, Gower, Carmarthenshire and the Brecon Beacons National Park.We have a wide range of outdoor activities available for individuals and groups both large and small, all catered to your needs. Whether you are looking for a taste of adventure activities, fun corporate events or challenging team building events we have the activities to suit your needs.All activities are provided by highly experienced and qualified Instructors. All hold the relevant and current First Aid awards. National qualifications held are those approved by the relevant governing bodies.

AUTHOR'S REVIEW

Hawk Adventures has been using South Wales as their playground for over two decades, and there really isn't anything about 'adventure' that they can't tell you about. Their experience and knowledge of the business, let alone the South Wales Region is unprecedented and very hard to sum up in 150 words. But I will go as far as to say that no matter what kind of activity your looking to take part in, whether it be for a team building event, stag party, or just as part of your holiday, every single member of staff here at Hawk Adventures is not only highly qualified, but more likely over qualified within all aspects of their field. They have a great website which will not only tell you about every activity they specialise in, but the profiles of every instructor is on that site and all available for you to check long before you book your activity with them, making them a very transparent business indeed.

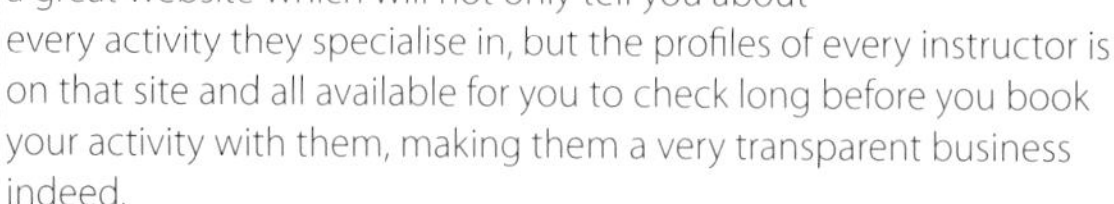

Garreg Wen, Golden Grove, Llanarthney, Carmarthenshire, SA32 8JR

The Spaceguard Centre

t: 01547-520247 e: mail@spaceguardcentre.com
www.spaceguardcentre.com

The Spaceguard Centre is the only organisation in the UK addressing the hazard of Near Earth Objects. NEOs are asteroids and comets that come close to, and sometimes collide with the Earth. Such impacts can have devastating effects – they have in the past and will in the future unless we use available technologies to prevent them. The aim of Spaceguard UK is to develop and maintain a world class facility for astronomical research and science education,with a specific emphasis on the Spaceguard project. We want to bring the wonders of the universe to everyone in a fun and understandable way.
Spaceguard UK operates the Spaceguard Centre located in Knighton, Powys, UK from where we provide timely information to the public, press, media and education about the threat of asteroid and comet impacts, and the ways in which we can predict and deal with them.

AUTHOR'S REVIEW

Forget Hollywood films such as Armageddon, Deep Impact, Deadly Skies and the like. The Spaceguard Centre is doing it all for real. During my visit to the Spaceguard Centre I was absolutely blown away to learn members of Spaceguard UK have already been active in promoting the assessment of the United Kingdom's contribution to the international NEO detection effort. The founders of this amazing space observatory high in the Welsh Powys hills have been scanning our skies for many years now and are very keen to pass on their knowledge to all visitors to the centre. Whether you are a keen enthusiast or not, you will leave the Spaceguard Centre feeling very glad you came and I'm sure planning your next visit back to this truly remarkable attraction.

Temple Street, Llandrindod Wells, Powys, Mid Wales, LD1 5DL

The Bear Hotel

High Street, Crickhowell, Powys NP8 1BW

T: 01873-810408 www.bearhotel.co.uk E: info@bearhotel.co.uk

A former coaching inn, The Bear at Crickhowell has been welcoming guests for 500 years and still extends the same warmth, comfort, cosy atmosphere, good food and wide selection of drinks as ev before. You can eat and drink with friendly locals in the historic bar – with its oak beams, wooden flc and open fires – or in the more intimate settings of our restaurants. In the summer, we'll serve you i beautiful gardens, surrounded by fragrant flowers and shaded by trees. Guests can stay in oak-bean rooms just as stagecoach passengers did or in more modern suites, some with spa baths.All of this i the charming town of Crickhowell, surrounded by the stunning scenery of the Brecon Beacons Nati Park, yet just over two hours from London and around an hour from Bristol, Cardiff & Birmingham.

The Dragon Hotel

Market Square, Montgomery, Powys, SY15 6PA

T: 01686-668359 www.dragonhotel.com E: reception@dragonhotel.c

The Dragon hotel was originally built as a Coaching Inn around 1630. The hotel is located in the hea of the attractive little town of Montgomery and is owned by a group of local families. It has built an excellent reputation for the friendliness and helpfulness of the staff, all of whom live in and around Montgomery. Our approach to our customers and guests is: classic and professional, but informal. A our bedrooms are en-suite. The Premium Rooms all have baths and showers. Other rooms have eith baths or showers. Please speak to our staff, when booking, if you have a preference. As would be expected with any 17th century building, the hotel has its own idiosyncrasies – including the odd 2 year-old creaking floorboard! This is all part of its character and charm and what sets it apart.

The White Horse

The Square, Clun, Shropshire, SY7 8JA

T: 01588-640305 www.whitehorseclun.com E: pub@whi-clun.co.uk

Come for a friendly, comfortable stay at our lively, country inn. You have four rooms to choose from colour coded and easy to remember. All rooms have TV, Shower, En suite and Tea making facilities. We specialise in local real ales and serve food predominantly from local suppliers. We are a great destination for people wanting to stay in this beautiful unspoilt part of the country. Situated in the Shropshire Hills an Area of Outstanding Natural Beauty (AONB). We are surrounded by beautiful countryside perfect for touring around on foot, bicycle or car. Close to the Market towns of Ludlow, Bishops Castle and Knighton, there is no shortage of high quality retail therapy. Knighton, Ludlow a Church Stretton boast impressive Golf Courses and Ludlow Racecourse is also within easy reach.

The Castle Hotel

Market Square, Bishops Castle, Shropshire, SY9 5BN

T: 01588-638403 www.thecastlehotelbishopscastle.co.uk stay@thecastlehotelbishopscastle.c

The Castle Hotel in Bishops Castle, Shropshire, has thirteen delightful en-suite bedrooms, three bus bars, a fine oak panelled restaurant and one of the finest hotel gardens in Shropshire. Situated in a quiet little edge-of-town square too, so no passing traffic! Red Kites soar above the castle top terrac gardens.The bedrooms are excellent quality, characterful & atmospheric bedrooms in the county o Shropshire, in which to base yourselves while you explore this beautiful part of England. Each room its own on suite and is individually decorated with lovely views of the surrounding Shropshire Hills designated area of Outstanding Natural Beauty (AONB) and the Welsh hills just a stones throw away offering some of the best unspoilt walking countryside in the land.

Cilhendre Fawr Farm Cottages

Wernddu Road, Pontardawe, Swansea & Gower Coast, SA8 3HY

T: 01792-862210 www.holiday-cottages-south-wales.co.uk E: info@holiday-cottages-south-wales.co.uk

Escape to the country on a beautiful holiday cottage break at Cilhendre Fawr Farm Cottages. The beautifully converted stone barn buildings are accredited 4 star luxury self-catering cottages situated in the breathtaking rolling hills of the South Wales Valley. You can expect some of the original barn features, stylish decor and immaculate furnishings for high quality comfort, as well as added luxury features which are sure to impress. Set in 49 acres of farmland the luxury barn cottages are perfectly situated for families, outdoor lovers and thrill-seekers alike, there is ample parking and safe playing areas for children. The cottages are close to the impressive Aberduilais Waterfalls and Brecon Beacons, the outstanding Afan Forest Park Woodland bike trails, breathtaking beaches of the Gower Peninsular.

Smithy Cottage

Brithdir Lane, Welshpool, Powys, SY21 8AW

T: 01686-640198 www.thehorseshoesberriew.com E: horseshoesberriew@outlook.com

Dating from the 17th century, this Traditional Country Inn situated in the Berriew along the A483 features a newly refurbished Bungalow built in a quiet location next to the canal. Our Accommodation also offers free Wi-Fi, so whether your visiting for Business or for the perfect romantic getaway Smithy Cottage has everything you could possibly require. he Horseshoes Berriew is managed by Darren and his dedicated team that are here to welcome you to our country inn their ambition is to provide a warm and friendly ambience, making it the ideal place for you to indulge, enjoy and relax during you're stay. Local to Welshpool town is the well known tourist attraction Powys Castle which also has a direct link across the canal path and is one of the most popular days out for those visiting the local area.

The Lion Hotel & Restaurant

Berriew, Welshpool, Powys, SY21 8PQ

T: 01686-640452 www.lionhotel-berriew.co.uk E: info@lionhotel-berriew.co.uk

Situated in the heart of the beautiful Welsh border country is the untouched village of Berriew, winner of Wales's 'best kept village' award. The centrepiece of this village is The Lion Hotel, a charming hostelry in the traditional style. The Lion's long standing reputation for good food, superb accommodation and friendly welcoming service makes it well worth the short detour off the main Welshpool to Newtown road. The luxuriously decorated rooms though in keeping with the hotel are well equipped with modern facilities. There are seven double rooms in total all with en-suite bath or shower facilities, there is also the option to stay in the four poster bed. Some of the rooms offer a view over Berriew's well kept churchyard whilst the others overlook The Lion's paved forecourt with views overlooking the village.

Hideaway white-rock Ranch

Bwlchgwyn Farm, Rhayader, Powys, LD6 5LE

T: 07504-535106 E: puppylover16@hotmail.co.uk

Bwlchgwyn Lodge is a timber building with disabled access, offering two King size bedrooms (Sleeps 8) and a twinned bedroom.The lounge also has 2 bed settees. The lodge boasts a large open-plan kitchen / dining room / lounge which looks out onto a covered veranda and across the beautiful Wye Valley and surrounding mountains. There is a large bathroom with a WC, hand rails, a sink, a bath and a separate shower. The bedrooms each have electric wall heaters while heat in the lounge area is supplied by a Warmlite oil filled radiator. Hot water is supplied by an immersion heater. Electricity is by pre-payment. Bed linen and towels are provided. A Welcome Basket will be awaiting you upon your arrival, containing a loaf of fresh bread, butter, Jam & marmalade, coffee, tea, milk and cereal. Bwlchgwyn Lodge is wheelchair friendly and has grab rails installed in the bathroom.The Lodge also has a hotub.

Tynllwyn Farm B&B

Groes Plaun, Welshpool, Powys, SY21 9BW

T: 01938-553175 www.tynllwynfarm.co.uk E:tynllwynfarm@btconnect.com

Tynllwyn Farm provides bed and breakfast accommodation for guests, and also offers an optional dinner menu. This must be arranged prior to arrival.We have five B&B rooms that include 2 double 1 king size and 2 twins. All our rooms are comfortable, finished to a high standard and have en sui facilities. Rooms include a TV and tea-making facilities.Communal areas include a large guest loun with a TV, comfy seating and open log fires in the winter. In the dining room we serve a farmhouse English breakfast. Guests are also welcome to enjoy evening meals if pre booked prior to arrival. W source ingredients locally where possible. We also have our Holiday Cottages with stunning views.

Beili Neuadd B&B & Bunk House Accommodation

Harmon, Rhayader, Powys, LD6 5NS

T: 01597-810211 www.beilineuadd.co.uk E: info@beilineuadd.co.uk

Beili Neuadd Bed and Breakfast and Bunkhouse accommodation has something for everyone. The farmhouse has been sensitively restored to retain its original charm and character with exposed beams, polished oak floorboards and wood burning stoves. It does however have all modern technology including Wifi. The beautiful 4 star Farmhouse B&B along with the 3 star Bunkhouse a a simple wooden chalet, provides a superb range of accommodation to suit all pockets to ensure that lots of visitors can enjoy the benefits of such a beautiful location and experience. Regardless of whether you are self catering or staying in the farmhouse, we aim to provide a relaxed, friendly environment where visitors are free to come and go as they like.

Bryndu Farm B&B

Llandefalle, Brecon, Powys, LD3 0NF

T: 01874-754227 www.bryndu.co.uk E: mary@bryndu.co.uk

Bryndu is a traditional working Welsh 17th century farmhouse in the Brecon Beacons and Black Mountains area, offering superb bed and breakfast accommodation, 4 poster beds, large en-suite bathrooms with bath and shower, LCD TV'S with DVD'S, holistic and beauty treatments available. T B&B is attentively run by its owners Mary & Wayne. The farmhouse has been lovingly refurbished to high standard and has a wealth of charm and character with exposed beams and stonework, and offers double and single room accommodation complete with en-suite facilities. Children are welcome but sorry no pets are allowed. Internet service is available to visitors.
Caravan & CampingOpen April – October. Open All Year

Bryndu Caravan & Camping Site

Llandefalle, Brecon, Powys, LD3 0NF

T: 01874-754227 www.bryndu.co.uk E: mary@bryndu.co.uk

Enjoy a break away in the peace and quiet of the stunning Brecon Beacons, Stunning Farm Accom dation; Caravan & Camping, Traditional Farmhouse B&B and luxurious self-catering Safari Tent. Set the gorgeous rural countryside in Mid Wales, Nr Brecon Beacons. Bryndu is a Traditional working fa set between the Brecon Beacons and Black Mountains. Family run, with a variety of accommodati onsite Holistic & Beauty Salon and outdoor Hot Tub. Experience the flavour and feel of the country on a working farm, far from the hustle and bustle of urban lifestyles. An ideal base for touring Mid Wales; Walking, cycling, pony trekking, fishing, canoeing, golfing, or just simply relaxing. Closely located to The Royal Welsh Show, Brecon Jazz and Hay-on-Wye Book Festival. April – October

Bryndu Wellbeing Safari

Llandefalle, Brecon, Powys, LD3 0NF

T: 01874-754227 www.bryndu.co.uk E: mary@bryndu.co.uk

Bryndu Holistic & Beauty Salon is run by Emma Gittoes. Emma Haines Holistic Beauty has been established since 2009 and is based in the main farmhouse. Emma provides a range of Holistic & Beauty treatments (see below). Emma has been very successful within her business winning 'Best Wedding Makeup Artist' 2014 & 2015 and was a runner up finalist for 2016 & 2017 in the Welsh National Wedding Awards. She recently won 'Masseuse of the Year' for the whole of Wales in the 2018 Hair & Beauty Awards, as well as being awarded the 'Silver Kite Award 2018' from the local Powys County Councillor in recognition for all her achievements.Please ensure you pre-book appointments with Emma, as she also offers her services to local clientele and does get booked up very quickly.

Pen-y-Bryn House Guest House

Llangorse, Brecon, Powys, LD3 7UG

T: 03336-002020 www.penybrynhousebrecon.com E: penybryn@activityuk.com

Pen-Y-Bryn House is a luxurious 5-star hotel in Brecon within the region of Bookends and Hay Castle. This 5-star guesthouse is within the region of Brecon Beacons National Park and Richard Booth's Bookshop. Pen-Y-Bryn House is a smoke-free property. Dining facilities at the hotel include a cafeteria. The hotel boasts a 24-hour front desk service. Other hotel amenities include garden and tennis court(s). Other services: dry cleaning/laundry service and tours/ticket assistance.
Room facilities include climate control and phone. Other room amenities include minibar. Bathroom amenities include hair dryer. Entertainment: In-room entertainment options at Pen-Y-Bryn House include flat-screen TV and satellite television service. Housekeeping services are also available.

The Red Lion

Llangorse, Brecon, Powys, LD3 7TY

T: 01874-658825 www.redlionllangorse.co.uk E: reservations@redlionllangorse.co.uk

Set in the beautiful village of Llangorse, nestled within the Brecon Beacons National Park, The Red Lion is all you'd expect from a country pub and more. The beauty of offering accommodation on a small scale is the personal service we can provide. When you call us to book we will be happy to discuss your needs with you and help you to select one of our variety of ensuite rooms all being ground floor with dvd tv and tea & coffee facilities. Breakfast is included.
Room 1 – Double room with triple bunk beds for under 16's
Room 2 – Four poster double room for that special night away
Room 3 – Standard double room

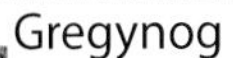

Gregynog

Tregynon, Near Newtown, Powys, Tregynon, SY16 3PW

T: 01686-650224 www.gregynog.org E: enquiries@gregynog.org

This large country house has a pretty Victorian face, and dates back to the 15th century. Gregynog Hall is set in 750 acres of beautiful, formal gardens and countryside. Private parking is free on site.
The traditional rooms are set in either the main house, a separate cottage, and in a converted historic stable yard. All come with a TV and tea and co ee-making facilities, and many have picturesque views of the grounds.Gregynog Hall has free Wi-Fi in public areas. There is a library with a wide range of books, including a large Arthurian literature collection. In the grounds, there are a variety of way-marked footpaths, as well as hides for birdwatching.
A full, home-cooked breakfast is available each morning, made from local Welsh produce.

The Elephant & Castle Hotel

Broad Street, Newtown, Powys, SY16 2BQ

T: 01686-626271 www.elephantandcastlehotel.co.uk E:admin@elephantandcastlehotel.co.

The Elephant and Castle Hotel is a privately owned hotel, bought by a local farming family. Over the 4 years we have completely refurbished the whole of the hotel to provide our guests with modern, quality accommodation and function facilitites, for business or pleasure.
Our friendly team of staff strive to ensure that your time with us is a memorable one, and we look forward to welcoming new and returning guests to our hotel. For luxury and relaxation stay in one o our Executive Riverside rooms, or our standard rooms within the hotel offer modern high quality ac modation with free Wi-Fi and free parking.

Trewythen Hotel

Great Oak Street, Llanidloes, Powys, SY18 6BW

T: 01686-411333 www.trewythenllanidloes.co.uk E: hayley@trewythenllanidloes.co.u

The Trewythen was re-opened in September 2012 by Glyn & Hayley Powell who are also proprietors the well-established Unicorn Hotel in Llanidloes.
The grand staircase leads up from the Breakfast room and conference room to a selection of single, double and family rooms, all tastefully decorated to complement and enhance the numerous perio features. A four-poster suite is also available.
We provide a Full Welsh breakfast using produce from local suppliers. Cereals, fruit juice, yoghurts a fresh fruit are also provided in addition to tea and coffee.
Free Wi-Fi is available throughout the hotel.

Pwllgwilym Cottages & B&B

Pwllgwilym, Llanafan Road, Cilmery, Builth Wells, Powys, LD2 3NY

T: 01982-552140 www.pwllgwilym-bandb.co.uk E: jane@pwllgwilym-bandb.co.u

Welcome To Pwllgwilym Bed & Breakfast, 4 star accommodation set in 60 acres of farm land, a short distance to the village of Cilmery, two miles from the old market town of Builth Wells.
We offer 3 spacious en-suite bedrooms... Each room has flat screen tv, fridge, tea & coffee facilities a hairdryer. Each room has a comfortable seating area, with free wifi available, non smoking rooms.
Pwllgwilym Selfcatering Holiday Cottages near Builth Wells was tastefully converted from the old fa Barn in 2006, a traditional conversion leaving the old beams, stone walls and adding traditional flag stone floors. The Barn consists of 3 spacious 4-star cottages which sleep from 4 to 17. Each cottage i comfortably furnished with a cottage feel, bedrooms have pine furniture, good kitchen facilities anc fully heated. The use of gas barbecue with each cottage, outdoor furniture, with ample parking.

The Old School House B&B

Pennant, Llanbrynmair, Powys, SY19 7BL

T: 01650-521486 www.theoldschoolhousewales.co.uk E: info@theoldschoolhousewales.c

Pennant is a small hamlet between Llanidloes, Machynlleth and Llanbrynmair, close to Snowdonia National Park and Aberystwyth, making this an ideal location for cycling, walking or just sightseeing Glyndwr's Way and Sustrans route 8 are easily reached from here. All our produce is locally sourced a we offer homemade preservatives and free-range eggs from the chickens in our garden (hopefully). Packed lunches and evening meals are available on request. Take time to relax in our rear garden ar spacious conservatory whilst we prepare you hearty, home cooked meals, leaving you nothing to d but enjoy the peace and quiet. TV and free Wi-Fi are freely available throughout The Old School Hou should you wish to stay in contact with the outside world.

Isfryn Cottage

Isfryn, Aberangell, Gwynedd, SY20 9ND

T: 01650-511463 www.isfryncottage.wales E: Isfryn@2spoons.co.uk

A very warm welcome to Isfryn from your hosts Steve and Linda. Isfryn (which means 'under the hill' in Welsh) forms a completely self-contained property, separated by 3ft thick walls of slate from Ty Hebron, the adjoining former Methodist chapel, which is now our home. Isfryn was built in the 1870s as a home for the chapel minister. To make you feel at home from the moment you arrive, you will be greeted by a welcome basket of goodies, many of which will be home-made by us. Having fully explored that, you can explore the rest of the cottage. All utilities are included. We provide you with two baskets of logs for the wood burner and you will be able to purchase further bags from us if you need them.

Alltybrain Farm Cottages & Farmhouse B&B

Llandefaelog Fach, Brecon, Powys, LD3 9RB

T: 01874-690214 www.alltybrainfarmcottages.co.uk E: rose@alltybrainfarmcottages.co.uk

Allt-y-Brain in welsh means hillside of the Ravens or "Crows Wood". Today the hills behind Alltybrain Farm are managed by the Forestry Commission and they lead to common land that forms a high ridge all the way from Brecon to Builth Wells giving intrepid walking and riding visitors spectacular views of The Brecon Beacons to the south, the Black Mountains to the east and the Eppynt hills to the north. We have two attractive high end four star graded Holiday Cottages each providing spacious accommodation for two people. We offer four star Farmhouse B&B accommodation in The Farmhouse. Alltybrain Farm Cottages and Farmhouse B&B is a place to stay for a quiet and peaceful holiday in the welsh countryside.

Blaen-Nant-Y-Groes Farm Cottages

Cwmbach, Aberdare, South Wales, CF44 0EA.

T: 01685-881457 www.tunnelcottages.co.uk E: stay@tunnelcottages.co.uk

On the edge of the Brecon Beacons, these 4-star stone cottages have free internet and private balconies. Blaen-nant-y-Groes Farm Cottages have a scenic location in Cwmbach, just a 15-minute drive from Merthyr Tydfil. The cosy cottages feature flag-stone floors and exposed beams, and each has a real wood-burning stove. All cottages have a private entrance and BBQ area with wonderful countryside views. Each cottage has a modern kitchen with a refrigerator, microwave and dishwasher. All Blaen-nant-y-Groes cottages feature a dining area, comfortable leather sofas and a TV. Set in 15 acres of grounds, the Blaen-nant-y-Groes Farm Cottages are a 30-minute drive from Cardiff. The Brecon Mountain Railway is a 20-minute drive away and Aberdare can be reached in a 10-minute drive.

The Rheolau Arms

15 Heol Rheolau, Abercraf, Swansea, SA9 1TB

T: 01639-730278 www.therheolauarms.co.uk E: sarahmorgangray594@btinternet.com

Welcome to The Rheolau Arms, our family-owned and run luxury bed & breakfast is situated at the foot of the Brecon Beacons. With views of the River Tawe, The Rheolau Arms is on the main A4067 Swansea & Brecon Road. Our guiding principle is to offer exceptional accommodation and service, to make our guests feel they are 'home from home' and to make their stay in the Brecon Beacons one to remember.We believe that there are a few prerequisites that a luxury bed and breakfast must have – relaxing decor, very comfortable beds, immaculate bathrooms, fresh linens, fluffy towels, welcoming guest areas, fresh flowers and a hearty breakfast with plenty of choice. These are the essentials that we combine with the highest standards of personal service. This is what The Rheolau Arms is all about.

The Forest Cottages

Gilfach Lane, Kerry, Newtown, Powys, SY16 4DW

T: 01686-621821 www. forestcottageskerry.co.uk E: info@forestcottageskerry.co.

Are you looking for a homely cottage in a peaceful environment where you can escape, relax and unwind ? Are you looking for onsite facilities which both adults and children can enjoy? The Forest Cottages offers you a warm welcome at their family run self-catering cottages in the beautiful Vale c Kerry on the border of Montgomeryshire and Shropshire. The Forest Cottages provides 3 quality cottages and a spacious log cabin two of which have private hot tubs in their secluded gardens. We welcome children of all ages and there is plenty to entertain them with an outside play area, tennis and games room, as well as tame animals to feed. Dogs are welcome in all but Forest Lodge. Holiday support our charity Dal Dy Dir which provides respite breaks for families with disabilities.

Checkers Pantry

Broad Street, Montgomery, Powys, SY15 6PN

T: 01686-669822 www.checkerswales.co.uk E: kathryn@checkerswales.co.uk

Checkers Pantry is open Tuesday to Saturday for delicious breakfast, light lunches, coffee and cake, w also have five gorgeous en suite bed and breakfast rooms if you fancy a stay in wonderful Mid Wales Checkers Pantry is is very informal - we do not take advance bookings unless your party is for 6 or more but if you have any queries please don't hesitate to get in touch. As a former Michelin-starre restaurant, we have lost none of our passion for quality ingredients and great food; we've just adde healthy dose of simplicity, comfort and family-friendly daytime opening hours. And you can now ta Checkers' food home with you! We have a selection of treats and ready-prepared meals to take awa We look forward to welcoming you to Checkers Pantry very soon!

Wye Glamping

Velindre, Brecon, Powys, LD3 0SU

T: 07974-000421 www.wyeglamping.co.uk E: info@wyeglamping.co.uk

Forget searching the garage and loft for all the camping paraphernalia you own, cramming the car with all your worldly goods, arriving in the dark and wet to put up the tent which you realise half wa through has a pole missing! Instead, stay in a spacious pre – erected bell tent or yurt. Sleep soundly on beds with real mattresses and duvets, cosy up in front of the wood burning stove with snuggly blankets, conjure up culinary delights in your sheltered kitchen area or barbeque and eat alfresco. Here at Wye Glamping the emphasis is on relaxing and enjoying the simplicity of being close to nature in comfort and style. Take a stroll through the countryside, splash in the stream, read a book whilst taking in the beautiful surroundings.

Tai'r Bull Country Inn

Libanus, Brecon, Powys, LD3 8EL

T: 01874-622600 www.tairbull.co.uk E: info@tairbull.co.uk

The Tai'r Bull Country Inn in Libanus, Brecon, is a country pub, restaurant and bed & breakfast, oozin rural charm and rustic character. Our picturesque surroundings in the heart of the Brecon Beacons provide the perfect backdrop for savouring the hearty, seasonal pub-food on our menu, and the carefully nurtured beers, lagers and fine wines gracing our bar. With a cosy log fire and various seating areas you'll be very happy soaking up the atmosphere in un-spoilt surroundings.
We have five en-suite bedrooms, newly refurbished with lovely oak beds and matching bedroom furniture. Rooms have tea/coffee facilities, flatscreen LCD TV, and Wi-Fi and have delightful views of Pen y fan mountain and surrounding countryside.

The Coach & Horses

Cwm Cronnan Road, Llangynidr, Powys, NP8 1LS

T: 01874-730245 www.thecoachandhorsesinn.com E: coachandhorses222@outlook.com

This old coaching Inn hidden away in the lovely village of Llangynidr is surrounded by the Brecon Beacons National Park and overlooking the delightful Brecon and Monmouth Canal. Chef patron Shaun Ellis is well known for warmth of his welcome and the excellence of his cooking. There is a range of tables for relaxed informal bar eating or the more formal restaurant features smartly laid tables, soft lighting and an elegant stone fireplace while mouthwatering dishes make inspired use of the finest produce from local and sustainable sources. The bar serves a range of drinks and traditional ales - the perfect place to relax in comfort and catch up on the day's activities with friends. Outside is a large, peaceful garden overlooking the canal with stunning views over the local countryside.

The Crown Inn at Clunton

Clunton, Nr Craven Arms, Shropshire, SY7 0HU

T: 01588-660265 www.crowninnclunton.co.uk E: enquiries@crowninnclunton.co.uk

You are assured of a warm welcome at this charming 16th century country pub and restaurant. Nestled in the lovely Clun valley in an AONB, we have Clunton Coppice to one side and the historic Bury ditches to the other, Clunton lies quiet as anywhere under the sun. Our award winning chef is passionate about great local, quality produce, most of which is sourced from suppliers within a thirty mile radius, and real home cooked seasonal food, bringing the flavours of the valley to the plate. Our offerings range from a glass of superb wine with a meal in our intimate restaurant, a hot drink after a country walk enjoyed by the wood burning stove, to fantastic local ales paired with a tasty Ploughman's.

The Castle Hotel

Market Square, Bishops Castle, Shropshire, SY9 5BN

T: 01588-638403 www.thecastlehotelbishopscastle.co.uk E:stay@thecastlehotelbishopscastle.co.uk

The Castle Hotel is a Shropshire hotel in Bishops Castle, one of the most charming and unspoilt market towns in England and conveniently close to the medieval towns of Shrewsbury and Ludlow. We are surrounded on all sides by the beautiful South Shropshire Hills (designated an Area of Outstanding Natural Beauty AONB), the Welsh borders, and in some of the best walking countryside in the country. The Castle Hotel is an eighteenth century inn with good food, panoramic views, fabulous gardens and one of the finest selections of real ales in Shropshire. We don't do Michelin at The Castle Hotel, but we certainly use many of the same local high quality suppliers. We're spoilt for them actually. We produce modern, good pub food that is hearty, flavoursome & fresh at great value!

Iechyd Da Health Foods & Produce

11 Broad Street, Llandovery, Powys, SA20 0AR

T: 01550-720703 E: jakeiechydda@hotmail.co.uk

Iechyd Da, is housed in what could be one of the oldest houses in Llandovery! Reputed locally as possibly being the first ever Lloyds TSB bank, this building that is now the towns most popular store for organic, fairt rade and just generally healthy food. With many locally sourced products in stock and available to order, it is not surprising Iechyd Da is such a hit with the locals. Also last but not least Jake the owners 'Artisan Bread' selection is to die for.

The Angel Inn

3 High Street, Llanidloes, Powys, SY18 6BY

T: 01686-414635

The Angel Inn in Llanidloes is a traditional coaching Inn built in 1748. The Inn has recently been full refurbished, but has retained all of its original character and charm, with both the Bar and Lounge full of the original oak beams. In contrast to the traditional and welcoming Pub feel, we have a fully modernised Restaurant at the rear of the premises providing a wide range of traditional and moder international cuisine; made using as much locally produced fresh ingredients as we can source. We have an outside decked Beer Garden where you can enjoy a drink in the sun or dine al fresco in the summer if you prefer. We offer a full range of beers and individually selected house wines with at le three cask ales on regular offer.

The Bridge End Inn

Bell Street, Talgarth, Powys, LD3 0BP

T: 01874-711936

The Bridge End Inn, a free-house pub and restaurant, offers you the chance to eat fresh, locally sour food and sample local beers. Featuring ales from Wye Valley Brewery and other local micro brewerie you are sure to find a tipple to suit your taste buds.

The recently restored pub sits on the banks of the River Ennig opposite the Felin Talgarth Mill, a restored 18thC corn mill. Pete the Chef is keen to stress that the food offering is not fast food but cooked fresh and at the same time fitting the budget of most families. Already gaining a reputation for the steaks, Pete is devising a unique menu of 'mix and match' that will be offering a huge range c taste for great value.

The Red Lion

Llangorse, Brecon, Powys, LD3 7TY

T: 01874 658 825 www.redlionllangorse.co.uk E: reservations@redlionllangorse.co.uk

Set in the beautiful village of Llangorse, The Red Lion is all you'd expect from a country pub and mo A family run business with a friendly, helpful team to see you have a comfortable visit with us. With variety of menus on offer including homemade, family favourites, traditional Sunday lunch, childrer and chef's specials with vegetarian and most allergies catered for. Upstairs you'll find our restaurant and functions room with access to our gardens which are children, wheel chair and dog friendly.

Cwtch Café

6A Broad Street, Builth Wells, Powys, LD2 3DT

T: 01982-551700 www. cwtchcafe.co.uk

Cwtch is an independently run cafe, offering home cooked food, delicious cakes and fresh coffee.
"If you haven't been here then you are missing out!" 5 of 5 stars-Reviewed 9 July 2015
I have been to this gorgeous café numerous times but kept forgetting to write a review. What can I the cakes are melt in the mouth and all as equally yummy making it hard to choose a favourite! Goc range of tea as well as spot on coffee. Lush breakfasts - locally sourced meat, clearly cooked to orde and nothing greasy in sight. Clean and tidy with friendly staff. Nice to see something different from chain doing well. Basically go and check it out :)

The Elephant & Castle Hotel - Riverside Restaurant

Broad Street, Newtown, Powys, SY16 2BQ

T: 01686-626271 www.elephantandcastlehotel.co.uk E:admin@elephantandcastlehotel.co.uk

Breakfast is served in our Riverside Restaurant. It is a lovely way to start your day looking out over the river whilst having breakfast. For lunch or dinner you will be greated as you arrive in the Cocktail Bar, and invited to take a seat and enjoy a pre-dinner drink in plush surroundings, whilst you choose from the delicious dishes on offer. We have a varied selection of wines to compliment our dishes.
Our Restaurant can accommodate up to 40 people and offers beautiful views of the River Severn.
Our team of professional Chefs offer superb homemade food in a picturesque setting. The menus are changed on a seasonal basis, and we use fresh local produce to create our dishes, which are all cooked to order. We can cater for special dietary requirements.

The Red Lion - Y Llew Coch

Dinas Mawddwy, Machynlleth, Powys, SY20 9JA

T: 01650-531247 www.yllewcoch.co.uk E: info@yllewcoch.co.uk

The Red Lion is the heart of Dinas Mawddwy with a fine, traditional yet lively atmosphere where this inn's history envelopes you from the second you walk in. An impressive fire place greets you, adorned like much is the building in relics of its fascinating past.
Owned and run by mother and son team Beryl and Berwyn Hughes, there is great food, real ale and accommodation available all year round. The food is what people really come for here, all made using local produce, prepared fresh each day. Local favourites are the variety of hearty homemade pies and the succulent Sunday lunch carvery which fills the place each weekends so it's advised to book to avoid disappointment.

The Horseshoes Inn

Brithdir Lane, Welshpool, Powys, SY21 8AW

T: 01686-640198 www.thehorseshoesberriew.com E: horseshoesberriew@outlook.com

The Horseshoes Berriew is a small, family run restaurant that prides itself on serving quality and wholesome food using locally sourced and produced ingredients wherever possible. We aim to provide all of this in a warm, relaxed and traditional environment. We can cater for large groups of people and are a family friendly run pub. We have a large selection of choices on our menu and we are positive there is something for everyone, however if you have any queries regarding the menu or dietary requirements, please don't hesitate to contact us prior to your visit. On those cold winter days pop in and enjoy some warming food in front of our log burning fire, alternatively during the summer months enjoy your food al fresco in our newly refurbished, dog friendly beer garden and let the children run around in our new childrens play area.

The Horse & Jockey

Chirbury Road, Churchstoke, Montgomery, Powys, SY15 6AE

T: 01588-620060 e: dave.powell147@hotmail.co.uk

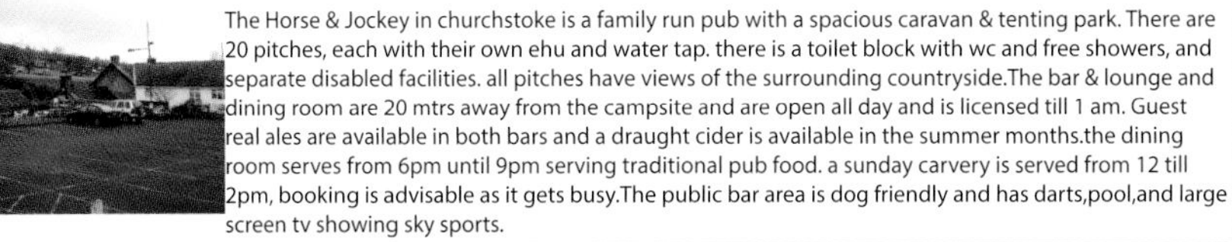

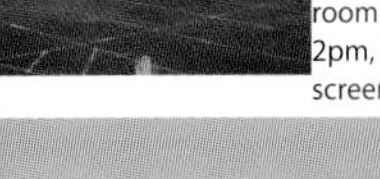

The Horse & Jockey in churchstoke is a family run pub with a spacious caravan & tenting park. There are 20 pitches, each with their own ehu and water tap. there is a toilet block with wc and free showers, and separate disabled facilities. all pitches have views of the surrounding countryside.The bar & lounge and dining room are 20 mtrs away from the campsite and are open all day and is licensed till 1 am. Guest real ales are available in both bars and a draught cider is available in the summer months.the dining room serves from 6pm until 9pm serving traditional pub food. a sunday carvery is served from 12 till 2pm, booking is advisable as it gets busy.The public bar area is dog friendly and has darts,pool,and large screen tv showing sky sports.

The Kerry Lamb

Kerry, Newtown, Powys, SY16 4NP

T: 01686-670226 www.thekerrylambpowys.co.uk e: admin@thekerrylambpowys.co.uk

We are a small, family run business that took over the Kerry Lamb in July 2017. Kerry is a beautiful village just outside Newtown, Mid Wales with good facilities and a very welcoming community. The has a bar and pool room, a relaxing restaurant / lounge area and a large beer garden perfect for chil out on sunny days. We offer a selection of traditional, affordable meals and a large selection of alcoh and non-alcoholic drinks. We can be booked for parties, meetings or events - even if this is outside o standard opening hours, do give us a call and we will do our best to accommodate you. At the Kerry Lamb we can cater for all your functions; weddings, birthdays, baby showers, christenings, funerals a more. Our buffet menus start from just £5 per head, or we can offer a more extensive menu if require

The Slaters Arms

Bridge Street, Corris, Machynlleth, Gwynedd, SY20 9SP

T: 01654-761324 www.theslatersarms.com e: hedd_jos@yahoo.com

Named after what used to be the main trade of the townsfolk of Corris, this grade II listed three-roon village pub is popular with locals and visitors staying at nearby hostels and campsites. The main bar some traditional features such as slate flooring and a decorative mantelshelf above a large inglenoo fireplace. A smaller dining room is to the left as you enter and a pub games room is at the rear. Walke families and well behaved dogs are welcome. We now serve lunch on a Sunday.(Booking is advisable Customers are welcome to sample the 3 ales on offer in the form of a 1/3 pint platter for the price of pint. Good value meals are served every day, takeaway food also available. Open mike folk music nig 1st & 3rd Tuesday every month. We also have a Camra accreditation.

The Bear Hotel

High Street, Crickhowell, Powys NP8 1BW

T: 01873-810408 www.bearhotel.co.uk E: info@bearhotel.co.uk

Eat at The Bear and leave satisfied – that's our aim. Our menu offers a wide range of locally sourced ingredients, well cooked to suit traditional tastes or those guests with an appetite for finer dining. The Brecon Beacons have become a centre for organic producers, and artisan food makers – many o whose products appear on our menu. You can choose where you want to eat – in amongst the chatt and laughter of the bar, the more intimate candle-lit surroundings of our table-service restaurants, c amongst the floral displays in our summer garden. You can reserve tables in our restaurant and we h a small allocation of tables in the bar which can be booked for meals before 7pm. All other tables are a first-come first seated basis, but if you are able to wait, we always try to seat everyone.

The Laughing Dog

Howey, Llandrindod Wells, Powys, LD1 5PT

T: 01597-22406 E: thelaughingdoghowey@gmail.com

All you'd expect from a thriving village local, from pub games in the fire-warmed bar to real ales from respected Welsh microbreweries such as Rhymney and Cwm Rhondda. Originating as a drovers stopover some 300 years ago and reputedly haunted, this pub is located in superb walking countrysi The varied menu combines the best of Welsh ingredients with influences from Europe and further af Start with five spice pulled pork, hoi sin sauce and Chinese pancakes; or lamb cawl with leeks, root vegetables, pearl barley and thyme; follow that with Glamorgan sausages, bubble-and-squeak with wine and onion gravy; beef and ale pie with home-made chips and peas; or chicken and coconut cur with roasted Scotch bonnet chillies.

SOUTH WALES VALLEYS

ıen one hears the words 'South Wales Valleys' the first words that always spring to everyone's ds are Rugby and Coal Mining, but the valleys are about so much more than that. It is true to say Rugby and Mining does play a part in so many people's lives within the valleys, but if you were ke a good look at the area, you'd see that the place has so much more going for it. Rolling hills, nt Welsh villages and some great tourist attractions really do make this part of Wales a great place sit.

s taken aback at how friendly people really are around the valleys. Not that I've heard any rent, but you could be forgiven for thinking, that because most people who live in the valleys are rong character working class people, that they could be guilty of being gruff and bad tempered, ever, after visiting the area and really getting to know the people who live there, it really couldn't urther from the truth.

ı there being so much to see and do here, it wouldn't be hard at all to plan your week's holiday nd all the attractions open for you to visit. With some great places to experience, places to eat offer good honest and wholesome food, not forgetting some lovely accommodation to stay in, it to the South Wales Valleys is a must. I am already planning my next visit to the area, as not only visit some fantastic places that could be visited time and time again, but I also made some great ıds along the way! So what are you waiting for, I think you've got some planning to do!

Rhondda Heritage Park

t: 01443-682036 e: iRHPreception@rctcbc.gov.uk
www.rctcbc.gov.uk

Rhondda Heritage Park, based at the former Lewis Merthyr Colliery, Trehafod, is regularly voted one of the top heritage and cultural visitor attractions in South Wales by tourists and provides a fun and interesting day out for the whole family to enjoy together. First port of call is The Visitor Centre which houses the Art Gallery, Level One Cafe, Gift Shop, and an indoor Period reconstructed Village Street displaying the commercial and domestic life of the valleys. Admission to this area is free except on special event days, which you can watch out for using the link. The Black Gold Tour Features a fully guided tour with ex miner guides that take about 45 minutes, and involves multimedia presentations, a tour of the pit head buildings and a trip underground to experience the life of a coal miner at 'pit bottom'! Tours are available at 11:15 and 13:30 daily. They're pretty popular especially during the school holidays so it is a good idea to book your tour before you visit. Rhondda Heritage Park is also home to the Energy Zone Children's Play Area.

AUTHOR"S REVIEW

The Valleys is a very complex story of both industry, family and passion and all of those stories are being told here at the Rhonda Heritage Centre. The minute I stepped foot through the doors of the parks main entrance, I knew I was going to enjoy my visit here, such is the magic of this place. You actually get to step back in time and take a journey, just to see for yourself what life would of been like, not only for the miners themselves, but for the lives of their families also. I loved the street scene and all the hard work that has gone into making sure you experience every attention to detail. Then the pinnacle of the visit in my estimation, is the underground mine tour. An experienced tour guide will be guiding you through the very tunnels that were trod thousands of times by thousands of brave souls.

Merthyr Tydfil

Lewis Merthyr Colliery, Coed Cae Road, Trehafod, CF37 2NP

Brecon Mountain Railway

t: 01685-722988 e: enquiries@breconmountainrailway.co.uk
www.breconmountainrailway.co.uk

Travel in one of our all-weather observation coaches behind a vintage steam locomotive through beautiful scenery into the Brecon Beacons National Park along the full length of the Taf Fechan Reservoir to Torpantau high in the Brecon Beacons on one of the most popular railways in Wales. At Pontsticill you can alight from the train and visit the Cafe, admire the view across the water to the peaks of the Brecon Beacons, go for a ramble alongside the reservoir and visit our new steam museum. There is a play area here for children. On your return to Pant, visit our workshop where old steam locomotives are repaired - follow the footpath to a picnic site which has an amazing panoramic view of the valley. Visit our 'Shunters Restaurant' which is fully licensed and buy a souvenir of your visit in our shop.
Special events are run all year.

AUTHOR'S REVIEW

The Brecon Mountain Railway is another one of those great railways that we have featured within our book. With amazing views and stunning locations you will be spoilt for choice when pointing that camera. Obviously it would be far better to be on the train when it's a sunny day but with the route being so spectacular it really is an all-weather railway. Whether you want to start your journey in the Brecon Beacons or its main station in Merthyr Tydfil depending of course where your accommodation that evening is and coupled with the fact that the car parking facilities are so good at Merthyr, it probably makes more sense to start there, the choice is yours. But whatever you decide be sure not miss out on this great little railway line.

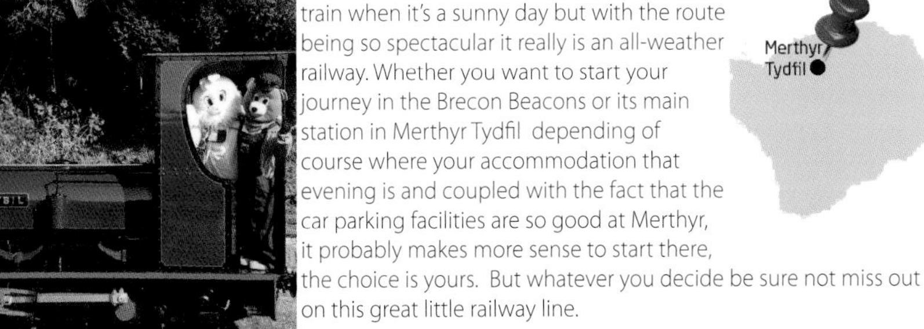

Pant Station, Merthyr Tydfil, Mid Glamorgan ,CF48 2UP

Llancaiach Fawr Manor

t: 01443-412248 e: info@llancaiachfawr.co.uk
www.llancaiachfawr.co.uk

Llancaiach Fawr Manor stands proudly, as it has done since c1550, overlooking the Glamorgan uplands. It is set within a restored period garden which provides the perfect opportunity to enjoy the passing of the seasons in this tranquil location. It is where the past and the present meet.

This superbly restored gentry manor house is no ordinary heritage attraction. History here is tangible. The costumed servants of the house are living and working in 1645 and allow you to share and engage in their world. Fires crackle, candles flicker and the sounds and smells of domestic life make your visit a memorable experience of the past. It takes a moment to attune your ear to the unfamiliar speech within the Manor itself, but within seconds of your warm welcome you become immersed in the time of the Civil Wars and the cares and concerns of ordinary people living in extraordinary times.

AUTHOR'S REVIEW

This attraction is very unique indeed. All though It is true to say there are houses of this nature dotted all across the UK, however, very few houses exist where there past inhabitants actually come to life and are free to walk around the house as if they would have done 300 years ago. Now don't be put off when I use the term past inhabitants! Although this house is one of the 10 most haunted houses in the UK, the historic interpreters are there to give you a taste of what life would of been like back then, but what occurs during the hours of darkness is a different matter! I couldn't get over how much in character the interpreters were! The minute you walk through the door you really would think you had just stepped back many years in time! It was fascinating to hear them speak just the same type of language that would have been spoken way back in William Shakespeare's time. I loved every minute of my tour of Llancaiach Fawr and cannot wait till I return.

Merthyr Tydfil

Llancaiach Fawr Manor, Gelligaer Road, Nelson, Treharris, CF46 6ER

Merthyr Castle Museum

t: 01685-727371
e:info@cyfarthfa.co.uk
www.cyfarthfa.com

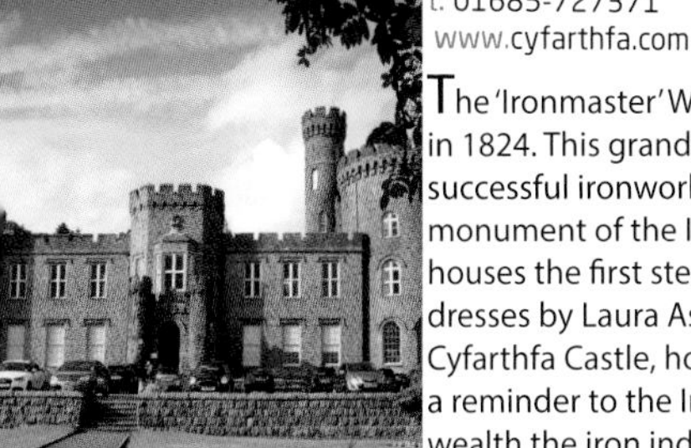

The 'Ironmaster' William Crawshay commissioned Cyfarthfa Castle in 1824. This grand, castellated mansion overlooked his immensely successful ironworks and has been called "the most impressive monument of the Industrial Iron Age in South Wales". The museum houses the first steam whistle, the first voting ballot box and dresses by Laura Ashley and Julien McDonald. The surroundings, Cyfarthfa Castle, home to William Crawshay II and family, serve as a reminder to the Ironmasters dominance over the town and the wealth the iron industry brought to the area. At the Castle you can admire the extensive fine and decorative art collections. This includes Swansea, Nantgarw and Wedgwood porcelain and art by Penry Williams, the Welsh Turner, and George Frederick Harris. Stroll through the atmospheric social and industrial history galleries which chart the rise of this once great ironmaking town. Learn about Richard Trevithick's Penydarren Locomotive of 1804, the first locomotive to pull a load along rails.

AUTHOR'S REVIEW

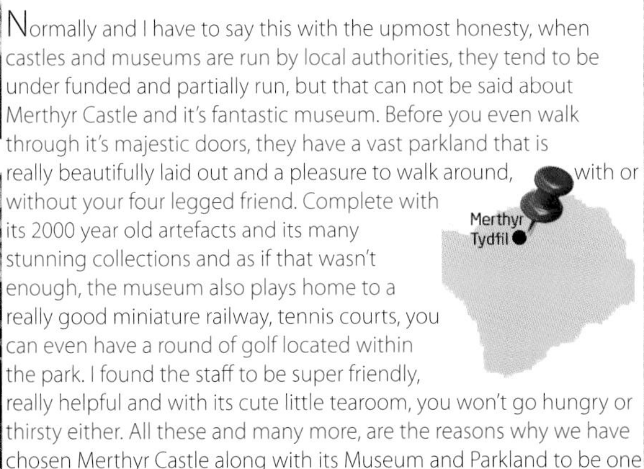

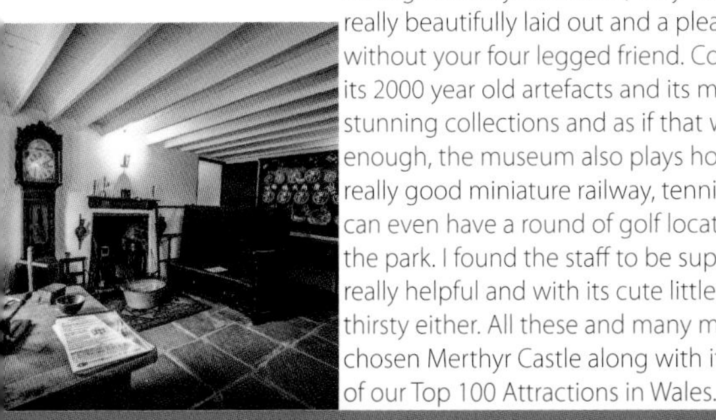

Normally and I have to say this with the upmost honesty, when castles and museums are run by local authorities, they tend to be under funded and partially run, but that can not be said about Merthyr Castle and it's fantastic museum. Before you even walk through it's majestic doors, they have a vast parkland that is really beautifully laid out and a pleasure to walk around, with or without your four legged friend. Complete with its 2000 year old artefacts and its many stunning collections and as if that wasn't enough, the museum also plays home to a really good miniature railway, tennis courts, you can even have a round of golf located within the park. I found the staff to be super friendly, really helpful and with its cute little tearoom, you won't go hungry or thirsty either. All these and many more, are the reasons why we have chosen Merthyr Castle along with its Museum and Parkland to be one of our Top 100 Attractions in Wales.

Cyfarthfa Park Brecon Rd, Merthyr Tydfil, CF47 8RE

The Royal Mint Experience

t: 0333-2412223 e: experience@royalmint.com
www.royalmint.com/experience

Take a tour and see behind the scenes of one of the UK's most fascinating attractions when you enter the Royal Mint Experience. First you will enter the factory where so much of the UK's money is made. This isn't just a show put on for visitors—the silver and gold streaming off the belts at the rate of 750 coins a minute will enter circulation and could be the pocket money your child gets next weekend! Here, for a fee, you and your family can strike your own coins or have your photograph taken next to caskets full of money. After your factory tour, head to the interactive experience where you can explore 6 zones explaining the Royal Mint's history, how coins and medals are made, coin collecting and even superstitions about money. You can learn why coins are put into Christmas pudding and why brides are traditionally meant to have silver sixpences in their shoe. Kids will be fascinated by all the ways money is used that doesn't include using it in shops!

AUTHOR'S REVIEW

Very few people actually know, let alone wonder where on earth all that spare change within your pockets and purses actually comes from, or at least, I didn't anyway up until recently. That was until I came across one of Britain's Biggest and shiniest hidden gems that is the Royal Mint Experience. Open 7 days a week, this attraction has a huge amount to offer, in both historical and educational terms and I was completely bowled over at how many rare and significant artefacts that are on display here. The staff are really friendly and go a million miles to make sure your visit is one that you'll really enjoy and if your visit is anything like mine, never forget. Also, a little tip, whilst your in the gift shop, why not bag yourself a bargain with one of their limited edition coins, believe me, they could be worth a pretty penny some time in the future, excuse the pun!

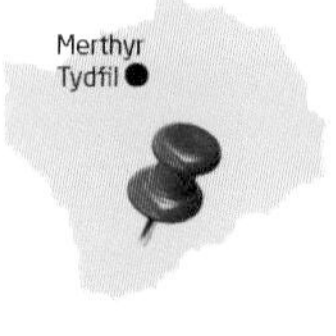

Llantrisant, Pontyclun, Mid-Glamorgan, CF72 8YT

ecret Garden

t: 01495-785237 e:info@thesecretgardenwales.co.uk

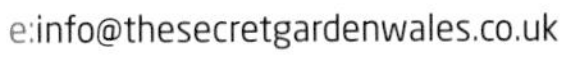

www.thesecretgardenwales.co.uk

The Secret Garden is a family run business that has been operating in South Wales for the last 20 years. With the largest range of plants and plant related items in the area you'll always find something new and exciting for your garden. Come and visit our brand new houseplant heated glasshouse. A wide range of houseplants from big foliage plants to the small delicate flowering ones to the beautifully scented indoor jasmines. The original farmyard is now the entrance to a fantastic garden centre with a massive range of plants of all types for your garden. Friendly and knowledgeable staff are on hand to make sure you find exactly what you want. Opened in 2006, our custom built glasshouse provides over 1000 square feet of covered area where you can find a range of tropical and exotic plants for the conservatory or the house , features ranges, glasshouse etc. Within the Garden Centre, Sally's Tea Rooms offers a delightful place for eating and drinking.

AUTHOR'S REVIEW

Throughout the many editions of the Top 100 Attractions range obooks, garden centres don't really feature that heavily. This isn't because I don't like them, it's merely because as a rule, gardens centres are just exactly what they say they are, centres for buying garden stuff. However dotted all over our fine land are garden centrers that really do stand out from all the rest. Secret Garden is just exactly one such garden centre. Situated only a stones throw away from Abergavenny and nestled perfectly within the South Wales Valleys, Secret Garden really did take me by surprise. From every day plants, to those of the exotic and tropical, around every corner there is something to wow every green fingered tourist. All garden centres worth their salt feature a place to grab a coffee, but here at the Secret Garden, Sally's Tea Rooms is the order of the day. Freshly baked cakes and the smell of great coffee, and that's before mentioning the great food on offer.

Merthyr Tydfil

Pentwyn Farm, Torfean, Mamhilad NP4 OJE

Ynys Hywel Activity & Nature Centr

t: 01495-200326 e: office@ynyshywel.co.uk
www.ynyshywel.co.uk

Ynys Hywel Activity and Nature Centre is hidden away in the beautiful Sirhowy Valley Country Park and provides an amazing learning experience outside the classroom or working environment. It's an extremely fun place to go, but it can also really help boost your confidence and set you up ready for whatever life throws at you. From half-day or full-day programmes to residentials, we cater for all corporate, local authority and individual clients to suit all groups and budgets, prices start from £10per person. What is more, all our packages are exclusive, meaning your group will have dedicated staff for your visit, so we can guarantee you our undivided attention to ensure that you all have the best time ever. Why not motivate, energise, boost morale or simply reward your staff or pupils with a bespoke day of activities at Ynys Hywel.

AUTHOR'S REVIEW 

Having featured this attraction in the last Top 100 Attractions in Wales Book back in 2015, Ynys Hywel has changed somewhat and I truly think for the better. Having loved the site last time, I absolutely love it this time and with a brand new team at the helm, great things are on the way for this activity & nature centre. Depending on how big a group you are, they can cater for all groups of varying sizes, from small families, to school groups, nothing is out of their remit. What I have always liked so much about Ynys Hywel, is that it allows families come together and be families, instead of being stuck on a mobile device of some sort, families can come and experience the outdoors and see just exactly what being a family means. The facilities are good, the food is great and the staff really know what they're doing, so what are you waiting for?

Cwmfelinfach, Newport, Caerphilly, NP11 7JD

Llechwen Hall & Restaurant

t: 01443-742050 e: enquiries@llechwenhall.co.uk
www.llechwenhall.co.uk

Set on a stunning hilltop location surrounded by magnificent views of the Welsh countryside, Llechwen Hall Hotel is one of the best kept secrets in the heart of the Cynon Valley. "Llechwen", a traditional Welsh word, translates as "White Slate" and it is thought that at some time in Llechwen Hall's history, the building's roof was constructed with beautiful white slate. Originating as a charming country house, Llechwen Hall first became a hotel in 1990. In previous years the hall has had a variety of uses, from being a farm house, to a private Welsh long-house and once, even a small primary school.

Current ownership of the hotel started in 2008 and since then Llechwen Hall has become a well established venue with a reputation for good food, friendly service, great weddings and overall a luxurious Country House Hotel.

After a significant expansion and refurbishment, the hotel has 44 stylish and charmingly appointed bedrooms.

All of the rooms are beautifully equipped with shower or bath facilities, and a lift grants access to the 1st floor guest rooms. There is a wide variety of accommodation styles, including: Standard, Executive and Four-Poster rooms, all with wide screen LCD televisions and complimentary WiFi to make sure you are kept connected.

Holding an AA Rosette for the past 5 years, there is an extensive A la Carte and Brasserie menu for all tastes and dietary requirements, including inventive vegan, vegetarian, and gluten free dishes.

The team of Chefs are passionate about using local produce, and are part of the Blas Cambrian Taste route from South to North Wales. The hotel also produces it's own organic honey, which is used in their dishes.

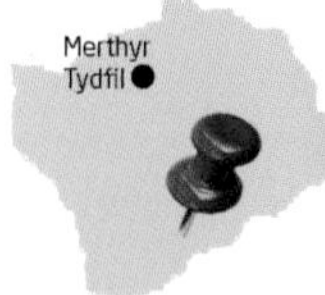

Llanfabon, Nelson, Pontypridd, CF37 4HP

Bedwellty House & Gardens

t: 01495 353370 e:bedwelltyhouse@aneurinleisure.org.uk
www.bedwelltyhouseandpark.co.uk

Bedwellty House and Park is a vibrant and historic venue managed by Aneurin Leisure, which combines classical elegance and state of the art facilities to provide an array of unique spaces, perfect for hosting an array of large and small scale events, making it the ideal setting for celebrations and corporate events of all sizes. Our Orchid House Tea Room provides a cosy and family friendly space in which to enjoy a range of delicious refreshments, homemade lunches and of course our famous Afternoon Teas.

Team Building

We understand that when a team has fun, they grow stronger and become more cohesive, so with that in mind we have a selection of puzzles and challenges designed to test existing teams as well as train new ones.

Civil Wedding Ceremonies & Civil Partnerships

If you're dreaming of having your wedding in an elegant and idyllic setting that will provide cherished memories for years to come, Bedwellty House & Park is the perfect venue for you.

AUTHOR'S REVIEW

The South Wales Valleys areas are abundant of new attractions, so many more than when I visited the area four years ago. One of those great attractions that went under my radar last time is Bedwellty House, Gardens & Parkland in the industrial town of Tredegar. Built in 1800, this house has well over two hundred colorful years under its belt, all of which can be learned about whilst on your visit. Once home to the political giant Nye Bevan, the politician responsible for many great things, one of which is the NHS, various Bevan memorabilia can be found dotted all over the house. Then there is the parkland, which I have to say is looking absolutely stunning, complete with its majestic trees, shadowing this beautiful home. All in all, I cannot recommend a visit to Bedwellty enough and a visit here isn't complete without a visit to its Orchid tearoom, which is great for afternoon tea or a light lunch.

Merthyr Tydfil

Morgan Street, Tredegar, Gwent, NP22 3XN

Bedwellty Park

At Bedwellty House & Park we offer a creative Educational Programme that covers a range of topics ıcluding the Victorian period which focusses on the life of Samuel Homfray, the Ironmaster and ccupant of Bedwellty House in 1851.

Our programmes are extremely flexible and can be covered as a whole day visit or a half-day ses-on; our sessions are tailor made to meet the requirements of each school, allowing us to adapt the ogramme depending on the number of children and the duration of the visit. In addition to this e are also happy to put together a specific programme if you would like to focus on a different pic to the ones already on offer.

s well as the Victorian programme, we also offer a range of other sessions, all of which are jam cked with hands on activities and crafts which the children can take home, including:
iry Fun
itable for Foundation Phase
rate Adventures
itable for Foundation Phase
bitats
itable for Foundation Phase & Years 3 and 4
onderful Woodlands
table for Key Stage 2
ssert Island Escapades
table for Key Stage 2
asonal Visits
ictorian Christmas Experience, Santa's Grotto and Breakfast with the Easter Bunny.

James' Place @ Brynawel

Brynawel, Queens Road, Merthyr Tydfil, Glamorgan, CF47 0HD

T: 07791-884237 www.jamesplaces.wales E: info@jamesplaces.wales

James' Place @ Brynawel Guest House Includes boutique hotel accomodation or a stylish self catering apartment set in a period Victorian House. Come and crash @Brynawel Pen Y Ty, fully equipped with ensuite and kitchen so you really can 'make yourself at home' Pen y Ty means top of the house, which gives this studio amazing character and superb views over the Merthyr valley. The studio is fully furnished with a super king sized bed, bistro table, desk, smart TV and sofa bed. The kitchen comes with everything you need (and probably somethings you don't!). The modern ensuite has a walk in shower, toilet and basin. Come and relax @Brynawel's Blue Room, tastefully decorated in a french style with blue toile de jouy wall paper and an antique cane bed. Our Blue Room has superb views over the valley.

The Coach House

2 Twyn Sych, Rudry, Caerphilly, CF83 3EF

T: 029-20884772 www.coachhouserudry.wales E: enquiries@coachhouserudry.wales

For over 20 years travellers have enjoyed our warm welcome in the heart of the Welsh countryside, the home of idyllic views and breathtaking scenery. 3 Star Bed & Breakfast with all the comforts of home. With a choice of continental style or cooked breakfast, our accommodation options include: Single, double, twin and family en suite rooms (each with TV and tea/coffee facilities) - Free WIFI - Central heating - Private parking - Pet friendly at management discretion (prior arrangement required). Our location gives easy access to many amazing cultural heritage sites, areas of outstanding natural beauty, Cardiff, the South Wales Valleys and the M4. We look forward to your arrival.

Studios at Glenthorne

The Grove, Merthyr Tydfil, The Valleys, CF47 8YR

T: 01685-722205 www.studiosatglenthorne.co.uk E: enquiries@studiosatglenthorne.co.uk

Based in Merthyr Tydfil, the heart of the Welsh Valleys and the gateway to the iconic Brecon Beacons, Studios at Glenthorne is a new take on the traditional B&B. Truly feel at home while you are away with all the amenities you need with in your hotel room. Each of our Studios come equipped with a kitche en-suite shower room, double bed, wardrobe, desk, bistro table, Wi-Fi and flat screen TV. Studios at Gl thorne are available for single and double occupancy, there is a sofa bed available for triple occupanc in the larger studios. There is no minimum booking restrictions and we also offer a delicious continen breakfast with granola, yoghurt and croissants with butter, jam, marmalade and fresh fruit juice, at an additional cost.

The Lamb & Flag

Wellfield Place, Glynneath, Neath Port Talbot, SA11 5EP

T: 01639-721995 www.lambandflagglynneath.co.uk E: thelambandflag@googlemail.c

The Lamb & Flag has re-opened its doors after the unfortunate blaze. Now fully refurbished along wi new function room, letting rooms and a bright and comfortable bar/restaurant seating area. We now offer a full and varied menu from delicious classics to daily specials. We also have a beautiful large garden with a very picturesque setting, and recently opened childrens play area.

We are situated 2 miles from Pontneddfechan, which is on the edge of the Brecon Beacons National Park, which boasts very many splendid waterfalls and some fantastic walks.ooms include Full English breakfast served between 8.30-9.30am.Arrival/Departure - The bedroom accommodation is available from 15:00 on the day of arrival, and must be vacated by 10:00 on the day of departure, unless specif alternative arrangements have been made. We don't supply hairdryers in the rooms.

The Prince of Wales Inn

Merthyr Road, Princetown, Tredegar, Caerphilly, NP22 3AE

T: 01685-844441 www. princeofwalesinn.freeindex.co.uk

The 'Prince' is a traditional pub incorporating many of the old values of local history in pictures and other items. A 40 covers restaurant is ideal for a party or reception and is also used for our popular Sunday Carvery. In the lounge Mondays and every other Friday around 20 good singers enjoy a great night with our keyboard player. The central log fire is a great attraction on a cold winter night with a few local beers and locally sourced steaks. Each room includes a TV and tea and coffee making facilities. The rooms also benefit from an en-suite bathroom. Fridges, electric heaters, and ironing supplies are available upon request. Guests at the Prince of Wales Inn can enjoy traditional bar meals in front of the log fire in the lounge bar. Dishes include Welsh steak.

Wern Ganol Guest House

Wern Ganol Guest House, Caerphilly Road, Nelson, CF46 6PS

T: 01443-450413 www.wernganolguesthouse.co.uk E: mail@wernganol.co.uk

Set in it's own grounds and enjoying panoramic views of open countryside Wern Ganol has been providing bed and breakfast accommodation in Caerphilly County for 40 years. With 6 comfortable en suite rooms on ground level, a large private off road car park and a pub across the road serving good food. Wern Ganol provides home from home comfort with a warm, friendly atmosphere and a great breakfast. Wern Ganol is an ideal location for business or pleasure. With local tourist attractions such as Caerphilly Castle, Llanciach Fawr, Castle Coch, and The Brecon Beacons National Park. Dedicated guests only fast free fibre wifi. Rooms are serviced daily between 10.30 am and 12.00 pm. All our rooms are situated on ground level with no steps. Large free off road car park.

James' Place @ Dowlais

28 High Street, Merthyr Tydfil, Glamorgan, CF47 8DP

T: 07791-884237 www.jamesplaces.wales E: info@jamesplaces.wales

James' Place Dowlais consists of 8 individually and creatively styled self-catering studios. They are ideally placed for exploring the Brecon Becons, climbing Pen-Y-Fan or visiting Bike Park Wales amongst many of the other great activities in the area or for working away from home. They are only a 5mins drive from the town centre and there is a bus stop right outside which can take you to the main train and bus station. Each studio has a separate but en-suite Kitchenette with all the essentials and Shower-Room. We also like to provide a few luxuries with Soap & Glory complimentary toiletries, a pint of milk and freshly baked home-made welsh cakes to welcome you to Wales.

Bedlinog Inn

High St, Bedlinog, Treharris CF46 6TG

T: 01443-710996 www.bedlinog-inn.co.uk

The Bedlinog Inn is a luxury bed & breakfast accommodation in the beautiful Welsh village of Bedlinog, South Wales. Our accommodation is second to none. On arrival, you will find a friendly and attentive service that will ensure you have an excellent experience staying with us at our luxury B&B. The Inn has been extensively refurbished to the highest of contemporary standards. For many guests, what makes staying at our B&B so special is the little details we offer our customers, to ensure your stay is the experience you want it to be. Whether it is the luxurious feel of the high quality bed linen and towels, the tailored range of complimentary drinks and small snacks available in all rooms, or the specialised toiletries, these luxury details are what set us apart from other B&B's. We know you will have good memories after staying with us.

James' Place @ The Brecon Becons

3 Pant-y-Dwr Llwyn-On, Merthyr Tydfil, CF48 2HS

T: 07791-884237 www.jamesplaces.wales E: info@jamesplaces.wales

This is our latest addition to James' Places which we are delighted and proud to offer as both family anc dog friendly accommodation! It has been creatively refurbished to make the most of the spectacular views and provides the perfect retreat for exploring The Brecon Becons, climbing Pen Y Fan, hiking through water fall country or even working away from home. The cottage can sleep 8 with a modern, stylish interior and a great outdoor space to make the most of the countryside. It is set in idyllic countryside far away from the "maddening crowds". The house has been extended at the back providing a spacious, open ground floor so you can sit back and gaze at the stars through the glass atrium or throw open the bi-folding doors to welcome in the countryside. We have searched high and low to find interi design touches that will bring a smile to your face.

James' Place @ Pontmorlais

3 Pant-y-Dwr Llwyn-On, Merthyr Tydfil, CF48 2HS

T: 07791-884237 www.jamesplaces.wales E: info@jamesplaces.wales

James' Place@Pontmorlais offers individually and creatively styled self-catering studios. They are ideally placed for exploring the Brecon Becons, climbing Pen-Y-Fan or visiting Bike Park Wales amongst many the other great activities in the area or for working away from home. They are right in the town centre a minutes walk from the main train and bus station.

Each studio has a separate but en-suite Kitchenette with all the essentials plus en-suite Shower-Room. We also provide a few surprising luxuries with Soap & Glory complimentary toiletries, a pint of milk an freshly baked home-made welsh cakes to welcome you to Wales.

The Grange Guest House

Pontycapel Road, Cefn-Coed-y-Cymmer, Merthyr Tydfil, Gwent, CF48 2PB

T: 01685-359750 www.thegrangecefncoed.wales E: stay@thegrangecefncoed.wa

The 150 year old Cefn-Coed viaduct, formerly the Merthyr to Brecon Railway and now part of the Taff Trail, provides a stunning backdrop to the house which is continued inside with spacious guest areas and 5 en-suite guest bedrooms. At The Grange we offer everything you need to have a stress free brea in the wonderful South Wales countryside. To have a great holiday you need a great night's sleep and all of our luxurious rooms are just the thing to wind down after a long day on the bike or exploring th local area. All of our rooms have super comfortable Hypnos beds, en-suites, Panasonic 32 inch flat-screen TVs. Fast, free wi-fi is available throughout the house. The quoted rates are per-room per-night and include our fabulous breakfasts.

Ty Shon Jacob Farm B&B

Coch-y-North Lane, Tranch, Pontypridd, NP4 6BP

T: 07950-961110 www.accommodationinpontypool.co.uk E: agneta@tyshonjacobfarm.co

We have the most beautiful, breath-taking riding country. If you are an experienced rider, we have ou own homebred horses for you to use on your rides round the mountains. There are many planned wa in the area. Pontypool Park, 180 acres of wood and parkland with features such as the shell Grotto an the restored Folly Tower, has a well equipped Leisure Centre with swimming pools, hydroslides, fitnes facilities, badminton courts, squash courts, gymnasium, bar, cafeteria, and a 265 meter Ski Slope, the second longest in Wales. Some units feature a seating area and/or a balcony. A continental breakfast available every morning at the property. The bed and breakfast offers a terrace. Guests can relax in th garden at the property.Big Pit National Coal Museum is 7.5 miles from Ty Shon Jacob Farm.

The Colliers Arms

Efail Fach, Pontrhydyfen, Port Talbot, Glamorgan SA12 9TY

T: 01639-643187 www.colliers-riverside.co.uk E: info@colliers-riverside.co.uk

The Colliers Arms is a warm and welcoming traditional village pub with excellent dining facilities. The Riverside Restaurant has French doors that open onto a balcony above the River Pelenna. It boasts an extensive menu and serves generous portions. The Colliers Arms is also renowned for its Sunday lunches. The Colliers Arms is situated on the B4287 halfway between Neath and Port Talbot. Pontrhydyfen is well known as the birthplace of the actor Richard Burton, but nowadays it is lucky to be situated in the Afan Forest Park with its many walks and cycle tracks. Glyncorrwg Ponds are a magnet for fishermen and also for cyclists.There are two other Country Parks in the area – Margam Park and Gnoll Park. There is also the bonus of a long sandy beach at Aberavon.

The Bunch of Grapes

Ynysangharad Rd Pontypridd, Mid Glamorgan CF37 4DA

T: 01443-402934 www.bunchofgrapes.org.uk E: info@bunchofgrapes.org.uk

We like to think the Bunch of Grapes is how a great pub should be, a friendly welcoming bar serving award winning ales ciders and bottled beers in front of a roaring log fire with a restaurant attached that also serves award winning food. 'A pub that was awarded 'Dining Pub of the Year' for the whole of the UK in 2016 as well as Britain's Best Sunday Dinner.' Using locally sourced seasonal produce with creativity and flair but without pretence. A pub where you are likely to walk in to a beer festival one day with a Welsh choir in full voice and return another to find a Welsh cheese and cider festival in the main bar. Where you can enjoy a home made pie and mash in the bar with a pint of Welsh ale while cheering on the Welsh rugby and then return with friends to a fine dining meal in the restaurant .

Bedlinog Inn

High St, Bedlinog, Treharris CF46 6TG

T: 01443-710996 www.bedlinog-inn.co.uk

The best of gastro pub food is balanced with a menu of pub classics in a contemporary setting that resonates with a traditional pub atmosphere. Whatever the time of year you will find something really tasty to complete your day's experience. The Bedlinog Inn's restaurant is an open plan design with contemporary wooden furnishings and ambient lighting. The best of gastro pub food is balanced with a menu of pub classics in a modern setting that has a traditional pub atmosphere. A diverse menu draws inspiration from classical, gastro pub dishes and is punctuated with weekly specials that are based on seasonal ingredients. Whatever the time of year you will find something really tasty to complete your day's experience.

Jols

30-31 High St, Merthyr Tydfil CF47 8DP

T: 01685-267878 www.jolsrestaurant.co.uk E: info@jolsfoodco.co.uk

Merthyr Tydfil is on the culinary map for the first time. People used to visit this great town for its industrial heritage and its position as the gateway to the Brecon Beacons. Now chef Jamie O'Leary is drawing visitors from all over the country wanting to try the delicious dishes at JOL's restaurant which is being compared to Michelin starred restaurants. Customers are surprised and amazed that Merthyr can for the first time boast of having a top class restaurant. For Jamie it is a dream come true."I grew up here and like everyone else I had to travel miles for a quality meal. My vision was to create something special here on our doorstep. I am delighted that people love coming here and that my food is winning a reputation far and wide."

Brynffynon Hotel & Restaurant

Llanwonno, Ynysybwl, Pontypridd, Rhondda Cynon Taf, CF37 3PH

T: 01443-790272 www.brynffynonhotel.com E: brynffynonhotel@hotmail.co.uk

Situated in the little hamlet of Hafod Ddreiniog, The Brynffynon is a traditional family run hotel in t tiny village of Llanwonno. Built in the 17th century as a small workmen's public house, its present o ers who purchased the Brynffynon in January of 2008 have endured to keep the rustic, traditional appearance whilst modernising key facilities to provide a warm, welcoming environmer The Brynffynon menu is driven by rustic, simple dishes, with the best ingredients we could find loc and seasonal too – made with care but delivered without lots of fuss. We'll be making fresh homer dishes every day, serving the most beautiful desserts and our aim is create a place where you'll fee at home, tucking into any combination of great food. Sit back with the comfort and heat of a real fi and why not try our daily selections of Welshcake, flapjacks, and fruit loaf!!!

The Crown Inn

Main Road, Llanwit Fadre, Pontypridd, CF38 2HL

T: 01443-218277

The Crown Inn in Llantwit Fardre known, fondly in the area as 'The Crown', has been serving the community as the 'local' since 1851 according to the census of that year. During the decades since, landlords and landladies have come and gone, the colour of the outside and the furnishings inside changed, but the pub still remains a major part of the community. fine food is available at reasonab prices, ranging from a simple lunch or a Sunday roast to a special evening menu and occasional eve There is also a separate specials board and children's menu. There is a special 'Steak Night' on Satur when you can get 10% off the price of any of our steaks. A function room is available for larger part Real ale is available at the bar along with a good selections of ciders, lagers and a great wine list, in ing a few cheeky numbers from the southern hemisphere.

The New Crown

Llanwonno, Ynysybwl, Pontypridd, Rhondda Cynon Taf, CF37 3PH

T: 01685-387925 www.thenewcrownmerthyr.co.uk E: info@thenewcrownmerthyr.cc

We are a vibrant town centre pub located on the High Street in Merthyr Tydfil. Having built up a gre reputation for our live music we are also proud of our quality food and drink offer and thoroughly e doing what we do. With a passion for quality and service we endeavour to make sure that you have great time every time you visit. We offer a contemporary menu featuring breakfasts, light bites, gril traditional classics as well as speciality dishes offering a taste of Portugal. A separate children's mer also available. We're well known for our live music and entertainment.

WE ARE OPEN Mon-Fri 9am – 12midnight - Sat 10am – 12midnight - Sun 12noon – 12midnight

FOOD SERVED Mon-Sat 12noon – 9pm (Unless stated at the bar otherwise) Sun 12noon – 7pm

The Crispy Cod

168 Gelli Road, Gelli, CF41 7NA

T: 01443 434888 www.thecrispycod.co.uk E:mathew@thecrispycod.co.

he Crispy Cod was founded by Mathew Williams in 2008. It was created with the concept of providi the freshest and finest food in the Rhondda Valleys.

The shop found amazing success within the local community and became the pinnacle of takeawa food. Above all the core belief of the freshest and the finest is at the heart of all food prepared and cooked at The Crispy Cod.

Mathew set his sights on building a restaurant that provided a warm and welcoming atmosphere v a 5* service. The sit-in restaurant in Gelli was a huge success and provided the local community wit gourmet experience.

It's very hard to know which county you are in whilst venturing round Wales, as one is just as stunning as the other, until of course you come to Cardigan, or Ceredigion as the locals would now like it to be known! With its gigantic sweeping sea cliffs, rolling hills, quaint villages and its vibrant nightlife, Cardigan Bay and the wider county of Ceredigion, is very unique indeed. I spent a few very pleasant days here, met some wonderful people, tasted some outstanding food and it didn't rain once either! Don't get me wrong though, I'm not saying it never rains here in Cardigan, but what I am saying is that no matter what the weather, Cardigan has something to offer come rain or shine.

If your considering driving from North Wales to South Wales, one would be forgiven for being tempted into driving via England, down the M6 to Birmingham, M5, M42, M40 corridor and then take The M4 direct to South Wales! However, we all have to be strong and not give in to our temptations. Let me take you a more refreshing way! Depending where in North Wales you are leaving from, let's say Llandudno ok! Here goes, A470, A487, A40! Thats it! 3 roads! Ok it may add about half an hour onto your journey? But boy it's worth it! Rolling hills, sweeping cliffs and with a cute town or village dotted along the way, you'll be spoilt for choice when it comes to the 'where do we stop for food' question? There's always been a strong rumour that Welsh people are rude and don't like the English or visitors of any description really, but that couldn't be further from the truth here in Wales, they love tourists and more the merrier in my experience!

The Silver Mountain Experience

01970-890620 info@silvermountainexperience.co.uk
silvermountainexperience.co.uk

Where history, myth and legend collide in a fantastic day out for the whole family. Set against the dramatic Cambrian Mountains, The Silver Mountain Experience is not your usual day out. Experience guided tour A Miner's Life, which takes visitors on a fascinating journey through the oldest part of the uniquely preserved silver-lead mine. Explore Welsh myth and legend in our theatrical experiences such as A Dragon's Tale and the mysterious Black Chasm (not for the very young or faint-hearted!). New attraction Time Lab features an interactive show for all the family, delving deep into the freaky facts and twisted tales linked to this unique silver mine. As well as our fantastic theatrics, you won't want to miss what else we have on offer. Discover our Mining Museum, let your imagination run wild in Woo Hoo Woods, go gem panning, den building, dig for fossils and much more. So what are you waiting for? Come and explore!

AUTHOR'S REVIEW

The Silver Mountain Experience is only several miles away from a couple of our other Top 100 Attractions, Devil's Bridge & Falls and The Vale of Rheidol Railway, which in my opinion could all be done on the same day. This award winning attraction really does have it all, as well as being 'Value for Money" the trip underground was both informative and educational, and the tour guide really did know his stuff which always makes a difference. It's now after my visit, very apparent why people are itching to film at Llywernog as did the BBC's 'Countryfile' team a few years ago. With loads to see and explore there's a lot to occupy yourselves with, and what makes it extra special is that apart from the underground tour you are pretty much left to your own devices. Which as you will see the kids love? As if that wasn't enough the surrounding area at Llywernog is breathtakingly beautiful so once you're done at the mine go and explore the surrounding area.

Aberystwyth

Ponterwyd, Aberystwyth, Ceredigion, SY23 3AB

Borth Wild Animal Kingdom

01970-871224
tracytweedy@hotmail.com
borthzoo.co.uk

On a little hill by the sea, overlooking the beautiful Ceredigion coastline, sits this haven for exotic animals and home for rescued pets.

Just a short walk from Borth railway station and the beach it's a place where you can get up close and personal to over 100 different species of animals, birds, reptiles and insects to learn about them and gain a better appreciation for all kinds of wildlife. Join us for an intimate animal experience and a day to remember for all the family. We want to bring you closer to these animals and give you a better understanding of how they would live in the wild if their habitat wasn't being destroyed. We actively support and raise funds for the Chinko Project which tries it's best to protect wilderness areas in Central Africa. The zoo will be undergoing major modernisation over the next few years with plans to open up the hill and give the animals larger, more interesting enclosures where they can live in comfort.

AUTHOR'S REVIEW

As human beings, we have always had a wild fascination with animals from all over the globe and here at the Borth Wild Animal Kingdom, you can get more up close and personal with that wild fascination. With all sorts of animals here, this zoo brings in and cares for rescued animals that wouldn't usually be housed in normal zoos, We have featured the zoo here in Borth in two previous Wales books and now with new owners, I am very confident that when I return after this third edition, knowing just some of their great plans, I'm sure they will of done great things here. Having met the Tweedy family and they're close team, I have every confidence that they will make a huge success of this attraction. Finally, the Borth Wild Animal Kingdom and Borth itself have a very special place in my heart and I couldn't recommend a visit more.

Aberystwyth

Devil's Bridge Falls

t: 01970-890233 e: visit@devilsbridgefalls.co.uk
www. devilsbridgefalls.co.uk .co.uk

Devil's Bridge Falls is a world famous tourist attraction just 12 miles inland from Aberystwyth. The 300ft waterfalls have attracted thousands of visitors since the 18th century, including William Wordsworth who wrote about the 'Torrent at the Devils Bridge'. The Nature Trail consists of a narrow, steep path which leads visitors through the ancient woods down to the bottom of the gorge and back up again. There are breathtaking views of the waterfalls along the way and an opportunity to see the 3 Bridges. A minimum of 45 minutes is required for this walk. A shorter 10 minute walk to see the 3 Bridges and Punchbowl is an easier option. Open all Year. Refreshments and Welsh Crafts are on sale nearby from Easter to the end of October. Enquire for entrance fee.

AUTHOR'S REVIEW

There are devils bridges all over the world from Europe to South America, built mainly in medieval times. But what makes this Devil's Bridge so different from the rest is that three bridges coexist here, each one built above the next. This attraction has been enticing tourists for hundreds of years and once you've visited too, you will see exactly why! As if the bridges weren't enough of an attraction there are the waterfalls to see as well. Devil's Bridge is served by Devil's Bridge railway station on the historic narrow-gauge Vale of Rheidol Railway, which opened between Aberystwyth and Devil's Bridge in 1902. The railway is also featured in this book and both attractions compliment each other nicely. When doing our research on the bridge and falls we wondered why the entrance fee for such an attraction was so low. After my visit, it became very apparent that the new owners of the site don't just see the bridge and falls as a money making scheme, and want as many people as possible to enjoy them like thousands of people have before them.

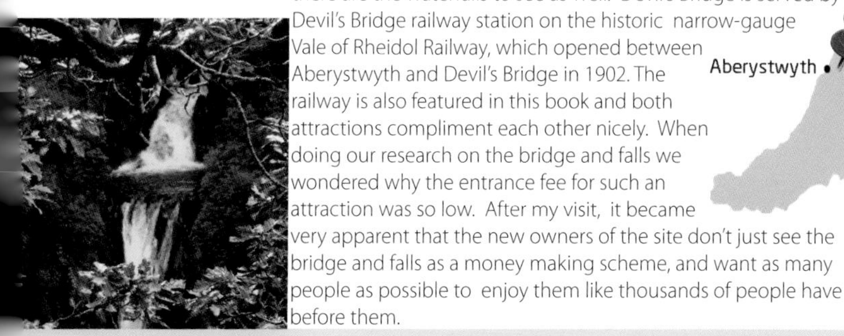

odlands, Devil's Bridge, Aberystwyth, Ceredigion, SY23 3JW

Aberystwyth Cliff Railway

01970-617642 manager@aberystwythcliffrailway.co.uk
aberystwythcliffrailway.co.uk

The northern end of Aberystwyth promenade, Constitution Hill, rises dramatically from the sea, providing spectacular and uninterrupted views of the town, Cardigan Bay, and on a clear day 26 mountain peaks spanning much of the length of Wales. The most relaxing way to enjoy this majestic panorama is to travel by train on the longest funicular electric cliff railway in Britain, which has been transporting visitors to the summit since opening in 1896. The recently refurbished summit train station has just been completed, providing much better protection from the elements and updating the structure to ensure a better visitor experience. Once at the summit visitors can experience the views afforded by the one of the world's largest camera obscura, which offers a bird's eye view of 1000 square miles of land and seascape. Aside from these two technological masterpieces there are fascinating historical displays, a kids play area, a well-stocked gift shop, and a cafe selling delicious home-made snacks.

ATHOR'S REVIEW

The Victorians really were an age of bold and innovating people. Building a railway that went up a cliff, or a mountain for that matter was no trouble to them. It is for that reason that we chose the Aberystwyth Cliff Railway as one of our Top 100 attractions in Wales. Being the longest funicular electric cliff railway in Britain, you really are in for a treat as you take your seat in the carriage of this unique attraction. Being quite scared of heights myself, I was full of trepidation before the carriage moved, but as we started to move, I really did feel quite at ease. As we made our way slowly up to the top, the views really were quite magnificent. Once at the top I was surprised to see that these old facilities have now been renovated to a very high standard, and with a lovely cafe style restaurant, lunch at the top is a must.

Aberystwyth

Cliff Terrace, Aberystwyth, Dyfed, SY23 2DN

The Yurt Farm

t 01974-821594 e info@theyurtfarm.co.uk
www theyurtfarm.co.uk

The Yurt Farm is a small eco friendly glamping site on our organic family farm in West Wales.
In a wildflower meadow we have handcrafted four yurts and a beautiful train carriage for you to stay in.
Help yourself to wood for crackling campfires under clear night skies or to keep your stove roaring. Fire up the pizza oven for an evening feast with friends. We provide everything needed to make your yurt holiday comfortable and enjoyable.
Watch dolphins in Cardigan Bay, walk in the Cambrian Mountains, watch red kites, cycle country lanes, meet the farm animals, taste really fresh vegetables from the farm shop and collect eggs for breakfast.
You'll love it... we do x

AUTHOR'S REVIEW

The Yurt Farm has to be Ceredigion's biggest and brightest of all of its hidden gems. Being a totally family run business, consisting of Thea, Laurie and their wonderful children, the Yurt Farm offers an escape from the usual reality of your normal life and within a setting that's as idyllic as can be. As if their state of the art yurts weren't enough of an attraction, dotted all over their 150acre Estate, are lovely little footpaths and farm trails that the kids will undoubtedly love to explore all day long. I had the good fortune to spend a small amount of time with Laurie and Thea and sampling their wonderful baked banana bread and after even that small amount of time, I was totally convinced I had to feature the Yurt farm as an attraction and not just as an accommodation provider in Ceredigion's 'Sleep Tight' section of this chapter.

Aberystwyth

The Yurt Farm, Crynfryn, Penuwch, Tregaron, Ceredigion, SY25 6RE

Libanus 1877

01970-617642 ibanus1877@icloud.com
libanus1877.com

Libanus 1877 recently opened in March 2017. We have transformed this beautiful building from a rustic Welsh Chapel to a modern, welcoming restaurant and boutique cinema. Inside you will notice that display the fantastic and intricate work of our local artist Muriel Delahaye.
We want you to experience delicious locally sourced cuisine and sit back in comfort in our boutique cinema.
Our boutique cinema has been installed with a 4K projector. We have 60 comfortable seats, positioned perfectly so that you can enjoy the film or live streaming from every corner of our cinema. We have also two seats which are catered for our customers who have accessibility needs.

AUTHOR'S REVIEW

Libanus 1877 was recommended to me by another attraction, that's when I knew this place was going to be special, I just didn't realise how special. After redeveloping the small art gallery also in the village, Peter Fleming Libanus's owner just didn't stop there. He set out to then restore this typically old Welsh Chapel and turn it into a first class restaurant serving top quality food. But Peter didn't even stop there, he then carried on to include within the buildings design, a state of the art 60 seater cinema that pulls in the crowds from far and wide, not just because of the films that it shows, but because it's absolute luxury. Libanus 1877 and it's owner have well and truly excelled themselves and thus why you now see it as one of our Top 100 Attraction in Wales. We love this little place and we're truly sure you will to, but don't just take our word for it, call in and have a look for yourselves.

Aberystwyth

Gerlan Chapel, High Street, Borth, Ceredigion, SY24 5JA

RSPB Ynys-hir

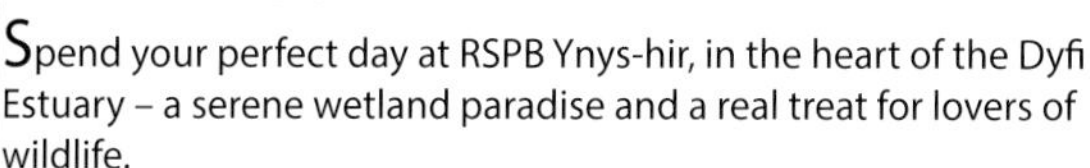

t 01654-700222 e ynys-hir@rspb.org.uk
www rspb.org.uk/ynys-hir

Spend your perfect day at RSPB Ynys-hir, in the heart of the Dyfi Estuary – a serene wetland paradise and a real treat for lovers of wildlife.

Trails will you take you through Welsh oak woodlands, reedbeds and down to the saltmarsh. In spring, the ground is carpeted in flowers, and birdsong fills the air. You might see pied flycatchers and redstarts emerging from the nestboxes. Summer brings wading birds, such as lapwings and redshanks, and some very special butterflies too. Then in the colder months, ducks and geese move in.

Pick up an explorer kit and have a go at pond dipping – children will have so much fun discovering all kinds of interesting creatures. After visiting the hides – find the ideal spot for a picnic or relax in our visitor centre, with a cup of coffee and home-made cakes.

AUTHOR'S REVIEW

Only a hop skip and a jump away from the Snowdonia National Park, is RSPB Ynys-hir. I would always suggest that when visiting an RSPB reserve, that you wear not only suitable clothing, but more importantly footwear, and I cannot stress this anymore than here at Ynys-hir. If I were you, and before you attempt to visit a particular reserve, to check the very informative RSPB website, which will always give you an up to date idea of both the weather, and if any diversions to trails that have recently been put into place. I guarantee you that once you've visited Ynys-hir, you will want to visit it time and time again, such is the magic of this reserve.

Aberystwyth

New Quay Honey Farm

01545-560822 info@thehoneyfarm.co.uk
thehoneyfarm.co.uk

There are lots of reasons to visit New Quay Honey Farm - a fantastic location in its own valley near New Quay, an Exhibition that shows you the life of the honeybee, with live exhibits behind glass; a shop selling honey from the Farm's 600 odd hives, mead made in its own meadery, and a tea room which serves locally sourced food of the highest quality; as well as the wildlife walk and picnic area. The honey Farm was started in 1995 to bring the beautiful honey of the area to a wider public and to share with visitors our fascination with the incredible life of the honeybee, the world's most studied insect. THE EXHIBITION spreads over the whole of the top floor of the converted chapel and shows the life of the honeybee and its importance in a combination of video displays, interpretation boards, and five live exhibits of actual full sized colonies of honeybees. THE SHOP sells a wide range of honey and honey products as well as books about bees, wildlife and nature, candles and other beeswax products. THE MEADERY also has a small exhibition and you can sample the meads in the shop. THE TEA ROOM serves many items made with our own honey, alongside the best the area has to offer, together with a great cup of tea or coffee.

AUTHOR'S REVIEW

Never before have I met two people so dedicated to what they do as Gerald & Mariana Cooper. It is clear to see that this is just, so much more than a tourist attraction to them. It is their life, their passion, and they want to share that passion with as many people as possible. We have Farm Parks in this book and they are the 'Crème De La Crème' of farm parks! But what makes the Honey Farm so unique is, it's all about one insect, an insect that we often don't think too much about, but we should, for honey is used in far more than we imagined and it's all to be learned about here at New Quay Honey Farm. Then there's the tearoom, which is a treasure trove of some of those products that are made from the very bees here at the farm. So for a completely unique and fascinating experience, plan a visit here, you will not be disappointed, and you won't be able to help yourself when it comes to taking a souvenir away with you!

Aberystwyth •

Cambrian Safaris

t: 01974-261425 e: richard@cambriansafaris.co.uk
www.cambriansafaris.co.uk

Discover the Wild Tranquillity of Wales with us.
Cambrian Safaris offer tours of the Cambrian Mountains (all day or half day) or all of Wales in a Land Rover Discovery.
We aim to show you places you will want to go back to again and again.
Discover the 'Picturesque Hinterland' of Ceredigion's uplands, including locations used in the BBC series 'Hinterland'. Farming, forestry, moorland, small lakes, the historic estates of the Ystwyth and Rheidol Valleys and surrounding area with numerous old mines. Tour the wider Cambrian Mountains byroads, drover's roads and the Elan Valley reservoirs.
Your guide has extensive knowledge of local areas, so CONTACT US to arrange a tour for you to enjoy spectacular landscapes, local history, wildlife and one view after another. A relaxing day out with no pressure of time, we can pick you up from your accommodation if you wish. Tour All of Wales with us for 2 or more days.

AUTHOR'S REVIEW

Little is known nationwide, let alone worldwide about the Cambrian mountains, as they can sometimes get overshadowed by their big brother the Snowdonia mountain range. Thanks to a selective amount of people this is now being corrected. Two of those selective few are both Richard & Hester Smith, together they have both established 'Cambrian Safaris'. When I first heard about this great idea I had to investigate further. After spending some time with Richard, it was clear to me that not only would it be great to feature them in this new edition of the Top 100 Attractions in Wales book, but it would be a huge honour. I have not met anyone that is as passionate and enthusiastic as what Richard isabout this special part of Mid Wales. I can assure you, that the onlyway to see this area of Wales is by taking a Cambrian Safari.

Aberystwyth

Tan Felin, Llanafan, Aberystwyth, Ceredigion, SY23 4BD

Dà Mhìle Distillery

01239-851 998
damhile.co.uk
sales@damhile.co.uk

As you arrive at the farm, you will enter straight onto our yard, between the main house, the dairy of Caws Teifi Cheese, our cow shed and milking parlour, and of course the distillery. We will then take you around the distillery, showing you all parts of the process from brewing, through to distilling, bottling, labelling and the warehouse where we age the whisky in an array of rare casks.
Once you're here, nothing is too much trouble, all questions will be answered to the best of our abilities and you will be as close to the equipment as the distillers. We even invite you to put your head inside the still so long as we're not distilling at the time! If we are distilling while you're there, then you can taste the alcohol straight from the still. Created sustainably from the wood found on the farm (trees fall every year in the typical Welsh winters), our gallery was hand built by a team of locals and help from our neighbours, not a single crane was used to put the many Oak beams into the ceiling.
"The highlight of this tour is the tasting room, located on the top floor of the building, with the top of the still column protruding into the room from below. In the center is a rustic solid wood table with each of the spirits that Da Mhile has produced, from the original 22 year old organic Springbank commission, Loch Lomond Malt and grain releases, through to the gin, seaweed gin and orange liqueur."

AUTHOR'S REVIEW

Whisky has been distilled in Wales since the Middle Ages, that is a well known fact, but what isn't so widely known, is that from a small farm in Wales, organic seaweed gin amongst many other botanicals, are starting to not only win awards, but have caught the eye of Royalty no less. Here at DÀ MHÌLE distillery, you can take a tour around the distillery itself, learn all about how the process takes place and even have a taste of the many products that they very cleverly produced here in Ceredigion. On the day I arrived, I took a tour around the distillery itself and although I don't drink alcohol myself, I have to say I thoroughly enjoyed it. I think the tour is value for money, very informative and offers a huge insight into the very clever world of distilling. So whether you drink or not, the tour has something to offer everyone.

Aberystwyth

Glynhynod Farm, Llandysul, Ceredigion, SA44 5JY

Gwenhwyfar Garden

t: 01239-810593 e: gorslwyd@aol.com
www: gwenhwyfargarden.com

Gwenhwyfar Garden is a place of inner & outer transformation, where both the seeds and weeds of life's journey, are sown & woven together, birthing the richness each precious life has to bring to our world. As children in a garden, we look and wonder at each flower, helping each soul recognise the beauty and meaning in all life's experience, learning from the richness and meanings common in indigenous cultures, though somehow lost from our own ancestral ways. We bring together those ancient threads to weave a sound blanket within which you can explore your right to heal. Your retreat is tailored to meet your needs. In times of crisis, you deserve a compassionate and understanding safe space within which to heal. Our aim at Gwenhwyfar Garden is provide a compassionate and healing space within which, we can tailor to meet your individual needs. To enable equal access, we have a number of bursaries every year for those with low income. We also have a number of energy exchange options.

AUTHOR'S REVIEW

As I travel throughout Wales and uncover the many great attractions that there are to visit, I stumble upon many that are so special, it is sometimes very hard to put into words just how special they are, take Gwenhwyfar Garden for instance. Thinking I was initially coming to see a normal but quite high end accommodation provider, I was greeted by its owner Jenni Chapter. I have to say that Jenni is no normal human being. I know that may sound strange to hear, but she isn't. From the minute we met, I knew she was one of life's special people and one who is completely selfless, selfless to of created this amazing garden and retreat that people can come and enjoy whenever they need to. Gwenhwyfar Garden isn't the biggest Garden in the world, but it has a big personality and when visited, you get to take a piece of that special personality home with you.

Gorslwyd Farm, Tan-y-Groes, Ceredigion, SA43 2HZ

Cardigan Island Coastal Farm Park

01239 623 637
info@cardiganisland.com
cardiganisland.com

Cardigan Island Coastal Farm Park is located in the southern part of Cardigan Bay on a picturesque headland overlooking the Teifi estuary, Pembrokeshire Coast National Park and of course the nature reserve of Cardigan Island which is home to an array of bird life and just 200 metres offshore. Part of Clyn-Yr-Ynys Farm, the Farm Park was set up in 1993 and it is very much a family run business.
Say hello to our various farm animals; enjoy our fenced clifftop walk to the headland from where you can watch Atlantic grey seals or spot dolphins; browse in our gift shop, with a selection of toys as well as local and Welsh crafts; children will enjoy our indoor and outdoor play areas; have a bite to eat in our cafe and enjoy the scenery; or stay a little longer at our campsite.
We hope you enjoy your visit!

AUTHOR'S REVIEW

We have some of Wales's most famous famous attractions within this book, but we also have some of the countries biggest hidden gems. Take the coastal farm park here in Cardigan for instance. There is a wide variety of your usual every day run of the mill farm animals, but then and this is what took me completely by surprise, is the huge amount of animals that you wouldn't usually associate with a farm park, like grey seals and bottlenose dolphins, making this coastal farm park one of its kind. I absolutely loved my visit here and the views of the island are just truly spectacular. Another thing worth mentioning, is the camping and caravanning park which is situated adjacent to the coastal farm park. With excellent onsite facilities, staying here means you get to wake up and witness one of Wales's best coastal views, whilst sat having your breakfast.

Aberystwyth •

SA43 1PR

Fantasy Farm Park

t: 01974-272285 e: fun@fantasyfarmpark.co.uk
www: fantasyfarmpark.co.uk

At Fantasy Farm Park there is a heated indoor play area for toddlers, with ride on equipment, inflatable slides, ball pit and the usual bright and colourful soft play frame with features for the smalls (and the not-so-smalls) to go nuts on! Facilities include a couple of cool castle themed bouncy castles, double level climbing maze and huge crooked orange slide! Ideal for under 7s. Outside they have a petting zoo with a nice range of old favourites for the smalls to coo at, where they can get hands on at certain times with some of the cuddlier species on display. Everyone will love taking a spin around the go kart track and for older types there's also a rodeo bull so why not get down with your cowboy (or girl) side and challenge your parents to a contest on it?! Family restaurant on site with children's menu too so if you don't bring a picnic (or you crave a hot coffee!) then you're still sorted.

AUTHOR'S REVIEW

Anybody who's anybody, attraction wise is in my book, from Cardiff Castle to Portmeirion. Zip World to the Snowdon Mountain Railway. But it's not just the big attractions that we are proud to endorse, it's the small guys also, take The Fantasy Farm Park by the way! This nnocent but fun place is one of our hidden gems that we are proud to endorse! With its educational 'Animal Barn' to the peaceful, calm and serene 'Nature Trail' The Fantasy Park is a must for anyone visiting Ceredigion. This is a true family run business, run totally with families at its core values and the parks owners Lloyd and Diana have worked tirelessly to make this attraction one that gets people returning time after time and believe me, they certainly do! The staff are friendly and they really do go that extra mile, what more could you ask for out of a Top 100 attraction. No seriously, you'll love it here and every family that I saw here on the day I visited, really did look like they were having a great time! I know I did!

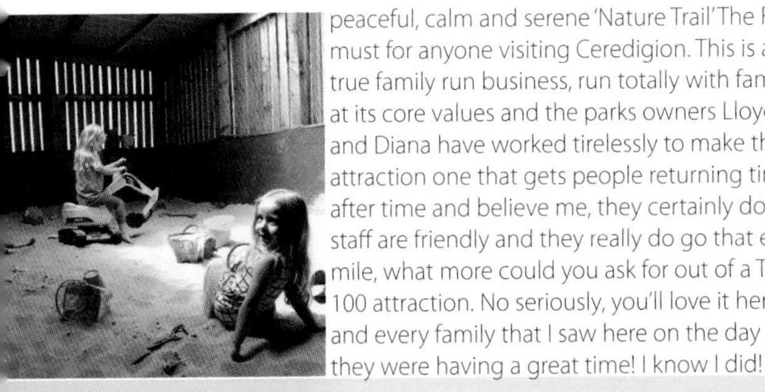

Aberystwyth

Llanrhystud, Aberystwyth, Ceredigion, SY23 5DA

Maesglas Uchaf - Bed & Breakfast

Ysbyty Ystwyth, Ystrad Meurig, Ceredigion SY25 6DD

T: 01974=282571 www.maesglasbandb.co.uk E: info@maesglasbandb.co.uk

Maesglas Uchaf (Welsh translation: highest green field), is a modern chalet bungalow, on the edge of the village of Ysbyty Ystwyth. The location and elevation ensure outstanding scenic views in every direction. The village of Ysbyty Ystwyth is situated about 15 miles inland from Aberystwyth; Devil's Bridge is 5 miles to the north and Tregaron 8 miles south. Our guest bedrooms, both on the first floo are spacious and comfortably furnished. They provide views of the Ystwyth Valley and open countryside, are centrally heated and double glazed. Each has a comfortable seating area with television and a hospitality tray providing: a selection of tea's, hot chocolate, filter coffee and biscuits

Gwesty'r Marine Hotel & Atlantic Apartments

Marine Terrace, Aberystwyth, Ceredigion SY23 2BX

T: 01970-612444 www.gwestymarinehotel.co.uk E: info@gwestymarinehotel.co.uk

Located on the picturesque promenade of Aberystwyth, the Marine Hotel is a relaxed, friendly hotel close to the town centre. We aim to provide all of our guests with excellent facilities, home-cooked traditional food and a warm service. The hotel has deluxe Jacuzzi suites with wonderful views over Cardigan Bay. There is a range of bedrooms to suit all needs, such as disabled friendly and special pet friendly bedrooms. ALTANTIC BALLROOM to seat 240, sea view DINING ROOM seating 120. Wedding conference facilities up to 400 persons, parking & free WiFi. Croeso cynnes i pawb. If you are looking accommodation in Aberystwyth town, then the Marine Apartment & Studio is the perfect self-cateri accommodation for you! Both apartments are modern and airy, and have a high standard.

Blue Grass Cottages B&B

Brynglas Farm, Chancery, Aberystwyth, Ceredigion, SY23 4DF

T: 01970-612799 www.bluegrasscottages.co.uk E: blue.grass@lineone.net

Blue Grass Cottages B & B Suites offers you 'Bed and Breakfast' with a difference - your own luxury, warm, cosy cottage suite with the breakfast being served within. We are situated on a small working farm, just a short drive from Aberystwyth - in the hamlet of Chancery - in the heart of Cardigan Bay. T Granary Cottage Suite has a Twin bedroom and a single bedroom. The Stable Cottage Suite has a Kin bedroom and a single bedroom. Free Wireless internet throughout : 4K Smart TV lounge/dining room Fully equipped kitchen. :Tea/Coffee facilities with fresh milk. En-suite bathroom with shower over the bath : Complimentary toiletries.Hair dryer : Alarm Clock : Radio and CD player. : Ample off road parking. Soar Cottage Suite has a double, twin and a single bedroom.

Bryncarnedd Country Cottages

Clarach Road, Aberystwyth, Ceredigion. SY23 3DG

T: 01970-612444 www.aberholidaycottages.com E: info@aberholidaycottages.com

Bryncarnedd was once a busy dairy farm, providing milk for Aberystwyth and the surrounding area. Since its demise, the farmhouse and its surrounding buildings have been sympathetically converted into self catering holiday cottages. The 10 cottages, named after traditional farm buildings, vary in size sleeping from 2 to 10 persons, with 1 to 3 bedrooms – and each one uniquely decorated and furnished with luxurious fittings to provide the perfect accommodation for your holiday away. Most of the cottages have en-suite bedrooms, some of the cottages have patios and gardens, while others have Jacuzzi baths to relax and enjoy. All of the cottages have an open plan layout, enabling you to cook, eat and live in a bright and airy environment, making the most of you valuable time together.

Myrddin Townhouse

Brynglas Farm, Chancery, Aberystwyth, Ceredigion, SY23 4DF

T: 01970-612799 www.bluegrasscottages.co.uk E: blue.grass@lineone.net

Our beautiful Townhouse is situated in a quiet cul-de-sac next to the Marina and just around the corner to South Beach in the coastal town of Aberystwyth. It is conveniently located for the castle and walking into the town for the shops, cafe's, restaurants, pubs, railway and bus stations. The house can sleep up to 11 people in 6 bedrooms - 2 King, 1 double, 1 single and 2 twin rooms - 1 being on the ground floor. 3 bathrooms - one on each floor. Games Room - suitable for children and adults. 4K Smart Television lounge with log effect fire. Separate dining room. Fully equipped kitchen. Rear enclosed courtyard garden with outdoor furniture and BBQ. Garage use for storage purposes - kayak's, canoe's, beach items etc. Free on street parking.Towels are supplied, beds made up ready together with day to day stuff.

The Hafod Hotel

Devil's Bridge, Aberystwyth, Ceredigion SY23 3JL

T: 01970-890232 www.thehafod.co.uk E: hello@thehafod.co.uk

Our Bar, Brasserie and Hotel is located in an exceptional location. Situated only steps away from the World Famous Devil's Bridge waterfalls and a two minute walk to the award winning Rheidol Valley steam train. The mountains are all around where you can step into the wild landscapes of the Cambrian Mountains and enjoy the nearby breathtaking views of the Elan Valley. All close by are walking trails, horse riding, fishing, biking, Kite feeding, steam trains and beaches. We have 16 bedrooms, including one suite, one family room and three twin rooms. Spend a relaxing night enjoying the views over the gorge with the waterfalls in the distance. We are very proud to offer our guests local, seasonal produce all prepared by our Head Chef, Elena. Elena is passionate about preparing creative, fresh produce and particularly enjoys making yummy desserts.

Llety Teifi Guesthouse

Pendre, Cardigan, Ceredigion, SA43 1JU

T: 01239-615566 www.lletyteifi-guesthouse.co.uk E: lletyteifi.co.uk@outlook.com

Llety Teifi has 10 en-suite bedrooms available as guest accommodation. Each bedroom has been designed to offer our guests a comfortable stay, full sized beds with leather or suede headboards, crisp cotton linen, fluffy towels and a Welsh welcome tray with tea and coffee making facilities and biscuits. The in room facilities include complimentary Broadband internet connections, flat screen freeview T Vs, Clock radios, irons, ironing boards and hairdryers – CD Players and refrigerators are available from reception for you to use during your stay. Each bathroom has a heated towel rail and a power shower ensuring a refreshing start to the day. The deluxe bedroom has an oversized chrome bed and the bathroom has the added luxury of a corner Jacuzzi bath. What an excellent way to spoil yourselves!

Cwmwythig Guest House

Capel Bangor, Aberystwyth, Ceredigion, SY23 3LL

T: 01970-880640 www.cwmwythigbedandbreakfast.co.uk E: pwllcclai.holidays@talk21.com

Located 4 miles east of Aberystwyth, just off the A44. Come and relax at this beautiful farmhouse overlooking the Rheidol Valley with it's panoramic views and quiet countryside. The dining area is traditionally furnished with a Welsh oak dresser, where you can enjoy a hearty Welsh farmhouse breakfast. You can sit and relax in our spacious lounge with television and DVD player.
We have two ground floor bedrooms that are beautifully furnished and well appointed, one double en-suite room and a twin bedroom with private bathroom. Upstairs there is a twin en-suite bedroom; a double bedroom; and a triple bedroom. The family bathroom has a corner bath and a shower cubicle. All bedrooms have a television, tea and coffee making facilities and free internet access.

Cwmwythig Holiday Cottages

Capel Bangor, Aberystwyth, Ceredigion, SY23 3LL

T: 01970-880640 www.cwmwythigbedandbreakfast.co.uk E: pwllcclai.holidays@talk21.com

Cwmwythig Farm offers Bed & Breakfast and luxury Self Catering Cottages just a few miles from Aberystwyth on the West Wales coast.

Located in the quiet countryside with panoramic views, a perfect spot to relax and unwind or to use as a base to go off exploring the region. The cottages have been converted to a high standard from old stone barns.

We are a family business and a working dairy farm with Holstein Friesian Cattle. You are welcome to watch us milking the cows and feeding the calves.

Woodlands Caravan Park

Devils Bridge ,Aberystwyth, Ceredigion, SY23 3JW

T: 01970-890233 www.woodlandsdevilsbridge.co.uk E: enquiries@woodlandsdevilsbridge.co.u

The Woodlands is a well established, family run caravan park set amidst some of the most beautiful scenery Mid Wales has to offer. It is situated in Devils Bridge, a small village nestling at the top of the Rheidol Valley, 12 miles inland from the coastal town of Aberystwyth. It is an ideal base for touring Mid Wales, walking, cycling, mountain biking, birdwatching, fishing or just relaxing and taking in the fresh air. The Touring Park is quiet and picturesque, and is away from the static caravans. It has both level hard ground and grassy pitches. Electric hook ups and TV aerial points are available if required.

The Starling Cloud

Boulevard De Saint Brieuc, Aberystwyth SY23 3TL

T: 01970-623743 www.starlingcloudpubaberystwyth.co.uk

E: StarlingCloud.Aberystwyth@marstons.co.uk

Welcome to The Starling Cloud—a family-friendly, new-build pub and lodge serving restaurant-style food in a relaxed setting. Our 27 rooms include family rooms, double rooms, and accessible ground-floor rooms. Whether it's our famous rotisserie chicken, flame roasted to crisp and tender perfection in our rotisserie oven, or a pub classic done well, you're sure to find something to tempt on our carefully-curated menu. As a real ale pub, we also serve a selection of fine cask ales, well-kept and served along-side our draught products, wines, and soft drinks. For our younger visitors, we have a secure outdoor children's play area, an indoor play zone, and a colourful children's menu featuring plenty of favourites

Penybont Bed & Breakfast & Holiday Cottage

Llangorwen, Clarach, Aberystwyth, Ceredigion, SY23 3DW

T: 01970-820159 www.penybontbb.co.uk E: john@penybontbb.co.uk

The Penybont B&B is located in peaceful countryside just 2 miles from Aberystwyth. Just one mile fro the beach at Clarach Bay the Penybont offers rooms with free Wi-Fi and free parking.

Rooms at this 19th-century Welsh cottage have TVs with Freeview, hairdryers and radios, and are en-suite. They also include tea/coffee making facilities. Traditional and continental breakfasts are serv daily.

There is also a two-bedroom, self-catering cottage with an open plan living room and fully equipped kitchen, with laundry facilities and an WC.

The University of Aberystwyth and Aberystwyth Railway Station are within a 5-minute drive of the be and breakfast. There is a good selection of shops, restaurants and bars in the city centre.

Cardigan Island Caravan & Camping

Gwbert-on-Sea, Cardigan, Ceredigion, West Wales, SA43 1PR

T: 01239-623637 www.cardiganisland.com E: info@cardiganisland.com

Cardigan Island Coastal Farm Park is located in the southern part of Cardigan Bay on a picturesque headland overlooking the Teifi estuary, Pembrokeshire Coast National Park and of course the nature reserve of Cardigan Island which is home to an array of bird life and just 200 metres offshore. Part of Clyn-Yr-Ynys Farm, the Farm Park was set up in 1993 and it is very much a family run business. There are a variety of friendly farm animals to see including pigs, sheep, goats, rare breed cattle, ponies, chickens, rabbits, guinea pigs and Dilwyn the donkey. There is also Llinos the llama and Bruce the emu from far-off lands. A small colony of Atlantic grey seals breed in the many caves located within the cliffs of the Farm Park, and can be seen virtually every day the park is open.

Brig y Don

Coronation Drive, Gwbert, Cardigan, Ceredigion, SA43 1PP

T: 07814-035728 www.brigydonwales.co.uk E: relax@brigydonwales.co.uk

Brig y Don, Welsh for 'crest of the wave' is a beautifully appointed house that takes full advantage of its spectacular cliff top location. It sleeps upto 8 people in 4 bedrooms all with en-suite facilities. The views from all the living areas and master bedroom provide an ever changing backdrop to your holiday that will always be remembered. *Uninterrupted panoramic sea views across Cardigan Bay to Poppit Sands and the crests of North Pembrokeshire

* Beautifully designed and immaculately furnished luxury holiday cottage * All bedrooms have en suite facilities * Spacious patios to enjoy al fresco dining and memorable sun sets

Enclosed, family friendly garden.

Four Seasons Hotel

Portland Street, Aberystwth, Ceredigion, SY23 2DX

T: 01970-612120 www.fourseasonshotel.net E: info@fourseasonshotel.net

Located in the middle of Aberystwyth, the Four Seasons Hotel is perfectly situated for those looking to explore the town and local area. The hotel is only 200m from the Victorian promenade, and 500m from the Pier, where during the summer you can dine outside and enjoy the views, or during the winter months enjoy the breath taking displays by the local starlings. The Four Seasons has a courtyard terrace at the rear and a traditional restaurant open all year round. The cosy bedrooms all have a fresh feel and modern decor, creating a bright environment for you to relax during your break away or the perfect atmosphere for you to work if you are staying on a business trip. All bedrooms feature a flat screen TV, as well as tea and coffee making facilities and private bathroom.

YHA Borth

Morlais, Borth, Ceredigion, SY24 5JS

T: 01970-612120 www.yha.org.uk E: borth@yha.org.uk

Overlooking Cardigan Bay with the chance of seeing dolphins and seals and just 20 metres from a beautiful sandy beach, this Edwardian house is perfect for a UK coastal holiday and is ideal for cheap family breaks or school trips in Wales. Don't miss the amazing petrified forest which is visible at low tide. FREE WI-FI available in communal areas for guests! YHA Borth has 60 beds and both private and en-suite rooms available. This Edwardian house oozes character and is perfect for family coastal breaks in Wales.

Nine of our 11 bedrooms have sea views.

Cardigan Bay Guest House

63 Marine Terrace, Aberystwyth, Ceredigion, SY23 2BX

T: 01970-600420 www.shelleyguesthouse.co.uk E: shelley-guesthouse@hotmail.co.uk

The Cardigan Bay Guest House is perfectly situated on Aberystwyth promenade. The majority of our rooms offer uninterrupted sea views where dolphins can be seen on a regular basis.
We have 13 rooms in total. They are located on 3 floors. Ideal for reunions, celebrations etc.
Facilities in the rooms include: flat screen TV (most rooms), hair dryer, free broadband and hospitality tray.
Breakfast can be purchased for an additional £4.50 per person.

Celtic Bay Guest House

62 Marine Marine Terrace, Aberystwyth, SY23 2BX

T: 01970-600420 www.celticbayguesthouse.co.uk E: shelley-guesthouse@hotmail.co.uk

Celtic Bay Guest House is a dog-friendly establishment on the seafront in Aberystwyth which offers se catering facilities, a large kitchen, dining room and a lounge with television. All rooms have television and tea and coffee making facilities using fine organic coffee and infusions. Many rooms have wonderful sea views and en-suite facilities. Free Wi-Fi is available throughout the property and parkin is available either outside the property (subject to availability) or at the North Road Car Park (1 minute walk away). The property has a selection of double en-suite, twin and single rooms and the property is also available for guests wishing to book the whole of the property for large family events and reunions.

Black Lion Hotel

Glanmor Terrace, New Quay, Ceredigion, SA45 9PT

T: 01545-560122 www.blacklionnewquay.co.uk E: enquiries@blacklionnewquay.co.u

The Black Lion Hotel is New Quay's Family Friendly Historic Inn. With stunning sea views and gardens with play areas why not enjoy a relaxed meal. We have nine spacious en suite rooms with five having fantastic sea views. Complete with crisp white bedding, beautiful local made furniture including slei beds and tea and coffee tray for your convenience. Breakfast is included in your room price and is se from 8-10 am [earlier if requested] in the hotel restaurant overlooking the sea. The emphasis is on gc quality and good value food, prepared in our own kitchens and locally sourced. Everything from our home made lasagne to our delicious burgers is made in house and our top quality Welsh Black and R Eye Steaks are all Celtic Pride.

Over the Rainbow Vegetarian Country Retreat

Plas Tyllwyd, Tanygroes, Nr Cardigan, Ceredigion, SA43 2JD

T: 01239-811155 www.overtherainbowwales.co.uk E: info@overtherainbowwales.co.u

A restored Georgian mansion providing a haven of rural seclusion tucked away down a long farm tra close to the pristine Cardigan Bay coast and Pembrokeshire National Park. You can stay B&B for some well earned time out, or hire the venue exclusively for small group holidays, residential retreats, fami celebrations and wedding receptions. Enjoy a relaxed stay in a country house nestled amongst acres woodland and gardens with idyllic views across the rolling Welsh countryside. Here you can comple unwind and relax just watching the stars and listening to the silence.We offer well appointed, sumptuous centrally heated bedroom accommodation including single, double or twin ensuite roo with décor reflecting influences of female myths & legends from around the world. Guests also have use of a communal guest lounge and large dining room. A warm welcome awaits you.

3 Pen Cei, Guest House

3 Pen Cei, Quay Parade, Aberaeron, Ceredigion, SA46 0BT

T: 01545-571147 www.pencei.co.uk E: stay@pencei.co.uk

Aberaeron is a charming seaside town charcaterised by pastel coloured Regency properties. The award winning 3 Pen Cei Guest House is situated on the harbour front only metres away from the historic Aberaeron Harbour and the stunning Cardigan Bay coast. Spoil yourself in the sumptuous beds, luxury bedlinen and quality facilities with its eclectic mix of old and new.
Aberaeron is blessed with many good restaurants providing the finest food from locally sourced ingredients. A warm Welsh welcome awaits you, and John and Lesley are at hand to tell you about the delights and opportunities for activities ranging from walking, cycling, angling and sea fishing.
3 Pen Cei is an ideal base for experiencing a taste of Wales.

Highcliffe Hotel

School Road, Aberporth, Ceredigion, SA43 2DA

T: 01239-810534 E: reception@highcliffehotel.co.uk

Set in the peaceful West Wales village of Aberporth this idyllic 16th Century traditional hotel provides a tranquil and relaxing get away from the hubbub of the modern world.
Origionally built as a ship owner's residence in 1820, this family run hotel is perfect for walkers, couples and families as it is located just 150yards from two golden sand beaches.
The hotel sits on a stretch of coastline in Cardigan Bay with some of the best coastal walks in Ceredigion. Be ready to relax with a home cooked meal in our cosy bar or restaurant and enjoy a glass of wine or two!
The Highcliffe provides an ideal base for a seaside holiday or for those touring Wales.

The Seven Stars

Llechryd, Cardigan, Ceredigion, SA43 2NR

T: 01239-682115

Seven Stars Inn in Llechryd offers cosy accommodation and a full Welsh breakfast in this small village around 3 miles from the picturesque town of Cardigan. There is a large bar and restaurant, as well as private parking and free Wi-Fi. Rooms at Seven Stars are decorated in a modern style and all have a TV. Each has tea and coffee facilities and an en suite bathroom. The property has a large beer garden and terrace area to enjoy meals from the restaurant or drinks from the bar. In addition to breakfast, the guest house can also prepare packed lunches on request. Llechryd is approximately 8 minutes' drive from Cardigan, which has several places to eat out, as well as many small shops and well-known stores. Among the area's other attractions, Pembrokeshire Coast National Park is less than 30 minutes' drive.

Fron Farm Fishery B&B

Bontnewydd, Ceredigion, SY23 4JG

T: 0800-050 241 www.fronfarmfisheryholidays.co.uk E: info@fronfarmfisheryholidays.co.uk

Fron Farm Fishery is a family run B&B close to Aberystwyth, Mid Wales, nestled in the beautiful Welsh countryside, enjoy our beautiful scenery. With a 30 minute drive to the coastal town of Aberystwyth, 30 minutes from Lampeter and 30 minutes from Aberaeron. An Ideal location if you are visiting the local universities and don't want to stay in the town. Relax in our large spacious lounge with a roaring fire. We offer two large double bedrooms, both with en-suite all on the ground floor. Our guest rooms are accessed by the level hallway. Both bedrooms are large, light and airy and are decorated to a high modern standard offering en-suite facilities. Our beds are made up with duvets and cotton sheets. Our standard pillows are foam, however alternatives are also available.

Beachfront Apartment

25 Bath Street, Aberystwyth, SY23 2NN,

T: 01970-639270 www.aberaccommodation.com E: maesymor@hotmail.co.uk

Beachfront boutique serviced apartment. Newly refurbished on aberystwyth seafront relax in comf and enjoy the view from the lounge looking out to the beach and promanade and the famous starl by the pier. Lounge with 50 inch smart tv, kitchen fully equipped with fresh milk in fridge and ice ir freezer. Various teas and coffee, hot chocolate , caffitere and horlicks. Double bedroom with docking station and radio. dressing gowns and slippers, bathroom with funky toiletries, flannels , flu towels, free wifi, water ,chocolate and biscuits.
WARM WELCOME TO ALL CROESO CYNNES

The Cliff Hotel & Spa

Gwbert, Cardigan, Ceredigion, SA43 1PP

T: 01239-613241 www.cliffhotel.com E: reservations@cliffhotel.com

The Cliff Hotel & Spa is a large family-owned hotel where warm, friendly welcome, excellent facilitie and the highest standards of service and cleanliness ensure that your stay is a most pleasant one.At 73 en-suite bedroom hotel, we offer first-rate facilities for those looking for a break, romantic get-aw special occasions, family holiday, business travellers, conference organisers, those getting married o looking for a place to eat and drink in comfort.With expansive, beautiful hotel grounds, the Cliff Hot and Spa is located on the coast of Cardigan Bay overlooking Poppit Sands and Cardigan Island. This perfect holiday destination to explore the West Wales' beautiful Ceredigion and Pembrokehsire Coa With excellent spa facilities you can unwind and enjoy the facilities and treatments provided at the

The Royal Oak Hotel

38 High Street, Lampeter, Ceredigion, SA48 7BB

T: 01570-218615 www.royaloak.wales E: theroyaloaklampeter@gmail.com

Located in Lampeter, The Royal Oak Hotel offers a bar. Among the facilities of this property are a res rant, room service and a shared lounge, along with free WiFi. Every room is equipped with a terrace All units at the hotel are equipped with a seating area and a flat-screen TV. All rooms will provide gu with a wardrobe and a kettle.
A continental breakfast is available daily at The Royal Oak Hotel.
You can play darts at the accommodation, and the area is popular for hiking and cycling.
Aberystwyth is 24.2 miles from The Royal Oak Hotel, while Carmarthen is 23.6 miles away.

Caemorgan Mansion

Caemorgan Road, Cardigan, Ceredigion, SA43 1QU

T: 01239-613297 www.caemorgan.com E: guest@caemorgan.com

David and Beverley host our recently refurbished Luxury 5 Star Gold Guesthouse. Just a short drive f the beautiful Cardigan Bay coastline and set in a quiet location on the outskirts of historic Cardigan Our Mansion Guesthouse is ideally positioned for both the business traveller and the more discernir vacation customer Our bedrooms are fully fitted with Super kingsize beds, Egyptian Cotton linen, duvets, flat screen large LED TV, desk, Wifi and broadband network, Tassimo tea and coffee machine alarm/radio, superior towels and bathrobes. Our extensive gardens are undergoing landscaping an provide a quiet distraction from the daily grind. Your stay with us is sure to exceed your expectati and help to persuade you to return again and again to this beautiful part of Wales and Cardigan Bay.

The Red Lion Inn

Saint Mary Street, Cardigan, Ceredigion, SA43 1DD

T: 01239-800999 www.redlioncardigan.co.uk E: info@redlioncardigan.co.uk

The Red Lion Inn is situated in a quiet residenual part of Cardigan's old town in Pwllhai / St Mary Street 75 yards from the banks of the River Teifi. After becoming a free house The Red Lion has gone though a very high specification refurbishment. This entailed being closed for a period and the result of the refurbishment has given The Red Lion Inn four modern ensuite bedrooms, new cooking facilities, and a cousey dining area for breakfast.The bar area has been transformed, concentrating on sports, we have all the sports channels showing live sports on four 49" flat screen TV's, accompanied with surround sound. Also in the bar area are two dartboards and a pool table, there's also wood burner for the cold nights and to the rear a very secluded beer garden that is a sun trap during the summer months.

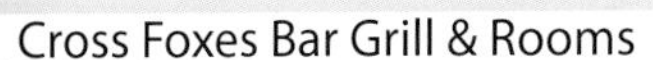

Cross Foxes Bar Grill & Rooms

Brithdir, Dolgellau, Gwynedd, LL40 2SG

T: 01341-421001 www.crossfoxes.co.uk E: hello@crossfoxes.co.uk

We are nestled at the foot of Cadair Idris Mountain and 4 miles from the historic town of Dolgellau, South Snowdonia. Our Grade II listed building offers you the perfect opportunity to relax, indulge and explore the Welsh Mountains, Coast and Heritage. We are graded as Gold (exceptional) by Visit Wales and recognised by the Good Food Guide. We have been awarded with a prestigious award by the Alistair Sawday's Special Pub with Rooms and voted by The Independent as one of Britain's Top 50 Country Pubs. We are very proud to offer our guests local, seasonal produce all prepared by our Head Chef, Kyle Wilkinson. Kyle is passionate about preparing creative, fresh produce and particularly enjoys making yummy desserts. With over 10 years, experience of working in high quality gastro pubs and recently shortlisted for the Welsh Culinary Association Awards, Kyle will be sure to not dissappoint you!

Nanteos Mansion

Rhydyfelin, Aberystwyth, Ceredigion, SY23 4LU

T: 01970-600522 www.nanteos.com E: info@nanteos.com

Located between the majestic sweep of Cardigan Bay and the rolling Cambrian Mountains, excellent road links take you along the scenic coast road to nearest town of Aberystwyth or deep into the breathtaking Welsh heartland. If the tranquillity of our location doesn't immediately touch your soul, then the opulent décor, sumptuous rooms, fine dining and discreet, attentive service will surely combine to cast aside the realities of everyday life. At Nanteos it's all about you. Somewhere to come and go as you please; where privacy is assured and where time, if you want it to, stands still. At Nanteos it's all about you. Somewhere to come and go as you please; where privacy is assured and where time, if you want it to, stands still.

Gwel y Mor Country Guest House

Gwel-y-Mor, Llanilar, Aberystwyth, Ceredigion, SY23 4PJ

T: 01974-241028 www.gwelymorcountryguesthouse.com E: gwelymor@hotmail.com

Gwel Y Mor Country Guest House is located in a stunning valley in Aberystwyth. Free WiFi access is available. Each room here will provide you with a TV and access to a patio and a terrace. Certain rooms have private bathrooms whilst others have shared bathroom facilities.

At Gwel Y Mor Country Guest House you will find a 24-hour front desk, a garden and barbecue facilities. Other facilities offered at the property include a shared lounge and an ironing service. The property offers free parking.Central Aberystwyth, with its famous castle, is 5 miles away. Brecon Beacons National Park is 42 miles from the property.

The Grosvenor

Green St, Cardigan SA43 1HY

T: 01239-613792

Located just across the road from the historic Cardigan Castle, The Grosvenor offers a great range c food and drinks to suit all tastes in a picturesque and convenient location for those visiting Cardiga Town. Relax and take in the views of Cardigan Quay and the River Teifi from our terrace or enjoy th comfort of our recently refurbished bar area. Open for lunch and dinner, we have an extensive mer ranging from sandwiches and snacks to pub classics such as beer battered cod and chips, or why n try our Sunday Carvery? We regularly host fabulous theme nights with live music and hold our gre value Steak Night every Friday. With a range of welsh beers and ciders available, The Grosvenor is t perfect place to relax and enjoy the laidback West Wales atmosphere.

Café Mariner

South John St, The Pier, New Quay , SA45 9NP

T: 01545-560467

Café Mariners is located in the idyllic fishing village of New Quay. Serving traditional fish and chips homemade specials, your usual favourites and all day breakfasts a good reputation has been gaine for quality food. Recently voted the best fish and chips in Ceredigion for 2012 a warm welcome aw you in Café Mariners and our take away fish and chip shop whether it's just a coffee, snack, ice crea or full traditional meal we cater for all.

Review 5 Star(Trip advisor)

Brilliant piece of cod!That was the best piece of cod I have ever had fried!! Thoroughly delicious. M Crispy And flavoursome. Well worth a visit and the curry sauce is summit else, 10/10.

The Blue Bell Deli & Bistro

The Pier, S John St, New Quay , SA45 9NW

T: 01545-560444 www.thebluebellnewquay.co.uk E: thebluebelldelibistro@gmail.

The Blue Bell Deli&Bistro is located in the most beauiful spot in New Quay. Sit back and enjoy the breath taking views from one of our balconies we only use the freshest ingredients to create wholesome delicious dishes. Our beautiful wine bar is perfect for parties, business meetings, funct & other festive events.

Please call for more details on buffet & afternoon tea pricing.We strive to produce the most flavour some & delicious dishes to tantalise your taste buds. Sourcing only the freshest and seasonal ingredients from our local producers.

The Hive

Cadwgan Pl Aberaeron, Dyfed, SA46 0BU

T: 01545-570445 www.thehiveaberaeron.com E: info@thehiveaberaeron.cor

The Hive Grill offers an American style menu with a European influence, with a variety of dishes on from burgers, steaks, fish and shellfish. The Hive kitchen is run by Jason Jones, our Head Chef who has a passion for using the freshest produce to prepare the style of food we all love to eat....

The Hive bar is open throughout the day from 10am in the morning, until late in the evening. Why try one of our cocktails whilst relaxing in our conservatory and watch the world go by. The Hive is t home of the famous Honey Ice Cream. Made on the premises by our master Ice Cream makers Kevi and Mateusz.

Uncle Albert's Cafe & Ice Cream Emporium

Gwynfryn, High Street, Borth, Ceredigion, SY24 5HZ

T: 01970-871166 E: gogsbrielle@hotmail.co.uk

Borth's centre for ice cream indulgence and wholesome homemade food. Our food is all made on site, entirely vegetarian, and we always have a vegan and gluten free selection. We serve breakfast, lunch, snacks, lots of salads, cakes, organic coffee and award winning Welsh ice cream. In 2013 we won the Gold Healthy Options Award from Ceredigion County Council.

Trip Advisor reviews*****Lovely surprise to find such a great cafe. Lovely quirky cafe with great coffee, food and ice cream. Very welcoming and just delicious food. If you are in the area there are some very boring typical sea-side cafes, so try this one instead:-)

The Summer Grill

8 Cadwgan Place, Aberearon, Ceredigion, West Wales, SA46 0BU

T: 01545-570120

The wonderful Summer Grill restaurant. The Summer Grill provides breakfast to all of our guests and offers a wide selection of cooked and continental options, including the popular vegetarian option Welsh Lava Bread.

Guests can enjoy a relaxed morning start in the extremely comfortable restaurant, with its own share of harbour views.

The Summer Grill is also open for evening meals from 5.30pm offering a selection of steak, fish and tapas. For more information call 01545 570033

Cletwr

Tre'r Ddol, Ceredigion, SY20 8PN

T: 01970-832113 www. cletwr.com E: cletwr@cletwr.com

It's cheering that so many who are driving through the parish along the A487 are stopping for a bite to eat and telling us they are pleased to find the cafe open again and serving such lovely coffee and snacks. The caffi now serves a range of excellent home-made cakes, as well as soup, sandwiches, breakfasts (meaty and veggie) and other light snacks. Ceredigion Tourism has given another seal of approval by appointing Siop Cynfelyn a tourist information point where visitors can get a range of tourist leaflets. We also offer "small plates, for small people" but actually we don't mind if you're 4 or 94, you're still welcome to try them out.Brought man's best friend with you? Well behaved dogs are welcome in our covered outdoor seating area.

Medina

10 Market Street, Aberystwyth, Ceredigion, SY23 1DL

T: 01970-358300 www.medina-aberystwyth.co.uk E: info@medina-aberystwyth.co.uk

The creation of Medina was inspired by people like the wonderful Ottolenghi, and by the foods Medina herself loves to cook and eat at home. She wanted to bring something different to Aberystwyth - somewhere where super fresh and simple food is put together imaginatively and displayed beautifully! Medina has a very informal cafe vibe, delicious fresh food served all day, great coffee, beautiful Chinese loose teas - and it's fully licensed of course. We serve a wide selection of dishes from delicious home baked breads and dazzling mezze to fabulous salads and spectacular desserts - and everything you see here is available to take away! We've gathered a selection of exciting products from far and wide including artisan beers and independently produced wines, jars of delicious spices and spreads.

Crwst

Priory Street, Cardigan, Ceredigion, SA43 1BU

T: 01239-611278 www.crwst.cymru e: contact@crwst.cymru

Crwst is a micro-bakery nestled in the beautiful Preseli Hills in a small home-kitchen. By 'micro' bake we mean a small production with a one man baker! Run by a Welsh couple born and bred in the are Osian & Catrin, Crwst proudly produces handmade organic breads and seasonal patisserie style bak As everything is baked from their home-kitchen, Crwst isn't your conventional 'walk in' shop. But yo can frequently find them at regular food markets and a variety of food fayres throughout the year tc sample their passionately handmade produce. You can also find Crwst at Cardigan Guildhall Market every Thursday and Saturday from 10am.

Carreg at the Cliff

Gwbert, Cardigan, Ceredigion, SA43 1PP

T: 01239-613241 www.cliffhotel.com E: reservations@cliffhotel.com

Join us in our newly refurbished bar and restaurant Carreg at The Cliff. Our experienced team have developed menus using the best fresh produce to ensure that your dining experience is second to none. Our A la Carte menus are changed each periodically to reflect the changing seasons and inclu speciality dishes as well as classic favourites and kids meals, ensuring that we always have somethin for everyone! At Carreg at The Cliff every effort is made to accommodate all dietary requirements. If experience food allergies or intolerances please contact our team to discuss your requirements
A buffet style breakfast is served every morning, including a great selection of cooked and continen options, available weekdays between 7:00am and 9:30am and weekends and bank holidays betwee 8:00am and 10:00am. Non-residents are welcome for breakfast, however, prebooking is essential.

Flatrock Bistro

Gwbert, Cardigan, Ceredigion, SA43 1PP

T: 01239-612638 www.gwberthotel.com E: reservations@gwberthotel.c

The Gwbert Hotel stands on the banks of the River Teifi at the estuary at Gwbert-on-Sea -renowned its salmon and sewin – it is one of the finest hotels in the locality. The Gwbert Hotel offers high stanc of accommodation with lift to most rooms. Our tastefully decorated restaurant – The Flat Rock Bistro with its panoramic views of the Pembrokeshire National Park, offers an extensive menu with dishes tastes and requirements.
A romantic weekend at the 'Domain of the Dolphin' is a must for all couples who wish to have a "get away from it all" weekend break. So don't settle for anything less. Book today and see what a differer a little attention makes!

The Stables Restaurant

38 High Street, Lampeter, Ceredigion, SA48 7BB

01570-218615 www.the-stables-the-royal-oak-hotel.business.site E: theroyaloaklampeter@gmail

A small family run hotel with restaurant and bar, showcasing great local fresh welsh produce at a gre price. Family and Dog friendly. Lampeter's best restaurant for free range WELSH and LOCAL Steaks, b ers, fresh fish and other great pub food.

Trip Advisor Review 5 Stars

Delicious burgers!

My partner and I come here often. The food is lovely and cooked very well. The staff are always frien and helpful. And all the meat is local which I love!

The Red Lion

The Red Lion, Saint Mary Street, Cardigan SA43 1DD

T: 01239 613482

The Red Lion is situated in Cardigan, 200 yards from Cardigan Castle and 11.2 miles from Newcastle Emlyn Castle. Each room is equipped with a flat-screen TV. You will find a kettle in the room. Rooms have a private bathroom fitted with a shower. The Red Lion features free WiFi throughout the property. After becoming a free house The Red Lion has gone though a very high specification refurbishment. This entailed being closed for a period and the result of the refurbishment has given The Red Lion Inn four modern ensuite bedrooms, new cooking facilities, and a cousey dining area for breakfast. The bar area has been transformed, concentrating on sports, we have all the sports channels showing live sports on four 49" flat screen TV's, accompanied with surround sound.
We cater for all, The Red Lion is a locals pubs, where friendly welcoming Welsh locals drink daily.

The Falcondale Hotel & Restaurant

Falcondale Drive, Lampeter, Ceredigion, SA48 7RX

T: 01570-422910 www.thefalcondale.co.uk info@thefalcondale.co.uk

The Falcondale is an impressive hotel, restaurant and wedding venue in Ceredigion, Mid Wales. It is nestled at the top of the Teifi Valley, hidden away a mile outside the University town of Lampeter. Guests of its luxury accommodation can expect to be awoken by the sound of birdsong and fall asleep to rustling trees and hooting owls. For 11 consecutive years our restaurant on the outskirts of Lampeter has been awarded 2AA rosettes. You can expect menus crafted and inspired by local producers and are updated daily allowing us to showcase the quality produce Ceredigion and surrounding counties have to offer. Whether it's popping in for a heavenly homemade afternoon tea or a special occasion, or just a good cooked meal, our menu has something to offer every food fanatic.

The Welsh Black Inn

Bow Street, Aberystwyth, Ceredigion, SY24 5AT

T: 01970-828361 www.thewelshblackinn.weebly.com e: thewelshblackinn@gmail.com

The Welsh Black is a 2 star Inn in the pleasant village of Bow Street, which makes it an ideal place to stay if you are exploring the Ceredigion coast or the nearby coastal town of Aberystwyth. We have 3 en-suite rooms available for bed & breakfast, 1 twin and 2 doubles, with t.v and tea/coffee making facilities. The Welsh Black is available for morning coffees, business lunches, family meals, snacks, afternoon teas and of course,whatever evening meal is required. The restaurant can seat 30 people. The whole bar can be used for larger parties, plus there is outside seating with a large car park to rear of the pub. Food is available at the following times :-Monday to Saturday - 12.30 - 2.30pm and 5.30 - 9.00pm, Sunday - 12.00pm - 3.00pm and 6.30 - 8.30pm.

Ffostrasol Arms

Ffostrasol, Llandusul, Ceredigion, SA44 4SY

T: 01239-851348 www.ffostrasolarms.co.uk e: info@ffostrasolarms.co.uk

The Ffostrasol Arms is a homely, traditional pub near Llandysul in rural Ceredigion. Arthur & Betty have created a warm, friendly atmosphere, welcoming locals & visitors alike. We also cater for functions, from weddings & large parties to day trips & conferences, often held in our spacious conservatory.We have a range of meals to suit all tastes. All food is cooked fresh to order, therefore we apologise for any wait during busy times. We use local suppliers where possible. Children's menus are available on request. Relax by the roaring open fire in the winter & enjoy the outdoor seating during the summer. We have two pool tables & a dart board and free Wifi is available throughout the pub. Well-behaved dogs are welcome in the pub area, but not in the restaurant.

Creme Pen Cei

The Pier/South John St New Quay SA45 9NN

T: 01545-561307

This bright and colourful Ice Cream parlour in my opinion helps to put New-quay on the culinary map. With an amazing and mind boggling selection of both Ice Creams & Sorbets, there is more th enough selection to satisfy anybody's palate. But that's not all Crème Pen Cei does well. They also have a wide selection of Panini's, baguettes, Salad boxes and the best coffee in town! We at Top 10 Attractions give a massive thumbs, and will stick our neck out and guarantee this food for thought selection will not disappoint!

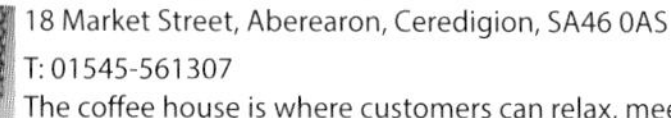

Naturally Scrumptious

18 Market Street, Aberearon, Ceredigion, SA46 0AS

T: 01545-561307

The coffee house is where customers can relax, meet friends or hold the all important business meeting!Enjoy freshly ground coffees, fresh leaf teas, ice-cold frappes or indulge yourself with a cu our Spanish drinking chocolate. Choose from a fabulous array of hand baked cakes and freshly bak patisserie. Why not be wicked and add a blob or two of local organic double cream!Dine in with Naturally Scrumptious, our menu reflects the seasonal produce we offer through our delicatessen (looks and tastes fab!). he coffee house is open throughout the day .You can alternatively make the most of our takeaway coffee service. Naturally Scrumptious delicatessen offers a taste of the world inside and you will be greeted with a fantastic show of delicatessen foods. Whether you are puttin a dinner party, having a tapas night or you delight in eating fine cheese and charcuterie, then Natu Scrumptious is the place for you, with Heather & Paula always on hand to offer advice & inspiration

yr Eos & Mansion Kitchen

Rhydyfelin, Aberystwyth, Ceredigion, SY23 4LU

T: 01970 600522 www.nanteos.com E: info@nanteos.com

yr Eos serves thoughtfully cooked and beautifully presented cuisine with a hint of Welsh character. Head Chef Gerwyn Jones believes in using locally sourced ingredients from producers who take pr their products. He brings years of experience to the Nanteos kitchen having worked under Gareth at Ynyshir. Dinner daily 6pm to 9pm . Tasting Menu available Monday - Saturday.

Enjoy breakfast at Nanteos served in the historic mansion kitchen, surrounded by the original iron ranges evoking memories of times gone by.Offering a wide selection of both cooked and continer fayre, we are delighted to offer breakfast from 7.30am to 10am. Our well-stocked library bar offers chance to relax with a cocktail inspired by the Nanteos' history or a glass of local Llaethliw wine ma

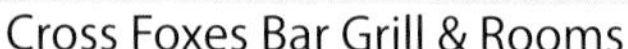

Cross Foxes Bar Grill & Rooms

Brithdir, Dolgellau, Gwynedd, LL40 2SG

T: 01341-421001 www.crossfoxes.co.uk E: hello@crossfoxes.co.uk

We are very proud to offer our guests local, seasonal produce all prepared by our Head Chef, Kyle Wilkinson. Kyle is passionate about preparing creative, fresh produce and particularly enjoys maki yummy desserts. With over 10 years experience of working in high quality gastro pubs and recene shortlisted for the Welsh Culinary Association Awards, Kyle will be sure to not dissappoint you!. Ou Butcher supplier has recently won 'Best Butcher in Wales' Award and we are very proud to be incluc in the 'Good Food Guide'. Come and try our delicious food where we have a range of Menus to suit occasions:

PEMBROKESHIRE

PEMBROKESHIRE

nbrokeshire is one of Wales's most popular destinations, not only to the likes of us tourists, but for turies now it has been a special location for artists, pilgrims and for many outdoor pursuits nusiasts. Pembrokeshire is also famous for being home to Britain's smallest city (St David's) this rming city was founded by St David, patron saint of Wales around 1500 years ago and is still to this full to the brim of welsh charm and its wide array of art galleries and independent shops, really es this corner of the county an interesting place to explore. Pembrokeshire is also famous for the ount of blue flag beaches it has dotted around its coastline, a coastline that spans a vast 275 km! only has it won dozens of blue flag awards, but a huge number of green coast awards also! Just en you couldn't be blamed for thinking there were no more awards to be won, Pembrokeshire has ervedly won well over a hundred seaside awards too.

ng the only coastal national park of its kind, and one of only three national parks in this great ntry of Wales, the others being the Snowdonia National Park and thirdly the Brecon Beacons, all of ch are featured in this book. This section of the book features plenty of great places to visit, castles have been the birth place to great kings, to theme parks, safari parks and animal farms alike. brokeshire really is a unique setting, and certainly one to spend your holiday in! For those rested in the movies, there are so many famous film locations to explore and if you really do your arch, you'll be able to uncover some places that have been featured in films such as the world ous Harry Potter franchise.

Thousand Islands Expeditions

t: 01437-721721 e: sales@thousandislands.co.uk
www.thousandislands.co.uk

Exciting jet boat trips or traditional leisurely cruises with wildlife guides onboard. Witness some of the most powerful currents in Britain, pass beneath some of the highest cliffs in Wales, see spectacular breeding colonies of hundreds of nesting seabirds. Ramsey is home to one of the UK's largest Atlantic Grey Seal colonies, seal pups are on Ramsey's beaches during September and October, look for our resident Harbour Porpoise feeding in the fast moving water in Ramsey Sound. Get the best of both worlds and see the RSPB Nature Reserve of Ramsey Island by land and sea, spend the day exploring the Island on foot and take a guided cruise . Venture offshore on one of our jet boat trips searching for whales and dolphins and see the spectacular Gannet colony on Grassholm Island or an exhilarating jet boat trip across to Skomer Island to watch the Puffins and Shearwaters.

AUTHOR'S REVIEW

Thousand Islands really have got it all when it comes to making sure your trip to South West Wales is one not to be forgotten! They really do run a slick operation, from buying your ticket right down to embarking and disembarking their vessels. Every care is taken to make sure you are totally comfortable and safety is absolutely paramount! I personally feel the reason there are not more boats in this area popping up is because simply put, they have a hard act to follow!

Cross Square, St Davids, Pembrokeshire, SA62 6SL

RSPB Ramsey Island & Grassholm

t: 01437-721721 e: info@thousandislands.co.uk
www.rspb.org.uk/ramseyisland

Ramsey Island is the most dramatic and rugged of all the Pembrokeshire islands and is a wild and beautiful place. Ramsey is a Special Protection Area for chough and the grassland, kept short and grazed by our flock of up to 200 Welsh mountain sheep, provides them with the perfect feeding ground. The island also has its very own sheepdog. In spring and summer look for peregrines and ravens nesting on the impressive west coast cliff. You can also scan the stone walls for wheaters and little owls or peek at the grey seal pups which litter Ramsey's beaches from mid-August onwards. In Autumn, revel in the sight and smell of some of the finest coastal heathland in Wales and catch a glimpse of feeding porpoises in Ramsey Sound. There is a small shop on the island and refreshments are available. Book your boat trip onto the island with Thousand Islands Expeditions.

AUTHOR'S REVIEW

Grassholm Island is a tiny white speck of land, 7 miles from the coast. As you approach the island, you begin to understand why it's white. It's home to 36,000 pairs of breeding gannets, the only gannet colony in Wales and third largest in the UK.
The island comes alive in early spring, with gannets returning to the island from late February onwards. The air is filled with males returning with nesting materials keen to establish territory ready to attract a female.
Grassholm has a strict no landing policy due to the national and conservational importance this Island holds. You can get a boat trip around Grassholm with Thousand Islands Expeditions.
info@thousandislands.co.uk

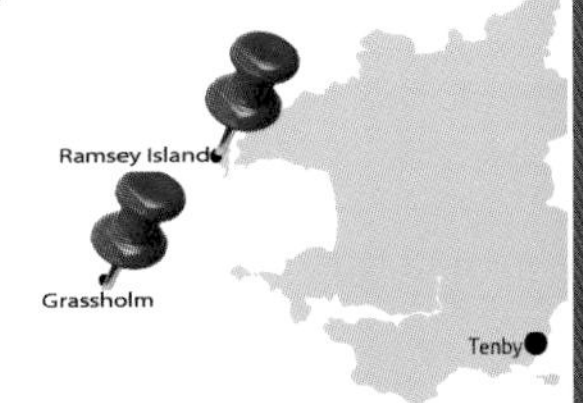

Image 1©L Morgan RSPB Cymru

PEMBROKESHIRE

St Davids, Pembrokeshire, SA626PY

Pembrokeshire Llamas

t: 07539-892519 e: pembrokeshirellamas@gmail.com
www.llamas.wales

Lead one of our llamas on a guided tour through the valley of Rhydwilym. Discover the beauty and secrets of the valley, whilst learning about the long history of the area. Not suitable for young children unless they are good walkers! Optional refreshments after the trek. The trek will take in beautiful views of the valley and beyond to the Preseli hills, and afterwards you are most welcome to sit with the llamas where we can supply you with tea and cake. Depending on the season, there is a chance you will spot one of our many resident red kites who spend the day soaring above Glanrhydwilym. Trainers / walking boots are usually fine for most of the year unless we have had an unusually rainy few days – in which case wellies might be a safer option. Generally there is very little mud on the treks, but it is always a possibility when going through the woods, so always wear something that you don't mind getting a bit muddy!

AUTHOR'S REVIEW

This is the third edition of the Wales book now and Pembrokeshire always continues to surprise me. Being a new kid on the block, Pembrokeshire Llamas has been a huge hit with all of its many visitors. This family run business has been put together by Matt & Alexandria and they couldn't be more suited to this business. They are friendly, warm and even though they are relatively new to tourism, they really do understand what people want and they provide it through their Llama Treks. Llama Trekking doesn't really feature abundantly within my books, the reason being, they are either done very well, or not that well at all and with the addition however of this trekking centre, you can obviously guess that it has to be a good one! Matt & Alex have great plans for the site and I'm really looking forward to my next visit, which can't come quickly enough for me.

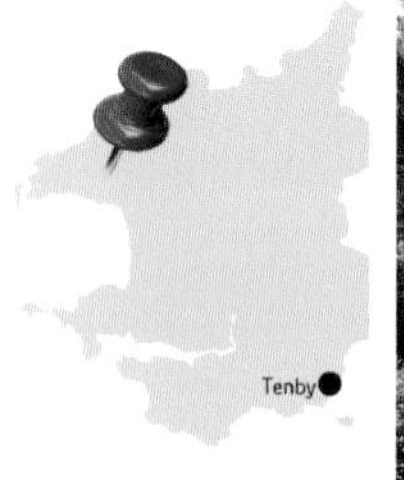

Glanrhydwilym, Rhydwilym, Llandisslio, Pembrokeshire, SA66 7QH

Picton Castle

t: 01437-751326 e: info@pictoncastle.co.uk
www.pictoncastle.co.uk

Picton Castle and Gardens is a fairy tale castle with enchanting gardens, just a few miles from Haverfordwest. As well as being an important part of the county's history it, it is a popular destination for locals and tourists alike and attracts thousands of visitors each year. Picton Castle provides the perfect setting for a fairy tale wedding day with its fine entrance gates and long carriage drive sweeping up to the Castle forecourt.Situated close to the Cleddau Estuary, known locally as the 'hidden waterway', Picton Castle comprises 40 acres of some of the most beautiful woodland gardens and grounds in West Wales.Stroll beneath some of the largest and oldest trees in West Wales and discover woodland walks, ferns, a maze and abundant feasts of wild flowers that blend with unusual woodland shrubs from all corners of the world.Please note that castle tours may be restricted when wedding ceremonies take place in the Great Hall. Secret Owl Garden – Wales' largest collection of owls in the woodlands at Picton.

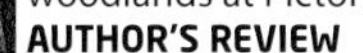

AUTHOR'S REVIEW

Picton Castle really is one of Wales's hidden gems. Despite being one of Wales's national treasures it still remains independently run which in today's economical climate is probably just as challenging as many other challenges that have faced the Castle in the past 700 years. What made me fall in love with Picton so much, was that the castle is steeped in history from the Norman invasion right down to the Cromwellian civil war, this castle has seen it all! Yet here it is, still standing as majestic and charming as it did when it was first built. Unlike many other properties in Wales, Picton offers tours seven days a week and are thoroughly enjoyable. If its just the gardens that your interested in you won't be disappointed! The gardens here at Picton are of a very high standard and in my opinion, add to the value of your ticket.

Haverfordwest, Pembrokeshire, SA62 4AS

Clerkenhill Adventure Farm

t: 01437 751227 e:dl@clerkenhill.orangehome.co.uk
www.clerkenhill.co.uk

We can ensure a great and relaxing day out here at Clerkenhill for the whole family. Take a stroll along our safe adventure farm trail through the spooky woodland with lots of interesting swings and slides and sights along the way, watch out for giants, bears and spooks! There is even a beach, but beware of the sharks! Have a chat with the animals around the park.
Watch the children laughing and playing in the numerous large play areas which include giant tube tunnel slides, our big adventure castle and relax in our summer house!
Clerkenhill is a family run park and is the ideal day out for all the family. Enjoy the Adventure Castle, Trails, Frizbee Golf, Crazy Golf and Animals around the park!

AUTHOR'S REVIEW

Clerkenhill has what a lot of farm parks of its type doesn't, and that is uniqueness! The farm park plays host also to the very popular Frizbee Golf Course. I have to be honest before my visit to Clerkenhill I had never heard of Frizbee Golf, but soon got up to speed on the craze and can truly see why it is loved by so many people. As this attraction goes from strength to strength, If you're looking for a truly fun day then I can seriously recommend Clerkenhill as one not to be missed.

Clerkenhill Adventure Farm, Slebech, Haverfordwest, SA62 4PE

CQB Adventures Pembrokeshire

t: 07917 684195 e: cqb.adventures@outlook.com
www.facebook.com/CQBAdventures

Pembrokeshires Premier Paintball & Laser Tag Experience. 10,000 sqf Indoor Military Themed Combat Zone, in Haverfordwest. Games are selected depending on whetherwe are running Junior or Senior sessions.

Capture the enemy flag

In order to demoralise the enemy your force is tasked to capture the enemy flag which is flying over their base camp. This is not an easy job as the enemy are a tough force and will fight to the last man.

Total Elimination

Your unit for this mission are Special Forces. The briefing is simple. "Total elimination of the enemy" Possible tactics you might think about for this operation is to send in two attack groups supported by a sniper team.

The General

It is vital that you escort your commanding officer to your HQ.

AUTHOR'S REVIEW

Come rain or shine, Pembrokeshire always has something to suit all ages and here at CQB Adventures, they are a testament to that statement. Whether your male or female, hours of fun are on offer here and I was really impressed with the centres whole set up. Based on the show-ground in Haverfordwest, apart from the sign on the door, you could be forgiven for thinking you've come to the wrong place, however, once inside, you can see that the centres owner, really has put a lot of thought and effort into putting this Paintball arena together. Now you don't have to take my word for it, all you have to do is read the hundreds of outstanding reviews on their Facebook page alone, by people that have experienced first hand, just how good this particular Paintball arena is. No matter though, CQB Paintball Adventures get a huge Top 100 Attractions thumbs up!

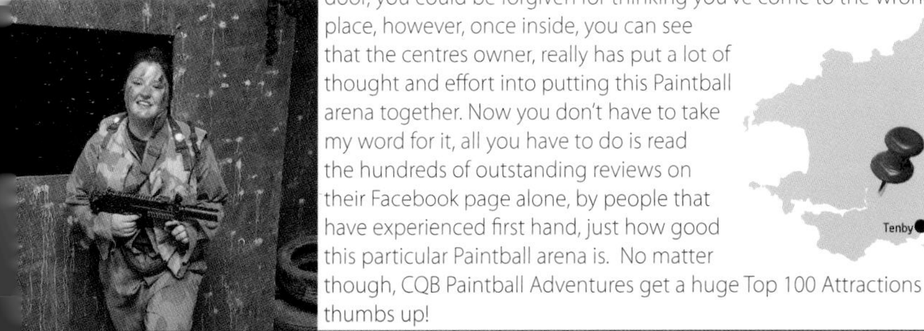

Withybush Road, Haverfordwest, Pembrokeshire, SA62 4BW

Cwm Deri Vineyard

t: 01834-891274 e: admin@cwm-deri.co.uk
www.cwm-deri.co.uk

Cwm Deri Estate is a working smallholding, which first opened to the public in 1992 and the vineyard is now one of Wales' foremost visitor attractions. Visit for a few hours or why not stay with us for a bit longer on our CL site or Static Caravan ?
For the very best of Welsh produce, whether it's wine, liqueurs, alcohol-free wines, preserves, cheese, cakes or ice cream, Cwm Deri has something to appeal to all the family, whatever their age.
Enjoy a tasting of our wines and liqueurs, either in our shop or on our patio and terrace, with a commanding view over the vineyard, animals and beyond to the National Park. If you enjoy superb freshly prepared and home-cooked food then you must try our stunning conservatory restaurant.
Relax with your drink and take a leisurely lunch or afternoon tea, secure in the knowledge that Cwm Deri's younger guests will be happily occupied in Pets' Corner. Free Wifi is available!

AUTHOR'S REVIEW

This is now the second edition of the Top 100 Attractions in Wales book, and believe me when I say this, Pembrokeshire is most certainly a different county since I first researched my initial op 100 Attractions, take Cwm Deri Vineyard for instance. Although open to the public since 1992, the vineyards of Wales completely went under my radar, until I heard about this hidden gem nestled perfectly within the rolling hills of the Pembrokeshire National Park. With Wine Tasting and Making, Vineyard Walks, a fabulous Pets Corner, top notch locally prepared food In their wonderful restaurant, and then just when you think there couldn't be possibly anything else to offer here, I hear about the Guide-to-the-Estate-Walks. When all's said and done, Cwm Deri Vineyard is one of the biggest smallest attractions in this book, hence why we have given it 'Hidden Gem' status!

Tenby

Martletwy, Pembrokeshire, SA67 8AP

The Reptile Experience

t: 07940-793845 e: info@reptile-experience.co.uk
www.reptile-experience.co.uk

The Reptile Experience is an exciting and fun "hands on" interactive education centre set in the beautiful seaside village of Saundersfoot near Tenby.

This popular all weather attraction brings the exotic and fascinating life of the rainforests and deserts of the world to visitors of all ages.

Your adventure into the magical realm of the natural world begins the moment you step through the door to be greeted by dragons, giant lizards, giant snakes, tortoises and turtles, frogs and assorted "creepy crawlies".

Encounters are scheduled by our experienced zoo keeper staff, so please call or message 07940793845 to check availability and book your unforgettable family adventure. Our adorable, reptile ambassadors enjoy meeting with our many visitors and a great deal of enjoyment is had by them too!

AUTHOR'S REVIEW

This attraction isn't your stereo typical type of tourist attraction, but don't read between the lines with that statement, as we at Top 100 Attractions absolutely love the Reptile Experience. which is situated here in the quaint seaside village of Saundersfoot. Although you wont hear a lot about Ian Clayton, the owner of the Reptile Experience, he is the only reason this fantastic attraction exists. He has dedicated his whole life to making sure that every visitor, young and old, has an absolutely fantastic experience and believe me, he achieves that every time. A visit to the Reptile Experience will give you one of those very rare chances to hold and get close to some of the worlds rarest and endangered reptiles on our fragile planet. I found the entrance fee to be more than reasonable and the attraction is very easy to find, but don't just take my word for it, go and see for yourself!

Tenby

Tenby Boat Trips

t: 07980-864509 e: info@tenbyboattrips.co.uk
www.tenbyboattrips.co.uk

We leave Tenby Harbour daily on one hour cruises to explore the hidden bays on the Atlantic side of Caldey Island. Two highly qualified and experienced local guides share an in depth knowledge of the island's wildlife and surrounding waters.

ISLAND CRUISE

1 hour 15 minute passage taking in some of Pembrokeshire's most dramatic offshore islands. Cruise Caldey Island sound to the famous smugglers caverns before crossing to the protected bird reserve of St. Margarets Island.

SUNSET CRUISE

July & August – A 2 hour round trip passage down the coast and into the Atlantic Ocean to watch the sunset with a sundowner of your choice. The boat is also available for private hire. Please contact us for details.

AUTHOR'S REVIEW

As I walked down the quay on Tenby's very busy harbour, I saw dozens of very excited people all queuing up to take a trip aboard one of the various Sea Cruises that Tenby Boat Trips offers. Although, not an attraction in their own right, they allow you access to one of Pembrokeshire's most famous landmarks, Caldey Island. The trip itself out to and around this heavily protected island, only takes just over an hour and worth every penny and my favourite part was the Cathedral Caverns, as they stand dominantly upon approach. Although this is the trip that I took, this popular boat company offer a small number of other options, from their popular Seal Safari, to their relaxing Sunset Cruises, whichever trip you chose, I guarantee a wonderful experience will be had by all aboard one of these boats, made even better by their highly experienced and knowledgeable crew.

Tenby

Tenby Harbour, Tenby, Pembrokeshire, SA70 7BN

arew Castle

t: 01646-651782 e: enquiries@carewcastle.com
www.carewcastle.com

Magnificent Carew Castle has a rich history spanning 2,000 years. Set in a stunning location, overlooking a 23-acre Millpond, the Castle is one of the most architecturally diverse castles in Wales. From the west the Castle is a Medieval Fortress, with imposing towers and impregnable walls, yet the view from the north is of an Elizabethan mansion with splendid mullion windows. The site also incorporates an impressive 11th century Celtic cross, the only restored tidal mill in Wales, a Medieval bridge and picnic area, all linked by a one-mile wheelchair accessible circular walk which enjoys uninterrupted views of the Castle. Well behaved dogs on short leads are welcome. There's plenty to see and do with an action-packed, family friendly events programme throughout the year. To find out more about events at the Castle please visit www.carewcastle.com

AUTHOR'S REVIEW

What denotes a Top 100 Attraction you may be asking yourself? We pride ourselves in the research we do, and our main two criteria is visitor experience set against value for money. We also take a few other things which we call TIC's! (taken into consideration) Although these TIC's are not deal breakers, they do play an integral part in choosing our attractions, take Carew Castle for instance. When you visit an attraction, and you have the memory of that attraction at the forefront of your mind at least one or two weeks after you've visited it, then that's a Top 100 Attraction! Carew has everything we look for in an attraction. As I stood on the bridge overlooking the castle, a warm feeling came over me, and the hairs on the back of my neck stood on end when I realised just how much history surrounds this great place, 2000 years of the good, bad and most certainly the ugly of what life has to offer.

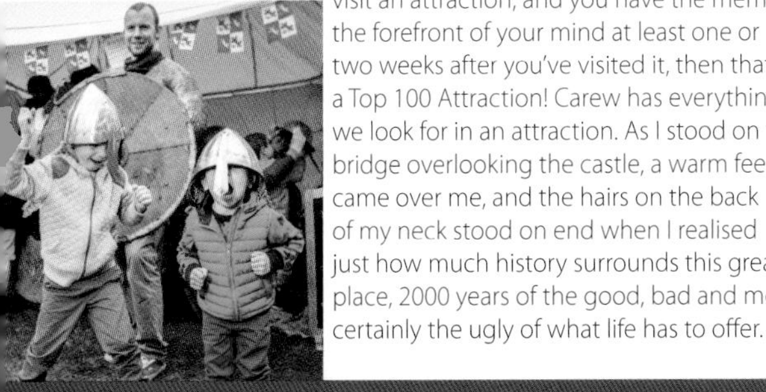

Carew, Tenby, Pembrokeshire SA70 8SL

Upton Castle Gardens

t: 01646-689996
www.uptoncastle.com e: prue@uptoncastle.com

Three of the original towers survive and there is evidence of a drawbridge and port cullies entrance while one wing contains the remnants of what was probably the great hall. The inhabited part of the castle mainly dates from the 17th and18th century with later additions of two further towers in the 19th century. The small medieval chapel dated by Time Team as 12th century contains several early effigies.. In the grounds of the chapel is a stone preaching cross listed by CADW as a historic monument. Mr Stanley Neal bought Upton Castle in the 1920s and was responsible for the laying out of the formal gardens and terraces and the planting of the Arboretum. It is thanks to him that we have the mature gardens bursting with rare plants that we see today.. At Upton there are several gardens within a garden which in all extends to about 35 acres.

AUTHOR'S REVIEW

Although Pembrokeshire is very popular for its more high profile attractions such as Oakwood Theme Park, Folly Farm and St. David's Bishop's Palace, it is also now with help of books like mine, becoming just as popular for its 'Hidden Gem' attractions such as Upton Castle Gardens. The picturesque Norman castle itself isn't accessible to the public as it is a family home, but to have it there as a backdrop to these idyllic gardens is truly fabulous. Walking around here it is quite easy to imagine you are anywhere in the world. I have visited some of the biggest gardens within the UK & Ireland that didn't manage to me make feel as content as the ones here at Upton Castle Gardens. I think also worth mentioning is that hidden deep within the woods here at Upton is a self catering cottage. Creek Cottage is available to rent throughout the year.

Tenby

Cosheston, Pembroke Dock, Pembrokeshire, SA72 4SE

Nolton Stables

t: 01437-710360 e: info@noltonstables.com
www.noltonstables.com

We are located in Pembrokeshire, on the West Coast of Wales in the middle of the stunning expanse of St Brides Bay. To the south is Broadhaven, Marloes and Skomer Island. To the north is Newgale Beach and the St Davids peninsular. The county town of Haverfordwest is 15 mins drive away.

We have over 60 horses and ponies with something to suit every rider. There is a short hack across our fields to the beautiful beach of Druidstone Haven which is the main location for Beach Riding. When the tide is in then there are plenty of countryside tracks and paths to explore.

The Stables is also home for fun activities of Zorbing and a Segway Course, and lessons can be taken in our indoor school.

There is extensive accommodation available close to the stables with our own self catering cottages and the historic Glebe House B&B.

AUTHOR'S REVIEW

Wales is full of businesses that have been passed through the generations for decades, and at Nolton Stables, that age long tradition has continued to not only flourish, but to grow also. Having been highly recommended to me via another business, I started to do my research, and believe me when I say this, that me being impressed is just to put it mildly. Nolton Stables is a very slick operation indeed, and has not only got something to offer experienced riders, but they also accommodate learner riders to boot, excuse the pun. Having now just expanded, this means the experience that one can expect to find here is hugely heightened and with the addition of the Zorbing and Segway, this truly has become a one stop shop for fun in Pembrokeshire, if not the whole of Wales. Nolton Stables deserves its place in this book, but don't take my word for it, take a trip to Pembrokeshire and see for yourself.

Tenby

Nolton, Haverfordwest, Pembrokeshire, SA62 3NW

Sea Trust Ocean Lab

t: 01348-874737 e: info@seatrust.org.uk
www.seatrust.org.uk

The Sea Trust is a non-profit community interest company, working to better understand and help protect local marine wildlife, and to raise awareness in the local community. We aim to inspire people to care about their local marine wildlife by opening their eyes to the stunning diversity of wildlife around the Welsh coast and engaging them in its protection.

We carry out daily porpoise photo-identification and 'click-count' porpoise activity surveys from Strumble Head and the northern Breakwater in Fishguard Bay, courtesy of Stena Line. A high percentage of the porpoise population in this area has some kind of marking, meaning we can carry out land-based photographic surveys on harbour porpoise – a first of its kind study in the UK.

We also run educational events for schools and the public, such as sea shore safaris and marine plastics workshops.

AUTHOR'S REVIEW

I was so pleased to learn that the Sea Trusts Ocean Lab was still here in this under represented corner of Pembrokeshire! The management and team all work very hard to make sure that not only does their hard work benefit the Pembrokeshire coast, but also the wider West Wales area. On the day that I had my guided tour around the Ocean Lab, I was greeted by one of their younger members of staff. Not only was he friendly and enthusiastic, he really did know his stuff, which took me completely by surprise, because as a young guy, you'd think his knowledge would of been quite limited, on the contrary, not only was his tour informative, his passion for the ocean lab and the great work that they do here just oozed out his every word, which made me want to stay longer! I can't recommend this attraction enough.

Tenby

The Ocean Lab, The Parrog, Goodwick, SA64 0DE

Slebech Park

t: 01437-752000 e: enquiries@slebech.co.uk
www.slebech.co.uk

Slebech Park is set at the centre of a 600 acre privately owned estate with a commanding position over the upper reaches of the Daucleddau Estuary, deep in the Pembrokeshire Coast National Park. This a location that is off the beaten track so much so that it is often described as being on the 'hidden waterway' yet it is actually very accessible and easy to find once you have been given the code! Slebech Park has 15 bedrooms situated in a Grade II 18th century Coach House built round a central courtyard. Each bedroom is unique but is decorated to the same simple but chic theme that is designed to promote the stunning landscape outside and the lawns running down to the waterside. The surrounding hills roll down to the estuary with its never ending supply of wading birds. This is an intensely relaxing place where you can simply sit and watch the slow ebb and flow of the tide. The scenery is constantly changing with the changing tide. Here you can enjoy real countryside with not another building in site and on a clear night you can star gaze to your heart's content.

AUTHOR'S REVIEW

Slebech Park along with its grand hall, is steeped in history and around every corner there are so many amazing things to see. I still, weeks after visiting Slebech Park have fond memories of the stunning views on offer of the banks of the tidal daucleddau river estuary. In recent years Slebech Park has been an inhospitable place, which goes against the parks history. For centuries the estate along with its magnificent hall have been welcoming weary travellers who needed a bed for the night, but now the new owners of the estate have made it their absolute mission to open every door to the public, and with the help of the Pembrokeshire National Park, have opened up their grounds for people to roam and enjoy the many acres of countryside heaven. With some of the highest quality accommodation Pembrokeshire has to offer, Slebech Hall has a wide selection of rooms to suit anyone's tastes.

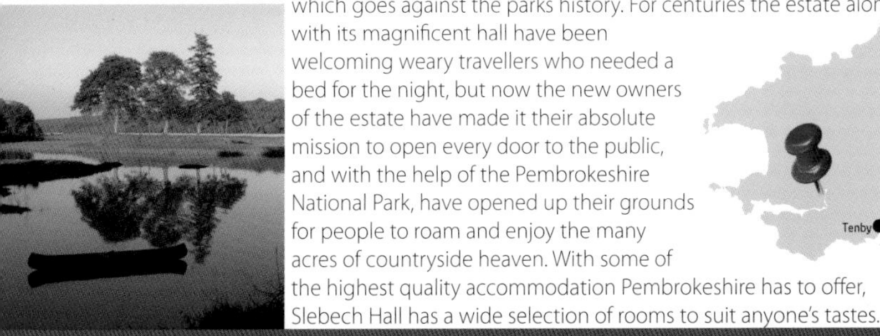

Slebech, Haverfordwest, Pembrokeshire, SA62 4AX

Oakwood Theme Park

t: 01834 815 170 e: info@oakwoodthemepark.co.uk
www. oakwoodthemepark.co.uk

Set in 90 acres of spectacular Pembrokeshire countryside, Oakwood is Wales' biggest family adventure with more than 40 exhilarating rides and amazing experiences to discover.

Don't miss Megafobia - famed as one of the wildest wooden coasters on the planet, it's the jewel in Oakwood's crown! If your up for getting drenched, then don't miss Drenched – one of the tallest, steepest and wettest water ride in Europe! Speed is one not to miss with it's awe-inspiring beyond vertical drop!

Oakwood's also home to classic family rides such as Bobsleigh, the Treetops Rollercoaster, Snake River Falls and the Pirate Ship.

Themed areas from 'Spooky Street' featuring The Creepy Crawler roller coaster, to Neverland – favoured by all little visitors. Enter the magical world of Peter Pan in this awesome £4m family-themed area. The Neverland area spreads across more than three acres and features 10 rides and attractions. Among the rides are 'Skull Rock' pirate log flume, complete with 12-metre-tall sculpted skull, the 'Lost Boys Adventure', 'Neverland Chase', 'Tink's Flying School',' Crocodile Coaster', 'Jolly Roger' mini galleon. 'Hook's House of Havoc' soft play and the 'Sights of London' taxi ride featuring Big Ben, the Tower of London and Nelson's Column.

With so much to do and see, enjoy a family day out at Wales' biggest family adventure!

AUTHOR'S REVIEW

Oakwood has to be Wales's Premier Theme Park. With plenty of rides to keep you occupied all day, you are guaranteed not only value for money, but lots of great memories. After being recently taken over by Spanish theme park giants the Aspro Group, the management at Oakwood have got massive plans for the theme park and although it would be a far better place to visit on a non rainy day there is one thing that is for certain, that no matter the weather the fun goes on all day at Oakwood.

Tenby

Canaston Bridge, Narberth, Pembrokeshire **SA67 8DE**

VERLAND

ter the magical world of Peter Pan in this awesome £4m family-themed area, which spreads oss more than three acres and features 10 rides and attractions.

ıong the rides are 'Skull Rock' pirate log flume, complete with 12-metre-tall sculpted skull, the st Boys Adventure', 'Neverland Chase', 'Tink's Flying School', 'Crocodile Coaster', 'Jolly Roger' mini leon. 'Hook's House of Havoc' soft play and the 'Sights of London' taxi ride featuring Big Ben, Tower of London and Nelson's Column.

ere is also 'Journey to Neverland' a stunning, interactive walkthrough area which takes visitors o the Darling family home and above the streets of London before arriving in 'Neverland' itself. cusland is designed especially for younger visitors and features tea cup rides, the Clown Coast- and children's playground. Oakwood Theme Park, Canaston Bridge, Narberth, Pembrokeshire 67 8DE. Book online at www.oakwoodthemepark.co.uk for great savings on admission prices.

PEMBROKESHIRE

Folly Farm

t: 01834-812731 e: info@folly-farm.co.uk
www.folly-farm.co.uk

Folly Farm is ranked in the top 1% of businesses on TripAdvisor having being awarded its travellers' choice award and voted the 10th best zoo in the world. Its award-winning zoo is now home to giraffes, flamingos, penguins, African lions, lemurs, meerkats, rhinos, tapirs, bongos, squirrel monkeys, bats and a sloth...plus many more. Alongside the zoo sits the Jolly Barn with all your favourite farmyard friends, including miniature pigs, ponies, giant rabbits, sheep, donkeys, goats, chickens and ferrets, plus the ever-popular 'Cwtch Corner' and the opportunity to milk a goat! The Jolly Barn is also the gateway to the rare breed paddocks, the piggery and land train tractor ride.

The fun continues in the magical indoor vintage fairground containing 16 lovingly restored fairground favourites like the Golden Gallopers, Dodgems, Caterpillar, Chair-o-planes and the Twist plus a whole host of indoor and outdoor adventure play areas, including the legendary 'Black Bart's Pirate Cove'. Spread over 120 acres and with around 50% of Folly Farm's attractions located undercover, there is plenty to see and do whatever the weather.

For more information visit www.folly-farm.co.uk or follow them on Facebook at www.facebook.com/FollyFarm

AUTHOR'S REVIEW

We have featured several farm parks within this book and one that has to be amongst the best is Folly Farm. Folly Farm are previous holders of the coveted Best Family Day Out in Wales Award, and has all the makings of being one of the best family attractions located within the British Isles. As well as being a family friendly farm park the park also houses its very own zoo, indoor vintage funfair, and a wide array of indoor and outdoor adventure play areas. Folly Farm truly is an adventure park within an adventure park.

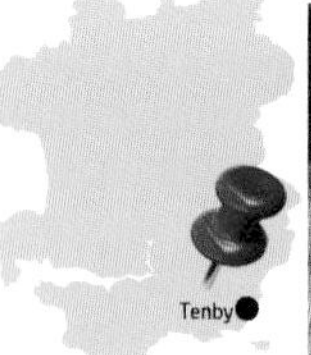

Folly Farm, Begelly, Kilgetty, Pembrokeshire, SA68 0XA

Gwobr
Aur
Gold
Award
2018
FOLLY FARM
Rated the 10th best zoo in the world on TripAdvisor
2018
CERTIFICATE of
EXCELLENCE
tripadvisor
Pick your own adventure
Explore the
Zoo
Experience the
Barn
Fun at the
Fairground
Come and
Play
www.folly-farm.co.uk

PEMBROKESHIRE

The Secret Owl Garden

t: 01437-751725 e: info@secretowlgarden.co.uk
www.secretowlgarden.co.uk

If you would like to really get up close and spend some quality time with our owls you can arrange a place on one of our flying experiences. We offer both group taster sessions and private experiences, keep reading for more details on how to join in the fun! Our private owl experiences of flying fun where you will get to fly three different species of owl through the beautiful woodland gardens. The experience is completely private so you can spend maximum time enjoying your time with the owls and means we can completely tailor the experiences to individual requirements. Just let us know when you book if there is any additional support you need while you're with us.

You will fly a small, medium and a large owl so that you can get to feel the difference in weight, see their different styles of flight and hear the different noises that they make. Even our really big owls are super friendly so that they can be flown by the smallest of people. During your experience there will be plenty of photo opportunities as you call the owls down to your gloved hand as many times as you like.

AUTHOR'S REVIEW

Celtic Holiday Park has always been a favourite of mine, now that The Secret Owl Garden is there, it has just got all the more special to me. Ran by Emma & Alex Hill, these two are no stranger to me as we have also featured their other success story, The British Bird of Prey Centre based at the National Botanic Gardens In Carmarthenshire. This couples sheer devotion to all things two winged is clear to see as I walked around each aviary and the Owls themselves look so happy, I don't think they'd want to be anywhere else! On the day I arrived, there was a special Harry Potter event on and being a big Harry Potter fan myself, I loved to see all of the staff dressed up. All the staff have smiles on their faces, they are polite and go out of their way to answer any question thrown at them and the joint entrance fee isn't that expensive, so has to be on your itinerary when visiting Pembrokeshire!

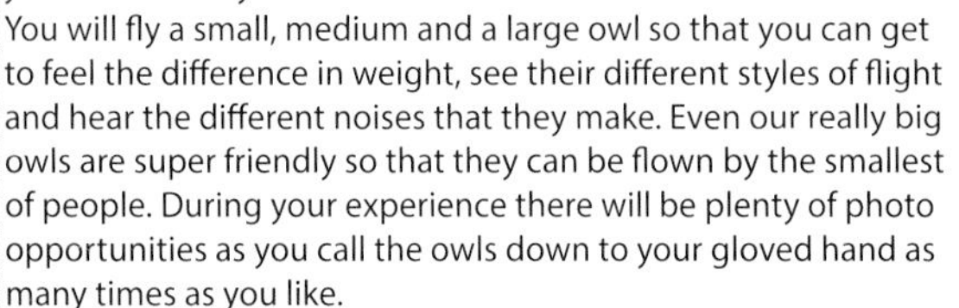

Celtic Holiday Parks, Noble Court, Redstone Road, Narberth, SA67 7ES

Manorbier Castle

t: 01834-870081 e: manorbiercastleoffice@gmail.com
www.manorbiercastle.co.uk

Manorbier Castle is a romantic Norman Castle in a fairy tale setting by the sea. It is privately owned and within 100 yards of the beach. The castle is approached up a long sweeping drive, over a wooden bridge, across the moat into the inner bailey. Within the castle walls are beautiful gardens, the old vaulted chapel which is licensed for wedding ceremonies, the keep, towers and a private house, built into the castle walls. With such a splendid setting overlooking a beautiful unspoilt beach, families love to explore Manorbier Castle and bring a little bit of history to life. The impressive Great Hall, Chapel and Turrets are dotted with life size figures – see children of the Tudor period and some prisoners in the dungeon. Enjoy delicious light bites and refreshments in the stylish cafe. Before you leave, take a moment to sit in the walled gardens designed by Daphne Shackleton one of Irelands foremost plantswomen, and just soak up the wonderful atmosphere that time has passed by.

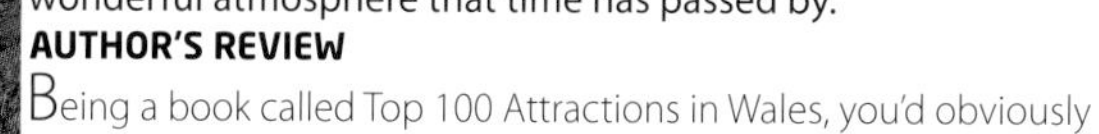

AUTHOR'S REVIEW

Being a book called Top 100 Attractions in Wales, you'd obviously expect some of the biggest and best attractions in Wales to be featured within its pages, and you would of course be absolutely correct. But at Top 100 Attractions, we actually specialize just as much in hidden gem attractions as we do the more obvious ones, this brings me nicely onto Manorbier Castle. Nestled perfectly in the picturesque village of Manorbier at the south of the county, Manorbier Castle, although not seeing a huge amount of military activity, has quite a large amount of historical importance. Being home to knights, important scholars, and princes alike, Manorbier Castle is one of those castles that you just cannot help but fall in love with straight away, in fact speaking of love, the castle has now become a perfect location to marry your beloved, as well as being a location used by film directors.

Manobier, Nr Tenby, Pembrokeshire, SA70 7SY

Castell Henllys

t: 01239-891319 e: enquiries@castellhenllys.com
www.castellhenllys.com

Castell Henllys is the only Iron Age Village in Britain reconstructed on the exact site where our Celtic ancestors lived 2,000 years ago. Here you can walk in the footsteps of the Demetae tribe.
Our exciting events offer you the chance to train as a warrior, watch a woodsman at work, huddle around a roundhouse fire to hear tales from a bygone age and learn lessons from the past that can help us to conserve the landscape we live in today.
The hill fort sits on an inland outcrop with stunning views of the surrounding countryside which today forms the heart of the Pembrokeshire Coast National Park. Our Visitor Centre is based on the Celts' ancient roundhouses and was built using local materials and sustainable technologies. The Castell Henllys experience is better than ever, with the addition of an interactive Visitor Centre.
So before you head up to the fort, you can enjoy:
Interactive exhibitions * Café and gift shop * Children's play area
Barefoot Trail * Riverside picnic site.

AUTHORS REVIEW

We have visited many different types of attractions during the course of our selection process and every single one has earned its right to be one of the Top 100 Attractions in Wales. None more so than Castell Henllys! Perched on a spur of land near the Pembrokeshire coast, this attraction has got everything you would require to make a great Welsh tourist attraction! Value for money, uniqueness, and great for all ages and that's just for starters. I have been to this attraction quite a few times and on every occasion I seem to spot something I hadn't noticed before. As you walk around the Iron Age fort it isn't hard to imagine what life would have been like on the west coast of Wales way back 2400 years ago. You get to sample also the same harsh daily life that would have been their only form of survival, in what would have been very grim times for the human race. All this and more comes to life here and I feel the team at Castell Henllys have done an amazing job of recreating just how fundamental being a close knit community would have been to these early Celtic people.

Tenby

Pantglas, Crymych, Pembrokeshire, SA41 3UR

Oriel y Parc Landscape Gallery

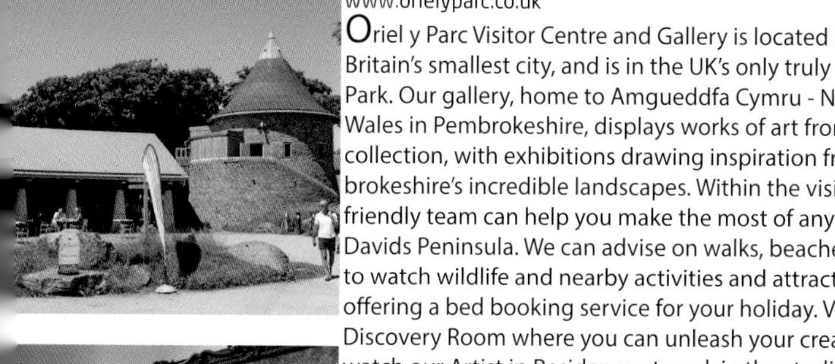

t: 01437-720392 e: info@orielyparc.co.uk
www.orielyparc.co.uk

Oriel y Parc Visitor Centre and Gallery is located in St Davids, Britain's smallest city, and is in the UK's only truly coastal National Park. Our gallery, home to Amgueddfa Cymru - National Museum Wales in Pembrokeshire, displays works of art from the national collection, with exhibitions drawing inspiration from Pembrokeshire's incredible landscapes. Within the visitor centre, our friendly team can help you make the most of any visit to the St Davids Peninsula. We can advise on walks, beaches, great places to watch wildlife and nearby activities and attractions, as well as offering a bed booking service for your holiday. Visit our Discovery Room where you can unleash your creative side, or watch our Artist in Residence at work in the studio. We also have a gluten free friendly café serving breakfasts and lunches using local fresh produce. Also available are indulgent coffees and specialist teas with a range of delicious cakes. We also have outside seating in our courtyard.

AUTHOR'S REVIEW

St David's is a very unique place, to me, it's a village, small town and a city all in one. With a varied amount of attractions locally, there is something for everyone here and of all ages. One such attraction in the Oriel Parc Landscape Gallery, which is part of the Pembrokeshire Coast National Park. With a great cafe, gift shop, along a varied amount of exhibitions throughout the year, the gallery has become a hub, the very epicentre of St David's and along with the cathedral and bishops palace, I can't suggest visiting St David's without visiting this Visitors Centre. I found the staff to be helpful, friendly and even though the centre can get very busy at times, which I witnessed on the day I visited, they all seemed to cope perfectly. You can't miss Oriel Parc, it's just on the left as you enter St David's, however, you'll have to find somewhere to park first.

Tenby

St Davids, Pembrokeshire, SA62 6NW

Manor House Wildlife Park

t: 01646-651201
book online at www. manorhousewildlifepark.co.uk

Manor House is Special - everybody loves this low-key and charming park. ITV's 'Anna's Welsh Zoo' is filmed at Manor House, and here you get to meet TV star Steve the Gibbon, his mate Lisa and their young son Bryn... watch this wonderful family as they swing through the trees in The Valley of the Apes. Zebra, Camel, Scimitar-horned oryx, Ostrich, Meerkats and so much more! Nothing beats the joy of hand-feeding a wallaby, especially when there's a joey in the pouch!You can wander freely in the Lemur Walkthrough with four endangered species of lemur, sit still and they'll come right up to you. And let's not forget Tommy the Tapir - everybody loves Tommy! Passionate about animals and want to get closer? Then the 'Shadow a Keeper Experience' is for you. Work with a keeper inside enclosures, feeding and caring for rare and endangered species - it's a life-enhancing, life-changing experience. People say our keepers should be bottled, they're so good, so knowledgeable. (Must be pre-booked on 01646 651201. Cost is £60 for one, £100 for two - this experience supports our conservation work.)

AUTHOR'S REVIEW

This conservation-led park has something for everyone. from the huge carved dragon on the front lawns and little scooters and cars for the young, the Hay Play Barn and Willow structures to Dolly and Macauley the world's naughtiest macaws! The real-food cafe is a special treat: with a seasonally-changing menu, everything is cooked in-house from scratch, real tea and the best coffee around! A great day out in Pembrokeshire! We especially loved walking with the animals in the African Village and Meerkat Mountain - see the new Meerkat Family close up.

Manor House Wildlife Park, St Florence, Near Tenby SA70 8RJ

Valley of the APES
THE African Village
LEMUR Walk-through
WANDER WITH THE Wallabies
f
a zoo for all seasons

PEMBROKESHIRE

Celtic Quest Coasteering

t: 01834-891373 e: info@celticquestcoasteering.com
www.celticquestcoasteering.com

We are Coasteering specialists and we're the only provider dedicated to it 100%. This means we have intimate knowledge of Abereiddy, one of the best locations in Pembrokeshire. Exploring the right hand side the bay, its got the lot, small to BIG cliff jumps, scramble climbing, water features and more. We're normally in the water for 2-2½ hours and finish the session in the Blue Lagoon (Red Bull Cliff Diving World Series location 2012 & 2013). Amid so many outdoor centres in Pembrokeshire, how is Celtic Quest Coasteering any different from the rest?

Our concept is to make coastal exploration accessible to all (aged 8yrs+) Whether you're after an adrenaline filled adventure activity or maybe you're not confident in water, we will tailor the activity to suit your needs and abilities. With a wealth of experience and oodles of enthusiasm our coasteering Guides will introduce you to the often inaccessible sections of the Pembrokeshire Coast National Park, at an affordable price!

Author's Review

In the ever changing world of attractions, there are new ones popping up all the time. Our job at Top 100 Attractions is to research every single one of them, and where appropriate, recommend them to you. Wales is becoming the adventure capital of not only the United Kingdom & Ireland but throughout Europe too. Celtic Quest Coasteering is one of the leading companies that makes that statement ever more true. It is a well known fact that the brain genes of a dolphin are closest matched with human brain genes, this couldn't be any better demonstrated than by the team here at CQC. This fearless bunch really do know what they're doing. From the coastline they work at every day, to the waters they venture in throughout the year, Cleo and her team really are the best in the business. I do not make that statement lightly, I make it after days of research into this award winning tourism provider.

Tenby

Abereiddy Beach, St David's, Pembrokeshire, SA62 6DT

Ramsey House

Lower Moor, St David's, Pembrokeshire, SA62 6RP

T: 01437-720321 www.ramseyhouse.co.uk info@ramseyhouse.co.uk

A warm welcome awaits you at Ramsey House in peaceful St. Davids, in the heart of Pembrokeshire. Ramsey House offers you the ideal combination of professional hotel management and the warmth of a luxury 5 star family-run boutique bed and breakfast accommodation, to the highest standards. Our three double and three twin rooms are all you would expect from a modern, yet extremely comfortable, luxury guest-house - and then some more.

* Award winning Luxury Boutique B&B with fine dining.* Peaceful location in the heart of Pembrokeshire, close to the coastal path.*Complimentary Wi Fi. * Off road parking.
* Adults only.

Vilu Reef Holiday Cottage

Swans Well, Broad Haven, Pembrokeshire, SA62 3JU

T: 07770-761688 georgebevan504@gmail.com

Vilu Reef is 1 bed upside down cottage situated in a village location on one of Pembrokeshire 's most beautiful golden sandy beaches. Finished to a very high standard with oak floors and oak furnishings throughout. The high quality open plan kitchen with soft close doors, dishwasher and fridge freezer has a full size oven and oak dinning table perfect for the summer evenings eating in.The cottage also has a utility room providing a washing machine and tumble dryer.The lounge has a leather sofa with more oak furnishings sky tv and dvd player with 2 large windows over looking Broad Haven and St Brides Bay .The view encompasses the bay to St Davids, Solva and The Bishops light house. There is a grassy garden with a table and chairs and charcoal barbecue for outside dining.

Bower Farm Bed & Breakfast

Little Haven, Haverfordwest, Pembrokeshire, SA62 3TY

T: 01437-781554 www.bowerfarm.co.uk E::bookings bowerfarm.co.uk

Stunning panoramic sea views. Relaxing, Friendly, Working farmhouse run by local family. Secluded, walking distance of sandy beaches, coast path and restaurants. All rooms en-suite & fridges. Couples, families, business people & dogs welcome. Our historic family have been living and working in this area continually since the sixteenth century and our local knowledge is at your disposal, with recommended routes to suit individual tastes. We have a working sheep farm with horses and poultry. Birds, flowers (some rare) and wildlife abound! Our home cooked food and friendly, relaxed atmosphere will fill you with cheer and warm your heart. Your host is a raconteur of repute! Even if you are just coming to west Wales on business, our relaxed easy going atmosphere will help unwind overnight and how much nicer to stay in a home rather than a hotel.

Popevilla Cottages

Popehill, Johnston, Haverfordwest, Pembrokeshire, SA62 3NX

T: 01437-890032 www.popevillacottages.co.uk E: stay@popevillacottages.co.uk

Popevilla Cottages are two newly converted Pembrokeshire barns, on a smallholding 5 minutes from the county town of Haverfordwest, and 20 minutes from the old county town of Pembroke. The Popevilla cottages are centrally located for the visitor to roam the wonderful rugged coast line of north and south Pembrokeshire. Also within easy access to the Preseli Mountains. The cottages are semi detatched single storey Pembrokeshire barns, with double glazing throughout, but still retaining many original details. The property is accessed via a layby from the A4076, into the front of the property via a wooden gate into a gravelled forecourt. There is a NO SMOKING and no pet policy in the cottages.

Morawelon Camping & Caravanning

Parrog, Newport, Pembrokeshire, SA420RW

T: 01239-820565 www.campsite-pembrokeshire.co.uk E: morawelonparrog@gmail.com

Morawelon Camping and Caravanning is a beautiful, family-run campsite opened in the early 1920s. It is nestled between the backdrop of Carningli (Mountain of Angels) and the stunning waterfront sea views of Parrog and Newport sands (often called Traeth Mawr, which is Welsh for big beach). We are perfectly situated for an unforgettable holiday on the Pembrokeshire coastline. Our holiday bungalow is located in 2 acres of private grounds and offers panoramic views over Newport bay and Parrog beach. You can get a spectacular view of Carn Ingli (Mountain of Angels) from our south-facing patio. If you would like to visit Parrog beach, it is only a 2 minute walk. Morawelon Camping and Caravanning offers hook-up points, undercover wash up area & chemical waste disposal point.

The Golden Lion

East Street, Newport, Pembrokeshire, SA42 0SY

T: 01239 820321 www.goldenlionpembrokeshire.co.uk E: info@thegoldenlion.co.uk

The Golden Lion is gloriously located in one the most attractive villages in North Pembrokeshire, a designated Area of Outstanding Natural Beauty. As a family run Inn we put in extra care to ensure that every detail of your visit is of the highest standard and at the same time, creating a relaxed and friendly atmosphere. We have 13 comfortable, light and airy en-suite rooms. All individually decorated, the style is clean simplicity – cool whites and creams, honey-hued oak, and original artworks come together to make a contemplative mix of the contemporary and the traditional. Relax in crisp cotton sheets, snuggly duvets and Welsh woolens.

The Trewern Arms

Nevern, Nr Newport, Pembrokeshire, SA42 0NB

T: 01239-820395 www.trewernarms.com E: tom.beard@trewernarms.com

The Trewern Arms near Newport is a picturesque 16th century Inn with 10 recently refurbished ensuite bedrooms, situated on the banks of the River Nevern. It is the perfect base to explore the Pembrokeshire National Park. Whether its seeing Carningli & the beautiful Preseli Mountains or walking the breathtaking coastal path. The hotel boasts a lovely riverside restaurant, the Wheelhouse bar, and Twm path function room, where you can find some of the best quality produce Pembrokeshire has to offer, we try to use local suppliers where possible some of which are based in Cardigan, Fishguard & Newpor Rooms are fitted with a TV. Certain units feature a seating area where you can relax.

The Ferryboat Inn

Manor way, Dyffryn, Fishguard, Pembrokeshire, SA64 0AE

T: 01348 874747 www.ferryboatinn.co.uk E: bookings@ferryboatinn.co.uk

We offer great hotel style accommodation near the Pembrokeshire Coast National Park and the Fishguard ferry port to Rosslare Ireland (600m from B&B) We have proven to be one of the most popul accommodation providers in the area either for a 1 night stay or short break holidays. The Ferryboat offers 7 comfortable and stylish en suite guest rooms (doubles, kings, singles and twin including two ground floor rooms one of which is designed for wheelchair access. Free secure wireless internet, free view LCD TVs, toiletries and fluffy towels. We have our own forecourt car park for 8 cars. We also offer a vast selection of delicious breakfast choices cooked to order, to cater for all appetites. So whether you are passing through or joining in one of the numerous activities or attractions our beautiful area has t offer we look forward to meeting you.

Canaston Oaks Luxury Farmhouse

Canaston Bridge, Narbeth, Pembrokeshire, SA67 8DE

T: 01437-541254 www.canastonoaks.co.uk e: enquiries@canastonoaks.co.uk

Canaston Oaks is family run, lovingly restored from an original Pembrokeshire longhouse to luxury award winning farmhouse accommodation. You don't have to take our word for it: we are delighted that Visit Wales has given us Gold Award status for the last ten years, including this year. The ten individually designed bedrooms offer variety in outlook and facilities. There is a large breakfast room with outside space to sit and relax and enjoy a glass of wine in the evening. We have a generously stocked honesty bar with a variety of wines, local beers and ciders, soft drinks and snacks for our guests use. Why not take a bottle back to your room and relax and watch the sunset? Please note that we prefer you use our honesty bar: if you bring your own alcohol we do make a corkage charge to cover our costs.

Rhoslan B&B

7 Erw Las, Fishguard, Pembrokeshire, SA65 9BS

T: 01348 875106 www. rhoslanbedandbreakfast.co.uk e: rhoslan@swabyltd.com

Rhoslan bed and breakfast Fishguard is a bungalow close to Fishguard,or 'Abergwaun', in a quiet cul-de-sac with elevated views out to Fishguard Bay. We're only minutes walk from town and easy reach of the Pembrokeshire Coastal Footpath. This is a great spot for seeing both sunset and sunrise. Another place for this is Pwllderi near Strumble Head, only a 10 minute drive away.

Rhoslan caters for double or twin bed accommodation, in a spacious, newly decorated and refurbished room with a good sea view. Guests have sole use of a newly fitted shower room which is directly opposite your bedroom. The room is close beside the front door and porch, which are for the sole use of guests while in residence. Breakfast is served in the room with the best views of the garden.

East Hook Farmhouse B&B

East Hook Farm, Mount Lane, Haverfordwest, SA62 3LN

T: 01437 762211 www.easthookfarmhouse.co.uk e: jen.patrick@easthookfarmhouse.co.uk

East Hook Farmhouse B&B is situated 3 miles west of Haverfordwest, 4 miles from Broad Haven and Pembrokeshire Coastline. Situated 1 mile off the main road Haverfordwest to Broad Haven, set amongst beautiful landscape. Surrounded by green fields its an absolute heaven for peace & quiet. Ideally situated to visit the beauty spots of Pembrokeshire, St Davids, Fishguard ,Preseli Hills, Tenby, Saudersfoot, The Islands, Skomer, Skokholm, Grassholm and Ramsey. Ideal for birdwatchers and walkers. Enjoy the high standard of 4 star Visit Wales graded B&B. Six bedrooms tastefully decorated with period and antique furniture. Super King beds large spacious bedrooms catering for all your needs. Homemade biscuits on your beverage tray.

Slebech Park Estate

Slebech Park Haverfordwest SA62 4AX

T: 01437 752000 www.slebech.co.uk e: enquiries@slebech.co.uk

At Slebech Park we offer a range of rooms to suit different requirements from our small but well appointed Granary Rooms to our Bedroom suites, all individually designed with a little more space to relax and unwind in. We are very pleased to say that the Estate came runners up in the AA Unique Serviced Accommodation awards in May of 2018.Proud to be a little different from the norm. Whether you are looking for a base for a well earned holiday with four or five days exploring the Pembrokeshire Coast or are on quick business trip looking for somewhere quiet and relaxing to work between meetings there is something for you at Slebech. A stay with us is not just about our rooms, but the experience of staying on a unique Estate with over a thousand years of history.

The Paddock

Lower Haythog, Bethlehem, Haverfordwest, Pembrokeshire, SA62 5QL

T: 01437-731531 www.thepaddockwales.co.uk E: joss@thepaddockwales.co.uk

The Paddock is an exclusive well placed 5 star country home in a stunning central location in the heart of Pembrokeshire on a working farm. Joss, who is Cordon Bleu trained and has over 20 years experience, will cook and serve you the most delicious home cooked meals – breakfast – dinner. Our house is a new build faced with traditional Welsh stone. It has been decorated and furnished to an extremely high standard and is full of up to date modern luxuries. The Paddock is a wonderful place to stay - with a homely relaxing feel, high quality luxury, fantastic food, great hospitality and good value for money. The three luxurious bedrooms- one can be converted to a twin; they have all been tastefully decorated and furnished to a very high standard and offer superior accommodation.

Newhouse Farm Holiday Cottages

Little Treffgarne, Haverfordwest, Pembrokeshire, SA62 5DD

T: 01437-741111 www.newhousefarm.net E: cheryl@newhousefarm.net

We are situated in the heart of the countryside, providing a convenient base from which to explore all of the beautiful county of Pembrokeshire.The 19th century, Visit Wales 3-star stone cottages at Newhouse Farm are all individually styled to reflect their unique characters and offer a rural hideaway in a peaceful setting, our aim is to provide a comfortable home from home, perfect to return to after a long enjoyable day.There are wonderful beaches and coves within easy reach for surfing, swimming or just beachcombing, castles and museums dripping with history and bracing walks for the more energetic. You can go diving or coasteering

Lamphey Hall Hotel & Restaurant

Berea, St Davids, Pembrokeshire, SA62 6DX.

T: 01646-672394 www.lampheyhall.co.uk E: andrewjones1990@aol.com

Tucked away on the far South-Western corner of the Welsh coast, and nestled in the village of Lamphey Lamphey Hall Hotel is a bespoke hotel that dedicates itself to fine food, rest and relaxation. The hotel is very much a family affair, in ambience and character and our guests regularly compliment us on the warm welcome and friendly atmosphere, which combined with good service and fine food, guarantee a memorable experience. Classic in style, Lamphey Hall offers individually designed rooms with furnishes that compliment the hotels character. All rooms are en-suite with sparkling new bathrooms. The recipe is straight forward, imagination, inspiration and the finest local ingredients. Welsh beef, Salt Marsh Lamb, Seabass and Lobsters from the local bays are all used when available and in season.There is the traditional setting of the main restaurant with its warm period features, open fire & piano.

Coach Guest House

11 Deer Park, Tenby, Pembrokeshire, SA70 7LE

T: 01834-842210 www.coachhousetenby.co.uk E: joycelynandmike@coachhousetenby.co.

A warm and friendly welcome awaits you at Coach Guest House Tenby, we are located right in the heart of Tenby, situated just outside of the historic town walls and a few minutes walk from Tenby's 4 award winning blue flag beaches. We boast 7 en-suite rooms with doubles and family rooms available all with TV, Mini Fridges, toiletries and Tea & Coffee making facilities. We have complimentary private parking included for your stay. Tenby town centre is only a short walk away with it's many award winning restaurants & pubs. Every effort is taken to ensure your stay with us is both enjoyable and a trip t remember. We very much look forward to welcoming you to Coach Guest House.

Cliff House Guest House

Wogan Terrace, Saundersfoot, Pembrokeshire, SA69 9HA

T: 01834-813931 www.cliffhousebbsaundersfoot.co.uk E: cliffhousebb@btinternet.com

Cliff House is a welcoming and very comfortable 4 star Guest House that was built as the home for a local shipbuilder in 1840. The house has panoramic views of Sauundersfoot Harbour and Beach, Monkstone Point and across Carmathen Bay towards the Gower Peninsula. Cliff House is only a one minute walk away from the beach, harbour and village centre. Free parking is provided for all guests. All rooms are delightfully furnished and well equipped with en-suite shower rooms, flat screen TV's, tea and coffee making facilities and free WiFi. A sitting room leading to a balcony overlooking the sea and a bathroom with both a bath and shower are also available for all residents.

Llys Meddyg *

East St, Newport, Pembrokeshire, SA42 0SY

T: 01239-820008 www.llysmeddyg.com E: info@ llysmeddyg.com

Nestled under Carningli (Mountain of the Angels), on the Nevern estuary, and within the Pembrokeshire Coast National Park, you'll find breathtaking beaches, rivers, woods and mountains all a stone's throw from your door. Refuel with the finest food made from locally-sourced ingredients in our Dining Room or Cellar Bar, and rekindle with log fires, down duvets and Welsh woolly blankets in our luxury accommodation. Our Georgian townhouse offers a unique blend of old and new, with elegant furnishings, deep sofas and a welcoming fire. ll our rooms are large, bright and comfortable with contemporary en suite facilities, double bed and stunning interiors. Originals and prints by some of our most celebrated local artists adorn the walls including John Knapp-Fisher, Peter Daniels, Linda Norris, Graham Hurdwood and beautiful ceramics by Adam Buick.

Roch Castle *

Church Rd, Roch, Haverfordwest SA62 6AQ

T: 01437-725566 www. rochcastle.com E: stay@rochcastle.com

Spectacular and dramatic, Roch Castle offers five Star AA and Visit Wales Guest Accommodation, with award winning breakfast in Pembrokeshire. Dinner is offered at two Rosette Blas Restaurant at Twr y Felin Hotel, just a 20 minute drive away in St Davids, with complimentary transfers available each evening.

All rooms are furnished to the highest standard and fully equipped with aromatherapy toiletries, towels and bathrobe, slippers, Sky TV, iPod dock, iron and ironing board, extra pillows, fridge and tea and coffee facilities. Your bed combines the highest quality Sealy mattress with hypo-allergenic Comforel topper, duvet and pillows and 300 thread count linens, ensuring a delightfully satisfying night's sleep.

The Grove Hotel *

High St, St Davids, Haverfordwest SA62 6SB

T: 01437-720341 www.grovestdavids.com E: grove@sabrain.com

Offering stylish and comfortable rooms that accommodate the needs of our most discerning guests. relax and enjoy your stay after your day exploring our local area, and indulge in our mouth-watering menu. Stay in one of our 11 beautiful bedrooms, or if you're looking for an extra special getaway, you can book our stunning suite. All our rooms come with en-suite bathrooms, tea and coffee making facilities, free w-fi and a TV. No visit would be complete without man's best friend so we are happy to accommodate dogs on request. We're very proud of our fantastic menus. indulge in quality dishes, with ingredients and products sourced from suppliers we can trust.

Boulston Manor

Boulston, Haverfordwest, Pembrokeshire, SA62 4AQ

T: 01437-764600 www.boulstonmanor.co.uk E: info@boulstonmanor.co.uk

The beautiful tree lined driveway that sweeps its' way along the Western Cleddau to Boulston Manor is the first indication that you are leaving the rest of the world behind you and entering a place where peace, tranquility and relaxation are at the top of the agenda. This is bed and breakfast in Pembrokeshire at its finest set in the truly inspiring surroundings you can get on a country manor house estate.There are three beautifully appointed guest suites at Boulston Manor, two doubles and a twin/triple suite, each bearing the name of a famous horse race, an indulgence of the owners, a testament to their love of all things equine. The guest rooms are en-suite and have everything you would expect of such a fine Country House Bed & Breakfast including, television with 'Freeview', tea & coffee making facilities, hairdryer, complimentary bath robes and ample power points.

Ferry House Inn

Hazelbeach, Llanstadwell, Milford Haven, Pembrokeshire, SA73 1EG

T: 01646-600270 www.ferryhouseinn.co.uk E: info@ferryhouseinn.co.uk

THE FERRY HOUSE INN is set in heart of Pembrokeshire, in the village of Hazelbeach, overlooking the beautiful Cleddau Estuary and has been run by our family for over 40 years. An ideal base for holidays and business, we are centrally located for exploring the surrounding country and attractions that i nclude golden beaches, ancient monuments, spectacular scenery and family theme parks, this is an area that has something for every visitor. Newly refurbished ensuite accommodation with a three star rating from the Welsh Tourist Board. We have six comfortable rooms with double, twin, family and single occupancies available, most rooms benefit from lovely views of Hazelbeach and the Cleddau Estuary.

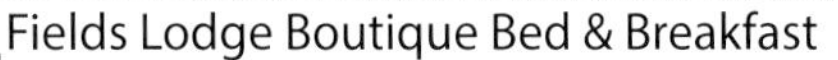

Fields Lodge Boutique Bed & Breakfast

Fields Lodge, Herbrandston, Milford Haven, Pembrokeshire, SA73 3TE

T: 07740-699871 www. fieldslodge.co.uk E: info@fieldslodge.co.uk

Our 4 star quality bed and breakfast pembrokeshire accommodation is designed for peaceful relaxation, from deep comfortable beds to local and organic produce; rewarding you after a day out in Pembrokeshire . Fields Lodge Bed and Breakfast in Pembrokeshire is the perfect spot for a getaway, indeed a recent guest commented we are "one of Pembrokeshire's best kept secrets". Our bed and breakfast Pembrokeshire based accommodation reflects our desire for you to be happy, relaxed and pampered.When on a get away break we would expect organic toiletries, deep comfortable beds and modern touches such as flat screen tv and ipod chargers, so we have provided them for you. So if you are looking for easy access to the Coast Path, and are as committed to quality as we are… we would love to hear from you…

St Brides Bay Holiday Cottages

Nine Wells, Solva, Pembrokeshire, SA62 6UH

T: 01437-720027 www.stbridesbaycottages.com E: enquiries@stbridesbaycottages.com

St Brides Bay Cottages is based in the picturesque fishing village of Solva, North Pembrokeshire, in the heart the stunning Pembrokeshire National Park. We've been letting holiday cottages for over 40 years during which time, as a Visit Wales Accredited Agency, our business has evolved into one of the best-loved holiday cottage letting agencies in North Pembrokeshire.We're a small, friendly team of people committed to making your holiday in the St Brides Bay area unforgettable – for all the right reasons. Because we hand-pick all our holiday cottages individually, we can help you find the perfect self-catering cottage whether you're looking for a coastal cottage with stunning sea views or a rural retreat with log burning fires, fishing, biking and country walks straight from the door.

The Corner Piece Inn

Fishguard Road, Rudbaxton, Haverfordwest, SA62 5PG

T: 01437-742185 www.cornerpiece.wales E: ajangel1974@gmail.com

Located on Fishguard Road, The Corner Piece Inn is a family orientated, friendly pub-restaurant with a homely atmosphere. We also have a loyalty scheme to help reward our fantastic customers. Come on in and see us, have a chat over a drink at our lively bar. Hungry? Our variety of menus offer something for everyone to enjoy with food served all day and lunch available every Sunday! We have a number of different eating options available, including a restaurant, bar, lunch and Sunday menu. Our superb food includes many great choices for everybody, whether you're looking for chicken curry, fish and chips or a hearty homemade pie, at The Corner Piece we have it all! We also have a children's menu and vegetarian options available, so there's something for everyone!

Freemasons Arms

Spencer Buildings, Dinas Cross, Newport, Pembrokeshire, SA42 0UW

T: 01348-811674 www.freemasonsdinas.co.uk E: info@freemasonsdinas.co.uk

Great food Live sports

Really friendly and welcoming landlord/lady, beer is great and food even better. Great prices too compared to the nearby Pubs of Newport. We have now become regulars even though we live in the Rhondda valleys!

Trip Advisor 5 Star Review Dog friendly bar

Lovely evening at this cosy little pub ...great choice of gins ...friendly staff and welcoming landlord definitely recommend especially if you have a well behaved ĺdog ...food good and exceptional service.

Slebech Park Estate

Slebech Park Haverfordwest SA62 4AX

T: 01437-752000 www.slebech.co.uk e: enquiries@slebech.co.uk

At Slebech Park the food is designed to compliment our stunning natural location. Our Slebech Park kitchen team is passionate about local produce, some of it from our own extensive Organic Vintage kitchen gardens. We offer a relaxed and "Graceful" dining experience in our restaurant which has unrivaled views over the natural beauty of the tidal DauGleddau river estuary.

We are proud to showcase the finest of Welsh culinary arts and the fine produce on offer, complemented by a warm Pembrokeshire welcome, sprinkled with a little bit of classical service in this our beautiful country of Wales. Our restaurant has been awarded 2 AA Rosettes for our Fine Food's & Service in 2016, 2017, 2018.

The Royal Oak

West Street, Newport, Pembrokeshire,SA42 0TA

T: 01239-820632 www.theroyaloaknewport.co.uk e: info@theroyaloaknewport.co.uk

The Royal Oak is an 18th Century free house with restaurant offering good food, drink and a takeaway service. The Royal Oak is situated at the centre of the historical town of Newport. Newport is an idyllic little town on Pembrokeshire's north coast. Newport has very loyal visitors with many spending the entire summer in Newport every year and with good reason. Newport is an undeveloped haven with a laid back way of life that acts as a perfect antidote to the excesses of modern life. At The Royal Oak, we take pride in our food & service. Our varied menu, ranging from bar snacks, selected authentic Indian curries to our imaginative British traditional food is consistently a big draw – especially our Sunday lunches.

The Canteen

Market Street, Newport, Pembrokeshire, SA42 0PH

T: 01239-820131 www.thecanteen.co.uk E: admin@thecanteen.co.uk

The Canteen is situated on the market street in Newport, Pembrokeshire. We serve food throughout the day, including our tasty brunch menu, with delicious illy coffee and range of tea pigs teas. For lunch and dinner, you can choose from our unique selection of stone baked pizza, handmade Welsh burgers and fresh salads.We can cater for special dietary requirements with Gluten free and vegan options available. We also offer takeaway pizza so you can enjoy a slice on the beach or at home. We also stock a full range of wines, local craft beer from Bluestone Brewing and Cider from Gethin's.
We always have a range of tasty desserts and milkshakes available to finish off your meal. Bring your friends or family and enjoy a delicious meal in our unique and relaxing environment.

The Salutation Inn

Felindre Farchog, Crymych, Pembrokeshire, SA41 3UY

T: 01239-820564 www.salutationcountryhotel.co.uk E: wydbrenda62@outlook.com

The Salutation Inn is a 16th century coaching inn which has been tastefully modernised to give 21st century comfort to our guests. The original parts of the old inn now blend perfectly with the modern and well appointed bed and breakfast accommodation, bars, and spacious restaurant. Our recently refurbished Denley's Restaurant is light and airy and offers views of the River Nevern.
The restaurant is available for use for functions, parties, wedding receptions and get togethers and can seat upto 45 people. Special menu's can be pre-ordered for groups of over 14 people. The Inn with its 8 comfortable bed & breakfast rooms is an ideal base for local leisure activities such as walking the Pembrokeshire Coastal Path and Preseli Hills.

Hotel Mariners

Mariners Square, Haverfordwest, Pembrokeshire, SA61 2DU

T: 01437-63353 www.hotelmariners.co.uk E: hotelmariners@hotmail.co.uk

The Hotel is situated within the attractive and ancient town of Haverfordwest within walking distance from local shops, supermarkets and leisure facilities. We have 27 en-suite bedrooms with quality furnishings and the use of TV with Sky Sports, tea and coffee making facilities, hair dryer and radio. Within the Hotel we have our own restaurant and bar where real ales are available and you can enjoy a quick bar snack or a more substantial menu with homemade and local produce freshly prepared and cooked by our chef. Customers please check with the Hotel if food is available during Sunday evenings through the Winter months .The Hotel restaurant and bar welcomes both residents and non-residents.Real Ales available, enjoy a quick bar snack or a more substantial menu with Homemade and Local produce.

The Creative Common

The Coach House, Goat Street, Haverfordwest, Pembrokeshire, SA61 1PX

T: 01437-779397 www.thecreativecommon.co.uk E: hello@thecreativecommon.co.uk

Your friendly neighbourhood coffee shop, serving up exceptional speciality coffee and loose-leaf teas We're also serving up wholesome food and treats – all from awesome local suppliers. Our own unique blend of coffee beans, roasted right here in Pembrokeshire and freshly ground to order. The finest organic Welsh milk, hand delivered by our milkman each morning. Lovingly crafted cake, homebaked in a little Pembrokeshire cottage kitchen. Details matter. We're much more than the sum of our parts. Yes, we are a coffee house. Yes, we are a place to work. But we also have heart. We have time. We have space. Linger a while, and see what unfolds. Kick off your shoes and cosy on our big ol' sofa. Read a book. Plug in and get some work done. Say hello to the person sat next to you (you're bound to have something or someone in common – this is Pembrokeshire after all).

Morawelon Restaurant

Parrog, Newport, Pembrokeshire, SA42 0RD

T: 01239-820565 www.campsite-pembrokeshire.co.uk E: morawelonparrog@gmail.com

Morawelon Cafe bar and restaurant provides a stylish and relaxing place to relax with an a-la-carte menu, hot and cold snacks and a variety of tea, coffee and cold drinks along with scrumptious cakes. We are fully licensed to serve alcohol and have a range of Welsh beers. The restaurant has panoramic views of Newport Bay. A spacious south-facing patio at the back of the restaurant provides a dramatic view of Carn Ingli. Dogs are welcome on the patio and fresh drinking water bowls are placed out for them each day. Soft whipping ice cream and lollies available. Booking advisable for tables. As a family-run business, you can be sure of great service and top-quality cooking. We use healthy and tasty ingredients to make sure that our food remains of a consistently high standard.

The Golden Lion

East Street, Newport, Pembrokeshire, SA420RW

T: 01239-820321 www.goldenlionpembrokeshire.co.uk E: hello@goldenlionpembrokeshire.co.uk

The Golden Lion is gloriously located in one the most attractive villages in North Pembrokeshire, a designated area of Outstanding Natural Beauty. Our mission is to deliver the absolute best in local cuisine and service in a relaxed and friendly atmosphere. Our team of talented and enthusiastic Chefs prepare an evening menu based on seasonal local produce with our favorites being Welsh Black beef fillet, locally caught sea bass and carefully prepared lobster – fresh from the harbour just down the road. Polish off your feast with a posh pudding or one of our traditional familiars such as sticky toffee pudding or homemade crumble. Our spacious restaurant – recently refurbished in Welsh slate and oak – is perfect for families and groups, with plenty of cosy corners for the romantically inclined.

Saint Brides Inn

St brides Road, Little Haven, Haverfordwest, Pembrokeshire,SA62 3UN

T: 01437-781266 www.saintbridesinn.co.uk E: malcolmwhitewright@hotmail.co.uk

Situated opposite the car park in Little Haven, you will find the Saint Brides Inn where home prepared and cooked food are offered, utilizing fresh local produce where possible and served in peaceful and tranquil surroundings, with the emphasis on good fresh food and friendly service.Opposite the pub is our pretty sun trapped beer garden where meals are served al fresco, or where you can just enjoy a refreshing drink or perhaps a coffee.The menu is ever changing, both for lunch and dinner and dependent upon the availability of fresh ingredients. In addition to an extensive but sensibly priced wine list, you will find cask ales in excellent condition, no juke boxes, pool tables or fruit machines but rather just a warm atmosphere.

The Rising Sun Inn

Pelcomb Bridge, St David's Road, Haverfordwest, Pembrokeshire, SA62 6EA

T: 01437-765171 www.therisingsunwest.co.uk E: therisingsuninn@hotmail.co.uk

The Inn has an excellent reputation for value for money home cooked meals. Fine Steaks, Vegetarian and Children's meals. There is a wide selection available on the restaurant's extensive menu. All prepared with top quality and wherever possible locally sourced produce. Our Function room caters for all types of occasions in the recently refurbished Pembrokeshire Suite. There is a separate lounge/bar area with comfortable seating, a pool table, fruit machine and Freeview television enabling you to enjoy a drink away from the restaurant. For those sunny days and evenings, the sites got plenty of outdoor seating at the front of the pub or in the pubs well-maintained beer garden. In addition, our caravan parks/campsites idyllic location provides a perfect location for one night stays short breaks or longer holidays in order to explore the many delights on offer in Haverfordwest and the beautiful county of Pembrokeshire.

The Hive

Cadwgan Pl Aberaeron, Dyfed, SA46 0BU

T: 01545-570445 www.thehiveaberaeron.com E: info@thehiveaberaeron.com

The Hive Grill offers an American style menu with a European influence, with a variety of dishes on offer from burgers, steaks, fish and shellfish. The Hive kitchen is run by Jason Jones, our Head Chef who has a passion for using the freshest produce to prepare the style of food we all love to eat....
The Hive bar is open throughout the day from 10am in the morning, until late in the evening. Why not try one of our cocktails whilst relaxing in our conservatory and watch the world go by. The Hive is the home of the famous Honey Ice Cream. Made on the premises by our master Ice Cream makers Kevin and Mateusz.

Anna's Welsh Zoo

Manor House Wildlife Park, St Florence, Near Tenby SA70 8RJ

T: 01646-651201 www.manorwildlifepark.co.uk E:gate@manorwildlifepark.co.uk

Specialising in Italian pizzas, all made on-site and with the highest quality, locally sourced ingredients, our real food cafe is a must. Some people come just for our delicious stonebaked Neapolitan Pizzas! Home-made cakes, big city quality coffee, decadent fairtrade hot chocolate, Suki leaf teas... need I go on? Why not treat yourself!

Lamphey Hall Hotel & Restaurant

Berea, St Davids, Pembrokeshire, SA62 6DX.

T: 01646-672394 www.lampheyhall.co.uk E: andrewjones1990@aol.com

The recipe is straight forward, imagination, inspiration and the finest local ingredients. Welsh beef, Salt Marsh Lamb, Seabass and Lobsters from the local bays are all used when available and in season. There is the traditional setting of the main restaurant with its warm period features, open fire, piano, paintings and chandeliers. You may prefer our Bistro for a more relaxed atmosphere, both rooms are sure to impress! With wonderful food, a selection of settings and the added benefit of plenty of parking, as well as on site accommodation, you will have nothing to worry about on the day other than to enjoy yourself. Warm Hospitality, careful preparation, you can taste the anticipation! Freshly Prepared Meals are served every day and evening. Always offering an excellent selection of fresh caught fish on our daily specials to compliment our extensive Menu. Vegetarians are sufficiently catered for .

Ferry House Inn

Hazelbeach, Llanstadwell, Milford Haven, Pembrokeshire, SA73 1EG

T: 01646-600270 www.ferryhouseinn.co.uk E: info@ferryhouseinn.co.u

THE FERRY HOUSE INN is set in heart of Pembrokeshire, in the village of Hazelbeach, overlooking the beautiful Cleddau Estuary and has been run by our family for over 40 years. An ideal base for holidays and business, we are centrally located for exploring the surrounding country and attractions that i nclude golden beaches, ancient monuments, spectacular scenery and family theme parks, this is an area that has something for every visitor. Our service comes with a smile and we will always do our utmost to ensure our guests enjoy the food and atmosphere.Diners at The Ferry House Inn can choose between our lunch menu, bar menu or chef's specials which change daily. Il offer freshly made home cooked food using locally sourced ingredients whenever possible.

CARMARTHENSHIRE

Carmarthenshire is too Wales as Kent is to England, the true garden of Wales. Before visiting this area f Wales, I truly thought that to be just a cliché that people come out with from time to time about laces that had a lot of green landscapes in them, I couldn't have been more wrong! With reathtakingly beautiful mountains, fresh, green landscapes and hidden forests that take you all the vay down to those enviable golden sandy beaches, Carmarthenshire truly is Wales's secret Oasis.)ne can now see why they chose this idyllic location to play home to the National Botanic Garden f Wales. I spent a good few nights in the county and got to explore all of our great attractions in this ounty, which at first I was wondering why someone would chose this region to stay in as part of a /elsh holiday.

hink I now know why visitors chose to visit this area, Carmarthenshire is a busy, bustling Welsh ounty and truly is the epitome of Rural Welsh life. With the Millennium Coastal path nearby and the ational Wetland Centre just a mile or so out of the town centre, there is just as much to do here as ere is in any other Welsh county. So on the face of it, Carmarthenshire really does get a huge thumb from us all here at Top 100 Attractions. I also cannot wait to work on our next welsh book as there as an awful lot that I didn't get to see! The likes of Llanelly House, Pembrey Country Park, and of ourse the Millennium Coastal Path, all help to make your visit to Carmarthenshire a very memorable ie. So no matter what you like to do, I'm sure you'll find it here.

The British Bird of Prey of Centre

t: 01437-751725 e: info@britishbirdofpreycentre.co.uk
www.britishbirdofpreycentre.co.uk

The British Bird of Prey Centre is a specialist collection of British raptors, focussing on the welfare and conservation of our native species of birds of prey. We are based in The National Botanic Garden of Wales, so you can visit us during you day in the gardens. Our aim is to give everyone the opportunity to interact with, and learn about, the birds of prey that can be found here in the UK and in doing so inspire communities to ensure their longevity. Plan your visit and find out about all of our daily events and activities at The British Bird of Prey Centre and The National Botanic Garden of Wales. Come rain or shine there's loads to do for the whole family! Browse through all of our amazing birds of prey and learn a little bit more about them. Each one has its own unique character and skills. Click on your favourite bird to find out how you can sponsor them.

AUTHOR'S REVIEW

The British Bird of Prey Centre, formerly known as Pembrokeshire Faconry was a very rare addition to our book, now, it's one of Carmarthenshire's biggest attractions! They used to be all over Pembrokeshire with their birds, now Alex and Emma Hill, like Noah, have created something far greater and have literally devoted both of their lives to this centre and after meeting them both again myself and finding out more about this new venture, they actually reminded me why it was that I started to write these books. Both Emma and her falconer husband Alex, not only know an huge amount about every bird that is within their care, they absolutely love every single one of these birds as if they were a child of theirs. Their passion and dedication is so clear to see and was a deciding factor in me actually choosing them as one of my Top 100 Attractions in Wales.

Stradey Castle

t: 01554-774626 e: info@stradeycastle.com
www.stradeycastle.com

Stradey Castle has been home to the Mansel Lewis family since it was built in the 1850's. This Grade 2* Victorian House, set in a secluded location outside Llanelli, is now open for Heritage Tours, Filming, Concerts, Parties, Photoshoots and Wedding Receptions. We are in the process of obtaining a License for the House to become a venue for Wedding Ceremonies. You can visit Stradey Castle on one of our regular Heritage Tours, held at 2.30pm on the 1st and 3rd Sundays of the month between April and September, or as part of a privately arranged tour. Booking is essential. For decades, Stradey has proved to be a wonderful and popular concert venue. The performers make use of the grand staircase in the hall where one of the House's two grand pianos are located.Stradey is becoming a popular venue for receptions and parties such as birthday teas and private lunches in the dining room. These can be accompanied by a tour of the House.

AUTHOR'S REVIEW

Some of the many castles we have in my books are well known, prominent and foreboding, but Stradey Castle isn't one of them. This Victorian castle perfectly fits the era and as you walk around the gardens and look back at the house, this is very much clear to see. Perfectly designed and still remaining with the first family that built the castle, Stradey Castle is a fine example of just how clever the Victorians were. First and foremost, Stradey is a family home and this is still very much clear to see as you walk round many of its rooms, speaking of which, tours around the castle will always be done by a family member and because of this, tours are really by appointment only. All in all, I guarantee that whether your a historic house lover or not, once you've visited Stradey Castle, it will leave a special place in your heart.

Swansea

Pwll, Llanelli, Carmarthenshire, SA15 4PL

Aberglasney Gardens

t: 01558-668998 e: info@aberglasney.org
www.aberglasney.org

Spectacularly set in the beautiful Tywi valley of Carmarthenshire, Aberglasney Gardens have been an inspiration to poets since 1477. The story of Aberglasney spans many centuries, but, the house's origins are still shrouded in obscurity.
Aberglasney Garden has probably been the most facinating garden restoration project underaken. The garden covers an area of 10 acres and destined to become one of the finest gardens in the U.K.
Explore the ancient formal gardens with its pools, parapets, cloisters and arches, and then discover the rare and unusual plants that are turning the rest of the garden into a plantsman's paradise. The Mansion, Garden and Shop are open Every Day except Christmas Day. (The shop is accessible to visitors without the need to pay admission to the garden).

AUTHOR'S REVIEW

Aberglasney is home to one of the most prettiest and probably the most historic gardens in Wales, dating back as far back as 1477. I have visited gardens all over the United Kingdom and all are just as impressive as the next, but the gardens here at Aberglasney really are quite special. Of course, you don't have to take my word for it, poets through the ages have been inspired by Aberglasney, and now beginning to inspire travel authors such as myself. With a wide variety of events in the gardens Calendar to chose from, there is always something going within the house and gardens. Friday nights through the summer are especially popular, as this is the night where food and live music come together like a well tuned violin. The catering needs are supplied by the team at the very popular Aberglasney's Tearooms, and they do not disappoint!

Llangathen, Carmarthenshire, SA32 8QH

Llanelly House

t: 01554-772857 e: bookings@llanelly-house.org.uk
www.llanelly-house.org.uk

Discover out about the past residents of the house and how they shaped the town and the industrial landscape of South Wales. Step back in time to the 18th Century with Sir Thomas and Lady Stepney. See them come to life and experience how the Georgians lived. Then move on to Victorian times and witness the scandalous 'upstairs downstairs' tales that haunt the Victorian areas of the House today. Showcasing award winning technology to breathe life into the dramatic stories of the Stepney & Chambers Families. We have welcomed many groups and organisations on private visits to Llanelly House. Why not combine your special Guided Tour Experience with our Signature Afternoon Tea, or a Lunch hosted within your own historic private dining space? We can even arrange "Character Teas" that include a Mini Tour with our Historic Characters & our lovely Afternoon Tea.

AUTHOR'S REVIEW

Although Llanelly House has stood on this site for over 300 hundred years, the house that we are now proud to call one of our Top 100 Attractions in Wales, reopened its doors to a new set of visitors in October 2013. I have to say, a tour around the house is no ordinary tour. With state of the art special effects, and interactive members of the household, the hairs on the back of my neck really did stand firmly on end. The staff and management, in fact all of those who are responsible for bringing this very special building back to life, have surpassed all expectations. One thing also worth mentioning, is that you don't actually have to be taking a tour to visit the cafe and restaurant, and the food here really is the envy of Llanelli. There is absolutely no way I can do justice to Llanelly House in just a little over 150 words, so all I can suggest is you need to see it all for yourself, you will not be disappointed!

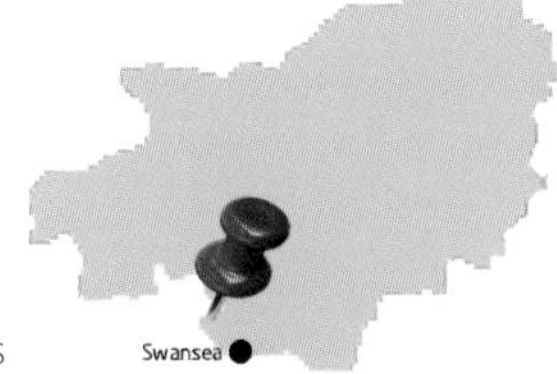

2-4 Bridge Street, Llanelli, Carmarthenshire, SA15 3UF

CARMARTHENSHIRE

WWT Llanelli Wetland Centre

t: 01554-741087 e: info.llanelli@wwt.org.uk
www.wwt.org.uk/visit/llanelli

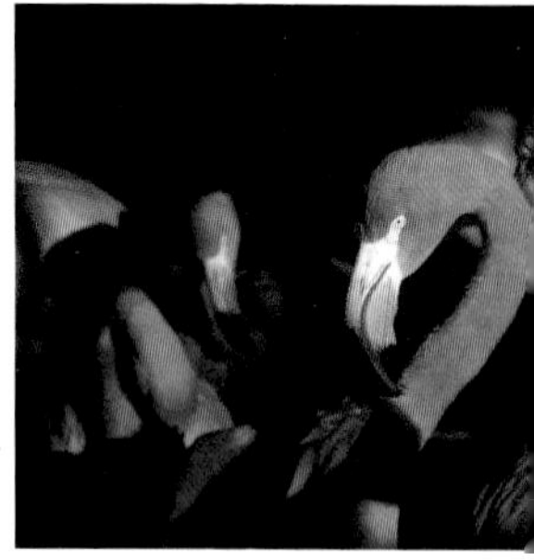

Get ready to explore 450 acres of amazing wetland habitat and discover incredible wildlife at WWT Llanelli. Whether you're a serious birdwatcher, or simply looking for a fun family day out, there's something for everyone here - 363 days of the year!
* Free car parking and room for bikes.
* Handfeed some of the world's rarest wetland birds.
* Seasonal highlights – plenty to spot!
* A fabulous flock of Caribbean flamingos to brighten up your day.
* Fully accessible hides and visitor centre.
* Wheelchair and pushchair friendly paths.
* Outdoor play areas and indoor soft play.
* Well-stocked shop to browse for the perfect gift.

Better still, every penny spent at WWT Llanelli goes to conserving wetlands and helping endangered species around the world!
Visit our website for more info.

AUTHOR'S REVIEW

WWT Llanelli Wetland Centre truly is one of the jewels in Wales'crown. Designated as a Site of Special Scientific Interest (SSSI) this internationally important Ramsar site is home to countless natural treasures including rare plants, thousands of migratory birds, spoonbills, kingfishers, owls, butterflies, dragonflies and elusive water voles. Restoration work was first started by Sir Peter Scott, son of the famous explorer Scott of The Antarctic and founder of the Wildfowl & Wetlands Trust. As I was being shown around the centre and reserve it quickly hit me how important the work of WWT is. Not only do sites like this matter because of the many threatened species that call them home, they also show visitors, including children, how important it is to respect our environment. An annual membership that gives free admission to all WWT sites is available, giving great value for money.

Llwynhendy, Llanelli, Carmarthenshire SA14 9SH

Hawk Adventures

t: 01558-668878 e: info@hawkadventures.co.uk
www.hawkadventures.co.uk

Providers of Outdoor Activities since 1990, we are dedicated to providing exciting and enjoyable adventure activities, corporate events and team building events. Our outdoor activity centre is perfectly placed in the beautiful Brecon Beacons and we deliver the activities across a wide range of locations throughout South Wales, Swansea, Gower, Carmarthenshire and the Brecon Beacons National Park.We have a wide range of outdoor activities available for individuals and groups both large and small, all catered to your needs. Whether you are looking for a taste of adventure activities, fun corporate events or challenging team building events we have the activities to suit your needs.All activities are provided by highly experienced and qualified Instructors. All hold the relevant and current First Aid awards. National qualifications held are those approved by the relevant governing bodies.

AUTHOR'S REVIEW

Hawk Adventures has been using South Wales as their playground for over two decades, and there really isn't anything about 'adventure' that they can't tell you about. Their experience and knowledge of the business, let alone the South Wales Region is unprecedented and very hard to sum up in 150 words. But I will go as far as to say that no matter what kind of activity your looking to take part in, whether it be for a team building event, stag party, or just as part of your holiday, every single member of staff here at Hawk Adventures is not only highly qualified, but more likely over qualified within all aspects of their field. They have a great website which will not only tell you about every activity they specialise in, but the profiles of every instructor is on that site and all available for you to check long before you book your activity with them, making them a very transparent business indeed.

Garreg Wen, Golden Grove, Llanarthney, Carmarthenshire, SA32 8JR

Caws Cenarth Cheese

t: 01239-710432 e: info@cawscenarth.co.uk
www.cawscenarth.co.uk

Glyneithinog, our home, is set in beautiful countryside overlooking the river Cych. Located just a few miles from Newcastle Emlyn, Cenarth and Boncath, you leave the tourist trail far behind as you meander through country lanes to find us. In our visitor center you can discover how cheese is made from the viewing gallery, watching the cheesemakers below hard at work making Caws Cenarth's finest offerings. The best time to visit is between 12.30 and 3pm if you want to see the cheese being made – but we are open from 10am to 5pm, Monday to Friday, including Bank Holidays, and 9am to 1pm on Saturdays. You'll also be given a chance to taste each and every one of our cheeses in our shop and learn more about the history of making cheese. Large groups are welcome – but best ring in advance to let us know you're coming.

AUTHOR'S REVIEW

Wales has produced some of the worlds best cheese for centuries, however it is only since Caws Cenarth came on the scene that the world finally knew about it. Gwynfor and Thelma Adams along with their very talented son Carwyn, have in my opinion drawn a line in the sand when it comes to cheese making, and it is a line many would struggle to cross. Not only can you visit the farm where the magic is created, you can take a tour and learn some of the spells that go into making this wonderful cheese. There is also a special trail for children which really impressed me as a lot of thought went into making sure that children get the most out of their visit too. The final act of your visit is to join Thelma or one of the family for a tasting session. Secretly I could of carried on tasting all of the different cheese's but my diet wouldn't allow. There is a reason why our future king 'Prince Charles' is a huge fan of Caws Cenarth Cheese and I'm sure after your visit, you will be too.

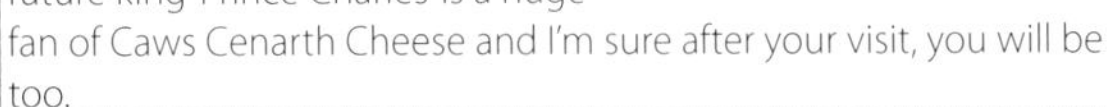

CAWS
CENARTH
CHEESE
CAWS
CENARTH
Cryf
CAWS
CENARTH
Ffili
CAWS
CENARTH
CHEESE
CENARTH
BRIE
Cwmni Caws Eryri
SNOWDONIA
CHEESE COMPANY

Coaltown Coffee Roastery

t: 01269-400105 e: info@coaltowncoffee.co.uk
www.coaltowncoffee.co.uk

We are a specialty coffee roastery. We focus on sustainable and transparent trade with small farms from across the coffee growing regions of the world, and aim to uphold quality at every stage of our production. We are driven by remaining ethical, and by our desire to roast delicious coffee that's full of personality. Unlocking the unique flavours within the world's finest coffee begins in the roaster. Hand-roasted in small batches, our Head of coffee is able to judge the timing and temperature to perfection, delicately drawing out the complex flavour notes from raw green beans. We carefully study how the beans turn from green through to straw yellow and then finally to rich, sumputuous brown, ready to be brewed into perfect cup. Our HOC has been trained within the guidelines set out in the Speciality Coffee Association (SCA) education programme.

AUTHOR'S REVIEW

Coaltown Coffee don't only have their own coffee outlets, but they are now the "go to" trainers when it comes to training barista staff, training not only on how the perfect cup of coffee is brewed, but how it should be served also. Visiting the Roastery here in Carmarthenshire isn't just about experiencing good coffee, it's also about understanding it, so if your a coffee lover, you need to visit Coaltown Coffee and if you're really lucky and they're not too busy, you may even be able to be lucky enough to get a guided tour around some of their roasting machines and have a sneak preview of the complicated process that goes into ensuring you get that perfect cup of coffee every time. I was originally going to feature Coaltown Coffee in our food for thought section for Carmarthenshire, but that would of been a crime, as they are so much more than just a place to grab a bite to eat, but don't just take my word for it, go see for yourself!

Swansea

The Roastery, Foundry Road, Ammanford, Carmarthenshire, SA18 2LS

t: 01269-400 105 e: info@coaltowncoffee.co.uk
www.coaltowncoffee.co.uk

AUTHOR'S REVIEW

Forget Costa, Starbucks or any of those multinationals that claim to be the best coffee providers in the world, in my opinion, when it comes to coffee, there is no family in the United Kingdom that know their coffee any better than Scott James and his family! When a number of people along my travels told me about Scott and what he has created in a small town in South Wales, I struggled to believe it, until I visited their state of the art Roastery in Ammanford, Carmarthenshire that is. But what also came as a huge surprise, Scott is only 24 years old, but don't let his age fool you, as scott and his coffee genius family, supply clients such as Selfridges, House of Parliament, just to name but a few and the list is becoming endless as the word gets out, such is how good this coffee is.

CARMARTHENSHIRE

Espresso Bar

t: 01269-400 105 e: info@coaltowncoffee.co.uk
www.coaltowncoffee.co.uk

Being their first Coaltown Coffee venue, the Espresso Bar means an awful lot to the James family. Here you'll be able to get yourself your favourite coffee in intimate surroundings, but if you are just looking for coffee on the go, that's fine also. The staff here at the bar are friendly and really do know their coffee and will be more than happy to chat to you and answer any coffee related questions you may have. Also worth noting, you can also buy bags of coffee at the espresso bar, so that you can take a little bit of the magic home with you. Finally, we at Top 100 Attractions really do love what Coaltown Coffee have brought to the world of coffee and we know that you will too, just be sure to tell them we sent you!

4 The Arcade, Ammanford SA18 2LN

National Botanic Garden of Wales

t: 01558-667149 e: info@gardenofwales.org.uk
www.gardenofwales.org.uk

Our mission to inspire, educate and conserve has not only made us a beautiful place to visit but a fascinating and relevant one too. We have an amazing collection of over 8000 different plant varieties, spread across 560 acres of beautiful countryside. We've developed a stunning range of themed gardens that appeal to a wide range of visitors, from those who just love the sight and smells of owers to those who want to know about medicinal plants or the latest DNA research into plant evolution.We are very family friendly. There is always plenty of activities for families to do in school and bank holidays, and we have a year round diverse programme of events that appeals to a wide range of visitors. We have the world's largest single span glasshouse, designed by Lord Foster, that has the best display of mediterranean climate zone plants in the Northern hemisphere.

AUTHOR'S REVIEW

The National Botanic Garden is truly Wales's answer to England's Eden Project. I was in awe of the place when last visited, I defnitely wish I had more time to have seen everything, but at least now I have an excuse to go back! What we at Top 100 Attractions absolutely adore is attractions that help us to learn and understand our natural habitat, but with the slick way the team at the National Botanic Garden do it, is very hard to beat. There is always something happening here and you will truly need to set aside a whole day to see everything, which in our estimation is fantastic value for money. Also with a couple of cafes and a good food restaurant you needn't worry about what's for lunch?

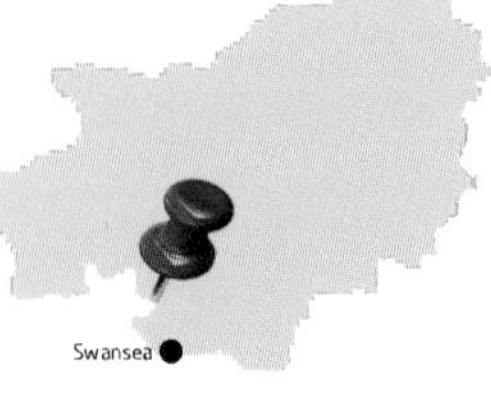

The Roastery, Foundry Road, Ammanford, Carmarthenshire, SA18 2LS

Merlin's Hill Centre

t: 01267-237808 e: alltyfyrddin@yahoo.co.uk
www.merlinshill.com

Discover the secrets of Carmarthenshire at The Merlin's Hill Centre at Alltyfyrddin – a farm steeped in history, shrouded in mystery and rich in wildlife on land that has been farmed for over 2000 years. Follow in the footsteps of Merlin the wizard and walk up the nature trails to the Iron Age Hillfort Site. Experience breathtaking views of Carmarthenshire and beyond, a landscape shaped by its rich heritage and where legend mingles with historical fact. Listen for Merlin's ghostly wailings, for legend has it, he is still imprisoned within this hill. Down on the farmyard, discover the area's history and traditions in the heritage centre and learn about farming – past and present. Watch the cows being milked in the afternoon. The Merlin's Hill Wool Collection – made from the wool of the Jacob Sheep that graze this hill – can be bought in the gift and book shop. Picnic area. Ample Parking.

AUTHOR'S REVIEW

Throughout the United Kingdom, Merlin, King Arthur's Guardian has left his mark and lots of Counties try and stake their claim to him and his mystical ways. However, here in Carmarthenshire it is strongly claimed that this Welsh county was where Merlin was born and ultimately where he returned to die. However, no matter what you believe, you'll be able to make your own mind up once you've visited the Merlin's Hill Centre just a few miles out of Carmarthen. Along with the history of Merlin and his cave, is a small farming museum which really did take me by surprise. Even though it's a small exhibition, together with its exhibits, it tells the story behind the history of farming in Carmarthenshire and its owners Gareth & Sharon have put a lot of work into each exhibit and with its entrance fee being very reasonable, it's definitely worth a visit.

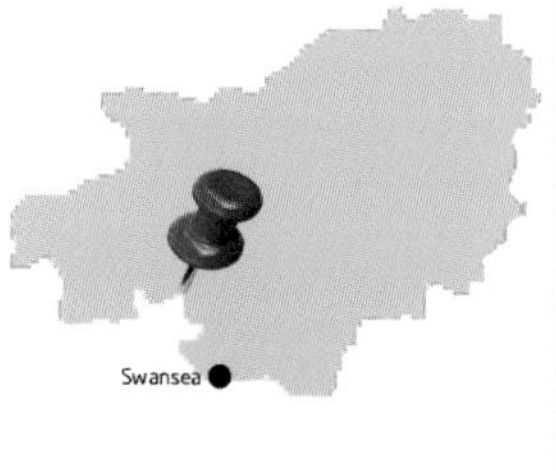

ltyfyrddin Farm, Abergwili, Carmarthenshire, SA32 7ER

Ffos Las Racecourse

t: 01554 811092 e: info@ffoslasracecourse.com
www.ffoslasracecourse.com

Ffos Las goes further than just being a racecourse, it is also an events and conference venue, and is a fantastic location for corporate events, weddings, functions, concerts and other occasions. The venue now boasts, conservation areas, solar farms, beautiful lakes, bridleways and the Diamond Jubilee tree plantation along with the racecourse. In 2018, Ffos Las was bought by Arena Racing Company (ARC) from the founder of the racecourse, Dai Walters. The venue is also suitable for music events and has seen the likes of Madness, Jason Donavan and boyband Blue take to the stage to perform to racegoers. It is argued that Ffos Las is best known for its annual Ladies Day which is held every August and is a known tradition in the West Wales area.
The most valuable race at Ffos Las is the Welsh Champion Hurdle which was moved from our sister track, Chepstow in 2011.

AUTHOR'S REVIEW

Ffos Las racecourse, is a true Welsh success story that will be talked about for many years to come. The course was built at the site of an open cast coal mine after mining operations ceased, but as you visit the racecourse you would never even know it was there. Ffos Las, is Wales's third racecourse but by no means comes last. With state of the art everything, this modern racecourse has everything to offer the modern day punter. On the day I visited Ffos Las, I was allowed to walk around the course, and it was only then with no one else around, I realised just how much has been put into this site, and how every attention to detail has been focused on meticulously. With the new race meeting itinerary now confirmed for 2020, now is the time to check your diary and make a definite date to visit, what is set to be a great racing year here in Wales.

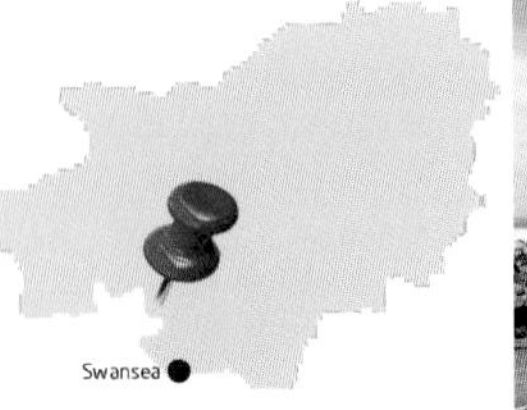

Ffos Las Racecourse, Trimsaran, SA17 4DE

The Old Stable Cottage

Llanddarog, Carmarthenshire, SA32 8NS

T: 01267-275330 www.butchersofllanddarog.co.uk E: enquiries@butchersofllanddarog.co.uk

A luxury, two bedroom cottage located in the village of Llanddarog just outside Carmarthen in South Wales. Located next to The Butchers Arms, it has one of the county's best pubs on it's doorstep - perfect for a leisurely lunch, sumptuous evening meal or a take away to enjoy in the comfort of your own cottage. In close proximity to all of South Wales' best attractions The Old Stable Cottage is the ideal base for your Welsh break. We offer several packages when staying at the Old Stable Cottage from single nights to fortnight breaks. To view current availability and prices please view the cottages4u website, should you wish to book your break through us directly or require any further information don't hesitate to contact us.

Jabajak Vineyard Restaurant with Rooms

Banc y llain, Llanboidy, Whitland, Carmarthenshire, SA34 0ED

T: 01994-448 786 www.www.jabajak.co.uk E: info@jabajak.co.uk

Jabajak is a 5-star Restaurant with bed and breakfast accommodation, set within a vineyard, on the border between Pembrokeshire & Carmarthenshire, 2 miles from the A40. We offer top quality local food, a warm welcome, attentive service and luxury bed and breakfast accommodation; perfect for romantic getaways, short breaks, corporate travellers, idyllic weddings or relaxing meals with friends. Treat yourself to a short break or fabulous meal, amongst the pure fresh air of Jabajak. We're a lush retreat, in breathtaking countryside, hidden in the rural heart of West Wales...yet only a few minutes from the main A40! The traditional Welsh country house was once a working farm, stables and drovers' staging post.

Kidwelly Farm Self-Catering Cottages and B&B

Penlan Isaf, Kidwelly, SA17 5JR

T: 01554-890266 www.kidwellyfarmcottages.co.uk E: kidwellyfarmcottages@live.co.uk

A traditional farmhouse on a hill overlooking the ancient town of Kidwelly with views of the countryside and sea, and ideally situated to explore Carmarthenshire. Wake up to the smell of a real farmhouse breakfast, made from local produce.The bedrooms are family sized with superking size beds, single beds, comfy chairs and sofas and ensuite bathrooms. They have all the facilities needed for your stay – stunning traditional Welsh blankets on the beds, tea & coffee making, TV, DVD player, mini fridge and microwave. Y Felin is a self-catering barn conversion holiday cottage that sleeps 8, with original oak beams and a wood burner. It has four bedrooms, two kingsize and two twin, one with a disabled access en-suite shower wet room and the others with a bath/shower rooms.

Kidwelly Farm Glamping

Penlan Isaf, Kidwelly, SA17 5JR

T: 01554 890 266 www.kidwellyfarmcottages.co.uk E: kidwellyfarmcottages@live.co.uk

Our glamping luxury four berth safari tents are a new venture which opened Easter 2017. The tents are in large secluded pitches providing privacy and plenty of space and freedom for children. Enjoy the peaceful haven of the countryside, relax on your veranda surrounded by nature and take in the stunning views of green fields and the nearby coastline. Watch the daily life of a working farm, walk along the brook and through the woodlands and enjoy sightings of buzzards and red kites. Make the most of the dark night skies of West Wales for star gazing.The campsite overlooks the ancient town of Kidwelly with its magnificent medieval castle and church, there is a footpath from the campsite down to the town through the woods. Purchase award winning sausages from the local butcher for the barbeque.

Allt y Golau Farmhouse B&B

Allt y Golau Uchaf, Felingwm Uchaf, Carmarthenshire, SA32 7BB

T: 01267-290455 www.alltygolau.com E: alltygolau@btinternet.com

Croeso Cynnes Cymreig - a Warm Welsh Welcome awaits you at one of the best bed and breakfasts in Carmarthenshire. Allt y Golau is a Georgian farmhouse just ten minutes from the National Botanic Garden of Wales and Aberglasney Gardens. This delightful Georgian farmhouse has been furnished and decorated to a high standard by the present owners, and enjoys panoramic views over the Tywi Valley to the Black Mountains beyond. Guests are welcome to take a relaxing walk through two acres of mature garden. Many thoughtful extras are provided in the comfortable bedrooms, and there is a separate lounge. Breakfast is provided in the cosy dining room and served around a communal table.

Llwyn Helyg Country House

Llanarthne, Carmarthen, Carmarthenshire, SA32 8HJ

T: 01558-668778 www.llwynhelygcountryhouse.co.uk E: enquiries@llwynhelygcountryhouse.co.uk

Llwyn Helyg is an award winning Country House situated in South Wales at the heart of the Tywi Valley, less than half an hour west of Swansea and midway between the bustling Market and County Town of Carmarthen and Llandeilo. The Bedrooms offer unrivalled luxury with 'And So To Bed' Beds and premium 'Vi-Spring' Mattresses, all with bespoke designed marble and granite furniture. All rooms have 42" Panasonic Flat Screen TVs with DVDs and Tea and Coffee facilities. Quality fluffy Dressing Gowns and Slippers are provided along with Hairdryers and Ironing Facilities.All En Suites are fitted with genuine Jacuzzi Whirlpool Baths (each with Sanitising Units for maintaining excellence in hygiene) and Grohe Rainshower Shower units.

The Plough at Rhosmaen

Rhosmaen, Llandeilo, Carmarthenshire, SA19 6NP

T: 01558-823 431 www.ploughrhosmaen.com E: info@ploughrhosmaen.com

A charming four star boutique hotel and award winning restaurant set in the beautiful Towy Valley at the edge of the Brecon Beacons. Surrounded by castles and country houses with the National Botanical Garden of Wales and Aberglasney House only minutes away. Relax in the tranquil surroundings of the Towy Valley in our beautifully appointed accommodation. You could not ask for more, captivating view from all our 23 well appointed en suite rooms equipped with everything you would expect for your stay - queen sized beds, free WiFi, sofas and disabled facilities - all impeccably serviced with our unique attention to detail. We were delighted to win the Gold Award for our accommodation in the Carmarthenshire Tourism Awards 2015/16.

Stradey Park Hotel

Stradey Park Hotel, Furnace, Llanelli, SA15 4HA

T: 01554 -58171 www.stradeyparkhotel.com E: reservations@stradeyparkhotel.com

Tucked in the Welsh hillside, standing proud over our world famous Gower and Carmarthenshire coastline, the 4 star Stradey Park Hotel & Spa in Llanelli waits to welcome you into the family. With first class service prepare to be spoilt as we take great delight in making your stay in Llanelli the first of mar Whether you are joining us for a family break, romantic weekend, corporate event, or spa treatment within our award winning Parc Spa you will find nothing is too much trouble to guarantee your comfo View our accommodation special offers, with prices to suit all budgets. Accommodation rates include a full buffet breakfast.Stradey Park Hotel & Spa, Llanelli offers guests free parking and complimentary hi speed WiFi in both public areas and guest rooms.

Bryn Hebog Bed & Breakfast

Lower Penddaulwyn, Capel Dewi, Carmarthen, Carmarthenshire, SA32 8AY

T: 01267 290289 www.brynhebog.co.uk E: info@brynhebog.co.uk

Bryn Hebog is a small bed & breakfast with three letting bedrooms which are all en-suite. On your arrival at Bryn Hebog, you will be offered a complimentary tray of tea or coffee which will be served to you in the conservatory, which is available for guests exclusive use at all times. Feel free to wander and explore the grounds or sit on a bench and take in the views. We have three bedrooms, a King-size, a Double and a Twin. Whichever room you choose you will find an en-suite shower room stocked with fluffy white towels and a selection of toiletries.In all rooms you will find luxury bed linen, freeview TV's, clock radios, hairdryers and a welcome tray with tea, coffee and hot chocolate making facilities.

Baytree Cottage B&B & Self Catering

Maesglasnant, Carmarthen, Carmarthenshire, SA31 2LS

T: 01267-236110 www.baytree-bedandbreakfast.co.uk E: baytreecottage@sky.com

At Baytree Cottage we offer friendly, stylish accommodation, just 2 miles from Carmarthen. Very easy to find us, just off the M4/A48. Our B&B is a newly traditional built house set in its own grounds, which combines taste with all the home comforts you could wish for, full of charm and character. The 'Potting Shed' self catering accommodation is designed for your comfort, and has all that you'd need for a relaxing and enjoyable stay. Baytree bedrooms are light spacious with a comfy sofa, television, and a tea/coffee tray for your comfort. Crisp white bedding on a king size bed, and in the large power shower room, all the towels are white and fluffy. Baytree Potting Shed, homely stylish feel, fully self-contained, with all the home comforts you would wish for. We are open all year round.

Bronhaul Farm Cottages

Bronhaul Farm, Bancyfelin, Carmarthen, Carmarthenshire, SA33 5NQ

T: 01267 211 303 www.bronhaulfarm.co.uk E: info@bronhaulfarm.co.uk

Bronhaul is a haven of tranquility in the rolling green shires of West Wales. It's a diverse and abundant valley of ancient woodlands, babbling brooks, flourishing gardens, rolling pastures and fertile wetlands. For many years, and for many people who've spent time here, Bronhaul is a place of retreat, natural beauty and biodiversity, deep peace and reflection, escape, inspiration, regeneration. Bronhaul offers relaxing farmstays in our characterful self-catering cottages, simple 'back-to-nature' camping holidays in our bell tents and the healing benefits of time in nature on our land-based retreats. We're also a small-scale working family farm, passionate about local food, sustainable living and working with nature. Come and join us! Experience the farm life, volunteer, learn skills for sustainability, play, imagine, immerse yourself in wild nature, eat local food, explore what wild West Wales has to offer .

Alltyfyrddin Farm B&B

Alltyfyrddin Farm, Merlins Hill Road, Abergwili, Carmarthenshire, SA32 7ER

T: 07866-880641 www.merlinshill.com E: alltyfyrddin@yahoo.co.uk

Alltyfyrddin offers 3Star Farmhouse Bed and Breakfast accommodation in five bedrooms - single, double, twin and family rooms. All have en-suite facilities and are tastefully decorated, furnished with your comfort in mind. Enjoy a choice of delicious breakfasts made from local produce. Spedial diets can be catered for by prior arrangement. Alltyfyrddin is an ideal base for visitors to explore the beautiful beaches, mountains, gardens and castles of West Wales. Alltyfyrddin B & B also provides a relaxing haven for business guests. All this just 2 miles from Carmarthen. We look forward to welcoming you to Alltyfyrddin. Alltyfyrddin B & B is a farm steeped in history, shrouded in mystery, and rich in wildlife.

The Ivy Bush Royal Hotel

Spilman Street, Carmarthen. SA31 1LG

T: 01267 235111 www.ivybushroyal.co.uk E: reception@ivybushroyal.co.uk

Commanding a spectacular position at the gateway to the Golden West, the Ivy Bush Royal has long welcomed leisure and business guests in considerable comfort and style. Once a favoured retreat for Lord Nelson and Lady Hamilton, the hotel has been sympathetically modernised to blend its old world charm with modern facilities. There are 70 comfortably furnished bedrooms, 2 family rooms and a suite. Fresh local produce is used extensively in our seasonal menus and beef from local farms feature prominently with succulent results. A comprehensive wine list complements the food with wines from all over the world and local beers are readily available.

Browns Hotel

King Street, Laugharne, Carmarthenshire, SA33 4RY

T: 01994-427 688 www.browns.wales E: info@browns-hotel.co.uk

Brown's Hotel, built in 1752, is an iconic literary address, the social hub of Laugharne and the favourite watering hole of poet and writer Dylan Thomas, who famously left the bar's phone number as his own.We offer luxurious rooms, the famous bar and our new Penderyn Restaurant.Brown's is a hotel of characters – the locals and staff are always up for a chat – and following in Dylan's footsteps President Carter, Burton & Taylor, Mick Jagger, Pierce Brosnan, Cerys Matthews and many others have made their way up the three stone steps to the bar. We take great care to create an incomparable visitor experience and each room has its own 1950s themed retro-styled furniture and tastefully designed colour scheme, which, together with our specially commissioned wall art showing lovingly re-created scenes from the post-war period, help to create some of the finest hotel rooms in Laugharne and a real 'Wow' factor.

The Red Lion Inn

Llandyfaelog Kidwelly Carmarthenshire SA17 5PR

T: 01267 267530 www.redlionllandyfaelog.co.uk E: info@redlionllandyfaelog.co.uk

Let us welcome you to The Red Lion in Llandyfaelog, a family friendly pub and restaurant with function room near Kidwelly Carmarthenshire. We have available five beautiful en-suite bed and breakfast rooms at The Red Lion Llandyfaelog, near Kidwelly in Carmarthenshire. Available room comprise of four double rooms and one single. Each room has been tastefully decorated and offers a high standard of accommodation in Carmarthenshire.

Room amenities include en-suite, tea & coffee, free Wi-Fi Internet, digital television and hair dryers. We have 4 double rooms, a single room (twin available upon request).

Pantysgyfarnog Bed & Breakfast

Llangynog, Carmarthen SA33 5DE

T: 07788-800210 E: georginaclaire666@gmail.com

Located in Carmarthen, Pantysgyfarnog offers 4-star accommodation with a garden and a terrace. This 4-star guest house offers a shared lounge and room service. The guest house has a hot tub, luggage storage space and free WiFi.

The rooms in the guest house are fitted with a kettle. All rooms include a wardrobe and a TV, and certain rooms are equipped with a balcony.

A variety of popular activities are available in the area around the property, including cycling and hiking.Carmarthen Castle is 8.1 miles from Pantysgyfarnog.

Valans

29 High Street, Llandybie, Carmarthenshire, SA18 3HX

T: 01269-851288 www.valans.co.uk E: enquiries@valans.co.uk

n 2004 we stumbled across a property in the village of Llandybie. A former florists, It had a lovely charm. Being ever optomistic we saw past the rotten floor boards and leaky roof and in it's place we visualised a restaurant; somewhere for locals and visitors alike to relax and enjoy. Work soon began and after eight months of refurbishment Valans was born. A warm welcome and good honest food is whats waiting when you visit us. We don't do pretentious, stuffy service and we won't try and bamboozle you with cooking terminology straight out of a chemistry book.

Croes y Ceiliog Cafe & B&B

Llanwrda, Carmarthenshire, SA19 8HD

T: 01550-777800

The Croes Y Ceiliog Inn is located on the edge of the beautiful Brecon Beacons National Park in the pretty village of Llanwrda in Carmarthenshire. We are a pub, café and bed and breakfast with traditional charm and attractive original features The Croes Y Ceiliog Inn represents the very best of an old Welsh country pub, where traditional values and atmosphere still survive. With comfortable, well equipped accommodation all rooms are a good size. We offer double rooms and a family room each with a tea/ coffee making tray and the usual extras to make your stay comfortable and enjoyable. A full Welsh breakfast is included in the price of the stay. The Croes Y Ceiliog stocks real ale, cider and a huge s election of fine wines. Food is served on most days including Sunday roasts.

Wrights Food Emporium

Llanarthne, Carmarthenshire, SA32 8JU

T: 01558-668929 www.wrightsfood.co.uk E: maryann@wrightsfood.co.uk

Wright's Food Emporium a café and food store in South West Wales.
...refillable wine / Maryann's freshly baked bread / run by people who know and love food / breakfast / refillable olive oil / artisan cheeses / craft beers / help and advice on tap/ the pork belly cubano / seasonal fruit and veg / sopressata / Mutti canned tomatoes / Welsh farmhouse apple juice / toasted welsh rarebit / refillable Welsh rapeseed oil / proper coffee / loads of tastings / Pembrokeshire poussin / pie of the week / Hallet's cider / small estate European wines... and many more reasons to be cheerful.

Ginhaus Deli

1 Market Street, Llandeilo, Carmarthenshire, SA19 6AH

T: 01558-823030 www.ginhaus.co.uk E: kate@ginhaus.co.uk

Ginhaus deli is located in the very beautiful little town of Llandeilo and is run by Mike and Kate Kindred. Mike and Kate first met in the Three Tuns, a very popular and much loved local drinking pub (everyone in Llandeilo has fond, if not slightly hazy memories of the Tuns!). Many years later and they are happily married with three little Kindreds and they are back in the Tuns...which has now been lovingly transformed into the wonderful Ginhaus deli.
Pop in and smell the cakes being baked, to taste samples from the extensive cheese counter, to marvel at the impressive selection of gins, to enjoy the relaxing atmosphere or just to say hello!

The Fox & Hounds at Bancyfelin

High Street, Bancyfelin, Carmarthenshire, SA33 5ND

T: 01267-211341 www.foxandhoundsbancyfelin.co.uk e: foxandhoundsbancyfelin@gmail.com

The Fox & Hounds is a hidden gem in the heart of Carmarthenshire. we are just of the A40 - stop off when you are heading to Carmarthen or when you are going on holiday to Pembrokeshire! An extraordinary Welsh pub with rich sporting heritage surrounded by glorious Carmarthenshire countryside. In the summer months, one can be found in the beer garden relaxing in the days sunshine or socialising in our public bar with our friendly locals.The food menu offers flavoursome and hearty dishes using local, fresh ingredients which are complemented by a great range of well-kept traditional ales, craft beers, local gins and fine wines. Are you travelling with your pets? We are dog friendly in our bar area.

The Warren

11 Mansel Street, Carmarthen, Carmarthenshire, SA31 1PX

T: 01267-236 079 www.warrenmanselst.co.uk e: enquiries@warrenmanselst.co.uk

A family run Cafe/Restaurant & Bar serving Simple, Honest & Wholesome food focussing on Local, Seasonal & Organic produce. The Warren is a quirky & unique venue set in the heart of Carmarthen town which opened its doors in 2016 after a successful Crowdfunding campaign raising over £20,000 from the local community. The Warren is also a venue for events such as Pop-Up Supper Clubs, Charity Quizzes, Live Music & Open Mic Nights. Founder Deri Reed built his reputation with his first business "Ethical Chef" which traded at Glastonbury Music Festival winning "The Green Traders Award." in 2014. Deri also won "Best Street Food" from The Wales Food Awards in 2016 before deciding it was time to secure a permanent location in his hometown of Carmarthen.

The New Curiosity

20a King Street, Carmarthen, Carmarthenshire, SA31 1BH

T: 01267 232384 www.thenewcuriosity.co.uk e: info@thenewcuriosity.co.uk

The New Curiosity restaurant is the first venture for husband and wife partnership Daniel and Rachel Williams. Daniel with over twelve years experience as a chef has worked in many a prestigious kitchen and also regularly appears on S4C's daytime programme "Prynhawn Da" giving cooking tips and demonstrations. "My first true passion is food, be it eating or cooking. I feel extremely fortunate to have the opportunity to live and work in an area with such an abundance of fresh quality produce, be it fish from the Towy river to the fantastic Gower Salt Marsh Lamb. I truly believe that we must make the most of our fruitful lands and we make every effort to use these commodities." We offer both light and forma lunches, a la carte evening meals which can be enjoyed in the relaxed atmosphere and understated modern decor of the grade listed building.

Waverley Vegetarian Restaurant

23 Lammas Street, Carmarthen ,SA31 3AL

T: 01267-236521 www.waverleyhealthstores.co.uk E: waverleyhealthstore@gmail.com

Established in 1847, The Waverley Stores are a family run health food shop providing the local community with a wide selection of quality health foods including wholefoods (such as dried fruits, rice and grains), herbal teas, toiletries, supplements and a lot more.We at The Waverley Stores pride ourselves on supplying a range of tasty organic fruit and vegetables. As well as locally grown vegetables, when in season. We are happy to offer our customers an order and collection service for those who don't have time to shop.For those looking for delicious vegetarian cuisine, we also have a restaurant providing tasty wholesome vegetarian, vegan and gluten free options.

The Red Lion Inn

Llandyfaelog Kidwelly Carmarthenshire SA17 5PR

T: 01267-267530 www.redlionllandyfaelog.co.uk E: info@redlionllandyfaelog.co.uk

Let us welcome you to The Red Lion in Llandyfaelog, a family friendly pub and restaurant with function room near Kidwelly Carmarthenshire. Come and enjoy a refreshing drink in the beer garden or bring the family for a delicious home cooked meal. Sample our hearty Sunday lunch in Carmarthenshire or choose from our appetising selection of dishes in the restaurant. If your looking for a function room in Carmarthenshire then The Red Lion can help.Our function room is a great choice for a celebrations. So whether your planning a birthday, christening, wedding reception, family get together, concert, charity evening or a meeting The Red Lion has the facilities and catering to help you.

The Tearooms at Aberglasney

Llangathen, Carmarthen, Carmarthenshire, SA32 8QH

T: 01558-667959 www.aberglasney.org E: tearooms@aberglasney.org

No trip to Aberglasney is complete without visiting the Tearooms, idyllically located overlooking the Pool Garden. The Tearooms are cosy inside while the terrace is a real suntrap. It's the perfect place to enjoy good homemade, freshly prepared lunches or of course a quintessential afternoon tea including homemade cakes and pastries. You'll also find a selection of wines, beers and ciders on the menu alongside great ice cream.Wherever possible all the ingredients used are local and when it comes to fruit and vegetables this means Aberglasney's own Kitchen Garden is put to good use. From crisp fresh salads to apple crumble, it's an opportunity to enjoy a taste of Aberglasney, so look out for information of what we've grown and used on the daily specials board.

The Bistro at Llanelly House

Bridge Street, Llanelli, Carmarthenshire, SA15 3UF

T: 01554-772857 www.llanellyhouse.org.uk E: bookings@llanellyhouse.org.uk

A warm welsh welcome awaits you from the team in our Llanelly House Bistro. Call in for a late breakfast, morning coffee or snack on your way to the shops, or linger over lunch if you have more time. Come try our locally sourced, Welsh inspired delicious breakfasts.

Come to Llanelly House, Wales' finest Georgian building, discover the legacy of the Stepney family. Visit the café and restaurant, taste our delicious food in 18th century surroundings. Enjoy our unique shop, set in Sir Thomas Stepney's study showcasing the best and finest Welsh gifts.Llanelly House has a choice of exciting tours, find out about the Stepney family and how they shaped the town and the industrial landscape of South Wales, includes scandalous tales from upstairs and downstairs.

Y Polyn

Capel Dewi, Carmarthen, Carmarthenshire, SA32 7LH

T: 01267-290000 www.ypolyn.co.uk E: hello@ypolyn.co.uk

We're not trying to be cutting edge or post-modern here. You won't find foams, gels and technical wizardry on the plate. What you will find is beautiful produce cooked simply and with respect. Saltmarsh lamb, Welsh beef and free range, rare breed pork are highlights of the well balanced menu. We're very keen to avoid pretention at Y Polyn. Tables are mismatching bare wood, tablecloths are banished, staff wear jeans and you get to pour your own wine. Almost everything we serve has been made on the premises.- We work hard at sourcing great produce, much of it local.
- We put ingredients together in tasty combinations that work, some of these may be familiar to you.
- We offer our own bread and bottled water at no extra charge. - We don't pour your wine for you and we don't have tablecloths. - The atmosphere is relaxed, friendly and very informal.

Cresselly Arms

Pontargothi, Carmarthenshire, SA32 7NG

T: 01267-290482 www.cresselly-arms.com e: cressellyarms@hotmail.com

The Cresselly Arms Bar and Restaurant, with its beautiful riverside garden is located on the bank of the river Cothi, which runs into the river Towy. We are in an idylic location, overlooking the bridge which gives the village its name, Pontargothi, in Welsh that means the bridge over the river Cothi. Our picturesque location is ideal for breaking your journey, meeting with friends in our stylish bar, or enjoying a delicious home cooked meal in our riverside restaurant.

You can choose to sit inside, overlooking the river or, when the weather is good enough, outside on the riverside deck or in the garden.

Butchers of Llanddarog

Llanddarog, Carmarthenshire, SA32 8NS

T: 01267-275330 www.butchersofllanddarog.co.uk E: contact@butchersofllanddarog.co.uk

We are a traditional Welsh pub in the heart of the country village of Llanddarog just off the the A48 between Cross Hands and Carmarthen.

Our aim is to serve good quality homemade food, using locally sourced produce at reasonable prices. In addition to the lunch and evening menus, both of which can be viewed on this website, we also provide lunch and evening specials that are changed weekly. A vegetarian specials menu is available and, as all our meals are freshly cooked, we can cater to most dietary requirements - if choice is what you are after, then we are the place for you!

The Ivy Bush Royal Hotel

Spilman Street, Carmarthen. SA31 1LG

T: 01267-235111 www.ivybushroyal.co.uk E: reception@ivybushroyal.co.uk

The Ivy Bush Royal has long welcomed leisure and business guests in considerable comfort and style. Once a favored retreat for Lord Nelson and Lady Hamilton, the hotel has been sympathetically modernized to blend its old world charm with modern facilities. Fresh local produce is used extensively in our seasonal menus and Welsh Black beef from a local farm feature prominently with succulent results. A comprehensive wine list complements the food with wines from all over the world and local beers are readily available..Air conditioned, with friendly service from experienced staff, the restaurant is open daily for all meals with traditional Sunday lunches featuring prime roasts are especially popularBreakfast buffet with an abundant array of hot & cold foods.

Cafe at No. 4

4 Queen Street Carmarthen SA31 1JR

T: 01267-275330 www.cafeno4.com E: daveatcafefour@hotmail.com.

Located in one of the oldest and most historic towns in Wales, Carmarthen. Hidden away lies the small and modest boutique restaurant Café at No 4. Starting life as a quiet Cafe, has now evolved into a bustling exclusive restaurant. Since 2013, Andrew Luck & David Jenkins have continuously poured in their hearts and determination into creating an establishment that is constantly growing. They have created a new and exciting addition to Carmarthen's constantly growing dining scene. Café at No 4 also host a Taster Menu evening on the last Wednesday of each month offering an insight into new and exciting dishes coming from the kitchen. Cafe at No4 is open from 18.00hrs on Thursdays, Fridays & Saturdays. We are proud to be one of few venues chosen to be in Western Mail/Wales Online's latest article of their trip around our county of Carmarthenshire.

Emlyn Arms Llanarthne

Lanarthne, Carmarthenshire, SA32 8JE

T: 01558-668989 www.emlynarms.co.uk E: info@emlynarms.co.uk

Formerly The Paxton, the Emlyn Arms is steeped in history and situated in the heart of the picturesque Towy Valley. Recently refurbished, it blends the style of yesteryear with modern accommodation in just the right measure. We pride ourselves on the range and quality of food and drinks available, we have a wide selection of wines and spirits, real ales, ciders and draught beers. Also a selction of soft drinks, and freshly brewed tea or speciality coffee.

For the glorious sunny days there is an outside seating area, and for the winter nights a cosy bar area, with a large flat screen TV, and a roaring log fire, what could be better?

The Black Ox

High Street, Abergwili, Carmarthen, Carmarthenshire, SA31 2JB

T: 01267-237370 www.blackoxgastro.wales E: contact@blackoxgastro.com

The Black Ox Gastropub is a charming neighbourhood restaurant and bar, situated in the heart of Abergwili - a true getaway to gourmet. Inspired by seasonal produce and the province's local suppliers, we only serve you the highest quality of food and drinks. All of the team are extremely proud of our Gastropub status, and our wonderful team of chef's are always producing the finest content on a daily basis. You can find us situated at the heart of the warm community of Abergwili, Carmarthenshire. Visit us for a vibrant, family-like atmosphere that we are sure you will love. Whether you want our high quality food or our refreshing choice of drinks, The Black Ox are sure to please. We're very proud of our fantastic menus. Indulge in quality dishes, with ingredients and products sourced from suppliers we can trust.

Pethau Da at Mansel Street

2 Mansel Street, Carmarthen, Carmarthenshire, SA31 1QX

T: 01267-236300 www.pethauda.co.uk E: post@pethauda.co.uk

We're a local, friendly, Welsh company who relish in providing home made food of the highest standard. Using local produce and ingredients we prepare everything here at 'PethauDa'. 'Pethau Da' opened in Mansel Street during the summer of 2017 and we're now open daily,evenings on the weekend, and during some special celebratory occasions. Our aim is to provide a very special welcome and fine food to our customers in a relaxed and homely environment – the perfect place to unwind. Pop over for breakfast, lunch, supper or call in for a cuppa and chat – a unique welcome and fine home made food awaits you.With everything prepared and produced locally it's a feast well worth witnessing and tasting.

Maryellens@139

139 Rhosmaen Street, Llandeilo, Carmarthenshire, SA19 6EN

T: 01558-823444 E: maryellens.139@outlook.com

Great coffees, homemade cakes and lovely lunches...If we look full to capacity downstairs, we've got upstairs seating too... not to worry if you cant stop we can get you some lunch or lovely treats to take-away (even if you just need a caffeine fix to go!)

Google Review 5 Star

Popped in for a sandwich and pot of tea, I had a chicken and bacon sandwich, lovely thick chicken and very tasty bacon. My Wife had a cheese and tomato sandwich, not actually on the menu but they were happy to accommodate. We both thoroughly enjoyed our food, lovely surroundings and the staff were friendly and efficient.

Stradey Park Hotel

Stradey Park Hotel, Furnace, Llanelli, SA15 4HA

T: 01554 758171 www.stradeyparkhotel.com E: reservations@stradeyparkhotel.com

Whatever your taste you'll find something to satisfy at Stradey Park Hotel & Spa, Llanelli, as we embark on a mission to offer you the ultimate dining experience. Whether you are sitting down to a business lunch, a romantic dinner for two, Afternoon Tea or traditional Sunday lunch with all the family, you'll delight in our cuisine. Our new Copperplate Bar & Grill in Llanelli, enjoys stunning panoramic views of the Gower Peninsula and Carmarthen Bay making it the perfect setting for a romantic meal, special celebration or simply an opportunity to unwind. Food is sourced locally wherever possible to bring you the finest dishes using the freshest ingredients. Our delicious new menu provides something to tantalize everyone's tastebuds.

The Plough at Rhosmaen

Rhosmaen, Llandeilo, Carmarthenshire, SA19 6NP

T: 01558 823 431 www.ploughrhosmaen.com E: info@ploughrhosmaen.com

A charming four star boutique hotel and award winning restaurant set in the beautiful Towy Valley at the edge of the Brecon Beacons. Surrounded by castles and country houses with the National Botanical Garden of Wales and Aberglasney House only minutes away.arrival.

A subtle blend of modern and traditional culinary styles coupled with a warm inviting atmosphere. The Plough Rhosmaen has an excellent nationwide reputation for it's commitment to using the best local ingredients, cooked in new and exciting styles and a menu with choices of the old favourites or dishes a little more imaginative, complemented by an extensive wine cellar and a great range of coffees to finish.

The Falcon Hotel

111 Lammas St, Carmarthen, West

T: 01267 234959 www.falconcarmarthen.co.uk E: reception@falconcarmarthen.co.uk

Located in the heart of Carmarthen, the historical Falcon Hotel has been the hotel of choice for visitors to this bustling market town for generations. Dining at the Falcon Hotel is always special and the restaurant has earned an excellent reputation for the quality of its delicious food, making it popular with non-residents as well as guests staying at the hotel. In fact, the restaurant attracts regular diners from all over Carmarthenshire and further afield who realise they are assured of consistently good food and first class service every time. Head Chef Lazar, create delicious dishes using fresh local produce and served in good, hearty sized portions. The new seasonal menu offers guests a great selection of traditional favourites with a modern twist. Setting high standards for the quality of their cuisine has ensured a large percentage of loyal customers that visit Carmarthen just to dine here.

Browns Hotel *

King Street, Laugharne, Carmarthenshire, SA33 4RY

T: 01994-427 688 www.browns.wales E: info@browns-hotel.co.uk

The staff and management at Brown's Hotel are delighted to announce the opening of their Laugharne restaurant. 'Penderyn Restaurant' reflects the close relationship between our iconic hotel and the award-winning distillery in the foothills of the Brecon Beacons.

The decor reflects the distillery colours, namely black and gold and there are pictures of the distillery adorning the walls. The chef is David Fry-Thomas who has conjured up a delightful menu with the focus on good local ingredients.We serve evening meals from Wednesday to Saturday and also a Sunday lunch menu. Check out Trip Advisor for our 5-star reviews! from the post-war period, help to create some of the finest hotel rooms in Laugharne and a real 'Wow' factor.

SWANSEA & GOWER COAST

f I was writing this introduction page a few years ago, you can be rest assured that it wouldn't be s many words as what it is today! Swansea, over the past ten years has gone through somewhat of facelift. With buildings going up almost every few months, this small city in Wales has now been ransformed into a city that could give any region in the UK a run for its money. Now throw the Gower eninsula into the mix, now that's a recipe that even Gordon Ramsey or Delia Smith couldn't of come p with. These areas ten years ago were nice places to visit, now all these years on, they're fabulous laces to visit. Why could that be, you may ask yourselves? We'll let me enlighten you. The county ouncil in Swansea along with the Gower rural district council, really have had a great vision of what's eeded to bring tourists to the locality.

ogether with every business within the tourism sector of those areas, they have transformed that retch of coastline into somewhere that is able to attract people from all over the world. The area can ow, not just be known for being home to notable people such and Catherine Zeta Jones, Sir nthony Hopkins and Dylan Thomas, but now be known for being one of the best places in Wales to pend your valuable holiday time. Speaking of Catherine Zeta Jones, no trip to Swansea or the Gower oast is complete until you've visited the Mumbles. I have some fond memories of my time in wansea and the Gower coast and I hope I'm responsible for the fond memories you're going to have nce you've been there too and if you've never tasted cockles and lava bread, believe me, it's to die r!

Perriswood - Archery and Falconry Centre

t: 01792-371661 e: info@perriswood.com
www.perriswood.com

Perriswood is a family run business situated in the heart of Gower overlooking the stunning Oxwich Bay.
We provide a range of activities that can be enjoyed by all generations and families. Whether you are looking to try something new; relax and take in the surrounding scenery; have fun with the family; or celebrate a special occasion… Perriswood is the place to be!
Archery sessions are available all day everyday, on our outside range with the fabulous view, or inside if the weather is too bad, and are suitable for the whole family (from 6 years old) and for all abilities. Visit our Archery page for more information. With 38 birds of prey at the centre we offer displays and experience days where you will have the opportunity to meet and hold the birds. Our ever popular Rifle Range at Perriswood is available for participants of 14 years and over, bringing yet another country pursuit for the family to try.

AUTHOR'S REVIEW

No trip to the Swansea area is complete without a visit to the Gower!.. Complete with blue flag beaches, unique coastlines and Catherine Zeta Jones's hometown 'The Mumbles' you'll have no time to get bored!.. But one place that needs to be on your itinerary is Perriswood Archery and Falconry Centre! Whether your looking for an indoor or an out-door attraction, Perriswood simply has it all! From Archery to Shooting and not forgetting the Falconry Centre there is always something to keep you busy! It is set to be a great year for Perriswood Archery and Falconry Centre and with their weekly pass available to everybody, you don't have to cram it all into one day.

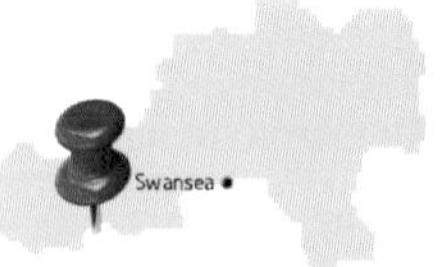

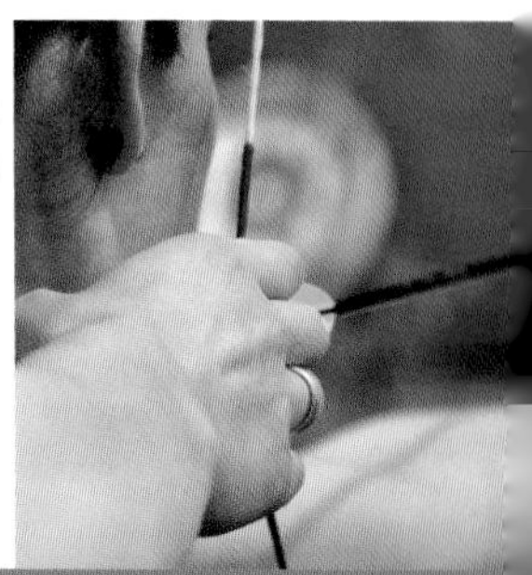

Perriswood Farm Penmaen, Gower, Swansea, SA3 2HN

1940's Swansea Bay

t: 01792-458864 e: mail@1940sswansea.co.uk
www.1940swanseabay.co.uk

Hidden away just two minutes from the busy M4 near Swansea, South Wales is the WWII experience 1940s Swansea Bay. The indoor street scene takes you past an RAF Plotting Room and into an air raid shelter where you hear the sound of bombs falling. Walking past a bomb damaged shop you pass a wartime front parlour then into the Three Lamps pub for a 1940s sing-along on the piano! As well as 1940s vacuum cleaners, washing and sewing machines on display there are also clothes and uniforms for the youngsters to try on. The gift shop has replica Ration Books and Identity Cards and also serves teas so you can have a Spam sandwich and Camp coffee! Open daily to the public daily from 10am to 5pm, guided tours from an Air Raid Warden are available for groups as are evening visits.

Here at the 1940's Swansea Bay Museum you get to taste life and soak up the atmosphere of how life in Swansea and the rest of the UK would have been way back in the 1940's. At first when I arrived at this attraction, I was a little bit unsure of what to expect with this attraction being smack bang in the middle of an industrial estate, but the museums location really is quite fitting to the message the museum is trying to give. Complete with its own set of trenches and guard posts it is very easy to allow yourself to be transported back in time where Vera Lynn would have been at number one in the top 40 and ration books would have been just as important to you as your Gas Mask! The owners of this attraction have put everything they can into making your experience here one never to be forgotten and for that we here at Top 100 Attractions applaud them. It goes to show that it's not just money you need to create an attraction of this nature but devotion, patients and in this attractions case a love for all things 40's!

Swansea

Elba Crescent, Crymlyn Burrows, Swansea, SA1 8PT

Gower Brewery Tour

t: 01792 371661 e: info@gowerbrewery.com
www.gowerbrewery.com

If you'd like to gain an understanding of how we make our ales, what ingredients we use and why - and you fancy a good evening out with friends or colleagues - why not come on a brewery tour… **A nice evening out!**We run tours for between 10 -20 people. Our tours are run during the evening and start about 6pm - 7pm. You'll be here for around an hour, which is plenty of time to have a look around and discover how we make Gower Gold so tasty! We'll give you a history of Gower Brewery, an explanation of the brewing process and raw ingredients, and follow it all up with a tasting session! If you would like a tour for a smaller number of people then just get in touch and we can arrange something for you. Brewery tours need to book in advance. Brewery Tour Vouchers can also be purchased. It doesn't end there!After you tour, why not head to The Greyhound Inn, just 4 miles down the road, and round the evening off with a home cooked meal. Or if you would like to sample a few more of our ales, The Kings Head Inn – our 4-star B&B, is located approximately 8 miles from the brewery.

AUTHOR'S REVIEW

I have featured a number of distillery tours in my books, but this is the first brewery tour that I have had the pleasure of being able to endorse. Micro brewery's are starting to appear all over the United Kingdom and are starting to put real ale back on the map. The Gower Brewery is an award winning brewery that really are becoming a force to be reckoned with. The Gower Brewery is the only micro brewery that I have come across that does a tour around their brewery, and now they have moved to new premises the tour has just got a whole lot better. With more to see, a tasting session and the ability to leave with some of your very own beer, I think this tour is absolutely fabulous. I recommend popping into their website and getting more up to date information, and give them a call to book a place on the tour.

Crofty Industrial Estate, Swansea, SA4 3RS

Dylan Thomas Birth Place

t: 01792 472 555 e: info@dylanthomasbirthplace.com
www.dylanthomasbirthplace.com

Just imagine... socialising, eating dinner and spending the night in arguably the most famous house in Welsh literature - the house where one of the most celebrated poets and writers of the 20th century was born, spent the first 23 years of his life and first put pen to paper.

Well, you and your family and friends can now do this yourselves! Thanks to the tireless efforts of a team of dedicated Dylan Thomas enthusiasts, his birthplace and childhood home at 5 Cwmdonkin Drive in the Uplands suburb of Swansea - the second city of Wales - has been fully restored to its 1914 condition when it was bought as a new house by the Thomas family. This house played a huge part in shaping the style and output of Dylan Thomas, and we guarantee that there will be something that you will see or touch that will provide memories for a long time to come time to come.

AUTHOR'S REVIEW

The country of Wales has been famous for many things, but as a rule literary wasn't at the top of the list, until 1914 that is. When Dylan Thomas was born, his parents David & Florence were I'm sure, completely unaware of just how successful their undistinguished son would become. Here at the birthplace, they have now lovingly and carefully restored Dylan's family home back to the way it would of been for 23 years of his life. In fact two thirds of his writings were written here, and from his little back bedroom, he would of transported himself into his stories and poems, that would later make him one of not only Wales best writers but throughout the world. As I walked from room to room, I was completely in awe and I must of said the word wow a hundred times! One reason to say wow, was that you can actually rent the house for the weekend and stay in any one of the restored bedrooms, you cannot get anymore unique than that!

5 Cwmdonkin Drive, Swansea, SA2 0RA

Llangennith Surf School

t: 07855-420 062 E: surf@llangennithsurfschool.com
www.llangennithsurfschool.com

Llangennith Surf School is located at Llangennith beach South Wales, a stunning three mile stretch of sandy beach right in the heart of the Gower. The atmosphere here is second to none with a friendly crowd and chilled out vibe, it's not hard to see why Llangennith is such a sought after location to surf and kick back.
Our fully qualified British surfing association coaches and Great Britain lifeguard staff will give you a totally unique surfing experience, with quality individual attention and ensure your safety, you wont be a number on a lesson with us , our staff are passionate about what they teach and love to see you feeling the surfing spirit just as they do.
One wave can change your life and learning to surf or improving your ability is great fun and a super healthy activity. Once you have had a surfing lesson with us, you will know that you have come to the right place, this is not a business to us, it is a way of life.

AUTHOR'S REVIEW

The Gower Peninsula is fast becoming one of the go to places in Wales to relax, seek out adventure and just generally get away from it all and one of the companies who've set their sights to help you do that, is the team at Llangennith Surf School. So, if you've always wondered what it would be like to learn to surf, or have dabbled with it before, no matter your level of experience, these guys really go that extra mile to make sure you feel totally relaxed and your going at your own pace. Each lesson is geared up to suit your level of experience and the level of professionalism that these guys show is second to none and this is why we have chosen them to be one of our Top 100 Attractions in Wales this time round and I have no doubt that you'll love every minute of your lessons and the experience you will gain from them.

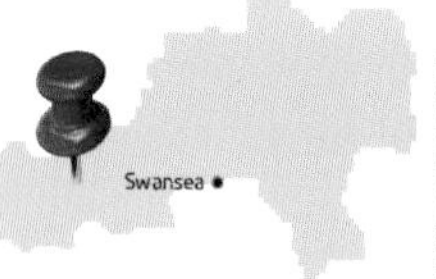

Hillend, Llangennith, Gower Peninsula, Swansea, SA3 1JD

Hawk Adventures

t: 01558-668878 e: info@hawkadventures.co.uk
www.hawkadventures.co.uk

Providers of Outdoor Activities since 1990, we are dedicated to providing exciting and enjoyable adventure activities, corporate events and team building events. Our outdoor activity centre is perfectly placed in the beautiful Brecon Beacons and we deliver the activities across a wide range of locations throughout South Wales, Swansea, Gower, Carmarthenshire and the Brecon Beacons National Park.We have a wide range of outdoor activities available for individuals and groups both large and small, all catered to your needs. Whether you are looking for a taste of adventure activities, fun corporate events or challenging team building events we have the activities to suit your needs.All activities are provided by highly experienced and qualified Instructors. All hold the relevant and current First Aid awards. National qualifications held are those approved by the relevant governing bodies.

AUTHOR'S REVIEW

Hawk Adventures has been using South Wales as their playground for over two decades, and there really isn't anything about 'adventure' that they can't tell you about. Their experience and knowledge of the business, let alone the South Wales Region is unprecedented and very hard to sum up in 150 words. But I will go as far as to say that no matter what kind of activity your looking to take part in, whether it be for a team building event, stag party, or just as part of your holiday, every single member of staff here at Hawk Adventures is not only highly qualified, but more likely over qualified within all aspects of their field. They have a great website which will not only tell you about every activity they specialise in, but the profiles of every instructor is on that site and all available for you to check long before you book your activity with them, making them a very transparent business indeed.

Swansea

Garreg Wen, Golden Grove, Llanarthney, Carmarthenshire, SA32 8JR

Pennard Golf Club

t: 01792-233131 e: manager@pennardgolfclub.com
www.pennardgolfclub.com

Pennard is a classic rugged links course situated 200ft above sea level leading to it being known as "The Links in the Sky". It is blessed with free draining ground, which remains playable all year round with tight lies, running fairways and firm fast greens. Along with the unique golf course, there are fantastic views of the famous Three Cliffs Bay over to Oxwich Bay. If at any time in your round you are not scoring well, look at the views and we are sure it will bring a smile to your face and regain your confidence for what lies ahead. The front nine is a classic mix of strong par 3's and 4's with a solitary par 5. This warms you up for the challenge on the spectacular back nine. From hole 10 the course and views just get better! The topography gets more severe and challenging with hole after hole moving out towards the Three Cliffs Bay over to Oxwich Bay.Stop for a moment and take in the view from green 16. You won't be disappointed. We are sure you will enjoy Pennard golf club.

AUTHOR'S REVIEW

With well over a hundred years of history and situated within one of the most beautiful areas of Wales, Pennard Golf club here on the Gower Peninsula, is one of this area's biggest hidden gems. It's is true to say that no member of the Royal family has ever played here, but to their loss in my opinion. This slickly run golf club has all you could want or need from this type of attraction, the staff are friendly, the facilities are of the highest standards and to top the lot, the fees are not that pricey either. What I also like about this club, is the fact that they welcome visitors of all persuasions, whether you're a novice or a keen golfer, everyone's welcome here at Pennard and together with a great food offering, the views from their eighteenth hole are truly breathtaking. All in all, you'll have a great experience here, but don't just take my word for it, go see for yourself!

Swansea

2 Southgate Rd, Southgate, Swansea, SA3 2BT

The Castle Hotel

The Parade, Neath. South Wales. SA11 1RB

T: 01639-641119 www. castlehotelneath.co.uk E: info@castlehotelneath.co.uk

The Castle Hotel is steeped in history. It is reputed that Lord Nelson and Lady Hamilton frequented the hotel on a number of occasions. In more recent years Richard Burton and Elizabeth Taylor have also stayed at the hotel. The Castle boasts a highly acclaimed restaurant with an extensive menu and a cosy wood paneled bar. All rooms at the Castle Hotel have a Private Bathroom with Bath and Free Toiletries. A Full English / Irish breakfast is served every morning. Staff are on hand 24-hours to ensure your stay as comfortable and enjoyable as possible. We offer a wide range of dishes on our a la carte menu, along with our daily Chefs specials menu. Book a table at the Restaurant and enjoy a meal of locally sourced quality food prepared by our talented chiefs.

The Estuary (Bar with Rooms)

Belle Vue, Pen-clawdd, Penclawdd SA4 3YE

T: 01792 850777 www.theestuarygower.co.uk e: info@theestuarygower.co.uk

The Estuary (named due to its proximity to the Loughor Estuary) was opened in July 2019 after extensive refurbishment. Originally known as the Railway public house it was once the focal point in the thriving village of Penclawdd, famous for its cockle industry and busy mining port in the 1800's. There are five double rooms, featuring King Size beds, each with en suite facilities and luxury toiletries. Three of the rooms have balconies with patio furniture and offer stunning views of the Salt Marsh and Loughor Estuary. They are well equipped with flat screen T.V.'s, Tea making facilities, Nespresso coffee machines and complimentary Wi-Fi. The chic Estuary Bar has a contemporary feel with copper and beach wood, has nautical vibes and luxe seating. It serves local beers from the award winning Gower Brewery, an extensive Gin menu and wines from around the World.

Island House

Gwynfe Road, Loughor, Swansea, SA4 6TE

T: 01792-899217 www.evanroberts.co.uk E: Gordon9@gordon9.plus.com

Situated in the old village of Bwlchymynydd, Loughor in easy walking distance of Pisgah Chapel and Moriah Chapel. Island House was built in 1870 and remained in the Roberts family, throughout the Revivalist period, until the 1950's. The Ellis family acquired the property in 1987 and is only the third family to have lived in the property. It has been very tastefully refurbished to a very high standard, whilst retaining all the original features including beamed ceilings & open fireplace. A traditional family home Bed & Breakfast establishment suitable for families, couples or single persons. Island House is fronting onto the Loughor Estuary Park ideal for walks. All bedrooms have digital freeview TV, tea, coffee and hot chocolate making facilities, whilst the guest lounge also has a DVD player.

Cwmbach Guest House & Cottages

Cwmbach Road, Cadoxton, Neath, Swansea, SA10 8AH

T: 01639-639825 www.cwmbachguesthouse.co.uk E: l.morgan5@btinternet.com

Cwmbach Cottages is one of the quieter places to stay in South Wales. We offer traditional Welsh hospitality and a warm welcome to all of our guests. Nestling on a hill side location surrounded by mature woodland just half a mile above the village of Cadoxton, Cwmbach Cottages is ideal for walking or relaxing holidays and we cater for both long and short stay breaks, including weekends. There are a network of foot paths within 100m of the Cottages leading to Graig Gwladys Country Park and the near by Aberdulais Water Falls. In addition, within the grounds of Cwmbach Cottages we have 3 self catering lodges capable of accommodating 2 to 6 people. We are located just 10 miles from Swansea and The Gower Coast.

Tides Reach Guest House

388 Mumbles Road, Mumbles, Swansea, SA3 5TN

T: 01792-404877 www.tidesreachguesthouse.com E: info@tidesreachguesthouse.com

Tides Reach is an elegant, comfortable and spacious house facing the sea and overlooking the promenade, with uninterrupted views to Mumbles lighthouse and Swansea Bay. Tides Reach is an ideal base from which to explore Mumbles, Gower, City of Swansea and surrounding areas. Tides Reach Guest House offers a variety of uniquely decorated and furnished rooms – 2 standard doubles, a superior double, family room and two with sea views. Every room features crisp white sheets and down duvets and pillows. All rooms have high ceilings and decorative detail and are decorated to a high standard with elegant furnishings and thoughtful touches to ensure that our guests feel at home during their stay.

Clyne Farm Centre

Westport Avenue, Mayals, Swansea SA3 5AR

T: 01792-403333 www.clynefarm.com E: info@clynefarm.com

Whether you are looking for a little hideaway for two or enough cottages for a special family celebration for fifty we have the place for you in our self catering 4 star cottages and barns. Try your hand at a variety of activities including horse riding and Challenge Valley – 'The Muddiest Assault course in the World' or just relax watching the view from our hill overlooking Swansea Bay and the Gower Peninsula midway between Swansea and Mumbles. Our rental costs include bed linen, electricity and heating, and towels. We also provide a 'starter pack' of essentials like toilet paper, black bags and washing up liquid and can arrange food orders at the start of your stay. We have plenty of space for tents but limit our camping numbers at Clyne so it never feels full. Our campsite overlooks Swansea Bay and has panoramic views yet we are close to Swansea and the Gower beaches.

Gower Accommodation

Shepherds, Parkmill, Gower, Swansea, SA3 2EH

T: 01792-371538 www.goweraccommodation.co.uk E: info@goweraccommodation.co.uk

The accommodation consists of four self-contained cottages (plus the apartment which is listed separately).Three Cliffs, Oxwich and Rhossili Cottages each have 2 bedrooms and will sleep 4 plus a child in a travel cot. Tor Bay Cottage has one bedroom so will sleep 2, plus a third person in a put-me-up bed or / and a child in a travel cot. Travel cots can be supplied at no charge - please indicate when booking that one is required.Bed linen and utilities are included in the price of your stay. Car parking is available outside the accommodation. Towels are not included but can be arranged for a small fee which covers laundry.On the ground floor, each cottage is has a well equipped kitchen area with electric oven, hob, microwave, and fridge with freezer compartment .

Parc Le Breos Guest House

Parkmill, Gower, Swansea, SA3 2HA

T: 01792-371636 www.parclebreos.co.uk E: info@parclebreos.co.uk

Parc-Le-Breos is a beautifully appointed Victorian hunting lodge, a stunning Gower Bed and Breakfast. The guest house and restaurant is set in the grounds of a Norman deer park in the heart of the Gower peninsula, only 20 minutes' walk from Three Cliffs Bay. Tastefully furnished throughout, you will find fresh flowers, pitch pine floors, crackling log fires and a distinctly laid-back style - Perfect for couples a families alike.As a relaxed and informal family run farm bed and breakfast, we aim to provide you with real home from home for the duration of your stay in Gower. A full Welsh breakfast (or something ligh if you prefer) is included .We are also pleased to offer wholesome home cooked meals in the evening and have a great wine list offering wines from around the world - even some from Wales!

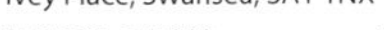

The Grand Hotel

Ivey Place, Swansea, SA1 1NX

T: 01792-645898 www.thegrandhotelswansea.co.uk E: info@thegrandhotelswansea.com

The Great National Grand Hotel Swansea is located in the heart of Swansea City Centre, next to the train station, and within walking distance of Swansea's many attractions.

Our 3 star hotel in swansea is located just minutes from Liberty Stadium, Swansea University and the beautiful beaches of the Gower Peninsula. Our Swansea Hotel has been a landmark Hotel since the 1930's, largely due to its ideal city location and unique design. The Grand Hotel in Swansea enjoys some of the best facilities any luxury hotel in Wales has to offer. The interior is created with style and elegance in a comfortable and welcoming environment making our Swansea hotel a popular choice for all. We have various room types of accommodation available to guests - Classic Double, Superior Double, Classic Twin, Classic Triple, Classic Family Rooms and Executive Rooms.

The Mirador Boutique Town House

14 Mirador Crescent, Uplands, Swansea, SA2 0QX

T: 01792-466976 www.themirador.co.uk E: info@themirador.co.uk

Here The Mirador Town House lay bespoke; tailor made for your requirements. It is within these hotel walls, you will discover a subtle break from reality, be it business pressure - or pleasure. Its uniqueness is apparent and appealing, its divergence is different from anywhere else, yet it remains unquestionably bespoke: Custom made for a discerning customer. For the past 4 years running; The Mirador Boutique Town House Hotel in Swansea has been awarded the TripAdvisor 'Certificate of Excellence' and Top Rated 'Simply The Guest' Awards by LateRooms.com! It is the perfect retreat for travellers and guests alike to rest in one of our boutique double bedrooms or King-Size bedroom suites. If you are looking for hotel accommodation in Swansea, step up and reserve a room at The Mirador and benefit from our luxury beds as well as our FREE high-speed Wi-Fi, all-in-one wide-screen DVD TVs and CD alarm clocks.

Leonardo's Guest House

380 Oystermouth Road, Swansea, SA1 3UL

T: 01792-466976 www.leonardosguesthouse.co.uk E: info@leonardosguesthouse.co.uk

Leonardo's is a family-run guest house which offers a high standard of bed & breakfast accommodation. Boasting an idyllic setting at the edge of both the Gower peninsula and Swansea City Centre, our B&B is a perfect location for easy access to Swansea University and surrounding areas. Our Bed and Breakfast is positioned facing almost due south, along the shore of Swansea's five miles beach, which stretches to the picturesque Mumbles and its Light House. We have cosy and clean guest bedrooms, some of which have a spectacular sea view.Breakfast is available and is served in a Mediterranean themed dining room where you can choose from our highly rated traditional English or Welsh breakfast, full or light continental breakfast and of course espresso, filtered coffee and flavoured teas.

The King Arthur Hotel

Higher Green, Reynoldston, Gower, SA3 1AD

T: 01792-390775 www.kingarthurhotel.co.uk E: info@kingarthurhotel.co.uk

Touched by legend on exquisite Gower, The King Arthur is a delightful traditional country inn. With its log fires and cosy restaurant, it has a relaxed and friendly old pub atmosphere. The King Arthur is found nestling under Cefn Bryn, Gower's highest point. The hotel is family run and consists of two bars, a restaurant, eighteen ensuite rooms, a small barn conversion cottage and our breath taking banqueting hall Avalon. Rooms at The King Arthur Hotel come with a TV, a writing desk and tea and coffee making facilities. They comprise a bathroom fitted with either a bathtub and shower. From conferences to birthday parties, christenings to afternoon teas, our versatile function room Avalon is the ideal place for your occasion.

Wynberg House

1 Eversley Road, Sketty, Swansea, SA2 9DB

T: 07415-189917 www.wynberg-house.business.site E: wynberghouse@gmail.com

Located across from Singleton Park, Wynberg House is located in Sketty Swansea and is 2.2 km from Grand Theatre. Among the various facilities of this property are a terrace and a shared lounge. The property is 2.3 km from Swansea Beach and 2.9 km from Swansea Marina. The units at the bed and breakfast are fitted with a seating area. The rooms at the property share a large separate shower/ wet room. The deluxe room has an ensuite and a lounge with access to the garden.
At Wynberg House each room comes with a wardrobe and a flat-screen TV. Including wi-fi, kettles, and complimentary tea, coffee and snacks. Breakfast is included! It includes à la carte or Full English/Irish breakfast daily at the property.

The Gower Hotel

11 Church Lane, Bishopston, Gower Peninsula, Swansea, SA13 3JT

T: 01792-234111 www.thegowerhotel.com E: info@thegowerhotel.com

The New Gower Hotel – with its 14 luxurious rooms, dog-friendly lodges, fully stocked bar, & on-site restaurant Monroe's – provides the perfect space for you to work, rest & play. Our personalised service makes The New Gower Hotel the perfect venue for celebrations, events, corporate meetings, or relaxing retreats. With our fantastic mix of boutique hotel rooms & dog-friendly lodges, there's a space for everybody at The New Gower Hotel. Whether you need to accommodate the whole family, require an intimate setting for you & your loved one, or you're simply looking for a cosy home-away-from-home, our friendly & helpful staff will find the perfect room for you. From the opulent & aptly named 'Room With Bath', to the more tranquil St. Teilo overlooking the local church, each room at The New Gower Hotel has a character of its own.

Ynysmeudwy Arms

Ynysmeudwy Road, Pontardawe, Swansea, SA8 4QJ

T: 01792-832111 www.theynysmeudwyarms.co.uk E: info@theynysmeudwyarms.co.uk

Historically unique, the Ynysmeudwy Arms is the perfect hideaway to relax and unwind. With our beautiful outdoor space and play area, our inn is a wonderful spot for the whole family to enjoy, surrounded by all the natural beauty South Wales has to offer. We have seven ensuite comfy and cosy guest rooms, beautifully finished and served with a warm welsh welcome. A location that offers all, from beaches and coastal walks, to mountain hikes and cycle treks, we're an ideal comfy base for adventures to unique and outstanding areas of natural beauty. Quintessentially welsh, our inn offers warm hospitality, with close proximity to sights found nowhere else in the world, from the stunning Brecon Beacons to the fabulous Gower Peninsula.

Norton House Hotel

Norton Road, Mumbles, Swansea, SA3 5TQ

T: 01792-404891 www.nortonhousehotel.co.uk E: enquiries@nortonhousehotel.co.uk

Norton House Hotel offers the best facilities in Mumbles and the surrounding areas, all from a quaint Georgian setting in a central location. Despite our hotel's period charm, we also deliver all the modern conveniences that the big brand hotels offer. In fact, you can have it all on your upcoming stay in this picturesque village! Catch up with your emails thanks to our free hotel Wi-Fi, whilst indulging in your favourite tipple at our residents' bar.
All our rooms have now been refurbished. We are pleased with the finished rooms and can offer some of the best accommodation in Mumbles and the Gower.
Enjoy a break, wedding or dining experience like no other at The Norton House Hotel.

The Towers Hotel & Spa

Ashleigh Terrace, Jersey Marine, Swansea Bay, SA10 6JL

T: 01792-814155 www.towershotel.co.uk E: info@towershotel.co.uk

The Towers is a large family-owned hotel where a warm, friendly welcome, excellent facilities and the highest standards of service and cleanliness ensure that your stay is a most pleasant one. Our 70 en-suite bedrooms are all air conditioned with SKY TV and internet access. Three of our executive suites have private lounge areas, ideal for a small meeting or just simply a quiet, private place to relax in peace. Our award-winning Tower houses three bespoke suites, ideal for romantic getaways and special occasions such as weddings and anniversaries. Each is individually decorated with beautiful views of the expansive hotel grounds, surrounding wooded areas and coastline. Our newly built Annex has 26 luxury en-suite rooms, many with picturesque outlooks. Seventeen of these are double/twins making them ideal for groups and very popular with sports teams.

Myrtle Cottage B&B

52 Bishopston Road, Bishopston, Gower, Swansea, SA3 3EN

T: 01792-736910 www.myrtlecottages.co.uk E: jackieroblin1@gmail.com

Myrtle Cottage B&B is located within a few miles (5 km) of Brandy Cove and Caswell Bay Beach. This 4-room, 3.5-star bed & breakfast welcomes guests with free breakfast, free in-room WiFi, and free self parking. Start your day off right with a free full breakfast, served each morning from 8:00 AM to 9:30 AM. A flat-screen TV comes with digital channels and Netflix, and guests can stay connected with free WiFi. The bathroom offers hairdryers, free toiletries, and slippers. Guests staying at Myrtle Cottage B&B enjoy free WiFi in public areas, a terrace, and a garden. There's free parking, and a shuttle from the airport to the hotel (available 24 hours) for GBP 120.00 per vehicle. Staff members are on hand to provide dry cleaning/laundry services and luggage storage.

Hael Farm Cottages

Hael Farm, Hael Lane, Southgate, Swansea, SA3 2AP

T: 01792-232797 www.haelfarmcottages.co.uk E: jon@haelfarmcottages.co.uk

Hael Farm cottages based in the Gower Peninsula in South Wales was designated an Area of Outstanding Natural Beauty (AONB) in 1956. It is also designated a Landscape of Outstanding Historic Interest in Wales, and the Gower Heritage. It may only be 16 miles long and 7 miles wide but the Gower has a rich diversity of landscapes, fauna and flora, archaeological sites, and historical features through the ages ranging from castles to churches and from agricultural to industrial relics which chronicle Man's occupation of the Gower Peninsula from Stone Age to present day.Port Eynon Beach Cottage and Oxwich View can be let as one cottage sleeping 14, connected by a communicating door on the first floor, with a large dining area sufficient for 14 guests to eat together.

The Dillwyn Arms Hotel

Herbert Street, Pontardawe, Swansea, SA8 4EB

T: 01792-863310 E: thedilwyn@gmail.com

A charming family-owned inn, the Hotel Dillwyn Arms Hotel offers comfortable accommodations and tasty home cooking just twenty-minutes from Swansea in the heart of historic Pontardawe.
All guest rooms at the three-star Hotel Dillwyn Arms Hotel feature hospitality trays, radios and private bathrooms. There's a spacious function room for guest events, complimentary parking and Wi-Fi throughout. Pet-friendly accommodations are also available for a fee. The hotel's restaurant and fully-licensed pub offer traditional menus featuring a popular Sunday Lunch and live music. Nearby alternatives within five miles include The Orchard Cafe, Organica and Charlo's Seafood.

Cariad Cafe

1–2 Bellevue, Penclawdd, Swansea, SA4 3YE

T: 01792-851185 www.cariadcafe.com E: info@cariadcafe.com

Cariad Cafe is based in Penclawdd on the Gower Peninsula. We pride ourselves on providing good quality, home-cooked food, using local Welsh produce wherever possible. We serve breakfasts until 12, lunches after 12, and ice creams, cakes, coffee and tea all day. The cafe serves a range of breakfasts to suit any appetite, including a Welsh Breakfast containing the famous Penclawdd cockles and laverbread - not to be missed! For lunch there is a choice of sandwiches, baguettes and salads; as well as a soup of the day. For a more filling meal try our lasagne, builder's brunch, or one of a many daily specials.
A wide selection of home-made cakes and treats are available throughout the day, including gluten free options. Ice cream sundaes are a firm favourite, as well as cones or tubs to take away.

The Rake & Riddle

Gowerton Rd, Penclawdd, Gowerton, Swansea, SA4 3RB

T: 01792-872886 www.therakeandriddle.com E: info@therakeandriddle.com

We welcome sandy feet and wet hair, so whether you've been for a countryside walk or spent the afternoon surfing, we'd love you to join us! Having obtained the lease for the Berthlwyd/ Sea Garden in November 2016 we wanted to create a new dining experience for the area. We decided that the name for the pub needed to have local influence and so were inspired by the cockle industry. The Rake and Riddle are the traditional cockle gathering tools that have been used for over a century in the village of Penclawdd. Our objective was to combine modern flavours with traditional quality with emphasis on using local produce. We feel that we have developed a great casual dining venue at the Rake and Riddle. Our menu reflects traditional pub favourites that we have identified through our teams many years.

Cwtch Cafe

Unit 4, St David's Square, Swansea, SA1 3LG

T: 01792-654070 E: cwtchcafeswansea@live.com

Cwtch is an independently run cafe, offering home cooked food, delicious cakes and fresh coffee.

"Welsh Breakfast!" 5 of 5 stars-Reviewed May 2018

We visited the "Cwtch" for Welsh breakfast on Monday 12th February. The "breakfast" was a substantial meal which included cockles and laverbread. For any tourists to Wales, laverbread is a local delicacy made from seaweed and very much an acquired taste – something not to be missed. Our breakfast was very tasty, a pleasant atmosphere, many of the customers were regulars and the staff were attentive. We enjoyed reading the wall hangings which decorate the "Cwtch" including a typical Welsh question "Whose coat is this jacket?"

The Plough & Harrow

88 Oldway, Murton, Gower, Swansea, SA3 3DJ

T: 01792-234459 www.ploughandharrow.eu E: reservations@ploughandharrow.eu

After a long time looking for the perfect place I came across the Plough & Harrow, just inside The Gower peninsular, in the village of Murton. For me the place was perfect, not only back in Wales but my home town of Swansea. Two minutes from Caswell bay and a short drive from the city centre, with a car park and a cosy country pub interior, it ticked every box.Less than two years later we were crowned Gastro-pub of the year at Cardiffs Food Awards Wales and in London at the Pub and Bar awards we were named Best Pub in West Glamorgan. So from humble begins we have started well and then began our third year in style by being awarded an AA rosette for culinary excellence! From here we look to keep building to give Gower the best Pub it's ever had!So come along, meet us, watch us grow and share in our story...Nick & Team X

Dilly's Kitchen

3 Dilwyn Road, Sketty, Swansea, SA3 9AQ

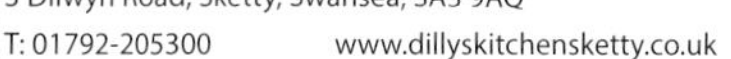

T: 01792-205300 www.dillyskitchensketty.co.uk E: info@dillyskitchensketty.co.uk

We at Dilly's Kitchen (Mike the father-in-law and Tom the son-in-law) have tried to create something different. Mike had a dream, so he worked on for 10 years hoping to begin his dream one day, then Tom came along being a Chef for 7 years, put the final piece together. So after marring Laura (Mikes step daughter) they teams up and started to work on Dilly's Kitchen. Tom beleaves in using local produce that supports the community, as we all know times are though, and Mike likes to chat alot. Putting these two together created a shop, but not just any shop its a Country Kitchen! Were we invite you to come in and have a chat, while enjoying food that is made from fresh local ingredients. If you havent got the time to chat, then we offer you to take away ready cooked meals to heat up once you get home. Taking away lifes stresses of cooking.

The King Arthur Hotel

Higher Green, Reynoldston, Gower, SA3 1AD

T: 01792-390775 www.kingarthurhotel.co.uk E: info@kingarthurhotel.co.uk

The pub consists of a main bar with its original stone work, reclaimed timbers and open log fires in the winter. The Gower Room, our family room is a nautical themed room displaying local maps, original artifacts and photographs of Gower's nautical history. Finally a cosy traditionally decorated restaurant. We are renowned for our warming home cooked food suited to all tastes. Choose from dishes on the main menu or "specials" board including seasonal game and locally caught fish. All meals are served in the restaurant, Gower room, main bar and fine summer days at outdoor tables on the green. We try to source as much local and welsh produce as possible for our menus.To complement your meals we offera varied and reasonably priced wine list with a good selection available by the glass.

Monroe's Restaurant

11 Church Lane, Bishopston, Gower Peninsula, Swansea, SA13 3JT

T: 01792-234111 www.thegowerhotel.com E: info@thegowerhotel.com

The New Gower Hotel – with its 14 luxurious rooms, dog-friendly lodges, fully stocked bar, & on-site restaurant Monroe's – provides the perfect space for you to work, rest & play. Our personalised service makes The New Gower Hotel the perfect venue for celebrations, events, corporate meetings, or relaxing retreats. The New Gower Hotel's on-site restaurant Monroe's, offers fine dining in the heart of the peninsula. Executive chef Mark Evans – along with his talented team – provide guests & non-guests of the hotel with spectacular dishes using only the finest, locally-sourced ingredients.

Monroe's is open to both guests & non-guests of the hotel serving both lunch & dinner, as well as drinks within the bar area.

Norton House Hotel

Norton Road, Mumbles, Swansea, SA3 5TQ

T: 01792-404891 www.nortonhousehotel.co.uk E: enquiries@nortonhousehotel.co.uk

Enjoy chic modern furnishings, and an ambience to match, plus an exciting menu of locally sourced ingredients right here at Norton House Hotel.

The Bistro offers a unique dining experience 7 days a week, with two A La Carte sittings and an Early Bird menu served from Monday to Sunday.

Why not try our traditional Sunday Lunch served 12.00pm-2.30pm.

Our restaurant is open for Breakfast, Lunch and Dinner. Meals are freshly prepared from locally sourced produce and we pride ourselves on well trained friendly staff with the experience to deliver service with great attention to detail.

The Towers Hotel & Spa

Ashleigh Terrace, Jersey Marine, Swansea Bay, SA10 6JL

T: 01792-814155 www.towershotel.co.uk E: info@towershotel.co.uk

We love food. And we certainly don't mind the odd drop of good wine. We are equally at home creating a sophisticated, discreet ambience and gourmet dinner for two, as we are with serving up a healthy dinner for a top sports team or a sumptuous five-star buffet for a wedding or conference. Open for breakfast, lunch and dinner seven days a week, our skilled chefs specialise in new European cuisine and traditional Welsh Fayre, using the very best in local seasonal produce delivered fresh each day. We can also confidently and creatively cater for vegetarians and those with other dietary requirements. Our extensive wine list has been carefully selected to bring you the best from both the New and Old . Private dining and bar facilities are also available - please contact us to discuss your requirements. For those who'd like to experience local hospitality, enjoy a drink in our welcoming bar.

The Dillwyn Arms Hotel

Herbert Street, Pontardawe, Swansea, SA8 4EB

T: 01792-863310 E: thedilwyn@gmail.com

A charming family-owned inn, the Hotel Dillwyn Arms Hotel offers comfortable accommodations and tasty home cooking just twenty-minutes from Swansea in the heart of historic Pontardawe. All guest rooms at the three-star Hotel Dillwyn Arms Hotel feature hospitality trays, radios and private bathrooms. There's a spacious function room for guest events, complimentary parking and Wi-Fi throughout. Pet-friendly accommodations are also available for a fee. The hotel's restaurant and fully-licensed pub offer traditional menus featuring a popular Sunday Lunch and live music..Less than ten minutes' drive reaches the picturesque grounds of the Pontardawe Golf Club, while historic Neath Abbey, Gnoll Estate, Swansea Community Farm, Liberty Stadium, and the sparkling shores of Gower Coast.

Gower Gelato – affectionately known as G.G.'s

Belle Vue, Pen-clawdd, Penclawdd SA4 3YE

T: 01792 850777 www. ggsgelato.co.uk e: info@ggsgelato.co.uk

G.G.'s is the brainchild of Emily and Chris Mabbett who are entrepreneur's and ambassadors of an up and coming new era for the village of Penclawdd. Many years ago there was a famous ice cream parlou in the village which is still reminisced about to this day by the locals. It opened its doors in July 2019 serving mouth-watering homemade Gelato to a secret recipe in a vast variety of flavours including Vanilla, Strawberry, Chocolate, Bueno, Oreo, Ferrero Rocher and many more besides. Their signature Sundaes and Freak Shakes are a sight for sore eyes and the Mega Sundaes are mind blowing and a challenge for anyone! Also, on offer are homemade crepes with delicious toppings and focaccias filled wit Italian delights and more! Speciality teas, Gower coffee, soft drinks and soda floats complete the menu.

Slice

73-75 Eversley Road, Sketty, Swansea, SA2 9DE

T: 01792-290929 www.sliceswansea.co.uk E: sliceswansea@hotmail.com

slice is owned and run by business partners Adam Bannister and Chris Harris. Experienced chefs, the pair have been cooking together since college and subsequently in high end restaurants around the country. With an eye for detail in both their food and service, they aim to deliver the best experience possible in their small, 16 seater restaurant on Eversley Road. Since opening in 2014, Slice has gained entry to the Michelin Guide and Good Food Guide. In 2015 Adam won the Welsh title on the BBC's Great British Menu and is competing again in 2016. If you or any of your party have any special dietary requirements let us know when you book. Whether you're vegetarian or vegan, or have sensitivity to gluten or dairy, we will prepare dishes specifically for your needs.

BrewStone

33 Uplands Crescent, Uplands, Swansea, SA2 0NP

T: 01792-470480 www.brewstone.co.uk E: uplands@brewstone.co.uk

We are a bar and restaurant located in the lively Uplands Crescent in the heart of Uplands Swansea. BrewStone is a day and night venue that offers a unique wood fire focused menu, craft beers, and cocktails. We aim to provide good quality, local products in a warm and welcoming atmosphere. After opening in 2014 in the budding area of Uplands, Swansea, our intention to contribute to the re-development of the inner city is ongoing, where students, business people and locals cross paths. We aim to perfect wood fire cuisine with our hand stretched pizzas, craft the cocktails worth chatting about, and creating the ideal atmosphere for a get together. The long narrow nature of BrewStone Uplands is celebrated with a dramatic linear ceiling. This narrow and extended ground floor space allows BrewStone to achieve what can only be described as a modern and approachable environment.

The Front Room

618 Mumbles Road, Mumbles, Swansea, SA3 4EA

T: 01792-362140 E: thefrontroommumbles@yahoo.co.uk

The front room is a café as relaxing and comfortable as your own front room! Situated on the sea-front in Mumbles, opposite Southend children's playground, we offer delicious home-cooked food, gorgeous coffee, cream teas and scrumptious home-baked cakes. Our food is freshly prepared using quality ingredients which are locally sourced. We offer a good selection of vegetarian and gluten free options. Children are made very welcome with their own menu, a big box of toys and crayons. Whether it's for a cuppa with friends, a family meal or an afternoon treat...come and cosy up in our front room.

Pant-Y-Gwydr

Oxford Street, Swansea, SA1 3JA

T: 01792-455 98 www. pantygwydr.com E: theph@me.com

Based in the heart of Swansea, the Pant-y-Gwydr serves French cuisine prepared using both traditional and original recipes, with an emphasis on the sauces on which much French cooking is based. The menu contains French classics (French fish soup, frogs legs, tournedos Rossini) and frequently-changing seasonal specials that include Welsh lamb, Welsh aged beef, local, wild fish and Scottish scallops wherever possible. We set great store by the authenticity of our produce: snails from Burgundy, Piment d'Espelette from South-West France, French wines, Welsh beer and spirits. All of our dishes, without exception, are made in-house and the majority of our suppliers are based in Swansea or in South and West Wales.

Gilligan's Restaurant

100 Eversley Road, Sketty, Swansea,, SA2 9DF

T: 01792-203767 www.gilligansrestaurant.com E: gilligans100@gmail.com

Our aim at Gilligan's Restaurant is to produce good quality, wholesome, tasty meals at affordable prices, where you can dine in a relaxed, comfortable atmosphere and bring along a bottle of your favourite wine or beer to enjoy with your meal, but please note our BYO policy does not include any spirits, liqueurs or soft drinks. We are fully licensed so if you prefer not to 'bring your own booze' we have a good range of wine, beers and spirits and soft drinks available, and of course the indulgent liqueur coffees to finish your evening. In addition to our main menu we have a DAILY SPECIALS BOARD with more starter options, main courses including Vegetarian and 'fish of the day' dishes and a couple more desserts to choose from too. If you have any specific dietary requirements, please let us know .

The Beach House Restaurant

Oxwich Beach, Gower, Swansea SA3 1LS

T: 01792-390965 www.Beachhouseoxwich.co.uk

At the Beach House we pride ourselves on offering a relaxed dining experience with the highest standards of service and professionalism. We want you to feel a warm welcome and leave looking forward to your next visit. Our beautiful restaurant enjoys a stunning natural setting located right on the soft golden sands of Oxwich Bay which enjoys magnificent coastal views. Our Head Chef and native Welshman Hywel Griffith is passionate about local produce and his team prepare dishes with skill, experience and creativity. W
e want all our guests to be happy with their whole dining experience at the Beach House. Achieving such a aim isn't easy but we will be working hard to make it happen.

The River House

Kings Road, Swansea, SA1 8AW

T: 01792-649060 www.riverhouse.co.uk

Located next to the river and sail bridge in the vibrant SA1 waterfront, The River House Lounge and Restaurant has become one of the best landmarks in Swansea. With a sophisticated cocktail bar and terrace area which overlooks Swansea's River Tawe and Marina, the Lounge serves light meals all day, as well as high end cocktails, fine wines and Champagnes. It's the perfect place to meet friends, business colleagues or to just relax in comfort and watch the world go by.The Award Winning restaurant offers a fine dining experience and is now widely recognised as one of the best restaurants in Swansea and South Wales. The restaurant also serves one of the best Sunday lunches in Swansea. With scenic views of the river, sail bridge and harbour, it is one of the best locations in Swansea. Fresh, local ingredients are used to provide high quality food to produce our seasonal menus.

Verve37

37 Uplands Crescent, Swansea, SA2 0NP

T: 01792-643701 www.verve37.co.uk e: mail@verve37.co.uk

Verve37 is an AWARD WINNING wine bar and restaurant in the heart of Uplands. If you are looking for a relaxing venue to unwind after a stressful day, or simply want to catch up with some friends and have a bite to eat over a glass of wine or a coffee, Verve37 provides the perfect venue.

At Verve37 we serve a selection of draught and bottle beers from around the world and a comprehensive wine and champagne menu served by the glass or bottle.

Verve37 has a lively bar, with areas to chill, a restaurant, a garden terrace and a private function room for those special occassions.

Mad Hatter's Cafe Bistro

29 Newton Road, The Mumbles, Swansea, SA3 4AS

T: 01792-363838 www.madhatters.co.uk e: info@madhatters.co.u

Mad Hatter's is an enchanting and elegant cafe/bistro run by a local family, serving the Mumbles community.A wide selection of delicious food is freshly prepared on the premises. We only use produce that is locally sourced and serve heavenly fair trade coffee by Ethical Addictions. You can enjo homemade food, with gluten free, vegan and vegetarian options available. From Tuesday to Saturday evenings our Bistro menu boasts the best of local food. Or why not just relax at the bar with a cocktail or chill in our tub chairs while you enjoy live music and some tempting nibbles. he cafe is beautifully decorated with the illustrations of John Tennie drawn by British artist Arran Gregory (Google him - he's pretty awesome!), producing a magical ambience in which to enjoy your tea.

GLAMORGAN'S HERITAGE COAST

Home to the most Southerly point in Wales, people have been visiting and living in the Vale of Glamorgan and its surrounding areas for 200,000 years now and once visited, it's not hard to see why! Still, not without seeing its share of hard times however, that hasn't stopped this area becoming a fantastic tourist destination. I think the fact that the BBC has filmed two series of its hit show 'Being Human' coupled with 'Gavin & Stacy' also being filmed in the seaside town of Barry, only goes to show that this area of Wales really has got what it takes to pull the tourists in from further and wider areas. The outstanding yellow-grey cliffs on the Glamorgan Heritage Coast which stretches in-between Llantwit Major to Ogmore by the Sea are unique only to the Celtic seaboard (Cornwall, Wales, Ireland and Brittany) as they're formed of Liassic limestone - totally unique for a Celtic nation.

They were formed 200 million years ago when Wales (as well as Cornwall and Ireland) lay below a warm, shallow, equatorial sea during the start of the Jurassic period. Today the cliffs contain elements of Jurassic age sea-creatures (although not land dinosaurs - the Celtic nations were all underneath the sea), such as ammonites. I do not think you need any more convincing that the Vale of Glamorgan has its fair share of stories, places to see and things to do than any other place in Wales. What makes this place so unique however is its versatility to be a great place of history, an amazing outdoor pursuit's area, or just simply somewhere to unwind and take it all in! Whatever you choose to do, Glamorgan has to be on your itinerary of places to visit whilst visiting the great country of Wales.

Warren Mill Farm Park

t: (07768) 839885 e: wmfarmpark@gmail.com
www.warrenmillfarm.co.uk/farm-park

Visit Warren Mill Farm and discover a 17th century farmhouse set in 40 acres of rural countryside!
This beautiful lakeside setting is home to very friendly farm animals that visitors can meet and greet such as rabbits, guinea pigs, rare breeds of sheep, goats, pigs, miniature ponies, llamas, alpacas and their newest addition water buffalo and lots more!
Fishermen can make the most of the Warren Hills Fishery with its 4 and a half acre natural mill pond with an abundance of fish including carp, bream and perch. Both the fishery and the farm park have access to food, drink and toilets.
A small, friendly farm in a stunning open space!
Children's play area at the farm park.

AUTHOR'S REVIEW

Warren Mill Farm Park is a new addition to our Top 100 Attractions family here in Wales and although I chose the attraction for its great attributes, it has a huge amount of hidden gem qualities also. Open all year round, this farm park offers huge value for money and with so many animals to see and pet, there is a sense of innocence with the site as well. All the animals at Warren Mill, appear to be greatly cared for and the pens and enclosures that play home to these wonderful creatures are in the best condition, which just adds to the confirmation that these animals are not only well cared for, but very much loved by the farms parks owners. Warren Mill Farm Park also boasts an extensively stocked Fishery with a high quality of infrastructure to boot. All in all, I'm sure your going to have a great time here, so what are you waiting for?

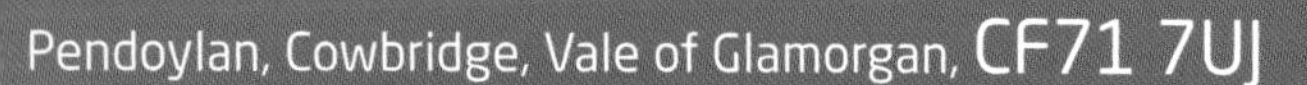

Pendoylan, Cowbridge, Vale of Glamorgan, CF71 7UJ

Coney Beach Porthcawl

t: 01656-78811
www.coneybeach.co.uk

Coney Beach Amusement Park is at the heart of Porthcawl and sits on Sandy Bay, which is one of seven bays at this historical South Wales seaside town. The Parks' own beach is nearly a mile long and a magnet for surfers and bathers alike with lifeguards on duty during the summer months and with donkey rides, bouncy castles and trampolines ideal as a safe family destination. Alongside the Megablitz, one of the largest roller coasters in the area, are all the attractions you will ever want from a traditional seaside fair, with arcades, shooting gallery, side shows, dodgems, the Sizzler Twist and lots more thrill, family and children's rides. As well as the fair there are cafes, restaurants, a bar and nearby function room which can be hired for private events.
Entrance to the Park is FREE and opens throughout the summer season.

AUTHOR'S REVIEW

Next year, 2020 will be a very big year for Coney Beach Pleasure Parkas they will of reached their 100th birthday, which for this type of attraction, is very rare! There is nothing you can teach his family about running a fairground, as they have literally done it all, from entertaining American and British troops returning back from World War 1, to touring throughout the British Isles with their popular fairground rides. I think another thing worth mentioning is the spectacular Beach that is attached to this attraction and the parks owner Patrick Evans, is very passionate about ensuring its cleanliness, this is paramount to him. Along with making sure his visitors have a fantastic time, Patrick tells me there are now going to be a whole range of water sports available on the beach, making it a hive of activity. I really like Coney Beach, it was like being a kid again, visiting here and I know you'll love it!

Porthcawl

Amelia Trust Farm

t: 01446-782030 e: general@ameliatrust.org.uk
www.ameliatrust.org.uk

Based in the Vale of Glamorgan, the Amelia Trust Farm is a countryside sanctuary for all to enjoy. As a registered charity, we believe no one should be excluded from society. We have a long and proud history of providing therapeutic support to disadvantaged and vulnerable people in a Care Farm setting. During term-time we run a programme for young people who are struggling in mainstream education perhaps because they have suffered abuse or neglect or are statemented with neurodevelopmental disorders such as ADHD or autism. They think that society has given up on them and feel worthless and that life has nothing to offer them. Without the right type of care and support this highly vulnerable group enter adulthood without the life skills people need to cope let alone succeed. We also extend our caring and nurturing environment to adults with learning disabilities and we are open to the general public throughout the year. With woodland walks, animals to see, play areas and a café there is plenty to do and enjoy.

AUTHOR'S REVIEW

It is fair to say that the Vale of Glamorgan is a strong farming comunity within South Wales and here at Amelia Trust Farm, they open up the doors to allow you to see just how strong that community is. However, being a strong farming community isn't the only purpose of this farm park and being a social enterprise, behind the scenes, the Amelia Trust do fantastic work in helping vulnerable and disadvantaged people. Complete with wonderful woodland walks and trails, a wide selection of animals to see and pet and a great little cafe, all go to show just exactly why Amelia Trust Farm has our family fun hidden gem award. Being a registered charity, this farm relies solely on donations and its entrance fees, or quite simply the place wouldn't exist, so for every visitor they get here, it all goes to ensure that this great little attractions future, is all the more stable.

Five Mile Lane, Barry, Vale of Glamorgan, CF62 3AS

Wiggleys Fun Farm

t: 01656-743246
e: info@wiggleysfunfarm.co.uk
www.wiggleysfunfarm.co.uk

Wiggleys Fun Farm is situated in the middle of the lovely countryside, yet easily accessible just 5 mins from Junction 36 of M4. Wiggleys Fun Farm is an all weathered attraction, it has themed indoor and outdoor play areas, farm animals, pets corner, woodland walks and duck ponds. There's a cafe where you can sit back and relax indoors or outside on our patio area.
Indoors - Wiggleys Adventure Play, Wigglets Play for Toddlers, Babies Barnyard, Race Track, Party Rooms, Wiggleys Farm Coffee Shop, Dining Area, Toilets. Outdoors - Adventure Play, Toddlers Area, Swings, Ball Game Activities, Animal Paddocks, Pets Corner, Sun Terrace, Woodland Walk, Duck Ponds, Picnic Areas for visitors who bring their own food, Hand Washing Facilities
Opening TimesMonday to Friday 10am - 6pm, Saturday & Sunday 10am - 5pm, School Holidays 10am - 5pm

AUTHOR'S REVIEW

Wales is an absolutely beautiful country with plenty of outdoor attractions on offer throughout every county. But one thing we have to think about when choosing our Top 100 attractions, is what happens if it rains. What we liked initially about Wiggleys Fun Farm, is that come rain or shine, there is still lots of fun to be had, and with so much to do here indoors or out, you cannot get bored. We judge all of our attractions on visitor experience, set against value for money, and Wiggleys has got both of those in abundance. With a great sizeable car park, and very reasonable admission prices, an indoor cafe that has a great selection of food, not forgetting amazing coffee, they literally have all you need for a fab day out. All in all we at Top 100 Attractions absolutely love Wiggleys, and we know you will too!

Aberbaiden Road, Bridgend, CF32 0BQ

Fonmon Castle

t: 01446-710206 e: fonmon_castle@msn.com
www.fonmoncastle.com

Fonmon is one of the few mediaeval castles which are still lived in as a home. Since it was built by the St. John family c1200, it has only changed hands once. In 1656, during the English Civil War it was bought by Colonel Philip Jones, a direct ancestor of Sir Brooke Boothby, the present owner.

Today Fonmon welcomes visitors in many different ways both as a wedding and events venue and through Public opening and tours:

The Castle is open to the Public from April to September. There is no need to book. Public opening times for individuals, families and groups of less than twelve are on Tuesdays and Wednesdays between midday and 5pm. Public guided tours are at 2pm, 3pm and 4pm. Access to the garden and grounds is free.

Last entrance to the garden is at 4pm.

Assistance dogs only allowed.

AUTHOR'S REVIEW

Wales is one of those one of countries that has an abundance of natural tourist attractions as well as many great man made attractions. But in amongst all of them are some hidden gems to uncover, that's where my book comes in very handy as I have already done the job for you. One of those hidden gems that I speak so much about is Fonmon Castle. Usually in the UK, castles of the thirteenth century are in ruins and are being cared for by CADW or the English Heritage, not Fonmon though! One of the many amazing things about this property is the fact it has remained in the same family for over 700 years. Tours around this property only take place on Tuesdays and Wednesdays ordinarily, however for groups of twelve or more, arrangements can be made. I really loved my tour here at Fonmon, you will to!

Fonmon, Nr Barry, Vale of Glamorgan, CF62 3ZN

Bryngarw House & Country Park

t: 01656-725155 e: info@bryngarwhouse.co.uk
www.bryngarwhouse.co.uk

There's no better way to explore Bryngarw Country Park than by putting on your wellies and following the Keepers quest. Collect your map and star talisman from Cedars Tea Room and see if you can find the Keepers of the Meadow, Woodland, River and Garden; the ancient guardians of the story of the land. Once you've found them, use the magical talisman to 'awaken' each Keeper and hear the stories of Bryngarw's wildlife and landscape brought to life. With an annual programme of courses, guided walks and events, you will not only explore the wildlife but learn about the folklore and traditional uses of our native plants and trees, the origins of our seasonal festivals and have a chance to experience first-hand some of the traditional customs and crafts of our ancestors. One of South Wales' most scenic wedding venues set in 113 acres of country parkland. The perfect backdrop for all-year-round wedding photographs.

AUTHOR'S REVIEW

One of the main reasons I decided to write my Top 100 Attractions range of books, was not because of the large number of huge attractions in the world, but more as a consequence of how many hidden gem attractions there are! Bryngarw House & Country Park are a fine example of that previous statement. One hundred and thirteen acres of amazing parkland and gardens is what awaits you here at this attraction, and the team of rangers, in fact all of the team at Bryngarw have dedication oozing from every pore as they are clearly passionate about every single acre. Another great feature at Bryngarw is the 'Keepers' audio trail. A lot of work has gone into the keepers story and located around the whole of the park these keepers will take you on a journey of discovery that show you just how important nature and human beings are completely at one with each other, or at least should be!

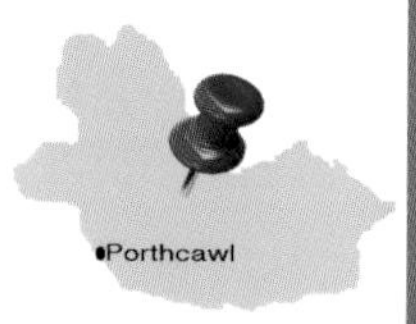

Brynmenyn, Bridgend CF32 8UU

Margam Country Park

t: 01639-881635 e: margampark@npt.gov.uk
www.margamcountrypark.co.uk

Margam Country Park is full of surprises. With an industrial past and breath-taking landscaped gardens, it's the perfect place for heritage hunting and natural play.

Winner of Green Flag Award and voted the Nations Favourite Park in the 'National Peoples Choice' Awards, the Park provides something for everyone.

From walking to cycling, orienteering to coarse fishing. A varied range of seasonal events and activities are programmed throughout the year.

The dog friendly Park boasts Margam Castle, 17th Century Orangery, monastic ruins, a Rare Breeds Farm Trail, 800 acres of Parkland with Deer Herd and two children's playgrounds.

Margam Park Adventure allows visitors to enjoy a host of activities from Mountain Biking to kayaking - all from one incredible location. The Park is also home to the only Treetop Challenge in Wales.

All visitors are able to enjoy the wonderful environment that the Park provides.

Visit our website for our Seasonal opening times.

AUTHOR'S REVIEW

Margam was the original site for a cistercian monastery, then being acquired after the dissolution of all monasteries in the UK in 1540 became the family seat of Sir Rice Mansell. It's now however home to Margam Country Park, and plays host to another one of our Top 100 Attractions 'Go Ape'. As I walked around the estate I could easily of been walking around the grounds of Hogwarts from the 'Harry Potter' films. With Deer walking within yards away from where I stood its easy to see why this park has made it into our Top 100 list. With remains of the abbey still intact it's no wonder why people like to spend all day here. Entrance into the park is totally free but there is a small car parking fee. But no matter what, a visit around the park for the day is priceless.

Port Talbot

Margam Country Park,Port Talbot, South Wales , SA13 2TJ

The Princess Royal Theatre

t: 01639-763214 e: artsmarketing@npt.gov.uk
www.princessroyaltheatre.com

The impressive Princess Royal Theatre is a multi-purpose venue situated in Neath Port Talbot.
Events include the annual pantomime, professional and amateur shows, concerts, children's shows, opera, musicals, live comedy, ceremonies and presentations, major conferences, seminars, exhibitions and fairs.
As well as programming a seasonal range of quality live entertainment events, the theatre is regularly used by local amateur dramatic groups and society's for their own productions.
The Princess Royal Theatre is available to hire with a capacity of 798 for full theatre events and almost all needs can be catered for.
Visit our website for a full list of our upcoming events or to download our Seasonal Events Leaflet.

AUTHOR'S REVIEW

The Princess Royal Theatre is located within the Port Talbot Civic Centre and I have to say that this impressive building does not disappoint. The theatre is formed in one of the wings of the civic centre and hosts many famous headline acts and some not so famous, but one thing you can always be assured of, is a great show. The theatres designers thought of everything when designing this theatre and their disabled facilities are second to none. I know this isn't one of the usual Victorian theatres of days gone by, but this is a theatre for the next generation, with excellent facilities and having said all that, the theatre prices for a lot of their shows are very reasonably priced also. On the day I visited, I found the staff to be very friendly, helpful and I can say with some vigour, that if this theatre was in my area, I'd be there all the time!

Civic Centre, Port Talbot, SA13 1PJ

Kenfig Nature Reserve

t: 01656 815070 e: margampark@npt.gov.uk
www.bridgend.gov.uk

Kenfig Nature Reserve is one of Wales's top sand-dune reserves, with plants like wild fen orchids, birds and insects depending on this habitat for their survival. The reserve is one of the last remnants of a huge dune system that once stretched along the coastline of southern Wales from the Ogmore River to the Gower peninsular. Glamorgan's largest natural lake, Kenfig Pool, is set on the edge of this beautiful sand dune nature reserve with spectacular views across Swansea Bay to the Gower.
The Reserve is home to a wide variety of rare and endangered species of plants and animals, including the Fen Orchid. The dune system makes up part of the largest active sand dune system in europe. Kenfig NNR is a favourite refuge for wildfoul all year round and is one of the few places in the UK where the bittern can be seen during the winter - the area is a very popular place with birdwatchers. The area is managed to ensure the dunes don't become overcome by dense grassland and scrub woodland which would result in the loss of much of the important and diverse wildlife. The reserve is managed so that the delicate balance of habitats is maintained and visitors can freely wander the area without harming any of the reserve and its features. Disabled access is encouraged yet access to the dune systems is difficult for wheelchair users.

AUTHOR'S REVIEW

Great variety of walks for able bodied and disabled people to Kenfig Pool or for able bodied to the secluded long golden sanded beach. Either stroll down dunes to Sker Beach which is stunning and usually deserted or visit the jewel in the crown the 'pond' - I have visited here many times in the past few years when I have been staying nearby. Sometimes Iseen up to 20 dogs all playing, swimming and running around together - great to see them all socialising - why keep a dog on a lead like they are pack animals! Toilet facilities at car park always clean and usually an ice cream van to refresh you after your walk. Free car parking as well - will certainly be visiting again and again.

Ton Kenfig, Pyle, Bridgend, CF33 4PT

HL Homes Serviced Accommodation

Unit 1, The Precinct New Road, Porthcawl, CF36 5DL

T: 01656-772449 www.hlhomes.co.uk e: enquiries@hlhomes.co.uk

We have a range of fully furnished properties, all of which are equipped with WiFi, on a self-catered basis for anyone looking for short term accommodation. Whether you are on holiday or working in the area, we can accommodate you with all of the comforts of a home from home! If you are looking at our range of serviced accommodation, get in touch so we can help. We will provide you with a dedicated point of contact who can tell you everything you need to know about our properties so that we find the one that's just right for you. At HL Homes we just love to be green! We use an array of multimedia platforms and e-services so you can book or view availability online. We've created a bespoke agency that can offer you an array of properties on a short term basis for complete flexibility. All of our homes have WiFi and are well equipped with all that you will need for a comfortable stay.

The Old Barn B&B

The Croft, Penmark, Vale of Glamorgan, CF62 3BP

T: 01446-711352 www.theoldbarnbedandbreakfast.co.uk

E: enquiries@theoldbarnbedandbreakfast.co.uk

The Old Barn B&B dates back to the 17th Century when it was used as farm buildings for the adjacent Croft. This charming, recently converted self contained barn combines many original features such as oak beams and slate floors with up to date facilities the modern traveller has come to expect. We have provided modern facilities to make your stay as enjoyable as possible. There is a TV with Freeview, radio / alarm clock, free Wi-fi, coffee and tea making facilities and hair dryer in each room, and an iron in the kitchen. You are welcome to use the kitchen facilities during your stay.
Children are very welcome and we have a cot and high chair available.

Coed-Y-Mwstwr Hotel *

Coychurch, Bridgend, CF35 6AF

T: 01656-860621 www.coed-y-mwstwr.com E: enquiries@coed-y-mwstwr.com

Idyllically nestled amongst flourishing Welsh woodland, The Coed-Y-Mwstwr Country Hotel in Bridgend is the kind of escape weekday desk-huggers spend their days dreaming about. Fill your lungs with clean air without sacrificing any luxurious home comforts as we strike a perfect balance between town & country. From enjoying views over the woodland canopy with a glass of fizz in hand, to immersing yourself in the lively bars & shops just a short drive away, our Victorian mansion is a real hidden gem. We passionately believe that during your stay you feel as relaxed as you would in your own home, our goal is for you to leave our hotel feeling calm, rejuvenated and ready to take on the world.

St Mary's Hotel & Golf Club *

St mary's hill, Pencoed, Vale of Glamorgan CF35 5EA

T: 01656-861100 www.stmaryshotel.com E: reception@stmaryshotel.com

This luxurious 16th century converted farmhouse retains its original character with beamed ceilings and stone walls. There is a 3-star luxury privately owned 30 hole golf complex and the property is a 2-minute drive from the M4 (J35). The rooms have a seating area and a desk. St Mary's Hotel Golf & Country Club has a bar and a restaurant for guests to enjoy. St Mary's has 24 en suite bedrooms furnished to the highest standard. In the oldest part of the building we have retained many of the original stonewalls and fireplaces dating back to the 16th Century. Our main executive suite has a four poster bed, oak flooring, panoramic views and is set high in the rafters of the old house.

New Farm Accommodation

Port Road West, Barry, Vale of Glamorgan, CF62 3BT
T: 01446-735536 www.newfarmbarry.co.uk E: hello@newfarmbarry.co.uk

Situated in the heart of the Vale of Glamorgan, New Farm Bed and Breakfast is the ideal location, whether you are off to sunnier climes, exploring south Wales or purely as a base to spend days visiting the many attractions that exist in this beautiful part of the country. An established business having served visitors for some 30 years; you can be assured of a warm Welsh welcome at this family friendly run bed and breakfast. The seventeenth century farmhouse is at the centre of the farm and has had an interesting history, now providing our valued guests with comfortable accommodation whether it be for those in the area on business or as a base to explore whilst on holiday in the principality or for an overnight stay before jetting off from Cardiff Airport.

Ballas Farm Country Guest House

Heol-Y-Sheet, Stormy Down, Pyle, Mid Glamorgan, CF33 4RY
T: 01656-741794 www.ballasfarm.co.uk E: stay@ballasfarm.co.uk

Standing in its own grounds Ballas Farm Country Guest House, is set in eight and a half acres of beautiful pasture and woodland. There are 4 guest rooms all with en-suite facilities. Two rooms are on the ground floor. An attractive dining room, which will seat 10 people. Assisted by family, Liz Hopkins welcomes guests to enjoy, relax and unwind in a newly refurbished farm house in the countryside. The tasty home cooked breakfast sets the morning off to a good start. Ballas Farm is within easy access of the A48 and J37, M4 making Cardiff and Swansea and very accessible for people exploring Wales. Cardiff Millennium Stadium, is approx 25mins drive away.Ballas Farm has been awarded a Certificate of Excellence by Trip Advisor and Simply the Guest, Top Rated by Laterooms.

Hazelwood House

Wildmill View, Tondu Road, Bridgend, Mid Glamorgan, CF31 4LJ
T: 01656-647780 www.hazelwood-house.co.uk E: info@hazelwood-house.co.uk

Purpose built and meticulously maintained our luxury guest house, minutes from Bridgend town centre, has received the highest reviews on Tripadvisor from our guests. Designed with the guest in mind, and offers the highest standard of Guest House accommodation in Bridgend, similar to what you would expect to find at a quality hotel. Built to Gold Business Standard and having received our four star rating from both Visit Wales (formerly the Welsh Tourist Board) and The AA, our guest house offers accommodation in eight spacious en-suite bedrooms, a discrete dining room and a lounge area housec in the conservatory. Residents also have access to the carefully tended garden which is set in 2.5 acres c natural parkland alongside the river. The guest house area has been designed to be completely separat from our home, so whilst you can expect a friendly welcome, you will also be afforded the privacy and freedom you would expect from a small hotel.

Cowbridge Cabins

The Lodge, Llwynhelig, Cowbridge, Vale of Glamorgan, CF71 7FF
T: 01446-772344 www.cowbridgecabins.co.uk E: info@cowbridgecabins.co.uk

Nestling within 2000 acres of Penllyn Estate Farm, and just ten minutes' walk of the historic town of Cowbridge with its array of pubs, restaurants and fantastic boutiques and beautiful beaches nearby, Cowbridge Cabins enjoys a fantastic location.There are six cabins to choose from; one family and five double / twin rooms - comfortable, secure and homely, at very affordable prices especially for a town c Cowbridge's status, which offers a diversity of choice. The town boasts of a superb range of pubs, wine bars and coffee shops unique in their character and styles; where eating out is always a treat!

As well as booking a cabin, you are welcome to walk around the farm, to the lakes and in the woods nearby. There are lots of businesses established on the farm so there is always plenty to look at.

Lilypot Log Cabins

Lilypot Farm, Bonvilston, Vale of Glamorgan, CF5 6TR

T: 01446 781880 www.lilypotlogcabins.co.uk e: lilypotlogcabins@gmail.com

Nestled in the beautiful Vale Of Glamorgan, Lilypot is perfectly situated for exploring nearby Cardiff and the surrounding beaches, woodlands and more. We are close to Cardiff Airport and 10 minutes drive from Cardiff City Centre. Peaceful countryside surroundings with beautiful views, close to stunning beaches, picturesque hills and challenging mountain walks. Lilypot Luxury Log Cabins sleep 6 and have fully equipped kitchens. Our log cabins are specially designed and made in Finland to suit our exacting demands on quality. Each one is hand built on site and finished to a high standard with excellent insulation, underfloor heating throughout for cosy nights in. take a walk through our neighbouring woodlands, do some fishing, horse riding or relax and enjoy the natural beauty of the surrounding countryside.

Great House Hotel & Restaurant

High Street, Laleston, Bridgend, Mid Glamorgan, CF32 0HP

T: 01656 657644 www.great-house-laleston.co.uk e: enquiries@great-house-laleston.co.uk

A unique blend of historic original features contribute to The Great House's mature and warm atmosphere character. The flagstone floors, oak beams, inglenook fireplaces, mullioned windows, stone archways and dovecote in the south wall combine with modern excellent facilities, services and friendliness. Each of our 13 bedrooms has a character of its own, from four-poster to king-sized sleigh beds. They reflect the warmth and friendliness throughout the house to create an entirely unique and unforgettable hotel experience.There are numerous thoughtful touches: fluffy white towels, bathrobes for your comfort during your stay, choice of pure mulberry silk duvets or wool blankets and sheets, elegant furnishings, a complimentary daily newspaper of your choice, and luxury toiletries.

Court Coleman Manor

Pen-y-Fai, Bridgend, Mid Glamorgan, CF31 4NG

T: 01656 720212 www.court-colman-manor.com e: experience@court-colman-manor.com

Court Colman Manor Hotel has so much to offer; with our convenient location and unique setting, it's the ideal place for your business meeting or wedding. With the benefit of a civil ceremony licence along with all the facilities to make any important celebration a memorable one, there's truly no greater venue. Situated in the beautiful South Wales countryside, Court Colman Manor Hotel is ideal for anyone looking to simply get away from it all. Our rural accommodation near Cardiff and Swansea guarantees an escape from the hustle and bustle to our tranquil countryside location. With 29 bedrooms, we are large enough to offer all the amenities of a quality hotel, yet small enough to get to know our guests. Our staff are always on hand to deliver the finest hotel and service experience – our team are a big part of what makes staying with us so special.

Moorshead Farm Cottages

Moorshead Farm, Siginstone, Cowbridge, CF71 7LP

T: 01446 773261 www.moorsheadfarm.com e: enquiries@moorsheadfarm.com

John and Sian invite you to enjoy your stay at the four holiday cottages converted from farm buildings adjacent to our 15th Century Farmhouse in the picturesque rural vale of Glamorgan.

Ony 3 miles away from the historic market town of Cowbridge or the heritage coast at Llantwit Major, we are just a short walk away from a good country pub. We have two,one bedroom cottages and two with two bedrooms.

All have fitted kitchens and electric heating as well as woodburning stoves and TV/DVD. Ample parking is just outside the cottage and bedding ,electricity and logs are incliuded in the price. Many pubs and restaurants are within easy reach of Moorshead.You can even walk to a few.

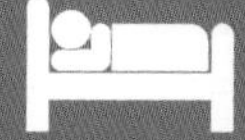

Limpert Bay Guest House

Limpert House, The Leys, Gileston, South Glamorgan CF62 4HX

T: 01446 751073 www.limpertbay.co.uk E: info@limpertbay.co.uk

When you visit the stunning Vale of Glamorgan and need a warm and cosy place to rest your head for the night, look no further than Limpert Bay Guest House. Situated on the beach in Gileston, South Glamorgan, our guest house offers a homely and welcoming overnight accommodation for guests. For more than 10 years we have been a home away from home for many visitors to the area. We often have guests who are exploring Cardiff, which is located around 25 minutes away, and visitors who have just arrived at Cardiff Airport, which is four miles away. With competitive prices, ample on-site parking, and a hearty breakfast served up in the morning, there is no reason not to stay with us. Breakfast is served between 7:00 a.m. and 8:30 a.m. between Monday and Friday, while it is available between 7:30 a.m. and 9:30 a.m. on Saturdays and Sundays.

Blanco's Hotel

Green Park , Port Talbot, SA12 6NT

T: 01639 864500 www.blancoshotel.co.uk E: info@blancoshotel.co.uk

Blanco's Hotel & Restaurant offers spacious and inviting surroundings, designed to offer guests the best in hotel accommodation. All 63 rooms are beautifully appointed, tastefully decorated in muted, relaxing colours and heavenly beds are adorned with crisp, fresh, white bed linen. Generous bathrooms with fluffy towels all combine to create a real feeling of a luxurious home from home. Each of the five deluxe room suites have been individually designed to make you feel pampered and cosseted. So put your feet up, relax and unwind in your private room. Blanco's Hotel is luxurious, elegant and sophisticated and conveniently located in a central location in Port Talbot. Blanco's Hotel & Restaurant is just 2 minutes off Junction 41 of the M4, 5 minutes from Junction 40 of the M4 and only 15 minutes from Swansea city centre.

The Golden Mile Country Inn

Corntown, Vale of Glamorgan, CF35 5BA

T: 01656 654884 www.thegoldenmile.co.uk E: info@thegoldenmile.co.uk

Tucked away in a peaceful corner of the Vale of Glamorgan, The Golden Mile Country Inn is in a rural setting with beautiful countryside views. Our 4 guest rooms combine both style and comfort and you will find attention to detail that anticipates your every need.

The Golden Mile Country Inn enjoys beautiful rural views and will offer guests peace and quiet to encourage a good night's sleep

All rooms are en-suite and offer

- Tea/Coffee Facilities
- Complimentary Wifi access
- HD television

Alexandra Guest House

44 Coity Road, Bridgend, Vale of Glamorgan, CF31 1LR

T: 01656 650761

Alexandra Guest House in Bridgend has been providing quality accommodation for over 25 years righ in the heart of the town. Ideally placed within a 2 minute walk of the town's centre, bus station and tra station. Just 2 miles away is the Mc ArthurGlen Designer Outlet and junction 36 of the M4 providing quick access to Cardiff or Swansea. Alexandra Guest House has 9 spacious rooms to offer, ranging fror single to family rooms with either twin or double beds. All rooms are on a Bed & Breakfast basis offerir a full British breakfast or continental option in our dining room. We can easily cater for individual dieta needs and can also provide children's meals. Rooms have full tea & coffee making facilities along with complementary biscuits. Freeview TV is also available in every room.

The Golden Mile Country Inn

Corntown, Vale of Glamorgan, CF35 5BA

T: 01656-654884 www.thegoldenmile.co.uk E: info@thegoldenmile.co.uk

Tucked away in a peaceful corner of the Vale of Glamorgan, The Golden Mile Country Inn is in a rural setting with beautiful countryside views. Our contemporary restaurant serves delicious wholesome food using fresh local produce. Our cosy elegant pub offers a great selection of ales, as well as an extensive wine list and a wide choice of cocktails. We are family friendly and offer a safe play area and cater for children's needs. We offer a wide range of innovative and traditional cuisine – something for everyone. Our philosophy is to use only fresh locally sourced produce of the highest quality, focusing on seasonal ingredients.Our menu offers a selection of light-bites, gastro pub fare and exciting main courses of the highest quality to satisfy the most discerning taste buds.

The Rock Inn

98 John Street, Porthcawl, Glamorgan, CF36 3DT

T: 01656-782096 www.rockinnporthcawl.co.uk E: info@rockinnporthcawl.co.uk

Here at the Rock Inn, we pride ourselves on delivering a great customer experience within our fantastic recently refurbished pub. Our staff are looking forward to serving you with our new fantastic range of drinks and substantial new menu of pub classics. We have everything covered. Enjoy relaxing in our bar trying our new cask ales whilst watching the live sports events, out in our landscaped court yard enjoying the sun with a refreshing bottle of prosecco, or having a cosy catch up in our soft seated lounge. Our new menu will certainly not disappoint and our various food offers will ensure you come back throughout the week. The little ones are catered for also with a children's menu to keep them full and activity packs are available to keep them entertained.

Corner House Inn

Llangywnwyd, Maesteg, Glamorgan, CF34 9SB

T: 01656 734964 www.cornerhousellan.co.uk E: enquiries@cornerhousellan.co.uk

Wayne and Gill welcome you to their Country Restaurant and Inn. Our menu features all fresh local produce resulting in what is probably the finest local cuisine available. We pride ourselves on the relaxed atmosphere in our house and our concept that your table is yours for the evening. Our bar has a selection of traditional ales and a wide range of lagers. We have a great selection of main menu dishes ranging from chicken, steak and seafood dishes, to homemade specials, ribs and vegetarian dishes, we also have a great range of kids items to choose from so all the family can eat! We pride ourselves on the service we offer our customers.Please feel free to drop us a line, either to tell us how well we are doing or how we could improve our service. Don't forget, if you are impressed tell others, if not then tell us.

Court Coleman Manor - Bokhara Brasserie

Pen-y-Fai, Bridgend, Mid Glamorgan, CF31 4NG

T: 01656 720212 www.court-colman-manor.com e: experience@court-colman-manor.com

The Independent's food critic, Roopa Gulati, placed Bokhara Indian Brasserie in the Top 10 Indian restaurants in Britain, an accolade which is testiment to our dedication to authenticity and excellence. We combine fresh ingredients with Indian spices to produce authentic and delicious dishes. Tandoori cuisine in particular requires very specialist training and, as our kitchen is open, discerning diners are able to watch their meals being skillfully prepared by our expert team. The creation of Tandoori naan is a visual pleasure all in itself. We offer a comprehensive array of dishes combining fresh ingredients with Indian spices to produce authentic and delicious cuisine. Whilst we are known for our Indian speciality, we also offer a host of great non-Indian dishes of equally excellent quality.

Mr Villas Fish & Chip Restaurant & Oyster Bar

4 Bron-y-Mor, Barry, Vale of Glamorgan, CF62 6SW

T: 01446-730662 E: mrvillas2015@gmail.com

Mr Villa's Fish and Chip Restaurant and Oyster Bar is celebrating its first anniversary at the Knap in Barry so it was an appropriate time to see what it has to offer. The owners, Beppe and Christine Villa, have 35 years of experience in the restaurant trade with sea food dining their speciality. The restaurant provides a wide range of fish dishes, but non-fish too. It has the bright, cheerful décor of a seaside fish restaurant in blues and whites, colourful vintage travel posters and bleached white wood panels. I've always enjoyed sea food courses because they tend to be filling without being too heavy. There's a wide choice of starters and main courses on the menu for meat as well as fish lovers, along with a 'specials board'.

The Six Bells Penmark

Rhoose, Barry, Vale of Glamorgan, CF62 3BP

T: 01446-710229 www.sixbellspenmark.co.uk E: mail@sixbellspenmark.co.uk

Step in through our doors and be welcome into a traditional country bar with heavy wooden beams, open log fires and hints of fresh homemade food floating through the air. From the outside, it's old-fashioned style, array of colourful flowers and hanging baskets paint the perfect picture for a calming escape from the hustle and bustle of day to day life. Locals love us and the word is spreading on social media! Dining here is high quality and traditional with a reputation built on getting the pub classic just right. James is a true believer in traditional values and all of our meat is locally sourced from personally selected Welsh farms including our own Rosedew Farm. Our carefully selected wine list offers an array o choices to compliment the delicious flavours of our menu.

Isabella's Restaurant

9 Well Street, Porthcawl, Mid Glamorgan, CF36 3BE

T: 01656 782330 www.braseria-isabellas.co.uk

Sonia and Geraint have co-owned Isabella's Restaurant since March 2012. We are a family run brasserie restaurant, with rustic décor and a Mediterranean ambience. We strive to deliver you great service and an atmosphere to match. The restaurant boasts an open kitchen and specializes in fresh meat and fish. On display we have a wonderful counter where customers come down to order and pick out what they want. All food is ordered on a daily basis ensuring we have the freshest produce. Where possible we use local. Recently we have begun to enjoy award success. Winning 'Best World Cuisine Restaurant' at The Food Awards Wales 2018. And an award for being recognized as a 'Top 20 Restaurant', at The Restaurant Awards Wales 2018. We have also been recommended by the Western Mail as a 'must try' restaurant along the South Wales Coastal Path.

Arboreal

68 Eastgate, Cowbridge, Vale of Glamorgan, CFf71 7AB

T: 01446 775093 www.arboreal.uk.com E: info@arboreal.uk.com

We are a Cowbridge based Cafe Kitchen Bar. Arboreal captures the relaxed nature of our environment and stays true to its concept by cooking food from our open wood oven. We love our coffees, world wines, cocktails and fresh juices. We are a Michelin Guide Eatery and as a small independent we really like to look after our customers. We believe in fresh, seasonal and honest food so we kept our menus simple and delicious.We tasted heaps of wine before deciding on our list and took pride in mixing classic cocktails.We designed an interesting and comfortable environment for our customers by using an inspiring mix of old, new, bespoke and recycled products.We wanted our customers to feel relaxed so we chose staff that shared our vision.And then...we opened. Now a couple of years down the line, w remain passionate about quality, keep our ethos simple and our expectations high.

Poco Poco

14 Wyndham Street, Bridgend, Mid Glamorgan, CF31 1EF

T: 01656-667999 www.pocopoco.co.uk e: info@pocopoco.co.uk

Poco Poco Tapas Bar and Continental Restaurant offers an unrivaled dining experience with a European atmosphere. Friendly and relaxed, the Mediterranean ambiance provides the perfect setting for a romantic meal or a get-together amongst friend. A fusion of continental flavours can be found in our tapas selection, a la carte menu and daily specials. Our range of vibrant and sumptuous Tapas draw influence from around the globe. Alongside the classics such as Albondigas (Spanish style meatballs) and Fish Cakes are contemporary creations like crispy chorizo and savoury dates wrapped in parma ham and soaked in amareto. The a la carte menu boasts an array of delicious dishes, such as chargrilled sea bass with chilli infused butter and a pesto dressing. To complement your meal we have a top wine list featuring the world's finest varieties, including cavas and champagnes.

The Prince of Wales Inn

Ton Kenfig, Bridgend, Mid Glamorgan, CF33 4PR

T: 01656 740 356 www.princeofwalesinn.co.uk e: davestone.sh@hotmail.com

The Prince of Wales Inn, formerly known as Ty Newydd Tavern, can be found on the outskirts of the small Welsh village of Kenfig in Bridgend. The inn boasts four quirky, characterful rooms: The Lounge, the dog friendly Snug, the Restaurant and the Old Town Hall. The medieval-style Old Town hall is available for hire for all kinds of private functions, including weddings, christenings, funeral wakes, birthday celebrations or business meetings. Our pub is open 7 days a week and we serve homemade food, freshly prepared on the premises, including real chips, pies and rustic pizzas, with a good selection of vegetarian and vegan dishes. We are famed for traditional Welsh dishes, including Welsh brunch, laverbread, Penclawdd cockles and faggots.

The Vale of Glamorgan Inn

51 High St, Cowbridge CF71 7AE

T: 01446-772252

This is the best pub in the vale. No darts music gambling machines pool or other distractions. Just good beer good company and more characters than a dickens novel. If you like atmosphere get there as soon as you can. Good atmosphere, great staff. The real deal. Get there on a Friday and you may get to meet local thespian Jeff grist?

A small pub in the main street in Cowbridge. We looked at the menu board and we all decided to have liver,bacon and mash potatoes. When our meal arrived it was nicely presented and very hot. The liver,bacon,onions were served with mashed potatoes, cabbage,carrots, broccoli, beans and a very tasty gravy. I would definitely recommend visiting this pub for a freshly cooked meal at lunch time.

The White Hart Inn

Wine Street, Llanwit Major, Vale of Glamorgan, CF61 1RZ

T: 01446-796956

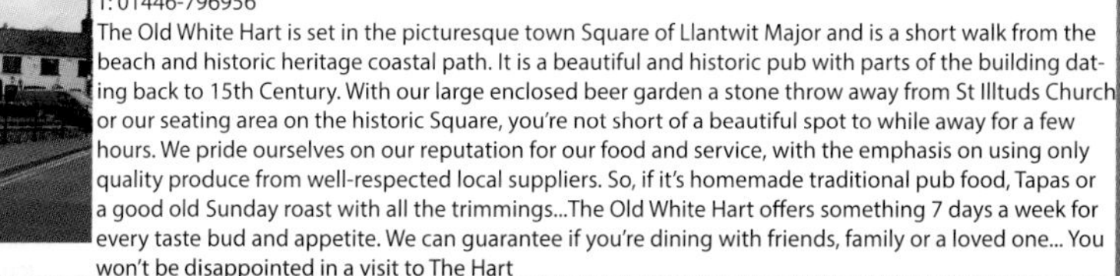

The Old White Hart is set in the picturesque town Square of Llantwit Major and is a short walk from the beach and historic heritage coastal path. It is a beautiful and historic pub with parts of the building dating back to 15th Century. With our large enclosed beer garden a stone throw away from St Illtuds Church or our seating area on the historic Square, you're not short of a beautiful spot to while away for a few hours. We pride ourselves on our reputation for our food and service, with the emphasis on using only quality produce from well-respected local suppliers. So, if it's homemade traditional pub food, Tapas or a good old Sunday roast with all the trimmings...The Old White Hart offers something 7 days a week for every taste bud and appetite. We can guarantee if you're dining with friends, family or a loved one... You won't be disappointed in a visit to The Hart

Blanco's Hotel

Green Park , Port Talbot, SA12 6NT

T: 01639 864500 www.blancoshotel.co.uk E: info@blancoshotel.co.uk

Our spacious contemporary restaurant, with its intimate booths, is perfect for enjoying a simple, informal lunch or a relaxing post-work drink. Seasonal and innovative menus blend British & European cuisine. Succumb to a mouth-watering Traditional Sunday Roast, home cooked to perfection. Discerning diners can enjoy an a la carte menu, available seven days a week offering quality, smart cooking with professional, efficient service. Excellent food and great wines, in your chosen company, will contribute to a memorable day or evening. Take time for yourself at Blanco's. We are licensed to carry out civil ceremonies and Blanco's is a popular choice for modern couples who like the idea of having the ceremony and reception in one place, and the ease it allows. The perfect end to a perfect day must be a stay in the Honeymoon Suite, with a huge bed and spa-style bathroom.

The Star Inn Wick

Ewenny Road, Wick, Nr Cowbridge, Vale of Glamorgan, CF71 7QA

T: 01656-890080 www.thestarinnwick.co.uk E: thestarinn.wick@gmail.com

Welcome to the Star Inn, a traditional country public house comprising of a cosy bar and separate lounge/restaurant area, both offering plenty of character and real log fires for those cold winter days. We opened in October 2012 and have since earned our place in the CAMRA Good Pub Guide and also a Highly Commended Third Place in Camras Pub of the Year 2018 competition for our outstanding real ales.We have recently refurbished the restaurant area for our 6th anniversary and together with a brand new menu we are very pleased with the results! (Also due to the increased number of spaces in the restaurant we have now converted the upstairs dining room into a pool room!) The kitchen is open Wednesday - Saturday for lunch (12.00-14.30) and evening meals (18.00-21.00). Sunday Lunch is available between 12.00-16.00. We look forward to seeing you again soon!

Scoops Portcawl

The Promenade, Coney Beach, Porthcawl, CF36 5TS

www.coneybeach.co.uk Find us on Facebook and Instagram

Location, Location, Location! At It's all about the view! Scoops Icecream & Coffee Bar sits over the beach with unrivalled views of the coastline and beyond from our balcony and conservatory. Scoops is a family business which has been serving award winning Welsh Icecream from Sub Zero since 2005. We have over 40 flavours to tempt you served on a selection of specialty waffles, wafers and tubs. We also use this famous local brand in our crepe creations, wondrous waffles and sublime sundaes. Fuel your thoughts with a locally roasted coffee, specialty teas from Twinnings and our moorish hot chocolates all made with milk and cream from a herd just outside Porthcawl. Compliment your hot drink with a sweet treat! A selection of desserts are always available and if your feeling peckish enjoy a freshly made panini, sandwich, baguette or a salad. Eat in or takeaway. Open daily throughout the summer season.

The Blue Anchor Inn

East Aberthaw, Nr Barry, Vale of Glamorgan, CF62 3DD

T: 01446-750329 www.blueanchoraberthaw.com E: enquiries@blueanchoraberthaw.com

The Blue Anchor Inn was one of the first pubs in South Wales to produce quality bar meals back in the 1980's. Since then we have gone from strength to strength, winning awards including the South Wales Food Pub of the year for 5 years, 2016/17, 2013, 2011, 2008 and 2006. We are Egon Ronay recommended and are included in the Michelin Eating out in Pubs guide since 2007 (the only South Wales entry in the guide), as well as the AA Pub Guide 2012, where we appear as Pick of the Pubs for the Vale of Glamorgan. The Blue Anchor offers the choice of eating in our Restaurant or, more informally, downstairs in the bar. Wherever you choose to eat, our menus all have at their heart locally grown or reared produce, prepared to the highest standards by our expert team of chefs. Our team are specialists in producing quality, locally sourced and innovative dishes.

WYE VALLEY & VALE OF USK

I have to be totally honest with you when writing this piece, that before going to visit some of the great places within this section of the book, I had never visited the Wye Valley area before. I knew of and had heard about the places that make up both the Wye Valley and the Vale of Usk but didn't know that collectively that that's what they were called. But I can honestly say with true conviction, that once visited, these places are certainly not places to be forgotten in a hurry. There are so many historical connections with this area of Wales and that can be readily seen in our selection of tourist attractions for this section of the book. From museums to castles, magical gardens to stately homes and a historical ship thrown in for good measure, this area is steeped in that much history, you'll begin o forget which year you're in.

hepstow racecourse is a huge pull to the area, along with its sister racecourse Ffos Las in armarthenshire, both of which are attractions in this book, they make up most of the Welsh race neetings and they also play host to a number of special events. I mention this only because for ecades this racecourse has continued to bring people from all over the UK to its race meetings, and I idn't want you to think that it was only historical events or places that the Wye Valley was renowned or. For centuries, people have seen the Wye valley as a very special place, they have taken to boating olidays and trips up the Wye river in their millions so much so, that now the Wye river has been iven the status nationally as a Special Area of Conservation.

West Usk Lighthouse

t: 01633-810126 e: info@westusklighthouse.co.uk
www.westusklighthouse.co.uk

The West Usk Lighthouse is a cosy bed & breakfast and small wedding venue (voted best in the region) situated near the City of Newport, Gwent, at the junction of the Severn and the Usk Estuaries which overlooks the Bristol Channel.
Built in 1821 by Scottish architect, James Walker, it is unique among lighthouses having all the accommodation situated within the building itself creating a distinctive design that is bigger in circumference and shorter in height.
The interior tends to be described as quirky and comfortable rather than luxurious. All the rooms are wedge-shaped with en-suite facilities. We have a stone spiral staircase, which runs though the centre of the lighthouse and beneath that is the rain collecting well - which is now our wishing well and wine cellar! The entrance hall is slate bedded and at the bottom of the stairs we have our resident Dalek (with an interesting story) and a TARDIS on the roof (changing room for the hot tub). They are an added bonus for Doctor Who fans.If you do stay with us, do not forget to have a dip in the hot tub situated the roof garden.

AUTHOR'S REVIEW

Wales has a whole multitude of varied accommodations to stay ales in, from Shepherds Huts, Gypsy Caravans, you can even stay in an African Safari Tent if it takes your fancy. But to be able to stay in a lighthouse that has also been featured on TV, really is a unique experience. I chose to feature the USK Lighthouse as one of our attractions because of the rare experience that can be gained from your stay here, and I promise you faithfully, that once stayed here, never forgotten. The owners of this lighthouse have not only a invested a huge fi nancial input into the lighthouse, but also their time and a huge amount of care and attention into each and every bedroom. They really do care about every single one of their many visitors and every effort goes into making your stay here one that you will always cherish.

Newport

West Nash Road, Nash, Newport, Gwent, NP18 2B

Newport Wetlands National Nature Reserve

t: 01633-636363 e: newport-wetlands@rspb.org.uk
www.rspb.org.uk/newportwetlands

This nature reserve offers a haven for wildlife on the edge of the city, but is a great place for people too with a RSPB visitor centre, a café, shop and family activities and trails. It's the ideal place to relax and enjoy a lovely slice of homemade cake and a hot drink whilst enjoying the view from the café window, followed by a browse in the retail area. There's lots to discover about the wildlife and heritage of this special area, including spectacular views of the Severn estuary to enjoy all year round. The reed beds provide food and shelter for a wide range of birds, such as the Cetti's warblers, bitterns and bearded tits. Ducks, geese and swans visit the reserve in large numbers during the winter, along with waders that can be seen on the foreshore, including curlew, dunlin and oystercatchers. We can also offer a variety of fun and informative activities and guided walks for a wide range of local interest groups. Newport Wetlands National Nature Reserve is owned and managed by Natural Resources Wales in partnership with RSPB Cymru and Newport City Council for the benefit of wildlife and people. Image 1 & 3 by Jeremy White, Image 2 by Nick Evans.

AUTHOR'S REVIEW

Although I have said it before, this site is an incredibly special place. Despite being situated right next door to a power station, thousands of birds call this home, along with a huge variety of other wildlife. Otters, water voles and stoats, as well as dragonflies, damselflies, moths and butterflies all cohabit here perfectly well. There is also a huge diversity of flora, including several species of orchid, which fill the reserve with colour throughout the spring and summer. So whatever time of year you visit, there will always be something to get excited about! Newport Wetlands National Nature Reserve is a fantastic place to bring the children, they will absolutely love the large range of activities that are regularly on offer.

West Nash Road, Nash, Newport, Gwent, NP18 2BZ

Walnut Tree Farm Park

t: 01633 680905 e: hello@walnuttreefarmpark.com
www.walnuttreefarmpark.com

Rain or Shine, There is Loads To See & Do * Farmyard Animals and Rare Breeds: Make friends with our farm animals and learn about rare breeds including the really cute Kune Kune pigs.
Rabbits and Guinea Pigs: Meet and play with the rabbits in their large pens
Tractor Rides: Explore the farm on our tractor and trailer
Large Play Areas: Adventure playground and large indoor and outdoor play areas. Child friendly activity areas with swings, slides, climbing frames and loads of wood chippings!
Soft Play Areas for Toddlers: A safe toddler friendly area for the little ones to have fun.
Go-Kart Racing: Pedal power racing around our purpose built circuit.
Horse and Pony Rides: Explore the farm on accompanied horse and pony rides.
Country Walks: Over 80 acres of country walks including 3 fishing lakes.

AUTHOR'S REVIEW

I had been told about Walnut Tree Farm Park by another attraction, so for this to happen, I thought it had to be good, so off I set on my travels and what I discovered was that I was wrong, the place isn't just good, the place is amazing! Being a family run business, the owner Philip Scrivens and his family, have invested not only a fortune into the site, but their love and hard work can be seen around every acre of this attraction. I spent some time with the owner, finding out all about the farm, why he created it and where he is taking it into the future and the two most important things I detected from Philip, was his outstanding love for all of his animals and making sure all of his visitors have a great time. He needn't worry about the second though, I witnessed a lot of happy people on the day that I visited the farm, the facilities were good, staff were friendly and the admission price reflects everything I've just said, ten out of ten!

Newport

St Brides, Newport, Gwent, NP10 8SQ

Llanvihangel Court & Gardens  

t: 07806 768 788 e: Enquiries@llanvihangelcourt.com
www.llanvihangelcourt.com

Welcome to Llanvihangel Court, a Tudor manor house and much loved family home, set on the edge of the beautiful Black Mountains and the Brecon Beacons. The house has a wonderful position in the landscape, set between fields and formal gardens and within easy reach of the market towns of Abergavenny and Hay-on-Wye, with their food and literary festivals. The rich history of the house and its beautiful grounds attract many visitors and guests throughout the year, for guided tours, weddings, accommodation, events such as theatre, music, story telling, as a film location, and much more. Llanvihangel Court has a fascinating history and you can explore this yourself by visiting the house on one of our guided tours. Tours take place during the summer months, which gives you an opportunity to enjoy the gardens and surrounding countryside. We provide free car parking for visitors. Please feel free to contact us if you have any further queries.We hope you enjoy finding out some more about the house and its history, when you can visit and the services we offer.

AUTHOR'S REVIEW

Over the years I have investigated and visited many old houses, castles and stately homes. Once visited, many of them found a way into my heart; Llanvihangel Court & Gardens was indeed one of them. Room after room of pure history is what you will find once on a tour of this house. Once I had been shown round by its owner I just wanted to go round and round again. It's very strange how a house can do this to you, and to be honest it is hard to explain. But we knew choosing this house to be in our book was a must, and when you make a visit here you'll know exactly why! Because this house is so fragile, the house isn't open all the time, so It is very important that you phone ahead to find out tour times and assure a place on a tour, but I guarantee once visited never forgotten.

Newport

Llanfihangel Crucorney, Abergavenny, NP7 8DH

Wye Valley Canoes

t: 01497-847007 e: info@wyevalleycanoes.co.uk
www.wyevalleycanoes.co.uk

The Wye Valley Canoe Centre sits on the banks of the River Wye four miles west of Hay-on-Wye. We are located on the bridge at Glasbury and have a fleet of Canadian canoes, single kayaks and double kayaks. You can paddle for a few hours or a few days. You start with us at the Wye Valley Canoe Centre in Glasbury and paddle downstream. When you reach your destination you telephone us and we collect you and your canoes with a minibus and trailer. It is a beautiful stretch of river, and ideal to spend time with friends or family enjoying the peace and quiet of a really unspoilt stretch of water. After a couple of hours you reach Hay where you can stop for lunch or we can collect you from there. For the more intrepid a full day will take you a couple of hours further on to either the Toll Bridge or The Boat Inn. If you need a complete break then try camping or B&B'ing it down the Wye for a few days and reach Hereford, Ross or Monmouth or a few place in between with a bit of canvas or the phone number of a B&B with a four poster.

AUTHOR'S REVIEW

The Wye Valley Canoe Centre was one of those attractions that I had to take at least four double takes whilst visiting it. With so many sides to this business, there truly is something on offer for every type of tourist. Firstly let me tell you about the canoes themselves. As you steer your trusty vessel down the River Wye, you really could be in any part of the world, the mighty Amazon first springs to mind, and Wye Valley Canoes will tailor make any type of trip you fancy. Then there are the Mountain Bikes that are on hire here at the centre. For a relatively small amount of money, you could be cycling through the Wye valley on either a top of the range mountain bike, or even a 50cc Piaggio Vespa Scooter, the choice is yours! With a Posh Bunkhouse, four Comfortable en-suite rooms, and an amazing cafe, Wye Valley Canoes is truly a one stop shop when it comes to exploring a truly hidden part of Wales!

• Newport

The Boat House, Glasbury, Glasbury Bridge, Hereford HR3 5NP

Hidden Valley Yurts

t: 01600-860723 e: amanda@hiddenvalleyyurts.co.uk
www.hiddenvalleyyurts.co.uk

Hidden Valley Yurts is in an Area of Outstanding Natural Beauty. Our 80 acre valley is a stunning mix of species rich wild flower meadows, ancient woodland and coppiced hazel which provides a habitat for a wide diversity of wildlife. Dormice, badgers and foxes share the land with our alpacas. Rare butterflies, birds and insects abound and the gently babbling brook which runs through the valley attracts kingfishers, herons and dippers.. Our 5 real Mongolian yurts are located in a beautiful, South facing wildflower meadow alongside a stream. With a large, communal kitchen, bathroom, dining tent, the site can accommodate up to 31 people in total and provide an ideal venue for both individual families or for friends and family groups to book the whole site. Tthe natural simplicity of a camping holiday with nature on your (Mongolian) doorstep but without having to pitch your tent. The felt lined yurts have wood burning stoves.

AUTHOR'S REVIEW

Within this latest edition of the Top 100 Attractions in Wales book, I really had to up my game when it came to the new additions of hidden gem attractions. I truly sense that with the inclusion of Hidden Valley Yurts, I have more than upped my game. The sites new owners Mike and his partner really have taken this site to a whole new level and it was clear to see that no expense has been spared here in achieving that. For those visiting the area of the Wye Valley & Vale of Usk, you really are spoilt for choice when it comes to choosing which attractions to visit within a forty to fifty mile radius, as there is so much to see and do. But being located at Hidden Valley Yurts, you can just stay here and get away from it all, I think also worth a mention is their luxurious lake house, for those not wanting to clamp it up, this is a perfect alternative. Hidden Valley Yurts is nestled within some of the most beautiful Monmouthshire countryside and they really do make our tagline of 'Same Country Different World' ever more real.

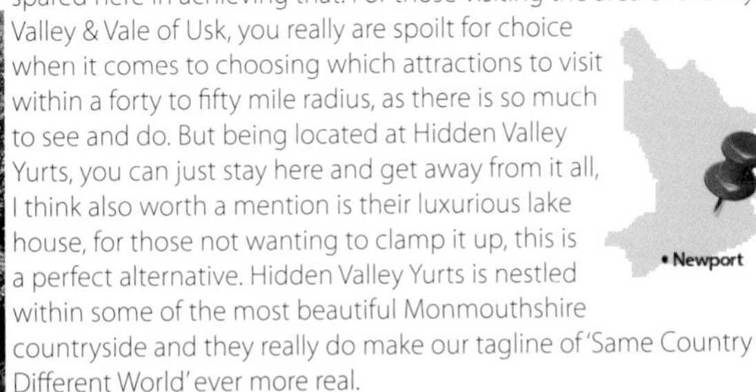

Lower Glyn Farm, Llanishen, Chepstow, Monmouthshire, NP16 6QU

Wyndcliffe Court Gardens

t: 01291-621242 e: info@wyndcliffecourt.co.uk
www.wyndcliffecourt.co.uk

The gardens at Wyndcliffe Court are designed in a series of formal spaces or "rooms" featuring sculpted topiary, a sunken garden, a summerhouse, walled gardens, fountains, a lily pond and an Archery lawn leading on to wooded walks. Designed by H. Avray Tipping, friend of Gertrude Jekyll and Editor of Country Life magazine they were completed in 1922 and are probably the best example of their type in Wales. They are worth a visit in their own right, but also make a wonderful setting for two contemporary garden sculpture shows "Elegance and Form". Wyndcliffe Court Gardens are 5 minutes from Chepstow and Tintern Abbey, nestled in the hills above the Wye Valley to the north of the village of St. Arvans. Situated on a high blu , the house and gardens o er views over the Severn, the coastal plain and the Bristol Channel. The Gardens are ideally located. 20 minutes from Newport, 30 minutes from Bristol and Cardi , 40 from Gloucester and around 2 hours from London, with excellent public transport links.

AUTHOR'S REVIEW

In this new edition of the Top 100 Attractions in Wales book, we have introduced 'Hidden Gem' status, an award which couldn't be better explained than here at Wyndcli e Court. Visiting here in the summer of 2018, and being completely honest by saying I am not a true garden expert, or fan for that matter, I wasn't too sure what to expect. However, one need not worry as these gardens are designed for everyone in mind. The gardens are designed in a series of rooms, and you don't need to be green fingered to appreciate them, especially with the addition of hundreds of sculptures around every corner which will leave you in awe as you explore. One of the many special features of Wyndcliffe Court Gardens is their Vintage Tea Room, now this is most certainly where my expertise comes in, homemade cakes, real tea and delicious sandwiches is the usual fare here, and their real lemonade is to die for.

Off Penterry Lane, St. Arvans, Chepstow, Monmouthshire, NP16 6EY

Parva Farm Vineyard

t: 01291-689 636
www.parvafarm.com E: parvafarm@hotmail.com

This award-winning vineyard was planted in 1979 on a sunny, south-facing slope overlooking Tintern and the beautiful River Wye. It is believed to be the site used by the monks of Tintern Abbey to cultivate vines hundreds of years ago. The old vines produce high quality wines, many of which have won awards both nationally and internationally. White, rose, red and sparkling wines are made as well as a Welsh Mead and fruit wines which are made with locally grown, or wild, fruits and berries. The Farm shop also sells local cider, perry and ales as well as preserves, honey and garden plants which are grown at the vineyard. A selection of gifts are also available. A self-guided tour of the vineyard may be taken all the year round. Although there is more to see in the summer months, it is interesting at any time and the views over the Wye valley are spectacular. A free wine tasting may be taken in the shop after the tour. Guided group tours and tutored wine tastings are also available but need to be booked in advance.

AUTHOR'S REVIEW

Some can be forgiven for thinking that if you want to visit a vineyard, you'd at least have to travel to a region of France. Top 100 Attractions can confirm that this is no longer true, and the reason we are so confident, is that we have uncovered an amazing little vineyard which has now been awarded our hidden gem status. Parva Farm Vineyard, is an award winning vineyard based comfortably within the Wye Valley and is more than probably based on the site that would of been used by the monks of Tintern Abbey, you can't get any more special than that! The site is so special, TV networks have all clambered here to film programmes such as 'The Hairy Bikers' and the BBC'S Countryfile, along with its veteran presenter John Craven. With a well stocked and attractive little shop, you can take a wine tasting session shortly after taking your tour around this wonderful vineyard.

• Newport

Dewstow Gardens & Grottoes

t: 01291-431020 e: info @dewstowgardens.co.uk
www.dewstowgardens.co.uk

Dewstow Gardens & Grottoes is one of the lesser well known attractions in South Wales, but also one of the most interesting. The gardens are a wonderful place to wander in themselves, with beautifully landscaped paths and decorative beds, waterfalls and pools and beneath all this, a labrynth of tunnels and grottoes Imagine discovering a lost garden with tunnels and underground grottoes buried under thousands of tonnes of soil for over 50 years. That's what happened at Dewstow Gardens & Grottoes. Built around 1895, the gardens were buried just after World War Two and rediscovered in 2000. The gardens contain many ponds and rills, but interestingly a labyrinth of underground grottoes, tunnels and sunken ferneries. The rock gardens are made up of a mixture of real stone and faced stone using various types of Pulhamite. Dewstow Gardens & Grottoes is a great place to visit for families and groups. There are many tunnels and underground grottoes to explore. . Why not make this a must during your visit to South Wales?

AUTHOR'S REVIEW

If I didn't know better I could of easily been forgiven for thinking that Dewstow was the setting for Lewis Carroll's 'Alice in Wonderland' . Dewstow House was built before 1804, when John Proctor (d. 1837) lived there. Dewstow Gardens were built after 1895 and buried after World War II. Rediscovery and large scale restoration of the gardens began in 2000. There is a labyrinth of tunnels interconnecting underground grottoes, ponds, tropical glass houses, rock garden and an alpine garden that help to make this attraction not one to be missed. If I'd of had time I could easily of spent hours at this very special place! So if I were you, I'd pack a flask! You could be there for sometime!

• Newport

Caerwent, Monmouthshire, South Wales, NP26 5AH

White Castle Vineyard

t: 01873-821443 e: robb@whitecastlevineyard.com
www.whitecastlevineyard.com

Our aim is to produce Quality Welsh Wines. We are very passionate about what we do here at White Castle Vineyard and are always striving to be as good as we possibly can be. We feel very privileged to have a vineyard here in Abergavenny. White Castle Vineyard is a small Welsh vineyard situated near the market towns of Abergavenny and Monmouth it is owned and run by Robb and Nicola Merchant. Having purchased the 12 acre small holding in 1995 they converted the milking parlour into their home a year later, however it was 2008 before the dream of owning a vineyard become a reality, the 5 acre gently sloping, south facing field was purchased, soil tests were performed and vines ordered.
May 2009 saw the planting of 4000 vines, the varieties of vines planted were Pinot Noir, Regent, Rondo, Seyval Blanc & Phoenix, now there was no turning back, May 2010 saw a further planting of 800 vines this variety being Siegerrebe. Robb & Nicola have attended Plumpton College East Sussex to study viticulture, this training giving them the skills needed to produce quality Welsh Wines.

AUTHOR'S REVIEW

Wales is fast becoming a real mover and shaker when it comes to vineyards and the wine they produce and there is one couple that really have shaken the apples from the trees, excuse the pun, they are Nicola & Rob Merchant of the White Castle Vineyard, Nr Abergavenny. Being keen wine drinkers themselves, Robb and Nicola really have become somewhat connoisseurs of their craft and their new vineyard tour is fast becoming a big hit with other wine drinking experts. They have become that trusted within their field, they have supplied and been involved with providing wine for even foreign dignitaries from around the world within foreign office events. I really like this little attraction and I know you will too. Their reception area and shop, together with the successful operation they run from there is a slick and professional operation and you couldn't be in safer hands on this vineyard tour.

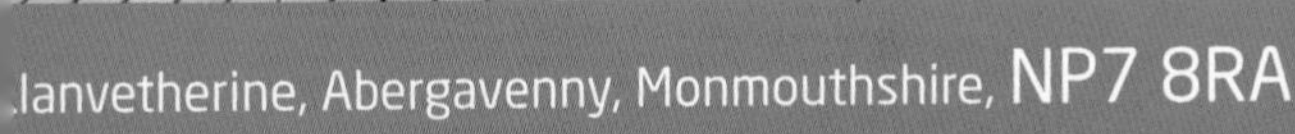
Llanvetherine, Abergavenny, Monmouthshire, NP7 8RA

Newport Medieval Ship

t: 01633-274167 e: newport.ship@newport.gov.uk
www.newportship.org

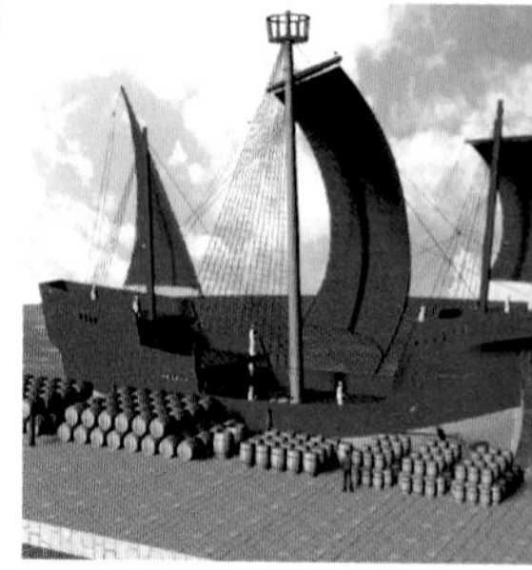

The Newport Medieval Ship is a fifteenth century merchant vessel unearthed in the heart of Newport in 2002. Work on the Riverfront arts centre was paused while excavations could take place, and the timbers have since been undergoing a lengthy conservation process so the ship can be displayed to the public. The conservation process for the Newport Ship has differed from that undertaken for famous ships like the Mary Rose and Vasa in that the timbers were all separated during the excavation phase. This means that each timber can be treeated simultaneously in large tanks, whereas the Mary Rose and Vasa both had to be sprayed continuously with preserving chemicals.

There are plenty of things going on at the Ship Centre. As well as guided tours we seek to inform our visitors about medieval life and time. From coin striking to visiting groups. Come down and learn more. If you can't make it to one of our open days you can contact us to arrange a guided tour of the project using the contact details found on our contact us page. Please bear in mind that the project is still actively working and our guides are volunteers, so while we do try to accommodate every request made it may not be possible to get your first choice of dates.

AUTHOR'S REVIEW

The Medieval Ship in Newport, is a truly unique attraction. For those who have never been lucky enough to see archaeology up close and personal, then you will absolutely love this place. In the unusual setting of a huge warehouse, the team are working on the recording and conservation of this fantastic find. sSee for yourself the hard work that is taking place to care for this important vessel. The ship centre staff and volunteers are extremely knowledgeable, full of interesting facts and bursting with enthusiasm. The re-enactors present on open days, bring the medieval experience to life. Take the family and enjoy a fun filled journey through the past.

Newport

Unit 20, Estuary Road, Queensway Meadows, Newport, NP19 4SP

Raglan Farm Park

t: 01291-690319
www.raglanfarmpark.com

Since the Williams Family threw open their barn doors to the public in June 2016, Raglan Farm Park has quickly grown to become a firm favourite for young and old alike. There's so much to do...and so much room in which to do it! We have over 25,000 sq foot of undercover indoor space, with 7 'soft play' themed areas. Play areas cater for age ranges from 18 months to 11 years. Outside there are zip wires, swings, slides, roundabouts, trampolines, 'ride-on' tractors and go-carts! There are 'astro-turf' paths around the park, so, even if the ground is damp, you won't be! We are proud to announce that, in 2108, we were awarded the 'Visit Wales' quality visitor assurance standard too. New for 2019, a classroom, where we now host visits with an educational theme. We can tailor this to suit your requirements. Topics covered include 'The Seasons', 'Where does our food come from?', 'Planting and harvesting crops', as well as some practical exercises... It won't be all work though! There'll be the opportunity to 'let off steam' in our play areas. Subject to approval from the school, we will supply a leaflet with some questions for the children to try and answer.

AUTHOR'S REVIEW

I've visited a huge number of farm parks, some huge, some really small. But one thing they all have in common, is their love for their animals and this can't be seen any better than here at Raglan Farm Park, in Wales's Wye Valley region. The Williams family have put their heart and soul into this business and this very rustic farm park deserves more than a standing ovation. On the day that I visited, I saw first hand just exactly how much they're love they have for they're animals, is at the heart of everything they do, as whilst I was on my tour with the owner, he got called away to do an emergency delivery of a lamb, but I wasn't the only one lucky enough to experience this, as they do live lambing most days of the lambing season. I know your going to have a great time here, but don't just take my word for it, go see for yourself!

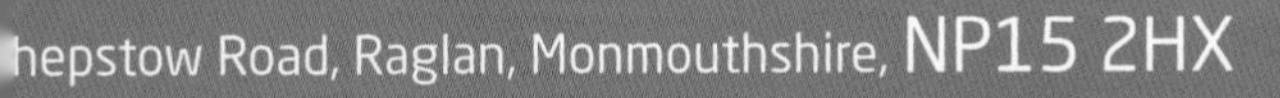

Chepstow Racecourse

t: 01291-622260 e: info@chepstow-racecourse.co.uk
www.chepstow-racecourse.co.uk

Chepstow Racecourse is home to the most prestigious horse racing in Wales, the Coral Welsh Grand National which takes place around Christmas time every year. Winners of this race have gone onto to win even bigger races such as Native River, who went onto win the Cheltenham Gold Cup. The racecourse is situated in the heart of Chepstow, and looks over the picturesque Piercefield Park. The racecourse isn't just home to 30 jump and flat race meetings but is also the perfect location for non-racing events such as weddings, special occasions, conferences and much more.
The racecourse has also held some fantastic music events throughout the summer months and has seen iconic performances from the likes of Tom Jones, Madness, All Saints and Will Young. The racecourse really does have something for everyone from our family days to our jump season opener weekend in October where future equine stars can be spotted.

AUTHOR'S REVIEW

Chepstow Racecourse has to be not only Wales' most premier racecourses, but one of Britain's also. The course itself is held in very high regard amongst the racing community and racegoers alike, not only because of its fantastic facilities, but also because it can host both flat and jump racing, which for a course as big as this, is no mean feat. Chepstow itself, has in and around 32 exciting race meets every year and his home to the prestigious Welsh Grand National. But the course isn't just famous for its horse racing, it also hosts a lot of concerts and all the big names in the music of our modern time have played here. Just when you thought that was it, you're totally wrong! Chepstow Racecourse has several separate events that offers fun for all the family and that just adds to the experience of visiting such an attraction.

• Newport

Chepstow, Monmouthshire, NP16 6BE

The Knoll Guesthouse

145 Stow Hill, Newport, Gwent, NP20 4FZ

T: 01633-263557 www.theknollguesthouse.co.uk E: theknoll@btinternet.cor

If you are looking for a home from home, then look no further because we'd like to share our house with you. The Knoll is a private house guesthouse retaining many of its original Victorian features and period elegance. The property was once a large family home and our philosophy is to treat you as ou personal guests (albeit paying ones) in this same residence today.
We're known for the warmth of our hospitality, the comfort of our beds, the freshness of our linen an our splendid breakfasts – quality accommodation at reasonable prices. We are designated 3 Stars, consistently score well on unsolicited internet guest reviews and are rated 8.5 out of 10 with Booking com.

The Old Black Lion

145 Stow Hill, Newport, Gwent, NP20 4FZ

T: 01497-820841 www.oldblacklion.co.uk E: info@oldblacklion.co.uk

The Old Black Lion Inn is privately owned and personally managed by the resident proprietor Dolan Leighton who looks forward to welcoming you as her guest. An historic 17th Century Inn, it is situated close to what was known as the Lion Gate, one of the original entrances into the medieval walled town of Hay-on-Wye. The Old Black Lion has 10 quality en-suite bedrooms situated in either the Main Building, the Coach House or the Cottage. The rooms provide all modern amenities with direct dial Telephones, WiFi internet access, Hairdryers, colour TV's, Tea & Coffee making facilities and our famous Teddy Bears to keep you company.We are particularly proud of the atmospheric beamed Cromwell Suite with its own galleried seating area.

Brynhonddu Country House B&B

Bwlch Trewyn Estate, Pandy, Abergavenny, Monmouthshire, NP7 7PD

T: 01873-890535 www.brynhonddu.co.uk E: stay@thelychgate.co.uk

Brynhonddu is located on the Eastern Edge of the Brecon Beacons National Park within a large managed estate and we take our responsibility to the environment very seriously.Brynhonddu provides comfortable accommodation within picturesque surroundings and is ideally situated for Walking, Touring and Activity Breaks. Set in the foot hills of the Black Mountains in the Brecon Beacor National Park, within the Welsh Border area known historically as the Welsh Marches.Brynhonddu Country House is an award winning 3* Bed and Breakfast and is Registered with Visit Wales, part of the Welsh Assembly Government. All of our rooms are comfortably furnished with Tea/Coffee makin facilities and TV. We endeavour to provide only natural products sourced from our own chickens and from local producers wherever possible for our guests' breakfasts.

Hardwick Farm Bed & Breakfast

Hardwick, Abergavenny NP7 9BT

T:01873-853513 www.hardwickfarm.co.uk E: carol@hardwickfarm.co.uk

We're a lovely, welcoming B&B on a working Welsh dairy farm a stone's throw from Abergavenny. We're a hop, skip and a jump from great restaurants, market towns, historical sites and the great outdoors of the Black Mountains in the Brecon Beacons National Park! Dairy farmer Carol Jones runs the bed and breakfast – she's been voted one of Wales' friendliest B&B hosts and she will welcome you and make sure you have a great stay and hearty farm breakfast. There are wonderful views of the Black Mountains from the farm B&B's windows. Walkers are welcome, as are cyclists and other outdo enthusiasts as well as visitors to the area attending Abergavenny Food Festival and the Abergavenny Cycling Festival.

The Clytha Arms

Clytha, Nr Abergavenny, Monmouthshire, NP7 9BW

T: 01873-840206 www.clytha-arms.com E: contact@clytha-arms.com

Award winning pub & restaurant, just outside of Abergavenny. Set in its own large grounds, The Clytha Arms is family run, warm & welcoming. Locally we have golf and fishing available on request. We have over 2 acres of land, open spaces and gardens. We are based right at the mouth of several national park walks & a very good cycling area. We have three rooms, including a large four poster room, all en suite (bath and shower taps) with TV, DVD and specialist tea/coffee facilities. We can also offer a private room for small conferences with video facilities and refreshments as required. All prices are inclusive of breakfast (per room), and government tax. Full Welsh breakfast with Vegetarian alternatives, as recommended by Susan Novak in the Good Pub Food Guide.

The Whitebrook Restaurant with Rooms

Whitebrook, Nr Monmouth, Monmouthshire, NP25 4TX

T: 01600-860254 www. thewhitebrook.co.uk E: info@thewhitebrook.co.uk

Chris Harrod, chef patron, and his wife Kirsty, manage a stylish restaurant with rooms. Their emphasis is on an experience of excellence throughout. They have already won a clutch of awards, including a Michelin star and 4 AA Rosettes. he Whitebrook has eight comfortable rooms, where you can enjoy total relaxation amidst the peace and tranquillity of the surrounding Wye valley.

Four of the rooms have been refurbished and redesigned to a high standard of contemporary style and luxury, with large ensuite rooms with large double ended bath and walk-in shower.

We are also graded five stars by the AA and Welsh Tourist Board for restaurants with rooms.

The River Cafe Accommodation

The Boat House, Glasbury, Glasbury Bridge, Herefordshire, HR3 5N

T: 01497-847007 www.wyevalleycanoes.co.uk E: info@wyevalleycanoes.co.uk

The Wye Valley Canoe Centre sits on the banks of the River Wye four miles west of Hay-on-Wye. We are located on the bridge at Glasbury and next to our café The River Café. We have 5 en-suite rooms above the cafe. The rooms are simple, modern and warm, guests come down to a large cooked breakfast with local juices, and coaltown coffee. All rooms are en-suite. These rooms are simply furnished and not a piece of floral wallpaper in sight. Rooms 1 to 4 have a TV. Free Wi-Fi is available. We now have a contemporary 'posh' bunkhouse in the Chapel next door for groups of up to 14. The Chapel is a bunkhouse for adults, ideal for family and friends get-togethers, work outings, book club get-aways or hen and stag parties.

The Kings Head Hotel - Restaurant - (Regency 59)

60 Cross Street, Abergavenny, Monmouthshire, NP7 5EU

T: 01873-853575 www.kingsheadhotelabergavenny.co.uk E: info@kingsheadhotelabergavenny.co.uk

The King's Head Hotel small family-run hotel in the centre of Abergavenny, with a friendly and relaxed atmosphere. You will receive a warm welcome and we will make sure that your stay is both a comfortable and enjoyable one. We pride ourselves on the standard of our rooms and offer the little touches that you would expect to find in a much larger hotel. Each one of our 14 en-suite bedrooms comes with modern shower and toilet facilities, flat screen TV's and tea and coffee making facilities. We have been awarded 4 stars by the Welsh Tourist Board. Regency 59 is the newly refurbished restaurant at the Kings Head Hotel. It is open daily serving tasty pub lunches in the day and expansive Indian and Nepalese cuisine in the evening.

The Bridge Inn

Methyr Road, Llanfoist, Abergavenny, Monmouthshire, NP7 9LH

T: 01873-854831 www.bridgellanfoist.com E: thebridgellanfoist@outlook.com

The Bridge is a friendly pub located next to the River Usk in Abergavenny offering home cooked food, good beers and plenty of live music. The Bridge Inn has four modern en-suite bedrooms all of which offer a comfortable nights stay. They are located above the pub and some rooms provide views of the surrounding hills and/or the River Usk which is literally on our doorstep.
Breakfast is provided in the rooms and consists of a continental breakfast hamper of croissants, muffins and cereals. In addition there is a mini fridge containing fruit juices, yoghurts, fresh milk and water. All rooms have tea and coffee making facilities too. If you would like to check availability or book any of these rooms please contact us and we'll reply as soon as we can.

Craigo Barn Holiday Cottage

Craigo Farm, Trelleck Road, Tintern, Monmouthshire, NP16 6SN

T: 01291-689757 www.craigobarn.com E: holidays@craigobarn.com

Less than a mile from the stunning Cistercian Abbey on the beautiful river Wye, Craigo Barn provides an excellent base for exploring the Wye Valley & Forest of Dean, either by foot, bike or car. Peacefully nestling in wooded hills and with direct access to many walks from the doorstep. Craigo Barn has been skilfully renovated to provide a tranquil all year round retreat. The barn sits in the grounds of Craigo Farm, recognised by Gwent Wildlife Trust as an important environment for wildlife with its carefully managed traditional hay meadows. Craigo barn offers an idyllic, cosy & comfortable holiday cottage in a beautiful environment, fully equipped for all seasons with central heating and free wifi.

The Wye Valley Hotel

Main Road, Tintern, Monmouthshire, NP16 6SQ

T: 01291-689441 www.thewyevalleyhotel.co.uk E: wyevalley.hotel@ukgateway.net

The Wye Valley Hotel is a family-run country inn in the riverside village of Tintern, at the heart of the Wye Valley, a designated Area of Outstanding Natural Beauty. Upstairs are eight comfortable en-suite rooms (including a family suite) while downstairs you'll find a cosy public bar with open fires and a large dining room (complete with its own bar and dance-floor). As well as a fine range of beers, wine and spirits, we offer meals that are freshly prepared and full of flavour, often featuring local produce and ingredients. We are CAMRA accredited and proud to have received consecutive TripAdvisor Awards for Excellence, as well as 5 star hygiene ratings.There is free Wi-Fi throughout the hotel and ample parking outside. Children, walkers, cyclists and dogs are all welcome.

The Royal George Hotel

Tintern, Chepstow, Monmouthshire, NP16 6SF

T: 01291-689205 www.theroyalgeorgetintern.co.uk E: contactus@theroyalgeorgetintern.co.uk

Located in the charming village of Tintern. The Royal George is an elegantly refurbished hotel with a wonderful cosy and dog friendly pub and exquisite restaurant. we pride ourselves on using locally sourced produce and seasonal menus to showcase the very best of the Wye Valley.
The Royal George has 14 stylishly decorated en-suite bedrooms, each with their own individual flair. We offer 4 dog-friendly rooms fully equipped with everything your furry friend will need on their travels, our pub also offers dinner for dogs too! set in the beautiful historic village of Tintern The Royal George is a perfect place to stay whilst exploring the local area providing a laid-back luxury approach to accommodation with superb on-site dining and a deliciously tempting breakfast.

Rectory Cottage @ The Old Rectory

The Old Rectory, The Bryn, Abergavenny, Monmouthshire, NP7 9AP

T: 01873-840007 www.rectorycottagewales.co.uk E: stay@rectorycottagewales.co.uk

Rectory Cottage is a two bedroom self-catering modern cottage let in the grounds of an 18th Century Old Rectory. Bed & Breakfast accommodation is available in the main house in a double room with private bathroom (adjacent, not en-suite). The cottage is in an excellent location between Abergavenny, Raglan and Monmouth. The accommodation consists of one double bedroom and one small bunk bedroom with adult sized beds. he cottage has a private patio area with seating, a BBQ and a wok firepit. The patio leads onto the secure back garden with a trampoline and other outdoor toys for your children's use. The cottage is well equipped with a 37" flat-screen television, DVD player and plenty of board games, cards and toys.

The Coach & Horses

Roman Road, Caerwent, Caldicot, Monmouthshire, NP26 5AX

T: 01291-420352 www.caerwent-coachandhorses.co.uk

The Coach & Horses in Caerwent has three newly refurbished rooms available throughout the year for people who require a weekend break in the South Wales Valley's to an extended break or even local events such as golf tournaments at any of the local golf courses or even horse racing at Chepstow racecourse.The Coach and Horses offers full access to the rooms via the pub which is also accustomed for disabled people. Each room has it's own unique view across the South Wales landscape enhancing the quiet tranquil beauty needed to get away from fast paced life. Breakfast is served between 8 am & 10 am in the restaurant every morning. A choice of cereals, toast or even a full Welsh breakfast accompanied by fresh juice , tea & coffee is available.

Swanmeadow Holiday Cottages

Pantygoitre Farm, Llanfair Kilgedin, Abergavenny, Monmouthshire, NP7 9BE

T: 01873-840207 www.swanmeadow.co.uk E: pantygoitrefarm@gmail.com

Swanmeadow enjoys a magnificent location in the beautiful Monmouthshire countryside. We are just 5 miles from the market town of Abergavenny, nestled deep in the Usk valley overlooked by the Brecon Beacons and Black Mountains. Creel Cottage and Fisherman's Rest are two barn conversions finished to extremely high standards giving a feeling of luxurious country living. Exposed oak beams, exquisite stonework and exposed natural stone floors give that true country feeling. Swanmeadow Lodge is a rare opportunity to stay in a genuine and traditional fishing lodge situated just metres from the riverbank to be close to the fishing or just to holiday in total seclusion a perfect destination for walking, bird watching or painting.

The Dragons Back

Pengenffordd, Talgarth, Powys, LD3 0EP

T: 01874-711353 www.thedragonsback.co.uk E: info@thedragonsback.co.uk

The Dragons Back Pub and Bunkhouse, is the highest pub in the Brecon Beacons National Park, a Country Inn with plenty of accommodation, b&b rooms, bunkhouses, Shepherds hut, Tardis and a campsite. Located in a glorious valley, over 1000ft above sea level in The Black Mountains – part of The Brecon Beacons National Park. We have a large variety of accommodation to suit most tastes and budgets :- – Four B&B rooms with a total of ten beds.

– Three bunkrooms one of six beds, one of ten & one of twelve beds – 28 beds in total.

– A small basic campsite that can accommodate up to 40.

– Finally we have a Shepherds hut that can sleep two – this is a new addition.

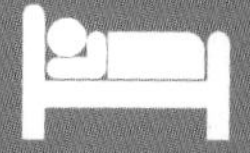

Tudor Farmhouse Hotel & Restaurant

High Street, Clearwell, Monmouthshire, GL16 8JS

T: 01594-833046 www.tudorfarmhousehotel.co.uk E: info@tudorfarmhousehotel.co.uk

20 chic bedrooms featuring fresh neutral colours, roll top baths, monsoon showers, Nespresso coffee machines and flashes of exposed stonework and ancient beams. All beds are equipped with gorgeous pocket sprung mattresses, duck feather pillows and duvets and 300 count linen sheets. We encourage our guests to Bring Your Own Device – BYOD. We have free superfast fibre-optic wifi throughout the hotel. Our best rooms. Our three spacious Suites are all unique and located in the prime locations with comfortable lounge areas, double beds, crisp quality linens, Nespresso coffee machines, luxurious roll top baths and monsoon showers (The Cottage has a fitted bath and a shower). Two are doubles only and two have a sofa-bed and would be suitable for a family of four.

Royal Lodge *

Symonds Yat East, Ross-on-Wye, HR9 6JL

T: 01600-890238 www.royalhotel-symondsyat.com E: info@rhhotels.co.uk

The Royal Lodge in Symonds Yat East is a comfortable Lodge situated on the banks of the River Wye, nestled in the picturesque Wye Valley, an area of Outstanding natural beauty And Special Scientific Interest in South Herefordshire. Our guests can be sure of a relaxing & peaceful break with our tranquil gardens, heart warming food in our cosy restaurant with a locally sourced Ale and range of Organic wines from our well stocked bar. The Lodge boasts the perfect venue for any event with our accommodation, restaurant & large function room complete with stunning riverside views; we can cater for weddings, corporate team building, conferences, product launches, christenings, Painting and drawing parties, wakes and group events.

The Beaufort Raglan

High Street, Raglan, Monmouthshire, NP15 2DY

T: 01291-690412 www.beaufortraglan.co.uk E: enquiries@beaufortraglan.co.uk

We have taken extra care to ensure that when you stay in one of our 16 en-suite rooms, you are certain of a good night's sleep. Our rooms reflect the age and character of each building and are decorated with individual attention. In the main hotel building the rooms are larger and have unique character and they have been refurbished in rich medieval colours whilst the Coach House rooms are slightly smaller with a "New England" feel to them. All rooms have crisp white linens and soft fluffy towels and whether staying for business or pleasure our rooms provide comfort and luxury to all our guests. We also have suites available with several bedrooms sharing a bathroom in a self contained space which may suit family groups.

St. Pierre Marriott Hotel & Country Club*

St Pierre Park, Chepstow, NP16 6YA

T: 01291-625261 www.marriott.com

The striking natural beauty of South Wales is yours to experience at our country hotel. Housed within a historic 14th century manor home in Chepstow, St. Pierre Marriott Hotel & Country Club is surrounded by 400 acres of parkland in the beautiful Wye Valley. Stretch out in our immaculately designed rooms, which offer luxury bedding, high-speed internet and a flat-screen TV, or book one of our suites for breathtaking country views. Additional hotel amenities include a heated indoor pool and a fully equipped gym, as well as a tranquil on-site spa. Perfect your swing on one of our two golf courses, including the Championship Old Course and enjoy challenging play with wonderful views. Stop by our outstanding hotel restaurants for seasonal cuisine, a cocktail or a delightful afternoon te

The Coach & Horses

Roman Road, Caerwent, Caldicot, Monmouthshire, NP26 5AX

T: 01291-420352 www.caerwent-coachandhorses.co.uk E: coach-horses.caerwent@outlook.com

The Coach and Horses prides itself on providing real pub food sourcing meat & vegetables from local Welsh farms. All of our pies are homemade and filled with the finest cuts of Welsh meat. Our chips are made from potatoes from a local farm and are of a good portion size. Our locally sourced cuts of beef are a real treat for anyone who loves a good steak! Sunday lunch is always a treat at the Coach and Horses. We serve a variety of meat including locally sourced Chicken , Lamb, Beef and Pork served with a variety of locally sourced fresh vegetables, roast potatoes , homemade yorkshire puddings and finished off with the best homemade gravy!! The public bar in the Coach and Horses has everything you would expect from a traditional pub with the addition of traditional Welsh Ales.

Shepherds Parlour

9 High Town, Hay-on-Wye, Powys, HR3 5AE

T: 01497 821 898 www.shepherdsparlour.com E: jess@shepherdsparlour.com

We are a small coffee shop in the beautiful, eclectic, bustling town of Hay on Wye. Come & visit us for home-made cake, delicious coffee & lunches and of course, we are the home of the fantastic, locally made ice cream dream that is Shepherds Ice cream. We are thrilled to bits to be able to make scrumptious lunches from fabulous ingredients, sourced ethically and locally. We are delighted to work closely with all sorts of food producers and growers to put the best of the best on your plate.
This is a team effort. The cakes are made in our on-site kitchen, at our kitchen a few miles away in Clifford or by Tam in Dorstone. The salad is grown in Dorstone too by Judy, as is the fruit for the jams and cakes. This is no little endeavour & we are extremely grateful for all the love & care which goes into growing & preparing these delicious things for us.

The Three Tuns

9 High Town, Hay-on-Wye, Powys, HR3 5AE

T: 01497-821855 www.three-tuns.com E: hello@three-tuns.com

Located in the historic market town of Hay-on-Wye on the England/Wales border, the Three Tuns Pub and Restaurant is reputed to be the oldest surviving house in the town and in recognition of its importance has a Grade II listing. The original building is believed to be a 16th Century three bay cruck truss timber frame building, now largely encased in stone. It has a huge central Inglenook chimney and a wealth of period features including the original dog leg staircase. The pub welcomes loyal locals, along with visitors from further afield, serving a selection of local beers, cask ales and great wines by the glass. The restaurant offers an Italian-inspired menu which is available throughout the day to enjoy in front of a crackling fire during winter or on our sun-soaked terrace in the summer.

The Old Black Lion

145 Stow Hill, Newport, Gwent, NP20 4FZ

T: 01497 820841 www.oldblacklion.co.uk E: info@oldblacklion.co.uk

Our team of talented chefs make serve up a mouth-watering menu every day, and use the finest seasonal and local produce to create new specials on a weekly basis. So, however often you drop in, you'll always find something new to try on the menu. We have two dining areas, in the Main Bar or in the cosy Den which has easy chairs as well as dining tables. There is a pianist playing in the Bar most Friday evenings to make it an extra special occasion. Whatever you choose to eat, we've got the perfect wine to accompany your meal too. Choose from our carefully selected wine list, or opt for a refreshing craft beer, lager, Herefordshire cider or cask ale instead. If you have any questions about food ingredients we are able to provide sources and information on allergens to allow informed choices to be made for those with specialised dietary requirements.

Regency 59

60 Cross Street, Abergavenny, Monmouthshire, NP7 5EU

T: 01873-853575   www.kingsheadhotelabergavenny.co.uk   E: info@kingsheadhotelabergavenny.co.

The King's Head Hotel small family-run hotel in the centre of Abergavenny, with a friendly and relaxe atmosphere. You will receive a warm welcome and we will make sure that your stay is both a comfortable and enjoyable one. Regency 59 is the newly refurbished restaurant at the Kings Head Hotel. It is open daily serving tasty pub lunches in the day and expansive Indian and Nepalese cuisin in the evening. We welcome both residents and non-residents in the evening so booking is recommended especially at the weekend. Head Chef Krishna Bhandari brings his Michelin starred experience and skills, from London to Abergavenny. Regency 59 offers a multi-sensory dining experience. Inspired by classic Indian and Nepalese dishes, our menu is bursting with flavour.

The Clytha Arms

Clytha, Nr Abergavenny, Monmouthshire, NP7 9BW

T: 01873-840206   www.clytha-arms.com   E: contact@clytha-arms.com

The Clytha Arms is in its 25th year of trading with Andrew & Bev at the heart of this country pub, wit its warm friendly atmosphere open log fires, sofas and settles make for an inviting comfortable pub & restaurant. The Clytha Arms was voted Country Pub of the Year 2016, 2015, 2014 and 2011 while highly commended in 2012 by The Campaign for Real Ale (CAMRA). We are also celebrating 22 years of being featured in the CAMRA Good Beer Guide.

You can pop in for a pint and tapas or full three course Sunday lunch with our extensive wine list. Whatever takes your fancy. Head Chef is Andrew Canning, assisted by daughter Sarah and her partn Roger Cottrell.

Marches Delicatessen

6 Nevill Street, Abergavenny, NP7 5AD

T: 01873-268080   www.marchesdeli.co.uk   E: info@marchesdeli.co.uk

With a wide range of artisan produce from Monmouthshire and the surrounding area you can be sur there is always something new to try. Why not order one of our gift hampers full of all your favourite Sit back and relax in our Monmouth coffee shop and sample some delicious home made goods befc you take home your shopping. The delicatessen showcases a selection of fine artisan foods as well as some favourite beers, wines and spirits from across Monmouthshire and the Marches region. The majority of our food is sourced directly from producers. This allows us to see firsthand the passion ar dedication which goes into making the exceptional produce we sell.

The Whitebrook Restaurant with Rooms

Whitebrook, Nr Monmouth, Monmouthshire, NP25 4TX

T: 01600-860254   www. thewhitebrook.co.uk   E: info@thewhitebrook.co.uk

Chris Harrod (ex-Le Manoir aux Quat'Saisons) delights in the abundance of produce that can be four simply by opening his front door - every dish on his menu, from breakfast through to dinner, feature a foraged ingredient.

Within 11 months of opening, The Whitebrook was awarded a Michelin star and the restaurant has since won an AA Wine Award for Wales and Inspectors' Choice (Restaurant with Rooms) at the AA Hospitality Awards 2017 and become one of only 39 restaurants in the UK to hold 4 AA Rosettes. Along with a place in the 2017 Waitrose Good Food Guide Top 50 UK Restaurants, these prestigious accolades put The Whitebrook amongst the very best restaurants in the country.

The Hardwick

Old Raglan Road, Abergavenny, Monmouthshire, NP7 9AA

T: 01873-854220 www.thehardwick.co.uk E: info@thehardwick.co.uk

Do you have a special occasion or reasons to celebrate coming up? Or maybe you just want to treat yourselves to an extra special dinner. If so why not enjoy the Hardwick experience in the comfort of your own home. We have a selection of menus for you to choose from, which will then be cooked for you in your own kitchen by one of our experienced team. They will be accompanied by a member of our waiting staff who will prepare the table, serve dinner and make sure your wine glasses are topped up throughout. Recently awarded five stars by Visit Wales, all our rooms are off a central courtyard, just a few yards from the restaurant. Complete your gastronomic experience with a luxurious nights stay and a tidy full Welsh breakfast.

Cafe Sprokwobbles

22 Bridge Street, Usk, Monmouthshire, NP15 1BG

T: 01291-672048

Sprokwobbles is a Cafe Deli situated on Bridge Street in the picturesque town of Usk. To one side there is a Deli where you can buy local produce, from Cheese to Chutney and Honeys to a single egg. The other side features a quirky cafe which welcomes four legged friends and a pretty garden courtyard for sunnier days.

Trip Advisor 5 * Review

Lovely cafe.

Visited for a quick coffee during the Usk Choral Festival. Sat in the naughty corner and had the tastiest lamb pie and house salad. Nicest little cafe I've been to in a long time, will definitely recommend.

The Beaufort Raglan

High Street, Raglan, Monmouthshire, NP15 2DY

T: 01291-690412 www.beaufortraglan.co.uk E: enquiries@beaufortraglan.co.uk

We are located in the heart of Raglan village and provide quality food, accommodation and meeting space. If you are seeking history, the local area has myriad castles including Raglan, Grosmont, Skenfrith and Chepstow - the oldest surviving post-Roman stone fortification in Britain.

The Beaufort is an ideal place to to relax and unwind and is perfect to use as a base to explore the sights of South Wales. We are passionate about seafood and serve some of the freshest in the Usk Valley. Everything we serve is responsibly caught and purchased daily from local markets. Our extensive selection of wine is unrivalled in the area. We have wines that can be paired with any of the items on our menu and we would be delighted to recommend a match.

The Wye Valley Hotel

Main Road, Tintern, Monmouthshire, NP16 6SQ

T: 01291-689441 www.thewyevalleyhotel.co.uk E: wyevalley.hotel@ukgateway.net

Our dining room, with waitress service and linen tablecloths, can seat a comfortable 50. Whether you are a large group or dining à deux, sit down, take up your napkin and let us serve you. Every Sunday lunchtime we serve a three joint carvery roast. This is very popular, so early booking is recommended. We love to cook with freshly prepared, locally sourced produce and seasonal ingredients – from plump trout to game, lamb and tender steaks. Like fish and chips? We use local ales for the lightest beer batter to coat fresh cod. Our hand-cut chips are thrice-cooked (for the crispiest wedges with the fluffiest insides). Sue takes her puddings seriously – making utterly delicious cheesecakes and tarts.

The Greyhound Inn & Hotel

10 Strand Street, Usk, Monmouthshire, NP15 1LE

T: 01291-672505 www.greyhound-inn.com E: enquiry@greyhound-inn.cor

The Greyhound Inn and Hotel offers everything you would expect from the best of country inns. We are a traditional, 18th century stone-built village pub with accommodation near the picturesque small town of Usk, in the heart of rural Monmouthshire, South Wales. Whether you come to stay, to eat a meal or a bar snack, or just pop in for a drink, you are always assured of the warmest of welcomes. Nessie and her team of chefs pride themselves on the taste and quality of the food from our kitchens. We use fresh, local ingredients whenever possible, offering an extensive variety of meal and snacks to suit an equally wide range of tastes. It's good, honest, home-cooked, traditional fare of the kind most of us love to eat but that's now so often missing from the menus of many fancy restaurants.

The Hunters Moon Inn

Llangattock Lingoed, Abergavenny, Monmouthshire, NP7 8RR

T: 01873-821499 www.hunters-moon-inn.co.uk E: thehuntersmooninn@btconnect.co

Nestled in the tranquil village of Llangattock Lingoed on The Offa?s Dyke Path, The Hunters Moon Inn is a traditional British Pub that has been trading since the 13th century. It is owned and operated by the Bateman family who have recently purchased it to return to its former glory. Offering bed and breakfast, real ales, a friendly local bar, bar food and evening restaurant, focusing on quality local suppliers. Our aim is to offer honest, freshly cooked food, superb beers and wines, in a friendly and beautiful setting. Whether you want a coffee and a sandwich or a full sit down meal, a real ale or a G&T, the hunters moon staff will be happy to serve you. The bar has free wifi. Dogs are welcome in th bar and can run around in the beer gardens.

The Lion Inn at Trellech

Church Street, Trellech, Monmouthshire, NP25 4PA

T: 01600-860322 www.lioninn.co.uk E: debs@globalnet.co.uk

The menus range from traditional pub grub, through to the exotic and unheard of; with children and vegetarians being catered for. Sourcing the majority of the produce within 10 miles of the pub. For example, the meats come from the local communities of Shirenewton, Raglan & Trellech. A "standard menu is provided within the pub along with a number of "specials" menus.

The specials boards change regularly and often feature dishes that offer new eating experiences for more adventurous diners. Regular favourites include Beef Stroganoff, Chicken in a creamy Tarragon sauce, Kangaroo steak, Ostrich with a creamy garlic sauce, Pork steak with a cider sauce and Duck.

The Cripple Creek Inn

Old Abergavenny Road, Nr Raglan, Monmouthshire, NP15 2AA

T: 01291-690256 www. thecripplecreek.com E: enquiries@thecripplecreek.cor

Nestled in the heart of the Usk Valley, The Cripple Creek Inn offers a warm welcome and an unrivalled dining experience since 1996. This charming pub has an extensive à la carte menu, which features homemade dishes produced using the finest locally reared beef, pork and lamb, fresh dairy products and seasonal vegetables, along with fresh fish delivered daily. Carolyn continues to manage the restaurant with their daughters Jayne and Lisa, alongside a dedicated and friendly team of staff. If you're a fan of tradition and love good, honest country cuisine, The Cripple Creek Inn may be just what you're looking for.The Cripple Creek Inn boasts three unique dining areas, providing the perfect setting for any occasion.

CARDIFF & AREA

When we selected all of our Top 100 Attractions, we had a lot of things to take into consideration, such as, value for money, disabled facilities, food outlets, visitor experience, just to name but a few. But like all the other regions in this book, not one of our attractions, accommodation providers or restaurants have paid advertising fees to be selected and each one is in here on merit. As far as tourist attractions in Wales are concerned, Cardiff's are all very compact and certainly if you don't have transport, still very easy to get to. Cardiff has millions of visitors each year on just weekend visits alone, without including people visiting as part of their holiday break. So as you can imagine, accommodation at times can get very scarce.

It's always a good idea when planning to visit Cardiff to check your accommodation availability first, that way you don't end up staying somewhere that ordinarily wouldn't suit, or at worst, end up disappointed that you didn't get any accommodation at all. Having said all that, Cardiff now has twice the amount of hotels, guesthouses and other accommodation types that it did ten years ago, so you should be able to find something to suit both yourself and your pockets. I couldn't get over how cosmopolitan Cardiff now is, and the people are so friendly and they genuinely love to have so many people visiting their great city every year. Whether it be rival rugby teams, people there for concerts or even if you are just visiting for the day, you will be very surprised how geared up the Cardiff people are to accommodate your every needs. Cardiff also has a huge range of places to eat, so you won't fall short of finding somewhere to satisfy your culinary needs.

Insole Court

t: 02921-167920 e: enquiry@insolecourt.org
www: insolecourt.org

Nestled in the leafy Cardiff suburb of Llandaff, Insole Court is a mansion house with a rich history and an even brighter future. Saved by the community, the 160-year-old house has undergone essential refurbishments and the ground floor is now open to visitors. Alongside this, the Court has the brand new, Stable Yard room hire facilities for community, business and private functions and the Potting Shed Café, serving freshly baked cakes, brunch and lunch 7 days a week.
Upstairs in the mansion, visitors can experience a permanent heritage exhibition, "This House is a Stage".The experiential walk-through audio drama brings local history to life in the form of a dramatic rendition of the rise and the fall of the Insole Family who built and inhabited the mansion, spanning an entire century from their arrival in Cardiff in the 19th century.

AUTHOR'S REVIEW

Having visited many stately homes and mansions throughout the British Isles and Ireland, I was convinced that I had seen everything, but I was wrong! On the day I visited Insole Court, I was completely taken by surprise! Surprised and shocked that I thought I'd seen all of what Cardiff has to offer and then here it was, hidden within a leafy suburb of Cardiff, was this great house with over 160 years of pure history and upstairs in this mansion house, plays host to various exhibitions, details of which can be found on their website, which you can find the address also on this page. The restoration project that saw this house brought back to its former glory has taken a lot of hard work and it just shows you what can be achieved when you have local support behind you! I really like this house and I'm sure you will too, the staff are all really pleasant and all really do go out of their way to ensure your visit here is one not to be forgotten.

CARDIFF

Insole Court, Fairwater Road, Llandaff, Cardiff CF5 2LN

Whizzard Helicopters

t: 02920-461361 e: info@whizzardhelicopters.co.uk
www. whizzardhelicopters.co.uk

Take an exhilarating flight over some of the most spectacular scenery in Britain, usually the reserve of the birds soaring overhead.
We offer two flights from Cardiff, fancy exploring other parts of the country by helicopter? We also offer flights, flying lessons and pilot training from our base in Welshpool and pleasure flights from Snowdonia, Manchester, Liverpool and for something a little different on holiday why not take one of our pleasure flights on the Island of Majorca. If you would like to have exclusive use of the helicopter then you can either choose one of our suggested flights or hire the aircraft for 15 mins, 30 mins or an hour and decide where you wish to fly to in that time and take the flight whenever you like. Our new Base at Cardiff Heliport is now open for helicopter flight training as well as charter and pleasure flights. Give us a call to discuss your future career!

AUTHOR'S REVIEW

Whizzard Helicopters are probably one of the most unique and thrilling attractions within this book. With flights throughout Mid Wales & Snowdonia, just to name a few, I couldn't imagine any better way to see these stunning parts of Wales. Even though they do set flights over each area, another great thing I liked about Whizzard Helicopters, is they can tailor make a journey to suit your requirements. Whizzard's professional and well trained pilots are just about the best in the pleasure flight business, and they really do add to the experience, and with state of the art helicopters you really couldn't be in better hands. Despite an attraction being big, we still look for visitor experience set against value for money when choosing our Top 100 Attractions. Whizzard Helicopters doesn't only have both of these criteria, they also offer a once in a lifetime and unrivalled experience, who could ask for more?

CARDIFF

Foreshore Road, Cardiff Bay, Cardiff CF10 4LZ

Caerphilly Garden Centre

t: 029-20861511 e: info@caerphillygardencentre.co.uk
www.caerphillygardencentre.co.uk

We are a family run garden centre a short drive from Caerphilly town. We are proud of our lovely centre and we are sure you'll like it too. Come and explore our vast plant area, our unique gift section which contains Yankee candles and Bomb cosmetics. we also have a great range of barbecues and garden furniture. Our plant area has recently had a full rebuild and is full of seasonal plants and shrubs to satisfy any gardener from novice to expert. The Palms restaurant has a fantastic selection of tempting treats and home cooked meals from a simple tea and scone to a Sunday roast with all the trimmings. We are stockists of Yankee candle products and Bomb cosmetics, our gift department is packed with great gift ideas and presents for any occasion, even if you just fancy treating yourself. We offer a vast range of furniture and Barbeques, stone ware and aggregates, as well as Garden products to suit any need.Our fully trained members of staff are always on hand for help and advice.

AUTHOR'S REVIEW

Garden centres all over our great land are getting more and more popular by the day and here on the outskirts of Cardiff, there is only one that I would even remotely consider endorsing and that's here at the Caerphilly Garden Centre. This award winning garden centre has got all you would want from a business of this nature and more. Another thing that I liked about this attraction, is that it is still family run and not been allowed to be swallowed up by the bigger garden centre chains. I won't bore you by telling you all about the hundreds of really interesting items that CGC sells, but what I will say is they have a really really good cafe called the Palms Restaurant. Using fresh produce, the Palms has a great little menu and you would be really stuck not to find something to suit you on there.

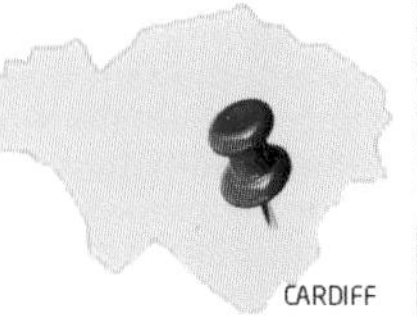

Penrhos, Nantgarw, Cardiff, CF15 7U

Cefn Mably Farm Park

t: 01633-680312 e: mail@cefnmablyfarmpark.com
www. cefnmablyfarmpark.com www.moodysow.com

Cefn Mably Farm Park is a huge all weather family farm attraction & soft play in one. Set in rolling countryside between Cardiff and Newport. We offer a wonderful mixture of farm animals and soft play areas - the ideal place for action packed days out with the kids, birthday parties, schools, and groups. The park is designed for families with toddlers to teens. The fun begins as you enter the indoor soft play barn where the children can let off steam while the adults can relax using WiFi with a coffee and a slice of home made cake on a comfy leather couch. Once you and the kids are worn out from feeding the animals on the farm and playing on the electric go-carts and real

diggers, you can visit our new farm shop and butchery to pick up a good old fashioned 28 day matured steak for your tea and some home made smoky bacon for your breakfast.

AUTHOR'S REVIEW 

Children have been enjoying the farm park at Cefn Mably for many years now, and is now seeing the children that were, bring their children that now are, to enjoy this great attraction. Recently redeveloped by Rhys Edwards and his wife Alyona, Cefn Mably has been transformed into a children's farm park wonderland that even adults can enjoy.

CARDIFF

With a newly introduced play barn and farm shop selling local produce within a few miles of the farm park, Cefn Mably really is the epitome of all farm parks and it's great to see they've stuck to their original ideals and more.

Techniquest

t: 029 20 475 475 e: info@techniquest.org
www: techniquest.org

Enjoy a great family day out in Techniquest, Cardiff Bay – the UK's longest-established science centre. Fire a popgun, sink an oil rig or launch a hot air balloon as you play with more than 120 hands-on exhibits. See the stars as never before in Wales' only digital Planetarium, and take part in live demonstrations in the Science Theatre. Friendly staff are on hand to make sure you get the most from your visit. Take a break in the coffee shop and complete your Techniquest experience with a visit to the shop with its quirky gift ideas, toys, books and souvenirs. Everything is under one roof with easy wheelchair access, disabled toilets and a lift to all floors. Throughout the year there are special events including stargazing evenings, animal weekends, rockets, dinosaurs and MORE! Plus, all the sights and sounds of Cardiff Bay are right on the doorstep!

AUTHOR'S REVIEW

Techniquest in Cardiff really made a lasting impression on me. Not only were the staff really knowledgeable about everything to do with science, but they were quite slick in the way they put it across. I liked the way none of the staff talked down to those who may not know all there is to know about science. This attraction isn't just for school children, or those wishing just to learn about science. The team at Techniquest (Cardiff) have really gone out of their way to make this an attraction for all ages, and for that very reason we were unanimous that both Techniquest (Cardiff) & Techniquest (Glyndwr) made it into the Top 100 Attractions in Wales line up.

CARDIFF

Stuart Street, Cardiff, CF10 5BW

Cardiff Sea Safaris

t: 029 2048 7663 e: info@cardiffseasafaris.co.uk
www.cardiffseasafaris.co.uk

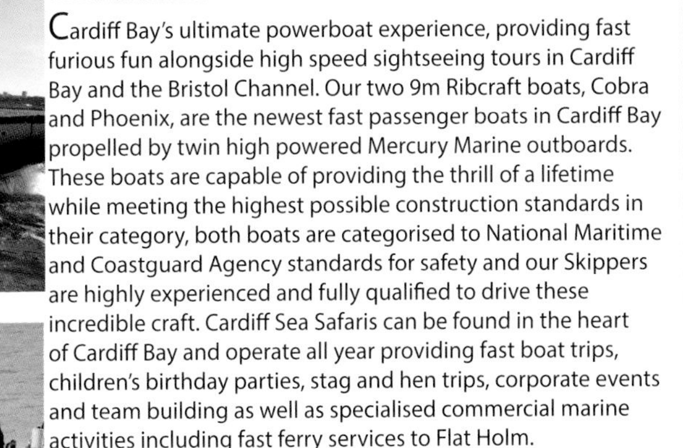

Cardiff Bay's ultimate powerboat experience, providing fast furious fun alongside high speed sightseeing tours in Cardiff Bay and the Bristol Channel. Our two 9m Ribcraft boats, Cobra and Phoenix, are the newest fast passenger boats in Cardiff Bay propelled by twin high powered Mercury Marine outboards. These boats are capable of providing the thrill of a lifetime while meeting the highest possible construction standards in their category, both boats are categorised to National Maritime and Coastguard Agency standards for safety and our Skippers are highly experienced and fully qualified to drive these incredible craft. Cardiff Sea Safaris can be found in the heart of Cardiff Bay and operate all year providing fast boat trips, children's birthday parties, stag and hen trips, corporate events and team building as well as specialised commercial marine activities including fast ferry services to Flat Holm.

AUTHOR'S REVIEW

Cardiff Sea Safaris was recommended to me initially by another attraction within this chapter, the World of Boats. When another attraction recommends an attraction to us, this usually indicates the attraction has to be very good. When I did my research on Cardiff Sea Safaris I was very impressed, and all this before I had even met the owners. What sets this company apart from others I have seen in the past, is the various trips they offer. There is basically a trip for everyone, whether you're looking for a quick blast around the Bay of Cardiff, or a relaxing coastal and island tour, CSS have got something for everyone. Knowing also what is involved in financing these type of boats, I think the prices that are charged is very reasonable indeed, all of which are clearly laid out on their website the address of which can be found above.

CARDIFF

Departure Address

Lower Board Walk, Mermaid Quay, Cardiff Bay, CF10 5BZ

Sayers Events

www.sayersamusements.co.uk E: info@sayersamusements.co.uk

Whatever your requirements for your event, we can provide the full funfair package! Do you require just one ride or a full range? We can do it all! Norman Sayers Amusements have decades of experience and many satisfied customers. Make your occasion special and memorable with our complete funfair operation.

We have worked with numerous local councils, providing them with a full funfair service. We can provide a bespoke service for you, adding a different element to each event.

Catering is one of the many services we provide. Do you need a unique food stall? We can cover all of your event catering requirements, from bespoke German-style food to a whole market for a mass audience at outdoor events.

If you are organising an event, there is no better place to come than Norman Sayers Amusements. We take care of everything from the catering, licensed bar and amusements to the running of the event. No matter what sized event you are planning, we can help. We are professionals when it comes to large scale public events.

AUTHOR'S REVIEW

When it comes to fairgrounds and events, there is only one family in South Wales that Top 100 Attractions is happy to endorse, that's the Sayers family. With Barry Island being virtually on life support, this family have taken their state of the art fairground to Cardiff and really have put the harbour bay area of Cardiff on the map. Now granted, it's not a permanent site at the bay, but no matter where they move to in the Cardiff area, Top 100 Attractions can update you on the Top 100 website. The Sayers family have been entertaining people for decades and their site at the Bay in Cardiff really did impress the hell out of me. For me, it wasn't only the fun of the fair that impressed me, it was also their catering facilities. Spotlessly clean, friendly staff and all at reasonable prices seems to be the norm with the Sayers family. Most definitely, a trip to Cardiff isn't complete without visiting one of their fun fairs.

CARDIFF

Llanerch Vineyard

t: 01443 222716 e: info@llanerch-vineyard.co.uk
www.llanerch-vineyard.co.uk

Our laid-back, luxurious atmosphere and our perfect location, just 20 minutes from Cardiff, make our restaurant, bistro, boutique vineyard hotel rooms, self guided vineyard tours and cookery classes popular with locals, day-trippers and holiday-makers alike.Whether you are a keen wine connoisseur and want to sample our signature Welsh wines, or are looking for a unique weekend getaway, Llanerch Vineyard hotel has the perfect combination of relaxation and sophistication to help you unwind and immerse yourself in the beautiful Welsh countryside. Llanerch vineyard offers an informal yet informative vineyard tour and wine tasting. The tour gives a brief history of the vineyard, Welsh wine and wine tasting, followed by a guided tour and a sample of three different still wines. We recommend combining your tour with either lunch, dinner or afternoon tea. Please speak with our reservations team to discuss the best option for your group.

AUTHOR'S REVIEW

Started from the ground upwards, Llanerch Vineyard has become a huge attraction in the area. Firstly, I'd like to tell you about their tours. Informal and educational, the tours offer an insight as to why Welsh Wine is starting to turn heads in the wine industry. The tour lasts for around an hour and a half and definitely goes well with an afternoon tea or lunch at the venue. At the time of writing this review, the tours only run from April to October, but it's always best to either phone ahead or check on their website for any changes. They have a beautiful restaurant and amazing accommodation at the vineyard and along with their state of the art cookery school, this all really adds to the experience of your visit no matter for how long you plan to stay, whether for a few hours or a few days, you won't want to leave!

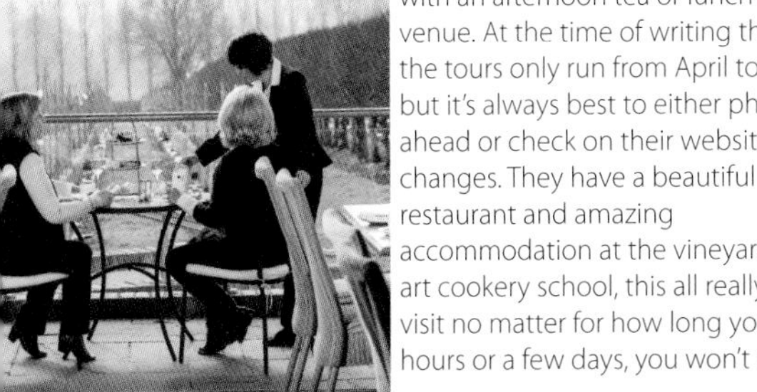

Llanerch Vineyard, Hensol Road, Pontyclun, CF72 8GG

Cardiff Story Museum

t: 029-2034 6214 e: cardiffstory@cardiff.gov.uk
www. cardiffmuseum.com

A fun, free museum for all the family exploring the city's story and heritage. The perfect place to start your visit to Cardiff! The Cardiff Story is the first museum where Cardiffians and visitors alike can discover the story of the city through the eyes of those who know it best – its people. The museum tells the tale of how Cardiff was transformed from a small market town in the 1300s, to one of the world's biggest ports in the 1900s, to the cool, cosmopolitan capital we know today. With activities for all ages, it is housed in one of Cardiff's most historic buildings – the Old Library – in the heart of the city centre, and is free entry. The Cardiff Story Museum is a great starting point for any visit to Cardiff, and gives an introduction to the city's history through engaging, interactive displays. It uses the stories of the people who have lived and worked in the city over past centuries to bring history to life. The museum runs a full event and temporary exhibition programme – details can be found on our website or by giving us a ring.

AUTHOR'S REVIEW

The Cardiff Story Museum is most definitely a must on any visit to Cardiff! What I liked so much about the museum is the fact you can stay as little or as long as you like, but no matter how long you stay, there is literally something to interest everyone here. From stories about Cardiff, to the struggles of the coal faces, it's all here in what I would call one of Cardiffs most informative museums and if that's not appealing enough, you get to visit this museum for free! I found the staff to be knowledgeable, courteous and anyone I asked questions of, they all seemed to go out of their way to not only give me an informative answer, but they were very thorough in their explanations. Finally, the museum is easy to find, well laid out and Cardiff is more the better for having this voice to tells its rich historic story.

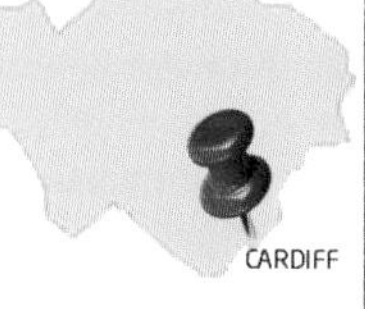

The Old Library, The Hayes, Cardiff CF10 1BH

Senedd Tours

t: 0300-2006565 e: contact@assembly.wales
www.assembly.wales

The Senedd is not just a building for Members, it is your building. It is the main public building of the National Assembly, the main centre for democracy and devolution in Wales. It is an open building – a building into which you can walk, have a cup of coffee in the Oriel on the upper level, and go into the public galleries from the Neuadd on the centre level. And it is not just visitors that come here to see and enjoy the Senedd – we have also had performers, singers, exhibitions and all sorts of activities going on here, because it is a public building.
It is also a sustainable building, built of traditional Welsh materials such as slate and Welsh oak and other sustainable materials. It is also sustainable in the way it is heated; for example, the earth exchange system uses heat from the bottom of the old dock, on which the Senedd stands, before it became the area which is now Cardiff Bay.

AUTHOR'S REVIEW

During your visit to Cardiff, a tour around the National Assembly for Wales Building has to be on your itinerary. Senedd tours are on offer daily and they really do give you an insight into the everyday goings on, in not only a Welsh politicians life, but for the hundreds of people who go to work in this building everyday. Once passed the airport style security, your free to grab a coffee etc from the cafe and take in the views of Cardiff Bay. Once your tour is ready to go, you'll be taken on a journey around this very impressive building. The National Assembly building isn't just a building where people sort out the politics of the day, but also a building that is very much in the hearts of Welsh people as it's where all the decisions are made that affect their daily lives. All in all I found the tours here informative, interesting and great value for money.

CARDIFF

Senedd Building, Cardiff Bay, Link Road, Cardiff, CF10 4PZ

Viola Arena

t: 029-2078-9630
e: info@violaarena.com
www.violaarena.com

Viola Arena is the brand new ice skating rink in the very heart of Cardiff's Sports Village. The arena boasts 2 spectacular ice pads used for a wide range of recreational and professional skating sessions, activities and events as well as a large cafeteria and bar. The ice rink is available for fantastic birthday parties, school bookings and private hire. We hold specific family disco sessions, toddler play sessions and much more!We have regular NISA Learn To Skate courses which are available to absolutely anyone and everyone! These courses are available to start at any point and are a great way to not only have fun but also improve fitness, balance and confidence.Private tuition is available to all ages and abilities. Our Viola Skate Academy is always looking to welcome new members. During half term and holidays we hold learn to skate crash courses which have proven to be incredibly popular. These courses include a 30 minute lesson every day, meal deal and all day skating pass! The best way to spend a half term by keeping active and making friends!

AUTHOR'S REVIEW

Cardiff is vastly becoming the go to place for events and with so many arenas and event spaces popping up all over the city, the calibre of event that happens here in Cardiff, is getting higher and higher, take the Viola Arena for instance. Putting the events held at the arena to one side for a moment, come rain or shine, the Viola Arena is most definitely somewhere you should come and experience. This state of the art building has a lot to offer to not only experienced skaters, but those who have always wanted to give it a try. Viola Arena is also to the elite Cardiff Devils Ice Hockey team and their games are most definitely worth a watch, whether your an ice hockey fan or not, every game offers an experience unrivalled by other sporting fixtures. I was really impressed by the slick running of the arena and I can't recommend it enough.

CARDIFF

Ice Arena Wales, Olympian Drive, Cardiff, CF11 0JS

VIOLA
ARENA

Cardiff Ski & Snowboard Centre

t: +44 (0)29-20561793 e: info@skicardiff.co.uk
www: skicardiff.co.uk

Located in Fairwater Park, only ten minutes from Cardiff City Centre, Cardiff Ski and Snowboard Centre was built in 1969 by Cardiff City Council. The original slope measured 90 metres and was the one of the first dry slopes in Great Britain.
In 1984 the Centre went through significant changes as the management of the slope was taken over by the governing body of snow sports in Wales- Snowsport Cymru Wales. The Centre not only gained a new management but also added 10 metres to its length and is currently a 100 metre long slope. Cardiff Ski and Snowboard Centre relies strongly on volunteers along with the fundamental full time members of staff. All of the instructors are experienced, nationally qualified, CRB checked, first aid certified and most importantly enthusiastic characters with a love of the sport. Our main area of expertise is introducing people to snow sports and sharing our passion for skiing and snowboarding. We provide activities for all levels and ages in individual, group and recreational settings. We run over 11,000 sessions a year and we provide special deals for schools and businesses.

AUTHOR'S REVIEW

Ever wondered what it's like to put all the gear on and ski on or off piste, well now you can here at the Cardiff Ski & Snowboard Centre. I was really impressed at the set up here and the level of expertise on offer. Based in a leafy suburb of Cardiff, this attraction is totally different to what Cardiff generally has to offer. With state of the art equipment and knowledgeable staff, CSSC was one of the first of the original slopes here in the United Kingdom, built in the late 60's, the centre is now being part of the Welsh governing body of all snow sports, so your in really good hands here. Now with the addition of Snowboarding to the mix, you can learn all of the skills that come along with this sport and who knows, maybe you could one day be a snow sport champion!

CARDIFF

198 Fairwater Road, Cardiff, CF5 3JR

Cardiff International White Water

t: 029-20829970 e: info@ciww.com
www.ciww.com

Whatever activity you're looking for – from White Water Rafting to Indoor Wave and Air Trail, Cardiff International White Water (CIWW) has it covered.

Our white water course boasts variable flows so people of all abilities can enjoy the thrill of rafting, which is one of our most popular, sociable activities. Using an inflatable raft, you'll work as a team to navigate the thrills and spills of the white water.

If bodyboarding is more your thing, try our adrenaline-pumping simulated surf machine. Suitable for complete beginners, as well as board sport enthusiasts, Indoor Wave gives visitors the chance to hit the waves in the city, regardless of the weather.

Or perhaps you're an adventure-seeker but not a fan of getting wet? If so, Air Trail was made for you! Grab your harness and tackle obstacles such as Monkey Swing, Barrel Crawl and Zip Wire, while towering above the white water course.

All training and equipment is provided; age and height restrictions apply.

AUTHOR'S REVIEW

Ideally located close to the heart of the city, it's no wonder CIWW is one of Europe's leading white water centres. If you're an experienced rafter or a novice kayaker, the centre has it all – White Water Rafting, Canoeing, River Boarding, Gorge Walking – just take your pick.

What I was so impressed with is how versatile the facility is – whether you're an Olympic athlete or a complete beginner on a stag party, you'll be met with the same welcome and level of professionalism. If you've never tried anything like this before you really must give it a go! Ben and the team are always on hand to make sure you get the most out of your visit.

CIWW, Watkiss Way, Cardiff Bay, CF11 0SY

Cardiff Castle

t: 029-20878100 e: cardiffcastle@cardiff.gov.uk
www: cardiffcastle.com

Cardiff Castle enjoys a rich and complex history spanning 2000 years and sits at the heart of the city. From the arrival of the Romans in the 1st Century AD, through the Norman Conquest to the lavish Victorian Gothic Revival. In the 19th Century, through the joint vision of the famously rich 3rd Marquess of Bute and his architect William Burges, each room was reimagined with an extravaganza of painted murals, intricate stained glass, imposing carved fireplaces and gilded ceilings.
Also worth a visit is Firing Line: Cardiff Castle Museum of the Welsh Soldier - a permanent exhibition telling the story of 1st The Queen's Dragoon Guards and the Royal Regiment of Wales over the last 300 years in a modern and interactive environment.
The Castle Visitor Centre is free to enter and houses the city's tourist information centre, a comfortable café, gift shop, and exhibition of the Roman wall remains.
Want to explore the rest of the Castle? Paying visitors can collect an audio guide to discover the castle grounds, battlement walk and impressive Norman Keep. Cardiff Castle is open all year, guided tours of the apartments and other specialist tours are available. The Castle hosts a range of events throughout the year including historical displays, festivals, and outdoor theatre, cinema and concerts.

AUTHOR'S REVIEW

Cardiff Castle, truly is the great bastion of all Welsh castles. I had been here on a couple of occasions before my latest visit, and thought I knew what to expect, I was totally wrong! There is even more to see and do, than the last time I was here, and the new Keep Terrace Bistro is the perfect setting to break your visit before making your way downstairs to the Cardiff Castle Museum of the Welsh Soldier. Whether it's lunch you require or just a simple cake and coffee there is something on offer to satisfy any pallet. I would easily set aside three hours to see everything here within the castle, but, if you're like me and love to read everything you might want to make that four hours.

CARDIFF

Castle Street,Cardiff CF10 3RB

Holm House Hotel & Restaurant

Marine Parade, Penarth, Cardiff, CF64 3BG

T: 029-2070-6029 www.holmhousehotel.com E: reception@holmhousehotel.co.uk

For coastal luxury, it doesn't come better than the elegant and sophisticated suburb of Penarth in South Wales. We invite you to experience the genuine warmth and intelligence of our service, as well as the luxury and attention to detail you'll find throughout the property. Holm House is designed to ensure you relax, unwind, enjoy the seaside location, and feel completely at home. Holm House invites you to experience our 12 unique and individually designed seaside rooms and suites. The interior design of each room is focused on supreme comfort and beautiful furnishings. Crisp white and yet soft bed linens and voluminous pillows await. The small design touches evoke the coastal location, and ensure a luxurious residential feel created specially to make you feel at home.

NosDa

53-59 Despenser Street, Cardiff, CF11 6AG

T: 029-2037 8866 www.nosda.co.uk E: info@nosda.co.uk

NosDa has the best location for a hostel in the Welsh capital. On the River Taff, NosDa is opposite Wales' most iconic building, the Millennium Stadium (Cardiff Castle and Cardiff Central Station are just a stone's throw away). NosDa means 'good night' in Welsh and that is exactly what we are promising. We are the only hostel on the River Taff with a licensed bar and not only that, NosDa is an established live music venue too. What better place to stay than a typically Welsh hostel with local bands, Welsh food & drinks, and local artists bringing you closer to the Welsh culture. NosDa is experienced in group accommodation and offers a variety of room types to suit all needs. We have a great communal kitchen and plenty of common space to chill out, watch TV, read a book or catch up on emails. Meet your fellow travellers whilst tasting some of our local ales and ciders!

cathedral 64

64 Cathedral Road, Cardiff, CF11 9LL

T: 029-2019 1138 www.cathedral64.com E: info@cathedral64.com

An elegant Victorian town house, cathedral64 offers luxury boutique bed and breakfast in Cardiff on "one of the best streets" in Wales and so convenient to the city. Rob and Sian want to welcome their guests to their newly refurbished home and offer a contemporary home away from home experience – a drink on arrival, stylish accommodation and a Welsh breakfast – a stay that offers the highest level of comfort of a relaxing home.

the house is situated on Cathedral Road, in the very centre of Cardiff, and offers an elegant alternative to corporate hotels. guests can stay in any one of the three unique bedrooms, conveniently situated allowing access to all of the offerings of the Welsh Capital.

Ty Carreg Fach Holiday Cottage

Castle Barn, Ty Isaf Farm, Castle Road, Tongwynlais, Cardiff, CF15 7JQ

T: 07827 785404 www.tycarregfach.co.uk E: info@tycarregfach.co.uk

Cradled within a peaceful valley near Cardiff, Ty Carreg Fach is part of an original Welsh stone barn nestling on the edge of Forest Fawr on the Taff Trail. This beautiful property boasts views of hillsides dense with trees. The surrounding area is steps from beautiful woodland and a host of outdoor delights nearby - the Taff Walking & Cycling Trail and Castell Coch. The Garth Mountain, several golf courses, Caerphilly and Cardiff castles are all within 5 miles, as is Cardiff City centre. The owner's large private garden is accessible to all guests and there is private parking on site. Ty Carreg Fach has two bedrooms, living / dining area and a bathroom.It sleeps four and is equipped with all the essentials required for a comfortable break - coffee machine, fridge, microwave, toaster & table wear. Breakfast is served on request, either in Ty Carreg or in the owner's farmhouse kitchen.

Old Post House

Greenwood Lane, St Fagans, Cardiff, CF5 6EL

T: 029-2056-5400 www.oldposthousecardiff.co.uk E: info@oldposthousecardiff.co.uk

Old Post House Bed and Breakfast South Wales is family owned and run business. Chris and Faye Price have excellent knowledge of the local area with roots in the village for over 25 years. They pride themselves on being welcoming and accommodating and will do their up most to ensure that all their guest have a wonderful and memorable stay. A grade II listed building, steeped in history. The former village's Post Office and Police Station has now been converted into a fantastic bed and breakfast in South Wales. It boasts six beautifully furnished bedrooms with indulgent toiletries and comfortable plush beds. Perfect to ensure you have a wonderful stay.

Three Horseshoes

Moulton, Nr Barry, Vale of Glamorgan, CF62 3AB

T: 01446-710428 www.3horseshoespub.co.uk E: 3horseshoespub@gmail.com

The history of The Three Horseshoes has always been synonymous with a family atmosphere and good food. It has always been unique in providing quality and service, whether just visiting for a coffee and using the Playbarn or attending a special event. Whatever your needs, we hope that The Three Horseshoes can fulfil them. With newly appointed on-suite bedrooms, this well established hostelry has been family run for 25 years. It is in the perfect rural location, just 5 minutes from Cardiff, 5 minutes from the airport and 5 minutes from coast. Offering a daily menu of fresh local produce, all meals are prepared daily on site by a team of chefs. Also on site is an indoor children's play barn, large outdoor beer garden and play area. Come and enjoy a cosy and relaxing atmosphere, with a drink in front of a roaring fire.

Llanerch Vineyard

Hensol, Vale of Glamorgan CF72 8GG

T: 01443-222716 www.llanerch-vineyard.co.uk E: info@llanerch-vineyard.co.uk

All the rooms at Llanerch Vineyard carry a five star rating, are beautifully appointed and are in close proximity to our restaurant and function venues. Accommodation in the main farmhouse comprises two luxury suites: The Cariad and The Junior, both with separate sitting rooms, deluxe bathrooms and attractive views overlooking the vines, and a farmhouse room, which overlooks the main courtyard. Adjacent to the farmhouse are a further seven ground floor rooms. Two are Superior Studios, named Orion and Perle, which each have a lounge area, and the remaining five are elegantly furnished, comfortable courtyard studios which may be interlinked on request. We would be delighted to provide any further information to assist you in making a reservation at Llanerch Vineyard.

Ty Mynydd Lodge

Ty Mynydd Lodge, Heol Isaf, Radyr CF15 8AF

T: 029-2140 9790 www.tymynyddlodge.co.uk E: tymynyddlodge@gmail.com

This original lodge, was the gatehouse to Ty Mynydd, the home of the Dahl family, where the world famous children's author, Roald Dahl spent part of his childhood. We have lovingly restored the property and now share it with our guests...Located in Cardiff, Ty Mynydd Lodge offers free WiFi. The property is around 3.7 miles from Cardiff University, 4.3 miles from Cardiff Castle and 4.3 miles from Principality Stadium. St David's Hall is 4.3 miles away and Motorpoint Arena Cardiff is 4.3 miles from the bed and breakfast.All rooms in the bed and breakfast are equipped with a flat-screen TV. The rooms are fitted with a private bathroom with a shower.
A cooked or continental breakfast is available every morning at the property.

Sandringham Hotel

21 St Mary's Street, Cardiff, CF10 1PL

T: 029-2023-2161 www.sandringham-hotel.com E: sandringhamsales@gmail.com

In the heart of Cardiff city centre, this family-run hotel offers free high-speed Wi-Fi and a full cooked breakfast each morning. Cardiff Central Rail Station is a 5-minute walk away.
Each room at Cardiff Sandringham Hotel has an LCD flat-screen TV with Freeview channels.
The restaurant and bar at the Cardiff Sandringham Hotel hosts live jazz in the evening, from Tuesday to Saturday. There is also a 24-hour reception.
The Principality Stadium and Cardiff Motorpoint Arena are both 5 minutes' walk away. St David's Shopping Centre can be reached in 1 minute on foot.

Restaurant James Sommerin

The Esplanade, Penarth, CF64 3AU

T: 029-2070-6559 www.jamessommerinrestaurant.co.uk E: pr@jamessommerinrestaurant.co.uk

My wife and I would like to welcome you to our restaurant with roomson the seafront in Penarth. Enjoy a unique, relaxed dining experience you won't forget. Our 9 beautifully decorated rooms each have a character of their own. 5 rooms benefit from amazing views over the Severn Estuary with floor to ceiling windows and Queen sized beds.
They reflect the warmth and friendliness throughout the building. All rooms have en-suite bathroom facilities, Smart televisions, fluffy white towels, duvets and sheets and elegant furnishings".
We have a fully accessible disabled room with en-suite wet room. We are able to offer some of our rooms as either a Double or Twin bed configuration; this may not show on the online booking system.

Tadross Hotel

271 Holton Road, Barry, Vale of Glamorgan, CF63 4HT

T: 01446-701800 www.tadrosshotel.com E: tadrosshotel@hotmail.co.uk

This large Victorian building has character. 40 minutes from Cardiff city centre and 20 minutes from Cardiff International Airport, and less than 2 miles from the beach.
The location of the Tadross Hotel is ideal for those who want easy access to the capital city of Wales, but without the rush, crush or expense. It offers en suite rooms and free on-site parking (with CCTV).
The en suite rooms are of various sizes and include TV and tea/coffee. Cutlery can be provided if you would like to eat in your room.

Riverside Bed & Breakfast

1 Coldstream Terrace, Cardiff, CF11 6LJ

T: 029-2021-0378 www.riversidebandb.co.uk E: irenahinc@yahoo.co.uk

We are family run B&B which offers comfort, friendliness and cleanliness. it is also our home. Riverside been open since 2006. We enjoy meeting people from all different parts of the world. We enjoy very much looking after my guests and talking to them, we make everybody feel very welcome. Riverside B&B is located right in the City Centre opposite the River Taff and the Millennium Stadium.
Cardiff offers startling range of unique attractions, top class entertainment and quality shopping with the difference all this is just within short walk from Riverside Bed and Breakfast.
You will also find lots of restaurant which offers excellent foods, theatres, galleries and museums.
If you are looking for a place to stay Riverside B&B is the right place.

No.10 Cardiff

10 Cathedral Road, Cardiff, South Wales, CF11 9LJ

T: 029-2009-1900 www.number10cardiff.co.uk E: reception@number10cardiff.co.uk

No.10 Cardiff is a beautifully restored and luxurious Georgian Town House located within 10 minutes' walk of the city centre. Close to Bute Park and the River Taff, it is the ideal base for a city break, busines meeting or wedding venue. Each of our 21 stylish rooms boasts an eclectic mix of bespoke hand-picke furniture and finishing touches that will treat you to a truly luxurious stay in the Welsh capital. All roon are en-suite and include fresh towels daily and complimentary toiletries. Coffee/ Tea making facilities are available with freshly-baked shortbread biscuits to greet you on arrival. All rooms also include free Wi-Fi, Flat Screen TV, hairdryer and iron/ironing board to ensure your utmost comfort and convenienc

The Jolyon's Boutique Hotel

Bute Crescent, Cardiff, CF10 5AN

T: 029 -20488775 www.jolyons.co.uk E: info@jolyons.co.uk

This premier Cardiff Hotel offers superb luxury accommodation in Cardiff opposite the Millennium Centre. Since its opening in October 2004 Jolyons Hotel has proved to be a very popular addition to this vibrant area of Cardiff. The Jolyons Boutique Hotel Cardiff has six individually-designed bedrooms lavishly furnished, with king-sized beds, WiFi facilities, free-to-view television, beverages, some with views of Cardiff Bay. Sumptuous en-suite bathrooms, including one with a whirlpool bath and one with a wet room appointed to the highest standards, with extra large fluffy towels, bathrobes and toiletries.

Lincoln House Hotel

118-120 Cathedral Road, Cardiff, CF11 9LQ

T: 029-2023-5558 www.lincolnhotel.co.uk E: reservations@lincolnhotel.co.uk

The Victorian hotel in the heart of Cardiff Imagine all the benefits of Victorian splendour in a hotel just minutes from Europe's youngest, most vibrant capital. Welcome to Lincoln House Private Hotel in Cardiff, South Wales.Whether you are visiting the Welsh capital for business, sport, culture, relaxation or for the city's busy nightlife, our traditional bed and breakfast offers some of the best-placed accommodation in Cardiff. Built in 1900, this Victorian Town House has been caringly restored and developed to provide today's guest with all the comforts of modern living in an authentic Victorian atmosphere.Lincoln House Hotel in Cardiff - an oasis of tranquility on the very doorstep of an energetic and lively capital city.

Ty Rosa B&B

118 Clive Street, Cardiff, CF11 7JE

T: 0845-643-9962 www.tyrosa.com E: info@tyrosa.com

Ty Rosa B&B oozes style and quality and your every whim is catered for. From the moment you step over the threshold a warm Welsh welcome awaits whether you are lesbian, gay, bisexual, transgender (LGBT) or straight, as we are even hetero-friendly. Complimentary wireless Internet (WiFi) access and comfortable launge are just two of the amenities on offer. There is also ample, free car parking and a bus stop on the street directly outside. We are the best. Our guest rooms, which are named after Welsh castles, have been lovingly and caringly decorated to make you feel comfortable and relaxed. Snuggle up in a luxury bed, in a room complete with matching wardrobe and bed-side cabinets.

Manor House Hotel & Restaurant

Sully Road, Penarth, Cardiff, CF64 2TQ

T: 029-2070-9309 E: sandiliz@manor555.fsnet.co.uk

With a traditional restaurant, pretty gardens and a patio, Manor House Hotel offers stylish rooms and free parking. Situated just outside Penarth, the hotel is a 10-minute drive from Cardiff centre.
The individual rooms have fresh, modern decor and private bathrooms. Some rooms have a private patio area, and all feature a TV, cosy seating area and tea/coffee making facilities.
A varied evening menu is served in the cosy bar or bright and airy conservatory restaurant. Delicious full English breakfasts are also served daily, with light continental options available. Just 10 minutes' drive from the beach and pier at Penarth, Manor House is 2.5 miles from Cardiff Bay and Docks. Barry, with its beach and harbour, can be reached in just 15 minutes' drive.

The Exchange Hotel *

4-5 Mount Stuart Square, Cardiff CF10 5FQ

T: 029-2010-7050 www.exchangehotelcardiff.co.uk E:ieuan.davies@exchangehotelcardiff.co.uk

Located 450 yards from Cardiff Bay, The Exchange Hotel offers 3-star accommodation in Cardiff. This property is situated a short distance from attractions such as Motorpoint Arena Cardiff. Free WiFi is available and University of South Wales - Cardiff Campus is 0.9 miles away. Each room offers tea and coffee making facilities, a safety deposit box, a hairdryer and ironing facilities. A spa bath is featured in the en suite bathrooms. A buffet breakfast is served each morning at the property. At the accommodation you will find a restaurant serving British cuisine. Vegetarian, gluten-free and vegan options can also be requested. Popular points of interest near The Exchange Hotel include Principality Stadium, St David's Hall and Cardiff Castle.

New House Country Hotel *

Thornhill Rd, Cardiff, Caerphilly CF14 9UA

T: 029-2052-0280 www.newhousehotel.com E: enquiries@newhousehotel.com

They say you can't have your cake and eat it, but we disagree. Towering majestically over the city of Cardiff, The of New House Country House Hotel is the kind of retreat that city slickers spend their weekdays dreaming about. Far enough from the city of Cardiff to feel the calming effects of the country, but still close enough to dip into the hustle & bustle when cocktails call, we strike a perfect balance between town & country life. The unique Manor House and grounds, planning expertise and signature Town & Country Collective personal service will all ensure that your wedding day will be just as you dreamed it would be. The New House offers a full range of options from intimate civil ceremonies to large exclusive-use weddings.

Mayfair Guest House *

134 Newport Rd, Cardiff CF24 1DJ

T: 029-2048-0500 www.mayfaircardiff.com E: kathyjolley14@googlemail.com

Mayfair Guesthouse is situated just 10 minutes walk from Cardiff city centre. We offer modern, clean and comfortable accommodation in single, double/twin, and family rooms, all of which have flat screen wall mounted televisions with built in Freeview (many channels/radio), and complimentary tea &coffee making facilities. ROOM ONLY
At the rear of the building we have a large secure car park which is protected with CCTV, and security lighting. Close to the Millennium Stadium, Cardiff Motorpoint Arena (formerly the CIA, Cardiff International Arena), Cardiff Castle, Mermaid Quay, Cardiff Sports Village and White Water Rafting in Cardiff Bay, many of Cardiff's Universities, plus many other attractions.

Barkers Tea House

High Street Arcade, Cardiff, Cf10 1BB

T: 029-2034-1390 E: charlotte@coffeebarker.com

Serving exquisite afternoon teas for those special occasions, splendid brunches, lunches and breakfasts. Not forgetting mouth watering milk shakes and cakes. Barker Tea House accommodates indoor and outdoor seating, as well as a cosy upstairs with antique arm chairs to fall back and relax into.
From quick lunches, to long brunches with your nearest and dearest. Barker Tea House is an experience you won't forget. Finest Tea, Hand Made Cakes, Scones & Clotted Cream. Splendid Breakfast, Brunch, Lunch & Afternoon Tea. Barker Tea House open every day.

"Excellent" 5 of 5 stars-Reviewed 18 July 2015

Barker tea house is superb!! I visit it quite often, whether it's for a catch up with friends or to just have a sit down for half an hour with a cup of tea and a muffin while shopping.

Coffee Barker

Unit 13, Castle Arcade, Cardiff, CF10 1BU

T: 029-2022-4575 www.coffeebarker.com E: charlotte@coffeebarker.com

Coffee Barker provides breakfast, dinner and tea to coffee lovers and city dwellers alike. Inspired by the coffee houses of New York's West Village and bistros of St. Germain in Paris, Coffee Barker brings the flavour from these metropolitan hotspots to a corner of Cardiff's City Centre.

"Coffee at its best savoured in real comfort"5 of 5 stars

Brought my daughter here for lunch. We had fantastic jacket potatoes with lovely toppings. Atmosphere fab and staff charming. Very reasonable price and super comfy chairs. They have just got it all right.

Gin & Juice

3-5, High Street Arcade, Cardiff CF10 1PY

T: 029 2022 1556

One of Cardiff's most renowned food and drink institutions, Barker, have just opened their latest venture, a new bar called Gin and Juice in the Castle Arcade. As the name suggests, it's a gin and juice bar serving up delicious gin cocktails and raw, energy-boosting juices. With a comfortable and laid-back style, the venue will specialise in healthy and nutritious food and drink with raw press juices and smoothie bowls. In the evening, however, it transforms into an elegant bar where customers can get a number of fantastic gin cocktail such as a Singapore Sling, a sloe gin Negroni and even an espresso gin martini. Alongside the main bar and dining area, there is also a small snug, which will be made available for hire from next year.

Vegetarian Food Studio

115 Penarth Road, Cardiff, CF11 6JU

T: 029-2023-8222 www.vegetarianfoodstudio.co.uk E: enquiries@vegetarianfoodstudio.co.uk

When it comes to vegetarian food, Cardiff has been described as "a bit of black hole". This, however, is no longer the case with the Vegetarian Food Studio gaining several awards and national recognition fc its pure and authentic vegetarian menu. We are located on Penarth Road, a short walk away from the city centre is our friendly family run restaurant which offers an extensive range of pan-Asian vegetaria dishes which has earned us an army of devotees. The Vegetarian Food Studio offer three main services The first being the restaurant. The second and third services are catering for events and weddings. If you have any food catering requirements we can help. We are vegetarian Indian food caterers with all the capabilities and facilities to deliver a first class food service for your event.

Wally's Delicatessen & Kaffeehaus

38-46 Royal Arcade Cardiff Wales CF10 1AE

T: 029 2022 9265 www.wallysdeli.co.uk E: steve@wallysdeli.co.uk

Wally's is the premier delicatessen in Wales and the South West of Britain, specialising in fine foods from around the world. We have been trading in Cardiff for over 70 years and also have a comprehensive array of our products on our website. When you visit Wally's Delicatessen why not pop upstairs to Wally's Kaffeehaus, our Viennese-style Coffee House, where we aim to offer a taste of Vienna in the heart of Cardiff. If you are planning a visit to Wally's Delicatessen & Kaffeehaus, please note that we are normally open from 8.30 am to 5.30 pm from Monday to Saturday and from 10.30 am to 4.30 pm on Sundays.

Bully's Restaurant

5 Romilly Crescent, Cardiff, CF11 9NP

T: 029 2022 1905 www.bullysrestaurant.co.uk E: info@bullysrestaurant.co.uk

Over 15 years, Bully's has developed a reputation as one of Cardiff's little gems. AA Restaurant of the Year Wales 2014 and 2 AA Rosettes. Bully's uses seasonal produce from Welsh providers, complemented by a unique French wine list sourced from small, passionate growers. Bully's is a great place to eat, combining an intriguing atmosphere with excellent, interesting food. The mission is not only to have great tasting food, but to provide efficient and friendly service because customer satisfaction is paramount. "We combine menu variety, atmosphere, ambiance, special theme nights and friendly staff to create a sense of 'place' in order to reach our goal of overall value in the dining experience."

Porro-(Llandaff & Wellfield Road)

T:(029) 2056 5502 - llandaff@porro.co.uk - 22 High Street, Llandaff, Cardiff, CF5 2DZ

T:(029) 2022 1905 - wellfield@porro.co.uk - 57 Wellfield Road, Roath, Cardiff, CF24 3PA

www.porro.co.uk

Opened in 2015, Porro is the second venture from the team behind The Potted Pig. We serve a varied and constantly changing menu of modern British food with Italian influences. As with The Potted Pig, we serve food we love cooking and eating. Porro embraces the Italian philosophy of celebrating simple, quality ingredients. We make every effort to keep our menus seasonal, which means using as many locally sourced products from independent and local suppliers as possible. There are however some things which can only be sourced from Italy! Our wine and drinks menu has been carefully selected to match our menus and is reviewed on a regular basis. We carry an excellent range of independently sourced wines as well as a fantastic array of bottled lagers, ales and ciders.

The Potted Pig

27 High Street (underneath Zizzi), Cardiff CF10 1PU

T: 029 2022 4817 www.thepottedpig.com E: info@thepottedpig.com

Opened in 2011 The Potted Pig has made it's home in a former bank vault underneath the city. We serve a varied and constantly changing menu of modern British food with a few French and New-York grill inspired influences. The menus are based on food we love cooking and eating rather than a single concept. At The Potted Pig we make every effort to keep our menus seasonal, which means using as many locally sourced products from independent and local suppliers as possible. Our wine and drinks menu has been carefully selected to match our menus and we carry an excellent range of independently sourced wines as well as a fantastic array of bottled lagers, ales and ciders.

Cafe Du Chat Noir

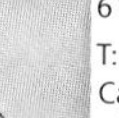

6 Wellfied Court, Wellfield Road, CF24 3PB

T: 029-2048-8993 E: cafeduchatnoir@yahoo.com

Café Du Chat Noir is run by Dorothee Henry and Stuart Bolter-Shone. French cuisine is the raison d'etre of this place and it certainly delivers. You can pop in just to partake of the extensive tea collection with some patisserie – the tea, incidentally was knowledgeably explained to a customer whilst we were perusing the menu. It's so great to eat somewhere where the produce and ingredients are the centre of the experience .

Trip Advisor 5 Stars -Amazing lunch

First time visiting this small and charming cafe; i'll definitely be coming back. The service was amazing with a friendly atmosphere. Good range of french cuisine and hot drinks to choose from which won't break the bank. Had the croque madame which was excellent.

The Corner House

Caroline Street, Cardiff, CF10 1FF

T: 029-2022 8628 www.cornerhousecardiff.co.uk E: enquiry@cornerhousecardiff.co.uk

Nestled amongst the busy shopping district of Cardiff city centre, The Corner House is a premium pub, bar, and restaurant that offers the perfect spot to rest your feet after a long day exploring the city. Perfect for lunch, dinner and drinks, this unique establishment will allow you to enjoy an expansive range of carefully selected menus incorporating a whole host of British pub food and Mediterranean inspired dishes.Expertly prepared by our superbly talented chefs, using the freshest, locally sourced ingredients, there are also a number of daily specials and offers available, which are sure to hit the spot, no matter what the occasion!

The Old Cottage

Cherry Orchard Road, Lisvane, Cardiff, CF14 0UE

T: 029-2076-5961 www.oldcottagecardiff.co.uk E: enquiry@oldcottagecardiff.co.uk

The ultimate escape from the hustle and bustle of everyday life, The Old Cottage near Cardiff should be your first port of call for a delicious lunch, dinner or drinks in truly special surroundings. A great place to unwind with friends, indulge in a delicious three-course meal or tuck into a midweek treat, this premium pub, bar, and restaurant offers a wide choice of carefully selected dishes, as well as an eclectic selection of wines, real ales, and lagers that are perfect for washing down your favourite meals.Boasting traditional and modern interiors, lots of stylish corners to relax, socialise, and indulge in, as well as a lovely outdoor space for a spot of al fresco dining, The Old Cottage is able to accommodate all of your dining requirements, no matter what the occasion.

Three Horseshoes

Moulton, Nr Barry, Vale of Glamorgan, CF62 3AB

T: 01446-710428 www.3horseshoespub.co.uk E: 3horseshoespub@gmail.com

The history of The Three Horseshoes has always been synonymous with a family atmosphere and good food. It has always been unique in providing quality and service, whether just visiting for a coffee and using the Playbarn or attending a special event. Whatever your needs, we hope that The Three Horseshoes can fulfil them. With newly appointed on-suite bedrooms, this well established hostelry has been family run for 25 years. It is in the perfect rural location, just 5 minutes from Cardiff, 5 minutes from the airport and 5 minutes from coast. Offering a daily menu of fresh local produce, all meals are prepared daily on site by a team of chefs. Also on site is an indoor children's play barn, large outdoor beer garden and play area. Come and enjoy a cosy and relaxing atmosphere, with a drink in front of a roaring fire.

The Kings Arms

Church Road, Pentyrch, Cardiff, CF15 9QF

T: 02920-890202 www.kingsarmspentyrch.com e: hello@kingsarmspentyrch.com

The Kings Arms is a 16th Century grade II listed Welsh longhouse pub situated in the leafy village of Pentyrch on the outskirts of Cardiff. Menus inspired by chef patron Helena and Owen using only the freshest ingredients and where possible harvested by our local food heroes. Enjoy well cared for Cask ales, continental & craft beers along with an extensive wine list in a wonderfully relaxing environment for eating out - with al fresco dining in the summer and crackling log fires in the winter. In short; a good old fashioned country pub with a warm welcome!Our menu is simple, affordable and fun, because that's the way we feel your dining experience should be. Our chefs change the menu monthly to make the most of the season and keep a small menu interesting for our regular diners. Each dish is prepared from scratch with care and skill. We are able to do this because, for us, the guest is King.

Holm House Hotel & Restaurant

Marine Parade, Penarth, Cardiff, CF64 3BG

T: 029-2070-6029 www.holmhousehotel.com E: reception@holmhousehotel.co.uk

There is nothing more delicious and inviting than dining at Holm House. The best cuisine begins with the finest ingredients, so you can expect to enjoy a menu which is focused on the very best of local and seasonal produce. We even have our own kitchen garden which supports everything being fresh and straight to the table. Whether it's a hearty full breakfast to fuel a sea front walk, a crisp flavoursome salad at lunch, or leisurely graze through dinner; taste, quality and presentation are paramount. The consistency of our dining experience, and special cuisine themed dinners throughout the year ensure that both guests and locals return time and again to savour the work of our Chefs. Both the dining room, and expansive sea view terrace provide the sunny, cosy or candle lit ambience.

Llanerch Vineyard

Hensol, Vale of Glamorgan CF72 8GG

T: 01443-222716 www.llanerch-vineyard.co.uk E: info@llanerch-vineyard.co.uk

Llanerch Vineyard has great pleasure in offering you a choice of dining experiences, in either the Cariad Bistro or the Cariad Restaurant.The Bistro, provides a relaxed and informal dining experience in the heart of the old farmhouse. The restaurant is a charming, light and airy space providing a more formal fine dining experience in the evenings and the perfect location for an afternoon tea at lunchtime. Further information about the wonderful variety of dining available at Llanerch Vineyard can be found on other pages in this section, or, if you prefer, please get in touch and we will be happy to deal with any query you may have. Once a month Llanerch Vineyard invites some of its fantastic wine suppliers from around the world down to host a wine dinner in Calon Lodge.

Ty Nant Inn

Tynant Road, Morganstown, Cardiff, CF15 8LB

T: 029-20843009 www.sabrain.com E: tynant@sabrain.com

Picturesque pub on the edge of the taff trail and just a stone's throw from the M4 and A470. Our menu, jam-packed with freshly prepared grills sitting alongside generously portioned pub classics, a range of delicious sharers and starters, plus a satisfying selection of tempting desserts. delicious! We hope you enjoyed your visit, and would love to know what you thought. Why not leave a review on TripAdvisor, or read what others have said. **Trip Advisor Review:******* ***Favourite Local Pub***:As a family we regularly visit the Ty Nant and the food is always enjoyable and good value for money. The service is excellent and all members of staff make you feel welcome from the minute you arrive. This will always remain my local pub of choice for a family meal and is a recommended visit for anybody in the area.

The Plymouth Arms

Croft-y-Genau, St Fagans, Cardiff, CF5 6DU T: 029-2056-9173

www.vintageinn.co.uk/plymoutharms E: plymoutharmscardiff@vintageinn.co.uk

The inn takes its name from Elizabeth Lewis, heiress of a major local landowner in the area, who married the Third Earl of Plymouth in the early 1700's. The Plymouth Arms' location provided easy access to Cardiff and was a popular stop off point for people travelling there in traditional handsom cabs. A country pub oozing rural charm and rustic character, our picturesque surroundings provide the perfect backdrop for savouring the hearty, seasonal pub-food on our menu, and the carefully nurtured cask ales and fine wines gracing our bar. Whether you are planning dinner with friends or Sunday lunch with family, book a table online and enjoy some quality time with those you love the most. Our lovely Grade II listed pub has great character. It's almost on the doorstep of the National History Museum and St Fagans Castle which has a commanding position above the River Ely.

Cafe Castan

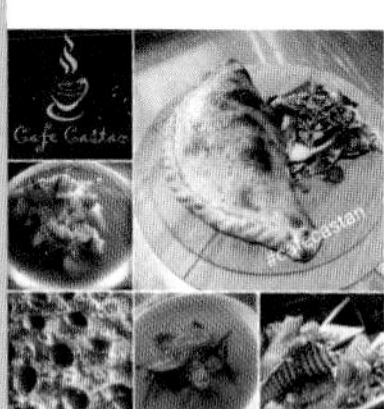

Llandaff Fields, Pontcanna, Cardiff, CF11 9QJ

T: 029-2022-0283 www.cafecastan.co.uk E: plymoutharmscardiff@vintageinn.co.uk

Café Castan has been open since March 2012 and has become the hub for many activities, on, and around the park. Our success has come from offering a good variety of homemade dishes to suit a wide audience. We continue to change and improve our menu to suit our customers. There are seasonal variations on the menu but most dishes are available throughout the year. Our emphasis is on providing quality for an affordable price. From January 2018 we will only use biodegradable food packaging replacing the traditional one-time use containers. All our hot drinks will be served in Edenware® cups. The material used is a double walled cardboard made from recycled paper lined with a plant-based starch to make it liquid proof. Traditional take away cups are lined with plastic and cannot be recycled.

The Early Bird

38 Woodvile Road, Cardiff, CF24 4EB

T: 029-2132-0520 www.earlybirdbakery.co.uk E: hello@earlybirdbakery.co.uk

Contrary to popular belief, we believe that brunch is the most important meal of the day. Our tempting breakfast treats are prepared from scratch using the best locally sourced ingredients. Everything from brioche buns to baked beans are made in house, providing a great learning opportunity for our team of young apprentices. We aim to give them the best possible start in their careers by helping them gain both skills and confidence. That's why we're called The Early Bird- we're going to help them catch the worm! Our team of bakers is knocks up a range of beautiful bakes using locally milled flour, organic Welsh dairy and free range eggs. We're famous for our fluffy brioche doughnuts and cinnamon swirls. Our coffee is carefully selected from ethical supply chains and hand roasted our stone based ovens.

The Gwaelod-y-Garth Inn

Main Road, Gwaelod-y-Garth, Cardiff, CF15 9HH

T: 029-2081-0408 www.gwaelodinn.co.uk E: gwaelodinn@outlook.com

The Gwaelod-y-Garth Inn (or just the Gwaelod as the locals call us) is one of South Wales' Premier Country Inns just a few miles outside Cardiff, offering a relaxing mix of Real Ales, Home Cooked Food and convivial company. Since Richie and Barbara took over the premises, it has re-established its rightful place in the heart of the community. The restaurant seats up to 60 diners, and a separate room seating 20 is available for private functions. Limited seating is also available in the downstairs bar. Specials are also available on a daily basis. The pub also has an onsite brewery - The Violet Cottage Brewery, or the "Brew with a View" - there is always at least one home-grown beer on tap.

The Esplanade, Penarth, Vale of Glamorgan, CF64 3AU
T: 029 2070 2512 www.thefigtreepenarth.co.uk E: enquiries@thefigtreepenarth.co.uk

Author's Review

Penarth is just a hop, skip and a jump from Cardiff, and in many ways reminds me of Colwyn Bay in North Wales, I think it could be said that Penarth is the posh brother of Colwyn Bay. The streets are the same, with similar style architecture, in fact the businesses are almost identical. There is however, a business that has no twin, and that's the Fig Tree. The Fig Tree is perfectly ran and owned by Mike and his partner Sandie, they are the perfect recipe (excuse the pun) when it comes to owning and running a successful restaurant such as the Fig Tree. Having worked on opening other people's restaurants, in 2009 Mike decided it was now time that he too opened what would later become one of South Wale's best eateries, and having now eaten there, I can say with hand on heart, the meal I had that cold winters night, was one of the best I have had in all the years that I have been writing these books. Having only the ability to write 300 words on this page, unfortunately I cannot go into too much detail about each dish, but I will say my starter arrived without too much wait, despite being freshly prepared. I had a dish of home smoked Cornish Mackerel with pickled samphire and horse radish cream, absolutely delicious, no other word would suffice. After finishing my starter, and in no time at all, my main course was winging its way towards me, and with the open kitchen being behind where I was sat, the aromas of my dish were with me before the meal was. A tasty Lamb trio was beset before me and being a huge lamb lover, I felt like I had just entered the gates of heaven. A Grilled Carmarthenshire Cutlet, slow cooked Vale of Glamorgan shoulder & a homemade faggot with fondant potatoes & rosemary jus didn't stay on my plate for long. I remember as a child not liking faggots one little bit, then, they were out of a tin, this faggot that was on my plate was the real deal. Just when I thought I couldn't eat another morsel, my waiter asked me if I'd like a desert, how could. I hurt his feelings by refusing? So I went for the lightest dish on the desert menu, the lime posset. However after saying I couldn't eat another morsel, I could have gladly eaten another three of those.

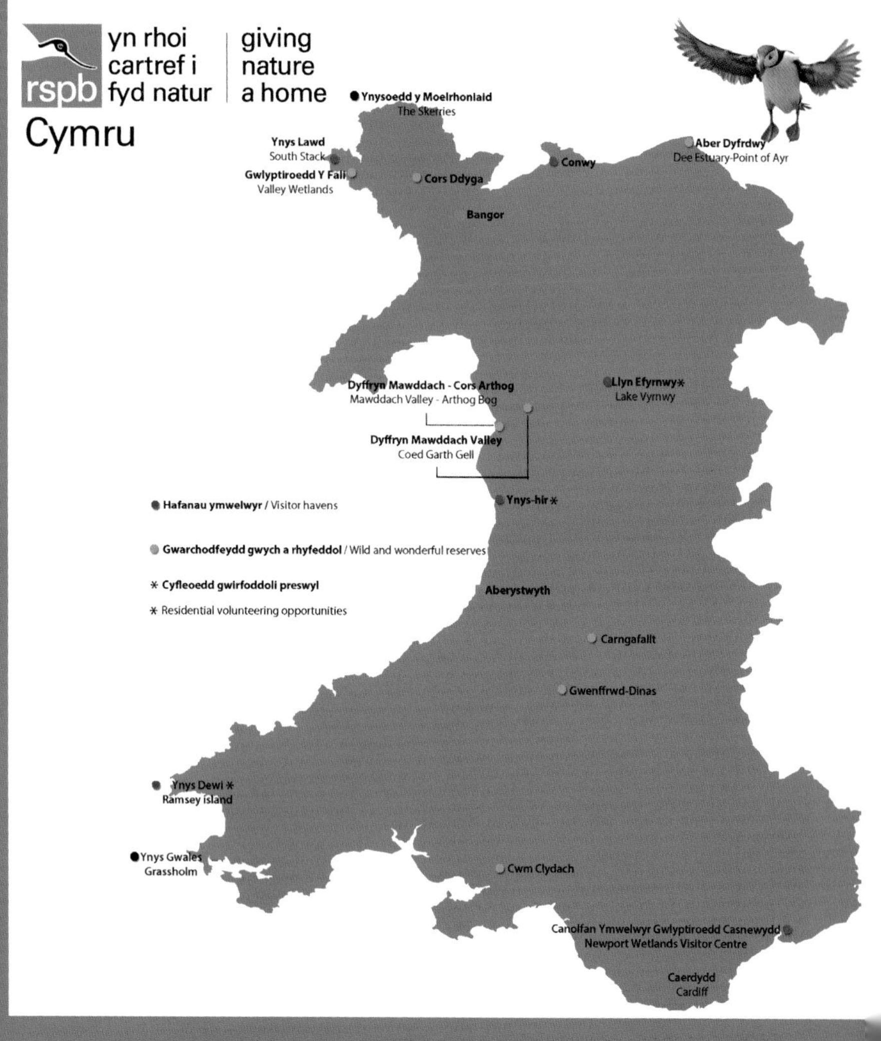
rspb
yn rhoi
cartref i
fyd natur
giving
nature
a home
Cymru
Ynysoedd y Moelrhoniaid
The Skerries
Ynys Lawd
South Stack
Gwlyptiroedd Y Fali
Valley Wetlands
Cors Ddyga
Conwy
Aber Dyfrdwy
Dee Estuary-Point of Ayr
Bangor
Dyffryn Mawddach - Cors Arthog
Mawddach Valley - Arthog Bog
Llyn Efyrnwy *
Lake Vyrnwy
Dyffryn Mawddach Valley
Coed Garth Gell
Ynys-hir *
Hafanau ymwelwyr / Visitor havens
Gwarchodfeydd gwych a rhyfeddol / Wild and wonderful reserves
* Cyfleoedd gwirfoddoli preswyl
* Residential volunteering opportunities
Aberystwyth
Carngafallt
Gwenffrwd-Dinas
Ynys Dewi *
Ramsey island
Ynys Gwales
Grassholm
Cwm Clydach
Canolfan Ymwelwyr Gwlyptiroedd Casnewydd
Newport Wetlands Visitor Centre
Caerdydd
Cardiff

RSPB Location Map

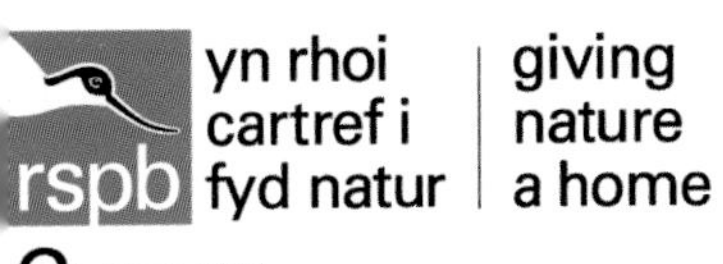

Cymru

RSPB CYMRU

The RSPB is the country's largest conservation charity. Together with our partners, we protect threatened birds and wildlife so our towns, coast and countryside will beam with life once again. Spending time outside discovering the incredible sights and sounds of our amazing wildlife is something we can all enjoy – together we can also help save it.

Give some time..and volunteer with us

Our volunteers come from all walks of life with a wide and diverse set of skills, passions and talents. They are involved in every aspect of our work. If you fancy giving us some of your time, whether you can give a month, a week or even just a day, you could end up leading guided walks, dreaming up ways to attract more visitors to reserves or throwing a coffee morning to raise money. You don't have to be a wildlife expert; we will provide training and are always thrilled to welcome new faces.

For more information call our Volunteer Development Officer on **01248 672850** or email us at **volunteer.cymru@rspb.org.uk**

Help us by becoming a member

Every gift you give, is a gift to nature - whether it's a one-off donation or becoming a member.

Whether you join as an individual, a couple, a family or as a youth member - your membership helps the RSPB save wildlife, protect wild places and connect people with nature. Each member gets: Unlimited FREE entry to more than 170 UK nature reserves, Nature's Home magazine every quarter and a welcome pack to help you make the most of your membership.

We spend 90% of our net income on conversation, engagement and advocacy work – we work hard to spend your money in the right places to secure a diverse landscape for our future generations.

For more information call our RSPB Cymru membership team on **02920 353274** or visit **www.rspb.org.uk/join-and-donate**

Sutherland House, Cowbridge, Road East, Cardiff CF11 9AB

Bodnant Gardens

Chirk Castle

Dolaucothi Gold Mines

Penrhyn Castle

Ymddiriedolaeth Genedlaethol National Trust

Only one attraction in Wales covers one fifth of the coastline, 11 of the 15 tallest peaks, 45,000 hectares of stunning landscape and includes castles, gardens, historic houses, bridges and a gold mine – the National Trust.

The Welsh countryside is enriched by fantastic attractions offering enjoyable days out and memorable experiences and so many of these inspiring places are cared for by the National Trust. You are never more than 40 minutes from a National Trust attraction, be it the imposing Penrhyn Castle in the North, majestic Chirk Castle in the East, romantic Powis Castle in mid Wales or the impressive Tredegar House in the South.

But the National Trust in Wales is not all about stately homes and fortresses, there are great days out to be enjoyed at Dolaucothi Gold mines, Aberdulais Tin Works and Waterfall and the intriguing Tudor Merchant's House. And the beautiful Bodnant Garden and Colby Woodland Garden offer so much more than simply stunning surroundings to relax and play in.

But by far the most incredible thing the National Trust offers, is unlimited access to all of this for the whole family for just over half the cost of one family visit to Alton Towers, and only £15.50 more than a family day pass to Chester Zoo.

And when you join the National Trust you can be sure that you are paying not only for access to all the 300 houses, 200 gardens, 40 castles and 76 nature reserves across Wales, England and Northern Ireland, but also helping the charity to look after our heritage and landscape forever for everyone.

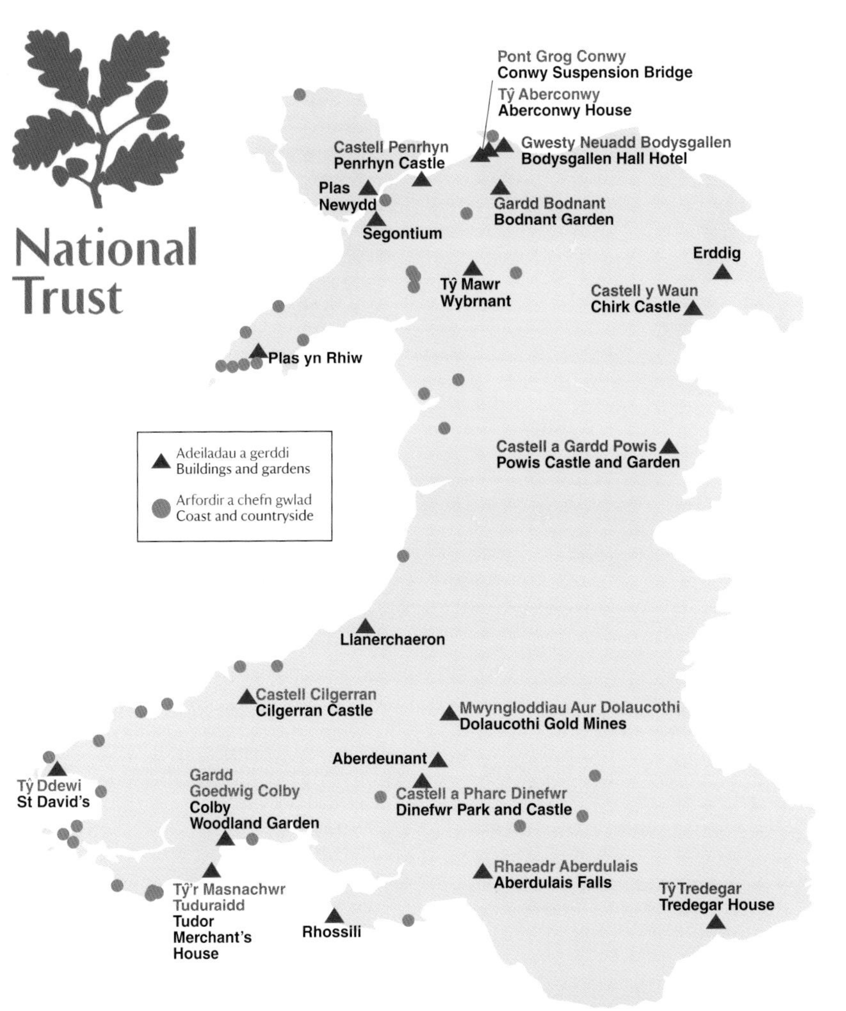

National Trust
Pont Grog Conwy
Conwy Suspension Bridge
Tŷ Aberconwy
Aberconwy House
Gwesty Neuadd Bodysgallen
Bodysgallen Hall Hotel
Castell Penrhyn
Penrhyn Castle
Plas Newydd
Gardd Bodnant
Bodnant Garden
Segontium
Erddig
Tŷ Mawr Wybrnant
Castell y Waun
Chirk Castle
Plas yn Rhiw
Adeiladau a gerddi
Buildings and gardens
Arfordir a chefn gwlad
Coast and countryside
Castell a Gardd Powis
Powis Castle and Garden
Llanerchaeron
Castell Cilgerran
Cilgerran Castle
Mwyngloddiau Aur Dolaucothi
Dolaucothi Gold Mines
Aberdeunant
Tŷ Ddewi
St David's
Gardd Goedwig Colby
Colby Woodland Garden
Castell a Pharc Dinefwr
Dinefwr Park and Castle
Rhaeadr Aberdulais
Aberdulais Falls
Tŷ Tredegar
Tredegar House
Tŷ'r Masnachwr Tuduraidd
Tudor Merchant's House
Rhossili

1. Amgueddfa Lechi Cymru, Llanberis
   National Slate Museum, Llanberis
2. Amgueddfa Wlân Cymru, Dre-fach Felindre
   National Wool Museum, Dre-fach Felindre
3. Amgueddfa Genedlaethol y Glannau, Abertawe
   National Waterfront Museum, Swansea
4. Y Ganolfan Gasgliadau Cenedlaethol, Nantgarw
   National Collections Centre, Nantgarw
5. Sain Ffagan Amgueddfa Werin Cymru
   St Fagans National Museum of History
6. Amgueddfa Genedlaethol Caerdydd
   National Museum Cardiff
7. Amgueddfa Lleng Rufeinig Cymru, Caerllion
   National Roman Legion Museum, Caerleon
8. Big Pit Amgueddfa Lofaol Cymru, Blaenafon
   Big Pit National Coal Museum, Blaenavon

NATIONAL MUSEUM WALES

Big Pit National Coal Museum

national museum wales
amgueddfa cymru

National Roman Legion Museum

St Fagans National History Museum

National Museum Cardiff

National Wool Museum

National Waterfront Museum

national museum wales
amgueddfa cymru

Big Pit National Coal Museum

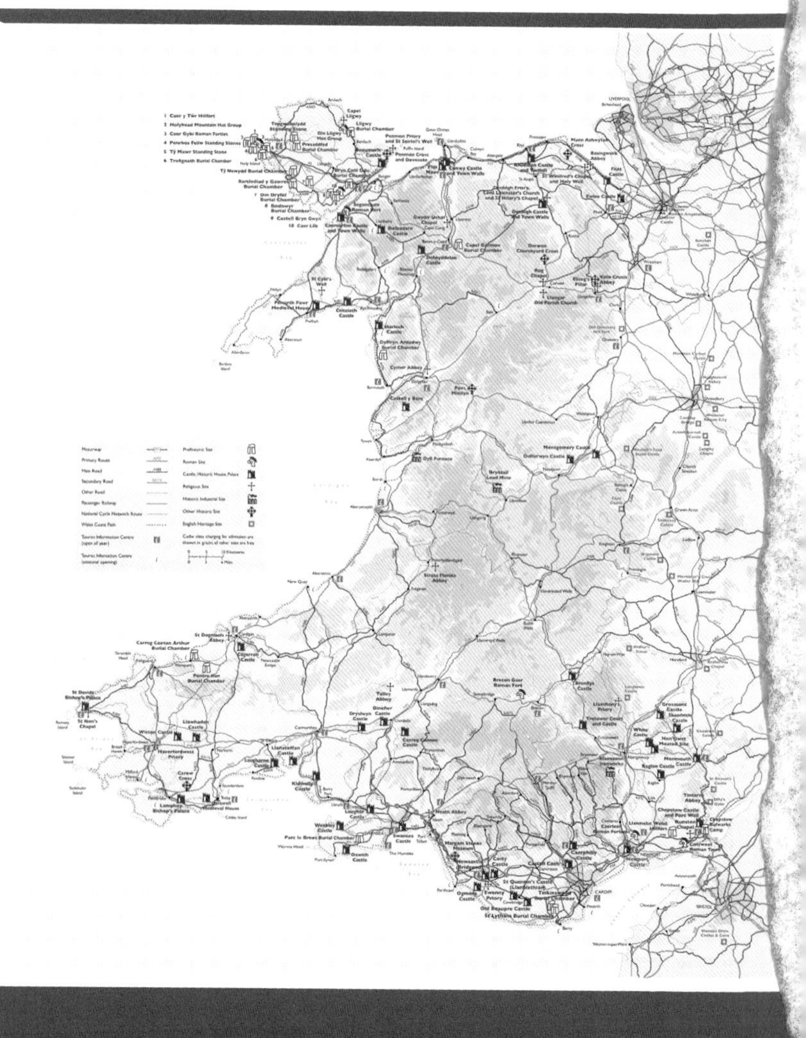
1 Caer y Twr Hillfort
2 Holyhead Mountain Hut Group
3 Caer Gybi Roman Fortlet
4 Penrhos Feilw Standing Stones
5 Tŷ Mawr Standing Stone
6 Trefignath Burial Chamber
Tŷ Newydd Burial Chamber
Capel Lligwy
Lligwy Burial Chamber
Din Lligwy Hut Group
Beaumaris Castle
Conwy Castle and Town Walls
Plas Mawr
Rhuddlan Castle
Flint Castle
Basingwerk Abbey
Denbigh Castle and Town Walls
Caernarfon Castle and Town Walls
Segontium Roman Fort
Dolbadarn Castle
Dolwyddelan Castle
Capel Garmon Burial Chamber
Valle Crucis Abbey
Criccieth Castle
Penarth Fawr Medieval House
Harlech Castle
Cymer Abbey
Castell y Bere
Montgomery Castle
Dolforwyn Castle
Dyfi Furnace
Bryntail Lead Mine
Strata Florida Abbey
St Dogmaels Abbey
Cilgerran Castle
Carreg Coetan Arthur Burial Chamber
Pentre Ifan Burial Chamber
St Davids Bishop's Palace
St Non's Chapel
Llawhaden Castle
Haverfordwest Priory
Carew Cross
Lamphey Bishop's Palace
Laugharne Castle
Llansteffan Castle
Kidwelly Castle
Talley Abbey
Dinefwr Castle
Dryslwyn Castle
Carreg Cennen Castle
Brecon Gaer Roman Fort
Bronllys Castle
Llanthony Priory
Tretower Court and Castle
Blaenavon Ironworks
Grosmont Castle
Skenfrith Castle
White Castle
Raglan Castle
Tintern Abbey
Chepstow Castle and Port Wall
Caerleon Roman Fortress
Caerwent Roman Town
Neath Abbey
Weobley Castle
Loughor Castle
Swansea Castle
Oxwich Castle
Parc le Breos Burial Chamber
Margam Stones Museum
Caerphilly Castle
Castell Coch
Newcastle Bridgend
Coity Castle
Ogmore Castle
Ewenny Priory
Old Beaupre Castle
St Lythans Burial Chamber
Tinkinswood Burial Chamber